PRELUDE TO GLORY

A newspaper accounting of
Custer's 1874 Expedition to
The Black Hills

HERBERT KRAUSE · GARY D. OLSON

(Preliminary research for this project was funded by a grant from the South Dakota Bicentennial Commission.)

Published By Brevet Press
Copyright © 1974 by Brevet Press
a division of BREVET INTERNATIONAL, INC.,
Northwestern Bank Building
Sioux Falls, South Dakota 57102

Library of Congress Catalog Card Number: 74-80769

Hard Cover Edition
ISBN: 0-88498-018-9

Soft Cover Edition
ISBN: 0-88498-019-7

First Printing 1974
Manufactured in The United States of America

Contents

Chapter	Page
INTRODUCTION	1
BISMARCK TRIBUNE	9
ILLINGWORTH THE PHOTOGRAPHER	33
ST. PAUL PIONEER	39
ST. PAUL PRESS	79
CHICAGO INTER OCEAN	97
NEW YORK WORLD	147
NEW YORK TRIBUNE	187
FINAL INTERVIEW	231
EPILOGUE	237
APPENDIX	239
Route Maps	240
Custer's Report	242
Grant's Report	248
Forsyth's Report	253
Ludlow's Report	260
Winchell's Report	262
Grinnell's Report	264
Zahn's Diary	266
Snow's Reminiscence	268
Wood's Reminiscence	271
ILLUSTRATION INDEX	273
INDEX	276

Acknowledgements

So many people have in one way or another helped in the preparation of this book that we wish it were possible to thank them all. Especially do we appreciate the encouragement and support given by Arnie Stenseth and the South Dakota Bicentennial Commission, together with the kindness and helpfulness of William Tillittson of the BISMARCK TRIBUNE; Frank E. Vyzralek of the State Historical Society of North Dakota; Dayton Canaday and his staff of the South Dakota Historical Society; Russell Fridley, Lucile Kane and the staff of the Minnesota Historical Society; Harold E. Anderson of Alexandria, Minnesota; George C. Chalou of the Old Military Branch of the National Archives; Raymond Dunmire and Willis Brenner of the Augustana College Mikkelsen Library; Capt. Trobjorne Saetre, m.v. THE ROYAL VIKING STAR; Dr. Arthur Huseboe, Dr. Thomas Kilian, Dr. C. J. McDonald and the entire Board of Directors of the Center for Western Studies; and last but certainly not least our secretaries who lightened the work load and served so cheerfully, Melissa McCool, Rennae Stiner, Garneth Oldenkamp Peterson and Mrs. Joeva Schaefer. Finally, a special thank you to Blake Kellogg for his arrangement of the Illingworth views and also Dr. Donald Jackson and his fine little volume CUSTER'S GOLD which first struck sparks to illuminate new aspects of an old problem.

The Center For Western Studies

PRELUDE TO GLORY is one of a number of recent projects of THE CENTER FOR WESTERN STUDIES, a study and research agency of Augustana College, Sioux Falls, South Dakota, concerned principally with South Dakota and its contiguous states, the Prairie Plains as well as certain related aspects of the Great Plains and the entire Trans-Mississippi West.

An integral part of Augustana College, the Center is fully owned and operated by the College. And while it does not conduct courses in instruction, it serves as a resource to the College, to other educational organizations, to the community, state and region as a center of information, and as a resource for teachers and research scholars. It is an agency through which studies, research projects and related activities are initiated and conducted, and by which assistance can be provided to interested individuals and groups.

The Center for Western Studies confines its interests to certain defined areas of study in the arts and sciences relative to the geographic region. Frequently, projects of the Center are highly interdisciplinary, involving a number of the prinicpal fields of concern. The Center is also actively engaged in the collection and preservation of printed materials and all types of documents useful in the study areas and for the preservation of the culture of the region. Collections of the Center are maintained in the College's Mikkelsen Library where rare items are subject to controlled use. The Center has been fortunate in securing several valuable collections which make it a major regional source for the history of the NORTHERN PLAINS.

A primary mission of the Center is to identify ways in which it can be helpful in improving the quality of life in the region surrounding the College. It works with individuals and groups on and off campus to achieve a better understanding of the region, its heritage and resources. The Center seeks to stimulate interest in the solution of regional problems through the application of knowledge in the areas of its concern. It is hoped that the publication of the Custer dispatches and allied documents, an example of the objectives of the Center, will help to illuminate some of the questions which still confront students of this region.

Introduction

The military order authorizing an expedition into the nearly trackless wilds of the Black Hills, issued by General Philip Sheridan that May day, 1874, through R. C. Drum, Assistant Adjutant General, was hardly exciting enough to agitate the coffee of any American reading his daily newspaper, whether in Boston or Chicago or St. Paul, Minnesota. Perhaps the editors of opposition papers, such as the Boston POST or the New York WORLD, superlatively sensitive to possible chicanery in the Grant Administra-

President Ulysses S. Grant

tion, might have sniffed a slight odor of chicanery in the news item. Or the writers for the Bismarck TRIBUNE, Dakota Territory, zealously anticipatory over the future of the Great Northwest, might have caught a whiff of strange throbbing in the item:

Brigadier General A. H. Terry
Commanding Department of Dakota,
St. Paul, Minnesota.
General:

The Lieutenant General Commanding directs that you send a column of ten companies of the Seventh Cavalry, under the command of Lieutenant Colonel G. A. Custer, to examine the country in and about the North Fork of the Sheyenne, shown on the maps as the Belle Fourche: also, the country south of it in the vicinity of Bear Butte, especially South and West of Bear Butte, commonly designated as the Black Hills on the map.

It would be agreeable to the Lieutenant General if you could send an engineer officer to determine the latitude and longitude of Bear Butte, or any other well-marked feature in the Black Hills which would serve as a good point of reference for that unknown section of country.

For the accomplishment of this purpose you are authorized to employ citizen teamsters for six weeks or two months, at the rate of $30 per month, as well as two or three wagonmasters, and one or two guides at usual rates of hire. Colonel Custer should be given full latitude to return in case he finds the performance of the duty unsafe, or the country impracticable for the movement of his column.

Very respectfully, your obedient servant,
R. C. Drum
Assistant Adjutant General.[1]

But for most Americans, the authorization in tone and wording was another triumph of official indefiniteness. The unique spell of the Black Hills was tucked away in two off-hand expressions. The emphasis seemed to be on the Sheyenne (Cheyenne) River and Bear Butte. But in May 1874, not many newspaper-reading Americans, still pucker-browed and disturbed over last year's depression and ensuing economic doldrums this spring, knew what Bear Butte was or stopped the munching of a cake to find out where it was. Besides, hadn't Captain William Raynolds visited Bear Butte in 1859 and delineated the mountain in his government report of 1868?[2] An expedition which might offer new opportunities to develop the western country would have been hailed with enthusiastic approval. The railroads were puffing freight loads of goods further and further west, now that the Union Pacific linked East and West; had linked New York and the Pacific a couple of years back. And now more engines were chugging at their steamy leashes on the spur lines and at tracks' ends, waiting for new roads to be laid to speed development further westward in Kansas, in Nebraska, in North Dakota. However regretful or humanitarian, the average American felt somewhat exasperately that sooner or later something would probably be done about the stubbornness of those Indians who seemed bent on blocking not only western expansion but the country's economic growth as well. Therefore an expedition to determine the latitude and longitude of Bear Butte as a "good point of reference" seemed more like another expenditure of taxpayers' money with little effect upon the price tag in the market. Searching for gold, now, as prospectors had in California—that was the adventure the fatigued old economy needed. But this authorization, bland, flat official orders with no mention of the opening of new settlement to whip up the lagging times; certainly no mention of even a hen's tooth of possibility of looking for gold, though gold was in the Hills for a certainty, as everyone knew; no hint of newspaper correspondents, of geological experts, of experienced miners accompanying the column; nor was an inkling given that the guides would be Arikara Indians, hiding ancient vengeance in their sheathed hunting knives.

Not that the complexities of the Black Hills were unknown in legend as well as in report. They were part of the dreams and the letters of young Louis Philippe reporting to his ailing father, Pierre LaVerendrye, the famous quester for the Western Sea and later writing to the Governor of New France when he told how on New Year's day, 1743, marching westward from the Missouri, he came in sight of "the Mountains," finding them "for the most part well-wooded with all kinds of timber," and beyond their dark mystery, according to his friends the Bow Indians, lay "the vast Sea"—the Great Northwest Passage, perhaps, the fabled Straits of Anian, but more likely the Great South Seas.[3] And the Black Hills, however vague geographically, took on legendary reality in Jacques L'Eglise's reports, he who had travelled up the Missouri to the Mandan country in 1790 and wrote about the Costa Negra to the west where pebbles in the dry washes lay shining among the stones.[4] And they were the mysterious hills of thunder where the white-boated turkey strutted, as Jean Valle told Lewis and Clark in 1805 when at the Sheyenne River the Captains heard the fur trader relate his seasons as a trapper on the Belle Fourche and in the Black Hills;[5] they were part of the story of the petrified forest full of petrified birds which sang petrified songs told on Jedidiah Smith's expedition to the beaver country in 1823 when the fur hunters passed through the southern Hills.[6] And they were in the El Dorado tales Father De Smet heard in his missionary wanderings in the Missouri country, from whence in his reports he recounted tales growing familiar around the campfires and fantastic in the bar-rooms, rolling over the tongues of trappers, traders and itinerant miners; men as quixotic as daring, who had slipped shadow-like into and out of the dark hills, returning sometimes with tales of gold lying in astonishing nuggets but also occasionally with samplings of actual pay dirt.

The surveys of Warren in 1857 and the northern reconnaissance of Raynolds 1859-60[7] dispelled some of the geological mists, but the scrutiny of the blue-dark mysterious canyons south and beyond, while it provided new information about the Hills, it also added to the glitter of their unknown potentials. A few men, seasoned with experience, studied the surveyors' maps. But government documents and maps of government surveys, often printed in small editions, were probably no easier to come by in 1874 than they are to the modern researcher in the present day. The average newspaper-reading American, still beholding brighter rainbows in legend and lore than in exact cartography and descriptive guide, was still unlikely to distinguish between the Black Hills of the Laramie Range and the dark outliers in the Sheyenne River Country. The newspaper in Bismarck, Dakota Territory, might trumpet that it knew the location of dry washes modelled with dust and the Laramie, Wyoming Territory news sheets might raise civic blood pressure in recounting the number of miners who told in the barrooms about their slipping into the Hills and beholding unparalled riches. However, whatever knowledge civic pride in Laramie and Bismarck held in its gesticulations about the fabled goldfields, as late as August 28, 1874—to anticipate events—only three days before Custer's return to Bismarck was awaited, the Chicago INTER-OCEAN wrote with pointed emphases, "lines of latitude and longitude are not well determined throughout the Black Hills country," but it assured its readers that with Custer's return, "the exact locality can

be learned from the engineers with the command."[8]

Whatever the dusty pitch of excitement in Bismarck, Dakota Territory, where the action was at its liveliest, in the rest of the newspaper-reading America only a small portion of readers were suddenly aware of an uneasy sensation like a subdued electric vibration when as in Chicago on July 4, 1874, the readers saw on the front page of the Chicago INTER-OCEAN, below the uninspiring stock market report the small dark capitals: Black Hills Expedition. The Expedition starts from Fort Lincoln. Rumor that it will be Interfered with by Hostile Sioux.[9] Under the small headlines a special telegram from Fort Lincoln, D.T., reported tersely that the command had left early on July 2.

What must have stirred mixed feelings behind more than one furrowed brow, remembering the May 15 authorization and its modest complement of teamsters and wagonmasters, was the electrifying addition that along with the ten companies of the Seventh Cavalry and the three companies of infantry, went 100 Indian Scouts under the command of the famous Bloody Knife, and a battery of Gatling guns.

But the reader of the INTER-OCEAN found nothing to suggest that in the military column were geologists or miners or experts in detecting the glint of gold in dry washes or grass roots. There was, however, that disquieting statement, welcome to many, disagreeable to others: "Probable that Strong Resistance will be made by the Indians . . . Startling rumors . . . gathering of tribes . . . under Sitting Bull . . . a missionary coming to the Fort, begging General Custer to give up the expedition to save bloodshed."

There was some assurance in the telegram's insistence on the government's right by treaty "to press through and explore all the contested Territory." And, the news release went on confidently, "General Custer is prepared to enforce that right." But the INTER-OCEAN added rather grimly, "A serious conflict may be expected before many days."[10]

Whatever the squeamishness about shedding blood, the newspaper reader may have folded his paper restlessly. If an El Dorado in the Black Hills were the adrenalin to invigorate the sluggish economic veins, perhaps it was worth a small skirmish or two. There were those treaties; and fair-play to all people was to be taken seriously. But this bellicose obstruction to progress, progress for the country . . . Well, a small skirmish . . . It couldn't be more serious than that, not with Custer and the Seventh. The newspaper was folded on the Custer item. So much for news in Chicago, at least on Independence Day, 1874.

In Chicago in the next few weeks the front pages offered little more than the sundries of a dull period. The Bleecher scandal, venal spots on the clerical gown and all, were being relegated to small headlines; the affairs of Jay Cooke and Co. were being scrutinized by a committee; crops were excellent in India, the possibility of revolt in Cuba growing; Bishop Hare of Minnesota duly noted the objectives of the Custer Expedition and expressed his indignation. The first dispatches from the column in Dakota were received with no explosions of public comment. The command was making rapid progress; on July 24 it was in Prospect Valley on the Little Missouri. No difficulties had encumbered them; no Indian hostilities—except small bands of Sioux lurking along the trail; Mr. Grinnell, of Yale found his first fossil and General Custer reported to General Terry that he had "sent pacific messages to all the tribes infesting this region before the expedition moved," a gesture sure to receive the approving reader's nod; but, the reader soon learned, "Custer's Indians were sure the Sioux meant war." "Should this be true" wrote Custer frankly, "they will be the party to fire the first shot." With such magnanimity, how could the expedition fail?[11]

Not all readers nodded in agreement, nor did newspapers. The New York WORLD thought there were "some queer things about the affair" and frowned over the preparations made with much secrecy; no appropriation had been asked of Congress; the War Department was "singularly reticent;" the officers were White House favorites; Custer was in command, Forsyth was his second and the President's son, Fred Grant, was third in rank. And the Boston POST wrinkled its editorial nose, scenting possible corruption in the affair: wasn't the expedition an invasion of Indian Territory and thus a flagrant violation of the treaty Bishop Hare had made with the Sioux? Which led the Chicago INTER-OCEAN, staunchly Administration, to observe acidly that there were among certain opportunist journals "the disposition to misconstrue every act of the administration."[12]

Meanwhile, Bishop Hare wired the Secretary of the Interior bluntly: "We are marauders in this case."[13] Such a bold statement from an eminent churchman, elicited a rejoinder from no less a personage than General Terry himself. "I am unable to see that any just offense is given to the Indians by the expedition to the Hills," he wrote on July 27. "Plunder is not the objective of the expedition; neither is it sent out for the purposes of ascertaining the mineral or agricultural resources of the Black Hills. It seeks neither gold, timber nor arable land." Having committed himself to specifics, Terry apparently suddenly found further explanation a bit sticky. "Two geologists, a few—two or three, I think—correspondents of newspapers, and a photographer; no person," he hastened to add, "except employees of the government have been permitted to accompany the troops." Why newspaper correspondents and a photographer were included to determine the latitude and longitude of Bear Butte was not made clear. As for the geologists, they were present "at the request of Professor Marsh of Yale College," added Terry as if with finger to lip, tentatively, "it is understood that their special object is the paleontology of the region."[14]

The next day, July 28, the Chicago Daily INTER-OCEAN had small headlines for its readers—Custer's First Report from the Front. It was happy to report successful progress; no Indian fights, only skulkers on the trail. The INTER-OCEAN printed the account on page two.[15]

Alert readers, comparing Custer's report with Terry's reply to Bishop Hare, appearing only the day before, might have wondered a little at statements like Custer's "a country of surpassing beauty and richness of soil. The pasturage could not be finer; timber is abundant, and water both good and plentiful." Cattlemen must have felt the vision of large

ranches in learning that despite steady marching of "over seventeen miles per day, one day making thirty-one miles; yet our mules and beef have constantly improved in condition, the beef cattle depending entirely upon the excellent grazing we have marched over." Later, as if in an afterthought, Custer adds, "Beds of lignite of good quality have been observed." True, lignite was not gold which Terry had included especially along with "Timber and arable land" as objects **not** sought by the expedition. But lignite might be suggestive of other minerals to come. And apparently Custer saw no harm in pointing out the mirages of opportunity quivering on the horizon.[16]

Bvt. Maj. Gen. George A. Custer

Actually, late July was near the tag end of the season when generally this part of South Dakota offers miles of soft tannish-colored dried grass; generally no heavy downpours are reported to renew the green growth and at the same time impede an expedition by turning the prairie soil into quagmires of gluey gumbo. In his report of August 2, Custer himself speaks of "the sun burned and dried yellow herbage to be seen on the outer plains." No great buffalo herds were spotted (gone to their autumn grazing grounds) but antelope were plentiful.

Was Custer drawing the long bow to the stretch in his report, despite Terry's explanatory limitations? Was Custer delineating visions beyond the contemplation of his superiors? Was this the entering wedge of a larger ambition?

At any rate, newspaper readers probably were at the moment titillated more by the Beecher case— which the St. Paul PIONEER termed the Famous

Three—and the news that a man near Rochester, Minnesota, had invented a boon to farmers—an automatic self-binder attachment which in one fantastic operation tied the mown grain into neat bundles. It would revolutionize farming, supporters averred. There was more hope for better times here than in the Black Hills adventures.[17] Often the readers turned to page four to find Custer. On August 12, 1874, on page four, the St. Paul DAILY PIONEER pointed out in its report on OUR POOR, that Ramsey County, Minnesota, spent $589.50 for coffins and burials and $153.25 for liquers, cash paid.[18] On the same page four appeared in headlines no larger than OUR POOR, "THE BLACK HILLS. Dispatches from Gen. Custer's Expedition. Dated August 3." Thoughtfully, the PIONEER corrected itself; the main dispatch from the west was actually dated August 2. The PIONEER reminded its readers that the old stories about the Black Hills, "the improbably ravines, dark and gloomy caverns, inaccessible hills" were purely "wild and exaggerated stories" which were now "put to flight by General Custer's description . . . His report reads like a description of fairyland, filled with bright-hued flowers . . . whose perfume filled the air; with lovely valleys, delightful natural parks, clear streams, etc., etc." The cavalry picked bouquets from their saddles and men and horses were gaily decked with flowers. After such panegynics, General Terry's prohibition on arable land and timber "apparently were impediments to progress." The PIONEER quoted Custer: "I know of no portion of our country where nature has done so much to prepare home for husbandmen, and left so little for the latter to do, as here." As if to tantalize the crowded tenants of the cities, those which Henry Fuller would name THE CLIFF DWELLERS, Custer rhapsodizes over the miracle that "not only is the land cleared and timbered for fuel and building, conveniently located with streams of pure water flowing through the length and breadth but nature oftentimes seems to have gone farther"—here the newspaper reader may have gulped in despondent envy—"nature seems to have placed beautiful shrubbery and evergreens in the most desirable locations for building sites."[19] Parenthetically, one is tempted to wonder whether this is a military man speaking as an intrepreneur or a military man speaking with political visions in his mind. Timber and agricultural bonanzas? Let the husbandmen in every American newspaper reader be stirred, for what great adventures might not further elusive unfoldings lead him? And gold? "Very little is said about the mineral resources of the country," the PIONEER wrote somewhat peevishly as if taken aback by the General's reticence, his guarded language in the remainder of the dispatches. "Gold," Custer said, "he would leave the subject with scientists who accompanied the expedition to report upon." Disappointed the PIONEER growled, "All reports of El Dorado are without foundation," and added glumly, "The only wealth of the county seems to consist of its beautiful scenery and fertile land." As for trouble with the Indians, sheer nonsense, said the PIONEER. The only camp of Indians was instantly surrounded by cavalry, invited to camp and graciously given flour, sugar, etc. And what did the hostiles do? They broke their promise, slipped away

and fled. The result? Pursuit and "a little scuffle" between Indian and a scout, "during which the scout's gun was exploded." The Indian got away; either he or his pony wounded; the pursuers found blood on his trail. And that was the only engagement the command encountered since it left Fort Lincoln. So Custer wrote in his dispatch; so the PIONEER assured its readers.[20] Meantime through the uncertainties of July and the doldrums of a dull August, the dispatches of the correspondents—Curtis of Chicago, Barrows of New York, Knappen of the Dakota Territory—came by horse to the telegraphs and by wire to the cities, and readers east of the wide Missouri opened their newspapers to paeans of delight over the freedom of prairie life and vicarious thrills of Indians' skulking menace; through reporters' eyes they got for the first time a sense of the mystery of these dark upthrusts in the prairies, their scope and magnitude, their waters, their forests, their verdant glades, their gnarled and toothy volcanic spires, their ragged shoulders until in a burst of journalistic fervor they saw as in the New York TRIBUNE, "Eden in the Clouds."[21] And their absorption, however, dormant must have steadily grown. They were spectators at a drama in a certain glamorous section of the country with reporters zeroing in on crucial events; readers saw the drama unfolding at a pace probably rarely experienced in journalism before. But it was Utopia contrasted with the price tag at the market place. The PIONEER PRESS in St. Paul had grumbled about the flowery descriptions and reminded its readers that the only El Dorado so far seen were beautiful scenery and fertile soil.

But this floral quiet splintered even in the sedate office of the Chicago INTER-OCEAN when on August 20 its readers stared in disbelief at the headlines: Startling news: a Battle in the Black Hills—Custer Expedition meets 4,000 Savages and a Desperate Fight Occurs. The Indians Repulsed with Heavy Loss—Custer Loss, Fifty Killed and Wounded.

The dispatch was date-lined Sioux City, Iowa, August 19[22] and allegedly came from Fort Sully. It was laconically brief.

But the very brevity of the report and the meagreness of details, though featured on page one, suggests that the INTER-OCEAN had its doubts about the sometimes trigger-happy journalism at Sioux City, Iowa. The INTER-OCEAN waited for its own correspondent, Curtis, to set the record straight. He did and it did.

On August 27 the news broke which readers especially in the West and Midwest but also in the East must have felt in their bones was coming. The telltale smoke of all the legends about nuggets in the streamlets turning the water gold, of riches glittering in the sands, had to have at least some embers of truth.

The Chicago INTER-OCEAN screamed: "Gold" on page one, August 27, and the mania set its teeth on bit and bridle.

Twenty-four hours later emotions still bubbled hotly. "The Gold Fever," trumpeted the INTER-OCEAN, "Intense Excitement in the City yesterday over the News from the Black Hills," crowning its scoop with a map entitled "The Black Hills country," replete with trails, railroads and a table of distances.

It reminded its readers that the story was exclusive in the INTER-OCEAN and chortled over its rivals. "The TIMES and TRIBUNE, devoid of enterprise, failed to send a special reporter with Custer's expedition, and hence they were without the important advices for which people were waiting."

Newsboys had been swamping the INTER-OCEAN offices. Nasal cries echoed on the streets. " 'Ere's yer INTER-OCEAN, tellin' all about the gold discoveries. 'Ere's your INTER-OCEAN; don't yer want a basket full of gold; tell ye all about it. INTER-OCEAN, Sir; lots of gold: want some of it?' "

It was a cry heard on many streets in America that August 27 and in the days following. Crowds besieged mining ofices for information. The INTER-OCEAN probably caught the spirit of this excited moment in reporting, "all classes were interested. Many wanted to start immediately . . . . The simple words 'Gold' acted like magic, and served to inspire a maddening desire to attain it not in the shape of coin but as nuggets or dust."[23]

Gold was indeed the magic word, yes. But the dispatches of the correspondents thoughtfully included in Custer's command, painting the Hills week after week as Paradise in the west, had laid the tinder, stick by inflammable stick. The necessary spark flashed and the tinder flamed, the west flamed; with wind-swept speed the country flamed. All classes were indeed caught in the heat. Anyone known to have travelled within a hundred miles of the region, whether in sight of the Black Hills or not, became an expert whose dubious knowledge and wisdom brought high rewards.

A reader familiar with the west, one John Goeway, interviewed by an INTER-OCEAN reporter, saw the gold strike and its consequences in one revealing thrust of insight. Asked the reporter, "Do you think the government will grant permission to miners going there?" Replied Mr. Goeway out of the prophesy of experience on the frontier, "If the miners are satisfied that there is gold there, all the governments in the world will not stop them working it. The whole United States Army will be powerless to prevent the influx of gold miners which will soon take place."[24]

In the shining haze of gold, who remembered the original provisions of the authorization for the expedition duly published in the newspapers? Or General Terry's limitations? Or the treaty with the Indians, dutifully published by the INTER-OCEAN in the "Gold Fever" issue? Few indeed. A man named P. D. Weare of Chicago told a reporter, "It's clear to see, from the fact of an official expedition being sent out, that they are going to work to destroy the Indians' title to the Territory."[25]

By strange coincidence at that very moment, the INTER-OCEAN found General Sheridan stating that "in the event of the gold diggings being within the Sioux Reservation there was one of two things mining parties could do; either obtain permission from the Secretary of the Interior to enter upon the reservation or apply to Congress to abrogate the existing treaty with the Indians, and make another with them." Then he added a clincher. "The Secretary of the Interior has no authority to act," he told the INTER-OCEAN. "Hence Congress can afford the only relief."[26]

Thus a perceptive reader might have noticed that the reading public was lured into the unknown and unpredictable areas of treaty abrogation probably without realizing that "abrogation" means "breaking;" and that Sheridan's suggestion was clear enough: the government might be ready to engage in the very acts of breaking promises which the American newspaper reader seemed to think was the customary untrustworthy behavior of the Indians.

Much later, the Bismarck TRIBUNE ironically ran two headlines which struck the nub of the problem. Heading its September 2, 1874 issue, it tried to have its cake and eat it too: "The Surrender of the Black Hills a Military Necessity. But the Treaty with Sioux must be Respected." A gesture, at least—or was it a mousehole of escape from a dilemna? For suddenly the question hung dangling in the air: were the new gold strikes actually in the boundaries of the treaty of 1868 or did they lie outside?

Lt. Gen. Philip Sheridan

The expedition had brought into sharp focus the thinking of the Commissioners responsible for the framing of the treaty. The crux of the debate, as far as the expedition and its incursion into the Black Hills is concerned, seemed to lie in article two where the United States "agrees that no person except those herein designated and authorized to enter upon the Indian reservation in discharge of duties enjoined by law, shall be permitted to pass over, settle upon or reside in the territory described in this article." But in what seems an astonishing afterthought, Terry writes in the St. Paul DAILY PIONEER of August 1, "that this possession was intended to exclude from the Reservation the military forces of the government, I cannot believe." And as one of the shapers of the treaty and participant in the conferences of the Commission privately and in sessions with the Indian delegates, General Terry ought to be knowledgable about the motives behind the intentions of the writers of the Treaty.

After noting that as common practice the Indian Bureau supported his view, "for, since April 27, 1869, three military posts have been established within the reservation . . . and at its last session, Congress appropriated $30,000 for the building of two more such forts," Terry comes to the quick of the question: "Can it be supposed that it was the intent of the treaty to set apart, in the heart of the national Territory, a district nearly as great as the largest state east of the Mississippi . . . within which the government should be forbidden to exercise those powers, which it everywhere else possesses, of sending its miltary forces where they may be required? —a district which, so far as military movements are concerned, should be a foreign territory?"[27]

It might have struck a sensitive reader as rather strange that Terry, referring to events in 1869, did not now in 1874 refer to article 10 where "the United States agrees that the country north of the North Platte River and east of the summits of the Big Horn Mountains, shall be unceded territory, and that no white person shall be permitted to set upon or occupy any portion of the same; or, without the consent of the Indians, to pass through the same; and further, the military forts now established in said territory, shall be abandoned."[28]

Were Custer's "pacific messages" to all the tribes "infesting this region," sent before the column moved and were they requests for permission to cross treaty territory? Was the text of any of the "pacific messages" printed? And was there any evidence of replies from the leaders of the tribes "infesting the region," granting or denying permission? Is Custer's attitude as to the quality of the "pacific messages" indicated in Custer's reply to a correspondent in an interview given at Fort Abraham Lincoln on September 1, 1874, and published in the Bismarck TRIBUNE, September 2:

"Reporter—I presume you were disappointed in not having a brush with the Sioux?

Custer—Yes, I was somewhat disappointed for, though I sent pacific messages and had taken every precaution to avert hostilities, I had reason to anticipate trouble, I was disappointed and am heartily glad of it."

Then he added words that seems to have a ring to them more resonant than one usually finds in the military: "Some thought I coveted an engagement— such was not the case, and I congratulate myself and the country on the safe return of the Expedition without bloodshed. An engagement, no matter how trifling, would have been magnified and misrepresented, and the good effects of the Expedition would have been to a great extent destroyed."

The reference to "misrepresentation," presumably by the news media and the pro-Indian factions, might have made the alert reader wonder why Custer entertained such fears, since there were thoughtfully provided for him—or did he instigate the provision?— an excellent corps of writers of various views to record in the national media the heroics or even the most "trifling engagement," and record it as accurately as human persuasion permits. Or was Custer thinking in terms of a letter he wrote to Mrs. Custer from Prospect Valley, July 15, 1874, "Keep press notices of the expedition . . . these will be interesting and of value later?"[29]

But now the hero was home; the dust of strange marches settled upon the consequences of the trip; the last dispatches were filed; the correspondents ended their work recording historic events occurring in the field. And now entered the tangled polemics of treaty-making and re-making and treaty-breaking, of charge and counter-charge. And the name of Custer dominated the national consciousness.

The dispatches of Custer's correspondents have been available since their first appearance in their respective newspapers. As nearly as we can ascertain, they are gathered in their entirety for the first time here. Their role in the Custer story has never been given full-scale scrutiny. Their possible influences via the news media in shaping American opinion on the Black Hills—Big Horn River Country, on the Indian policy, on the attitude toward the Indians needs a full length study. Actually, these dispatches seem to be the first large group of accounts to be published specifically about the Black Hills in the framework of the Indian problem. They gave eastern readers not only broad first hand coverage of

Brig. Gen. Alfred Terry National Archives

the march but also the journalistic intimacy and personal spontaneity of the "I was there" style often lacking in previous more considered and formal government reports of such reconnaissances. Through various reporters' eyes, Eastern readers had an opportunity to view the march across the plains and through the Black Hills day by day; they saw the leaders at work and play; they saw Custer as a leader, as a man and as a military strategist and could approve or disapprove the correspondents' characterizations; they had a chance to observe the reporters' reactions to the plan to enter Indian Territory protected by the Treaty of 1868 and the possible motives for violating the sanctity of restricted areas. In addition there were the reactions of the journalists themselves to Custer, to the Black Hills Country itself, its scenery, it mythic lore, its awesome peaks, its flora and fauna, its potentials as an inducement for western settlement, its reputation as a refuge for "red outlaws," its legendary gold prospects, its sacred nature, a locality revered by the Indians. The dispatches seem to indicate they were written without any but normal personal biases but no doubt each journalist remembered that his varied audience at home was exercised then (as now) at government efforts to deal with the Indian problem. The writers in the field were well aware of attitudes that ranged from violently anti-Indian to the indifferent to the dedicated pro-Indian. The bias at home might be revealed in the choice of the headline with which the correspondent started his dispatch. Since this was probably the earliest large collection of newspaper dispatches dealing with one facet of the Indian and related problems, here was the grist for the mills of those who advocated sympathetic understanding and those who proposed military regulatory methods. The dispatches of the correspondents who travelled with him undoubtedly helped to weave the colorful national glory and acclaim accorded George A. Custer and the Expedition of 1874. Perhaps 1874 has a place in the events which led to 1876 and Little Big Horn.

FOOTNOTES

1. For instance, cf. Chicago DAILY INTER-OCEAN, August 28, 1874, p. 1.
2. William Franklin Raynolds, REPORT ON THE EXPLORATION OF THE YELLOWSTONE RIVER. Wash., D.C., G.P.O., 1868, **passim.**
3. Pierre La Verendreye. JOURNALS AND LETTERS. Champlain Society. Toronto. 1927, 418-420.
4. Abraham Nasatir, BEFORE LEWIS AND CLARK, St. Louis, 1952. Vol. 2, p. 738.
5. JOURNALS OF LEWIS and CLARK EXPEDITION, 1804-1806, Thwaites ed. Vol. I, pp. 175-177.
6. JAMES CLYMAN, FRONTIERSMAN, ed. by C. L. Camp, Portland, Oregon. 1960.
7. Lieut. G. K. Warren, REPORT OF EXPLORATIONS IN NEBRASKA AND DAKOTA, IN THE YEARS 1855-56-57, Wash., 1875; W. F. Raynolds, REPORT ON EXPLORATION OF THE YELLOWSTONE RIVER, Wash., 1868.
8. Chicago DAILY INTER-OCEAN, Aug. 28, 1874, p. 2.
9. Chicago DAILY INTER-OCEAN, July 4, 1874.
10. Chicago DAILY INTER-OCEAN, July 4, 1874, p. 1.
11. Chicago DAILY INTER-OCEAN, July 28, 1874, p. 2.
12. Chicago DAILY INTER-OCEAN, July 28, 1874, p. 4.
13. Quoted by General Terry in Chicago DAILY INTER-OCEAN, July 30, 1874, p. 3.
14. St. Paul DAILY PIONEER, Aug. 1, 1874, p. 2.
15. Chicago DAILY INTER-OCEAN, July 28, 1874, p. 2.
16. Chicago DAILY INTER-OCEAN, July 28, 1874, p. 2.
17. St. Paul DAILY PIONEER, Aug. 1, 1874, p. 2.
18. St. Paul DAILY PIONEER, Aug. 12, 1874, p. 4.
19. St. Paul DAILY PIONEER, Aug. 12, 1874, p. 4.
20. St. Paul DAILY PIONEER, Aug. 12, 1874, pp. 4, 5, 6.
21. New York TRIBUNE, Aug. 17, 1874, p. 1.
22. Chicago DAILY INTER-OCEAN, Aug. 20, 1874, p. 1.
23. Chicago DAILY INTER-OCEAN, Aug. 28, 1874, p. 1.
24. Chicago DAILY INTER-OCEAN, Aug. 28, 1874, p. 2.
25. Chicago DAILY INTER-OCEAN, Aug. 28, 1874, p. 3.
26. Chicago DAILY INTER-OCEAN, Aug. 28, 1874, p. 3.
27. St. Paul PIONEER PRESS, 1874, p. 2, 3.
28. Chicago DAILY INTER-OCEAN, Aug. 28, 1874, p. 1.
29. Marguerite Merrington. THE CUSTER STORY. New York, 1950, pp. 273-274.

BISMARCK TRIBUNE

On June 24, 1874, the BISMARCK TRIBUNE announced to its readers that "N. H. Knappen lays his scalp on the altar of the TRIBUNE, and goes with Custer to the Black Hills as our special reporter." The reference to scalps was meaningful to the residents of this two year old settlement located on the Missouri River and at the end of the line of the Northern Pacific Railroad. Bismarck stood at the very edge of the northern frontier and not all Sioux tribesmen had yet conceded government ownership of the land. But to Bismarck residents like Colonel Clement A. Lounsberry, owner and editor of the TRIBUNE the town had a great future if only opportunities were seized boldly. The Custer Expedition, they were quick to recognize, was just such an opportunity. It would blaze a trail to the Hills from Fort Abraham Lincoln, just across the river from Bismarck, and when the existence of gold was confirmed, as they were confident it would be, Bismarck would be the outfitting and jumping off point for hordes of men with the smell of gold dust in their nostrils. Understandably then, the Custer Expedition was strictly front page news in the BISMARCK TRIBUNE.

The history of the BISMARCK TRIBUNE is nearly concurrent with that of the town itself. Townsite claims were first established in the spring of 1872 when the route of the Northern Pacific became known, and considerable building was done during that summer. But the real start of Bismarck coincided with the first train's arrival on June 5, 1873. The next day a small cylinder press and some printing supplies belonging to Colonel Lounsberry were unloaded, and a month later the first issue of the TRIBUNE appeared. Lounsberry apparently named his paper the TRIBUNE after the MINNEAPOLIS TRIBUNE where he had earlier worked as an editor and legislative reporter. After giving the TRIBUNE a proper launching in the summer and fall of 1873 Lounsberry returned to Minnesota during the winter months to conclude his business interests there. During his absence Amos Jordan edited the paper until he began a campaign to run some bad elements out of Bismarck and ended up doing the running himself. His successor as editor was a young man of seventeen from Wisconsin named Nathan H. Knappen. When Lounsberry returned in April he announced that Knappen was going east for a month's vacation and apparently he had earned it, for he commented that "Few can appreciate the difficulties Mr. Knappen has labored under during his editorial career . . ." While he had made "two or three mistakes," the proprietor approved of the work he had done, wished Knappen success and assured him that if he chose to return to Bismarck "a 'sit' is open for him."[1]

In May 1874 the TRIBUNE informed its readers that Knappen had returned to Bismarck, and was now "engaged in Life Insurance business having been appointed agent of the St. Louis Life Insurance Company for the line of the Northern Pacific."[2] Knappen was clearly an enterprising young man, for the next

month the TRIBUNE heralded the news that he was selling "White's Portable Fly and Mosquito Net Frames." Numerous complaints about the mosquito problem in the area would indicate that Knappen had found a good line to sell and Lounsberry confirmed this in saying that he was "having an immense sales both here and at the Fort."[3]

The TRIBUNE not only welcomed the idea of a government expedition to the Black Hills but did everything in its power to encourage the idea. After all, as the editor of the TRIBUNE reminded local residents, "These Hills are about 200 miles from Bismarck," and "they can be reached from Bismarck better than from any other point." And certainly the TRIBUNE helped make the lure of gold more irresistable. "As the Christian looks forward with hope and faith to that land of pure delight," proclaimed Lounsberry in June of 1874, "so the miner looks forward to the Black Hills, a region of fabulous wealth, where the rills repose on beds of gold and the rocks are studded with precious metal." The government had to that point succeeded in keeping citizens from exploring the region. But, in May 1874, the editor proclaimed, "the time has now come when the entire army could not much longer keep the country from being over run by the invincible white man—by the hardy pioneer."[4]

Knappen was more emphatic in proclaiming the discovery of gold than the other correspondents, and back in Bismarck Lounsberry worked to uphold his reporter's credibility. He pointed out that correspondents for the CHICAGO INTER-OCEAN, and the ST. PAUL DAILY PRESS, and Custer himself had confirmed the discovery of gold. And while these authorities seemed somewhat cautious in their statements, Lounsberry reminded his readers that "the TRIBUNE reporter had better facilities than any other." Knappen, the editor confided, had been instructed to "go with them, and take off his coat and dig, if necessary." And he assured readers that the miners of the expedition would be unable to keep any secrets from his reporter, "because he is one among them—sleeps with them, and eats with them."[5]

Firm confidence quickly gripped Bismarck that Custer's discoveries had assured the community's future. Several days before the expedition returned, the TRIBUNE reported that local merchants were already "laying in a stock of mining tools, and miner's outfits." These preparations were made upon expectations that an expedition would "undoubtedly leave this point this fall intending to winter in the Hills . . . ." While the TRIBUNE admitted that the Indians posed a certain menace to such an expedition it quickly assured readers that the Black Hills constituted a "neutral ground, and is seldom visited, and then only for hunting." But most importantly, declared the editor, "The very fact that Custer is in command at Ft. Lincoln guarantees immunity from the depredations of hostile bands to a country that the army would soon establish two new military posts —one enroute to the Hills on the Little Missouri and another near or in the Hills themselves. After all, reasoned Lounsberry, "The Government is responsible for the gold discoveries, and will feel bound to protect the settlers who will take advantage of those discoveries." All this, of course, was to prove that the very best route to the New El Dorado began at Bismarck rather than Yankton, Sioux City or Cheyenne.[6]

Three days after the expedition returned to Fort Abraham Lincoln the TRIBUNE reported that exploring mining parties were already outfitting "and men determined to do or die," were planning to spend the coming winter in the Black Hills. These eager fortune seekers, predicted the editor, "can no more be stayed than could be the onward current of the Mill Race flood." While the "hardy pioneer" could take care of himself and the Indians too, "if it is left to him to do it," the TRIBUNE felt that Congress had better purchase the Hills from the Indians "for the sake of decency . . . ."[7]

The TRIBUNE's prediction proved to be accurate and for about three years Bismarck prospered from the gold rush to the Black Hills. Outfitting miners and freighting supplies to the Hills was a booming business. But the boom was short-lived and Bismarck was soon left to seek less glamorous opportunities for growth and prosperity.[8]

Not everyone was overcome by the gold fever. N. H. Knappen, even after seeing the glories of the Black Hills and staking a claim, was able to resist the contagion. Two weeks after the expedition had re-turned the TRIBUNE announced that Knappen had severed his connections with the paper. At the end of September the "Personal" section of the TRIBUNE informed readers that Knappen, "a lively newspaper writer," had just become associated with H. S. Burke of the PERHAM NEWS in Minnesota. Several weeks later Lounsberry reported that Knappen had now secured an interest in the PERHAM NEWS, a paper which he described as "decidedly newsy and neatly printed, creditable in matter and make up."[9] Despite his promising start in the newspaper business things did not go well for Knappen. In August, 1876, he announced to residents of Moorhead that he had taken over the operation of the RED RIVER STAR. His introductory editorial indicated that the STAR was his fourth newspaper in one year. Knappen, determined to make a success of this paper, took in an experienced newspaper man as a partner and changed the tabloid's name to the MOORHEAD ADVOCATE. But failure continued to cast a shadow upon his efforts, and in June 1877 he lost the ADVOCATE to a mortgage foreclosure sale. In the June sixteenth issue of the ADVOCATE Knappen said farewell to Moorhead in an editorial headlined "Down and Out."[10] The final report by the BISMARCK TRIBUNE on Knappen's struggle for success was the fact that it had ended abruptly. On January 5, 1878, Lounsberry announced to his readers that Knappen had died in Albert Lea, Minnesota, on December twenty-sixth at the age of twenty-two years four months and six days.

So ended a brief but decidedly vigorous career in frontier journalism. Knappen suffered much failure and achieved few successes in his short life, but as Colonel Lounsberry aptly put it "few young men under 23 years of age have accomplished half so much." ". . . measuring his life by his deeds," concluded the TRIBUNE's editor, "has he not lived already an average lifetime?"[11] To history and probably Knappen himself the most exciting and important event in his short but intense lifetime was the summer he rode with George Custer to the Black Hills.

FOOTNOTES

1. BISMARCK TRIBUNE, Centennial Edition, July 11, 1973 p. 2A Minn. State Census, 1875, Maroon Lake Township, Ottertail Co., Minn. BISMARCK TRIBUNE, April 22, 1874.
2. IBID., May 13, 1874.
3. IBID., June 3, 1874.
4. IBID., June 17, 1874, p. 1 and May 27, 1874, p. 1.
5. IBID., Aug. 19, 1874.
6. IBID., Aug. 26, 1874.
7. IBID., Sept. 2, 1874.
8. George F. Bird and Edwin J. Taylor, Jr., HISTORY OF THE CITY OF BISMARCK, NORTH DAKOTA: THE FIRST 100 YEARS, 1872-1972, Bismarck, 1972, p. 27.
9. BISMARCK TRIBUNE, Sept. 9, Sept. 30, and Oct. 14, 1874.
10. BRAINERD TRIBUNE, August 18, 1876; RED RIVER STAR, Aug. 4, 1876; MOORHEAD ADVOCATE, June 16, 1877.
11. BISMARCK TRIBUNE, January 5, 1878, p. 1.

BISMARCK TRIBUNE
Issue of June 24, 1874

Personnel of the Black Hills[1] Expedition — Who are Going and for What.

The Best Equipped Expedition ever Organized in this Country.

Poor Lo[2] is Safe if he Behaves Himself — But he may stir up a Hornet's Nest.

CAMP CUSTER'S EXPEDITION NEAR FT. A. LINCOLN, JUNE 23d, 1874.

Special Correspondence Bismarck Tribune.

THE CAMP.

The expedition was placed in camp on the 19th inst.; in order to accustom the horses to the rope, the men to camp life, and to see that nothing is lacking to make the equipment complete. The men amuse themselves exercising their horses and caring for them, while the teamsters are accustoming their animals to each other. It is often the case with expedition of this kind; that at the end of the first day's march, some article of comfort or of vital importance is found wanting, but the few days camp life which Gen Custer, ever thoughtful of the interests of his command has chosen to give his men before starting, will enable them to correct any ommisions of this kind. The camp is pleasantly situated about two miles below Fort A. Lincoln and the men manage to enjoy themselves hugely though they are anxious to be under way.

ORGANIZATION.

The expedition consists of ten companies of the 7th Cavalry, five of which will be under the immediate command of Gen. Custer, and five under the command of Gen. Forsythe, of Gen. Sheridan's staff; two companies of infantry, commanded by Major L. H. Sanger; a battery of three Gatling guns and one Rodman, commanded by First Lieutenant Josiah Chance; a detachment of U. S. Engineers under Col. Ludlow, and sixty Indian scouts, commanded by Lt. Wallace.

THE STAFF.

Gen. Custer issued Order No. 1, on Friday, on assuming command of the Expedition, and announced

1. Who has not heard of the Black Hills and the rich treasures of gold and other precious metals supposed to exist there? Year after year expeditions have been formed or talked of to explore this region, but no reliable information has been obtained concerning it. The expeditions formed have been checked by Government interference or driven off by the Indians. Only a month ago, the Bozeman Expedition returned disorganized and to some extent disheartened, after a month's continuous fighting with the Indians, reporting barren results.

As the Christian looks forward with hope and faith to that land of pure delight so the miner looks forward to the Black Hills, a region of fabulous wealth, where the rills repose on beds of gold and the rocks are studded with the precious metal. Nuggets of pure gold as large as walnuts have been shown and evidence produced as undisputable as that on which the Christian founds his hope that they come from this promised land.

And hence it has come to pass that with the return of every spring-time bold men make their arrangements to explore this region, and the Government officials are kept constantly on the alert to prevent it, but the time has now come when the entire army could not, much longer, keep the country from being over run by the invincible white man—by the hardy pioneer.

Today there is forming on the banks of the Missouri, an expedition consisting of from seventy-five to one hundred of as brave boys as ever drew bead on a red-skin, to be led by the redoubtable Chris. Gilson, and sworn to visit the Black Hills and report. They come in squads from Yankton, from Moorhead, from Jamestown—from the east, the far west, and from the south, and early in June they will meet where provision has been made for crossing the river, and with pack-mules loaded with flour, bacon, ammunition, etc., take up their line of march for the Eldorado of the north.

Who is the brave leader of this band of hardy pioneers? we are asked, and reply, Chris. Gilson, who will live in history and song as one of the bravest men of his time. Those spirits who cannot help admiring the valor of Daniel Boone, or the pluck and persistence of Kit Carson will delight to revere the name of Chris. Gilson. For twenty-eight years Chris. has operated on the western plains, now a guide or interpreter, then occupying positions of higher trust.

For years he has been an attache of the 7th Cavalry—a sort of nephew of the regiment, but of late, Chris. has chosen to take his own course, and in this case he not only proposes to go independent of the 7th Cavalry, but in spite of it.

Gilson will be remembered as the man who in a single handed combat with a party of seven desperadoes, at Sargent City, Kansas, in February, 1873, killed Sam Wright, Thomas McLeland, and Jack Stutzman, shooting also an arm off of another, when the remaining three abandoned the contest. The citizens of Sargent for this act voted Chris their thanks and presented him with a $150 shotgun, and the railway managers gave him a pass for a year over their line of road. In November before, Chris had killed a companion of these roughs named Clayburn, as in this case in self defense.

Those who wish to go with him should apply to him at once at Bismarck. There is no fee, but parties joining will need a mule, gun, rations, etc.

About the 15th of June, ten companies of the 7th Cavalry under the command of Gen. Custer, two sections of artillery under the command of Lt. Chance, accompanied by Lt. Col. Fred Grant and Gen. Forsythe of Gen. Sheridan's staff, Col. Ludlow, and several practical miners will leave Ft. A. Lincoln for the same region. Their mission is a peaceful one. They go to explore the country, a corps of observation and will not interfere with the Indians unless attacked by them. The expedition will not be attended by expense to the Government, as the men and horses will require fewer supplies on the march than in camp.

The discoveries which will surely be made by this expedition will be of immense value to the people of this country. The land is known to be unexcelled for agricultural purposes and there can be no doubt as to the truth of the rumors relating to its mineral wealth. The Bozeman **Courier** has the following relating to the country, which cannot fail to be of interest:

(Cont. col. 1, page 12)

---

2. This is God's country. He peopled it with red men, and planted it with wild grasses, and permitted the white man to gain a foothold; and as the wild grasses disappear when the white clover gains a footing, so the Indian disappears before the advance of the white man.

Humanitarians may weep for poor Lo, and tell of the wrongs he has suffered, but he is passing away. Their prayers, their entreaties, can not change the law of nature; can not arrest the causes which are carrying them on to their ultimate destiny—extinction.

The American people need the country the Indians now occupy; many of our people are out of employment; the masses need some new excitement. The war is over, and the era of railroad building has been brought to a termination by the greed of capitalists and the folly of the grangers; and depression prevails on every hand. An Indian war would do no harm, for it must come, sooner or later. A gold excitement, founded as the Black Hills excitement will be, on the report of scientists and officers sent out by the Government, will give the restless spirits of our land something to do, and all something to think of. Then, give us the construction of the Northern Pacific and possibly the Southern Pacific, not to speak of the many roads which will seek connection with them, or the canals designed to give the West cheap connection with the East, and the bone and sinew of the country will find employment, and a new era of prosperity will dawn upon our country. Who does not recognize the necessity of our people? They must have something to do. Our cities are crowned with men out of employment, our factories are closed, our rolling mills idle—the industries of the country paralyzed.

Custer's expedition may be the pebble which dropped in at an opportune moment will set the mighty sea of American thought in motion, and produce not only the results mentioned, but greater results.

BISMARCK TRIBUNE
Issue of June 17, 1874

(1. cont.)

Parties who have returned from the Expedition to Tongue River all accord in one opinion—that the various valleys traversed by the expedition represent the finest country they ever laid eyes upon. The grass is sufficiently developed even this early in the season to cut, and they are of the opinion that fruits of every kind could be cultivated successfully. Grape vines, plum trees, and a variety of small fruit trees were found in abundance. Ash and timber of a like character was noticeable. Minerals of every kind abound in the ledges skirting the valleys, and from what prospecting was done, there is no doubt of the existence of gold in paying quantities in many of the localities visited. As an agricultural country it stands unrivalled. The warm season there is evidently much longer than we have here, and the valleys are susceptible to the cultivation of cereals of every description. Vegetables requiring longer seasons of warmth than the present settled portions of Montana afford, would thrive in the Yellowstone valley and the various tributaries putting into it. As a stock growing country it possesses superior advantages—mild, short winters, little snow and an abundance of grass.

Within a few short years, should the Northern Pacific Railroad fail to open up to settlement that desirable section the hardy pioneers of the West will make an opening for the more timid immigrant from the East. Even ignoring its known mineral wealth, it possesses other and sufficient attractions to make its acquisition to the uses of the husbandman one of the necessities of the age; and western enterprise will not allow such magnificent natural resources to remain undeveloped. Should the proposed military posts be established in that country, its speedy settlement would follow. The danger from Indians would be modified to make it safe for small parties to prospect and work the mines there, and settlements for agricultural purposes would be made in the numerous rich valleys putting into the Yellowstone.

It is to be regretted that the late expedition did not build stockades and hold the country. It would have been the nucleus of a general settlement of the country, and the red man, as in Kentucky, Indiana and Ohio would have been compelled by moral force to have given way before the grand tidal wave of white immigration from the East and West. Thousands of persons in both sections have been anxiously waiting the results of the expedition. Had the latter gotten a good foothold, tenable even for a short while, sufficient is known of the wonderful resources of the country have made it the signal for a grand rush, putting to flight the present impediment to its peaceful occupation.

BISMARCK TRIBUNE
Issue of May 27, 1874

the following staff appointments, viz: Lt. Calhoun, Acting Assistant Adjutant General; Captain A. E. Smith, Quartermaster; Assistant Surgeon J. W. Williams, Chief Medical Officer.

Dr. Williams is assisted by Acting Assistant Surgeons Allen, of Fort Rice; and Bergen, of Iowa.

Col. Fred. Grant, Aid de Camp on General Sheridan's staff, accompanies General Custer as an Acting Aid.

THE SCIENTISTS.

Several eminent scientists accompany the Expedition. Professor Winchell and an assistant will take the "testimony of the rocks." Professor Grinnell of Yale College, also accompanies and will look after fossils. H. N. Ross, and Wm. McKay, of this place, both practical miners and explorers, are expected to find the gold.

GUIDES AND INTERPRETERS.

Louis Agard, who intermarried with the Sioux, and who speaks the language fluently, and has been in the country 30 years, accompanies the Expedition as a guide and interpreter. Charles Reynolds, a widely known scout and hunter, also goes as a guide.

EQUIPMENT.[3]

Those who ought to know affirm that this is the best equipped expedition that was ever fitted out for service on the plains. It is provisioned for sixty days, and is armed with the new Springfield arm just adopted for the army. Gen. Taylor, who was president of the commission which adopted the arm, declares it the most perfect breech-loading gun yet manufactured. It was submitted to all the known tests, and was adopted after a year's investigation. General Terry says that on one occasion, five shots made at five hundred yards could have been covered by a man's hand. The calibre is reduced from 50 to 45, the ball more elongated, the charge of powder heavier, giving longer range and greater accuracy. The ammunition used by this gun is also used for the new Colt's breech-loading revolver with which the cavalry is also armed.

THE GATLING GUNS.

The Gatling guns will fire 350 shots a minute, and are good for 900 yards. The ball used by the

3. The allowance of transportation for companies serving with the BH E will be one wagon to each comp. In addition to the 100 rounds of ammunition to be carried on the person and in the saddle pockets—there will be six boxes of extra carbine am and one box of extra pistol am carried in the comp wagons.
Wagon for Exped.
Special Orders, No. 3, Hq. BH Exped. Ft. A. L., June 13, 1874. NA RG 393 Orders, BH Exped., 1874.

(Canvas Allowance)
For officers one wall tent to each company & one wall tent to every two officers. In addition there will be one "A" to each officers mess. For enlisted men shelter tents will be used at the rate of one tent to every two enlisted men; one "A" tent will be allowed to each comp. for use of the 1st Sergeant and one "A" tent to each company for protection of mess stores.
Spec. Order #2, Hq. BH Exp. Ft. A. Lincoln, June 12, 1874. Tents & Equipment NA RG 393 Orders, BH Exped., 1874.

Troops of this command during the coming season will wear the campaign hat as perscribed by S.O. No. 92 AGO series 1872.
The cavalry companies of this command will take their Guidons into the field with them this summer.
Troop clothing.
Spec. Orders No. 4, Hq. BHE, Ft. A.L., June 14, 1874. NA RG 393 Orders BHE, 1874.

Bvt. Maj. Gen. George A. Custer

Gatling gun, is a trifle larger than the old minnie rifle ball; the metallic cartridge is used. The cartridges are placed in a hopper and as a crank is turned, a rod is plunged into the end of the cartridge causing the explosion. The guns are ten barrelled, consequently at each revolution ten shots are fired. Should (Lt.) Chance open on the red devils with one of these guns they would think the infernal regions had broken loose on them. Then imagine the effect should the Gatling guns with their rain of leaden hail, be supplemented by the unearthly shriek of a three-inch Rodman.

CONFIDENCE.

No wonder that Gen. Custer is confident that the Indians cannot successfully cross his path. Armed as this expedition is, officered as it is, no body of Indians likely to be brought to bear on it, could seriously embarrass it. They can only harrass it by picking off here and there a straggling man; the favorite game of the savage, the ambuscade, is too well understood to be feared.

OBJECTS OF THE EXPEDITION.

Gen. Dandy informs us that when at Fort Laramie, a squaw brought into that post a nugget of pure gold as large as a hen's egg, which she claimed came from the Black Hills. Other specimens have been brought in by the Indians from time to time, and the Indians questioned concerning the country invariably tell of the rich minerals, or are so evasive as to create all the greater interest. "Running Antelope" in a conversation with Gen. Custer lately, said that the great objection the Indians had to the white man exploring the Black Hills was that they would want to take the country when they learned of its mineral and agricultural wealth. So it has come to pass that an impression has obtained throughout the country that this is a perfect Eldorado, and believing that an exploration should be made, which would give valuable information, this expedition was organized, and is sent out by the Government. Time and again, expeditions fitted out by private parties have been backed by the

Government, because if permitted to go on their own responsibility, they might not only trespass on the rights of the Indians, which this expedition will not do, but would be liable to be massacred by the wily savage. Indeed several parties have already been murdered in years agone, and of parties seeking to visit this region, not a man has returned. Yearly the disposition to visit the Black Hills, on the part of the restless spirits among our mining population, has been growing, but now that the Government has taken the matter in hand, they will bide their time.

PACIFIC MESSAGES.

Pacific messages have been sent to the Indians; they have been given to understand that this is not a measure of war, but of peace; that if they will let the expedition alone they will not be molested— their rights will not be interfered with. And Gen. Custer hopes they will take heed and let him alone.

THE INDIAN'S STRENGTH

Still the young men have left their reseravtions, and are gathering in the vicinity of the Black Hills; they are about 5,000 strong, and if they attack at all it will be in force.

GEN. CUSTER.

To Gen. Custer, of whom a coarse wood cut appears at the head of this article, more than to any other, does the credit of the organization of this expedition belong. The Gen. has faith in this country, and desires to promote its developments. He thinks it a burning shame that so vast a region, reputed so rich in minerals and agricultural resources, lying almost in the center of the continent, surrounded except on the north by civilization, should so long remain unexplored.

The General has had much experience with the Indians, he has studied their history and their customs; he understands their rights and appreciates their wrongs. He has been their friend and their prosecutor. He won, during the late War, a reputation of which he might well be proud, and it is peculiarly fitting that this work should be entrusted to him.

OTHERS.

The efforts of Gen. Custer to secure the exploration of this

South Dakota State Historical Society

Custer crossed the north fork of the Cannonball River in North Dakota on July 7, 1874. It is likely that this is the first photograph taken by St. Paul Photographer William H. Illingworth who accompanied the expedition. The contingent had stopped to camp. Livestock can be seen grazing in the upper left and the sun is still bright enough to illuminate the landscape.

country have been warmly supported by Gen. Sheridan and the commander of this Department, and while it is not an expensive one to the country, it is indeed an important one.

There is much more that I wish to say concerning this expedition, but my letter is already long, and I must defer. I promise you, however, that I will keep you posted, giving all incidents of interest that occur on the march, brief descriptions of the country, a faithful account of discoveries, &c. (sic).[4]

The expedition has been delayed a day or two in order to receive the new arms. It will probably move on Monday next.

K.

4. The Bismarck **Tribune** has kindly sent us a Chromo of Gen. Custer, which they publish and distribute as a premium with their excellent weekly. The **Tribune** is a lively paper published on the frontier and gives all the news in that locality together with information to all who intend visiting the gold fields in the Black Hills country. Terms $2 per year. Address **Tribune**, Bismarck, Dakota Territory.—Austin (Minn.) Independent.

BISMARCK TRIBUNE
Issue of October 28, 1874

BISMARCK TRIBUNE
Issue of July 8, 1874

THE CHASE FOR GOLD.

Interesting Gossip Concerning the Expedition—A War Dance—The Indian Couriers—Their Power of Endurance—A Politician Heard from—Starting—On the March—General Custer's orders, &c., &c.

CAMP CUSTER'S EXPEDITION
Near Ft. A. Lincoln, July 1, 1874
Special Correspondence
Bismarck Tribune

DELAY.

The new arms arrived yesterday, and were issued today, tomorrow we shall break camp and take up our line of march for the Black Hills. The delay of a week or more, caused by the non-arrival of the new arm, has been decidedly irksome to the civilians invited to ac-

Although each wet plate had to be individually prepared in a complex and time-consuming process, Illingworth seemed to follow the pattern familiar to many photographers of taking "just one more." He took this second and closer view of the Cannonball. Men can be seen swimming at the center right while others are on the far right shore. Captain of Engineers William Ludlow described the Cannonball as "a fine stream, 30 feet to 75 feet in width and one foot to two feet in depth flowing with swift current over a shaly bed through a well wooded valley . . ."

company the expedition; but Gen. Custer's hospitality has been boundless and the officers and ladies of the command have vied with each other in attentions to the "guests of the expedition" for so the scientific corps must be regarded, as they go on the invitation of the commanding officer, and without pay from the Government.

CORRESPONDENTS.

The newspaper corps, consisting of gentlemen representing the New York Tribune, Chicago Inter-Ocean, St. Paul Press, St. Paul Pioneer, and the Bismarck Tribune, have enjoyed themselves hugely, and anticipate no small amount of excitement while on the trip, and as newspapermen love excitement

as a duck loves water, they are reasonably happy.

AN AMATEUR SCARE.

In addition to the Scouts to accompany the expedition mentioned in my last letter, twenty-five Santees have arrived and will go with us. They are a fine looking set of fellows, and are a good deal more than half civilized. Sunday the Indians from the Fort were wandering over the country, and succeeded in getting up an amateur Indian scare, which of course appeared to be a big thing in print, when telegraphed east. If I mistake not, so soon as the cavalry is gone Fort Lincoln may anticipate genuine scares, for wandering bands of Sioux will surely come

down to steal stock, and make trouble in other respects.

A WAR DANCE.

As the good man is taught to pray before entering on any great and important undertaking; the Indian is taught to dance. And as we were expecting to move today the scouts had a big war dance last night. They made the night hideous with their yells. Imagine ye noble reds dressed only in war paint, feathers and breech clouts. A score or more braves gather, accompanied by their wives, children and sweethearts, and the disturbance begins. Knives, tomahawks, clubs, swords, pistols, or whatever they fancy for the purpose, are swung high in air, and crouching, cringing, springing, weaving, dodg-

Illingworth had his first opportunity to take a spectacular picture of the expedition when Custer camped at Hiddenwood Creek, North Dakota, on July 8, 1874. Illingworth set his camera on a cliff, facing north, with the creek in the immediate foreground and to the left. Tents flanked the wagons (center) on three sides, to protect them from hostile attack.

ing hither and thither, their movements are accompanied by those thrilling yells which have stricken terror to so many hearts.

POWER OF ENDURANCE.

It is wonderful how rapidly news is transmitted among the Indians, and it is in the accomplishment of this work that they show the most wonderful power of endurance. News is received that it is important it should go to some distant tribe or village, one or more Indians prepare for the work. A feast is made and they eat and dance; eating as much as a dozen white men wo'd (sic) eat; they call on their neighbors and eat again, and continue dancing and eating until nature exhausted forces sleep. After sleeping a few hours they eat again, and are then ready for business. They mount the fleetest pony in camp and are off, riding day and night, without food, water or rest for five days sometimes. Arriving at their destination, they state the news, and another round of feasting and dancing commences, to be followed perhaps by a tramp of two hundred miles more in another direction with the news to another tribe. By these couriers every movement of Custer is reported, and long before his command reaches the Black Hills the Sioux will be apprized, not only of his approach but of his strength.

ANTICIPATED TROUBLE.

The Sioux, through whose country this expedition will go, are strong and brave. They have always been the foe of the white man, and consequently have not been demoralized through intercourse with them. They can muster about five thousand young men, and if they attack Custer at all it will be in force. It is believed, however, that they will not attack or trouble us, except to hang around the outskirts of the expedition and pick off a man as they can, steal stock if opportunity presents, or draw a small detachment into ambuscade. But Gen. Custer has studied the Indian so long that he understands his mode of fighting as well as poor Lo understands it himself, and anticipates no danger.

FORT LINCOLN.

During the absence of the cavalry command, Col. Poland will have command at Fort Lincoln. The garrison is small, but it will keep constantly on the alert, and it is not believed that it is possible

South Dakota State Historical Society

This photograph was taken from the identical position as the one on the facing page. In a map he drew on the area, Capt. Ludlow described it as having alkaline soil and poor grass. He labeled the "country sterile." Two days later the expedition ran into hordes of grasshoppers. The shadow from one leg of Illingworth's tripod can be seen in the lower right hand corner.

for even a thousand Indians to do greater harm than the running off of stock herded into the vicinity. They might do that with Custer's entire command in the camp, though they failed in their attempt last spring.

The officers' wives remain at Lincoln, and do not apprehend the least danger. Mrs. Custer remains at the barracks in order that she may receive news from her husband, as couriers come in. Couriers will be sent in every week, and I shall be able to keep the Tribune constantly posted.

A POLITICIAN HEARD FROM.

Gen. Custer informs me that he receives letters from all parts of the country, in relation to the expedition, from men who volunteer all sorts of advice, and who want to go with the expedition for all sorts of reasons. One man, a lawyer, writing from Kansas, thought he ought to be allowed to go because he was a delegate to the Philadelphia Convention. But Gen. Custer, not being a politician, did not take any stock in him.

K.

———

BIG SLOUGH, JULY 3.

The expedition broke camp yesterday and took up its line of march for the Black Hills, making thirteen miles the first day.

THE ORDER OF MARCH.

First the Indian scouts, consisting of thirty-eight Santee and twenty-two Arickarees, mounted on native ponies, commanded by Lt. Wallace, one of the bravest and best officers in the command. The Santees are dressed in cavalry uniform, the others in their paint and feathers.

Gen. Custer and staff marching at the head of the column, is followed by the artillery, commanded by Lieut. Chance; the wagon train following, guarded by two companies of infantry. On the right flank march five companies of cavalry, commanded by Gen. Forsythe, of Gen. Sheridan's staff, and on the left five companies, commanded by Col. Telford, of the 7th cavalry. Gen. Forsythe and Col. Telford alternately furnishing a company of cavalry for rear guard.

Thus it will be seen that every precaution is taken to keep the command intact and be prepared at all times to repel assaults.

NO FIRING ALLOWED.

Gen. Custer has issued strict orders not to fire on Indians making their appearance unless they show unmistakable signs of hos-

South Dakota State Historical Society

This unusual outcropping of rock caught Illingworth's eye while he was taking photographs of Custer's Camp at Hiddenwood Creek. The process of preparing the glass wet plates was difficult enough, that once Illingworth had his equipment set up, he tended to make several exposures. Sometimes he would simply point the camera in a different direction from the same vantage point, which may have been the case here.

tility. No Indians have yet been seen.

BREAKING CAMP.

The scene in the morning, as the expedition breaks camp, is grand indeed—decidedly so to those of us who are not familiar with military movements. The several commands, as they take their positions in line, and spread out in some broad valley or plain, showing their full force to the best advantage, with the band playing, presents a scene decidedly enlivening, and which must strike the Indian, even, with wonder and admiration.

THE COUNTRY.

The country so far is decidedly rolling—the knolls rising to the dignity of abrupt hills or buttes. The country is not at all similar to that east of the Missouri river, and so far greatly inferior to it; but it must be remembered we are in the vicinity of the confluence of the Little Hart and Missouri rivers—a fact which may account for the roughness of the country. The country is well watered and the hillsides abound in a stinted growth of timber.

SUN STROKES.

Yesterday was exceedingly hot.

Five of the infantry surrendered under the intense heat, and one teamster fell from his horse, overpowered by it; but none are seriously affected.

CROSSING THE HART.

This was found to be no easy task, but the command was got across after two or three hours delay, and without loss of stock or material.

N.H.K.

**BISMARCK TRIBUNE
Issue of August 5, 1874**

CUSTER.

Progress of the Expedition—
The Country—Incidents of
The March—Ludlow's
Cave—Hunting, &c.

CAMP CUSTER'S EXPEDITION.
SHORT PINE WOOD
JULY, 15, 1874.

THE MARCH.

The march has been a hard one, over a country in the main uninviting though much of it well adapted to grazing. Some of the Valley's are exceedingly rich and beautiful. Such is the case in the valley in which we are now encamped.

WOOD AND WATER.

There has been but little wood on the route, scrubby stuff skirting the streams only (sic) We have found plenty of water; and pretty good except in the Grand River country where it was alkaline. Our marches have averaged about 18 miles per day, and at night we have always found wood, good grazing and water. One day we marched 31 miles. The animals are all in good condition and the men cheerful.

LOCATION.

Our present camp is about 225 miles from Bismarck — probably 175 in straight lines, as we made a detour of sixty miles to see a cave, of which the Indians told us such wonderful stories of which more hereafter. We are still in Dakota, though within a few miles of the Montana line.

INCIDENTS.

Little of interest has occurred on the march except hunting to relieve the monotony. An occasional accident to men or animals causes

South Dakota State Historical Society

Michael Smith was wagonmaster for the Custer Expedition. He had the distinction of being the only individual on the trip, with the exception of Custer, whom Illingworth photographed alone and closeup. Illingworth was undoubtedly mindful of good public relations with Smith. Illingworth had been provided with a specially enclosed wagon which acted as a portable darkroom. He was frequently allowed to travel at the head of the column or beyond it, in order to take pictures. Smith is well armed. He is leaning on his rifle and wears a pistol in a holster in front of his left thigh with the handle facing his right hand. It appears from the terrain that this picture could have been taken while in camp at Hiddenwood Creek in North Dakota.

delay; one of the horses was bitten by a rattlesnake but our very efficient veterinary adopted effective remedies and the animal was saved. The bite was followed by sweating, blindness, trembling and staggering. These reptiles abound in great numbers and live with the owls and prairie dogs, in the homes of the latter.

LUDLOW'S CAVE.

Our guides had told us much about a cave which was regarded as the home of the great spirit; and they said buffalo, elk, deer, antelope, and various other animals and reptiles appeared there in a translated state, but it turned out to be a very insignificant affair.

The cave is about twenty feet wide at the entrance and extends back several hundred yards — perhaps ten feet high, evidently made by the action of water in the lime rock, and on its walls are crude carvings intended to represent various wild animals made by Indians though perhaps by tribes other than those now occupying the country.

A SKULL.

Near the cave was a skull which the physician pronounced that of a white man, perforated by a bullet, whose it was, or when killed, are questions that will probably never be answered.

INDIANS.

No Indians have been seen on the route until within the past two or three days, when several parties have been noticed in the vicinity. The Indians seem to be gathering in our front, and we have noticed columns of smoke going up, which our guides say is a signal, and they regard an attack imminent. We do not fear the result however, should the Indians attack us, as we are strong enough to fight five times our number of the red devils.

STANLEY'S TRAIL.

Stanley's trail of last year, can be plainly traced, as our may be for many years to come. The tracks made by the wagons are the plainest, but the paths made by each file of infantry or cavalry are plainly marked.

HUNTING.

It is well known that Gen. Custer is extremely fond of hunting, and he has had much of it on this trip, so far. Every day the General may be seen in buckskin and broad-brimmed hat, accompanied by his faithful hounds. Every day the officers feast on antelope, which abound here in great numbers. It is almost impossible to keep the men from firing on the fleet-footed animals as they rush across the path of the command, and it can-

not be done at all times. A few days ago, the men in charge of one of the Gatling guns, left their piece for a chase after antelope. The team attached to the gun, became frightened, and away they dashed, "hell-to-split over the prairie." They soon struck a slough, however, and miring, were captured. The drivers were dismounted for a day, as a punishment for their neglect. Gen. Custer's pack of full blooded Scotch staghounds take an important part in the chase, and the few Englishmen in the command are supremely happy when they are in full chase after a jack-rabbit or an antelope.

FOSSILS.

Prof. Grinnell has found an important fossil, it was a bone about four feet long, and twelve inches in diameter, evidently a bone of the mastodon or some animal still larger.

PETREFACTIONS.

Some very fine petrefactions have been discovered, some weighing several hundred pounds; Gen. Custer will probably allow some of them to be brought into camp on the return.

CONCLUSION.

The expedition is now five miles from the Little Missouri, and about

Ludlow's Cave is located in North Dakota between the north and south forks of the Grand River. It was visited by the expedition on July 11, 1874. Custer named the cave in honor of Captain of Engineers William Ludlow. The Indian guides had attributed a good deal of wonder and mystery to the cave, alleging that it was a dwelling place for the Great Spirit. Correspondents with the expedition reported the cave walls to contain crude drawings of buffalo, elk, antelope, deer, beaver, fish, birds and reptiles. Numerous artifacts such as arrows, bows and flints were found in the cave. Custer, in writing to his wife Elizabeth, said, "I cannot account for the drawings of ships . . ." This view is from the mouth of the cave, looking out. It was described as being eight to 10 feet high, 12 to 14 feet wide and 230 feet deep.

Through the years this picture has carried the caption "locality not known." It appears, however, to be in Wyoming, south of Belle Fourche River, which would date it to about July 18 or 19, 1874. At this point the expedition was less than a week away from entering the heretofore unknown portions of the Black Hills.

five days' march from the Black Hills. We do not expect to be able to communicate with civilization until the return of the command— probably about the 1st. of September.   N. H. K.

(Author's Note: In 1874, because of telegraph delays and other communication difficulties, news dispatches from the field frequently reached newspaper offices out of order from the sequence in which they were originally written. To preserve the chronology of events, we have arranged the dispatches in the order of their writing, which means that some of the issue dates appearing at the top of pages and in the columns will be out of calendar order).

BISMARCK TRIBUNE
Issue of August 19, 1874

EL DORADO.
THE BEAUTIFUL LAND OF THE DAKOTAS.

What a Tribune Correspondent Saw in the Black Hills.

HILLS GLISTENING IN THE SUN, AS IF SET BY GEMS OF SILVER.

All is not Gold that Glitters, and yet Gold is Found.

CUSTER'S VALLEY,
BLACK HILLS,
AUG. 2nd, 1874

Special correspondence,
Bismarck Tribune.

On the 16th ult. (sic) the march was resumed from Short Pine Creek in a westerly direction, over the ridge into the valley of the Little Missouri, thence south up the river for about twenty miles and leaving it again on our right.

THE LITTLE MISSOURI.

This river rises in Wyoming and runs in a southwesterly direction through Western Dakota, and empties into the Missouri above Fort Berthold. It is a crooked and turbid stream, its banks covered with a fair growth of timber.

The valley of the Little Missouri is pretty to the eye, but judging from the parched condition of the grass drouth prevails to an alarming extent. It could be easily irrigated, however, and in that case must be exceedingly productive.

Thirty miles were marched on the 16th, and a dry camp at night. The camps on the 17th and 18th, were made in the bad lands, which

The early morning shadow of photographer Illingworth, his camera and tripod can be seen in the foreground as he faced west to photograph Inyan Kara, in Wyoming. The peak, which towers 6,374 feet above sea level, was the most impressive topographic feature seen to that point by the expedition. Inyan Kara was first recorded by the Warren Expedition in September of 1857, and was presumed by members of the Custer Expedition to be 6,500 feet in height.

need no description. Here they are about five miles wide, however, and range north of the hills.

THE BLACK HILLS.

On the 18th, for the first time the Black Hills were seen. On the 19th, we camped on the Belle Fourche River, near the camp of Capt. Reynolds, which was made fifteen years previous to a day. The camp is on the Belle Fourche —the North Fork of the Cheyenne —and in the skirts of the Hills. Here we laid over Sunday, being delayed by a fearful rain storm which lasted from Saturday until Sunday afternoon.

From Bitter Creek to the Belle Fourche, a distance of about eight miles, the Hills were of a sand stone foundation, perfectly barren excepting a few pine trees, and were covered with a thin layer of black ashes, resembling fine coal, from which they take their name.

THE WESTERN PASS.

On the 21st, after ascending the ridge on the south side of the Belle Fourche we came into a beautiful tract of table land and after crossing this, reached the west pass into the Black Hills, which is a smaller but beautiful valley, which, though not extensive, would make the finest kind of farms.

With the exception of a small tract lying south of the Red Water Creek, which is red sand and marl, the soil is a deep black loam, extremely productive. Heavy dews fall — so heavy that good crops could be produced without a drop of rain, while the facilities for stock growing are unsurpassed.

Inexhaustible beds of gypsum, in some instances 25 feet thick, and as pure as crystal, are found here.

BEAVER CREEK.

This small stream empties into the South Fork of the Cheyenne, and derives its name from its inhabitants — the beaver. The valley is extremely beautiful and highly productive.

MT. INYAN KARA

was visited by Gen. Custer and staff, one of the reporters and the scientific corps, escorted by two companies of cavalry. Col. Ludlow with much difficulty reached the highest point of the mountain, leading his horse, and high on its

Minutes after the first exposure, Illingworth took a second picture of Inyan Kara. The Custer Expedition had camped five miles to the east of the famous mountain on July 22, 1874. Illingworth was up early on the morning of July 23 to photograph the peak while Custer ascended it with his staff and several members of the scientific corps.

flinty side cut the following name and character, viz: "Custer." "74".

The height of this mountain is 1,100 feet above its base and 7,700 feet above the sea, being 1,500 feet higher than any other point of land in the United States. The mountain covers about 12 square miles.

A PARADISE.

Floral Valley I believe is one of the most beautiful spots on God's green earth. Beautiful flowers are on every hand, from which cavalrymen gathered bouquets while on their horses. Springs from the mountain sides form beautiful rills which ripple along over their pebbly beds, the waters colorless, tasteless and pure.

When the band plays, the music dances on the mountain tops, dives into the caves, rushes through the valleys and is returned again by the charming echoes, and the noise of a rifle sounds like that of a cannon. No wonder the Indians regard this the home of the Great Spirit. My pen fails me in describing the flowers of this valley. Among them may be found geraniums, asters, the gorgeous lily, the modest daisy, the retiring violet, the coarse gaudy sunflower; and about fifty other varieties. Game abounds on every hand. Elk antlers are strewn over the prairies, as are buffalo horns at Bismarck.

This is indeed a beautiful land, a very paradise, and no wonder the untutored savage guards it with jealous care. The soul would be dead indeed, which could not appreciate the beauties of this region.

CASTLE VALLEY.

The march continues, the scenery changing from lovely to grand. High precipices rise on either hand several hundred feet; trout brooks spring from the mountain sides. The command feast on wild fruits of almost every kind. There are thousands of acres of raspberries, fine and luscious. The hills are pine clad, and magnificent, resembling castles, from which the name was derived. Through this valley Castle Creek flows into French Creek, a branch the South Fork of the Cheyenne.

CUSTER PARK.

This beautiful valley in which we are now encamped, exceeds in beauty, loveliness and grandeur all others. Travelers tell me that nothing known compares with it. The scenery is more interesting than that of the Yosemite, of the Yellowstone or Central Park. The Park is about fifteen miles long by three wide. I'll not attempt a description but leave that for abler pens.

NOT ALL GOLD THAT GLITTERS.

The micaceous rocks in the hill sides, as we approach this park, glisten in the sun, and the mountains sometime look as if set with silver gems, and in some instances the sky and landscapes are reflected as in mirrors, but all is not gold that glitters.

FOUND AT LAST.

In this valley gold was at last found, and though bed-rock has not been reached, the most skeptical must be convinced that it is here.

Messrs. Ross and McKay are confident there are rich diggings in this region as were ever discovered, but those who come out expecting to fill their saddle bags, haversacks, pockets, &c., with the precious metal, are disappointed, for the largest chunks are not on the surface. The explorers have secured in some instances as high as fifty cents from one pan. While the researches have not been extensive, enough is known to warrant the statement that the placer and quartz mines are rich beyond comparison, while there is every facility for mining. The country too is sheltered and operations can be carried on until late in the fall, and early in the spring.[5]

ACCIDENTS AND INCIDENTS.

On the 30th, Lt. Chance's horse fell with him, cutting a deep wound below the knee, making a fearful but not dangerous wound.

On the 17th M. Cunningham of H. Troop was taken with dysentery from which he died on the 21st. Nothing is known of Cunningham's relatives. He was a good soldier.

On the same day a dispute arose between privates William Rollins and James Turner, which resulted in the death of Turner, shot by Rollins. The trouble grew out of an old affair of two years' standing. Rollins found his horse tangled in the picket rope and blamed Turner, who had been on stable guard, for it. Hard words followed. Turner struck Rollins, who drew his pistol and shot Turner, the ball striking the left elbow, passing into the stomach and lost itself in the backbone, causing

5. The reports are now all in, and the news of the gold discoveries sent by the **Tribune** special is confirmed. Gen. Custer is very cautious in his statements, but he mentions one instance where fifty pieces of gold, the size of a pin-head, were taken from one pan. The **Inter-Ocean** correspondent, drawing his inspiration, to some extent, from Gen. Custer, who has requested the correspondents to be particularly careful about exaggerating, throws cold water on the discoveries, but mentions another instance where thirty-five cents were secured from two pans of dirt. Miners can put this and that together, and draw their own conclusions.

BISMARCK TRIBUNE
Issue of August 19, 1874

death in about eight hours. Those who saw the affray say Turner was trying to draw his revolver. Rollins gave up his, remarking that he had to shoot or be shot; but Turner on his death-bed insisted that he did not attempt to draw his revolver until Rollins' revolver was pointed at him.

Turner spoke of a brother-in-law at Jeffersonville, Indiana. He, too, was a good soldier, and was buried in accordance with military custom.

INDIANS.

The dusky natives have been seen in small bands, but they have not interfered with us; we have not even had a good scare.

As we came into this valley we struck a fresh trail and followed it about ten miles; came upon their camp of the previous night, in which the camp fires were still smouldering. Here the command halted and Lieut. Wallace was sent forward with his scouts. Only a few moments elapsed before one of the scouts returned and reported five lodges of Indians two miles away.

BOOTS AND SADDLES

was sounded, and Gen. Custer, with one company of cavalry, went dashing down the valley to where the scouts were secreted, and your correspondent, armed with a lead pencil followed.

Louis Agard, who speaks the Sioux language, was sent forward with a white flag, with instructions to inform the Indians of our presence and objects. A detachment of Indian scouts followed some distance behind, to support him in case of treachery on the part of the Sioux.

The Ree, it is well known, are hereditary enemies of the Sioux. Here they thought they saw a chance for a fight, and they decked their heads with feathers, painted their faces and were happy in thinking of the glorious scalp dance that would follow the fray.

"Do not fire a shot unless the Sioux attack you," was the stern order of the pale face chief which dampened the arder of the dusky scouts somewhat, for they knew too well what a violation of that order would cost.

Gen. Custer, followed by two or three, among them your correspondent, leaving the command in the valley, climbed to the crest of the hill overlooking

THE INDIAN VILLAGE.

How pretty the little village of clean white tepees nestling in the valley below appeared. The inhabitants, unconscious of our presence could be seen moving about — the children at play on the green.

The sides of the valley were covered with a dense growth of pine, affording shelter for a concealed foe. General Custer ordered up Col. Hart with the remainder of the command, as it was possible the flee tepees might be only a decoy. The precaution was a wise one, but unnecessary.

Again cautioning the Rees concerning an unprovoked attack, Gen. Custer ordered the scouts to advance on the village, presuming the approach of the scouts would create less alarm than would that of the cavalry.

The women and children were alone in the village. The Indians were hunting in the forests. All was serene for they had not heard of the advance of the white man.

The children were struck with consternation and fled to the bushes. The squaws were almost dumb with fright, and Agard's words did little to assure them.

SLOW BULL.

One of the men named Slow Bull was near, and bravely came forward, but he was alone, and what could he do to protect the village?

Agard pointing up the valley, said: "Here comes the white chief, the one in the blue shirt, galloping at the head of his command. Let him assure you of our good intentions." Coming upon the village at a rattling pace, Gen. Custer was the first to alight from his horse and greeting Slow Bull with the customary Indian salutation, "How," grasped Slow Bull by the hand, and smoked with him the pipe of peace; the squaws meantime, had become at ease, and the children returned to their play ground.

Slow Bull said he was a good Indian. He was certainly hospitable, and we were invited inside and introduced to his wives, one of whom was a daughter of Red Cloud, and the Indians were Unkapapas, from the Red Cloud Agency.

South Dakota State Historical Society

Custer was accompanied to Inyan Kara by two companies of cavalry; they, however, did not make the ascent. Illingworth moved closer for this exposure. Capt. Ludlow accompanied Custer to the summit. Ludlow reported in his journal that ". . . the Sioux fired the prairie to the south and west. After two hours of waiting, the smoke having only grown denser, we returned to camp."

MRS. SLOW BULL.

Mrs. R. C. Slow Bull was a very pretty looking Indian woman. Her long black hair was neatly braided, and her dark bright eyes and white teeth gave expression to a countenance indicating a warm heart.

She, with her neighbors, had been very much frightened, but when she found that their scalps were safe she resumed her gum chewing and became very sociable, and was really glad to welcome us and entertained us in a lively manner. Her tepee was the neatest and cleanest of the five. The family effects not needed for immediate use were packed away, neatly tied up in clean skins. The floors were carpeted with other skins, and on every hand was evidence of taste and industry — and vanity as well.

Mrs. Slow Bull is not only a fashionable woman, but domestic as well, and has an eye to business. After the ice was broken, she informed Gen. Custer that she had not a bit of coffee or sugar and the children had been crying for some days for both.

The General informed her that he would make the little ones happy by supplying this deficiency, when she chatted more sweetly, Agard acting as interpreter, your correspondent amusing himself reporting the conversation infinitely superior to the senseless gossip which is too apt to prevail in civilized society.

During the conversation, Mrs. S. B. took up one of her little ones, and studied its craniology with more minuteness than would be considered polite in good society, but it was no doubt quite necessary.

ONE STAB.

One Stab, the chief of the band, an old and shiftless fellow, came in and he also smoked the pipe of peace with us. And after a long interview between he and Gen. Custer, One Stab concluded to go with us and remains with us at the present time acting as our guide.

CONCLUSION.

We shall remain in this valley five days and then proceed to the head waters of the Little Missouri and return to Fort Lincoln.

Our camp is situated in latitude 43:36 deg. and longitude 103:30 deg.: about 180 miles south of Bismarck — in a direct line probably 240 miles southwest.   N. H. K.

(Mr. Knappen's letter continues at some length, detailing Gen. Custer's interview with the Indians and its result, but is omitted because its substance was given last week in Gen. Custer's official report. — Ed. Tribune.)

BISMARCK TRIBUNE
Issue of August 12, 1874

GOLD!
EXPEDITION HEARD FROM.
Custer at the Black Hills on the 2d inst.

THE MOST BEAUTIFUL VALLEYS THE EYE OF MAN EVER RESTED UPON.

Gold and Silver in Immense Quantities.

NO FIGHTING WITH THE SIOUX.

Two Privates Lost — One by Disease — One by Accident.

CUSTER'S BLACK HILLS EXPEDITION, AUG. 2. VIA FORT LARAMIE, WYOMING, AUGUST 3, 1874.

Special dispatch to the Bismarck Tribune.

We reached here yesterday; the command being in good health and spirits. We have lost two men since last report, both of them were privates. One of them was shot by a member of his company, and the other died of sickness. A small party of Sioux met with on the 27th; but we have had no fighting as yet. Charlie Reynolds carries dispatches from this point to Fort Laramie.[6] Since the command struck the Black Hills, we have been prospecting in a continuous line, in the most beautiful valleys man ever looked upon.

Here, in Custer's Valley, rich gold and silver mines have been discovered, both placer and quartz diggings; and this immense section, bids fair to become the El-Dorado of America.

The march will be renewed from here on the sixth, for the head waters of the Little Missouri, and from thence to Ft. Lincoln.[7]
        N. H. K.

7. BLACK HILLS
How do you like it?
Glorious, isn't it?
Count me in for the Black Hills.
There is no string on me; Black Hills or bust; say I.
Some one will surely organize a party.
Col. Wilson's hotel will be in demand; there ain't bed room enough in this town to hold the people who will come nor has Uncle Sam military enough to stop them from going.
It must be true; Knappen's word is as good as gold. I am off for the diggings.
The townsite contest can go to — — I'll find my money with a pick and pan.
Knappen's dispatch is worth a thousand dollars to me. I feel that much better off, no matter if it does prove false.
Such were the exclamations heard on every hand when, on Monday morning, the Tribune published an extra, giving news from the expedition. The greatest excitement prevailed. Men who for weeks had been despondent because of the grasshoppers, the drouth, the townsite trouble, and the universal dullness, brightened up and were themselves again, and a better feeling prevails in town than has been felt since the panic last fall, when the bottom fell out of everything that had Northern Pacific in it.
Why? Because Bismarck is the nearest railroad station to this new Eldorado. This is the nearest point for outfitting, the nearest point for supplies. Parties going to and returning from the Black Hills will pass this way, and everyone of them will contribute to our wealth. Bismarck will be a Cheyenne or Denver repeated, and will contain within the next three years from five to ten thousand inhabitants. Many fortunes will be made and lost, and Bismarck will be the town which will gather the gold.
No wonder Bismarck people were happy.
Then, too, we have our full share of floating population, who have been waiting for something to turn up. This gives them an outlet—something to hope for, something to do.
We hope by next week to receive full advices by mail, when the glorious news will certainly be confirmed, and details probably given.
        BISMARCK TRIBUNE
        Issue of August 12, 1874

6. Reynolds had just come in from Fort Laramie, on his way to Bismarck, and was interviewed by a Sioux City **Journal** man. He reports the distance from Fort Laramie to Custer's Valley, as 200 miles. Charley had made it alone, through an Indian country. He performed a similar service for Gen. Stanley, last summer, carrying dispatches 200 miles to Fort Benton.
The **Journal** says Charley is not at all excited as to gold, but says while he did not pick up any nuggets, and did not know that any of the expedition had, he knows that there is gold there, for he had seen the explorers wash surface dirt which yielded two or three cents to the pan, and it was the opinion of the practical miners along with the expedition, that if the earth should be removed down to the bed-rock, rich deposits of the precious metal would be found. When Reynolds left, no thorough researches had been made; only a little surface digging having been attempted, but enough had been done to indicate gold, and probably in great quantities, the indications, as the miners say, all being rich. Every member of the expedition is satisfied that the Black Hills are rich in gold and silver.
Gen. Custer, with five companies of cavalry, accompanied Reynolds to a point on the south fork of the Cheyenne, where he left him on the 3d inst. Reynolds traveled principally in the night, eluding the observation of the Indian war parties, watching the expedition, with which the country is full.
        BISMARCK TRIBUNE
        Issue of August 19, 1874

BISMARCK TRIBUNE
Issue of September 2, 1874

Black Hills Correspondence.
Custer's Gulch — The Tribune
Man and Others
Take Gold Claims — None
Disappointed at the Results of
the Expedition — "Poor Lo must
Fall" — Game Killing a
Grizzly — Custer, Bloody Knife
and Bear — Black Hills Region.

CAMP CUSTER'S BLACK HILLS
EXPEDITION, BEAR BUTTE,
LONGITUDE 103 DEG.,
LATITUDE 44 DEG.,
SATURDAY, AUGUST 15TH,
1874.

Special Correspondence
Bismarck Tribune:

On the morning of the 6th inst., the command took up its line of march for Bear Butte, where it arrived last evening. Bear Butte is about 160 miles south of Bismarck and 110 miles west, say 215 miles in a direct line.

Custer's Park is about 40 miles south west, though to reach that point we have marched 105 miles, tramping around through valleys and ravines.

EXPLORATION COMPLETED

The exploration of the Black Hills is now completed, but the General will probably

EXTEND HIS EXPLORATION

up the north fork of the Cheyenne, and to the head waters of the Little Missouri, then returning to Bismarck by another route — though, undoubtedly, a direct one. You need not look for us before the 31st inst:

GOLD AND SILVER.

Gold, silver, plumbago and iron, and immense beds of gypsum have been found — the two former in paying quantities.

On the morning of leaving Custer Park, in what will hereafter be known as

CUSTER'S GULCH,

the following notice might have been seen posted by the side of a shaft sunk by Mssrs. Ross and McKay:

Correspondents and soldiers alike were universal in their praise for Floral Valley. Dozens of species of wild flowers were reported growing there. Custer gave the valley, located in eastern Wyoming, its name because of the profusion of flowers. Correspondent Nathan Knappan of the BISMARCK TRIBUNE described it as ". . . one of the most charming little valleys in the world." The expedition passed through the valley on July 25, 1874, just before entering South Dakota. To the Indians the valley was known as Minne-Lusa, or "Running Water." Spring water in the valley was measured at 44½ degrees Fahrenheit.

District No. 1, Custer's Gulch,

Black Hills, August 5th, 1874.

Notice is hereby given, that the undersigned claimants do claim (4,000) four thousand feet, commencing at No. 8, above discovery, and running down to No. 12 below and do intend to work the same as soon as peaceable possession can be had of this portion of the territory by the general government, and we do hereby locate the above claims in accordance with the laws of Dakota Territory governing mining districts.

H. N. Ross, discoverer, 400 feet.

Mike Smith, below discovery No. 1
Walt. Comer   "   "   No. 2
W. J. Konnelly,   "   "   "   3
W. T. McKay   "   "   "   4
Dan Manning,   "   "   "   5
Henry Henning,   "   "   "   6
N. H. Knappen,   "   "   "   7
Dick Matherson,   "   "   "   8
Harry Roberts,   "   "   "   9
James Brook,   "   "   "   10
Tim. Hose,   "   "   "   11
Geo. Bosworth,   "   "   "   12
Pat Smith, above discovery   "   8
C. W. Freede,   "   "   "   7
F. Weddle,   "   "   "   6
Alex. McBeth,   "   "   "   5
C. Bassett,   "   "   "   4
Samuel O'Connell,"   "   "   3
George McCabe, "   "   "   2
James McGee,   "   "   "   1

This is a sluice diggings, and is estimated at $10 per day to a man.

NONE DISAPPOINTED.

No member of the expedition is disappointed at the result of the expedition and the belief is common among members of the expedition that there are not troops enough in this department to prevent the immediate occupation of the country by miners.

Why not occupy the

BLACK HILLS?

It is now well known that though the Black Hills country belongs to the Indians, it is not occupied by them, and is seldom visited by them. Because of their superstition it has been held as a sacred spot to them — as the

HUNTING GROUND OF THE GREAT SPIRIT.

and, just here, permit me to remark that the belief prevails among the command that if the Great Spirit should determine to seek a hunting ground, he would go no further than the Black Hills for it.

GAME OF ALL KINDS ABOUND,

and in unlimited quantities.

It is a fact recognized by all, that there are no finer grazing lands in the world, than are those in the valleys of the Black Hills, and none can see any reason why they should not be occupied by the adventurous white man. I dare say that none consider the rich deposits of gold and silver, the abundance of game, the soil, water and timbed—the fact that the country abounds in everything that will make a great State prosperous and wealthy, will for a moment agree with those who think that this country should still be left in the hands of the Indians, who like the

DOG IN THE MANGER,

will neither occupy it themselves or allow others to occupy it.

It is true the expedition was an affair of peace, not intended to bring on hostilities—nor has it brought them on—for not a shot has as yet been fired at the hostile Indians—none have made their appearance, but the news 'ere this is abroad in the land, and the restless spirits from all localities will flock to the frontier towns, and they will break for the Black Hills, and will reach them, too, and to prevent it would require a larger army than it would take to guard the Rio Grande, were every Mexican determined to supply himself with American stock.

And in the conflict which follows

POOR LO MUST FALL,

for though he has some rights that white men are bound to respect he has none that

INFATUATED GOLD HUNTERS

will respect.

The facts should be considered by the Government and immediate steps taken for the peaceable extinguishment of the Indian titles.

GAME.

I said game was abundant. So it is. There are deer, black and white tailed, elk, black and grizzly bears, mountain sheep, mountain lions and all manner of fur bearing animals.

KILLING A GRIZZLY.

Gen. Custer and Col. Ludlow, on the 7th inst, killed a grizzly which weighed about eight hundred pounds. Six or eight shots were fired before the old fellow surrendered. On receiving the first shot he cocked himself up on his hind legs, and showing his huge teeth, he grinned in defiance; but like all who fight Custer, he was compelled to surrender.

ANOTHER GRIZZLY.

On the same evening, the Santee scouts killed the mate to the one killed by Custer and Ludlow, which was even larger than the male, but before bringing her down, the noble Santees fired shots enough to extinguish the whole Sioux nation.

The one killed by Custer and Ludlow had claws fully five inches long, and teeth or tusks as long as a man's finger, which were set outside the lips, making an animal somewhat ferocious in appearance. I have rode inside the columns since I saw those jaws—would rather see old Sitting Bull than such a bear.

A PICTURE WORTH HAVING.

Illingworth took a photograph of the stricken monarch, with Gen. Custer, Col. Ludlow, and Bloody Knife the Sioux Guide, standing around it.

BEAR BUTTE REGION.

We entered the Hills from the west side, through the Western Pass, and sought an outlet through the northeast, which we found, though not without considerable difficulty.

The formation of this portion of the Hills is the same as that of the western portion. The lower range is covered with a black substance which resembles crushed coal— possibly lava—the upper range is of red sandstone. Bear Butte is about two and one-half miles outside the Hills. There is but little timber on it, and it is surrounded by prairie. Next to Harney's Peak, Bear Butte is the highest of the hills.

BEAUTIFUL LANDSCAPES

After leaving Custer's Park on the 6th, we marched for two days through a beautiful country— parks and valleys—of which the Black Hills are full; the landscapes in many instance arranged as if by art. On the 8th we marched through a forest destroyed by fire and storms—desolate enough, I assure you; but soon we struck another section as lovely as the loveliest. The 11th was spent hunting for an outlet through the Hills— the 12th and 13th in the same way, but yesterday we struck the prairie about twenty miles southwest from this point.

PARTING.

All regretted to leave the Hills with their pleasant groves, beautiful lawns, ice cold brooks, and luscious fruits and gems of gold and silver.

For no country has nature done so much as for this, leaving so little to be done by the husbandman. The open and timbered spaces are so divided that a person can obtain a farm of almost any dimensions, from an acre upwards, with the proper proportion of timber and prairie, with pure babbling brooks, in which the water is only 12 degrees above freezing the warmest days in summer.

Nature seems to have gone further, and has located choice building sites amid evergreens, flowers and shrubs.

The soil is deep black loam, between 3 and 4 feet deep, moist and exceedingly productive. There is every indication of an abundance of rain, while the ground is not torn by torrents.

MORE ABOUT GOLD.

The scientific corps accompanying the expedition, have examined mineral resources, although not thoroughly, as the halts have been brief, and it is the opinion of those who are in a position to know, that the minerals are as rich as any in the world.

I saw a prospect taken from one pan of earth which yielded fifty pieces of gold the size of pin heads. This was taken from a shaft in Custer's Gulch. Gold was found in the grass roots, and in the earth, in paying quantities, to a depth of eight feet.

Miners estimate that gold to the extent of one hundred dollars per day to the single man, can be secured from one locality prospected.

CONCLUSION.

All the officers of the command are well, except Lt. Chance, who is still lame, but is getting along nicely.

James King of H. troop, 7th Cavalry, died on the 13th of dysentery. He had been ailing for three days, but he refused to leave the ranks until the day previous to his death. King's friends reside at Des Moines, Iowa, and he is spoken of as a good soldier.

Two games of ball were played in the Hills, of which I have forwarded the score. They speak for themselves.

N.H.K.

BISMARCK TRIBUNE
Issue of September 2, 1874

BLACK HILLS.
The Tribune Correspondent Makes a Final Report. Return of the Expedition. Gen. Custer's New Command, &c.

FORT A. LINCOLN, D.T.
AUGUST 31ST, 1874

Special Correspondence
Bismarck Tribune.

On the morning of the 16th, the march was renewed for Lincoln, the command moving in a northwesterly direction for the further exploration of the Little Missouri, crossing the Belle Fourche 20 miles from Bear Butte.

Soon after breaking camp on the morning of the 16th, four hostile Sioux were seen, and Bloody Knife was sent forward to interview them. They said there was a war party ahead, and that in Prospect Valley the whole Sioux nation was waiting for us, but no Indians were seen and no signs excepting a small trail, which was some days old, leading east.

After leaving the Belle Fourche, no running water was found until we struck the Little Missouri, on the 18th. The weather could not have been better for marching, and good time was made. We laid over at the Little Missouri on the 20th, and on the 21st started down that that (sic) stream, following the east ridge to avoid the bad lands, striking the river at night, in order to get water, wood and grazing. On the 23rd we crossed the trails made by the surveying parties of the Northern Pacific in '71 and '72, following the latter through a portion of the bad lands, and thence across the country to Heart River, where

we struck the trail made by Gen. Stanley on his return from the Yellowstone last fall, and from there Custer made a straight road to the crossing of Heart River, 12 miles west of Fort Lincoln where we arrived last evening. It was the impression of all that we would halt at the crossing of the Heart and go in next morning, but on arriving there, the following order was promulgated, much to the surprise of all:

"The command will march at 1:30 for Fort Lincoln, laying here one hour. The order of march will be as follows: First the Indian scouts, commanded by Lt. Wallace, Gen. Custer and staff, the band, the right and left battallions, comprised of 19 companies of the 7th Cavalry, the wagon train, accompanied by two companies of infantry."

The surprise, unlike some of Gen. Custer's surprises, was an agreeable one to those interested, and the command came in from Heart River, 12 miles, like a train of cars, and of course astonished the anxious ones at Lincoln, as none expected the expedition would arrive until the next day.

It is useless for me to say that Custer's Black Hills Expedition has been a decided success throughout —the fact is well known by all, and may memories live in the hearts of the American people. Through the untiring energy of Gen. G. A. Custer, a Paradise hitherto unknown, rich in numerous minerals, has been make (sic) known to the world, and now all that remains to be done, is for Congress to open this beautiful land for settlement, and protect those who go there, from its present worthless inhabitants—the Indians.

Seventy-seven miles out we buried Sergeant Stempker, of L Troop 7th Cavalry, who died on the 26th of Aug. of dysentery. He had been a member of the company nearly four years, and was highly spoken of by all who knew him. I was unable to ascertain anything concerning his relatives excepting that his people lived in Boston, Mass.

Good grazing was found from the time we struck Heart River to Lincoln.

That section of country lying along the line of the Northern Pacific for one hundred miles west of

Bismarck is the best and most desirable farming lands that I have seen in Dakota Territory, excepting the Black Hills, fully as good as the Red River Valley. The valleys of the Heart River, Sweet Brier and the Big Muddy are not very extensive but contain a deep fertile soil, with plenty of water and considerable timber.

Our route home was somewhat out of the way, taken with a view to finding the source of the Little Missouri, which has heretofore been unknown, still by cutting off the bend made from Bear Butte to the Heart, it would afford a practical route to the Black Hills.

I am satisfied, however, that the route suggested by John W. Smith, the late purveyor of the Black Hills expedition, is the shortest and best route of any suggested from the Missouri. He suggests a direct line from Bismarck to Bear Butte, entering the Hills through the Northern Pass. This route is over a fertile an (sic) comparatively level country, crossing numerous streams, affording wood, water and grazing.[8]

Mr. Smith has resided at the lower agencies for many years and knows every route which has been suggested and he is satisfied that this is the route for exploring and mining parties to take.

On arriving at Fort Lincoln, Gen. Custer reported to the Adjutant General of the Department of Dakota, closing his remarks as follows.

After the Head waters of the Heart River were reached we moved almost due east to this post. We examined and located that portion of the Little Missouri hitherto unknown. We marched about one thousand miles and my command, with replenished supplies, is in good condition to take the field tomorrow.

On his arrival, the General must have been gratified to find an order awaiting increasing materially his command the middle District of the Department of Dakota, which embraces Forts Lincoln, Stevenson, Rice, Grand River Agency and Camp Hancock, with Headquarters at Lincoln.

The Headquarters of the 7th cavalry heretofore at St. Paul, will also be moved to Lincoln at an early day.

N. H. Knappen

8. There is a new, direct, and well marked trail from Bismarck to the Black Hills, made by the return of the expedition.

Gold in the grass roots, and at a depth of eight feet is not bad, particularly when the amount yielded is $100 per day to each miner.

The men who made the Black Hills gold discoveries reside at Bismarck, and will accompany the first expedition to the new El Dorado, which will be fitted out at Bismarck.

Bismarck merchants are already laying in a stock of mining tools, and miners outfits. An expedition will undoubtedly leave this point this fall intending to winter in the Hills where there is an abundance of game of all kinds.

BISMARCK TRIBUNE
Issue of September 2, 1874

(From the Cheyenne Leader, Aug. 29)

As the forthcoming official report of General Custer will fully establish the fact that the Black Hills country is rich with precious minerals, we deem it our duty to point out to those who intend to go to these new mines the safest, shortest, and most practicable way of getting there. Cheyenne is barely 220 miles from the Black Hills, via Fort Laramie and the Red Cloud Agency; it is not more than 200 miles, going direct from here to Red Cloud. At this agency there is a large military post affording protection to this frontier, and from Red Cloud to the Black Hills it is only fifty miles. The road from here to Red Cloud, either by Fort Laramie or by the old Red Cloud Agency on the Running Water or Niobrara River, is SETTLED A GOOD PART OF THE WAY by ranchers and stockmen, so that supplies, aid, and protection can be had on this line to within fifty miles of the mines. Those who wish to go to the Black Hills can find no other route so desirable in every respect as this. Those living east, south, and west, especially, will find it shorter, safer, and better than any other route. It is shorter for those living farther north toward St. Paul, than the route via Bismarck. People from the Eastern states, who go by St. Paul to Bismarck, will find that, after having made the immense detour of travel required to reach Bismarck, their serious troubles are just to begin. From the latter place to the eastern base of the Black Hills it is at least 300 miles, through what are known as the "Terres Mauvais," or bad lands of Dakota; utterly uninhabited, except by the most savage tribes of Indians, and completely unprotected the entire distance.

FROM SIOUX CITY

the route, all wagon travel, is fully 600 miles, nearly the whole distance through a hostile country, affording neither supplies nor protection. Bismarck is 500 miles northeast of Cheyenne, and emigrants going to the Black Hills via that place, are liable to encounter the severe storms which make that latitude so undesirable in the fall and winter months. From Cheyenne to the Black Hills it is only 200 miles, with good roads, a settled country, and military protection.

SIX DAYS' EASY TRAVEL

from this city will take the miner to his place of destination. From Sioux City it will require nearly a month of hard travel, and from Bismarck almost as long, to say nothing of the danger from hostile Indians the whole distance. Our readers have only to refer to any War or Interior map to be satisfied as to the truth of the statements here made as to distances, and as to this being the nearest point to the Black Hills, a point made easily accessible from all directions by the Union and Kansas Pacific Railways.

CHEYENNE HAS FACILITIES FOR OUTFITTING

miners and emigrants superior to any other place along the Union Pacific Railroad. It is from this place that all the supplies are shipped for the troops at Fort Laramie, Red Cloud and Spotted Tail, and large trains for this post are consantly moving over the road. Regular weekly mails leave this city for Fort Laramie, Red Cloud and Spotted Tail, bringing postal facilities to the very door of the reported gold region. Altogether there is no route proposed that can offer anything to compare with the route from Cheyenne, so far as safety, protection, supplies and distance are concerned.

The route up the Missouri River

TO BRULE CITY OR FORT RANDALL,

as recommended by the Sioux City papers, is one full of delays and uncertainties. Within a month's time the country between these points and the Black Hills is liable to be covered with snow from one to twelve feet in depth. The Missouri River itself will also soon be closed to navigation for the winter, and not be open again before April or May next year. The route from this city is open the year round, with the best of roads, plenty of wood, water, and grass, and one other great consideration which no other route can offer—a line protected by military posts almost to the base of the Black Hills. From whatever direction the tide of emigration may seek the new Eldorado, the road to the south, to Cheyenne, is bound to be the line of communication with the outside world. It is near two railroads, open to all seasons, and with mail facilities already extending to within fifty miles of the mines—200 miles nearer than any other postal communication.

THE ROUTE VIA BISMARCK,

is hardly worth considering; it is impracticable, except for large parties; it is exceedingly dangerous, much longer and more difficult in every respect. No one would, in his proper senses, think of undertaking to go in that direction, when a shorter, safer and better line is open to him. The road from here to Red Cloud; (fifty miles from the mines) is safe for everybody, no matter how small the party. It is traveled constantly the year round, by mail carriers, army officers and by immense freight trains. Arrived at Red Cloud, the miner is near his objective point. The richest discoveries made by General Custer were on the southwest side of Black Hills. The principal discoveries of gold were on the southwestern slope of Wyoming Territory, near the table mountain called Inyan Kara. People approaching from the east may find precious minerals on that side of the Hills but it is far more likely that they will have to pass around or through the mountains to the points indicated by General Custer, before they are rewarded for their labors. The above statement we are ready to substantiate by official reports of military officers who have been stationed in Wyoming and Dakota for years, and by the testimony of our old settlers, traders, and hunters, who have spent a life-time in this section of the country.

FROM A DENVER STANDPOINT.

Charles Reynolds, Custer's trusted scout, who has returned from the interior via Fort Laramie and Cheyenne, furnishes some interesting information. Mr. Reynolds, who has lived for years in Colorado, and is well known to many of the old residents, is a young man of quiet, reticent disposition, extremely anxious to say nothing but the unexaggerated truth, and to tell nothing of which he is not fully acquainted

Custer, in describing Floral Valley, is quoted by Correspondent Samuel Barrows in the NEW YORK TRI-BUNE as saying, "Its equal I have never seen." William Curtis of the CHICAGO INTER-OCEAN described it as ". . . a paradise, and every man of the expedition stood silently to enjoy and admire." Capt. William Ludlow recorded in his journal that it was ". . . filled with the greatest profusion of wild flowers in almost incredible numbers and variety." In this picture, an unidentified rider is standing behind his horse on the far right. In several Illingworth pictures, one or more individuals appear, apparently having accompanied the photographer to a site, either in advance of, or remote from, the expedition.

through personal experience. Mr. Reynolds, gives as a reason why the Black Hills have been so assiduously guarded by the Indians that the abundance of game of all kinds, and the un-surpassed stock ranges afforded by the well-watered and heavily-timbered valleys, afforded both protection and sustenance to the families of the Indians while the heads of the latter were out making raids on neighboring tribes, or on their regular visits to the various agencies for government annuities; added to which the Indians were aware that a knowledge of the rich mineral deposits that lay undeveloped within its limits would be a powerful incentive to stimulate white occupancy. Mr. Reynolds says that all through the hills were found fresh

TRACES OF LARGE INDIAN CAMPS

but the Indians took the precaution to move out of the route of the Custer invasion. The vague notions that have been entertained about where the mineral belt of the Black Hills is located must, in the light of information gained by the explorations of the Custer expedition, become revolutionized. Many persons, supposed to be well posted on the Black Hills regions, contended that the northwestern range or tier of the Black Hills was where the mineral wealth would be discovered, but the developments brought to light by the miners and explorers accompanying the expedition show that the previous metals are found, if not exclusively, at least in the

greatest abundance, on this side of the Black Hills range.

GETTING READY.

There is a perfect fever of excitement at Chey-enne over the news from the Black Hills region. It is the regular gold fever. A most fascinating mystery has existed for years regarding the character of the country. The news brought back, from time to time, by scientists and military expeditions, has always commanded, es-pecially in our mining districts, the most eager interest. The present excitement grows out of the Custer expedition. The Mills expedition, which is soon to leave Cheyenne for the Big Horn country, will serve to keep alive the ex-citement at least until winter. A party of pros-pectors, some of whom have but recently re-turned from the San Juan mines, are outfitting now at Cheyenne for the trip, and expect to go straight to the Black Hills, taking their scalps in their hands.—DENVER NEWS.

CHICAGO INTER-OCEAN
Issue of September 2, 1874

ILLINGWORTH THE PHOTOGRAPHER

William H. Illingworth

equipment was both bulky and heavy, the process intricate, the weather hot, and the travel long and hard.

In the spring wagon provided him, Illingworth packed his cameras, a supply of heavy glass plates, chemicals, and a portable darkroom. The entire collection of equipment probably weighed nearly 400 pounds. The procedure Illingworth and other photographers of his time followed while in the field went something like this. By some means, probably part way by wagon and the rest of the way on foot, he carried his heavy camera, darkroom tent and processing supplies to the site he had selected. After setting up the camera on its tripod and focusing it by means of the ground glass back, he would proceed to set up his portable darkroom. It was necessary to have the darkroom close to the camera, for with the wet

While the newspaper correspondents brought Americans a verbal description of the Black Hills and the expedition's personnel, it was William H. Illingworth who created a visual account through the magic of wet plate photography. Colonel William Ludlow, the engineering officer in charge of mapping and the scientific study of the region to be explored, hired Illingworth to make a photographic record of the expedition. In return for agreeing to provide the government with six sets of whatever photographs he might take while in the field, Ludlow furnished Illingworth with all equipment, supplies and rations, and arranged to have him included on the roll of civilian employees as a teamster drawing a salary of $30.00 a month. It was his skill as a photographer that Illingworth brought to Dakota territory that summer. The government provided him with everything else.

Ludlow's choice of photographer was in a technical sense an excellent one. Illingworth produced over seventy photographs of the country traversed, the expedition and the people on it. His choice of subject and view as well as the quality of the pictures themselves were exceptional. These were not easy achievements given the conditions under which Illingworth was forced to ply his trade. The photographer's

This ink sketch of Custer is in the photo archives of the Minnesota Historical Society, and was apparently drawn by Illingworth. It is likely that the sketch was made from a projected photograph—a sophisticated method of tracing. No portrait of Custer like this is with any of the Illingworth glass plates in the South Dakota State Historical Society collection. It may be possible that Illingworth took a portait of Custer while he was in Dakota Territory. There are Custer pictures somewhat similar to this but they are not credited to Illingworth.

Photographer William Illingworth captured this dramatic view of the Custer Expedition's two mile long wagon train as it entered Castle Creek Valley in the western part of South Dakota's Black Hills. In this instance, he proceeded ahead of the wagon train, climbed a high hill and obtained this spectacular picture. The exposure time for wet glass plates ranged from 10 to 15 seconds. Obviously the train halted for the picture—apparently just before it broke up for camp in the valley.

plate process, the negative had to be developed before the emulsion on the plate dried. In the dry heat of a Dakota summer Illingworth had to work quickly. The glass plate was prepared by first giving it a coat of collodion and potassium iodide and then immersing the plate in silver nitrate before the collodion became hard. The silver nitrate bath had to be timed very precisely or the plate would be ruined. Three minutes was sufficient time, but since the strength of the solution often varied Illingworth had to determine the exact timing by feeling the corner of the treated side with his finger. After removing the plate from the silver nitrate solution Illingworth had to move quickly. First, he clamped the plate in a light-tight holder, then ducking out of his stiffling tent his sweaty hands would insert the plate in the camera and pull out the cover slide. With a quick wipe of the brow he would then remove the lens cap and carefully count off ten seconds or so. Then to plunge back into the suffocating tent to develop the plate before the emulsion dried. Illingworth would first coat the plate with a ferrous sulfate solution, at

the exact moment wash it with water to halt the developing process, and immerse it in a fixing bath of potassium cyanide. After the plate was dry Illingworth had another delicate glass negative to care for until he returned to his St. Paul studio where he would produce the prints. The quality of his negatives was so good that it is possible to read the labels on the wine bottles in one of his pictures with the aid of a magnifying glass. Illingworth was obviously a man of great skill and energy to be able to produce such a large number of fine photographs.

Colonel Ludlow was undoubtedly pleased by Illingworth's conscientious work while in the field. But back in St. Paul after the conclusion of the expedition, Ludlow's estimation of his hired photographer changed dramatically. Instead of the promised six sets of prints, Illingworth gave Ludlow only one partial set, pleading a lack of money as his excuse. At the same time, however, Ludlow noted that the photographic firm with which he was affiliated, Huntington and Winne of St. Paul was advertising full sets of the prints for sale to the general public.

It is quite likely that this second picture of Castle Creek Valley, looking east, was taken shortly after the one on the preceding page. Illingworth would sometimes make an exposure in one direction, then turn his camera on its tripod and take a second picture of a different scene, in the opposite direction, from the same vantage point. It was in this valley that the expedition encountered Indians. Several of the newspaper correspondents mention seeing Indian trails. A very obvious trail from travois poles can be seen extending from the center right of this picture.

Ludlow promptly lodged an embezzlement suit against Illingworth in the St. Paul courts. When the photographer escaped conviction through a legal technicality, Ludlow urged the War Department to press charges. But in the end the Judge Advocate General decided to drop the matter. Illingworth's glass negatives remained in his possession until his death in 1893. Sometime later they were discovered in a St. Paul attic and eventually given to the South Dakota Historical Society.

Although a professional success, Illingworth did not have an altogether happy personal life. He was born in England in 1844 and came to Philadelphia with his parents as a child. In 1850 the family moved to St. Paul where his father established a jewelry business. Illingworth apparently assisted his father until he was about twenty years old when he traveled to Chicago to learn photography. In 1866, shortly after returning to St. Paul, he accompanied the Fisk emigrant expedition to Montana Territory. The thirty stereoscopic pictures he produced on that journey probably were the basis of the studio and gallery he opened in St. Paul the following year.

In 1893, Illingworth ended his own life with a bullet in his head. His son, seeking to explain the tragedy, stated that he had been despondent over ill health, but clearly Illingworth had additional reasons to be melancholy. Married three times, his first two wives died, and he had divorced the third shortly before his death.

Even though his life was short, Illingworth's contribution to history was significant. While most photographers never ventured out of their studios, Illingworth often hauled his cumbersome gear into the out-of-doors and recorded early views of Minneapolis, St. Paul, and other parts of Minnesota. Today the Minnesota Historical Society is the proud owner of many of these Illingworth photographs. Most important to our subject, however, is the fact that in the summer of 1874 he and his camera were with Custer as he explored the Black Hills.[1]

South Dakota State Historical Society

It is possible, and even likely, that this exposure was made by Illingworth just after he took the picture, from a high vantage point, of the wagon train entering Castle Creek Valley (see previous page). Limestone Peak stands in the background. Livestock graze in the center. A few tents have already been pitched near the head of the wagon train, and other preparations for camp are about to begin.

FOOTNOTE

1. Information on the life of William H. Illingworth and the photographic technique of his time came from the following sources: T. M. Newson, PEN PICTURES OF ST. PAUL, MINNESOTA AND BIOGRAPHICAL SKETCHES OF OLD SETTLERS, St. Paul, 1886, p. 234; Henry Hall, "Restless, Troubled Opportunist: Portarit of a Pioneer Photographer," RAMSEY COUNTRY HISTORY, IV (Spring 1967), pp. 9-11; and Donald Jackson, CUSTER'S GOLD: THE UNITED STATES CAVALRY EXPEDITION OF 1874, New Haven, 1966, pp. 60-63.

South Dakota State Historical Society

Some minutes later, Illingworth moved slightly to his left and shot the same landscape again, as on the preceeding page, but the scene had changed. By this time the wagons had dispersed, tents had been pitched and the men were settled down and ready for supper. Custer's camp was located northwest of the present village of Deerfield, parallel to Castle Creek and Highway 110.

Five horsemen can be seen to the center right of this picture. Apparently, Illingworth was accompanied by one or more men whenever he went away from camp to take pictures. Such action was prudent because of the possibility of attack by hostile Indians, and practical because of having assistance in hauling the bulky photographic equipment. Not infrequently, one or more individuals appear in Illingworth scenic shots. One can presume that someone was usually standing near him during those exposures where no person appears.

ST. PAUL PIONEER

Aris B. Donaldson

Although the ST. PAUL DAILY PIONEER arranged to have Professor A. B. Donaldson serve as its special correspondent with the expedition, it regarded his dispatches as at best second page material. The fact that the editor of the DAILY PIONEER buried the Black Hills news on the inside pages was not a reflection of the quality of the dispatches themselves. But it was intentional. If a Minnesota newspaper was to promote interest in any western area it was going to be western Minnesota, not Dakota Territory.

In 1874, Minnesota lay at the edge of the northern middle border frontier, and its residents were understandably proud of the progress they had made during sixteen brief years of statehood. They had wrested from the wilderness a booming state of flourishing cities, towns, and farms whose produce was being moved on an ever expanding system of railroads. The population of Minnesota had passed the half million mark in 1874 and a heavy flood of immigrants was continuing to pour into the state. Much of the credit for the rapid settlement of Minnesota belonged to the promotional activities of the railroad companies. But the frontier press clearly had earned a share of that credit as well. During the 1850's and 1860's enterprising editors had established newspapers in the towns that blossomed on the Minnesota frontier. By 1870 six dailies and seventy-two weeklies brought news to local residents and proclaimed the manifold virtues of Minnesota to outsiders.[1]

The history of newspapers in Minnesota began in 1849, the same year that territorial status was achieved—when James M. Goodhue, a Yankee printer, brought out the first issue of the MINNESOTA PIONEER in St. Paul. And although ownership changed hands several times and at least two mergers with other papers occurred, in 1874 the ST. PAUL DAILY PIONEER stood as a true descendant of the state's first tabloid. During the Civil War the DAILY PIONEER had been a Democratic paper, no easy role in a heavily Republican region. And after 1865 the paper passed through six different owners until 1874 it was purchased by David Blakely, a Republican. But whether Democratic or Republican in political persuasion, it was first and foremost a Minnesota paper.[2]

The DAILY PIONEER did not send a professional correspondent to accompany the Custer expedition to the Black Hills in the summer of 1874. Instead it made arrangements with A. B. Donaldson, who was to be the expedition's botanist, to write exclusive accounts of the trip for the PIONEER as well. As the editor of the PIONEER at one point told his readers, "Professor Donaldson is a gentleman of fine scientific attainments, a keen and accurate observer, and his statements possess the merit and reliability, which is not always found in letters of professional correspondents."[3]

Aris Berkeley Donaldson, born in Muskingum county, Ohio, on February 20, 1831, graduated from Ohio Wesleyan University with honors in 1855, and except for service with the Union navy during the Civil War taught school in Ohio until 1869. In that year he was hired as one of the nine original faculty members of the University of Minnesota when it opened its doors for the first time that September. He served as professor of rhetoric and English literature at the University until 1874 when he resigned to accompany the Custer Expedition. The next year Donaldson purchased the ALEXANDRIA (Minnesota) POST from L. S. Gilpin which he edited until his sudden death on November 27, 1883.[4]

Donaldson was always referred to as professor even after he had left the teaching profession. His obituary in the DOUGLAS COUNTY NEWS of November 29, 1883, calls him professor Donaldson and William Curtis of the CHICAGO INTER-OCEAN remarked in his dispatch of July 23, 1874, that Donaldson "alone, of the titled scientists/on the expedition/ is exclusively known as . . . the Professor." Indeed, Curtis was much intrigued by Donaldson and on at least two occasions described the Professor's special qualities. At the outset of the expedition, Curtis confessed, everyone had regarded this corpulent professor with his face wreathed in whiskers as "a singular curiosity in human nature." But after they came to know him, he continued, "the good old fellow's kind heart, unselfish motives, characteristic politeness and hearty enjoyment of everything make him a favorite everywhere, and, notwithstanding his pedantry, it cannot but seem that he is a great child enjoying a summer's holiday." As editor of the ALEXANDRIA POST Donaldson was also well loved by local residents. The writer of his obituary in 1883 described him as being unassuming but very capable, "a sincere Christian, and supporter of the Temperance Cause."[5]

Professor Donaldson's faithful and constant companion on his "summer's holiday" was a horse named Dobbin. Curtis described Dobbin as "a long, lank beast, very deliberate in his movements, but perfectly docile, and exactly to the Professor's taste."[6] Donaldson and his Dobbin ambled their way from Fort Abraham Lincoln to the Black Hills and back in July and August, 1874. The Professor gathered flowers, bulbs and plants, charmed and entertained his fellow travellers with stories and composed epistles which described the people around him, the daily events, the land and something of himself for the readers back in St. Paul. Donaldson's personality is clearly reflected in his dispatches. They contain careful observation, insight, imagination, good humor and more than a touch of a professor of rhetoric and English literature.

FOOTNOTES

1. George S. Hage, NEWSPAPERS ON THE MINNESOTA FRONTIER, 1849-1860, St. Paul, 1967, p. 124.
2. IBID., p. 126.
3. PIONEER, Aug. 14, 1874, p. 2.
4. A. B. Donaldson's Obituary, DOUGLAS COUNTY NEWS, Alexandria, Minnesota, November 29, 1883. E. Bird Johnson, Ed., FORTY YEARS OF THE UNIVERSITY OF MINNESOTA, Minneapolis, 1910, p. 31.
5. IBID.
6. Curtis letter to the INTER-OCEAN of July 27th.

ST. PAUL PIONEER
Issue of July 1, 1874

THE BLACK HILLS

The Favorite Stronghold of
the Red Man.

Something About the Objects of
Gen. Custer's Expedition.

Special Correspondence of
The Pioneer.

FT. ABRAHAM LINCOLN, D. T.,
June 26, 1874

THE SIOUX

The nation of Sioux Indians now comprises about 35,000 souls. It is divided into thirteen tribes. About one-third of the tribes may be regarded as friendly to the whites, one-third as semi-hostile, and the other third as uncompromisingly and implacably hostile.

This great nation, including all its tribes and bands, occupies the extensive reservations assigned them by the U. S. government. These reservations lie almost wholly within the Territory of Dakota, and west of the Missouri river. A considerable part of this reservation is but little known, and especially is this true of a portion situated in the south west quarter of the Territory, and known as the

BLACK HILLS.

This region, so mysterious and about which so much has been conjecturally said, lies between the North and South Forks of the Cheyenne River. It is somewhat triangular in shape, its base line separating the two forks and being near 100 miles in length. The other sides are shorter, their apex being in the angle formed by the junction of the two branches. It is known that the outer side of these hills is covered with heavy timber, and that from them flow the numerous streams which supply to North and South Cheyenne. It is believed that within are rich mines of precious metals, and rare plants and animals living, and fossiliferous, with which the scientist is unacquainted. It is the famed stronghold and favorite hunting ground of the red man. It is even dearer to him than the land of the "graves of his forefathers." He believes that the souls of the departed revisit these earthly abodes, and in spiritual forms pursue the spiritual game over the old, familiar hunting grounds. To the simple faith of the Indian, it is the most sacred spot of earth, to him the "holy of holies."

"Here the souls of the happy dead repair

From their bowers of light
to this bordering land.

And walks in the fainter glory there
With the souls of the living
hand in hand."

The Indian would preserve it inviolate and conceal all its mysteries; the white man would reveal its wonders, unlock its secrets, and satisfy the eager world with information. Superstition and ignorance here stand in opposition to truth and civilization. This will explain why this region has so long remained in terra incognito to all except the non-communicative savage. So eager the white man's desire to explore, and so determined the purpose of the Indian to prevent it, that attempt and resistance have frequently resulted in loss of life to both parties.

What private enterprise has failed to do, the government now proposes to accomplish. Hence the organization of the present

EXPEDITION TO BLACK HILLS

The purposes of this expedition are not military or aggressive. They are all peaceable and exclusively in the interest of science. Geographical, topographical and geological information is sought. To accomplish this, everything pertaining to the expedition is made auxiliary. The very strength and formidableness of preparation are to enforce a peace by rendering opposition futile and disastrous.

Of the peaceable intentions of the government all the tribes have been notified, and they have been assured that they will not be molested or disturbed in the least degree, provided they do not commence hostilities.

RUMORS AND
EXAGGERATIONS.

All sorts of reports, some of them utterly false and many others exaggerations huge, are being circulated here and printed elsewhere. It would be easy to write whole columns of these sensational and exciting stories. One hundred thousand Sioux warriors, armed with Henry rifles, dwindle to not exceeding 5,000 all told, as the utmost possible available force of all the hostile tribes, while in the whole nation there could not probably be found 500 Henry rifles. A white man stealing an army mule grows into a raid by yelling savages stampeding whole herds of long-eared quadrupeds. A single hostile Indian seen far away, is, by some perspective illusion, brought dangerously near, and by a mirage peculiar to western plains, is multiplied into hosts invincible.

ENEMIES LURKING NEAR,

but they are few and keep at safe distances, and from them no attack need be feared. Our scouting parties and picket guards may have some trouble, but further than this it is not probable that there will be hindrance to our peaceable advance.

DELAY.

In order to furnish the expedition with the most improved fire arms, it has been found necessary to wait here until Monday the 29th.

My next letter will give an account of the military organization of the expedition, its officers and appliances, and the accompanying scientific and reportorial corps.

ARIS.

ST. PAUL PIONEER
July 3, 1874

BLACK HILLS EXPEDITION

Letter from the Special Correspondent of The Pioneer.

Fort A. Lincoln—The Expedition—
Scouts—Correspondents—
An Enemy Slain.

Stormy Night—Sunday in Camp—
Clear Atmosphere— Col.
Fred Grant, Etc., Etc.

FORT ABRAHAM LINCOLN,
D.T.,
June 27, 1874.

To the Editor of the
St. Paul Pioneer:

Fort A. Lincoln is situated on the west bank of the Missouri, nearly opposite Bismarck. By the river it is 1800 miles above St. Louis, and 1200 miles below Fort Benton, the head of navigation; by Northern Pacific Railroad 450 miles from Duluth, and 560 from St. Paul. Its latitude is nearly 47 degrees and longitude 34 degrees west from Washington. Its altitude above the sea level is about 1700 feet. The adjacent country, on both sides of the river is rolling prairie, treeless, shrubless, and unimproved. A narrow skirting of timber grows along the lower river bottoms.

From here to the Black Hills, it is about 300 miles in a southwesterly direction. None but hostile indians (sic) occupy the intervening country. All the friendly Sioux are found along the Missouri; all the unfriendly, in the interior.

The military part of the expedition consists of ten full companies of the 7th U. S. Cavalry: the other two companies of the regiment are out with Maj. Twining on the international boundary survey. (A cavalry regiment contains twelve companies of 84 men each.) Besides the cavalry there are two companies of the 17th U. S. Infantry. The cavalry and artillery horses number near 1,000. The field pieces consists of three Gatlin (sic) guns, each capable of throwing 250 balls a minute; and one Rodman six-pounder. The artillery service will be performed by the cavalry force. The Gatlin gun is a newly invented piece of ordance, being patented in 1865. It is breech-loading — almost self-loading—and is operated by the simple turning of a crank. The balls are about the size of common carbine or rifle shot, are put in the common metallic case, and discharge through a number of revolving barrels.

SCOUTS.

Sixty Arickaree (commonly called Ree) Indians will accompany the expedition. Their agency is at Fort Berthold. They are deadly enemies of the Sioux. A company of twenty-eight Santee Sioux will also act as scouts. The Santee tribe is 2,000 strong, and is the only tribe of Sioux living out of Dakota. Their agency is in Nebraska, thirty miles west of Yankton, on the Missouri. This tribe has adopted the manners and habits of civilized people. They have cultivated farms, fixed homes, numerous schools, and many of them speak the English language.

Nineteen Santees accompanied Gen. Stanley last year on his expedition to the Yellowstone. Some of that nineteen are in the present

company. They came to this place under the charge of their Missionary, the Rev. S. D. Hinman of the Episcopal church. The valuable services of Mr. Hinman are best shown by the character of the men themselves. From Sioux City to Bismarck, they came all the way by rail, via St. Paul.

All these Indian scouts are enlisted just for this present expedition. They are uniformed, armed, mounted, and placed in charge of a Lieutenant. They will be out nearly all the time, only reporting at headquarters with information or for orders.

The expedition camp is on the river bank two miles below the Fort. The scientific corps is not yet in camp, nor fully organized. Of it and of the officers in charge of the expedition, anon.

CORRESPONDENTS.

The N. Y. Tribune, Chicago Inter-Ocean and ST. PAUL PIONEER has each a special.

YOUR CORRESPONDENT

SLAYS A DEADLY ENEMY.

This afternoon, growing a little weary of camp life, I strolled outside the lines and sauntered away off on the prairie. Thoughts of home and dear ones filled my mind, and scalping Sioux and every danger was forgotted, (sic) when, horror! there (sic) almost hidden in the grass, lay the most deadly foe my eyes had ever rested on, just ready to spring with a fearful bound upon me. Although unarmed, I dare not, for my reputation's sake, call for help or flee from danger. Often had my blood run cold at the recital of some deed of scalping and murder by the stealthy savage. But now, my time of action had come. Picking up a stick, or rather club, which, fortunately lay near, I administered several well-directed blows, completely crushing the head. I then cut off as a trophy—not the battered scalp, but the tail of the rattlesnake, bearing eight rattles, and will bring it home as the first specimen of the Black Hills expedition.

The time for leaving here has not been officially announced.

LATER LETTER.

FORT A. LINCOLN, D.T.,
June 29.

To the Editor of
The St. Paul Pioneer:

Late Saturday afternoon a steady rain came on, and gradually increased, until at times the very "windows of heaven" seemed open. It continued all night and until about 8 o'clock in the morning. A part of the time the wind was very high, and had not our tents been new and strong, and firmly staked and guyed, they must have been blown over, if not blown to pieces. The beating of the rain, the vibration of the tents, the flapping of the flys, the braying of mules, the neighing of horses, the thunder and lightning, and the fear of having our tents blown over, seemed to keep the whole camp wide awake. The Indian's dog-tent and the soldier's A tent were hardly proof against the violence of the storm, and wet blankets and clothing were hung out to dry all around the camp. But the wall tents kept all within dry.

SUNDAY IN CAMP

is no Sunday at all. All the seven days of the week are equally sacred and equally profane, but chiefly profane. The work of preparation moves steadily on, and knows no intermission even for for Sabbath hours. All day long the busy note of labor is heard. This annihilation of the Christian's day of rest and earthly care seems strange to those unused to such non-observance; but custom long continued is assented to if not approved, even though in contravention of the higher law.

THE CLEARNESS OF THE ATMOSPHERE

is, if possible, even greater here than in the far-famed State of sky-tinted waters. The well-defined, sharpened lines projected on the sky by the rolling prairies and distant buttes is marvelous beyond expression, and can never be duly appreciated unless actually seen. The outlines seem cut in relief upon the very face of the heavens.

COL. FRED GRANT

and several officers made a visit to Fort Rice, twenty-five miles below here, on Saturday, returning yesterday evening.

SPORTSMEN, HO!

This morning, early, a deer was caught in sight of camp, and the fat, savory venison is now hanging up at headquarters' mess. Deer and antelope abound all along the way to Black Hills.

If rumor is not wholly at fault, and if all signs are not deceptive, and if the expectations of all—the hopes of some, and the fears of others—are not disappointed,

THERE WILL BE FIGHTING

before this expedition returns. The Indians will commence hostilities. The most noted of all Sioux chiefs, Tatanka Syotanka, or Sitting Buffalo, is congregating his forces at Black Hills, and will oppose the advance. Time will show!

ARIS.

ST. PAUL PIONEER.
Issue of July 8, 1874

BLACK HILLS EXPEDITION

Complete Roster of Military and Scientific Corps.

Brief Biographical Sketch of the Commander.

Starting of the Expedition and General Order of March.

Letter from the Special Correspondent of The Pioneer.

IN CAMP, FT. A. LINCOLN, D.T., June 30, 1874

HAIL STORM.

Yesterday afternoon we were visited by a genuine hail storm. For about twenty minutes the wind was high and the rain fell almost in torrents, mingled with hail. Many of the pellets were fully half an inch in diameter. Birds were killed, horses and mules stampeded from the camp, and many tents flooded or blown over.

But the storm over, the sun came out, tents were righted, animals secured, and evening closed in with rainbows and beauteous clouds, and inspiring music by the regimental band.

Many of the interludes from camp duties are filled up with lively games, such as base ball, pony racing and dancing by the Indians, and universal card playing.

SCIENTIFIC CORPS.[9]

The chief officer is Col. Wm. Ludlow, of the Engineer Corps, U. S. A. To aid in the work is the well known State Geologist of Minnesota, Prof N. H. Winchell, of the University, and his assistant; G. B. Grinnell, a graduate of Yale, and one of its corps of instructors, and his assistant; and the well known artist of St. Paul, Wm. H. Illingworth, as photographer of the expedition, and his assistant.

To enable this corps the more accurately and successfully to accomplish its work, it is furnished with a great number and variety of instruments and appliances, such as odometers, aneroid barometers, geological and topographical instruments, the botanical and zoological apparatus, and astronomical instruments for determining latitude and longitude.

The following is the

OFFICIAL ROSTER

of commissioned officers on duty with the expedition:

Lieut. Colonel G. A. Custer, 7th Cavalry.
Major G. A. Forsyth, 9th Cavalry.
Major I. G. Tilford, 7th Cavalry.
Lieut. Col. F. D. Grant, A.D.C. to Lieut. General.
Captain Ludlow, Engineer Corps. U.S.A.
Lieut. I. Callum, 7th Cavalry, A.A.A.G.
Lieut. A. E. Smith, 7th Cavalry, A.A.Q.M.
Asst. Surgeon J. W. Williams, U.S.A.
Acting Asst. Surgeon J. Allen, U.S.A.
Acting Asst. Surgeon J. Bergen, U.S.A.
Captains N.K. Hart, F.W. Benteen, G. W. Yates, Thomas H. French, Owen Hale, M. Moyland, 7th Cavalry.
Lieutenants Thomas W. Custer, Thos. M. McDougall, E. S. Godfrey, D. McIntosh, E. G. Mathey, F. M. Gibson, B. H. Hodgson, G. D. Wallace, C. A. Varnum, H. M. Harrington. 7th Cavalry.

INFANTRY BATTALION.
Capt. Sanger, 17th Infantry.
Capt. Wheaton, 20th Infantry.
Lieut. Roach, 17th Infantry.
Lieut. Gates, 20th Infantry.

As the expedition is now receiving so large a share of public attention, it may be well to refresh

Custer's Expedition—Rolling Weather up North.

Special to The Pioneer:

9. BISMARCK, D. T., June 22—A special arrived last night bringing Lieutenant Fred. Grant, Colonel Ludlow, and others, who join Custer's Black Hills expedition. . . .

Weather very hot—mercury ranging from 98 to 102 in the shade for several days, but pleasant winds prevail.

ST. PAUL PIONEER
Issue of June 24, 1874

Photographer William Illingworth took a picture of this distant view of Monument Butte, northwest of Deerfield, while the Custer Expedition was camped on Castle Creek. It was while they were at Castle Creek that the expedition encountered a small band of Indians, camped nearby.

the memory of the reader by a brief mention of some of the salient points in the military history of its commanding officer,

GENERL CUSTER.

He graduated at West Point in 1861; was in the first battle of Bull Run as Second Lieutenant; afterwards aid-de-camp on Gen. Pleasanton's staff, and later on the staff of Gen. McClellan; made Brigadier General and assigned command in Sheridan's Cavalry Corps; placed in command of division at Cedar Creek and Winchester, and continued as Division Commander till the close of the war. His war record is alike brilliant and honorable, and his services invaluable to the nation.

At the close of the war a division of cavalry was organized and sent to Texas, under his command as Major General of Volunteers. This is the culminating point in his rank in the volunteer service, and is the highest. Before the close of the war, by regular promotion, he was raised to the rank of Captain in the regular army.

As Maj. Gen. Vols. he was mustered out in 1866. By the re-organization of the regular army in 1866, four new regiments of cavalry were added, and he was selected as Lieutenant of the 7th.

In June 1867 his regiment was sent by General Hancock from Fort Hays, Kansas, against the Cheyenne and Araphahoe Indians between the Platte and Smoky Hill rivers.

In November 1868 his regiment left Fort Dodge, Kansas, to join an expedition under Gen. Alfred Sully against hostile tribes in Indian Territory. Gen. Sheridan overtook the expedition at Camp Supply, and ordered Gen. Custer with his regiment to go further south. In carrying out this order, the Cheyennes were defeated in the battle of the Washita, their principal villages destroyed, their munitions of war and 800 of their ponies captured, and a number of their warriors, including the famous chief Black Kettle, taken prisoners. The regiment then joined the forces under Gen. Sheridan, and marched to Fort Cobb. On the way were recovered the remains of Mrs. Blinn and her child, captives slain by the Indians, and the bodies of Major Elliott and nineteen men who had been cut off prior to the battle of Washita.

In March 1869, he left Fort Sill, I.T., to compel the Cheyennes to return to their reservation. While on this expedition he effected the release of a number of captives taken the preceding year.

During the years 1870, '71, '72

there were no active operations against the Indians.

In 1873 he arrived with his regiment at Yankton, passed through the terrible snow storm there, marched to Fort Rice and joined the Yellowstone Expedition under Gen. Stanley. On this expedition, the Indians were defeated at Big Horn and Tongue rivers.

From this brief sketch it is safe to assert that there is little to know of Indian life and modes of warfare that Gen. Custer has not already learned, and that too by the actual experience of years on the frontier and in the wilderness. If thorough education, years of training, intimate knowledge of the West and its untutored inhabitants, and a noble ambition can crown this reconnoissance with success, then Gen. Custer is preeminently the man for leader.

LATER LETTER.

VALLEY OF LITTLE HEART
RIVER, D.T.,
July 3d, 1874

Yesterday at eight o'clock the Expedition made its first day's march, twelve miles. The route was mostly over billowy prairie, with here and there a narrow valley along the margin of some small stream. The soil is generally thin, and herbage scant. The grass is short, and a tree or bush is rarely seen. The Heart Valley is from one to two miles wide, and the soil deep and fertile, though slightly alkaline.

The General Order prescribing the manner of marching and encamping, and giving a number of variety of instructions and admonitions to be observed, has been issued from Headquarters.

The order of march is about as follows:

First—The Indian scouts, under Lieut. Wallace are to move in advance.

Second—The battery of Gatling guns, Lieut. Chance commanding.

Third — Ambulance and wagon train, the latter moving in four columns, when practicable, Captain Smith commanding.[10]

Fourth—Infantry Battalion in two columns, Lieut. Sanger commanding.

Fifth—On the right flank, a Battalion of Cavalry, Major Forsyth commanding. On the left flank, a

10. Custer to Elizabeth, July 15, 1874, from Prospect Valley, Dakota Territory, twelve miles from the Montana line, 103° 46′ west, 45° 29′ north.
Capt. Smith is the best Quartermaster I ever had in the field, and wins praise from all sides for his management of the trains . . .
Marguerite Merington, THE CUSTER STORY, p. 274.

Battalion of Cavalry, Major Tilford commanding. These batalions (sic) move opposite the train, and within 100 yards. Outside these battalions are flanking parties, consisting of three men and a non-commissioned officer from each company.

Ten Indian scouts are to be detailed daily, to move in front, and within 1,000 yards, and to be always in sight. Special scouting parties may be sent out by the commanding officer of the expedition.

In the rear of all, is one company of cavalry.

Two frontiersmen accompany the expedition, as hunters. Yesterday they killed and brought into camp two large, fat antelopes, and day before, one. We passed in sight of a number of these fleet and graceful animals. They are more numerous than deer. The buffalo is about extinct in this Territory; but his bleaching bones may be seen almost everywhere over these wide pasture lands and his deep worn trails may be traced for miles, wandering through the hills and along the valleys.

The General Order is very minute in all the details as to encampment. Nothing seems omitted that could contribute to safety and comfort. The following paragraphs are copied from the order, verbatim:

"As the utmost prudence will necessarily be observed to prevent surprise of individuals or of small parties by prowling Indians, no member of the command will go beyond the line of flankers while on the march, nor beyond the line of pickets while in camp, except by special permission of the commanding officer of the expedition, and then such parties will, when practicable, pass and re-pass the lines at the same point.

"As a pistol or rifle shot will be a signal of danger, the discharge of firearms within or near the lines, by day or night, is strictly prohibited. Firing at game from the column or from the vicinity of the camp is prohibited, except under circumstances warranting special permission. Hunting parties will only be organized under authority from these headquarters.

"As the object of the expedition is a peaceable one, care will be taken not to molest or in any manner disturb any Indians who may be encountered on the march, unless the latter first act in a hostile manner.

"As a matter of precaution, no party of Indians, however small, will be permitted to approach the vicinity of the picket lines by day or night. Officers and men are particularly cautioned against being drawn into the trap usually laid by Indians, by the latter exposing a small number and endeavoring to induce pursuit.

"This command is about to march through a country infested by Indians, more or less hostile, and even should the latter, as it is hoped, not engage in general warfare and the usual acts of hostilities, there is no doubt but they will endeavor to make captures of stock, and to massacre small parties found imprudently beyond the lines. To guard against this, the utmost caution and prudence on the part of every member of this command will be required.

"While it is hoped that these admonitions will prove ample, the Commanding Officer of the expedition will promptly apply correctives of the most summary character in all cases of violation of the orders contained herein."

The firearms of both the cavalry and the infantry are the very best.

The supply train of the expedition consists of a hundred and fifteen wagons, one hundred and ten of which are drawn each by six mules. These wagons carry on an average five tons each of provisions and forage, camp equipage and ammunition. One hundred and thirty-six head of beef cattle are driven along. The train will grow lighter and the herd less from day to day. The fine band of the 7th cavalry accompanies, and will often discourse to us inspiring music.

The days are sometimes very warm; but thus far, the nights have been cool, and we all enjoy refreshing sleep.

The order to move caused great rejoicing in camp, especially among civil attachies of the expedition, some of whom had been waiting at Fort Lincoln for over three weeks. This was the case with several newspaper correspondents.

It is now only 7 o'clock in the morning, and the courier will leave camp with the mail in a few minutes. This letter has been written since reville (sic) at 5. In the meantime we have had breakfast and prepared our baggage for the camp wagons.[11]

ST. PAUL PIONEER
Issue of July 29, 1874

BLACK HILLS EXPEDITION

Letters from the Special Correspondent of the Pioneer.

Full Particulars of the March from Bismarck to the Black Hills.

The Heat Intense but the Whole Command in Good Health.

Minute and Reliable Description of the Country Traversed.

Interesting and Important Geological Observations.

Prof. Donaldson's Letters.

FIRST LETTER

ON THE WAY TO
BLACK HILLS,
Camp No. 4, July 7, 1874.

To the Editor of the
St. Paul Pioneer:

Our second days march was through a country hilly, almost mountainous, rocky, sterile, treeless, shrubless and not well watered, To make an advance of six miles required a detour of fourteen miles. From the summit of a rocky butte by the wayside, Fort Lincoln could be distinctly seen, distant about fifteen miles, though, on account of the clearness of the atmosphere, it appears only three or four miles, and not a tint altered by reason of any blue or haze.

Through this clear air the sun pours down his intensest beams. The earth becomes heated as by internal fires. The stones and pebbles become so hot as literally to blister the hands; while to sit down, is but to experience the sensations of Gustamozin or Cortes' gridiron. The thermometer went up to 101 degrees in the shade. The extreme purity and dryness of the air is the only salvation for man or beast. At one point on the days march, there was a shallow pond of surface water, not over one rod wide nor more than three rods long and six inches deep. Yet even this hot, stagnant pool was

11. BISMARCK, D.T., July 3.—The Black Hills expedition, 1,000 men strong, left this morning. From all information derived thus far, indications are that hostile Indian bands have been congregating on the route and in the neighborhood of the Black Hills, to the number of from six to eight thousand fighting men, well armed and equipped, and with plenty of ammunition, and propose to give Gen. Custer a warm reception. No news is expected concerning the expedition until its return.

ST. PAUL PIONEER
Issue of July 7, 1874

(Author's Note: In 1874, because of telegraph delays and other communication difficulties, news dispatches from the field frequently reached newspaper offices out of order from the sequence in which they were originally written. To preserve the chronology of events, we have arranged the dispatches in the order of their writing, which means that some of the issue dates appearing at the top of pages and in the columns will be out of calendar order).

To make doubly sure that he obtained a good picture of Monument Butte, Illingworth moved slightly to the west and closer, before making a second exposure. During this period, Correspondent A. B. Donaldson of the ST. PAUL PIONEER wrote, "Mr. Illingworth still continues to photograph the scenery."

eagerly visited by all to quench the burning thirst, and from it canteens were filled for future use. One called out, "O, for an umbrella fifty cents a minute for an umbrella!"

All sighed for

"A lodge in some vast wilderness,

Some boundless contiguity of shade."

But cooling springs nor leafy shades came not for our wishing.

The surface of the whole country is strewn with shaley sandstone and granite boulders. Cactus of several varieties is common; but the floral decoration is most meager. The tops of the highest hills are covered with a handsome species of creeping cedar and myrtle. These hardy plans hold together and bind down the thin soil, which else would be scattered by the winds, to leave the rocky-pated

butte without their handsome wigs.

The genuine English hare, known among western sportsmen as the jack rabbit, is found here. There are 12 or 15 grey hounds with us; and it requires the utmost speed of these long-legged and fleet runners to capture the flying hare. Still we have seen the captures made several times, but not any case till after a long and exciting chase.

Antelopes have put in their appearance; but more of them when they more abound, as they will in a few days.

Our second camp is planteau (sic) from one to two miles wide, and five or six miles long. A small stream, a mere wet-weather brook, rises here and furnishes us with stagnant water. This table land is an oasis. Smoothly rounded hills from nearly the whole horizon. This graceful conteour (sic) is only

broken here and there by some jagged butte lifting its rocky head against the sky.

Only two days out; but the sun has set his mark upon us. Lips unprotected by a mustache awning— O how sore, blistered skins, noses red as lobsters boiled, ears that shame the glowing color of the turkey gobbler's gills, and the cruticle (sic) peeling off the whole face, make us even more hideous in appearance than our red brethren. When we get back we will be more swarthy than Mississippi raftsmen. Who will know us then?

As Dr. Sepany and Mr. Calhoun were sitting on an eminence, watching the passing columns, a sparrow lit upon the Doctor's knee, looked at him for sometime, apparently feeling no fear but only curious to interview the remarkable visitors, in order to report their arrival to her young ones.

After making the second exposure of Monument Butte, Illingworth swung his camera 180 degress to the southwest and took this picture of Custer's Camp sprawled along Castle Creek Valley. Note that a group of about eight wagons are formed in a circle on the right. Most of the other wagons are lined up in two long rows in the center. A row of tents protects the far southeastern end of the camp in the upper center. The camp extended for a length of well over a mile down the valley.

What a pity that all the beautiful birds are not alike fearless of the rational lords of earth. Cruel man!

The fourth of July passed without observance.

Our third day's march was through a better country, clothed in green by recent and heavy rains. The annual drouth (if there be such a thing) has not yet set in. There are no lakes or marshes or timbered lands to retain water or moisture; and in a few hours after a heavy rain the streams cease to flow, and hold water only in stagnant pools, and even these soon dry up, leaving the whole country arid as Sahara. Oh for tree planting!

We encamped on Dog-tooth Creek, between the Dog-tooth Spurs.

Our fourth day's march, although made on Sunday, was more than a Sabbath day's journey. Reville sounded at 3 o'clock and breakfast was over and wagons loaded, and we were under way at 5 o'clock. The day did not seem like Sunday; and it is safe to say that three-fourths of the command never once thought of the day of the week. Our army scarcely knows the Christian sabbath. In these days of innovation and radicalism, is there not cause for amendment in some military customs?

The country grows more interesting as we advance. The plains and vallies (sic) wide, and the ridges and buttes are correspondingly separated. The soil is richer and less stony. The horizon line would suggest a country broken and impassable. Rocky heights, pinnacles, serrate ridges, bony bluffs, pyramidal buttes, make the entire outline. But all these seem to open like gateways as we travel on passing us from plain to plain and valley to valley and the surface, which had appeared in the distance nothing but unevenness and desolation, is found to be nine-tenths level and fertile. It is something like sailing among the thousand islands of the St. Lawrence. That distance lends enchantment to the view, is here proved false and its converse true.

We crossed the trail made by Gen. Stanley last year, in his expedition to Yellowstone. His trail

From the position where the previous picture was taken, Illingworth moved south about a mile and took this picture facing to the southwest. Shadows would indicate that the time was about noon. The wagons which appeared in the distant center of the previous picture now stand in the foreground. Castle Creek, not shown in this picture, wends its way in front of the wagons. Tents protect the rear. Limestone Butte rises in the background. A small square wagon, similar to the one driven by Illingworth and used by him as a portable darkroom, stands in the center of the picture behind a tent with an open flap.

is just the same as we are making. and can be followed for years to come. It consists of four parallel wagon tracks, cut several inches deep and everywhere plain. These tracks are but a few yards apart. The flanking battalions also make trails, distinct enough now, but they will be less permanent than the wagon trails. From the quadruple columns of wagons great clouds of dust arise, which can be seen even when the train is out of sight.

It is tedious and difficult to get the train across some of the sloughs and ravines. The pioneer corps has a good deal of work to prepare the crossings. The muleteers appreciate the situation. Whipping, yelling and profanity

are then always in order. What a double and twisted, awkward and blasphemous jargon of oaths these men can spew and splutter and bellow out. The mule-whipping, swearing, whooping, hurrahing and howling can be heard at least a mile. Though out of sight, "over the hills and far away," it is easy to tell when the mule train is stuck, by the discordant and almost infernal sounds which smite the ear. Three or four of the drivers do not swear or whip their teams unmercifully. They are men. Let them be promoted! To relieve the tedium and awful monotony of these delays, the band often discourses most cheering and lively airs. The breaking of wagon tongues and the crippling of mules and sometimes

drivers, are also variations.

On the fourth day out, after crossing Dog-tooth Creek, and a dividing ridge, we descended to as fine a rich and well-grassed a prairie as the very best in any of the States. This plateau is not less than eight miles long and six wide. It gradually declines to Bear's Creek valley, our fourth encampment. The serrated, jagged horizon has given place to one of right lines and graceful undulations. All around the country presents every appearance of fertility.

One of the horses was bitten by a rattlesnake today, and but for prompt and effective treatment by the veterinary surgeon would have died. Soon after being bitten, he was dripping with sweat, became

Another view of Custer's Camp, along Castle Creek, was obtained when Illingworth turned his camera due west. Captain William Ludlow described the valley in his journal as ". . . luxuriantly rich and grassy, a fine stream meandering through it." He went on to say that, ". . . . the grass in places was as high as a horse's shoulder." This view is from Highway 110, north of the present Village of Deerfield.

blind, trembled, staggered and nearly fell. Had the bite not been near the fetlock, there would have been no salvation. Bandaging above the wound, bleeding, and bathing with ammonia were the remedies.

A.B.D.

SECOND LETTER

ON THE WAY TO
BLACK HILLS —
FIFTH DAY OUT.
(July 9, 1874)

The fifth day of our journey we marched thirteen miles, over fine, rich, well grassed, rolling prairie. The day will long be remembered for

ANTELOPE HUNTING

Mr. Illingworth went out alone to the distance of six or seven miles. From one elevation he saw antelope in every direction, in not less than three hundred in number were all in view at one time. He killed three, gave one to an Indian, brought in two, and could have secured more, but he had no means of carrying them. They can out-run the fleetest horse or grey-hound.

Gen Custer was out in advance, and captured one or two. At least fifteen or twenty were brought into camp. Scores of them ran right close to the cavalcade, and in many cases right through the lines; and even the order prohibiting shooting at game from the columns was not in all instances obeyed. Several men were dismounted for offence, thus augmenting the infantry at the expense of the cavalry.

Numerous hunting parties were permitted to go out, and a great deal of wild shooting was done and a great deal of Uncle Sam's ammunition was wasted. Whole volleys were fired, with no other results then the stampede of the game and the whirring of rifle balls unpleasantly near our head.

Some Indian scouts, in the advance column shot down a fine buck that was running near by and on which Gen. Custer, who was some distance ahead; had drawn a bead. The General quickly reminded them of their trespass by firing from his needle gun two whizzing shots over their heads. The effect was not lost. Instantaneously the redskins emptied their saddles and embraced their mother earth. They did not fire from the column any more and only greeted the friendly game with the customary "ugh!"

A herd of seven antelope, led by a fine buck ran across the advancing columns and within ten or fifteen feet of the battery of artillery. The temptation was too great for mortals to resist, and whole volleys were discharged contrary to orders. The cannoniers did not have time to unlimber their ordinance, but blazed away with their revolvers. The noble buck fell completely riddled through, while, marvelous to relate, the balance of the herd escaped. The driver of one of the four-horse teams drawing a Gatlin gun, left his post for a moment to salute the herd with his six-shooter. His team became frightened and ran away, and for a few minutes a Gatlin gun made a series of rapid evolutions over the plains of Dakota, in a manner wholly unrecognized in military practice. Before any damage was done, the war steeds ingloriously terminated their brilliant maneuver by miring in a slough. The driver escaped with no other punishment than that of being dismounted for the remainder of the day. Deer were seen for the first time, and one was killed by an Indian and brought into camp.

INDIAN INVOCATION.

On an eminence, about a mile to our left, a white flag was seen waving. A scout was sent to bring it in. It was about a half a square yard of light figured calico, tied to a cross piece on the top of a slender pole about ten feet long. From each end of the cross piece was suspended a plug of tobacco. The whole was evidently an offering to some deity, made doubtless, to secure protection of some kind, and most likely from this expedition.

"Lo, the poor Indian, whose untutored mind, Sees God in clouds and hears him in the wind."

PETRIFACTIONS.

Along the road today were many specimens of petrified wood, of large size and rare beauty and value. Some of them would weigh at least one thousand pounds. Prof. Winchell examined them and expressed the belief that for mineralolgical cabinets or museums some of these single fossils would be worth hundreds of dollars. If we return by this route, Gen. Custer

promises to bring back several of the finer ones.

After a march of thirteen miles, we encamped on the North Fork of the Cannon Ball River. It furnishes us plenty of good, running water, and along its banks sufficient wood can be gathered to supply our camp. It drains a large area, and has worn a channel wide and deep enough to float a Mississippi steamer. Mr. Illingworth took a stereoscopic view of the valley, showing the handsomely rounded and grassy hills, the perpendicular cliffs, the shining river fringed with box-elder, and the cattle herd quietly resting in the green meadow.

THE SIXTH DAY

we marched thirty-two miles. We rose at 3 o'clock in the morning and did not enter camp on the South Fork of the Cannon Ball till ten at night. The only water we found was in pools, and somewhat alkaline. By someone's blunder, the whole train was misled about one mile and had to turn about and countermarch that distance over a bad road. All came into camp weary and worn, hungry, thirsty and faint. Before the train arrived and supper was prepared and over, and the men ready for a short rest, it was nearly midnight.

At three o'clock in the morning the whole camp was alarmed by the needless firing of a picket guard, whose imagination converted an innocent antelope into a lurking savage. During the night one of the draft horses died from the effects of over-exertion. Even before the long march was ended, one weary soldier picketed his horse by the wayside and camped alone. Thirsty and supperless, he lay down. The solid earth was his bed and pillow, and the jeweled sky his only canopy. But sleep, "exhausted nature's sweet restorer," sealed his eyelids and soothed his spirit into forgetfulness. When the opening eye of day shone upon him, he buckled on his trappings, mounted his rested steed, and safely rode into camp. During that long day's ride, we passed through some fine country, a portion of which was table land, at least 2,500 feet high. The purity and clearness of the air reminds one of the glades of the Alleghanies.

Climatically, no place could be more desirable for a summer home.

At the close of the

SEVENTH DAY

July 8th, we pitched our tents in a broad and fertile meadow on the bank of Hidden Timber Creek, 103 miles from Fort A. Lincoln. Nothing worthy of the name of timber grows on this creek or anywhere else in all this vast region. The creek is so named because on its west bank, just opposite our camp, there is a rocky, concave bluff on which some bushes grow. The creek below and the rocks above keep off the fire. Within fifteen miles not enough could be gathered to boil a tea-kettle. The bleaching bones of the buffalo may be picked up almost anywhere, but a fire of buffalo chips will never again be kindled on the plains. Of coal, geologists tell us there is none. The veins of lignite are generally too thin and too poor to pay for the mining.

We crossed a table plain of not less than 26 or 27 hundred feet elevation. The horizon line was distant from 15 to 30 miles. Pinnacles and domes, serrate hills and broad valleys were all taken in at one sweep of the eye. What added materially to the grandeur and impressiveness of the scene, was the passing overhead of a heavy thundercloud. From it a few drops of rain fell, and between it and the earth the lightning made its fiery leaps and the reverberating thunder rolled. In the distance, several passing showers could be seen.

The whole days' march was through fine grazing lands.

In the evening, Mr. Illingworth moved his camera to the top of the opposite bluff and stereoscoped us all.

EIGHTH DAY.

After crossing Hidden Timber Creek, we wended our way out of the valley and over the hills. Rocky pinnacles and ledges were all around us. Passing the creek bluffs we descend to a rolling plain. Every elevation is covered with siliceous limestone, petrified wood or sandrock, literally paved and wedged in so that between the separate pieces a blade of grass can scarcely grow. The country becomes more sterile. Bare clay and sand and alkali and prickly cactus and sage brush are all abounding. It is hard to trail over a surface so broken into gullies. Our trail is indirect and serpentine.

At the foot of Wolf Butte is a village of prairie dogs. They peeped out of their little mounds, surveyed us with startled curiosity, yelped their little barks, and disappeared below. Singularly enough, just be-before reaching the butte, we saw the first prairie wolf. This butte is at least three thousand feet high. Its summit is a flat sand rock, about 25 feet across, and can only be reached on one side, and then by climbing an almost perpendicular wall 40 or 50 feet in height. On the other sides, the upper party of the ledge projects like a table leaf, or perhaps more like the capital of a column. The swallows, from their mud-built nests beneath the overhanging leaf, interviewed us in the most friendly manner.

On the sloping side of the butte, and partly imbedded in the earth, lies the petrified stump of an immense tree. It is the finest single specimen that we have found. On one of the flats, about a half mile to our left, several acres are covered with petrified wood, from the smallest chip to blocks of two or three hundred pounds weight. These petrifactions are of almost every color, black, red, white, blue and variegated, straight-veined and curled, and all highly polished by the sand driven across their surfaces by the ever blowing winds.

Four of five miles west of Wolf Butte is Bald Butte. This latter is a curiosity. Its name is descriptive of its character. It is round as a dollar, about 100 feet across and 60 feet high, and nearly perpendicular. It is chiefly composed of parallel and slightly inclined strata of different colored clays, black, brown, blue and white, overtopped by a reddish shale.

Notwithstanding the general sterility of the region traversed today, there are enough grassy spots to supply our beef herd and horses. While the loaded train jogs steadily on, the cavalry makes frequent halts, dismounts and unbridles, and grazes the horses.

THIRD LETTER

ON THE WAY TO BLACK HILLS,

NINTH DAY OUT.
(July 11, 1874)

At sunrise on the 10th of July we left camp on the Grand River. This is the largest stream on our route. We moved up the valley 24 miles, crossed the river three times, and a second time pitched our tents by its waters. The soil is generally thin, and weeds and cactus usurp the place of grass. Only a few bushes, here and there, can be found on its banks, and at the close of the day we have no fuel, except what has been brought in wagons for 15 or 20 miles. Evening finds us 166 miles, odometer measurement, from Fort A. Lincoln, just across the Missouri from Bismarck, yet in all this distance we have not seen more timber than would make probably 20 cords.

TENTH DAY.

As usual, reville calls us up at 3 o'clock in the morning and we leave camp between 4 and 5. While we miss the "forty morning winks," the band entertains us with that "which tames the savage heart and breaks the stubborn will."

Leaving the valley we gradually ascend the rolling prairie. From the top of a handsomely rounded butte on the right, the view is fine indeed. Some of the horizon lines can scarcely be less than 40 miles distant. The river is nearly lost to view, while hills beyond hills arise, in almost endless succession. One plateau of several square miles is literally covered with them. They are conical and from 50 to 200 feet in height. They resemble a village of ant hills greatly magnified or the tumuli of some ancient race. Towards the Southwest, the direction in which we are moving our way seems barricaded by a line of bluffs, almost mountains, presenting to us, as seen from this point for miles and miles nothing but an impassable wall, on the sides and crests of which a few hundred pines seem to be struggling for an existence. What savage warriors may be there lurking in rocky ravines?, yes waiting for their prey to pass by; what dens and caves, what canons and wonders of nature lie there unknown; let us advance and see. Before leaving this summit I stoop down to draw the picket pin at the end of the lariat by which my horse is tethered to graze, and find on the ground at my feet an iron ring and

staple. When and how did they come here? Had some roaming Sioux lately stood at this height, watching for our approach? and had he, when discovering us, precipitately fled, and left these behind? Many supposed evidences of the nearness of the hostile red man had been reported; is not this another? Two such things would be esteemed by Indians living way out here, as objects of no small value. They were never intentionally cast away. Thus I amused and speculated till the rearguard came by. Gathering up the lariat, I rose to fasten it to a ring in the saddle, but the ring and its staple were lost. So, I had found them!

In some places passed over today, the surface is white with alkali; the vegetation killed by it, and the water, if there be any, spoiled.

On one of the alkali flats is a village of prairie dogs, covering several acres. Owls were flying about over it. The dogs, owls and rattlesnakes live together in the same holes. This latter statement is made upon sufficient evidence.

Towards evening we passed, on our left, a high butte. Its summit is a platform of six or eight acres. Nearly at the extreme top is a stratum of quartzitic limestone "in position," the finest that has been found. The existence of this stratum is an important fact in determining the geology of the country. It is above the friable sandstone and soft clay. This formation originally extended over large areas. As the sandstone and clay became disintegrated and carried away, the limestone broke to pieces and fell down in blocks of all sizes, and in this irregular form covers a large extent of country, and more especially the hill tops. This entire region was once the level bed of an ocean. Aqueous action, either fluid or glacial, has resulted in giving to the country its present configuration.

Late in the afternoon we reach the rocky walls which, in the morning, had excited so much curiosity. The formidable buttresses do indeed stop our progress, and we encamp at their feet. The pines and bushes furnish us plenty of wood, but there is an insufficiency of water and but little grass. In such a place, one would expect to find plenty of cool, refreshing springs.

The entire contingent was most impressed by the discovery of a large pile of elkhorns on July 28, 1874, on Elkhorn Prairie, now known as Reynolds Prairie, located north of the present Village of Deerfield. ST. PAUL PIONEER Correspondent A. B. Donaldson described them as a ". . . votive offering to some diety." He went on to recount the pile as ". . . probably 12 to 15 feet high when first built, but has settled down until it is now only five or six. It was photographed by our artist." (Donaldson was referring to Illingworth). Capt. William Ludlow reported in his journal that ". . . the Indians disclaimed any share in its construction." He was apparently referring to "One Stab" and a group of Sioux whom the expedition had encountered on July 26th. Although two poles are pictured standing upright, a third can be seen lying on the ground to the left. The expedition's zoological report stated, "Three lodge poles had been set up in the form of a tripod, and supported by these was a pile of bones 8 or 10 feet high."

But there is only one, and it is nearly dried up, affording barely enough water to fill a few canteens. Oh that a Moses were here, to smite the rock in this thirsty land, that it might give drink to man and beast.

This brown sandstone ledge rises about 175 feet above the plain. On its top is a plateau of from 50 yards to one or two miles in width, and extending North we know not how far. Its boundaries are as noted and jagged as it is possible to conceive. Canons run up into it, and these have branches and sub-branches, some of which are mere fissures, almost caves; others widen out to 50 or 100 yards. The ledges are water-worn and honeycombed into all imaginable shapes. In some cases, holes are worn in the thin promontories, large enough to admit an army wagon. From these ledges, masses of rock, great and small, are constantly tumbling down, forming a talus which, in some cases, reaches the very crest.

One of the principal fissures has been greatly enlarged by the action of the water flowing through it. Its entrance is at the head of a wedge-shaped canyon. It extends back several hundred yards. It is 8 or 10 feet in height and width at the entrance, and gradually becomes less as it extends back, until it is merely a seam in the rock. Its sides are covered with rude Indian engravings, representing the buffalo, elk, antelope, deer and beaver, fish, birds and reptiles, and the sun, moon and other objects of idolatrous worship. In it were found arrows, bows, flints, bones, beads, a rude bracelet, and a rusty, flint-lock pistol. The latter was found by Gen. Custer. Concerning this care (sic), the Indians have a great many legends and superstitions. They are probably not worth repeating. One will serve as a sample: They believe that an old man, with a long, white beard and "without beginning of days or end of years" dwells in the cave, and that he may, occasionally, be seen. In honor of the topographical engineer of the expedition, Gen. Custer named the cave "Ludlow's Cave." It was stereoscoped by Mr. Illingworth.

The south point of this plateau commands a very extensive view. From it we can see Slave Butte, Hill of the Short Pine, Blue Clay Hill; pyramidal, sugar-loaf, and flat buttes, and many other objects of interest; but, chief over all, and bearing ten degrees west of south, distant 95 miles, we see a dim blue line, the crest of the nearest Black Hills.

A human skull, pronounced by Dr. Williams, Regimental Surgeon, the skull of a white man, was found in our camp. The lower jaw was gone. Whose, or how it came there, will probably never be known.

The geology of this interesting region will in due time, appear in the official report of Prof. Winchell. He kindly furnishes data for the following information, the result of observations and measurements made by himself: Beginning at the crest of a knoll which crowns the plateau—

1. A bed of siliceous limestone— 2 ft. thick
2. Whitish sandy clay—60 ft. thick
3. Reddish sandstone with irony concretions—40 ft. thick
4. Rusty, castellated sandstone— 40 ft. thick
5. White sand, with calcareous cement—15 ft. thick
6. Bedded blue clay—35 ft. thick
7. Unexposed interval—10 ft. thick
8. Lignite—5 ft. thick
9. Massive, white, sand (seen)— 10 ft. thick

Total vertical section, exposed in this place—217 feet thick.

By observations made in other places, about 15 or 20 miles distant. It is ascertained that the total thickness of stratum No. 9 is 50 feet; that beneath it is a course of obliquely bedded rusty sandstone, 3 feet thick; that beneath this latter is a hard or bedded clay, or somewhat gritty, 110 feet thick,—giving as a total vertical section, 370 feet.

All these strata are non-fossiliferous, except the lowest, which contain a few of the mammalian group.

It may be observed that Ludlow's Cave is in the stratum numbered 4.

A.B.D.

ST. PAUL PIONEER
July 28, 1874

THE BLACK HILLS.

The Latest News From Gen. Custer's Expedition.

Nearly to the End of the Journey. The Entire Command in Good Health and Fine Spirits.

(Authors' Note: In 1874, because of telegraph delays and other communication difficulties, news dispatches from the field frequently reached newspaper offices out of order from the sequence in which they were originally written. To preserve the chronology of events, we have arranged the dispatches in the order of their writing, which means that some of the issue dates appearing at the top of pages and in the columns will be out of calendar order).

ON THE WAY TO
BLACK HILLS,
CAMP IN PROSPECT VALLEY,
MT., July 15, 1874.

By odometer measurement, we marched 11 miles on the 12th inst., though in a direct line the distance could hardly be half so great. The country sterile and all drying up. We circled around knobs, marched and counter-marched along ravines, halted in the burning sun till weary, and at last found shelter in our tents. Our guides know the country as to wood, water, game and pony-riding; but their judgment as to practicable wagon routes cannot be relied upon.

Sometimes while delayed at crossing or in treacherous alkaline flats, and while the sun smites us with his powerful heat, we have found a resting place "in the shadow of a rock in a weary land." Such a rest and such a shadow. O, how grateful! O, how thankfully enjoyed!

The diamond atmosphere has changed to one of ordinary bluish tint, less suited to purposes of observation in this country of "magnificent distances." When the wind blows hard, the fine dust and alkali is lifted and mingled with the air, giving it a grayish tint, and painfully irritating the eyes and chapping the skin.

All the next day we travel over the poor, cactusy, alkaline flats, crossing a number of dry channels and finding no water except in stagnant pools. Hills of from 150 to 200 feet in height are standing here and there, and their bald weather-beaten sides only increase the dreariness of the scene. These hills or buttes are of all shapes, conical, sugar-loafed, pinnacled, dome-topped and flat-topped, and all girdled by belts of as varying and blended colors as the strata of white, black, blue, brown and red clays and sandstone of their naked sides. Traveling through such a country as this, with the thermometer at 100 in the shade, takes the enthusiasm all out of a neophyte; and after marching 15 miles, from 5 till 1 o'clock, we are all ready for rest in camp.

The next day brought us across the territorial line into Montana. The first nine miles the country grew not better, but rather worse. The same barren flats and naked hills. One of the latter is a cross between a federal castle and a mohammedan masque. It has square towers and minarets, buttresses and domes. In some other country than this, it would readily be taken for some ancient ruin.

Just before reaching our present station, we climbed a long hill, out of the bad land bottoms, and reached a broad and beautiful plain, which soon descended slightly to a broad valley, extending for many miles north and south. Except for lack of timber, it can hardly be equalled anywhere for beauty, extent and fertility. It fairly rivals the Vermillion valley of Minnesota, the Wabash of Indiana and the Sciota or Miama of Ohio. In its background of hills it wants nothing, while its elevation gives a purity and clearness to the air hardly surpassed on the continent. Here is sufficient wood for our purposes, soft water, boundless pasturage, and safety from attack. Gen. Custer has fitly named it "Prospect Valley," and given us all a day of rest.

We are now 226 miles on the way or 190 miles in a direct line. We have marched 13 days without resting for a single day, and have averaged a little over 17 miles per day. We are about five miles west of the 104th meridian, the territorial boundary between Dakota and Montana, and in latitude 45 deg. 30 min.

We are probably not less than 2,800 feet above the level of the seaboard. Our means of estimating altitudes are not the best, being only the aneroid barometer; while it is well known that even the mercurial barometer cannot be relied upon for such purposes.

Antelopes have been hunted more or less every day since we started. Mr. Illingworth is entitled to the laurel for his success. He brings in more game than any other man. He keeps our mess of seven all the time supplied. He must be the seventh son of the seventh son in direct descent from Nimrod.

A sensational reporter, who failed to discriminate between the true and false or who was inclined to exaggeration and fiction, would here find an ample field for his peculiar gifts. Rumor circulates a thousand wonderful stories in camp every day, and it is easy to invent another, making the "thousand and one." Many of these creations of fancy are so life like, that even here they often deceive, while at home and in print they would be accepted unquestioningly.

Thus far everything is favorable. There has been no sickness worth naming among men or animals. All stand the trip remarkably well. Every wagon has come through safely. No serious accident has occurred, and, excepting one horse, nothing has been lost. The entire command is in good health and fine spirits. A broad belt of unexplored country will be mapped, science will be furnished with valuable information, the curiosity of the American people to know the secrets of their own vast heritage will be gratified, and the world will approve an expedition undertaken for none other than the most laudable purposes.

But few Indians have been seen, and there have been no acts of hostility, and it is still hoped there will be none. While we "keep our powder dry," and are ever watchful, we still feel hopeful and cheerful, and trust there will be a favorable issue in all respects.

From this date till the return of the expedition, about the first of September, it is probable there will be no tidings back and forth between us and the great world of civilization.

At dark today, two Ree Indian scouts will start back with the mail. They can reach Fort A. Lincoln in four days. They will not return; nor do we expect that any messenger will come to us. This large command, in the heart of the continent of the United States, so completely isolated for two months!

The readers of these letters will criticise them charitably, remembering that they have been written in the midst of the confusion, inconvenience of camp life, and with the discomfort and weariness which one must feel to whom such a life is all so new.

A. B. D.

ST. PAUL PIONEER
Issue of August 15, 1874

THE BLACK HILLS

Full Account of Gen Custer's Exploring Expedition.

By Prof. Donaldson, Special Correspondent of the Pioneer.

Description of the Topographical Features of the Country.

Full Details of the Work of the Scientific Corps.

Magnificent Mountains, Forests, Parks and Floral Vales.

Indications of Gold Sufficient to Pay for Mining.

All the Incidents of Interest During the Long March.

* * * * *

BLACK HILLS EXPEDITION

Editor St. Paul Pioneer:

COURIRERS. (sic)

July, 25. — On the evening of July 15th, at 8 o'clock p.m., the messengers bearing the last mail left camp at Prospect Valley. Whether they reached Fort A. Lincoln in safety, we know not. They were two of the Ree Indian scouts, by name, Skunk's Head and Bull Neck. They were selected for this duty by their Chief, Bloody Knife. They were well mounted, and furnished with the best of revolvers and carbines, and plenty of ammunition and rations for four days.

They carry no forage, but will graze their horses. They were enlisted for six months and have squaws and papooses at Fort Lincoln, and were glad of the opportunity to return. They were lightly accortered to run the gauntlet of their foes. They were to travel only at night, and for that reason would return on our trail.

SHORT PINE HILL

On the morning of July 16th, the Scientific Corps and three reporters, escorted by a company of cavalry made a detour to the left, to visit the high table-land on Short Pine Hill. This table-land is five or six miles long, and nowhere more than a half mile wide. Except in the geological formation it differs but slightly from the plateau at Ludlow's Cave, already described. On the sloping sides of the ravines leading up to the plateau, there is some tolerably fine pine timber, in all 5 or 6 areas. From examinations made by Prof. Winchell, it is ascertained that the whole formation belongs to the tertiary period.

1st. A base of blue clay, 150 ft. thick, containing large fossil bones of turtles and saurians.

2d. Rusty sandstone, 50 ft. thick.

3d. Upper stratum, 150 ft. thick; arenaceous, indurated mail, varying to arenaceous limestone and sandstone; color, white, but weathering to a sort of pinkish hue.

From the south end of the plateau, we see, in the dim distance, Bear Butte and Harney's Peak, while nearer and towards the east are Slave Butte and Deer's Ears, and just in front of us and distant about 45 miles the Black Hills lift their huge forms in dark, irregular outline against the sky. To the west, the turbid Little Missouri meanders through a broad valley, and its course can be traced twenty or thirty miles by its skirting of willow and brushwood. The distant bluffs which bound the valley on the west are like those described in former letters, only, if possible, these are still more jagged and serrate, notched, domed, pinnacled.

LITTLE MISSOURI, IN MONTANA.

After leaving Prospect Valley, Eden Vale, a few miles marching brings us to the Little Missouri. From sterility or want of rain or both, the valley is almost utterly barren. A square mile would hardly afford grass enough to keep half a dozen sheep from starving. Here the cactus finds a congenial home, and divides supremacy only with a sagebrush and a species of sunflower, a coarse, rank weed from one to three feet high, which spreads its garish rays as if in every mockery of the prevailing desolation.

Taking in a supply of wood and water at the river, we leave this valley of disappointment, and, after 8 or 10 miles traveling find a little grass, and halt in sight of the Black Hills, at the end of a long, weary, weary day of 17 hours and 31 miles travel through heat and dust.

PRAIRIE-DOG AND RATTLESNAKE LAND.

The next day of 18 miles travel over undulating country presents nothing of interest. To add to the nothingness of the vegetation, a scragly (sic) brush plant called by the Indians "Grease weed," puts in an appearance and helps to suck up the little moisture from the heated earth and air. The better parts of this miserable region are settled by prairie-dogs and rattlesnakes. This command and a few estrayed grasshoppers are the only visitors.

FIRST CAMP IN WYOMING.

Our next camp is on a bluff, overlooking a bad-land valley, which is all worn and washed into breaks and gullies. The Black Hills now loom up grandly, distant only 10 or 12 miles. During the afternoon several rain clouds formed over them and dispensed their rich treasures of moisture and coolness. The hot and naked plains below received not one drop, nor even the shadow of a passing cloud. The last two camps were in the southwest corner of Montana; this one, on the bluff, is in the northwest corner of Wyoming.

Leaving our bluff camp, 15 miles marching carries us to the Belle Fourche (Beautiful Fish,) or North Fork of the Cheyenne. Some of the valleys passed over during the day look well enough at a distance, but are either barren or produce little else than worthless weeds and brush. Several irony-ridges were covered with pine and scrub white oak. In the bottoms of the Belle Fourche there are a few large cottonwoods. We crossed the

trail made by captain Reynolds in his explorations of 1859. Our camp on the river is abundantly supplied with wood and grass, and, the next day being a rainy Sunday, we did not move. A reconnoitering party, escorted by a company of cavalry, traveled about eighteen miles through the rain and fog, and returned to camp late in the evening, with no other result than that of being wet, weary and hungry.

IN THE BLACK HILLS.

Winding our way out of the valley of the Beautiful Fork, we traveled fourteen miles among the foot hills of the mountains. Some of the lands are very fine, soil rich and deep, and the grass long, thick, of excellent quality and clear of cactus and brushweeds. Groves of pine, here and there, gave to the whole country the appearance of highly cultivated and ornamented estates in the East.

The base of the Black Hills is 2,800 or 3,000 feet above the sea level. Several of the plains crossed today can hardly be less than 4,000 feet high. As units of comparison, it may be stated that Mount Washington, a peak of the White Mountains in New Hampshire and the highest point in New England, is less than 5,800 feet, while Black Mountain in North Carolina, the highest land in the United States, east of the Mississippi, is only about 6,000 feet. The Alleghanies, in New York and Pennsylvania and Virginia, are nowhere over 3,000 feet. Altamont, on the Baltimore and Ohio railroad, is only 2,800 feet.

The valleys which we have seen today, are from a half mile to a mile in width, of fine meadow land. From the oak-fringed margins of the streams, their grassy slopes extend gradually upward, growing steeper till they meet the border of pines of the tali at the foot of the bluffs. In some cases these wooded tali reach to the very crests and conceal the rockly ledges of non-fossiliferous white and brown sandstone. Most of the timber is inferior.

The sunset was of unusual splendor. The lines of stratus and each fleecy rack in the west, were tinged with orange, red and golden hues; while in the east, the purple twilight bow extended its broad arch of beauty modest in its fainter

glory; towards the south, dark mountains of cumulus were edged with brightest silver, a gorgeous pathway fit for steps of deity. But these short-lived splendors fade away.

"And comes still evening on till twilight gray.
Hath in her sober livery all things clad."

The stars come out one by one, and troop by troop, till all the constellations burn, and "music of the spheres" begins and "all the hosts of heaven rejoice." The band plays, and thus, with mingled earthly and heavenly music, terrestial beauty and celestial glory, the first day ends and the first night is ushered in to the strangers among the Black Hills.

Moving forward the next morning, the gently sloping valleys become steep hillsides, and the spurs encroach more and more upon us, until we are almost wedged in and scarce have room to move the wagon train in a single line down the narrow ravine till it emerges suddenly into

RED WATER VALLEY, WYOMING.

This valley is from one to five miles wide and about thirty miles long, with numerous lateral valleys extending up the smaller streams. Its surface is generally level, though in some places rolling and occasionally variegated by a bars, rounded knoll or bank or red marl or shale. In these knolls and banks there are inexhaustible beds of gypsum, in some cases 25 or 30 feet in thickness, perfectly pure and white except where surface stained, and in all cases easily rained. It scarce seems an exaggeration to say that there is enough gypsum in this valley to fertilize every acre of land in the United States and to supply the whole world with plaster-paris.

There is scarce any waste land in all this valley. It is an immense meadow. Under cultivation it could not fail to produce heavy crops of corn and all the cereals; while, enclosed as it is by a great bulwark of rugged, pine-covered hills, from 3 to 8 hundred feet high, its sheltered situation would doubtless make it a suitable locality for fruit growing. The soil is of a red color, caused by the decomposition of red marle and shales. We made two

South Dakota State Historical Society

Harney Peak is in the far distance. The expedition passed about five miles south of it on July 30. On the morning of July 31 Custer and a small party set out and ascended the summit. A note was written and placed in a copper shell which was driven in a rock seam. The note read: "Gen. G. A. Custer, Gen. G. A. Forsyth, Col. Wm. Ludlow, W. H. Wood, A. B. Donaldson, N. H. Winchell, Script, July 31, 1874." Although Illingworth approached the mountain he did not make the difficult ascent. The peak was named in honor of Gen. William S. Harney by Lt. G. K. Warren who made a topographical survey of the region in 1857. Its altitude is 7,242 feet above sea level, but was erroneously presumed to be 9,700 feet high at the time of the Custer Expedition. Even at 7,242 feet it is the highest peak in the United States east of the Rocky Mountains.

camps on the Red Water and spent about three days in the valley. There are fine springs, clear, cold and strong. One of them furnished an abundance of water for all the men, horses, mules and cattle of the expedition. Its temperature was only 45 deg. (13 degrees above freezing). These are about the first good springs that we have found in our march of 325 miles.

Some of the ledges and buttes forming the rim of this valley are perfectly bare all over and so red that no painter could redden them. Their glaring color contrasts strongly with the green meadow and hills around.

During our sojourn here, the thermometer has at times risen to 117 degs. in the sun.

THE LAST FOE.

July 28. — Private John Cunningham, of Co. E., died at our camp in Red Water Valley on the night of July 21st. Disease, chronic diarrhea combined with acute pleurisy.

Two privates of Co. M, Joseph Turner and Wm. Raller, (sic) old comrades, who had been four years and nine months together, have often quarreled and sometimes

fought each other. On the morning of the 22nd of July the old enmity, and a new quarrel resulted in Roller's shooting Turner. Turner was placed in an ambulance, rode 23 miles, and died just as we entered camp in the evening. A post-mortem examination, made by Dr. Williams, showed that the wound must necessarily have resulted in death, no matter what the subsequent treatment.

Roller is under arrest, and upon the return of the expedition will be immediately turned over to the civil authorities for trial.

Upon a little knoll, within the

At first glance this picture and the one on the facing page appear to be identical. Closer study indicates, however, that the mountain in the distance in this photograph is obscured from view because of haze. Illingworth was attempting to photograph the highest point in the Black Hills—Harney Peak. After failing with this exposure he succeeded with the next.

limits of the camp, a broad grave was dug. In the evening, at a quarter to nine o'clock, the whole regiment, by companies, was called into line to attend the burial.

1st in the procession was the band.

2d. An ambulance bearing the two dead.

3d. The companies of which the deceased were members.

4th. Other companies.

5th. Regimental and staff officers and civilians.

As the solemn cortege marched across the campus, the band played a mournful dirge. A hollow square was formed about the grave. Side by side the two bodies were lowered into the vault. By the light of a lantern the funeral service was read. A platoon of soldiers then

stepped to the edge of the grave and fired three successive volleys. The dead heeded not! A trumpeter then came up, and blew loud and long. No response came! He then blew the call, "Day is closed, light put out!" The grave was then filled. As the placid moon and twinkling stars looked down upon the solemn scene, slowly and sadly we left the dead alone, "to sleep the sleep that knows no waking."

To hide the grave from the desecrating savage, who would soon come prowling round, its surface was leveled off and a fire was kept burning upon it all the next day.

A thousand thoughts come crowding up for utterance," but we forbear, and leave the reader to moralize upon this painful drama of real life.

MT. INYAN KARA.

At an early hour in the morning, Gen. Custer and staff, the scientific corps, and one reporter, escorted by two companies of cavalry, left the upper camp on the Red Water, to visit Mt. Inyan Kara, in Wyoming, latitude 44 degrees 13 minutes, and distant from our line of march about five miles. Captain Warren visited it in 1859. He estimated its height at 6,600 feet, which is about 1,500 feet higher than any land in the United States east of the Mississippi.

It covers about twelve square miles. Its shape is that of a horseshoe. The shoe is a sharp-backed ridge, several miles in length, and very steep on both its sides. In the center of the shoe is the mountain peak, rising several hundred feet

The identical location of tree limbs in this picture compared to the previous one, indicates that Illingworth did not move his camera. He did, however, expose a second plate to obtain this view of Mount Harney. The Peak was first spotted by the expedition on July 26th from a high hill along Castle Creek 20 miles to the northwest. Custer and his group approached Harney Peak on July 30th and climbed it July 31, 1874.

higher than any part of the ridge, and separated from it by a horse-shoe-shaped rocky canon, from 500 to 700 hundred feet deep.

There is no granite or other primary rock in the mountain neither basalt nor trap. The whole is an immense upheaval of non-fossiliferous, sedimentary metamorphic rock. The strata are very much broken and are inclined at almost every angle.

On the west side of the mountain and about 300 feet down its rugged side, is a perpendicular, columnar wall, 250 feet and a half mile long. Except in its composition, it resembles the palisades of the Hudson. At its foot is a talus of immense masses, extending two or three hundred feet down to the bottom of the canon. The view of

the mountain from the side of the canon opposite this wall can hardly be surpassed.

The encircling, horse-shoe ridge is mostly covered with Norway pine. The inner mountain is almost bare of vegetation. As difficult and even dangerous as the ascent, Gen. Forsythe led his horse to the very top, and brought him down again in safety. In the hard, flinty album of the summit, engraven with a cold chisel and hammer, in large and distinct characters, Arabic and Roman, is a date and an autograph, thus,

"74.
CUSTER."

If the archeologist is puzzled over this inscription, let him consult the commandant of this expedition.

T h e Topographical Engineer, Col. Ludlow, measured the height of the mountain above its base, and found it to be 1,100 feet. He had no means of estimating the elevation of the base above the sea-level; but there is no reason to doubt the correctness of Captain Warren, in fixing the height at 6,600 feet.

The temperature of the summit is sensibly lower than that in the plain below, and we found it pleasant to sit on the leeward side of the crest and in the sunshine.

Of the extensive and magnificent views from the summit, we can say nothing; for unfortunately, on the day of our visit the air was so hazy that nothing could be seen beyond ten miles. A hazy air is unusual in this country.

On account of the obscurity of the air and the difficulty in approaching the mountain, Mr. Illingworth took but one view of it, and that from a distance of about two miles.

FORESTS, PARKS AND FLORAL VALES

Climbing the steep banks of the Red Water, we were soon traveling over a handsome prairie, gradually rising towards a pine forest. Entering this we found it sufficiently open to give an easy passage to the train. Presently was prairie again. Thus on alternating till we reached one of the most charming little valleys in the world. It is narrow, only a few hundred yards wide, and resembles a beautiful well mown lawn, winding in endless curves and sinuosities through its pine-wooded margins. Little coves indent the timbered border. No landscape architect could design a scene of more perfect enchantment. Rocky points sometimes take the place of trees, and thus give increased beauty and corresponding interest.

Leaving this valley we climbed the pine-clad hills to forest plains. Excepting an occasional clump of popple or willow, deciduous trees have disappeared. The pine timber is good, tall and straight, and thousands of acres grow along our line of march. It never can be made available other than for home consumption, except by the building of railroads. Logging streams are too far away. But, as might be expected, the Indian has not been more fortunate than the white man in saving the forests from destruction. Thousands of square miles have been burned over, giving to the burnt districts a sort of desolate and graveyard look. In some cases a new growth has sprung up; but a burned pine forest seldom reproduces itself. In some cases it requires great labor to open a road through the fallen timber.

Panthers have been seen, and as many as 12 deer in one herd, and venison again supplies the camp.

Continuing an easterly course, with much delay and no little difficulty and danger, we passed down a steep ravine to

FLORAL VALLEY,

so named by General Custer, on account of its profusion of wild flowers. We made two camps in this valley and were about two days traveling up it, a distance of twenty miles.

It is almost fac simile of the valley we passed through only a few miles back. The brook which flows through it is a fine, rapid stream of clear water, about four feet wide and one foot deep. It gurgles and ripples over its stony bed, falls in sparkling cascades down the rocks, flows beneath mossy arches, and gives joy and refreshment to all. A finer stream for trout culture could hardly be found on the continent. Its source of supply is two or three large springs, flowing from beneath the mountain's base. Their temperature is from 44 to 44½ degrees. The water seems perfectly pure and without taste, smell or color.

In this valley, every sound is echoed from the timbered borders and the mountain sides. The report of a rifle seems as loud as that of artillery on the plains. The music of the band was weird and fascinating; it seemed to come from genii, concealed in the graves and caves of the mountains' sides, and fancy suggested the haunt of the muses. No wonder that the Indians have strange superstitions in regard to such fairy dells, and think them the bones of departed spirits.

About noon of the first day in this valley it became cloudy. At first the clouds swept along the mountain tops; but they gradually lowered until they almost touched our heads; finally they filled the whole valley and shrouded us with mist and dampness. In the evening they rolled away and the sun set clear.

The elevation of our two camps can hardly be less than 5,000 or 5,500 feet. The nights are very cool. Not a fly, gnat or mosquito can be seen. Excepting butterflies there is scarcely an insect.

This must once have been and still may be the favorite grazing ground of the elk. Eight pair of magnificent antlers were picked up. Gen. Custer intends presenting several of them to the Smithsonian Institute.

Strange to relate, sand-hill

cranes visit this valley; some of them were shot, and several of them were captured alive. They will help to increase the menagerie, which already includes hares, prairie dogs, night-hawks, owls, one eagle, and a cage of rattlesnakes. Additions will be made.

The floral decoration is the very richest. Every order and species seem to vie with every other in giving brilliancy to the display. The gaudy sun-flower and the delicate hare-bell, the fair lily and the bright blue daisy, the coarse elecampane and the modest vilet, the gay lark-spur and the fragrant peppermint, roses and pinks, asters and phlox, bell-flower and caropsis, geraniams, golden-rod, purple coneflower, are part of Flora's contributions to these lovely dels. There are about 50 species in flower, about 25 have flowered and perhaps about 25 are still to bloom. It is hardly possible to exaggerate in describing this flowery richness, and what is written above is less than the simple truth.

Many of these species are undescribed by botanists; and among them is a lily of rarest beauty. Many bulbs have been secured and will be carried home. Everybody, even muleteers, were enraptured with the flowers. Everybody was making bouquets. All sorts of interjections were used to express wonder and admiration. Some said they would give a hundred dollars just to have their wives see the floral richness for even one hour.

CROSSING THE BACK-BONE OF THE BLACK HILLS.

Following up Floral Valley, and rising rapidly, a few miles brought us to the mountain's crest, the divide between the waters of North and South Forks of the Cheyenne, at an elevation of 7,000 feet, where there is a natural depression—the valley on one side interlocking with a valley on the other side. The timber margins still continue, but the tall, straight spire like balsam is sprinkled more thickly among the pines. These interlacing avenues are perfect parks in beauty. There is a net work of them all through the mountains. Trout brooks, springs of almost icy coldness, beautiful wild flowers and abundant pasturage, are common to them all. In some places the timber margin recedes up the mountain side, leaving all below smooth and grassy; in other places the timber extends down to the level plat. In the lower parts of these valleys, picturesqueness is often mingled with grandeur, and rocks upon rocks are piled, in every possible form; precipices rise several hundred feet above the tops of the trees growing at their base; gigantic promontories push themselves into the foreground, and sharp-backed ridges cleave the sky; while an occasional massive column towers high above all else surrounding it, alone, silent, solemn, inaccessible.

WILD FRUITS.

There are two varieties of currants, black and red; two varieties of gooseberries, both large, smooth, delicious fruit; several varieties of June berries and huckleberries; strawberries, large and luscious; raspberries, black and red, both fine. All these fruits are abundant, and the whole command feasted. If nature uncultivated does all this, what might not the skilled horticulturist attain?

The sheltered vales must be favored homes for all the year. Beneath the pine-clad mountains side, the winter storms would scarce be felt; spring would early unfold her robes of green; summer, refreshed by showers and ever flowing streams of cool, crystal water, display her lavish beauty; and autumn yield abundant fruit.

For grazing and the dairy, central New York or the Western Reserve in Ohio are not better suited.

Mr. Illingworth still continues to photograph the scenery. The views taken along Castle Creek, and of our camps there, are French Creek, a branch of the south fork of the Cheyenne. It is so named by Gen. Custer on account of the castellated appearance of the rocky ledges along its sides.

ELK HORN PARK AND ELK HORN MONUMENT.

Our interpreter having misunderstood the guide, we marched from our first camp on Castle Creek, about 5 miles eastward over the rolling prairie of Elk Horn Park, and there found that deep ravines and rocky canors (sic) prevented our further advance and forced us to return to a second encampment on Castle Creek, only

two miles below the first. These camps are all that could be desired for water, pasturage, fuel and scenery. On a hill, at the further end of Elk Horn Park, is a stack of several hundred Elk horns. It is doubtless, the Indians votive offering to some deity. It has been standing many years, and the horns are bleached perfectly white. It was probably twelve or fifteen feet high when first built, but has settled down until it is now only five or six. It was photographed by our artist; the background of the view is fine mountain scenery.

BEAVERS.

In the trapping season, come here to hunt the beaver. These industrious animals, skilled hydraulic engineers, have many dams across the mountain streams. They have populous colonies in all the best valleys. They have preceded the white man in discovering and settling this excellent and remarkable country.

VIEWING THE LAND-SCAPE O'ER.

From a mountain top, near our Castle Creek camps, a vast area of country can be seen:—thousands of square miles of dark forest; thousands of square miles of burned forest; a number of fine parks, including Elk Horn; glimpses into numerous valleys, grassy and green as well-watered lawns; many mountain peaks, including Harneys, bare, rugged, rocky, distant about twenty miles E.S.E., and Crow's Nest, a similar peak, about the same distance N.E. If not mistaken in our longitude, our camps on Castle Creek are in Dakota. By our line of march, we are 395 miles from Fort A. Lincoln. We have rested four days in camp, and have marched twenty-three days, averaging a little more than seventeen miles a day. There has been but little sickness and the whole command is now well. We are passing through the centre of the Black Hills and there have been no acts of hostility. Neither gold nor silver have been found, but the miners report the indications more promising.

INDIAN TRAILS AND CAMPS.

July 30.—For a number of days past, we have been crossing or following recently made Indian trails.

The latter was the case as we came down Castle Creek. We passed several camps, lately occupied. About noon, on the 27th inst., the advance came upon a camp where the fires were still burning. The party had evidently just gone down the valley. Gen. Custer sent scouts forward, two of whom, Black Medicine and Bare Arm, soon returned, reporting that there were five lodges (a lodge is a tepee or tent) encamped about two miles below us, and just around a point in the valley.

The General, with E Company, and Lieut. Wallace, with a detachment of Ree and Santee scouts immediately went down. By great caution they succeeded in approaching the camp and surrounding it without giving any alarm. The General then sent down Louis Agar, a French half-breed, who speaks the Sioux language, and two Sioux scouts, with a flag of truce. He next sent in several Rees under their chief Bears Ears, with peaceful messages. The General with the cavalry, and Wallace, with the scouts, then went in. Some of the Indians were quite self-possessed, others were greatly alarmed, and some of the women and children attempted flight.

The General, through an interpreter, had a long and peaceful interview. Some of the men who were out hunting were sent for and they came in. They were a hunting party of the Ogilalah tribe of Sioux, and have an agency with that of Red Cloud on the White River in Wyoming, about 80 miles south of here. They did not know that there were any white people in the Black Hills, and had not heard of the expedition. There were 25 or 30, all told. They were well supplied with clothing and camp furniture (well for Indians) and had a number of nice, fat ponies. They gave their visitors cool, spring water to drink and with them, "smoked the pipe of peace." Their chief men were Slow Bull, One Stab, and Long Bear. Slow Bull has two wives, one of whom is the daughter of the renowned Chief, Red Cloud. She is the mother of four children, one at the breast.

The General, very carefully and fully explained to them the object of the visit to the Black Hills; that it was done in friendliness and good will towards the Indians; that they intended no harm but only kindness; that the Great Father (the President) only wanted to know something about the country, and that after we had spent a few days here in exploring, we would all go back peaceably; that instead of injuring or molesting them he would do all in his power to show his sincere friendship; he invited them to camp by us and eat of our rations while we stayed in the country; he invited them to visit our camp, and told them not to be alarmed; he told them that if they knew the country and would go with him and show him the best roads, he would make them all presents; he invited them, under any circumstances, to come and get rations, of flour and meat, sugar, coffee and tobacco. In short, he said and did all that was possible to conciliate them and to open with them friendly intercourse.

Some of them seemed reserved and timid and showed some fear of the Rees, their bitter enemies; others seemed social and anxious for further acquaintance. The timid ones said they had been in the Hills about two months, and that their time was up, and that they must return at once to the agency to draw their annuities; the others thought there was no need of so hasty a return. Much more was said and all in the kindest manner possible, and the interview finally terminated by a promise on their part to come up in the afternoon and visit us and accept a present of rations. They further promised and contracted that, for the rations given them they would furnish two guides to show us the best routes through the Black Hills.

Our party then all returned.

In the afternoon, four of the men came up, and were received at headquarters with every mark of attention, respect and kindness including much hand-shaking.

However, they acted strangely, and before the commissary wagons had reached our camp; two of them slyly passed out and did not return. The other two seemed uneasy and did not want to wait for the presents, but proposed to come up in the morning and get them. The general then borrowed the rations from one of the companies,

the supply train still not having come.

To make assurance doubly sure, to prevent the possibility of molestation to any of the band by the Rees or any other of command the General sent word to Lieut. Wallace to select fifteen of his most reliable Santees and send them down with the two men carrying the rations, with orders to stay on guard at their encampment all night, to prevent molestation, and to come up with them in the morning to our camp to receive more rations.

Wallace requested the ration bearers One Stab and Long Bear, to wait a few minutes until he could select the friendly escort and guard. In the meantime, and while the detail was being chosen, the General went over to that side of the camp. But the ration bearers did not wait as Wallace requested, and he sent a Sioux scout to request their return. But to return, they refused. The General, not wishing his guard of fifteen to go down alone, but in company with the men carrying the rations, lest going down alone might cause alarm in the Ogilalah camp, directed the ration bearers to be brought back, and ordered several Santees to follow them and repeat the request, and explain the reason, and that if they still refused to, then take their ponies by the bridles and lead them back.

This order was obeyed to the letter; but Long Bear, refusing to return, one of the Santee sergeants took hold of the pony's bridle, as directed: whereupon Long Bear seized the sergeant's gun and attempted to wrest it from him. The sergeant only saved it by throwing himself from his horse; and, regarding Long Bear's act as the beginning of hostilities, he fired at him as he retreated up the hill from the valley. One or two other shots were fired at him.

One Stab returned to our camp, and is still with us. The scouts immediately hastened down to the Ogilalah camp, and found that the whole party had fled, evidently soon after the friendly interview. They had destroyed all their camp, equipage, chopped up their tent poles, cut holes in their kettles, and thrown away their dried meat. Their trail was followed for a long distance; but they had been many

hours on the way, were far ahead and traveled so fast that they could not be overtaken.

The fate of Long Bear is involved in mystery. But the next day, his saddle and blankets were found in the woods, having some blood on them. In another place his guncover and rations were found. Fifteen men have scoured the woods but have failed to find the pony or his rider. Whatever his misfortune may be, it is the result of his own indiscretion and double-dealing.

One Stab is treated very kindly. He knows the country and promises to guide us through it. He will remain a captive a few days; and, if he proves true, will be well rewarded. He seems contented, though stolid; but this latter is only Indian-like.

The sincere and earnest effort made to open and maintain friendly intercourse with this band of Sioux has been frustrated by their own folly, hostility and treachery. Outside of our own command, these Ogilalahs are the only human beings with whom we have had one word of intercourse since leaving Fort Abraham Lincoln.

BUILDING STONE.

August 2.—A large part of the rock formation is carbonate of lime (marble), of various degrees in hardness and fineness. It is sometimes all one color, white or dark, sometimes as veined and mottled as the Egyptian. Of that which is good, there is a sufficient quantity to supply the sculptors of the world and all the cemeteries, and to cover the Black Hills all over with a city of marble. A large part of the sandstone is well adapted for building purposes. There are whole mountains of mica schist; some of the harder and less shaley portions of which would probably answer for building stone. At any rate, it would make enough scythe whetstones to supply the world. There are whole mountain ranges of granite. Some of it is hard and fine and variable in color; other portions exceedingly coarse and friable, containing great sheets of mica and large crystals of tourmaline, and occasionally large masses of feldspar or quartz. Besides these principal kinds of rock, there are others, more or less valuable for building or other purposes.

FROM CASTLE CREEK TO CUSTER PARK

The direction from the former to the latter of those places is nearly south; distance 28 miles.

There is the same alternation of woodland and prairie, upland and valley, as described in former letters. Some entire mountains edges are made of micaceous shades. As the sun shines upon them they glisten like mirrors, and make the whole mountain's side appear like shining silver. As the angle of reflection changes, the brightness fades away, and nothing but the dull, black rock remains. The captain of one of the cavalry companies thought he discovered a great natural wonder, a hole in the top of the mountain, through which the sky could be seen; presently he saw another, then another; finally all disappeared. They were reflections from the shales.

The day we left Castle Creek, Headquarters moved in advance and selected an encampment in a green meadow, watered by a cool, babbling brook, and sheltered by a background of pine-clad mountains. The distance was 15 miles. But though most of the road was easy, a few bad places caused much delay. Some fallen timber had to be cleared away, a ravine had to be bridged, and up one steep grade the teams had to be doubled. The result was night came, and the train rested in a little valley three miles from headquarters. The command was divided, the greater portion being with the train, The advance prepared for a bivouac. Several deer had been brought in, and over the camp fires slices of the tender venison were roasted on the ends of forked sticks. This, with "hard tack" and the icy-cold water made our evening meal. The meat was delicious; but to an appetite sharpened by the day's ride through the cool, mountain air, almost anything is good. Beneath the deep foliage of the pines bright fires were built, and with no other mantle than the starlit heavens, we passed away the hours of night in telling stories, or in sleeping on the ground. After a while the moon rose, and its soft lambent fight chased the darkness from the valley, and the paler stars faded from the sky. At length, at about half

past three the lumbering train came in, and by sunrise breakfast was ready, and at seven o'clock we again moved on, through handsome groves, along valleys green, and over prairies, rich for tillage and grazing. On our left was a high, stony, granite ridge. Until today no granite has been seen. The ridge is almost perpendicular, and in most places entirely bare of vegetation. Its sharp back seems dislocated and vertebrae no longer united, but separated by fissures hundreds of feet in depth. A chamois might skip across these deep rents, but less agile mountaineers would need a bridge. These vertebrae are not usually sharp and angular but have been smoothed and rounded by the action of the weather. Still there is no regularity or symmetry in their forms, and they constantly change in profile as viewed from different points. This was a busy day for the landscape photographer. Evening found us encamped in one of the most charming and lovely natural parks in the world. Gen. Custer is probably the first civilized man whose eyes beheld this scene of beauty. After much entreaty, his modesty is far gave way reluctantly to consent to the the request of the topographical engineer that the name be

CUSTER PARK.

We have spent four days in this delightful retreat, have gone up, down, and across it, and yet its graces have not been half revealed. In my attempt at describing it, there is no danger of exaggeration. Expressions of admiration are heard from all. No one ever saw anything to equal it. The Yosemite Valley and the Mariposa Forests, the Yellowstone Park and the valleys of the Hudson, Mohawk and Connecticut, have grandeurs and beauties and richness in varying degrees; but here these elements are marvelously combined as scarcely to need a single thing to give perfection to this landscape design of the Infinite Architect. One man said, "I have visited Central Park in New York City a thousand times, but its beauties will not compare with these."

The length of this park may be approximately stated at fifteen miles, and its width three miles. In places, it may not be over a

mile wide, in others six or eight miles. No one can define its limits. It has no well marked boundaries. There are broad avenues leading out of it in every direction, among the enclosing ridges and peaks. There are endless curvatures in these avenues, with ever-changing and always new and beautiful views.

Some of the encircling ranges and peaks have smooth sides and rounded summits, and are covered all over with pine and balsam; others are perfectly bare and smooth, hundreds of feet in height, and almost inaccessible.

In several places great blocks of granite, almost as large as the Metropolitan house, lie scattered around the edges or inside the peak. Between and among these enormous masses there are narrow and angular paths, intersecting each other in a perfect network of intricacy. Be careful, lest in these deep cool, shadowy clefts you lose yourself. In other places the rocks are not so large, and among them pine trees grow. There are hundreds of these rock and grove islands; besides there are many shady, timber islands without the rocks. These little groves, from a clump of half dozen trees to several acres in extent, are sometimes on a level with the green enclosing lawn; sometimes they are on smooth hillocks, but everyone is a perfect gem. There are thousands of beautiful views in this park, no two of which are alike. The broad acres and the winding passages are all alike covered with thick, green grass, the product of a soil rich in all the elements of plant nutrition.

A very little labor would open carriage roads for miles and miles up the ravines and gulches of the mountains, while bridle-paths might be made to reach the grand canons and the lofty peaks.

Here is the hunter's paradise: squirrels, hares, wolves, panthers, bears, deer and elk are here. Let the disciples of Izaac Walton come here with the outfit of the "Complete Angler," and indulge in piscatorial sports and dreamy reveries along the banks of Custer Creek.

The lover of nature could here find his soul's delight; the invalid regain his health; the old, be rejuvenated; the weary find sweet repose and invigoration; and all who could come and spend the heated season here, would find it the pleasantest summer home in America.

A VISIT TO HARNEY'S PEAK.

From our first encampment in Custer Park to Harney's Peak is eight or ten miles in a straight line, nearly east. Gen. Custer and a small party, escorted by a part, only, of one company of cavalry, set out early in the morning to visit the peak. About half the distance, the road was good and scenery like that of the park. Then came the climbing of stony ridges, picking our way among burned and fallen timber, boring through the tanglewood of the gorges, and occasional flounderings through treacherous morasses. But all the way there was cool water and abundance of berries. Large and luscious service berries hung in such thick clusters that beneath their weight branches were bending down and almost breaking. Their were a few trailing blackberries or dewberries. But of raspberries there was no end. Acres and acres of the mountains' sides were covered with them. They literally reddened the ground. They were large and sweet and could be picked in clusters of from three to six. The bushes were not large, but they were loaded with the luscious fruit. They grow best where the forests had been burned, and were found all the way up to the top of Harney's Peak.

From the bottom of a deep ravine, we climbed and climbed upward, walking most of the way and leading the horses. At last we stood beneath the almost perpendicular peak which we supposed to be Harney's. Leaving the horses we had to scale the almost verticle wall for about 200 feet. Wedging ourselves into the clefts, and pushing ourselves up after the fashion of chimney sweeps, clinging to projecting points and straddling over ridges, we at last reached the top.

The view was worth infinitely more than all that it had cost us. Southwest of us, about 30 miles distant, we could distinctly see the valley of the South Fork of the Cheyenne, and beyond it for 20 miles the Bad Lands, reaching across to the White River, distant 50 miles, which could be traced by

the lines of timber on its borders.

Southward the plains beyond the Black Hills went stretching away, until in the far, dim, blue distance they were indistinguishable from the sky. South and southwest we could see the mountain ranges north and west of Fort Laramie, and possibly among them, Laramie Park.

Seven degrees east of north, true meridan, huge Bear Butte lifted its rugged form into the blue depths, distant 50 miles

Northward we could not see beyond the Black Hills.

We could see the green meadows and paradisiacal loveliness of Custer Peak. Eastward was not Adam's Eden, but another Eden "of God's planting" in the Black Hills, diversified by lawn and grove, and silvery brooks and ever-changing vistas.

But around us, for miles and miles away, what a waste of mountains. Naked granite everywhere. Ridges, walls, pinnacles all around us. Gen. Forsythe says: "This is the Switzerland of America." All say, "We never saw the likes for rugged desolation." Some of the ridges are cloven and weathered into needle-shaped columns, and were fitly named "Organ Peaks," from their resemblance to the pipes of an organ. There are many such organ peaks all around us. In this sublime cathedral of nature, let Aeolus play in gently summer zephyrs; and in winter let Boreas make the mountains tremble with the reverberating music from those tremendous columns.

On the top we ate our lunch, and from cool canteens we all drank to General Harney's health.

About three-quarters of a mile east of us is a peak (Harney No. 2) several hundred feet higher. We resolved to climb it. In due time we reach the top, and after a hurried glance start down again, calling to those below, "Stop! there is a higher peak beyond!" A council is held, and it is unanimously and enthusiastically resolved to visit No. 3 the true Harney's Peak, still eastward about one and a half miles, and not visible from No. 1, on account of the interveniton of No. 2.

Away we go! There is no time to lose. It is already late in the afternoon. Among trees, bushes and rocks we must go down at an

angle of nearly 45 degrees to the bottom of a ravine a thousand feet deep and a good deal more than a thousand up on the other side.

The escort remained behind. The rest of us somehow or other, got across and took our horses along. Gen. Custer walked and his orderly led his horse; Gen. Forsyth rode; the rest of us, by riding, walking, jumping, sliding, rolling, bumping, thumping, pulling and pushing got down and up again, and finally stood below the peak, an almost perpendicular wall several hundred feet high, where we left our horses, and then climbed up much in the same manner as at No. 1.

The rarified air, the exertion and the excitement run Prof. Winchell's pulse up to 136 and Gen. Custer's to 112 per minute.

The view is nearly the same as from No. 1, except that the horizon is further removed. Gen. Custer fired several percussion shots from his needle-gun. They could scarcely fail to strike against rock, and the sound of the explosion reached us in 16 seconds; the distance must have been several miles. A doe and two fawns crossed the mountain just below us.

We were 1,900 feet above the bottom of the ravine, 800 feet higher than peak No. 1, and probably 7,500 feet above the ocean level. Still there was, right by us and just above us, a square rock rising up about 75 feet, which we could not climb. Prof. Winchell made the attempt and partially succeeded, but a loose rock just above him made it dangerous to climb higher. He stood above us all. The following memoranda was written and closely folded and put inside an empty copper cartridge shell. The point of the shell was beaten into a wedge shape and then drived into a seam in the rock: "Gen. G. A. Custer, Gen. G. A. Forsyth, Col. Wm. Ludlow, W. H. Wood, A. D. Donaldson, N. H. Winchell, Script. July 31, 1874."

Besides this party, it is almost certain that no human beings ever before climbed these peaks. It is certain that no white man ever did; and it is well known that the noble, the royal, the genuine North American Indian is one of the laziest mortals on earth. He never climbs if he can help it, and when he happens to reach a high hill top, he

Correspondent A. B. Donaldson gives this decription of organ pipes near Harney Peak: "We never saw the like for rugged desolation. Some of the ridges are cloven and weathered and needle-shaped columns and were fitly named 'organ peaks' from their resemblance to the pipes of an organ. There are many such organ peaks all around us . . . in this sublime cathedral of nature. . ."

always heaps up a pile of stone as a memorial of his visit. No such monuments were found on any of these peaks.

We had not time to devise a scaling ladder to reach the highest point; but after making a few observations, gathering some fern leaves and geological specimens, we started down. Private O'Toole, the General's orderly, had attempted the ascent. He only climbed up about ten feet, then despaired and waited till our return. In coming down he slipped and lodged on a point and spread himself out on the rock like a letter X, and cried, "Oh! oh! oh! Lordy!" Presently he slid down the balance of the way, all unscathed, but vowing mentally to forever thereafter restrain all ambition.

It was nearly sun-down. The dark shadows nearly filled the ravines and sunlight only gilded the highest peaks. Joining the escort, away we went, Gen. Custer in front. Down, down, over the rocks, logs, bushes, everything. Mazeppas ride was nothing to this. It was not a mad ride, but a brave, daring one. Spotted Tail nor Sitting Bull with all their pain-begrimmed warriors yelling at our heels could not have made us ride faster. I plunged the spurs into patient old Dobbins' sides to make him keep up, and he became desperate and plunged along and I was afraid he would fall and break his neck and mine too. I got off and tried leading him; but nothing less than a pair of mules could have pulled hard enough to make him

keep up with our rate of marching. On his back again, away we go and keep the column closed. At last we get to the bottom of the great ravine, which the biggest ridge of Alleghanies would not more than half fill. Bushes, green and dead here crossed our path; but on we went, smashing down everything except the mountains. A whole herd of stampeded buffaloes could hardly have made more noise crashing through a thicket.

Darkness was not long in coming. We halted to see if all were up. The escort had fallen behind, and was out of hearing. We waited for them to come up. The order was given to keep the column closed. We still had a good many miles of marching to do through brush-wood and forest, and over several ridges before reaching the open country of the park. We knew the direction to the camp, but there was no road or trail to follow. We must steer by stars and compass, in the deep darkness, over a route that would be considered very difficult if not impassable even by daylight. The men said they could not keep us and lead their horses. The General ordered them all to mount and stay mounted, except when he ordered them to dismount.

On we go again! through forests and thickets, along the mountain sides, and over ridges. The rocks strike fire from the horses' shoes. Scarce a word is spoken. The clatter and clang of iron hoofs, the words "Halt," "Dismount," and "Mount," and the crackling of branches, are about the only sounds. The trees grow taller, and the shades deeper. We sometimes halt to see which is the north star. At length the clouds hide that from view, and occasionally a match is struck to take our bearings by the compass.

We came to a bog, overgrown with bushes, twelve or fifteen feet high. Gen. Custer's horse had done a full share of road breaking, and to relieve him another man and horse were placed in front. The pioneer got safely through, and the dismounted column was ordered to follow. All that could be seen was a black hole in the bushes, and then all was utter darkness till we got out on the other side. In the middle of the miry bog was a ditch. I felt, or rather stumbled my way into it, and out again. Dobbin did not better than his leader. He may have seen something; I am sure I saw nothing except when the bushes switched across my eyes there were showers of falling stars. Just as he floundered through the first ditch I sloughed down in a second one, and in trying to pull out I fell and was afraid of being run over by him and the balance of the column. With more vehemence than euphony I called wo! wo! and he halted. Then woe was me. Well fertilized with a coat of black muck I crawled out from between his forefeet and paddled my way out to terra firma, soiled but sound. Those more experienced in roughing it took the

horses by the tails and were led, or rather towed through.

Going on a little further we suddenly came to a jumping off place and halted. Gen. Putnam could not have gone down, and could not have gone forward if he were down. The moon was just rising. The rocky field before and below us was worse if possible than the lava beds of the Modocs. Turn about we did at a right angle (to the left,) and again marched bravely on.

We were soon on the borders of the park. The trees were tall and heavy and stood apart. The smokers lighted their pipes and cigars, the power of speech returned and we jogged merrily on, certain of reaching camp.

Soon we struck the open avenues, followed them down to the broader meadows, and looking away of the park four or five miles ahead, we saw a beacon burning on a mountain peak near the camp, to light us home. It is no use to say that we were not glad of the sight. We had been "lone and wandering, though not lost" for homes, and had nothing now to do but go straight home on easy and safe road.

Our ride had been a long one. It was dangerous for horses and not safe for men. Yet we were all safe. We were punched and scratched a little; but none were hurt and nothing was lost.

We all felt compensated a hundred fold for the hardships of the adventure. The satisfaction and knowledge of such a day's experience and observation is worth more than dollars and cents.

We rode up the valley through the chill and damp of midnight and entered camp about one o'clock. O how glad they all were to see us back in safety and in such fine spirits. Col. Grant said that he never before in his life felt so glad to see anybody! They had feared that were were lost or captured and had sat up watching for us. Such cordial and hearty greetings it is a pleasure to receive.

EXPLORING PARTY OFF FOR THE BAD LANDS

This morning at six o'clock, two companies of cavalry with three days rations, started on an exploring expedition eastward, and to the Bad Lands beyond the south fork

of the Cheyenne. They took no wagons, carrying their supplies and equipage on pack horses and mules. We will remain here in the park till their return.

Prof. Winchell and Mr. Grinnell went along. The former to work up the geology and secure fossils, the latter for fossils only. These two, with one assistant, were the only civilians in the party.

STEREOSCOPIC VIEWS.

These are busy days for **Mr.** Illingworth. He has no time for hunting now. From early morn till dewy eve he is fully occupied in securing views of this inimitable scenery. He will return with one of the finest collections of photographic art ever offered to the admirers of the sublime and beautiful.

INDIANS.

Not one word additional. One Stab is still with us. No Indians are seen.

THE MAIL OUT.

The courier, bearing our mails, will leave tomorrow morning, via Fort Laramie. He is a white man named Reynolds, thoroughly acquainted with Indian policy and life on the plains, and has carried out mails from other exploring expeditions. He will be attended for about a day and a half by an escort of cavalry, acting as explorers; he will then have about 80 miles to travel alone.

ALL WELL THUS FAR.

Up to this date, the expedition has been eminently successful. In valuable information collected, it will be second to none. If nothing untoward befalls it during the thirty days remaining, the whole country may be thankful that it was organized and prosecuted.

THE RETURN ROUTE.

It is the present expectation to commence the return march in a few days, go eastward by Bear Butte, then across into Montana, and down the Little Missouri, exploring its bad lands, and enter Fort A. Lincoln from the Northwest.

GOLD,

has been found, but whether or not in quantities sufficiently large to pay for the mining has not yet transpired. The indications become more promising daily, and prospecting still continues.[12]

D.

12. Prof. Donaldson is a gentleman of fine scientific attainments, a keen and accurate observer, and his statements possess the reliability, which is not always found in letters of professional correspondents.

The discovery of gold in paying quantities, the varied and exuburant flora, the abundance of game, grass, timber, and small fruits, mentioned in Gen. Custer's official report are fully described in detail by Prof. Donaldson, together with interesting incidents of the long march.

ST. PAUL PIONEER
Issue of August 14, 1874

ST. PAUL PIONEER
Issue of August 14, 1874

BLACK HILLS EXPEDITION
Through the Black Hills—Another Exploration—Beauties of Custer Par, Etc.

NEAR S. W. CORNER
OF DAKOTA,
11 o'clock p. m., Aug. 3
To the Editor of the PIONEER.

This morning at six o'clock, Gen. Custer and staff, with an escort of four companies of cavalry, rationed for three days, left camp at Custer's Park, to explore the Black Hills in a southwesterly direction, and conduct the mail bearer one day on the road to Laramie. By invitation of Gen. Custer, your correspondent accompanied the party.

Here we are, bivouacked for the night. All well thus far. No Indians and no trouble. The courier leaves in a few minutes. He will travel all night. He goes alone. He is well mounted and well armed. His horse is a fresh one. It was led thus far on the way.

The first twelve miles of our ride was through Custer Park. It is larger and more beautiful than my description makes it.

The last 25 miles was this side of the Hills and is mostly dry and sterile. Gypsum in inexhaustible quantities is here, and sandstone and limestone. This country is hilly and broken, and timber small and scarce.

We marched 45 miles today. Pack mules bore the rations and bedding. We will return by a new route. We hope Mr. Reynolds may get safely through to Laramie.

For the present adieu.

A. D. Donaldson.

ST. PAUL PIONEER
Issue of August 25, 1874

BLACK HILLS EXPEDITION.

More Letters from Prof. Donaldson.

The Most Distant Point Reached by the Expedition.

Discovery of a Herd of Three Hundred Elk.

Further Descriptions of the Black Hills Country.

Hunting Grizzlies and Elk in the Mountains—Getting Lost in the Fog.

Special Correspondence of the St. Paul Pioneer.

BLACK HILLS EXPEDITION,
Aug. 8, 1874.

The morning after the departure of the courier with our last mail, Gen. Custer and his party left their bivouac and in a few minutes reached the South Fork of the Cheyenne, crossed over and rode several miles down the westside. The last 20 miles before reaching the river is through a poor and hilly country. The soil, naturally thin is rendered almost barren by drouth. The timber gradually runs out. On the river only a few small cottonwoods grow. Southward the treeless, arid plains extend indefinitely.

While on the river, we were fully fifty miles from the train encampment in Custer Park, and not less than twenty miles southwest of the Black Hills. On that side it is hard to tell where the Hills end and the plains begin. From one to the other the transition is gradual. The river, where we saw it, is four or five rods wide, shallow and full of sand and gravel bars. The water is clear but strongly impregnated with gypsum and saline matter. It is not palatable when first dipped up, and when carried a little while in canteens becomes nauseating.

Several miles before reaching the river, cactus makes its appearance, and, in the bottoms, it and sage brush are the almost exclusive vegetation.

Along the gullies leading down to the river, two species of wild currants grow. Both are large, and the black one especially pleasant to the taste. Wild cherries are abundant. They grow in the ravines, on small bushes, are large and very black, are not bitter nor astringent, but sweet and luscious; so that even these waste lands may furnish valuable additions to our already large lists of cultivated fruits.

While on the river, we were about 475 miles, by our trail, from Fort A. Lincoln. This is the most distant point reached by any portion of the expedition. Leaving the river, we started for the train. There was but the slightest breeze, the sun poured down his heat upon us from a cloudless sky. For 20 miles there was not a drop of water. Man and beast suffered from thirst. Two horses gave out

While they were in the Harney Peak vicinity, Correspondent A. B. Donaldson wrote "These are busy days for Mr. Illingworth. He has no time for hunting now. From early morn till dewy eve he is fully occupied in securing views of this inimitably (sic) scenery." Donaldson accompanied Custer to the top of Harney Peak. The climb was difficult but in his dispatch Donaldson said, "The view was worth infinitely more than all that it had cost us."

and were abandoned. The pack mules were the only animals that did not languish. Beneath their big, unwieldy loads of bedding, provision and forage, they trotted nimbly and comically along, not caring for anything except to occasionally launch out their heels at some unwary horseman who unluckily rode too near, or to bray and snort discordantly, in harmony with nothing except the prevailing dreariness of the country.

At length we reach the edge of the Black Hills, find good pasture in a green meadow, and plenty of water; sleep soundly, sweetly, healthfully beneath the open sky, and early in the morning are on the way, twenty miles from the train.

But the scene is changed. All around is full of interest, attraction, beauty. Cold, running streams, and valleys green, and deepest shades; rocks, monuments, precipices, and towering mountains, fill the mind with wonder and delight. On the top of a wooded ridge, rising up in silent majesty and grandeur, full twice as high as the tall pines growing at its foot, there stands a perpendicular granite column, 20 or 30 feet in diameter, crowned by an immense capital, 40 or 50 feet in depth or breadth. It is a prominent landmark for twenty or more miles in all directions. It was named Turk's Head. Beside this giant Castle Rock is the merest pigmy.

As a lone and faithful sentinel, here it has stood for ages. Not the lightning bolt, volcanic throes nor marring elements have broken its silent vigils or marred its grand proportions. In ever—during majesty, (sic) it will keep "watch and ward" over the Black Hills till the foundations of the earth shall be broken up and "time shall be no longer."

Sergeant B. L. Clear, of K company has been seven years and seven months a member of the Seventh Regiment United States Cavalry. Gen. Custer and other officers of the regiment have known him for years. They all speak of him in the highest terms. They all have entire confidence in his truthfulness, reliability, coolness and good judgment. Some five or six miles before we reached the train, Clear was riding alone, two or three miles off, on one of the flanks. He says that he there saw a herd of not less than one hundred elk. The herd was approaching him, and was almost within easy gunshot, when the braying of his mule startled them, and they ran off in an opposite direction. Being so far away and alone, and his mule already tired, he did not think it best to pursue. There is no reason for distrusting this story. The fresh tracks of large herds have been seen by many. I have seen them. They are nearly as large as cattle tracks. Many small herds have been seen, and the Indians and others have killed and brought in a considerable number of both buck and cow elk. One of the Santees killed three large buck Elk in one day. Their meat was nearly all eaten, and their horns and skins were saved.

Deer are also abounding. One man killed and brought in five in one day. The Indians have whole wagon loads of the dried skins. Often, in our camps at night, we can hear the snarling, barking and howling of the wild beasts, in the mountains.

The exploring party, which set out to visit the Bad Lands south of the Cheyenne, failed to reach their destination. They were out a little over three days and were within two or three miles of the river. They traveled, in going and returning, 88 miles. In the direction they went, it is almost impossible to get out of the Hills. The mountains were so steep that some of the horses, while being led up, tipped over backwards. One of them had to be abandoned. Sometimes stones were accidentally loosened and came rolling down, greatly to the danger of all below. In one case, a man only saved himself by standing behind a tree. A large stone struck the tree and nearly cut it off.

Rather than climb these steps they attempted to reach the plains by going down the canon of Custer Park Creek. This canon is seven or eight miles long, and has perpendicular walls, from five to eight hundred feet in height. They followed it seven miles, through pools

and over its stony bed, till at length they came to a great rock, lying across the chasm, which forbid all further advance, compelling them to return and climb the ridge.

The night before leaving the lower camp in Custer Park, Gen. Custer returned to the chief, One Stab, his pony, rifle, and all his other things, gave him five days rations, bid him good bye, and had him quietly passed beyond our lines about nine or ten o'clock, so that he might put at least a nights travel between himself and danger from our blood-thirsty Rees. The old man, though 63 years old, is straight and tall, sits up gracefully in his saddle and rides well. He was glad to be free again, and ere daylight came was doubtless many miles on his way to the agency; nor long would he delay till the smoke of his own tepee should gladden his eyes and his arrival make happy the hearts of his squaw and papooses, and the wonderful story of his captivity and deliverance he related to his astonished countrymen. When our Rees found that he was indeed gone and out of their reach, they were moody and silent. The Chief, Bloody Knife, slunk to the rear of the marching column and scarce spoke a word all day, except to say that he felt ashamed and disappointed.

The Chief, Bears Ears, went to Gen. Custer and, after expressing his displeasure, resigned his office as one of the guides of the expedition. Mad Bull (appropriately named) made a great speech, showing that he and Bear's Ears should have been allowed to take out and kill and scalp the poor, old, emaciated, disarmed, unoffending captive. Gentle, magnanimous, noble, christian red men? Heroes and martyrs be they all.

By triangulation, the engineer corps ascertained that Harney's Peak is 4,200 feet above the level of our lowest camp in Custer Park. They suppose this camp to be about 5,000 feet above the sea, giving to Harney a total height of about 9,000 feet.

During our sojourn in the Hills there have been a great many fine rains and thundershowers, both by day and by night. The echo of the thunder, as it rolls, and rumbles and roars and trembles along the mountain gorges is deeply impres-

sive, and sublime. As thus "From peak to peak, the rattling drags among, Leaps the live thunder," the soul that is not utterly devoid of sensibility, must be awed into reverential silence, as seeing man's littleness and Deity's omnipotence. Storms on the plains have more of terror, more of danger, but less of grandeur.

These summer rains clothe the mountains and the vales between with the richest verdure, and cause the cool springs to gush forth in never-failing abundance. So copious and so life-giving are these rains, that two vallies where we have recently encamped, the millions of grasshoppers that covered the earth, and swarmed in the air, were not able to eat up the vegetation as fast as it grew, and the vallies were green and afforded excellent grazing. On the plains and in the States, one half such a grasshopper scourge would devour everything.

We encamped in Custer Park about seven days. There is but one sentiment in regard to it: In natural beauty it cannot be surpassed. It is the farthest point reached by the wagon train, and is distant from Fort Lincoln 425 miles. We commenced the return march August 6th, and followed the old trail back about thirty miles, and then struck off eastward through Elk Horn Prairie, in the direction of Bear Butte. After crossing a mountain ridge, a camp was located in a green meadow beside a cool mountain stream. The train was still several hours behind and Gen. Custer and Col. Ludlow, Bloody Knife and private Noonan, went up the valley a short distance, looking for a road out the next morning and also having an eye for any game that might be near. Presently Col. Ludlow saw a herd of deer and commenced counting them, one, two, three, four, five— when Bloody Knife exclaims motto! motto! (bear! bear!). Immediately the deer were forgotten and all parties paid their compliments to the bear in rifle shots. Bruin ran off some distance through the brush and among the trees. Finding himself wounded and hotly pursued, he came to bay and prepared for fight at close quarters. He reared his huge form up and his hind legs, with his back against a pine tree and his face to the foe, and with his fore paws very politely gestured to his lately made acquaintances to come forward to a friendly pow-wow and hand-shaking, and a still more friendly hugging. His courteous invitations were only answered by a cold lead, soon to be followed by a keen bloody knife in the hands of Bloody Knife, searching for the great jugulars through which flowed the tide of life. Bruin died. He was an old dark-brown grizzly. He was taken into camp that all might see the first grizzly bear ever shot by a white man in the Black Hills. He was placed on a big rock, his four captors just in the rear, and the group was photographed. You will want the picture.

Later in the afternoon, one of the Santees, Red Bird, killed another grizzly, and brought in the skin and part of the meat. The common, black bear and the large common bear are found here.

BADLY SCARED.

The killing of two grizzly bears in one afternoon would, of course, create intense excitement. Everybody was anxious to go out a hunting, and every one expected to be successful in the capture of the biggest game. Around the evening campfires, hunting stories were told and hunting parties were organized for the next day. Some were so excited that they hardly closed their eyes in sleep that night.

Reveille sounded at 3 o'clock in the morning, and soon the whole camp was active. The fires were rekindled and blazed up brightly, warming and drying the chill, damp, foggy air. Breakfast was soon prepared and over, tents were struck and loaded, and before it was fairly light the camp ground was deserted.

A fog had settled down over mountain and valley, and nothing could be seen beyond fifty yards distance.

Numerous hunting parties had started out, all full of animation and excitement, ready for deer, elk, grizzlies, or Indians. For some time the advance of the train and its direction could be known by the playing of the band. At length the playing ceased or the sound was lost in the distance. There was but little conversation, lest the sound of voices might startle the game,

and except an occasional gunshot, scarce a sound could be heard. For several hours we almost groped our way up the valleys, across the ridges, through the forests and thickets and over fallen timber. Our party was guided in part by the sound of the land and in part by a compass carried by Prof. Winchel (sic). We first started westward, then southward and finally swung around into an easterly course, the direction in which our days march was to be made. This detour brought us, as we supposed, about two miles from the train, on the left flank, the train to our right.

Confident of our being right, we were moving quietly along through a clean, grassy avenue only a few yards wide and bounded on each side by a handsome growth of young pines. Suddenly our horses pricked up their ears, as if they saw something ahead. We strained our eyes in vain to pierce the fog. We saw nothing, and rode on. Presently, directly in front of us and coming towards us, uprose, like apparitions out of the mist, three armed horsemen. They were a sergeant and two men out hunting. They thought the train was to the left hand and going westward; we thought to the right hand and going eastward. One or both parties must be wrong. The safest plan was to run no risk by going forward in either direction, but to return to the train at once. All of our party, except myself, did this. The sergeant was an experienced hunter and woodsman, and I thought it safe to follow him. My object was to find a pair of elk horns attached to the skull—detached horns could be found by the wagon load. I had declined the offer of a rifle, and did not expect to kill any game.

We followed the sergeant several miles, going a little north of west. We ventured to suggest that it was hardly possible that the train should move so far westward, that we had gone around a head of it, that it had crossed our trail in our rear and was going eastward, opposite the course we were traveling. But the sergeant was sure of being right and still pressed on. The fog lifted and we found ourselves going up a most charming little valley. Plenty of deer were seen and many shots were fired.

Some of them were wounded, but they all escaped, running off into the woods and thickets. The grass was loaded with moisture, and from every bush we touched there fell a shower of dew drops. From riding in the fog and under the trees and among the bushes and through the grass, we were almost dripping wet. As we rode along, the stillness of almost everything made every little sound the more impressive. There was not the slightest breeze. Occasionally we would hear the melancholy croak of the raven, or the dismal gurgle of the big blue crane as it flew over our heads; sometimes the whirring of the swift wings of wild duck, as, disturbed by our approach, it rose from the quiet waters of the beaver pond; sometimes the concert of many blackbirds, anon the twitter of a sparrow, the crow's dull caw, the distant drumming of the pheasant, or the sweet carol of some mother-bird over her nest of young ones. In some places the timber came quite down to the brook's edges, and the tall pines and spruces were festooned with long, pendant mosses, and the shade beneath was never broken by the entrance of a single sunbeam. Everything was cool and damp, and covered with the softest carpeting of moss. The cold water lay like purest crystal in the pebbly, rocky pools, fit mirror and fit boudoir for the innocent does and spotted fawns to make their toilet in. We passed slowly through these fairy dells. Still on we went. We saw elk trails, freshly made, and the big tracks of the ugly grizzly. We saw beaver's dams and ponds and houses; and trees which they had cut down to brows upon or use in dam-building. We were so interested and so charmed that hours and miles passed by uncounted. At length awakened as from some reverie or vision of delight, we saw that the sergeant was still leading us westward. He said he was right. We thought he was certainly wrong. He consented to go to the top of a peak near by; we went, but could neither see nor hear the train. We were in a perfect solitude among the mountains. He consented to go westward a while and see if we might perchance get some glimpse of the train. We went westerly for miles, down a valley parallel to the one we had gone up and just like it and leading into the same creek. We followed it down to its junction with the larger valley, the one in which was our last night's camp. The sergeant would return no further; said he was right and had been right all the time, would not stop to counsel or advice, but started due west with his men to meet the train by a short cut. We had followed him eighteen or twenty miles, and felt sure that he was mistaken. The morning hours were all gone, our horses were already tired and hungry, and to follow him was only to go further astray.

With his men, he started west, up the mountain side, and in a moment was lost to view. We were alone. We thought the case a desperate one and to be met by a desperate remedy. We could not control the sergeant, but could ourselves. We started down the valley alone. The silence which had before been simply impressive, now became terrible. We had miles and miles to ride alone, and must be careful not to overtask an already jaded horse. We might need all his wind and speed for some emergency. Down the creek for miles, at length we saw the trail made by the train, leading eastward from the valley through a narrow, rocky defile. We were near the camp of last night. It is said that hostile Indians watch us every hour of day and night, and that we are scarcely more than out of our camps till the Indians are in them hunting with the greediness of scavengers for what we throw away. What a place for an almost unarmed man to meet them! They having every advantage and he none. If such a meeting must occur, must we offer up ourselves an unresisting sacrifice or resist to the utter end? We chose the latter. We ungloved our hands, the better to use them, drew the revolver from its holster, placed a finger on the trigger, and thumb on the hammer, thought of home and its loved ones, besought a higher power to defend us, and rode down to the defile, the only place near in the steep mountains side through which it was possible to go eastward. We enter the defile, the trail is all dry and has been for hours, we watch every turn, every recess, every tree and bush, every place where a wiley savage

might be lurking. Thus we go for miles and miles. Occasionally, where the road is easiest, Dobbin strikes a canter. At last we catch a glimpse of the long line of white-tented wagons. But it is still miles ahead and before overtaking it we go down into a valley out of sight. Finally, making a turn around a point, we overtake the rear guard. My thankfulness was not unexpressed, though not to human ears. That I escaped is no proof that there was not danger. That the sergeant and his men at last turned about and reached camp in the dusk of the evening, does not prove that he and his whole party were not liable to be cut off. Remember Lieutenant Crosby, and Dr. Huntsinger and Major Elliott and his nineteen men. Don't get lost in the Black Hills. It is bad enough to be scared, but worse to be scalped. So good-bye, kind reader.

A.B.D.

THE BLACK HILLS.

Progress of General Custer's Exploring Expedition.

Twenty-Six Days Spent in Exploring the Hills.

No Coal but Iron and Gold that can be Mined with Profit.

Not Certain that a Single Hostile Indian has been Seen.

Extracts from Gen. Custer's Official Report.

Letter from Prof. Donaldson,

CAMP NEAR BEAR BUTTE,
Aug. 15, 1874.

To the Editor of the Pioneer:

From the camp where the two grizzlies were killed, eastward to the outer ranges of the Hills, for a distance of eighteen or twenty miles, the whole country was once covered with heavy pine forest. At least twenty and probably thirty years ago it was nearly all destroyed by fire. A young forest sprung up, in some places of pine, but generally popple; but it, too, has been destroyed by fire within three or four years. This doubly scourged region is the most drear of any part of the Black Hills. The very richness and unbrokenness of the forest caused its more utter destruction. Yet the springs and streams still flow and the valleys are rich with pasturage. In one of our camps, bounded on all sides by dead and burned timber, there was a spring of 46 deg. temperature, and yielding enough water to supply 10,000 people.

Just inside the eastern ridges, the General changed our course and marched the command, by easy stages, for several days down the valley of Elk Creek. The living timber made its appearance, and gives to the lower Elk Creek country a look of freshness and beauty that strongly contracts (sic) with the dreariness of the burnt districts. From the mountains lying on the east side of the creek, there are fine and extensive views on the plains. In the south, Harney's Peak can be seen, overlooking all around; in the northeast, Bear Butte seems near by, while further on, in the distant blue are Slave Butte and Deer's Ears.

On the lower bottoms of Elk Creek, we find white oak, birch, elm, ironwood, wild grapes, and wild hops. (These hops may be the same as the cultivated variety.) A reconnoitering party under Lieut. Godfrey traced the meanderings of this creek through the mountains and for several miles out on the plains. Like all the other creeks on the east and south side of the Hills, it leaves the mountains through deep gorges and canons. The lovely parks and valleys of the interior are most effectually shut in. Only indomitable energy and zeal could ever find a way for a wagon train into or out of these secluded retreats.

While on this creek, our Rees killed their first elk. In the evening they had an Elk Feast and Dance.[13] The entertainment was in the edge of the pine forest, and around the bright camp fires. Whole sides of the elk were set up to roast, on long pins stuck in the ground. It was well cooked. They decline salt on their fresh meat. While the meat was roasting, they danced to the music of sticks beaten on frying pans and tin wash basins. It was perfect in time, but lacked everything else to charm. We are apt to considering dancing as easy and graceful lithe and fascinating. But in the Ree's dancing, all these were wanting, and everything else, (except time) that could render it pleasing. They never straighten up; but keep the knees bent and body inclined forward, while the head is thrown up to stare around. Each one dances independently of all others, except that they justle against and stumble over one another. They jerk up their feet and stamp them on the ground as awkwardly and clumsily as bears, clowns, or Calibans. They make no vocal symphonies, but grunt and whoop-howl and groan. Some wore trousers and others leggins and breech cloths. Some wore shirts and others only blankets. They were bare-foot, or else wore moccasins, boots or shoes. On their heads were hats, or caps, or cloths, or only long, laughing, black locks. Their clothing was as diverse in color as in kind. Uneducated pigs or ourangoutangs could excel them.

But they are not employed as dancers. As scouts, they are invaluable. Under the guidance of the kind and gentlemanly young

13. Reported Battle with Four Thousand Indians—The Gattling Gun a Peace Maker.

Sioux City, Aug. 16.—A special dispatch from Fort Sully says the mail carrier just in from Fort Rice reports a messenger from Custer's camp brought news that Custer has had a fight with the Indians, who it is reported numbered four thousand. The Indians were driven off with great slaughter. The Gattling guns are too much for them.

Further particulars expected.
By Associated Press.

Sioux City, August 19.—A report comes from Fort Sully this evening that Indians to the number of four thousand attacked Custer's expedition on the 13th, and were repulsed with heavy loss. Custer's loss is reported fifty killed and wounded. This report is brought into Fort Sully by the mail rider, who states that he met one of Custer's scouts above Grand River and got the news from him.

ST. PAUL PIONEER
Issue of August 20, 1874

Lieutenant, Wallace, who has charge of them, they scoured the whole country over in advance of our marching columns. If any hostile Sioux had been anywhere in front of us or on the flanks, these ubiquitous and most cunning scouts would certainly have found them out. Where they scour the country, no ambush could be successfully laid. The Santees are more civilized, but not more useful. All these Indians had their peculiar work to do, and they have been taught to do it well. White men could hardly equal them in the capacity of scouts.

Strongly in contrast with the hideous dancing and music of the Indians, are the songs sung by the white men around our camp fires, "Fairy Bell," "Bonny Jean," "Lightly Row," "Over the Sea," "Poor Old Joe," and many others have been rendered in a style worthy of professional vocalists.

The Santees sing the most charming of our Sunday school songs, and sing them well. Sunday school songs, sung by Indians, in the Depths of the Black Hills!

On the 13th of this month another of our command was "mustered out." Private James King, of Company H, said to be a good man and an excellent soldier, died of chronic diarrhea. He was buried at our last camp in the Hills. In a grassy nook, beneath the shade of the evergreen pines, a lone grave was dug. In the morning, just as the golden rays of the rising sun began to tint the tree-tops and gild the light clouds in the eastern sky, his body was laid away. Captain Benteen, his company commander, read the funeral service. His comrades stood around the open grave and heard the solemn words. Big tears rolled down the bronzed cheek of many a soldier. It was a sad, sad funeral. The customary volley was fired, the band played a solemn requiem, and the trumper (sic) blew the call "Day is out, extinguish lights." King's day on earth was indeed out; but we trust that as bright and glorious celestial morning dawned upon his soul, as was that earthly morning which shown upon his comrades weeping around his grave.

On the 14th day of August we left our last camp in the Black Hills, and by ten o'clock the whole command was out on the plains, about 25 miles south of Bear Butte.

We had spent twenty-six days in exploring the Hills. The wagon train had been drawn through them 215 miles; 448 miles has been carefully explored. This long line of exploration is a broad belt, from five to twenty miles wide. It will all be carefully mapped by the Engineer Corps, and its geology written up by Prof. Winchell. Besides these long lines, Gen. Custer, in looking for roads and camping grounds, has traveled hundreds of miles more, while scouts and hunting parties have been almost omnipresent. From this expedition this region will be pretty well known. For a more careful and exhaustive exploration and research, especially of its mineralogical character, more time is requisite. There is no evidence of coal, but plenty of iron. Gold can probably be mined with profit. No very rich placers have been found, nor has there been any discovery of gold bearing quartz. Our prospectors did not have sufficient time. The best placers will yield from 25 to 100 dollars per day to each miner.

Thus far the expedition has been eminently successful. More has been accomplished than could have been expected, even by the most sanguine. By skill or inspiration, we have almost invariably had most desirable and beautiful localties for our camps.

It is not certain that a single hostile Indian has been seen. Many Indians visit the Black Hills but they have no permanent villages. Not a single permanent habitation has been found. In all our long line of travel and exploration, we have not seen the slightest evidence of any attempt to cultivate the earth.

Our camp today is five miles south of Bear Butte. We visited it today. Col. Ludlow estimates its height, along the creek bottoms, at 1,250 feet—250 feet less than Capt. Warren's estimate. From its summit, the course of the Belle Fourche and South Fork may be traced almost or quite to their junction. Slave Butte and Deer's Ears may be seen, the Bad Lands are in sight, and the plains stretch out almost indefinitely. The mountain is covered almost all over with shingle. Its ascent is not easy and would be far more difficult but for the many zigzag paths made by the deer and antelope. These paths lead to the top. It is hard to conjecture why these animals have so often climbed this mountain. On the whole of it, there is not enough grass to subsist more than half of one antelope. A few small pines grow among the shingle, and on the south end of the mountain are some fair sized trees. The whole mountain is an upheaval. Its base is an elipse, longer diameter, north-west and south-east, about one mile; shorter, about a half mile long. Its top is a sharp ridge, steep as the comb of a house, and about a half mile long.

Bloody Knife, Chief of the Rees, has selected six scouts, who will leave this evening with a mail for Fort Abraham Lincoln. They are well mounted and provisioned for five days. They will travel all of tonight. Then they may travel day or night according to circumstances. It is about 200 miles direct from here to Lincoln. They will not attempt to reach our old trail.

By courtesy of Gen. Custer, we are permitted to make the following extracts from his official dispatch of this date.

In speaking of leaving the Hills, he says:

"Nearly every one of us has loth to leave a region which had been found so delightful in almost every respect. Behind us the grass and the foliage was clothed in the green and the freshness of May; in front of us, as we cast our eyes over the plains below, nothing but a comparatively parched and dried surface, the sunburnt pasturage of which offered a most uninviting prospect to both the horse and rider."

* * * *

"No portion of the United States can boast of a richer soil, better pasturage or purer water (the natural temperature of which as it flows from the earth is but 12 deg. above freezing), and of greater advantages generally to the farmer and stock-raiser, than are to be found in the Black Hills."[14]

A.B.D.

14. Chicago, Aug. 28.—Lieut. Gen. Sheridan has issued an order notifying parties now reported to be organizing at various points on the border to visit the Black Hills in search of gold, that they will not be permitted to go, unless under authority of the Secretary of the Interior, or the Congress.

Some efforts are reported as being made here to organize an expedition for the Black Hills country.

ST. PAUL PIONEER
Issue of August 29, 1874

South Dakota State Historical Society

This valley, near Harney Peak, was named after the expedition's photographer—William Illingworth. Although the scenery is not unusual, Illingworth apparently felt that two exposures were merited. For this shot the camera was located slightly to the left of its placement for the picture on the facing page.

ST. PAUL PIONEER
Issue of September 3, 1874

BLACK HILLS EXPEDITION

Letters from the Special Correspondent of the Pioneer.

Journey from Bear Butte to the Little Missouri.

Return of the Expedition to Fort Abe Lincoln.

Description of the Country and Incidents of the March.

CAMP OF THE
LITTLE MISSOURI,
Aug. 21, 1874.

To the Editor of the Pioneer.

FROM BEAR BUTTE TO
LITTLE MISSOURI.

This march was made in five days, nearly thirty-one miles a day. Water was scarce most of the way, and the grazing often scant. The amount of grain issued to the animals is very small, wholly insufficient to keep them up, and grass is the main dependence. When grass and water fail, of course the animals do. Several worn out horses and mules have been abandoned and shot; while about fifty have been taken from the teams or from under the saddle and been turned into the cattle herd to be driven along.

The country passed over is very similar to that on the corresponding portion of the march outward, and has been described in the earlier letters of this series. We crossed the Belle Fourche much lower down and further out from the Black Hills. It is four or five rods wide, and on the ripples, about a foot deep. The water contains a good deal of alkali, and the bed of blue and white clay, over which it flows give it a milky color. On the lower bottoms, scarce anything grows except cactus and coarse rank weeds. Along the water's edge, there is a narrow skirting of cottonwood trees and bushes.

As a rule, the grass becomes thinner and poorer and more dried up as we recede from the Hills. Cactus and a small sage plant grows almost everywhere. Down some of the dry and dusty creek channels great torrents thirty feet deep, have at times, washed down. Not a single spring has been found.

Dried up as the country generally is, yet the antelope finds subsistence; and the same hunting scenes occur as on the outward trip. Antelope steaks, stews and roasts are common fare for nearly all the command. A great many fine buck heads and some entire skins have been carefully preserved as specimens, and will be mounted by taxidermists for public museums or private collections.

Except along the streams, the whole region is treeless and shrubless. What trees and shrubs do grow, make but poor fuel and are almost useless for every other purpose.

The surface is generally rolling, and we have marched with out deviation from straight lines. We passed westward of Stave Butte and within four or five miles of it. It was visited by a small party. It is eight or nine hundred feet above the surrounding plain. About two-thirds of the way up, it is composed of white and blue clays; above that, brown and white sandstone. Its summit is a narrow platform of rock, but a few feet in width and about a hundred yards in length. Except at three or four points, this table rock is inaccessible. The view from the summit is one of the finest to be had on the plains, embracing large portions of Dakota, Wyoming and Montana. A great many points of interest can be seen, among which are Ludlow's Plateau, Slim Butte, Deer's Ears, Owl Butte, Bear Butte, a wide extent of the Black Hills—from which rises up Custer's Peak, Terry's Peak, Sundance Mountain and probably the Harnies and Inyan Kara. Short Pine Hill, the distant Powder River Mountains, and the long winding valleys of the Belle Fourche and Little Missouri. If you are ever near Slave Butte, take your field glass in hand, go to the top on a clear day, spend several hours in looking around, and you will be well paid for the time and the climbing.

We traveled through the whole length of Prospect Valley. It was described in a former letter, and it may simply be added that its entire length is about twenty miles. We passed our old camps there, crossing our trail and bearing northward. We camped a second time in the valley, but lower down and near the Little Missouri. Our next camp was thirty-five miles distant on the head waters of the Grand River. During the night there was a fine, refreshing shower of rain, laying the dust and cooling the air.

The next day carried us to the Little Missouri. Here we lay over one day to rest. There is plenty of dry grass, but it seems nutritious and the stock graze it with keen appetites. The river is 75 to 100 yards wide. The water is clear, though strongly alkaline. It has nearly sunk away in the broad sandbanks and gravel beds. In a few weeks more of dry weather, it will probably cease to be a flowing stream; yet, in time of freshest, it is a broad, deep, rapid river. There is no verdure, except of the cottonwoods. The Indians say, that the Bad Lands begin eighteen miles below here. If so, we will see them.

On approaching the Belle Fourche, War Eagle, a young Ree Scout, reported that he had discovered a small party of strange Indians about two miles on our right. Gen. Custer permitted him, with Bloody Knife and Cold Ham, to visit the strangers, strictly forbidding all acts of violence. These three scouts approached very near before being discovered. The four startled Sioux warriors drew their

South Dakota State Historical Society

This picture, and its near twin, on the facing page is of Illingworth Valley, named in honor of the expedition's photographer. The trees on the far edge of each picture indicate a slight shifting of the camera position, from left to right.

arms for fight; but, on being assured of the peaceable intentions of our party, consented to a friendly palaver. All hands ate, drank and smoked together. The information given by the strangers seems so sensational and improbable as to be undeserving of credit or record. When our party left, the alarmed braves mounted their ponies and galloped off at full speed till lost to view in the distance.

At 8 o'clock on the evening of the 15th, from our camp at Bear Butte, six scouts started for Lincoln with our last mail. Whether they reached their destination in safety, you may know, but we do not. Their names were Lover, (the

leader of the party), Horn-in-front, Red Stone, Killed-by-the-Bear, and two others, each named Left Hand.

One of the most experienced, practical and useful men on the expedition is John C. Wagner from Pleasant Grove, near Rochester, Minnesota. He has traveled extensively in every State and territory west of the Mississippi, and bears recommendations from the Hon. Edmund Rice and General Green of St. Paul. He is familiar with life on the plains, in the mountains, and among the Indians. He knows all about freighting, by wagons and by pack trains. He is wagon master and packer for us. Packing is an art, and in it he is proficient. For his skill in managing the pack team to the South Fork, he was commended by General Custer.

Though the wind is almost constant on the plains, yet the temperature is much higher than in the Hills. We all sigh for the coolness, the freshness, the beauty, the pleasantness of the Black Hills, and wish that we could travel through such a country all the way to Fort Lincoln.

LAST LETTER.

FORT LINCOLN, D.T., Aug. 30, 1874.

RETURN OF THE BLACK HILLS EXPEDITION.

After touching the Little Missouri, we marched parallel to it for several days, camping on its branches, and following its general course in a northerly direction, about 100 miles down the east bank, till we struck the surveyed line of the North Pacific Railroad, on the edge of the Bad Lands. Except along the water courses, all this wide extent of country had been lately burned over by prairie fires. Whether these fires had their origin in our our camps on the outward march, lying from 20 to 50 miles eastward, or were intentionally or accidentally started by the Indians, cannot be told. The whole country was blackened and desolate; and the hungry mules, cattle and horses looked in vain from their accustomed pasturage. These fire-swept, treeless hills and plains were bad lands, though quite unlike the Bad Lands of the Little Missouri. These lands have, doubtless, been well described by persons who have carefully examined them. No description will be attempted here. They cover an area of not less than one thousand square miles, and through them the river flows. They are mostly steep, conical hills three or four hundred feet in heighth, and perfectly bare of all vegetation. They are made up of horizontal strata of clay, sand, and stone, of all colors. These many-colored, gorgeous zones give to the whole panorama the appearance of some vast and magnificent ruin of ancient pyramids, fortifications and cities. From here, the return to Fort Lincoln was nearly on the trail of

Gen. Stanley's last year's expedition to the Yellowstone (the line N.P.R.R.) down the valley of the Big Heart River, about 150 miles. The burnt district extended about 50 ms. eastward of the Little Mo. The balance of the way the grass was green and grazing excellent. Rains had been frequent, and all was fresh and growing. The valleys of the Big Heart is one of the finest sections of Western Dakota.

At one of our camps, a little more than 100 miles west from Fort Lincoln, the soldier's dreaded enemy, the chronic diarrhea, demanded another victim. After days and nights of pain, delirium, heroic resistance, the unequal contest ended. Twas eight o'clock in the evening and the camp was all still; the deep blue sky was sprinkled with stars; the bright, full moon was pouring its flood of light over the plain; the noiseless zephry was floating by. The silence was broken by the mournful note of the bugle, calling us to the side of a grave, freshly made in the green turf. With military honors, with solemnity, with sad hearts, we laid to rest the all that remained of Sergeant Chas. Sempker, of Co. L. The good man and the faithful officer calmly and peacefully sleeps alone, to be awakened only by the reville which shall call into one general assembly the dead of all the earth.

One of the beauties in journeying over the plains, is the exceeding splendor of the sunsets and sunrises. The latter we could never fail to see, as we rise at three in the morning and have usually traveled a good many miles before king of day unlocks the portals of the east and reveals his glorious majesty. Another beauty is the clearness of the atmosphere, bringing distant objects apparently near; and causing everything to stand out in bold relief. Another beauty is the marching of the cavalry companies and the gleaming of their bright arms, and the prancing of their gallant steeds; while the long line of white-tented wagons, and the straight lines of infantry, and the fantastic attire of the Indian scouts, all make a moving panorama which no one could fail to admire. Then is music, martial, mournful, merry, and inspiring, lends its charm to all.

For several days before reaching Lincoln, constant vigilance was required in order to prevent restive members of the expedition from going on to the Fort in advance of the command.

A bright and lovely Sunday morning dawns upon us, twenty-six miles west of Fort Lincoln. The last day's march in the long home-stretch has come. Fourteen miles finds us resting for several hours on the banks of Heart River, only twelve miles from Lincoln and just concealed from view by rising ground between. The train closes up solid, the stragglers all gather in, the company flags are all unfurled; and arrangements are all completed for taking the fort by surprise.

A long line of mounted men extends across the prairie, just below the brow of the hill. The bugle sounds the call to advance, and in less than one minute the long line mounts the hill and Lincoln is in view. Soon the sentinel on the watchtower sees us, and the news of our approach flies to every quarter and causes many a quick heart-throb at the suddenness of our approach. Soon all the points of look-out are occupied, and men on horseback and on foot come running at full speed down into the ravine to meet us. There were warm greetings then.

To a gallant young gentleman who had accompanied us on the expedition, it was creditable to see the quivering lip and swimming eye which he greeted his father, an officer at the Fort, who had galloped down to meet him.

Coming nearer, the ladies and children, beautiful ladies and sweet children (we had seen neither for sixty days) were out to cheer and welcome the long gone wanderers. The band played the most lively airs, and the expedition closed with the inspiring notes of "Garry Owen."

We had been out 60 days, almost in the heart of the continent, and had not heard one word of news from the great world of civilization. The distance traveled by the train is 880 miles; the number of days marching 48; the rate per day a little over 18 miles; the largest day's march, nearly 36 miles, the shortest, 3 miles. To this add:

	Miles.
Trip to Short Pine Hill	10
Trip to Mt. Inyan Kara	15
Trip to Harney's Peak	30
Trip to South Fork Cheyenne	100
Trip down Elk Creek to the plains	25
Trip to Bear Butte	10
Trip to Slave Butte	10
Total (your correspondent's journeyings)	1,080

Besides this, there were many short reconnoisances not included in the above.

General camp was pitched 47 times in 47 places. Twelve days the train did not move, and the principal part of the command rested.

No former expedition was ever so successful in the matter of transportation. Every wagon that started out has been brought back in good condition. The loss by breakage and leakage was only a small percentage. But a few horses and mules have been abandoned, and several died of disease not incident to the trip. On account of the great quantity of wild meat secured by hunting parties, the beef herd was not all needed, and a large number of the cattle were returned to Lincoln. The above results were mainly brought about by the indomitable energy and constant oversight of Capt. A. S. Smith, Acting Quartermaster and Commissary.

Lieut. Chance's guns were mute companions all the way. They have no voice of friendliness, and found no foes to terrify—not even one hostile Indian.

In one of the earlier letters of this series, some strictures were made upon the nonobservance of the Sabbath in the Army. But how soon we all fall into the habits of those around us, whether good or evil. Sunday soon became as secular as any other days. "We took no note of time, except of its departure." One of the best men on the expedition, a churchman, a moralist, a Christian, deemed it no offence to spend the whole of one Sunday in deer hunting; and more, was proud of the game secured. The writer hereof was not the hunter aforesaid, but would feel rich in the possession of all his virtues.

In an economical point of view,

the expedition has not been a costly one. The troops and transportation, though inactive in barracks, must be subsisted and men and animals must be lost, materials expended, and wastage and loss occur. More than this can hardly take place in the field, and in the present case, there was probably less in the aggregate of eqpenditure (sic) than if the expedition had not been made. Forage is very costly at Fort Lincoln and great quantities are required. On the expedition, but little was used. The grazing of the animals saved many thousands of dollars worth of grain and hay. The amount thus saved will probably equal all the extra outlay.

The expedition has been a complete success. It returned on time, and accomplished all its objects. In sixty days, nothing more was possible. Its results are full of interest and value to the artist, to the scientist, to the statesmen, to all. To the genius that conceived, and to the energy that executed the grand enterprise, the country owes something more substantial than mere compliment.

For kindness and urbanity, for diligence and ability, let every officer of the expedition be commended. To mention one name, we must mention all, but let it be said, to the "immortal honor" of Gen. Custer that he neither drinks intoxicating liquors nor uses tobacco in any form nor ever utters a profane word. To be free from the minor and the major vices, to be a perfect gentleman, to be a talented and chivalrous and successful officer, is to be worthy of all honor. Let the leader of the Black Hills expedition have this merited due!

One question, shall the grand and beautiful Eden just discovered "well-watered as the garden of the Lord," rich for horticulture, agriculture, and mining, be longer left as only an occasional hunting ground for the most obstinately depraved nomad that bears the "human form divine," and that too, when thousands through whose veins thrills the noble Anglo-Saxon, Scandinavian, and German blood demand it for their homes?

Patient and kind reader, one word more, then I will stop though not done. I have endeavored to be

simply a truthful writer. It costs something to trace down rumor and get facts. "Truth is a coy maiden" and must be sought. I have paid the cost, you have the truth. Unused to the saddle and to roughing it, my back failed the first day; and after that, for more than three weeks, existence was prolonged pain. Yet in pain I kept the saddle, climbed the buttes, "viewed the landscape o'er," and, by lying flat upon my back, tablet overhead, wrote many letters to **The Pioneer.** My infirmity grew worse, till at the first crossing of the Belle Fourche, it seemed that my last day was near and that soon I should be left under the wayside turf. But we then entered the Black Hills, the water was no longer alkaline but sweet and pure, the air cool and delightful, my health improved daily and to the paradisiacal hygiene of the Hills I am indebted for complete recovery and return in perfect soundness to thank you for your attention, and bid you adieu.[15]

---

15. From a careful examination of the letters of our special correspondent, Prof. Donaldson,—from the correspondence of other journals—from the official reports of General Custer—from the address of Prof. Winchell, geologist to the expedition, delivered before the Minneapolis Academy of Natural Sciences—from the published statements of the three principal miners, McKay, Ross and Smith, and from conversations with a number of the leading officers and other prominent members of the expedition, we feel authorized in coming to the following conclusions in reference to the Black Hills:

1. The climate is temperate and healthful, cool in summer, mild in winter; frequent showers, but few heavy rains and light snowfalls.

2. Springs of pure, cold water are abundant, and living streams meander through all the valleys.

3. The mountains are covered with a fair quality of timber, nearly all pine, more than sufficient for a perpetual supply.

4. Red, white, and brown sandstone, red and white limestone, granite and marble are there in great abundance.

5. The Valleys are open meadows, covered with rich, nutritious grasses. There are numerous undulating prairies, generally not large, varying from a few acres up to several thousand.

6. The soil of the valleys and prairies is all fertile; and considerable portions of the timbered lands would, when cleared, make excellent farms.

7. There is no coal, but some of the beds of lignite would make excellent fuel, and could be easily and profitably mined.

8. Pure gypsum, in inexhaustible quantities, would not only supply the home demand, but would be profitable for export.

9. Iron ore is rich and abundant; and smelting furnaces could doubtless be operated with profit, using charcoal or lignite for fuel.

10. Excepting corn, for which the summers are too cool, both soil and climate are remarkably well adapted for the cultivation of all the cereals, and all or nearly all the field and garden products.

11. Wild fruits of almost every variety possible in a northern climate are abundant; and, excepting the peach, all the cultivated varieties could be easily and profitably grown.

12. A finer region for grazing and the dairy probably cannot be found within the United States.

13. At present, it is the finest hunting ground in America, if not in the world. Badgers, swifts, hares, porcupines, wolves, beavers, two species of deer, black, brown, cinnamon and grizzly bears, panthers and elk, are on the streams and beaver ponds, wild ducks, geese, cranes, and other water fowl.

14. The native flora, in richness, beauty and variety, surpasses that of any known and equally northern latitude.

15. For picturesque and sublime scenery, it is inimitable.

16. Of the precious metals. We are neither sanguine nor skeptical. We believe the country neither an Eldorado nor barren. We have examined all the evidence, and we believe that gold may be mined with profit in the Black Hills, but there is not yet sufficient certainty of the fact. The expedition was limited to sixty days, and spent all the time possible in the hills, but that time was wholly insufficient for a thorough mineralogical prospecting of the whole country. The richest placers and quartz may not have been discovered. Yet it is probable that when the hills are open to settlement, many impulsive persons will go there, with glowing expectations of sudden wealth, only to find themselves bitterly, though perhaps not utterly disappointed.

We have seen no satisfactory evidence of the existence of either silver or quicksilver, and very strongly doubt that either of these metals have ever been or ever will be found in the Black Hills.

17. Strange as it may appear, it is nevertheless true, that the Indians make but little use of the Hills, very seldom visiting them, and then only for brief periods of hunting or grazing. For permanent occupancy, either in mining or other pursuits, no white man has a right to go there till the Indian title to the land is extinguished, and this extinguishment can only be effected by the United States.

In the defiance of treaty rights, of law, of military orders, it would be supreme folly for any parties to attempt going to the Black Hills. The whole power of the government would be used to enforce the treaties; and the savage vengeance of the Indians inflicted upon those who venture thus to trespass on their rights, would be forever unredressed.

Don't go to the Black Hills before they are opened to settlement by the United States; then, if gold-mining "does not pay" you will still find a pleasant and happy home among the thriving and varied industries of the busy settlers all around you, safe under protection of U. S. military posts.

ST. PAUL PIONEER
Issue of September 20, 1874

ST. PAUL PRESS

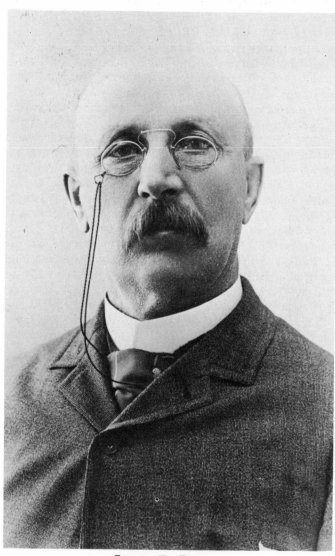

James B. Power

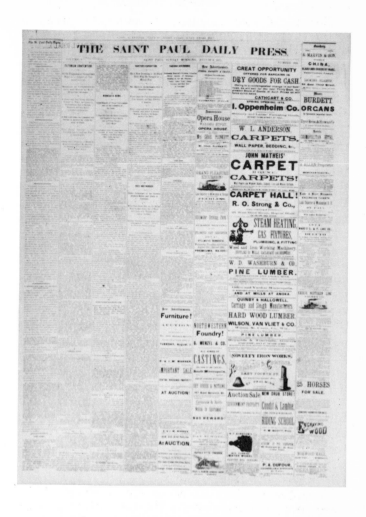

The ST. PAUL DAILY PRESS was the Republican rival to the DAILY PIONEER. But while these two papers were partisan competitors in politics they clearly did have one thing in common, they were both solidly partisan champions of Minnesota. Like the DAILY PIONEER, the DAILY PRESS almost without exception relegated the exciting news from Dakota Territory to the inside pages. The front page of the paper was reserved for what the editor felt were the more important stories of the time. During the two months of the Black Hills expedition the biggest front page news was the day-to-day developments in the Beecher-Tilton scandal in Brooklyn where charges against the prominent clergyman Henry Ward Beecher were being investigated by the council of his Plymouth congregation. Theodore Tilton charged that Beecher had seduced his wife and maintained an affair with her over a period of nine years. Day after day and week after week columns of page one newsprint were devoted to the details of testimony and rumor concerning the scandal. Other news deemed worthy of front page coverage included the serious grasshopper depredations of that summer, natural disasters like floods in Ohio, race problems

in the South, and beginning in August politics and more politics. Clearly the editor of the DAILY PRESS was not about to use his front page to promote the fortune and future of Dakota.

The DAILY PRESS was born in 1861 out of a merger of two lesser papers, the TIMES and the MINNESOTAN. The purpose of the consolidation was to create a Republican organ of sufficient stature to counter the strongly Democratic DAILY PIONEER. The editor who made the paper a success was Joseph A. Wheelock, a young though experienced and capable journalist. The DAILY PRESS prospered not only from good leadership, but also as a result of the growing strength of the Republican Party in Minnesota. It stood for Lincoln, the Union and abolition. And after it had secured the state printing contract from a Republican dominated legislature its future was assured. In the two decades following the war the DAILY PRESS remained stable in management and continued to prosper as its Democratic rival the DAILY PIONEER passed from hand to hand and struggled to exist. In 1875, the year following the Custer expedition, the two papers were merged to form the PIONEER PRESS. The policy of the newly created paper was avowed to be "independent of party." It would, declared its editor, "reserve at all times the privilege of supporting such platforms and such candidates as to the editors and proprietors seem best to accord with their conscience and views of the public weal." In reality, however, the new paper was basically Republican in sympathies as it continued under Joseph Wheelock's direction and editorial pen.[1]

The special correspondent reporting the progress of the Black Hills expedition for the DAILY PRESS signed his letters simply "Power." And that unadorned signature made the DAILY PRESS correspondent somewhat of a mystery figure. At the outset it seemed that this must be F. W. Power, who like Knappen, Donaldson, and the photographer Illingworth, had been signed on the expedition by G. B. Dandy, Quartermaster at Fort Abraham Lincoln, as a civilian teamster at a salary of $30.00 per month. While it is not entirely clear why these men were attached to the expedition in this way, it seems likely that this was a method whereby they could officially be included in the company and provided with place and provisions at government expense. The correspondents for the big Chicago and New York papers are noticeably absent from the quartermaster's list of civilian employees, and we know that these papers paid the cost of having their men included in the expedition.[2]

Since F. W. Power was the only Power on the expedition's roster of military and civilian personnel it seemed certain that this was the DAILY PRESS's reporter. But while having discovered his first two initials seemed at the time to be a major breakthrough it subsequently proved impossible to identify him further. F. W. Power it appeared was simply one of the countless young men seeking his fortune on the frontier, moving restlessly from one hopeful opportunity and place to another and finally settling somewhere far from Dakota.

Then the mystery deepened still further. While rechecking the pages of the DAILY PRESS a short editor's note was discovered in the September third issue announcing the arrival in St. Paul of "A number of prominent gentlemen who accompanied General Custer's expedition to the Black Hills." The editor mentioned the names of some of the most prominent like Major Forsyth, Colonel Fred Grant, William Illingworth and William E. Curtis. Noting that "There were others in the arriving party whose names have not been ascertained," the editor went on to tell of Curtis's plans to do an illustrated article on the expedition for SCRIBNER'S MONTHLY. Finally in a short paragraph at the very end of the article, he informed St. Paul residents that "J. B. Power, Esq., well known here . . . returned with the party as far as Brainerd."[3] "He, too, is well," announced the editor. There it was. Two men named Power had accompanied the expedition, and now the question was which one served as special correspondent for the DAILY PRESS.

James Buel Power was, indeed, well known to St. Paul for he was one of its most prominent residents. Born in New York in 1833 Power had entered the profession of civil engineering and moved west with the railroads. In the mid 1850's his work brought him to Minnesota where in 1861 he became the first head of the state land department. In 1871, after he had served in several state offices, the Northern Pacific Railroad hired Power to organize its land department. Thus, in the summer of 1874 James Buel Power was land commissioner for the Northern

Pacific, and he may well have accompanied the Black Hills expedition to spy out the country beyond the rail head at Bismarck.[4]

Evidence in the dispatches seems to suggest strongly that it was J. B. rather than F. W. Power that reported for the DAILY PRESS. First of all, it is clear that the man writing for the DAILY PRESS was not a full-time reporter. Unlike the other correspondents Power sent no reports from Bismarck prior to the departure of the expedition on July second. Nor is there a final report made after the return of the party to Fort Abraham Lincoln at the end of August. This would be perfectly understandable if a busy and important man like James Buel Power, "Esq." were the correspondent. Moreover, in his dispatch of August second Power comments that the sutler, John W. Smith, had "on hand some of the best [whiskey] that **our** noble city could afford, the taste and effect of which many of **our** readers can testify too . . ." This indicates that the correspondent was a resident of St. Paul, and in the 1874 St. Paul City Directory one can find J. B. Power but not F. W. Power. The available evidence, then, would seem to indicate that F. W. Power did, indeed, serve as a teamster while J. B. Power accompanied the expedition to scout the land for the Northern Pacific and when he had the time write dispatches for the ST. PAUL DAILY PRESS. If the Northern Pacific was represented, one can only wonder how many other interested civilians joined Custer on his military reconnaissance of the Black Hills.

FOOTNOTES
1. George S. Hage, NEWSPAPERS ON THE MINNESOTA FRONTIER, 1849-1860, St. Paul, 1967, pp. 125-26.
2. Report of Persons and Articles employed and hired at Fort A. Lincoln by G. B. Dandy Q.M. for the Black Hills Expedition, National Archives, Washington, D.C., RG 92, package 51, 1874; General Phillip Sheridan to Custer, Chicago, June 2, 1874, Marguerite Merington, ed., THE CUSTER STORY: THE LIFE AND INTIMATE LETTERS OF GENERAL GEORGE A. CUSTER AND HIS WIFE ELIZABETH, New York, 1950, p. 271.
3. ST. PAUL DAILY PRESS, Sept. 3, 1874.
4. Mr. & Mrs. J. B. Power's Golden Wedding, THE ST. PAUL PIONEER PRESS, March 28, 1907; J. B. Power's Obituary, PIONEER PRESS, Dec. 17, 1912.

ST. PAUL DAILY PRESS
Issue of July 28, 1874

CUSTER'S EXPEDITION.

The Military Forces Upon the Head Waters of the Little Missouri.

Two Hundred Miles have they Marched into the Bowels of the Bad Lands without Impediment.

Report of What has Transpired on the Route During the First Two weeks of the Campaign.

CUSTER'S BLACK
HILLS EXPEDITION,
CAMP LITTLE MO. RIVER,
July 15, 1874.

Special Correspondence of the St. Paul Press.

Since leaving Lincoln there has been no way of communicating with you, and, in fact, until within the past few days, there has been so much sameness about our march that it would not be of much interest to the outside world.[16] Our line of march has been southwest and west, over a rolling prairie, under the hottest of suns, the effects of which every one's face gave a good demonstration— in the way of sunburns, skin coming off, &c. We left Lincoln on the morning of July third, and marched some ten or fifteen miles. Everything passed off agreeably until reaching the "Little Heart River," where we found the crossing quite difficult, and remained until late in the afternoon before getting over. There is in the train some 150 wagons, all very heavily loaded, and they necessarily require considerable time to cross the rivers (as they are called.) Our marches so far have varied between 15 and 30 miles a day, and are determined by two things, wood and water. Could we find both of these articles, the average march would be say 18 to 20 miles per day. On one occasion we marched 31 miles before finding water; got into camp late that night, July 7th, and next morning were called out early by a shot fired by one of the pickets, at a supposed Indian, but which proved to be somebody's horse. This is the only time that anything suspected to be Indians were heard of. We forded the Cannon Ball and Otter rivers with little difficulty, and finally arrived at the Grand River

16. Gentlemen who reached this city from Bismarck on Wednesday evening, state that while nothing definite has been heard from Custer's expedition to the Black Hills, there are reasons for the belief that a considerable battle has already been fought with the Indians, who are determined to resist the advance of the expedition by every force and effort. Two of Custer's hunting dogs, which had accompanied him on the expedition returned to Fort Lincoln last week, and three Indians, seriously wounded have been returned to the agency at Grand River— two of the number arriving on Saturday, and one on Monday last. These Grand River Indians are said to be peaceable, as Indians usually are, but the people of Bismarck are unable to account for their wounds unless they had been engaged with the forces opposing Custer's march. It is generally believed at Bismarck that Custer will be compelled to fight his way to the Black Hills, as the Indians are bound to protect these (to them) sacred grounds at all hazards of life and limb. There is a belief prevalent among the Indians as well as among white men, that gold in great quantities exists in that mysterious region, and as Indians cannot utilize it conveniently, they are determined that white men shall not have that blessed privilege.

ST. PAUL PRESS
Issue of July 24, 1874

Cave, some 200 miles southwest of Lincoln.

From the description given by "Bloody Knife" and "Goose," we expected to find something grand, but on reaching them were very much disappointed. The cave is, as I said, about 200 miles from Lincoln, southwest, and about ten miles south of Grand River, in the sandstone rock. It is about 20 feet high by 12 to 14 feet wide, and extends in the rock some 230 feet, or rather that was as far as we could go. Inside of the cave we found rings, arrows, etc., left there by the Indians. "Bloody Knife" says they were offerings to the Great Spirit, the abode of whom it is. My opinion is that the God, or Gods, of the Indian could find a more agreeable place to spend his leisure time were they to try very hard. The country around the cave is hilly, with some little timber, but nothing worth speaking of. I neglected to say that the inside has various representations, of beaver, antelope, men, buffalo, all rather rude in design and execution. They were also said to be made by the Great Spirit. The artist, whether spirit or human, certainly was not a finished or accomplished designer. Gen. Custer intended camping there a day to explore the cave, but that was not easily done, as water was so scarce, and he determined to go on for a day or so before stopping, so easily next morning, at our usual hour, 8 A.M., we started to find a good camping ground.

We marched 12½ miles and found ourselves within two miles of our old camp. The ravines were deep, and a plenty of them, the country almost equal to the "Bad Land." We went in camp early, found good springs, in fact the best water since leaving "Lincoln." Most of the water is alkali, and to find a fresh cool spring is really a treat, for which each and every one is thankful. Monday we had an easy march with nothing of interest to relate except that Indians were really seen for the first time. Captain McDougall Co. E. 7th while out hunting on the left, some mile or two, saw about 20 Sioux, but not sufficiently close to exchange shots, or indulge in conversation.

General Custer has been expecting an attack for several days, but

Not specifically identified, this is another of the spectacular pictures of the Black Hills taken by William Illingworth. The St. Paul photographer would sometimes make several exposures in different directions from a single vantage point. The granite formations seem to indicate that this scene might be near the Needles or the Harney Peak vicinity.

it seems that they are waiting until we get in the Hills. Of one thing we feel confident that we can handle all of the Indians in and around the Black Hills. There is no danger of having a fight in and around the Black Hills. There is no danger of having a fight so long as the country is any way open. The men and officers both seem anxious to come in contact with a thousand or so. Should the Indians make their appearance at any time during the day I shall get under the ammunition wagon and there remain. Yesterday, 14th, we saw where a few Indians had camped the night before, and also saw a few on the bluffs some distance off. So far the men and horses have been holding out remarkably well. Lost only one horse belonging to Col. Ludlow's wagon. We find grass plentiful, and water

also, but most of the water is alkali.

Since writing the above, Lieut. Gates of the infantry informed me that several of his men had given out, on account of heat and bad water, but most of them returned to duty, and now we have only three sick men in camp, and most of them will be ready for duty again in a day or so.

With regard to the country, it is only fit for Indians, buffalo, grasshoppers and mosquitoes. We have not seen any buffalo yet, and very few signs of them. Mosquitoes are plentiful and also grasshoppers.

We are encamped at present in a very pretty valley near the Little Missouri, and in fact, it is the only place that I have seen fit for a white man to think of living, and this would only be agreeable for a month or so in summer.

After getting in camp yesterday we saw considerable smoke in the west, said by Bloody Knife to be an Indian signal calling the hunting parties in, and also those from the agency, Grand River, &c.

We are resting today, mending wagons, having horses shod, &c. We move tomorrow at the usual hour.

We have enjoyed ourselves considerably hunting. General Custer is fond of the sport himself; he has killed six antelope. Every officer in the command has indulged in the sport more or less, and each day hunting parties may be seen returning with antelope. We have had fresh antelope every day, for dinner and breakfast, being very fashionable we only eat two meals a day, breakfast and dinner, at 3 A.M. and 6 P.M. The officers are very sociable, and visit each other after getting in camp and talk over the day's march, etc. You will hear from us again just as soon as another scout returns.

I was unfortunate enough to lose my letter, consequently had to write this up very hurriedly today. We are not in Montana, as was supposed this morning, but still some 15 miles in Dakota. Latitude, 45 deg. 3'; longitude, 103 deg. 40'.

Respectfully,
POWER.

ST. PAUL DAILY PRESS
Issue of August 15, 1874

THE BLACK HILLS.

Notes of the St. Paul Press Correspondent Upon Gen. Custer's Expedition.

Description of What Was Seen Among the Hills and Valleys on the Sources of the Little Missouri River.

Some Parts of the Country Good, others Bad, but no Prospect Yet of an Overplus of Precious Metals.

Episodes in Camp Life—Solemn Scenes at a Funeral—Strawberries and other fruit, game and fish among the luxuries—Remarkable Flora—Geological Curiosities, &c., &c.

CUSTER'S BLACK HILLS EXPEDITION.

Lat. 43 degrees, 36 degrees, Long. 103 degrees, 30 degrees,
Aug. 2, 1874.

Special Correspondence of the St. Paul Press.

The next day after writing we started from camp at the usual hour, feeling very much refreshed, and ready to meet the noble red man, whenever he might feel in the humor of doing us that honor. Our march, for several miles, was the same old every day thing. Toward mid day our hearts were made glad by the news that Indians were in the neighborhood. Lieut. Wallace, commanding the Indian Scouts, was called out by one of the braves to see a few "Sioux" in the distance. I accompanied him to a hill about half a mile off, to get a sight of them—and there they were—about three miles off

South Dakota State Historical Society

Again the exact locality of this scene is not known but it is presumed to be in Custer Park. The name for the broad, long valley was used by the correspondents and the members of the expedition, but is no longer in use today. They were apparently referring to the area south of Harney Peak. Correspondent A. B. Donaldson of the ST. PAUL PIONEER said of its beauty, "No one ever saw anything equal to it."

we could see a few, but very poor satisfaction did it afford any one. After waiting awhile we turned our footsteps toward the column, who were then refreshing themselves and horses by partaking of the waters of the Little Missouri. Mr. Reynolds, who has spent considerable time in the west, also reported Indians, but afterwards concluded that is must be Lieut. Hodgson and party, who went out early in the morning with Col. Ludlow and Profs. Grinnell and Winchell, and the reporters for the **Inter-Ocean** and the New York **Tribune**, also accompanied the party. Our march for the most

part was through cactus and sage brush, while the hottest of suns shown on our devoted heads.

Headquarters—that is General Custer, the scouts and two companies of cavalry—marched on thinking to find a suitable place to camp, but finally concluded that good camping places were few and far between in this country, and at last rested their weary horses on a hill, with no water or wood and very poor grass, but the best thing that they could do. Capt. Chance with the artillery, next made his appearance. Then the wagons all came in good order over thirty-two miles marching. Then

Illingworth took this picture facing east from a location that is now near Highway 16, midway between Custer and Hill City, just northwest of the Crazy Horse carving. Although positive identification is difficult, it appears that men, horses and a tent may be located at the center left of this picture. It could be part of the Custer camp which was stretched along a valley south of Harney Peak.

stable call, and our noble horses had their corn, which constituted their supper—grass being out of the question, though Prof. Winchell insists that the soil is good enough for anything, only wants rain. Some one reported Mr. Knappen, reporter for the Bismarck **Tribune,** absent, or rather that he had not then made his appearance in camp. I walked over to Co. G, and found him all O.K., having just reached there. While resting he had fallen asleep on the road side in the shade of a "sage bush."

The country was so dry, and grass so scarce that we saw no antelope—in fact no game whatever. The river valley was certainly not very beautiful, sloping back to the hills some miles distant. West of the river the hills were

higher and presented quite a fine appearance, and induced one to believe that we were at last getting into the "Promised Land," (Black Hills) where gold, and not milk and honey, could be found, but alas, as for gold I feel confident that no such thing will gladden our weary and longing eyes, and that even greenbacks will be few in the party, having had a tendency to accumulate at the wagons of our best friend, Mr. John W. Smith, sutler for the expedition. And this Smith friend is certainly a gentleman of the first whiskey—always having on hand some of the best, that our noble city could afford, the taste and effect of which many of our readers can testify to— they, in other words, knowing how it is themselves. Not being a

drinkest (sic) I can only say so from hearsay—Mr. Gates — Lieutenant I should say — of infantry, has just been looking over the above statement, and thinks there must be some mistake. Judging from his standpoint, there is nothing more supposable, being fond of the aforesaid whiskey, he thinks everyone else must be so.

On the 17th we started out in high hopes of making the "Belle Fourche" that night, but disappointment was our lot; the Black Hills, although well in sight that morning, were still a considerable distance off. Prof. Donaldson insisted on it the country was only fit for rattlesnakes and Indians; that he intended advising the general government to give the Indians, their assigns, heirs, &c., the

South Dakota State Historical Society

This is a view of a portion of Custer's camp. It has long been identified as being near the Needles, in which case it would be in an area called "Custer's Park" by members of the expedition. It is possible, however, that this is part of Custer's camp located along French Creek, about four miles south of the Needles. It was from French Creek, that Custer launched reconnaissance parties to the south to find the south fork of the Cheyenne River and to the southeast to find the mouth of French Creek.

country forever, though our march was over a much better country that day. We found lots of game and a few rattlesnakes. Col. Grant came in contact with an old fellow who surrendered after some considerable resistance, but the colonel, having something of his father's disposition, determined to fight it out on that line if it took the whole summer. Capt. French, Co. M, 7th Cavalry, and Lieut. Chimer, commanding artillery, were both successful today hunting, each killing an antelope; also Mr. Illingworth, photographist, the latter gentleman proving conclusively that he can use a rifle as well as a camera, and has had the good fortune not only to get some good pictures but also to prove himself to be one of the best shots

on the expedition, which is considerable to say, as we have several. Gen. Custer, Capt. French, Lieuts. McDougall and Hodgson, are all considered fine marksmen.

Our camp tonight is quite pleasantly situated, with water near by. The first of the night mosquitoes trouble considerably. About midnight it commenced blowing, I was awakened by Lieut. H—calling out; "Get up, and let's keep our tent from blowing over." Col. Custer was not so fortunate. Lieut. Chimer, and Mr. Curtis, of the **Inter-Ocean,** might have been seen, each holding on to a tent rope, and calling out for some of their men to come to their rescue, as their tent was blowing away.

The morning of the 18th broke beautifully on the scene. Tents

might be seen a half mile from camp, caught by osage brush or cactus; hats were plentiful, and various other articles of apparel might be found scattered around. The Black Hills looked quietly down and seemed glad that we had been put to so much trouble. Sunrise found each man in possession of most of his property, and on the way across the "Bad Lands" that lay in our path. We crossed them after some little trouble, and found a beautiful valley, the prettiest seen yet. We feasted our eyes for awhile on this Eden of rest, where, the Sioux had wandered for many a day, "lord of the soil."

The 23d was spent in camp, washing &c. being the order of the day. General Custer and party found nothing of interest over at

Custer's "permanent camp" was located along French Creek, from August 1-5, 1874. Illingworth took this view by facing his camera to the north. The camp is located about three miles due east of the present City of Custer. He apparently was impressed by this view, as he moved slightly to the east and took two more exposures which can be seen on the following pages.

French Creek originates just southeast of the present City of Custer and meanders in an easterly direction for 20 miles, where it joins the Cheyenne River. The creek passes through the middle of what is now Custer State Park. It was along this valley that Custer camped. This Illingworth picture was taken from a location slightly farther to the east of the one on the preceeding page.

Hungyakara (sic); they reached camp quite early and engaged a good dinner.

Our march of the 24th was a tiresome one, the country being mountainous, and in some places almost impassable; the wagons had to be lowered by ropes, which required considerable time. We were repaid for the time and toil. The valley was beautiful, the soil fine; the productions of this beautiful spot were flowers of various kinds, and berries in abundance. We did not remain long in this earthly Eden. Our passage was obstructed by protruding rocks so to avoid as much as much (sic) trouble and work as possible we crossed the hills. Our road out of this enchanted valley was equally as rough as the passage down.

After a time we reached the top of the hill to find it thickly timbered, giving considerable work to the pioneer company, Captain Yates. We found, scattered around, elk horns, the largest I ever saw, some measuring over six feet. Gen. Custer, Captains McDougall, French and several others will decorate their parlors with some of the finest. Illingworth, the artist, shot a panther—wounding it —his rifle being too small to kill it. Beyonds the hill we found another valley more beautiful than the first, called, or rather named by some of the party, "Lost Water," by others "Floral Valley," either name being very appropriate; the first name suggested by a beautiful stream of clear, cool water that disappears in the

ground, and the next by the flowers that abound. There we found rose, lilly, (new; seems not to have been discovered before), two new geraniums, pink and white, blue bell, wild onions, flowering pea, aconite lupin, great variety of Compositae, several species of Leguminosae, dog-tooth, violet, etc. Dr. Williams, botanist, etc., will give a full account of flowers etc. In connection with this stream there seems to be a legend, (Indian of course) which is something as follows: Its source is in a beautiful cave, supplied with all of the luxuries of life, both artificial and natural, fruits of all kinds from every clime, wine the finest, foreign and domestic, on every hand fountains of champagne, walls of purest gold and floors of pearl.

Moving slightly farther to the east, Illingworth made this third exposure of Custer's "permanent camp" along French Creek. Illingworth was taking his pictures to sell to the public for stereoscope viewing and was therefore usually careful to feature an object in the foreground (such as the dead tree and branch above) to give added feeling to the sense of depth.

Those who are fortunate enough to enter this paradise are so enchanted that they desire to spend the rest of their lives there, and after life take it for their heaven. The disappearing is accounted for in pretty much the same way; that is, it flows into a cave just opposite of the above. One, the happy hunting ground, the home of the departed brave; the other, the last resting place of the unfortunate and the coward. In passing this beautiful spot one can but wonder at the goodness of the Supreme Ruler of heaven and earth, with what a liberal hand beauty has been scattered over the face of the earth, and the question arises, "Is there no appreciative being here—no one to look on, to see God's handiwork, to behold its

grandeur and beauty? Does not the red man see these things and offer up his thanks for them?

But I wander from my subject. Lt. Hodgson found a tent pole which is the subject of considerable interest, and some dispute, some saying that it is a relic of Reynold's and others of Warren's expedition, and some say that it was carried there by the Indians. Being behind that day I was agreeably surprised to find Lt. Hodgson and Capt. McDougall enjoying strawberries, fine large ones. The valley supplied the command with strawberries, gooseberries, raspberries and service berries. The streams we found were not only fresh and cool, but was well filled with fish, some large enough to eat. We did not pitch our tents

until late in the afternoon, consequently did not enjoy a supper of the finny tribe. We found indications of Indians, lodge poles, fresh trail, &c., all bearing evidence that the Indians had spent some time there, &c.

Respectfully,
POWER.

In the valley of French Creek, at Custer's "permanent camp" three miles east of the present City of Cust-er, Illingworth took three similar but interestingly different exposures. This is a closeup view of the camp. Smoke from three cooking fires appears in the distance. Tents surround the camp on four sides. A circle of wagons is formed in the center, apparently as a fortress of last resort, should the perimeters of the camp be overrun in a hostile attack. Much prospecting was done along French Creek and it was here that gold was discovered on August 2, 1874, leading Custer to name the area "Golden Valley".

ST. PAUL DAILY PRESS
Issue of August 16, 1874

THE BLACK HILLS.

Gen. Custer's Expedition Reaches the Point of its Destination.

Interview with the Red Inhabitants of that Newly Discovered Region.

A Few of them were Surprised at the Sudden Appearance of the White Man, but No Collision Occurred.

Discovery of Gold—Geological Formation of the Hills—Base Ball Among the Boys, &c.

CAMP NO. 27,
CUSTER'S BLACK
HILLS EXPEDITION,

Lat. 43 deg. 36 deg.
Long. 103 deg. 30 deg.
August 2d, 1874

Editor St. Paul Press:

I finished my last letter by giving an account of our life in the Floral Valley, Col. Grant dining on strawberries, &c. Our march on the 26th continued up this valley of flowers until it terminated at the top of the ridge, or divide. We entered then into another, where floral wealth was equal to the one just left, and watered by a stream equally as beautiful, and surrounded by hills more magnificent. We followed this "vale of delight" for some few miles, when we found another going to the right at right

angles with the one already described; but wishing to avoid Indians and Indian trails we took the left hand, leading almost directly east. All Indian trails seen on previous days were going south. We marched but a few rods when lo! what should we find but an Indian encampment, with all the evidences of having been lately occupied—that is within the past two days. There we found tepee poles, and the remains of antelope and deer. This valley seems to have been a thoroughfare for them supposed by some to be a trail from Red Cloud's agency to the hunting grounds. Gen. Custer's idea being to avoid all difficulties with the Indians, he had on nearly every instance

Illingworth carried his bulky photographic equipment farther away from the camp and moved slightly west before taking this second picture with his camera facing to the south. The rock and tree that were to the far left in the previous exposure are now just left of center, because of the increased distance of the camera from the camp. Smoke from the fires is thickening. Samuel J. Barrows writing in the NEW YORK TRIBUNE referred to the miners with the Custer Expedition, saying, "Ross and McKay, in a literal sense, found this their golden opportunity." Mining claims were established on August 5, 1874. The Gordon Stockade was built just east of Custer's campsite in the winter of 1874 by a group of prospectors who illegally entered the Black Hills, seeking gold.

crossed their trail—turned either to the right or left—in fact most anything to prevent the possibility of coming in contact with them, the expedition being one of discovery, and not to create any difficulty with the occupants of the Hills. One would judge from these trails that the Indian is an admirer of all that is grand and beautiful in nature. They always select the wildest spots for camp ground, surrounded by the most romantic hills and dales, and bounded on one side by the prettiest of rippling streams—a fit place for student or lover.

Our march continued some few miles down the valley, with fresh evidences of Indians on every hand.

On we went, determined to find an opening in the valley large enough to arrange our camp in the most secure way possible. The stream continued to rush along by our feet and the hills rise in all their majesty, on either flank—some of them the monuments (it seemed) of some departed brave; others representing castles and fortifications, etc., antique and beautiful in design. I was riding with the General, when one of his orderlies called his attention to smoke ahead. From that moment everything was in a state of excitement. The scouts were sent forward—Bloody Knife and several others—to ascertain the cause. We continued at a walk, as heretofore. They soon

returned and reported several fires on the hill just ahead. On reaching there we found every indication of its having been occupied only a few hours before—fire still burning, lodge-poles, and a fresh trail down the valley also giving evidence that the birds had flown. This camp did not appear to have been occupied by any great number, so we could form no idea why they had left, unless it was that they saw us coming down the valley, or that some of their hunters had just returned and informed them of our presence in the Hills. The General determined to remain here until morning; in other words to make it our camping ground, it being a beautiful spot for the

South Dakota State Historical Society

This picture is almost identical to the one on the preceeding page, with a notable exception. The small tree which appears in the foreground of the previous picture, just to the left of the large rock, has disappeared. Illingworth apparently removed it for his final exposure. A more general haze of smoke now rises from the camp, indicating that numerous fires have been lit. Writing in the CHICAGO INTER OCEAN William E. Curtis said, "All the camp is aglow with gold fever," then added, "Officers and privates, mule-whackers and scientists, all met on a common level, and the great equalizer was that insignificant yellow dust."

purpose. The General selected it, I have since understood, as a camping ground to spend several days, it being wide, with a good supply of wood, water, and grass. We had just dismounted and unsaddled our horses, and thrown our weary bodies down to rest inside of the pines that surrounded us, when our advance scouts returned and informed General Custer that they saw five lodges some three miles below. Not wishing to scare them, the General sent Egard (sic), one of our guides (a white man known to most of the Indians,— Sioux—in the Northwest, and on friendly terms with them) forward with a towel as a flag of truce, to inform them that we were in the

neighborhood, and that we had no intention of disturbing them, etc... and also, if possible, to secure one of them as a guide. A party of our Indian scouts, Santees (Sioux) and Rees, were sent down to protect Egard, in case they should show fight. General Custer, accompanied by Forsythe (sic), Lt. Calhoun, your correspondent, and the others, also Barrows, Curtis, and Knappen, escorted by a detachment of Co. E., 7th cavalry, commanded by Sergeant Clair, followed them closely, to prevent the Rees from doing any damage, they being hostile. The General, putting spurs to his horse, was soon at a point where he could see the encampment some two and a half

miles below our camp. From our position we could see very plainly, about half a mile below, the five lodges. Here the scouts had halted to await further orders from General Custer, as previously directed, and give Egard time to get down to the encampment. The scouts are mainly composed of Ree Indians, whose friendship for the Sioux is not the warmest, they having reason to remember how merciless and cruel they (the Sioux) have been to them this past winter, the fight at Berthold being fresh in their memory—a little affair that occurred just before the expedition left Lincoln, in which several of the Rees were killed, scalped, &c. The Rees, before going down, stripped themselves and saddles of everything, and painted their faces with war paint, loaded their guns and made all necessary arrangements for the fray; and, in fact, it was with the greatest difficulty that they could be restrained from an attack on the village at once, and gave every indication of being in a bad humor with the General because he would not let them go forward and slake their thirst for blood. Could they have followed their own inclination, every squaw and pappoose (sic) in the little village would have fallen victim to their vengeful knife.

"Do not dare to fire a shot unless the Sioux attack you," was Gen. Custer's reply to their mutterings. He said beware in a tone which implied a penalty not expressed, which the Rees did not care to incur. The Santees—mostly young men from below, of whom there are some twenty—are all well educated, and can scarcely be classed among the savages; are friendly, and all of them, or the most of them, read and write the English language very well, though one could well see that they were quite anxious to enjoy the excitement of a little fight. Cold Hand, Bloody Knife, Goose and the other Indians from Grand River Agency, are of the Uncpapa tribe. They pass to and from through the various tribes of Sioux Indians, and are friendly or hostile as the case may be, sometimes one and sometimes the other, as the occasion may influence.

The whole party, Gen'l Custer excepted were all in for a little fun. Little did the Indian dream that the white man would be there before he returned from the hunt, that morning, as he shouldered his rifle and left for the wood. The white man and red were far away, and they deemed themselves secure. Surrounded by hills, they had left squaw and pappoose to care for the teepees, to dry the meat and bead the moccasin; but Indian dreams of security, like those of the white man, are often only dreams. I must confess that the encampment looks beautiful, as we saw it through our glasses. The white buckskins newly tanned, that covered the lodge poles, were as white as an officer's tent before it comes on contact with storm or

sunshine. The squaws seated on the ground cutting up deer meat, others eating and some beading moccasins, the young Indians lying around in every attitude enjoying their freedom and the sunshine, and the dogs, lying in the shade of a teepee, were happy; but that happiness was soon to be broken in upon—the white chief was just over the hill awaiting the return of Engard (sic) the scout. Imagine the surprise of the Indian squaws, when, without any notice, Engard (sic) made his appearance almost at the door of the teepee, with rifle in hand, a white flag, and mounted on an Indian pony. In a few words he made known the object of his visit, but still the squaws and children did not seem satisfied, some of the children taking their flight to the woods. Slow Bull being in the neighborhood, soon made his appearance. Egard pointed out to him Gen. Custer, the white chief commanding, and General Custer had a long conversation with "One Stab" the principal chief, also Long Bear. They very much surprised to hear that we had been in the Hills so long; they knew nothing of it before; had not even heard that we were coming. On entering one of their teepees were presented to Slow Bull's squaw, a daughter of Red Cloud. She was not beautiful, certainly, though quite good looking—fine teeth, black hair of course, braided into two "tails." She conversed with Egard, and seemed willing to give more general information than any of the rest. The General told her if she would send up, that he would give her sugar and coffee, for which she thanked him. The General questioned "One Stab" about the best passage through the Hills etc. The old fellow offered one of his young men as a guide. The General then asked him to come up and camp near us, which he promised to do the following morning. Long Bear promised to go hunting with your reporter, which I dare say would have been his last hunt. After our conversation we took our departure for camp, there to await the wagons, which were some distance in the rear; but in the course of time they made their appearance in good order. The Sioux came also to get the coffee and sugar promised by Gen-

eral Custer—Slow Bull, One Stab, Long Bear, and others whose names I did not learn. They smoked and talked for some time but seemed to be rather uneasy and anxious to get back; so, after being supplied with sugar, etc., they took their departure without much ceremony. The General, not wishing to have them go off so, sent several of the Sioux, or scouts, after them, to tell them to return and he would send down some one with them to protect them from the Rees and to remain with them all night; but it was of no use, they could not be induced to return—something had excited their fears. The Santee, being determined to obey orders and bring him back, took Long Bear by the bridle of his pony, intending to lead him, but the Indian not fancying any such treatment, grasped the Santee's gun, saying at the same time that he had "just as soon die today as tomorrow," and endeavored to get the gun. The Santee let go his bridle and fell off his horse, by that means securing his gun. He fired at the Sioux as he disappeared, and it seems wounded his pony, but the Indian and the pony made good their escape, however. Poor old One Stab was not so fortunate, and was captured and brought back to camp. The General sent Bloody Knife, Goose, and other of the friendly scouts down to the camp, but the Indians were gone, with lodges, &c. Nothing remained to tell where they had gone. One Stab, when told, was very much surprised; said he had no idea they would leave, but supposed that the young men were uneasy. One Stab is still with us, and will accompany the expedition to Base Bute, and then return to his home. Nothing of interest has transpired since the above mentioned episode — some long marches and hard ones.[17]

Oh! I forgot to say gold has been discovered. The Hills around us are composed of quartz, hornblende, filspar, mica, tourmaline, mica schist, and granite sandstone of several varieties.

Since reaching our present camp the boys have played one game of baseball, but as this is written by fire light and in a hurry, I can't give an account. The command is in good health and spirits. Good night.   Respectfully, POWER.

17. Sioux City, Aug. 3—A dispatch to the JOURNAL from Fort Sully, D. T., states that four Indian runners arrived at Cheyenne agency today, direct from the hostile camp in the Black Hills. They saw Gen. Custer's command in camp near Bear Butte, at the Foote of the Black Hills, on the evening of July 31st. They report that the hostile Indians knew nothing of Custer's expedition, were peacefully disposed, and wanted to come into the agencies to trade.

ST. PAUL PRESS
Issue of August 4, 1874

ST. PAUL DAILY PRESS
August 9, 1874

CUSTER'S EXPEDITION.

He is Now Browsing in the Black Hills with No Savages to Molest him.

The March to his Destination over a Beautiful Country.

Which Lands the First Americans in the True, Genuine, and Only Eldorado of America.

Where Gold and Silver Lie Scattered Around, and which is Already Making Plethoric Knapsacks of the Boys.

Special Dispatch to
the St. Paul Press.

BLACK HILLS' EXPEDITION
CUSTER'S VALLEY, AUG. 2,
via
FORT LARAMIE,
Aug. 8.

We reached this place yesterday, after marching four hundred and forty-eight miles. The command is in good health and spirits. Two deaths have occurred since last report, both soldiers from M and H companies of the Seventh cavalry. One died from natural causes, and the other was shot in a personal difficulty.

Two accidents are to be chronicled; Capt. Chance of the artillery and Capt. MacIntosh of the 7th cavalry, were kicked by a horse. MacIntosh is well, and Capt. Chance is convalesent.

We surprised a party of Sioux Indians in Castle Valley on the 26th ult., but no fighting has as yet taken place.

One Sioux chief of said party is still with us as guide.

Our march has been through a beautiful country. Since reaching the hills we have wood, water and grass in abundance. Gold and silver are found in quantities that will pay.

Five companies depart tomorrow, and two are already out prospecting. From indications this is the Eldorado of America.

ST. PAUL DAILY PRESS
Issue of August 26, 1874

THE BLACK HILLS.

Record of the March of Custer's Expedition Through their Unknown Defiles.

Gen. Custer as a Bear Killer— Abundance of Game—Character of the Country—Bear Butte not Much of a Mountain after all—The Return Journey Commenced.

CAMP NO. 35,
CUSTER'S BLACK HILLS
EXPEDITION,
BEAR'S BUTTE, D.T.,
August 15th, 1874.

Editor St. Paul Press:

My last letter from Custer Valley gave an account of the Sioux camp seen a few days before. Gen. Custer and party (escort) returned to camp after a march of one hundred miles. They accompanied Reynolds some sixty miles on his way to Fort Laramie, and parted with him at 12 o'clock the first night out. The General went as far south as the Cheyenne, and found the country just the same as that already discovered, rocks, &c. They crossed beautiful valleys, with quantities of fruit—gooseberries, raspberries, and other kinds equalls (sic) as good—but a full account of the trip I am unable to give, as I remained in camp; my horse feeling rather too feeble to undertake an extra one hundred miles.

We spent the time in camp very agreeably, hunting and fishing. I saw the first bear, but did not get it. Ross and McKay busied themselves prospecting during the stay there, and found both gold and silver. They gave it as their opinion that the country is very rich and bids fair to "pan out well."

Gen. Custer sent for One Stab and informed him that he might go that night. The Rees were very much disgusted when they learned the next day that the General had let the old fellow go. The night was fearfully dark and rainy, and the fact of his going was kept secret from the Rees, or they would have had the old fellow's scalp. About 8 p.m. he mounted his pony and was escorted out of camp by a guard. So ended his stay with us.

The General and party returned to camp on the 5th inst., and early on the morning of the 6th we retraced our old trail, traveling all day over the most beautiful part of our trail, and encamped within four miles of Castler Creek, the Indian camp.

On the 7th we passed the old encampment and crossed Elk Horn prairie, traveling northwest. The road was a rather rough one, the wagons not getting in until quite late. Gen. Custer and the party who accompanied him were rather more fortunate, and got to the camping ground early in the afternoon. They found the valley filled with game, deer and a few bear. Bloody Knife counted some 15 or 20 deer, and saw two bears. Gen. Custer and Col. Ludlow made short work of one, putting some six balls into him before the old fellow would surrender. The bear did not show fight, but raised himself on his hind legs, and backed up to a tree, and stood there until the fatal bullet put an end to his earthly pilgrimage.

Gen. Custer and Col. Ludlow had a picture (photograph) taken of the bear and themselves, by Prof. Illingworth, of St. Paul. The picture is indeed a fine one. The bear is lying on a rock; Gen. Custer and Col. Ludlow, both dressed in buckskin, rifles in hand, are standing close by; Bloody Knife is a little in the back ground but shows well.[18]

"Red Bird," a Santee scout, succeeded in killing the mate to the one already killed, which was not quite so large, but both fine specimens of grisly. There has been considerable hunting since by the officers, and others who were at liberty to go, each one hoping that they might be the fortunate ones to kill a "bar." Our camps have been well supplied with water and wood. The only possible objection to staying in the hills is the cold nights, four and five blankets being scarcely sufficient to keep one warm. We have had frost several times; on one or two occasions I have been tempted to look out for ice.

On the 8th our march was a hard one. We only traveled 14¾ miles, but the wagon train did not get in until after 12, midnight. Our intention was to go to Bear Butte that night, but the country

18. Custer to Elizabeth, August 15, 1874, from Bear Butte Creek, Dakota Territory.
I have reached the hunter's highest round of fame . . . I have killed my Grizzly. We reached Lincoln about the 31st. There has been no drunkenness, no card-playing on this trip.
Marguerite Merington, THE CUSTER STORY, p. 275.

would not admit of it, so we camped within about 7 miles of the Butte.

The morning of the 8th the weather was so misty that we had to wait until the fog went off a little, but the sun was soon out and we went on our way rejoicing. Lieut. Hodgson, commanding Company B. was pioneer, and had a hard day's work of it, the trail being over the hills and valley, which were thickly timbered at one time, but now most of the timber is on the ground, there having been a fire that killed most of it, and instead of finding felspar, hornblende and tourmaline, we found mica schist, volcanic formation, quartz, metamorphic rock, potsdam sandstone and sandstone. Our camp was beautifully situated in a valley, in which we found deer and beaver. The stream that watered this sloping plain was well filled with fish, but as time was wanting we did not partake of them, but sought our tents, and were soon dreaming of "Bear Butte," which was just over the hill, as Bloody Knife informed us.

The 9th (Sunday) sunrise found us well on the way, in fact on top of the hill from which Bear Butte could be seen. After looking in almost every direction for some outlet by which we could go to the Butte, the General concluded to travel eastward, that being, in fact, the only way that he could, and although we could and did on several occasions see the plains, yet it was an impossibility to get to them with a train. So, as it was Sunday, and there being no good way to get out, the General only traveled some seven miles and camped in a continuation of the valley in which we camped the night before.

On the 10th we were compelled to travel some little southeast, the country being so broken that we found it impossible to go in any direction for any length of time. By nine o'clock we came to a halt, fortunately in a good place to camp. The valley was large, and the stream wide and deep, with sufficient fish to supply the entire camp. Most of us indulged ourselves with the sport, and succeeded in capturing a good supply of the finny tribe. Those of the command who were not fond of fishing went hunting. Several elk were killed. On the 11th we remained in camp, and sent two companies forward to make a road for the next day. The time was spent as usual in camp, some hunting, others fishing, and some indulging in the "natural game of 'draw'." That day, like all others, passed away, and "taps" reminded us that it was again time to commit ourselves to the arms of "Morpheus," which we did—some with our boots on, others without— quietly reposed until the morning of the 12th.

Our march on this day, although a short one, was quite interesting; the scenery was very fine. We followed the stream, which was flanked on each side with bluffs composed of sand and lime-stone, and presented quite a picturesque appearance, though not so grand and imposing as that around "Custer Valley."

We camped in the valley a pleasant place, and a beautiful camp. That night an order came around saying that the command would not move on the 13th until after 2 p.m., and that the officers would meet at headquarters next morning at 9. They met there and were photographed by Illingworth. At 2 p.m., as ordered, the command moved out, and marched only a few miles to get out of the valley and nearer the plains, so as to give us a good start for Bear Butte on the 14th.

We broke camp yesterday, 14th inst., earlier than usual, and soon after sunrise we were on the plains once more, traveling westward. We found the grass dried up, and traveling very dusty, but after a long and tiresome march of 31 miles we pitched our camp at the foot of Bear Butte, which, I heard one of the men remark,

"is not such a damned big thing after all."[19] The Butte is about 2 miles long and presents quite a fine appearance.

Tomorrow we start westward to the Little Missouri, and will soon be on our way homeward.[20]

> Your &c.
> P.

19. Sioux City, Iowa, Aug. 19.—A report comes from Fort Sully this evening that the Indians, to the number of four thousand, attacked Custer's expedition on the 15th and were repulsed with heavy loss. Custer's loss is reported at fifty killed and wounded. The report was brought into Fort Sully by a mail-rider who states that he met one of Custer's scouts above Grand River and got the news from him.

ST. PAUL PRESS
Issue of August 20, 1874

Special Dispatch to the St. Paul Press.
20. Fort Sully, Aug. 18—Two bands of Indians have just arrived from the Black Hills, They make the following report: They left the hostile camp on the seventh, and found the expedition encamped in what is known to the Indians as the Cow Pen, in the Black Hills. This was on the thirteenth. After remaining at that point over night they started for this place. They say that the main body of the hostiles, numbering about 5,000, were on the Big Rosebud. The first information the hostiles had of Custer's movements was given them by sixteen Indians who had stolen some stock near the crossing about the time the expedition started. Upon hearing of the expedition to the Black Hills the hostile camp was thrown into great excitement and confusion. Chiefs and head men began haranguing the camp, declaring for war to the end. One chief in particular (Four Horns) said the whites had violated the treaty, and the Indians who had heretofore been supposed to be friendly, now had no excuse for remaining at peace with a people who proved so treacherous. He also declared that he would intercept Custer on his return if he lost half the braves in the camp. It is doubtful about the hostiles being able to intercept Custer before he reaches the river, unless he should be detained by the roads.

ST. PAUL PRESS
Issue of August 19, 1874

Gen. Custer's expedition, in addition to its exploit of opening a pathway into what has heretofore been considered an impenetrable region, is acquiring celebrity as a most efficient aid to the menageries. During the trip to the Black Hills, Gen. Custer succeeded in capturing a number of living curiosities, among which may be mentioned an attractive nest of rattlesnakes,—one old and four young—which furnishes its warning rattle whenever the temporary cage is disturbed. The old snake seems perpetually coiled and ready for a spring at any trespasser in his dominion. The box has its fascination but a commotion will be produced if it is broken while on the way to New York. A very large porcupine is contained in another box in the company with a youthful and meek-looking badger, while a third cage contains a pair of hawks captured in the Black Hills, which appear to be natives of that region, as there are visible points of difference between them and the varieties found in Minnesota. The eyes of these birds are remarkably handsome and brilliant, and the plumage dark and brown in color. General Custer's little menagerie also boasts of its specimens of the Jack-rabbit, which is considerably larger than the animal commonly found in this region, and bearing a strong resemblance to the English hare.

This interesting collection of western snakes, birds and animals, arrived in this city on Saturday evening from Bismarck, and after remaining in the United States Express office over the Sabbath, was started on its way to New York Sunday evening—all in the best of health, cheerful spirits, and prepared to resent an indignity on the spot.

ST. PAUL PRESS
Issue of September 15, 1874

CHICAGO INTER OCEAN

William E. Curtis

"Ere's your INTER-OCEAN telling all about the gold discoveries. Ere's your INTER-OCEAN. Don't you want a basket full of gold? Tell you all about where you can get it. INTER-OCEAN Sir, Lots of gold, don't you want some of it?" So cried scores of news boys to an excited Chicago on the day first news of a gold discovery in the Black Hills reached the city. Mining offices and bullion dealers were quickly deluged by "anxious inquirers," many of whom were working men left unemployed by the severe economic depression which had descended upon the country a year earlier. A large edition of the INTER-OCEAN was quickly sold out, and the next day its editors gloated over his competitors'— the TIMES and TRIBUNE—lack of "enterprise" in not having sent correspondents with the Custer Expedition to obtain the "important advices which the people were wanting."[1]

The Panic of 1873 had dealt a particularly severe blow to Chicago which was in the process of bouncing back from the destruction of the great fire of 1871. New industries along with old had folded over night

and hundreds of the city's workingmen were suddenly without work or prospects. It had been the profound hope of many Chicagoians that Custer's exploration of the Black Hills in the summer of 1874 would discover gold and rekindle national prosperity like the California strike of '49. The "enterprise" of the INTER-OCEAN in sending a correspondent with Custer had been prompted in large part by this dream of economic panacea. It was also, of course, quite natural for an editor to try to scoop his rivals with a sensational story. And the fact that the INTER-OCEAN's motto was "Republican in everything, independent in nothing," meant that it would as a matter of course not only defend the rightness of such an expedition but have relative ease in getting its correspondent included.[2]

The INTER-OCEAN was the name given in 1872 to the former CHICAGO REPUBLICAN by its new owner Jonathan Young Scammon. It continued, however, to be Republican in policy if not in name. It was a newspaper for the solid respectable classes and stood squarely behind Republican and big-business policies such as the high protective tariff. Scammon explained to his readers on March 26, 1872 that the name INTER-OCEAN was "especially appropriate to the location of our commercial city upon the great interior ocean of the Western Hemisphere." And true to its new name the INTER-OCEAN built a wide midwestern circulation through extensive coverage

97

of frontier and agricultural news. Thus, even aside from the economic situation of 1874 and its political persuasion, it was consistent with its general outlook for the INTER-OCEAN to be interested in the expedition to the Black Hills of Dakota.[3]

The man sent west to cover the Custer expedition for the INTER-OCEAN was twenty-three year old William Eleroy Curtis. Young Curtis was just beginning what would be a long and illustrious career in journalism. He was born to Reverand and Mrs. Eleroy Curtis in Akron, Ohio, in 1850 and graduated from Western Reserve College in 1871. Printer's ink seeped into his veins during college days when he worked part time "at the case" and as a reporter for the CLEVELAND LEADER. In 1872 he landed his first full-time job with the INTER-OCEAN as a cub reporter and remained with that paper for the next twelve years. During his career with the INTER-OCEAN he established a reputation as an enterprising reporter of great literary ability and became one of the best-known newspaper correspondents in the West. But even the wide open spaces of the American West proved too confining for Curtis's talents and interests. In the year 1884 he resigned from the INTER-OCEAN to become the secretary of the South American commission created by President Arthur to promote better relations between the United States and Latin American Republics. The next year President Cleveland appointed him a full member of this commission and Curtis was soon taken up with what has been called the "Pan-American movement." He toured every Latin American country and later traveled extensively in Europe and the Near East, and the list of his publications grew longer with every trip. In the 1890's he first served as director of the Bureau of American Republics and later was in charge of the Latin-American and historical departments of the World's Columbian Exposition at Chicago. At the time of his death in October of 1911 he was the Washington correspondent of the CHICAGO RECORD-HERALD.[4]

In the same issue that carried Curtis's dispatch proclaiming the discovery of gold in the Black Hills the INTER-OCEAN let its readers know just where it stood on the question of the future disposition of the area. While the editor recognized that a treaty made it unlawful for whites to enter the Hills, he was confident that the "government would without doubt take speedy measures" to open it to settlement. Certainly, "It would be a sin against the country and against the world," he declared, "to permit this region, so rich in treasure, to remain unimproved and unoccupied, merely to furnish hunting grounds to savages." And yet he cautioned against "too speedy and unauthorized invasion" as leading to hostilities with the tribesmen. It would be far better he counseled, to await "proper permission." But he was realistic enough to recognize that the "temptation" of gold was probably "too strong to brook delay." Still, warned the editor, men would do well to reflect upon possible consequences before they surrendered to the gold fever. After all, he reminded his readers, the "headlong rush" in the early days of the California strike had brought "much disappointment and suffering to thousands."[5]

Two days after proclaiming the gold discovery, the INTER-OCEAN printed a sampling of comments on the event from other newspapers. Several papers protested against a probable violation of Indian treaty rights, but the NEW YORK INDEPENDENT by far was the most outspoken. In a leading editorial published as an open letter "To President Grant," the INDEPENDENT reminded the President that the treaty "absolutely protects the Indians." Nevertheless, it foresaw an invasion of the Black Hills within a year, "unless you, President Grant, keep the nation's promise. Will you do it," the paper demanded?[6]

In its own editorial the INTER-OCEAN commented upon this concern for Indian rights. While it assured readers that it was "no advocate of an unlawful entry" upon the portions of the Black Hills guaranteed the Indians by the treaty, it appeared that some segments of the region were not reserved to the Indians. And if settlers wished to enter those areas they should be able to do so. The INTER-OCEAN viewed it as unfair that "solicitude is often expressed for the rights of the Indians, while the rights of white settlers upon the frontier are passed over in silence." "It will be time enough," declared the editor, "for benevolent persons and philanthropic newspapers to demand the rights of the Indians should not be encroached upon when the whites become trespassers." Until that occurred, he concluded, "open letters to President Grant, and paragraphs advising General Sheridan as to his duty in the premises, had best remain unwritten."[7]

There was not long to wait until the trespassing occurred. And through the remainder of 1874 the INTER-OCEAN followed the events in Dakota very closely. It never openly advocated or even condoned unlawful entry of the Black Hills, but certainly it persisted in keeping the subject alive in the minds of its readers.

FOOTNOTES

1. INTER-OCEAN, Aug. 28, 1874, p. 1.
2. Edwin Emery and Henry L. Smith, THE PRESS IN AMERICA, Englewood Cliffs, N. J., 1954, pp. 508-509. Frank L. Mott, AMERICAN JOURNALISM, A HISTORY OF NEWSPAPERS IN THE U. S. THROUGH 260 YEARS, New York, 1950, p. 463.
3. IBID.
4. James Grant Wilson and John Fiske, ed., THE NATIONAL CYCLOPEDIA OF AMERICAN BIOGRAPHY, 6 Volumes, New York, 1888-92, pp 43-44. Allen Johnson, et. al., DICTIONARY OF AMERICAN BIOGRAPHIES, 20 Volumes, New York, Vol. IV, p. 620. CHICAGO RECORD-HERALD, Oct. 6, 1911.
5. INTER-OCEAN, Aug. 27, 1874, p. 4.
6. INTER-OCEAN, Aug. 29, 1874.
7. IBID.

CHICAGO INTER-OCEAN
Issue of July 1, 1874

THE UNKNOWN WEST

General Custar's (sic) Exploring Expedition to the Mysterious Black Hills

The Column to Start on the 25th from Fort Abraham Lincoln, Dakota

An "Inter-Ocean Reporter at General Custar's (sic) Head-quarters—The Preparations and Prospects

A Sketch of the New Northwest, Dakota and Minnesota—Fort Lincoln—A Description of the Post and Its Surroundings

From our own Reporter

FORT ABRAHAM LINCOLN, DAKOTA, GENERAL CUSTAR'S (sic) HEADQUARTERS, June 22, 1874

This, the most recently established, and now the most important, perhaps, of the frontier posts, we start on Thursday for the Black Hills. The expedition is nearly all gathered, the troops are in camp ready to move, and the great transportation train, containing sixty day's supplies, is standing a mile or two over the hill yonder, waiting for the word of the commander. Nature never designed, and the government never chose a more advantageous post than Fort Lincoln, for reasons almost innumerable. On the west shore of the Missouri River, upon one of those high bluffs that has turned the snaky course of that muddy stream, it looks far down the valley in both directions, and commands the approaches from all directions. The place is reached by

THE NORTHERN PACIFIC ROAD,

the western terminus of which is a lively little place called Bismark (sic), just across the river. Our party came over the road by a special train, kindly provided by General Mead, Superintendent, and the trip was one of the utmost pleasure. So much has been said of the road, and the magnificent country which it has opened, that I need not burden this letter with an extended description. The great forests of Minnesota, filled with little lakes and rapidly running streams; the wide, clear prairies of Dakota, broken occasionally by ridges of small hills, unbroken by timber land, and all ready for the plow of the pioneer, that pilgrim to futurity, give one a theme for volumes of description; and as they have been in the past, so they will be in the future talked about, till migration and settlement has made them as familiar and productive as the plains of Illinois or the dairy farms of Ohio. One has a small idea of the vastness of our country till he is whirled along thirty miles an hour, for days at a time, with an unbroken stretch of country before him, and all the inhabited world behind. The managers of the Pacific Road have already made and are perfecting glorious arrangements for imigration. All along the line, at distances of 100 miles or so, they have erected enormous hotels fitted and furnished to suit the fastidious, and kept on a plan that must please everybody. To Brainard, to Thompson's junction, to Morehead (sic), or to Fargo, the settler, can take his family, and leave them there as comfortably as at the old homstead (sic) in the East, till his claim is established and his own house is ready for their reception. The days of pioneer hardship are over; prairie schooners are almost obsolete, for the emigrant travels in a Pullman car nowadays with a dozen trunks and a car-load of furniture and carpets on the train behind him. On account of these arrangements, the class of settlers coming to this country is superior, socially, to the general herd, and one finds in the log cabins way up here accommodations as comfortable and surroundings as pleasant as are habitual in the oldest and most refined rural districts of the East. These are the people who develop a country; who carry civilization with them, without waiting for it to come as an aftermath; and now that a start is made, its settlement and development, with the natural advantages it offers, must necessarily be rapid and thorough. At present the settlement is confined almost exclusively to those who compose the population of the half dozen thriving little towns along the line; people who have come to be ahead of the crowd that is expected to follow; people who have been looking for health and have found it here; people who want to buy up lands in advantageous localities and establish towns, and that army of restless adventurers who always rush into a new country like hungry cattle into a cornfield. But they are fewer here than in almost any other section of the country that can be mentioned, and, as a consequence, a larger number of the better class come.

BISMARCK

is perhaps the liveliest town west of Duluth. Only a year old, it claims a population of 1,500 people, a newspaper, and the full quota of saloons, gambling bells, and kindred pernicious resorts. It derives its importance more especially from the neighborliness of Fort Lincoln, and is the source of all the supplies that cannot be found in a sutler's store. The river, which is very wide and rapid at this point, is crossed by a rotten ferryboat, and the steep, muddy banks of the Missouri receive the passengers. The barracks occupy fifty acres or more, and are all new, neat, and convenient. The grounds are laid out in delightful drives, and in the center a wide park is left for a parade. The garrison are very proud of their quarters, and are working hard to beautify the place, by setting out shade trees, grading the drives and adding tasty touches here and there. The officers' quarters are in neat cottages fronting the parade, and as many of them have their wives at the post, the society is quite large and cultivated. General George A. Custar (sic), the cavalry hero, is in charge of the post.

THE GARRISON

is the Seventh cavalry, and portions of the Sixth, Seventeenth, and Twentieth regiments of infantry. The officers of the post are General G. B. Dandy, Quartermaster; Lieutenant A. E. Smith, Commissary; Dr. Weeds, Surgeon; Dr. Williams, Assistant Surgeon; Lieutenant James Calhoun, Adjutant; Captains V. K. Hart, F. W. Benteen, William Thompson; George W. Yates; T. H. French, Owen Bale, William Maylan; First Lieutenants T. W. Custar, T. M. McDonegan, E. G. Mathey, Donald McIntosh, Frank Gibson, E. S. Godfrey; and Second Lieutenants B. H. Hodgeson, Harrington, George D. Wallace, and Charles A. Vanune, of the Seventh Cavalry; Captain Poland, and Lieutenants Badger and Bronson, of the Sixth Infantry; Captain Wheaton and Lieutenant Gates, of the Twentieth Infantry; and Captains Sanger and Grossman, and Lieutenants Chance, Burns and Roach, of the Seventeenth Infantry. In addition to the garrison there are a hundred or more Indian scouts from the lesser Sioux tribes, and the Reas (sic), which are almost extinct, who have taken refuge here, and are serving the government in a valuable capacity for their rations. The famous scout, "Bloody Knife," is their chief and leader. These troops, with the exception of a couple of companies who remain to guard the post, and with the addition of a couple of companies from Fort Rice, will compose

THE BLACK HILLS EXPEDITION.

General Custar (sic) will command, General Forsythe (sic) and Captain Calhoun having the charge of the wings. Lieutenant Wallace will command the scouts, and Lieutenant Chance the artillery, which consists of a battery of Gatlin guns. The train consists of about 150 supply wagons, ambulances, etc., under charge of Captain Smith, acting quartermaster. The remainder of the party consist of Lieutenant Colonel Fred. Grant; Colonel Ludlow, Chief Engineer of the department, with W. H. Wood, Assistant, and a squad of engineers; Professor Winchell, State Geologist of Minnesota, and an assistant; Professor Grinnell of Yale College, and an assistant mineralogists and botanists; Huntington & Co., photographers, St. Paul, and representatives of the New York TRIBUNE and INTER-OCEAN. The preparations are complete, the battalion is in camp a couple of miles south of the post, and on Thursday, the 25th inst., a start will be made. The route of the expedition is marked as nearly as possible on annexed map, which is a copy of one made in 1861 by General W. F. Raynolds,

of the Engineer Corps, after his explorations of the Yellowstone and Little Missouri Rivers. That expedition passed west and south of the Black Hills, but did not enter

THOSE LEGENDARY REGIONS

because of the determined opposition of the Indians and the danger attending it. But General Custar (sic) takes a force sufficient to meet and overcome all opposition, and will go through as he says, if he kills every Sioux this side of the Rocky Mountains. Around these Black Hills hover a mysterious interest. Twice before this an attempt has been made to enter them—the expedition of General Reynolds (sic) referred to, and one commanded by Lieutenant Warren, which went up from the south to Powder River, in 1859, but was not permitted by the Indians to enter. Why it is guarded so carefully is unknown, unless there be treasures hidden in those wilds which the Sioux wish to keep from the white man's rapacity; but they have been more jealous of this portion than of any other of their ancient heritage.

IS THERE GOLD THERE?

In General Raynolds' report he says: "Very decided evidence of the existence of gold were discovered in the valley of the Madison and the Big Horn Mountains and we found some indications of it in the neighborhood of the Black Hills, between the Forks of the Shayenne (sic). The very nature of the case, however, forbade that an extensive or thorough search for the precious metals should be made by such an expedition as I conducted through the country. The party was composed in the main of irresponsible adventurers, who recognized no moral obligation resting upon them. They were all furnished with arms and ammunition, while we were abundantly supplied with picks and shovels. Thus the whole outfit differed in no essential respect from one which would be required if the object of the expedition had only been that of searching for gold. It is thus evident that if gold had been discovered in any considerable quantity, the party would have at once disre-

garded all the authority of the officers in charge, and would have been converted into a band of gold miners. It was for this reason that the search for gold was at all times discouraged. The Sioux Indians of that region are said to possess large quantities of valuable gold ornaments, and officers tell how they have brought large nuggets of the pure metal into camp. General Custar (sic) goes prepared for a thorough examination, and he keeps back all adventurers and "prospecters" from his train, so that the secret of the Indians' jealous care will be discovered, and may be a rich treasure prove.

THE PROSPECTS OF FIGHTING

are growing, and it may be that something will be done toward Indian extermination before the return of the expedition. The scouts say a large body of Sioux have gathered a hundred miles or so to the South to resist the advance, and if they do, General Custar (sic) is prepared to give them a thorough threshing. The scouts are crazy for blood, and have their war dances every night at their quarters near the river. The soldiers also are anxious for a little something to relieve the monotony of marching, and are living in hopes of an attack. A strong garrison is left there to guard the post, for it is quite as probable that an attack will be made here as anywhere, while the cavalry is gone.

Curtis.

CHICAGO INTER-OCEAN
Issue of July 9, 1874

CAMPED IN DAKOTA

An "Inter Ocean" Reporter at the Headquarters of the Black Hills Expedition

The Reconnoissance Delayed until the Second of July— Final Preparation

General George A. Custer as He is, and Not as He is Commonly Supposed to be

The Commander and the Man at Home and in the Field—His Private Habits—Army Reminiscences

From Our Own Reporter

HEADQUARTERS
GEN. GEO. A. CUSTER,
BLACK HILLS EXPEDITION
IN CAMP NEAR FORT
LINCOLN, D. T.,
June 30, 1874

There may be no such word as fail in the lexicon of youth, but the word delay is written a great many times, with a great many synonyms. One would think that military precision would allow nothing but promptness, and that military discipline would allow no indications of impatience, but soldiers are human, and heirs like their fellow flesh to delays and disappointments. The Black Hills Expedition was ordered to start on the 20th of June. The commanding officer took five days of grace, and issued an order announcing the 25th for the march; before the day came he received instructions to await the arrival of a new issue of ordinance, which he did, and the arms came today—a new and improved pattern of the Springfield rifle, as handsome weapons as were ever handled by man.

THE COMMAND WILL MOVE.

Day after tomorrow we are to start, then, if nothing further opens to interrupt progress. It has been a severe test of the patience of everybody, this waiting with horses b r i d l e d and knapsacks packed, and a murmur of rejoicing was heard in the camp when the arrival of the new rifles was announced. We have been in camp just a week now, and have experienced all the ennui of tented life. The old soldiers of the war will remember how heavy time hung on their hands when they saw action before them, and the word they waited for was not said. The same yearning and groaning, wishing and hoping and swearing has been heard in this miniature army because of its delay; but now that the day has been positively set and rations issued, the discontent is over, and everybody is occupied putting the finish on his preparations.

THESE EXPEDITIONS INTO "THE UNEXPLORED TERRITORY BEYOND"

are more pretentious than people imagine. It is not the mere jaunt of a body of cavalrymen off into an adjacent region; it is not like those raids which were common in the war, that originated in a day, and were forgotten in a night, but it is an undertaking which requires months of preparation and careful planning. We are going into a country uninhabited except by wild men, where there is no known source of sustenance, either for man or beast; sixty days at the least is to be spent, and prudence requires that the necessities of life for that entire period be carried from the start. For this purpose a train of 150 wagons is organized, each drawn by six mules, making a herd of no less than 900. The cavalry battalion requires about 1,000 horses, and a herd of 300 beeves, which will be driven with the train, increases the live stock of the expedition to 2,200 head. In addition to the military there must be civilians employed as teamsters, herders, blacksmiths, saddlers, and otherwise, till there looms up in this expedition an affair of magnificent proportions. And just here for a moment let the reader imagine these 900 mules braying, the 1,000 horses whinnying, the 300 cattle lowing, and the 2,000 men groaning though

The dark and gloomy watches of the night because of these pestiferous mosquitoes, that make the valley of the Missouri

THE VILEST PLACE IN THE WORLD.

Its pure, bracing atmosphere; its clear, blue skies; its gorgeous sunsets cannot redeem it in the mind of a reasonable man, and although one galloping over these hills in the cool of the day may expand his lungs exhilarated, may exclaim enthusiastically upon the glories of the sky, and gaze fascinated at the fantastic shadows that the jutting bluffs along the river cast upon its bosom when the sun is low, yet all his romance fades with the pink and purple of the sky; all his enthusiasm evaporates, and his fascination is forgotten when the river's bosom is all shadow, for then the mosquitoes rise over the Missouri as the locusts over Egypt, devouring everything, and yet after a week of this General Custer, the Pharaoh of these plains, will not let Israel go. Off in the Sioux country, away from these Missouri bottom lands, they say there are none of these insects, and if we ever get there life will once more be enjoyment. Existence here is sufferance —and hard, hot breathing under netting and blankets. One lives with gloves and a head shield during the day, and sleeps in his shield and gloves, under blankets and bars during the night. Lift up your shield to speak to your neighbor, and in fifteen minutes after your lips and chin feel as mammoth as the Andes Mountains. Take off your glove to button your collar closer, or adjust your net, and your hand is a swollen and unseemly thing. If you assume coolness in thin linen, when the mercury is above ninety, as it has been everyday but one, you creep sorrowfully back to your wigwam and wrap your burning body in a blanket. Life is a mockery, a base imitation of that which it ought to be; and yet General Custer will not let Israel go.

He is a great man—a noble man is

GENERAL CUSTER,

and one of whom the most of the world—that part which does not know him—has a singularly wrong idea. I came here expecting to find a big-whiskered, swearing, ranting, drinking trooper, and I found instead a slender, quiet gentleman, with a face as fair as a girl's and manners as gentle and courtly as the traditional prince. Hunting for the drunken raider, I found a literary gentleman, in his library, surrounded by adjutants and orderlies, to whom he gave his military directions, while he wrote and read. His guest for four days, I never sat with a more courteous host, or generous entertainer, or polished conversationalist. With one of the sweetest, brightest women in the world for a wife, his home is that of a cultured gentleman, instead of a roystering cavalryman, as is generally supposed.

General Custer does not drink, notwithstanding t h e prevailing idea of his intemperance. He believes in and practices total abstinence. The good temperance teachers of the day can use him as an example rather than an object of regret.

General Custer does not swear. In his constant companionship for more than a week, under circumstances too, that have been unusually trying, I have not heard an oath from his lips; and what is more, he does not allow profanity among his subordinates.

General Custer does not smoke; does not use tobacco in any form. One would know it from the clearness of his complexion and the pearly polish of his teeth. Thus far and unreasonably has the world been mistaken, and it really does seem strange to find

A SOLDIER THAT NEITHER DRINKS, SMOKES, NOR SWEARS.

But what some one will ask, are his vices? His soldiers will tell you he has none, unless an almost inordinate love for the higher brute creation may be called such, for General Custer has the best dogs and the best horses he can procure within the limits of search. His leash of hounds is probably as large and well-bred as any in the country, and his own and the horses of his regiment, the Seventh Cavalry, are famous all over the States, while he has the reputation of being the best sportsman and the most accurate shot in the army.

A BRIEF OUTLINE OF HIS CAREER

will be appropriate in this connection. Leaving West Point, in July, 1861, he was sent immediately into active service in the Fifth Regular Cavalry, and was soon made aid-de-camp to General McClellan, with the rank of captain. In '63, only 23 years old, he was made Brigadier General of volunteers, and originated the idea of "Raids," which made him famous immediately. In 1864 he was made a Major General, and given command of the cavalry in Virginia. His record since that time is so well known as to need but the single reference that he, the youngest Major General in the service, captured more prisoners, more cannon, and more flags than any commander in the war of the Rebellion. At the close of the war he was made Lieutenant Colonel of the Seventh Cavalry, and was sent into Texas. His frontier fighting since that time has been as remarkable as his record

in the war, and now no man on the plains is more respected or feared by the hostile Indians than him whom they call

"THE LONG-HAIRED CHIEF".

This spring his golden curls have been sacrificed; he looks younger, more soldierly, although less poetical, and the coming reconnaissance will prove if he is shorn of his strength. At present General Custer is 34 years old—a slender, fair-haired, blue-eyed man. His wife, a charming lady, who has shared his marches and victories since early in the war, is as gentle and cultivated, and yet as soldierly as a woman can be, and her home is one green spot, if there be no others in the frontier life of the officers of the Seventh.

A few evenings since the writer, entering General Custer's library, saw a new phase of this man's character. He sat on a low stool by his desk, with a spelling-book in his hand; before him were two little girls, one white and the other colored, the children of his servants, whom he was affording the necessities denied by the lack of schools. Apologizing for my interruption, I was withdrawing, when he cried out in his hearty way:

"Come in! come in! and see my school!

GENERAL CUSTER'S SCHOOL

I entered the room, and in a pleasant, familiar way he went on with his teaching, having his scholars spell the words alternately, tell their meaning, and construct sentences: I have found that this has been his custom for several years, and all these little people of his household know of written words is what he has taught them.

Since I have been here I have heard anecdotes of his goodness and manliness, from his soldiers and others, that would fill columns. A motley class of beings are the human drift-wood that has gathered in the regular army; and a difficult class to please. The soldier nowadays is generally eccentric; is an oddity, or else an unfortunate; some causes beyond those ordinarily influencing men have driven him into the dog's life of a "regular" and he who can gain the universal respect of these many-minded, queer dispositioned

men, must be molded differently than the majority of us. General Custer is such a man.

A WEST POINT REMINISCENCE.

Getting three or four old comrades together, the conversation naturally turns on old times, and those of us who have been privileged the companionship of the officers of this expedition have had a rich feast of army reminiscence. Colonel Ludlow, chief of the engineers in this expedition, was a freshman at West Point. General Custer was about to graduate, and has the former to blame because he did not get a graduate's diploma. The fact has been recalled in the association of the past few days, and I will tell it as General Custer told it at dinner one day. He talks very rapidly—so that he repeats his words in a peculiar manner which I cannot reduce to writing.

WHY CUSTER DIDN'T GET A DIPLOMA.

"Why you see," said the raider, gesturing over a tureen of soup, "Ludlow was a greeny, but he had pluck; and one evening, when I was officer of the day, some upper classman pitched on to him, and he showed fight; the boys encouraged them until they got into a good square out-and-outer, just as I was going my rounds. Instead of sending both of them, as I should, to the guard house, you know, I pushed back some fellows that were trying to trip Ludlow, and said that there must be fair play. It was a good one, and Ludlow was getting the best of it, when the boys began to interfere again. I was just getting my hand in again, when old ——, Instructor in Artillery, came around, and instead of arresting Ludlow and the other fellow, he locked me up for allowing the fight to go on, and I was in the guard house when my class graduated. But they wanted soldiers at Washington just then, and they sent me on. I never went back there again.

THE SOLDIER BEHIND THE STUMP.

General (or "Sandy," as they call him here) Forsyth tells a funny story that developed at the reunion of soldiers when the Detroit monument was dedicated.

While Custer and other of the famous men of the war were receiving the people at the Russell House, an old fellow came up, and said:

"General Custer, how do you do. I suppose you don't remember me, as you never saw me but once."

"I am sorry to say I do not," replied the General.

"Don't you remember once down in Virginia, in a big fight there, you found a soldier behind a stump, and told him if he didn't get out of that and go to the front you'd shoot his d__n head off?"

"I don't remember saying any such thing," said the General.

"Yes you did," persisted the soldier; "I heard you; I was the man; but I wasn't afraid to go into that fight—I had broken my musket and was trying to mend it, and I knew some day I should have a chance to tell you how it was. And now, continued he, "I want to introduce my wife and children to you," and he brought up a blooming matron and a flock of fair-haired children.

I might fill a page with similar reminiscences, recalled and told around the mess table here, but prefer to give them to the public in doses rather than in a lump.

THE PROBABILITIES OF INDIAN FIGHTING

are very great, as reports constantly continue to come in concerning the rendezvous of the different tribes under "Sitting Bull," to interrupt the approach of the expedition. An Indian missionary came to General Custer the other day, to persuade him not to go out through the Sioux country, because, he said, there would be terrible fighting; but with all due difference to the Peace Commission, the Indians need a sound threshing, and they probably will get it.[21]

A QUEER CASE.

There wandered into the post the other day a richly dressed person, who said he had come up here to buy lands. Stopping at the post trader's, which is the hotel as well as commercial center and general resort, he showed strange freaks, which indicated that he was not right in his mind, and was closely watched. The second day after his arrival he started off on foot to-ward the west, saying he was going to the Yellowstone Park. The fact was reported to General Custer and a squad sent after him. He told them, when he was overtaken, that he was going to the Yellowstone country, and would be back in a few days. He was brought back and placed in the hospital, where he is now waiting developments. An examination of his sachel showed him to be the possessor of over $1,200 in currency; and among his papers were evidences that he had come here to purchase land. His name is suppose to be Emil Kluky, and his cards are addressed Joseph Kluky, No. 26 Wohlzeile strasse, Vienna. He has had correspondence with Henry Reimann, loan and land agent, Broad street, New York, in reference to investments. A telegram concerning his condition was sent to the latter address, but no reply has yet been received. He will be given into the care of the Austrian Minister in a few days if nothing further is heard concerning him.[22]

Curtis.

Special Telegram to the Inter-Ocean.
21. Fort Lincoln, D. T., July 3.—The Black Hills Expedition left here yesterday morning, under the command of General Geo. A. Custer, General Forsyth and General M. S. Tilson commanding the wings. The column consists of ten companies of the Seventh Cavalry, three companies of infantry, 100 Indian scouts under command of the famous Bloody Knife, and a battery of Gatlin guns. The train consists of 150 wagons and carries supplies for sixty days. The party will probably be gone until the 1st of October, making a thorough exploration of the legendary region of the Black Hills and establishing a site for the building of a fort and trading post there. It is probable that a strong resistance will be made by the Indians, as startling rumors are constantly arriving at this place of the gathering of the different Sioux tribes under Sitting Bull about seventy miles to the south. An Indian missionary came to this post a few days since with the information that the Indians intended to contest every foot of the march, and he begged General Custer to give up the expedition to save bloodshed. The treaty with the Sioux reserves the right of the United States to pass through and explore all the contested territory, and General Custer is prepared to enforce that right. A severe conflict may be expected before many days.
CHICAGO INTER-OCEAN
Issue of July 4, 1874

22. The disposition to misconstrue every act of the administration, which exists on the part of certain opposition journals, frequently leads them to indulge in the most far-fetched and unfounded conjectures. The Custer expedition to the Black Hills of Dakota is a striking instance in point. The New York WORLD, leading off as usual in the assault, thinks there are some queer things about the affair. The preparations, it says, have been made with much secrecy; no appropriation was asked of Congress; the War Department has been singularly reticent; hence, argues the WORLD, the expedition must be the work of "a ring." The officers are known favorites at the White House; Custer is in command, Forsyth is second, and Fred. Grant is third. What clearer evidence can there be of a "job" than these damning facts? The Boston POST also scents corruption in the Custer expedition, and stigmatizes this invasion of the Sioux territory as a direct and flagrant violation of the treaty which Bishop Hare has made with that tribe. Like the WORLD, the organ of the Boston Democracy, too, talks about "a ring" and White House favorites, "including the rapidly-promoted son of the President."

Now, nothing can have a more slender foundation to rest on than these insinuations about rings and jobs. If the preparations for the Black Hills expedition were made with any special secrecy,—which remains yet to be proved—if no appropriation were asked of Congress, and if the War Department has really been "singularly reticent" about the affair, this would be nothing exceptional. Military preparations are generally secret, neither is it usual to ask special appropriations, for every raid against the Indians, from Congress; nor is the War Department in the habit of proclaiming in advance, from the house-tops, what it proposes to do. Nor, indeed, are we aware that General Custer is a great favorite at the White House. The long and arduous services which this gallant Western sabreur has been performing on the frontier point him as pre-eminently fitted for the command of such an expedition as that against the Sioux, and his experiences as an Indian fighter had therefore far more to do with the appointment than his standing with the President. Stripped of these unwarranted allegations, there is, in reality, nothing more to justfy the stuff of the WORLD and consorts about "rings and jobs", than the Colonel Grant is attached to the command of the expedition.
CHICAGO INTER-OCEAN
Issue of July 21, 1874

CHICAGO INTER-OCEAN
Issue of July 29, 1874

CUSTER'S EXPEDITION

The Column on the March
Into the Black Hills and
Big Horn Country.

Organization of the Command—
The Troops, the Scouts, and
the Supply Train.

Indian Allies—Interviews and
Legends of the Country to be
Traversed—Specimens of
Ingenious Trailing.

A Desert Region—Heat and
Alkali Dust—An Oasis Here
and There in the Midst of
Desolation.

An Indian War Dance and Its
Dismal Suggestions—Savages
in Sight—A False Alarm—
Probabilities of Fight.

First Letter

From Our Own Reporter.

GENERAL CUSTER'S
BLACK HILLS EXPEDITION,
IN CAMP AT CANNON BALL
RIVER, DAKOTA, July 6, 1874

"How," said he.
"How," said I.
And with that, the usual greeting, I was welcomed by "Bear's Ears," who was to tell me his story. The place was a log cabin—a portion of what is known as "Indian Quarters" at Fort Lincoln; the time was near sunset, the light that came through the open door being just enough for me to distinguish the form of a rugged old man, with features black as a negro, and as bold and marked in their outlines as the familiar face of Robert Collyer. The expression on the face was one I can never forget; it was one that would haunt anybody, seen in the gloomy atmosphere of twilight, smoking sage and Killikinick tobacco. The evening before, at a war dance, I had been introduced to

"BEAR'S EARS"

by an interpreter as a man of extraordinary intelligence and remarkable history, and had asked him for the story of his life. There he was standing in all the glory of his war paint, a statue of naked bronze, and his eye shone with the inspiration that those absurd pow-wows awaken; he could not tell it then—he was thinking, he said, of the future, and must lead the braves in the war dance—but the next day would think of the past, and tell me his history if I would come at sunset. Now, he was a different picture, clad in one of those uncouth stable frocks, a pair of cavalry pants, from which he had cut long strips under the thighs to give his libs free motion, and a high crowned officer's hat, ornamented with plumes and bands of red flannel, from under which his long hair hung in a bushy mass. I could tell that he had been thinking of the past, for retrospection was written in every wrinkle, and his eyes seemed looking far away. He was not an ideal Indian, as far as appearance goes, but his life was a romance as thrilling and tragic as was ever written.

THE WARRIOR'S ROMANCE.

Forty years ago, he told me through the interpreter, he was living with his tribe, the Rees, in the upper Missouri, and loved a maiden whose name was Wa-ka-ta-na. Another youth, named "Wrinkle Hand," was his rival, and unfairly took advantage of him in the contest for a heart, so as to place him in disgrace among his people. Unable to bear the scorn and derision that was heaped upon him, and the loss of his love, one morning he saddled his pony and rode away to the lodge of the Sioux, the enemies of his people. Here he made solemn vows to the Great Spirit, and cut off two fingers from his left hand as

A SACRIFICIAL OFFERING.

He was with the Sioux for seven years, wandering over the plains of Dakota, and through the wild forests of the Black Hills, hunting and fishing and fighting, but all the time remembering the vows and the sacrifice. It was in the last moon of the seventh year of Bear's Ears' exile that he met Wrinkled Hand, his rival, in the Valley of the Cannon Ball. His time was come; his vows were fulfilled, and having cooked and eaten his enemy's heart, he rode back to his tribe, the Rees, took Wa-ka-ta-na for his wife, and told the story of his courage and vengeance till he became a hero.

THE REES ARE ALMOST
EXTINCT

now. Bear's Ears is one of the oldest of the tribe, and has left the forest for the protection of the whites, a cabin, and bacon and hard tack rations. Wa-ka-ta-na is a great, fleshy, dirty squaw, lugging water and building fires for the warriors. No wonder Bear's Ears loves to think of the past and its romance.

"Bear's Ears", is one of our guides,—one of the very few accessible Indians who have been in the Black Hills country—and I am writing from the valley of the Cannon Ball—the only really beautiful piece of landscape we have seen so far on our march. The river, a small, shallow, and very crooked stream, empties into the Missouri about twenty miles below Fort Rice, and we are a hundred miles or more from its mouth. Its name comes from the fact that all along its banks and bottom are accumulations of stone as smooth and round as a cannon ball. The Indians call it "Inyan Wakahap." General Sully made a trail along here in 1864, and on the War Department maps the country is very well defined. But here we leave all civilized traces, and tomorrow morning enter the unknown land.

ON THE MARCH.

We have been out four days, having started from Fort Lincoln on the 2d of July, just one week after the date originally appointed, and are rapidly becoming inured to the hardships of camp life and the march. The weather has been terribly warm and dry, the thermometer having ranged constantly from 94 to 103 in our tents at the middle of the day, but the nights have been deliciously cool and bracing, so that by early marching and rest in the heated hours we have been able to get on right well, and have marked our seventy-fourth mile. General Custer is a rapid leader, and, although our train is unusually heavy, he is hurrying forward so fast that we shall reach Slim Butte, the end of the first stage and the first point of interest, in about five days more.

THE MYSTERIES OF
SLIM BUTTE.

No white man has ever seen Slim Butte, and its attractions are at present quite indefinitely presented; but the Indians tell of beautiful scenery, remarkable caves, and rare minerals there. "Goose," our Sioux guide, of whom I shall have occasion to refer frequently, and whose remarkable history I have among the resources of my note-book, says there is one cave near the butte which the Indians regard as the abode of the evil spirits. It is entered, he says, only by a hole in the surface of the open prairie, and extends miles and miles—he cannot tell how far—being continually filled with the shrieks and wailings of the tormented damned. On the walls, he says, are carved great inscriptions in some unknown language, in letters as long as his arm, which even the medicine men of the Sioux have been unable to interpret, and to which have come also the wise men of all the tribes, but with no better success. Sometimes, says Goose, the letters and figures shine as if they had been rubbed with fire, and then the shrieks and groans are the loudest, their echoes reaching even to the open air. These inscriptions, the Indians think, are the edicts of the Great Spirit against those in torment, and they shine like fire whenever they are renewed.

THE ORDER OF MARCH

General Custer has adopted the same as is usual on these expeditions, the wagon train being in the center of a square formed by the advance guard, column of cavalry on each flank, and a battalion of infantry in the rear. General Custer himself leads, with his guides and the Indian scouts under Lieutenant Wallace, and carries a flag of red and blue, which he means to plant on the highest summit of the chain of Black Hills. The right flank is commanded by General Forsyth, of Chicago, and the left by Colonel Tilford, of Fort Rice. Thus it is seen Chicago is well represented in this expedition— represented by one of its most popular citizens and one of the noblest and bravest soldiers in the United States Army. But people do not appreciate General Forsyth till they see him in the field, and his admirers in society would congratulate themselves on their own good judgment could they see him among his soldiers on these hot, dusty marches—the model of patience, nerve, and soldierly courtesy.

CAMPAIGNING UNDER CUSTER IS NO SPORT.

People who sit in cool, dark parlors and shaded offices may envy us, but if they consider seven and eight and ten and fourteen hours in the saddle, under a sun that raises the mercury a hundred degrees on a parched, dusty plain, an experience to be envied, four days such as we have spent would convince them to the contrary. No one, so far, very fortunately, has felt fatally the terrible suffering, but the ambulances are full of poor soldiers who have fallen out by the way. The animals feel the heat and the want of sufficient water even more than the men, and whenever the train stops the air is hideous with the braying of the poor, thirsty, tired mules. The most of the "bottom lands" in this region are covered with a sediment of alkali, which is as fine as the finest powder, and sifts through veil or any other protections a person can wear, and sifted through is very painful, getting into the pores of the skin, and burning and smarting till one imagines himself in the process of cremation. The heat and wind parches and cracks our lips and faces, and this dust settling on the blistered flesh, is about as serious torture as the strictest disciplinarian can desire. But nevertheless we enjoy it—the experience, not the dust—and lie down on our blankets at night-fall with the mind quivering with new thoughts and the strengthened pulses throbbing with the fresh vigor this glorious atmosphere instills.

Second Letter

IN CAMP AT "HIDDEN WOOD," DAKOTA, Wed. Evening, July 8, 1874

A PICTURE OF CAMP LIFE.

For a background a sunset as gorgeously beautiful as any that ever glowed on Italian skies, and a high, jagged bluff, covered with clusters of trees, with a clear stream of water running at its base; in the foreground a smooth, grassy plain covered with tents, hooded wagons, and grazing horses; a band in the center playing familiar airs, and an atmosphere cool, fresh, and bracing— and you have a picture of our camp to-night. The day has been hot and

dusty, and we have suffered and panted through a march of twenty miles to enjoy this balmy evening and beautiful spot—the most beautiful in varied scenery of any we have yet seen. This place, the only timber in a radius of thirty miles, is called Pa-ha-che-cha-cha, or "Hidden Wood," by the Indians, because the hills so cluster around it that the trees cannot be seen two miles away—one of the few shady oases in this desert of prairie land, and very grateful, after a week's marching. A Wisconsin lumberman would laugh at the use of the word "wood" as applied to a cluster of timber that would not turn out 10,000 feet of planking, but let him live in this country a while and he would value even the stinted shrubbery that occasionally makes a feeble attempt at existence on the banks of some sluggish stream.

Our march today occasioned one of the most

REMARKABLE INSTANCES OF SCOUTING

the old campaigners with us say they have ever seen. This timber, as I have said, stands alone in a wide radius, and it was quite necessary for our comfort that we reach it. Goose, our Sioux guide, had told General Custer of its existence, and promised, if possible, to lead us here. The course, as he pointed it out with a spear of grass the evening before, was a little south by southwest, and he showed us far in the distance a sharply cut butte or hill, rising above the thousand of its companions against the haze sky. We were to pass to the left of that, he said. The march was a long, dry, and dusty one, nothing but ceaseless hills and valleys, one after the other, and so nearly alike in appearance that we wondered how our guide could do otherwise than lose his way. Seven hours or more passed, as they always do in marching, slowly and drearily, and as we approached a high, rocky cliff, beyond which we could see nothing but the sky, Goose grunted a few gutturals to one of his companions, who spurred his horse into a canter, while we filed slowly after him. Reaching Pisgah, he spread out his arms over space as some pulpit orators do when they wish to represent eternity in pantomime, and turning, beckoned stolidly to us to come along.

THE PROMISED LAND.

Surely enough, there it was, just below us, nestling in the lap of a rocky ledge—a cluster of trees about as big as a New England garden, and a bright little brook running around its roots. A sigh of joyful relief came involuntarily from everybody, but as it isn't soldierly to express emotion of any sort, we didn't say anything, except one of us, and he, an irreverent youth who attends the expedition with his brother, an officer, expressed the sentiment of all thuswise:

"The old cuss struck it, as sure as h__l."

General Custer looked at the youth, but couldn't reprove him—he expressed a solid fact.

OUR INDIAN SCOUTS.

These scouts are curious characters. We have nearly 100 of them, who form the advance guard—about forty Rees, fifty Santees, and a few Sioux. The Santees are regularly enlisted soldiers, are dressed in the regulation uniform, and most of them talk and write English, but the rest are the traditional aborignees — dirty, lazy, and singularly instinctive. They dress in the most fantastic fashion their imagination can suggest and their resources afford. Some have no clothes on—to speak of—although General Custer makes it imperative that something that cannot be mentioned politely be worn. Others have uniforms and blankets, ornamented and altered to suit the taste of the wearer, and their ideas of millinery or tailoring are exceedingly unconventional. Give one a pair of army pantaloons, for instance. The first thing he will do is to cut away a large portion of the rear; then he will sew stripes of red flannel along the sides and around the bottom, and will end up by hanging on a few brass buckles or shells, or beads.

A MAN SQUAW ON THE WAR PATH.

In the Ree tribe there is a mysterious-looking individual clothed in a woman's frock, but wearing a warrior's scalp braid and accoutrements. He — or she — is the drudge of the camp—does all the cooking, brings all the wood and water, and looks after as many ponies as his—or her—other duties will allow. The braves look upon him—or her—with an air of superiority that cannot be mistaken, and in none of the war dances or other manly pastimes is he—or she—allowed to take a part; but the poor, bedrudged indefinite drags out a miserable existence, neglected and forlorn, not even being allowed to ride with the column on the march, but being a perpetual straggler, generally having to lead three or four extra ponies belonging to the braves. I asked Bloody Knife about him—or her.

"The form of a man but the heart of a woman," he replied through an interpreter, and then went on to explain that the indefinite was a man, but had not the courage to endure the tortures a young man must subject himself to before he can become one of the braves. So he had to live with the women and do a woman's work. Suffrage was not extended to such as he.

"Why does he come with you?" I asked of Bloody Knife.

"He wants to get rid of that frock", said the interpreter, without putting the question to the chief. "If he takes a scalp it comes off him."

A NEW PRINCIPLE IN POLITICAL ECONOMY.

Let it be applied. If Susan B. Anthony wants to vote without having to pay a fine and costs, let her take a scalp; if Miss Willard wants to become State Superintendent of Instruction, let her take a scalp; if Mrs. Spaight wants to get the ear of the political almighty on the social-evil question, let her take a scalp. She can scalp Mrs. De Geer, for instance, or that pale, inoffensive, fawn-like little woman that follows her around; or she can go into the City Hall and scalp Mayor Colvin, and fling the gory hair at the Common Council.

A MODERN WAR DANCE.

Every night, before retiring, our Indians have a war dance. My tent is near their quarters, and I know it. To witness their singular ceremony once is quite interesting, but when one is kept awake half the night as a regular thing, and is expected to breakfast at 3 o'clock every morning, it loses its romance. The most imposing occasion of the kind was the night after the Santees joined the expedition, and the alliance of the tribes was celebrated. We were in camp at Fort Lincoln then, and a long, low, log cabin was used as Indian quarters. In the center of the room, on the ground, was built a fire, the smoke of which, mingled with the odor that may naturally be expected to arise from seventy or eighty unwashed, naked, and perspiring savages, made the place almost intolerable for ordinary beings, and even the poor hungry dogs that always haunt an Indian lodge left the room disgusted, but the braves puffed their killikinnick and breathed in the atmosphere with a relish. At the start two groups were formed, one of Rees and the other of Santees, either side of the fire. For a time they sat quietly smoking, till all the warriors were gathered, when some one brought in a drum and handed it to the Santees. They placed it in the center of their circle, and all who could reach began to pound its head with sticks, their pipes, fingers, and anything available, humming

A DREARY MONOTONE IN THE MINOR KEY.

All Indian music is in the minor key. It was soft in tone, and grew into a sort of moaning—like the wind in the branches of a leafless forest, and lasted five minutes or so, ending with a few subdued shrieks. The pipes were relit and passed from one group to the other, each warrior taking a whiff or two and sending it along to the next. Then the Rees took the drum and went through the same ceremony, but with a different theme to their chant. It was then repeated by the Santees, a little louder and faster, and the shrieks at its close more decided and numerous. Then two Rees went at it again; and the Santees for the third time, interspersing lively little whoops between the measures of the song, and pounding with decided emphasis on the drum. Then it was passed over to the Rees again, and two or three of the Santees rose to their feet, doing a sort of walk around, for which their brethren in the other group furnished the music. Then the others began to rise, one by one, and joined the dance, hopping up and down, first with one leg and then with the other, as if they were tramping down something, each uttering a whoop at short intervals until the groups were broken up, and the alliance was supposed to be formed. The pow-wow grew livelier, the drumming and moaning and whooping grew louder, and the atmosphere more vile as the dance went on, but a white man gets enough of it in a very short time, and I could not remain after they got well agoing. It was my first war-dance and in it I saw something of which I had often read, but not the realization of my anticipations. It was certainly a curious, a fantastic, a savage scene—naked men with painted bodies dancing around in a dim, gloomy, flickering fire light. It was a scene for a painter—on canvas it would be poetique, legendary—but, bah! the stench. The coming generation will not see war dances. The modern Indian hasn't animation enough to get up a pow-wow, and it's only the old, scarred braves who whoop as their fathers did. The modern Indian prefers peace to war; he prefers sleeping in the sunshine to hunting the antlered deer and the bounding antelope; he would rather steal than work. Shades of Cooper and Natty Bumpo! how the red man has degenerated.

SHALL WE HAVE WAR.

It is an open question whether Sitting Bull and his Sioux will attack us. Thus far we have had no trouble, and have seen no Indians, although a scout reported having seen several the other day, a mile or two from our column. The other morning about 2 o'clock the whole camp turned out at an alarm, and several shots were fired, but it only proved to be a mule that had strayed out of the picket line during the night, and was trying to stray back again.

Curtis.

CHICAGO INTER-OCEAN
Issue of July 30, 1874

CUSTER'S EXPEDITION

Still on the March into the Unexplored Hunting Grounds of the Hostile Sioux.

The Yellowstone and the Black Hills the Objective Points— Notes from the Dust-Covered Column.

"Buckskin Joe," the Mule Whacker—Cave Butte and the Mysterious Cavern—Savage Hieroglyphics.

Pre-Historic Fortifications— The Wagon Train Struggling Through the Desolation of the "Bad Lands."

The Destiny of the "Off Wheeler"—The Oath Alphabet of the Plains—Cactus— No Trouble as Yet with the Indians.

From Our Own Reporter.

CUSTER'S BLACK HILLS EXPEDITION. IN CAMP NEAR "THE CAVE," Dakota Territory, July 11, 1874

"BUCKSKIN JOE, THE MULE WHACKER"

"Under that old slouch hat," said an officer friend to me one evening, pointing to an old mule driver, "I think you will find a romance."

"Not a very inviting field to search in," I replied.

"But you haven't seen the face yet; when you see the face you will be more reasonable— see there!"

The man we were looking at took an old gray slouch hat from his bushy hair to wipe the perspiration from his forehead, and it was like lifting a curtain from a picture.

"That's Buckskin Joe," continued my friend, "the oldest man on these plains, I believe, and one of the most singular fellows I ever saw. He has had a very interesting life, and you had better interview him. His wife ran away and married a Congressman some years ago; but touch lightly on that, as the old fellow is very sensitive."

A few evenings after I made an attempt to interview "Buckskin Joe," the mule-whacker, with a romance under his old slouch hat.

We had been marching until sunset, and while I was lying around waiting for supper, I saw my man by a fire he had just kindled near his wagon. He sat on the ground, with his knees against his chest and his arms around them, watching the flame that was feebly trying to creep into the substance of the larger wood, and his face, intent on nothing, was a study a painter would have worshiped. With his long bushy white hair and beard, covering the whole of his face except the nose and forehead, and bushy white eyebrows that shaded a deep-set pair of shrinking brown eyes, he looked as much

LIKE THE POET LONGFELLOW

as any man I have ever seen—the features of a prophet and the eyes of a child. His attention was drawn to my approach, by the crackling of the dry branches which lay around, and looking up he bade me a polite

"Good evening."

"Will you let me light my pipe from your fire?" I asked.

Half unconsciously he stripped a little twig and put it into the flame, with a quiet "certainly."

I took the taper from his hand, and in exchange offered my tobacco pouch—a courtesy that is always extended on the frontier when two people meet; as much a matter of etiquette as shaking hands in the "States."

"No, thank you." said he with a shake of the head, "I seldom use it."

"I hope you don't object to the odor, for I wanted to sit by your fire and smoke till my supper was ready."

"Not at all," he replied with a wave of the hand that would have delighted Chesterfield; "make yourself as comfortable as possible"—and he rose, renewed the wood, and taking a camp kettle hung it on the tripod.

"They tell me you're the oldest man on these plains: have you ever been down this way before?"

OVER FORTY YEARS ON THE PLAINS.

"In '55," said he quietly, I went out with Harvey (sic), and our trail was fifty miles south of this —we went around the foot of the

Illingworth had a sensitivity for the spectacular, as evidenced by this picture of Custer's "permanent camp" on French Creek. Note the "T" shape arrangement of the tents from this vantage point. Smoke from cooking fires can be seen drifting over the valley. The picture on the facing page is virtually identical. Evidence of the permanent nature of the camp can be seen in the well worn wagon trail to the right of the tent row.

Black Hills and up the Cheyenne," and in answer to other questions he told me briefly and politely that for forty-one years he had been between the Northern Mississippi and the Rocky Mountains. His language was pure, grammatical, and well-pronounced; his voice was soft and musical—so soft sometimes that it tried my ear to catch his meaning. His was the manner of a man who was being bored, and whose good breeding wouldn't allow him to show it. But I kept at him, leading the conversation into different channels and occasionally placing him in a position where his politeness compelled him to reply, till he got quite sociable, and touching on that singular

taste that led men into nomadic lives like his, he said with a great deal of fervor:

"You don't know how it is, my friend; the open air and a team of mules is as much to my taste as your city home to you. I couldn't breathe in a city. I have been on the plains forty-one years, and now and then I have vowed that I would quit it, but before my team was unharnessed I'd be anxious to get off again."

"But you're getting pretty old for this business."

"Yes, I'm old—64 last January—but I am tougher now than most of the young fellows. I don't suppose I shall hold out much longer, though, and I'm

GOING BACK TO THE
STATES ONCE MORE
BEFORE I DIE—

this fall, if I have good luck. I ain't been in the States since '59, and I've got some friends I ain't heard from for nine years now, and maybe it wouldn't do much good to go down yonder; but I'd like to see how things look. There were only three bridges over the Schuylkill when I was there last, and now they tell me there's one at most every street."

"Were you from Philadelphia?" I asked.

"Yes. I ran away from my home in Philadelphia when I was 9 years old, and went into the Western part of the State, and worked for

South Dakota State Historical Society

In his journal Captain William Ludlow wrote "There is much talk of gold and industrious search of it is making." (sic) He went on to say, "I saw in General Custer's tent what the miner said he had obtained during the day. Under a strong reading glass it resembled small pin heads. . ." Lt. Col. Fred Grant, the President's son, and a member of the exposition said in his report, "Some gold and silver said to have been found—but to me it looked like the same pieces that were shown to me yesterday and the day before yesterday." Illingworth was apparently too busy exposing numerous photographic plates to take time to pan for gold.

nigh seven years; then I went back home and worked under the very same roof with my mother, she tending dairy and I doing chores, and she didn't know me all that time. I staid (sic) there a year or two, and then I came West, and hereabouts I've been — at Sioux City, Fort Dodge, and all around —teaming and trading with the Indians ever since, and I couldn't leave it now."

"But it seems queer to me," I suggested, "that a man can live so long in such a way without a wife and family."

"I have no family, but I was married once. I lost my wife some years ago," and he rubbed his eyes, saying something about smoke and alkali dust. Then he got up and moved around restlessly, took the kettle off the hooks, and lifted the lid. The old man had dug down into his memory as far as he dare go. He did not sit down again, but kept busying himself in the preparation for his meal, and I hadn't the heart to ask him any more questions. Who was the Congressman that stole his love away no one seems to know, but everybody seems aware of the fact, and all agree it was a man of national reputation. Some time, perhaps, Buckskin Joe's secret will be given to the world—and the reasons of his strange melancholy told.

One is continually meeting such men in frontier life—men who have found the civilized world too small for them, too crowded. They are generally intelligent, and have the air of well-bred gentlemen, but underlying their strange taste and inclination there seems in almost every case some sacred motive— too sacred for the world to know and meddle with.

FATHER DU SMETTE (sic), THE JESUIT.

Long ago, there used to travel through this country an old Jesuit missionary, named Father du Smette (sic), who is well remembered and frequently spoken of by our Indians. It was he, it is supposed, who gave to these hills the name butte, and applied the other French names to places where we find them. Many of the Indian names of streams and hills are corruptions of the French, with the syllables divided and broken. Fathere du Smette (sic) used to ride about the country from tribe to tribe, they say, in an old wagon, with a black cross nailed to the dashboard, which, when he died, some three years ago, the Indians cut up into relics, so strong was their faith in the old man's grace. Many customs among the Sioux, such as one which is found in some tribes of erecting crosses over graves, came of course from his example, and his teachings have become part of the religion of the race. There is something grand about such influence—a colossal gentleness which was omniscient in action and deified in memory. We measure greatness by notoriety—but how false a scale. Father du Smette (sic) was doubtless never spoken of by civilization, and no book, lest a romance of these plains be written, will contain his name; yet he touched a chord to which the heart of a whole race will vibrate as long as they remain as nature made them.

THE MYSTERIOUS CAVE.

We reached this place about midday yesterday, and so much had been told of its wonders and mysteries by our Indian guides that we were all eager with anticipation; and when, ten miles back, a high rocky bluff covered with scattering timber had been pointed out to us as the spot, we pressed ambitiously forward in its direction, and many were the queries and suggestions that passed from saddle to saddle on the probable result of our research. There was a radical change in the face of the country as we reached the place—a change that was grateful then, but regretted afterward—the grassy knolls becoming more abrupt and rocky, and showing at times great bare spots of clay. At last the Cave Butte was actually before us—a high hill broken into ledges and ravines, around which ran an almost unbroken palisade of sandstone. On the top were a few trees, and many of the ravines were filled with verdant underbrush. Reaching the bottom, our guides scattered, one galloping wildly up one ravine, and another into another, leaving us chagrined and puzzled at the foot. Here we rested a few

moments, while Goose, Bloody Knife, Bear's Ears, Cold Hand, and the other scouts, were rushing about over the rocks on their ponies. Finally, we saw Goose come to a stand still, and, in his stoical way, make an indifferent indication with his hand. This was enough, and General Custer, catching the gesture, spurred his horse up the ravine, followed by the rest of us, till we stood in a narrow gully,

WHERE THE SANDSTONE YAWNED.

Leaping from their saddles, everybody made a dash, anxious to be the first to reach the climax of a discovery that was almost sure, and twenty of us were at the mouth at the same instant. And here was the cave where the souls of the impious were imprisoned; the mysterious entrance, on the walls of which was spirit-writing and demonography. Alas for shattered hopes and blasted expectations! The cave was a crevice between two ridges of rock; the entrance was a crypt formed by overhanging sandstones, and the demonography was like the tracery of school children on the walls of a country school house. There were pictures of deer, elk, and antelopes, bears and wolves, ponies and dogs, and curious hieroglyphics that seemed to have been formed by some one scratching at random on the porous stone. There were marks, though, that were puzzling. About eight feet high on one of the walls was the

IMPRESSIONS OF A CHILD'S FOOT,

half an inch deep in the stone, and as perfect as if it had been molded by a skillful sculptor. Near it were a couple of hands in the same style of relief, one of them with the wrist upward, so that to have been drawn from life the model must have stood on his head, six or eight feet high in space. There were other marks quite as singular, and possessing quite as much interest to the curiosity hunter, but nothing that could be attributed to anything more than average human skill. Yet from Goose all these marks claimed a superstitious veneration. He stood at the entrance a few moments and looked at them silently, then turned away and

never came near the place again. Bloody Knife and the others also stood aloof, but some of the younger braves followed the crowds that went up afterwards, and loafed around while the explorations were going on.

Colonel Ludlow made a survey of the interior, following a narrow passage some 400 feet, until it became so small he could go no further. There are no chambers, and the walls are dry and porous.

In the crevices between the rocks at the entrance are found bows and arrows, beads, bracelets, rings, and other relics, placed there by the Indians as "medicine," or offerings to the Great Spirit for his blessing. General Custer seized upon an old flint-lock pistol as long as his arm; some one else picked up a gold ring in which the initials "A.L." were engraved—probably the booty of some raid—another person found an old knife, another a shaving brush, and everybody bore away some memento of the place. By-and-by, after poking in the sand, some one unearthed a human skull which the surgeons pronounced to be that of a white man, and it was passed around the company, with jests and jibes, from some, serious queries and philosophy from others, but curious silence from most of us. There were three holes in the forehead, just over the left eye, supposed to have been made by bullets, and it was evident that the former occupant of that ghostly tenement had been the victim of savage cruelty—probably some prisoner brought from the frontier and made a sacrifice to the spirits of the cave. There was some question about a name for the cave, for the Indians have none of distinction, calling it Wassum only—their word for hole in the ground—but General Custer will probably put it down on the map as the Cave of the Skull or Ludlow's Cave, immortalizing either the poor creature who died so mysteriously there or the chief engineer of this expedition. The high palisades around were called "Cave Butte," and a sharp pinnacle that shoots up a little to the north, like the dome of a mosque, "Temple Butte," it being known among the Indians only as "the place where the man was killed by a cow."

ANCIENT FORTIFICATIONS.

The sandstone ledges around the cave, or Cave Butte, as we christened them, are so regularly laid out, so even in their altitude, and so perfect in their connection with each other, as to suggest the possibility of artificial construction. Colonel Ludlow said there was too much good engineering shown in their arrangement to have been the work of nature, and his theory is that Cave Butte was once a fortified city, whose walls were of sandstone, with limestone interstices, for the two composites are found together. Imagine the highest point of a wide rolling prairie, rising 250 feet above the valleys around it, and 150 feet or more above its highest neighbor knoll, approached from all sides by valleys and ravines which seem to find their origin there; the top of the butte a perfect table land, covering forty acres of soil, very fertile compared with its surroundings, and only broken by slight gutters for drainage; around its edge, a continuous perpendicular wall of sandstone rock, similar to the palisades of the Hudson, jetting out into sharp angles, receding into recesses, and rising at times into parapets and pinnacles; the walls almost perfect, so nearly unbroken that it was difficult to find a place to climb to the top; around the central Butte towers and buttresses so that every approach is guarded, and every portion of the outer wall is protected from another point, and you have Colonel Ludlow's fortification. At a distance the singular structure looks like one of those old castles which line the rivers of Europe, and devouring time has knawed (sic) at the walls so long that in places they look almost as if they had been almost battered down.

WHAT THE SCIENTISTS FOUND THERE.

Professor Winchell says he has discovered indications of similar formations at the tops of many other high buttes, but this is the first time he has seen anything like regular strata, and the first time he has found limestone in place. His theory is more practical and less poetical than Colonel Ludlow's, and I have given the latter's first, that it may be accepted for a moment at least. Professor Winchell found stratas of silliceous limestone, calcaveous, and sandy clay, bedded blue clay, and lignite, all in their regular order alternating with the sandstone, which was found in several varieties, including the reddish with iron concretions, a castilated, an argilaceous, and white. He says very decidedly that the only hand that did the planning and finished the work of those grand battlements was that of nature's self, and that the only labor done was atmospheric—that while the rocks around it crumbled and were weathered down, the hill where the man was killed by the cow has stood the pressure.

A SOMEWHAT SINGULAR FACT

may be stated in this connection— that there is no fossils in this country. Four scientific gentlemen have been wandering about with bags and hammers for nearly a week and not yet have they found one of any importance. It seems that nothing ever died in this region, and one is inclined to the opinion that nothing ever existed here until foolish, restless man penetrated these barren plains. here are an abundance of remarkable petrefactions, but only of a vegetable substance. Huge stumps are frequently found, with the roots and bark as perfect as can be possible; logs of wood, and even tree branches, with their natural form and color in a perfect state of preservation. We shall soon enter the mineral region, if the information of the Indians is at all reliable, and will probably pass through a moss agate country.

The only game we see is antelope, and they are so plenty that the whole command has been kept in fresh meat for several days. One or two deer and a few ducks have been killed, but they do not abound.

Our course is now southwest, and we shall soon cross the line into Montana, following he valley of the Little Missouri down.

IN CAMP NEAR THE LITTLE MISSOURI MONTANA TERRITORY, July 14, 1874.

THE BAD LANDS.

When I say we are in the "Bad Lands," every man who has traveled much will appreciate the misery of our existence. What sort of an idea the words convey to the average reader I can hardly tell, but it can be no worse than the reality. Over a large track in the Northwest extends a strata of hard white clay, which, when it comes to the surface, is the ideal of barrenness. Such a tract extends from the point where we are now, a few miles east of the Little Missouri River, for several hundred miles west of that sream, and one can scarcely imagine a region more desolate. The surface is cut up into canons and ravines with perpendicular banks washed out by rains, for water cannot penetrate the clay, and wears it away only very slowly, for it is as hard, almost as marble. Its action in time, however, has left strange freaks in the shape of pillars and piles of clay in all sorts of fantastic shapes and resemblances. Here we find a castle standing coldly upright against the sky, as white and even as polished stone; again a bold abrupt object of an uncouth and undefinable shape, standing as if alone when the earth had sunk around it; there are others so grotesque and angular that we can imagine them almost anything they at all resemble; and again clearly defined, smoothly polished columns and obelisks, perfectly proportioned and delicately finished, suggesting a tribute to some great man or some holy memory. From where I write tonight I can see a row of these white clay hills far in the east that resemble pictures of the pyramids, and they are, I have no doubt, quite as hard and polished as the stone of the Pharaoh mausolem (sic).

HOW ROADS ARE MADE.

Traveling with our wagon train in this sort of country is next to impossible. The ground is hard enough, except when we strike an alkali "bottom," as we frequently do; but the canons and gulches are so frequent it keeps us digging and bridging all the time.

When we reach a gulch that cannot be spanned, a grade is made to its bottom and up again; when we meet a stream we cannot ford or a sluice that is bottomless, to bridge it is the work of a few moments. General Custer is a famous road maker, and to him, as to the great Napoleon, nothing is impassable. In our regular marching order following the scouts and the color guard comes the pioneer company, with a wagon full of spades, shovels, picks, axes, scythes and other tools. Reaching a place that has to be bridged, the General selects the most available point and with a shovel in his hand he directs and assists at the work himself. The modus operands (sic) of bridging is somewhat novel. If cobble stones and sod or willow branches and rushes will not make a road-bed the train master cries "poles," and every teamster brings the extra wagon tongue he always carries with him and lays it devotedly down at the General's feet. These poles are then placed crosswise— two or three layers of them, cobhouse fashion, and the crevices are filled with brush, sod, mown rushes, and every available substance three of four hundred bridge-builders can lay their hands on. The bridge done, the artillery and ambulances are sent across, being of the lightest tonnage, and when they cut through, repairs are made; then the mule teams are sent across; and did you ever see a lot of six-mule teams cross one of these bridges? It is

AN EVENT IN A LIFETIME.

The animals are driven by a single line and a long snake-whip, especially the whip. The line is attached to the left-hand bit of the "night leader," and he may be considered the rudder of the "outfit." The helmsman sits astride of the "night wheeler," and if he wants the team to "gee," he jerks at the line savagely, and it is a moral certainty that the mule will turn his head away from it and go "gee." If he wants to "haw" he pulls steadily on the line, drawing the mule's head around, and he goes "haw." There is nothing more easy in all the philosophy of life. The position of mule-wacker in an army train is about that of a roustabout on a river steamer or a marine in the naval service. His

chief requirements are to crack a black snake whip and swear— and such swearing, it would make the hair of a Chicago hackman stand on end. When I have told how a bridge is crossed, I shall tell a story to illustrate. Well, the mule-whacker "haws" and "gees," swears and cracks his whip, jerks the line, and digs his spurs into the animal he is riding till he has got the team in position, then with a dart, a few jumps, and final tug, under a frightful torrent of oaths and whip-lashes over the poor animals' heads, the other side is reached. The mules hop around a moment under the smarting of the cuts they have just received, and with a bray of relief tug on patiently just as good, meek people do when they have met one of the trials of life, passed through it, and come out purified. A wagon train crossing a creek or a gully is as good as a Fourth of July celebration, and reminds me strangely of one when I stand at a distance —the cracking, and shouting, and hurrahing that is always done, and I suppose is absolutely necessary: but its

VERY DISAGREEABLE TO THE "OFF-WHEELER."

The destiny of an "off-wheeler" is absolutely terrible. If fifty whacks are given to a team of mules in crossing a bridge, I find by a mathematical calculation that the "off-wheeler" gets forty-three of them. Half a dozen gentlemen with long black whips always stand at a crossing to assist the principal whacker. Their duty is somewhat the same as his, only they stand still, have the free use of both hands, and have a better "purchase" for their feet than saddle stirrups, so they can whack harder and more frequently than he—and the majority of their blows fall on the "off-wheeler." If I was an "off-wheeler" I should memorialize Congress to have the position of assistant mule-whacker abolished. You see these men— these assistants—stand in the middle of the gulch, and the wagons go down so quickly that the leading mules run under while their whips are in the air, but the "off-wheeler" gets along just in time to catch the downward stroke; and as the tug comes in going up the other side, the assistants generally gets time

to whack him again before he is out of trouble. While the wagons are waiting at one of these gulches —waiting for their turn to cross, you hear an occasional bray, about one-sixth as many brays as there are mules in the wagons. It is the off-wheeler. It is simply a short, subdued bray, but it means a great deal.

THE MULE WHACKER'S OATH.

I said I should tell a story, and were it not true it should never find a place in print through my agency, and I give it now with an apology, simply to illustrate how absolutely depraved these mule drivers are, and how awfully appropriate are some of their oaths. In crossing a gulch one day one of our drivers was killed by his mules balking and turning the wagon over him, and an old, experienced and skillful driver put in his place. A few hours later at another crossing the animals showed signs of balking again, and the man yelled out at them loud enough to be heard for half a mile around,— and it sounded more like the voice of a demon than the voice of a man—

"Hoop! Hoop, there! Gee, G_d d__n you! Do you want to send another ___ __ _ _____ to h__l?"

Traveling in the bad lands encourages such profanity as this, for our course today has been nothing but crossing gulches and bridging canons; and with all our digging and bridging we have had to go over nineteen miles in fourteen hours to make a distance less than ten miles from our camp last night.

We are just on the edge of the tract, and occasionally reach an oasis in the desert, where grass and running water can be found. But generally the earth is barren of vegetation.

NOTHING BUT CACTUS

being green enough to grow here, and of that we find vast beds, acres after acres of luxurious growth, on a soil as white and bald as the top of Long John Wentworth's head. And it is that miserable, thorny little species, insignificant in appearance, but with an influence when one steps or sits on it that is very persuasive. The little thorns will penetrate almost anything that opposes their perpendicular. Gloves and clothing are no protection whatever, and even boots are a vanity on a real good cactus bed.

THE FLORA OF THE COUNTRY we have passed over is exceedingly meager. Nothing rare or beautiful of vegetable life has been found, except the sweet briar roses that have a missionary sort of an existence here among the floral heathendom. But as we go further south we see indications of richer vegetable growth, and pine and spruce trees begin to be discernible on the distant hills. I shall be glad enough when we get off the prairie and out of these cactus beds; and that deliverance will be soon. We are now in Montana, and tomorrow or next day reach the Belle Fourche River, which bathes the feet of the Black Hills, and when that is crossed we have reached the legendary country—the unknown land. Strange to say, we have had

NO TROUBLE FROM THE INDIANS.

Last winter, when Sitting Bull sent an embassy to General Custer to protest against this expedition, he gave as one of his reasons for not wishing the whites to make an anabasis through his country, that he was going into Montana to fight the Crows this summer, and that he didn't want to change his plans. Until yesterday we supposed that he had concluded this engagement, but it seems from late developments that we are being watched. Yesterday afternoon half a dozen of our people returning to our camp, which had been deserted for an hour or more, surprised a couple of stray Indians making a reconnoissance, but the latter made no demonstrations, and General Custer has forbidden any offensive operations. Today large fires have been seen on the hills in that direction, and putting the two facts together our scouts say that the strange Indians were spies, who have signaled their tribes, waiting below us. If such is the case, we may have fighting; but General Custer does not fear any serious trouble.

An Indian courier goes out with these letters tomorrow morning— an immense raw-featured fellow, with squirrel fur braid in his hair

South Dakota State Historical Society

This picture bears the original caption "Spectre Canyon". It is presumed to be in the general vicinity of French Creek and because of the vantage point may have been taken about the same time as the exposures on the previous pages. An enlargement seems to indicate tents to the right edge of the clearing.

and breech - clout of bead - embroidered flannel around his loins. A safe and pleasant journey.

Curtis

CHICAGO INTER-OCEAN
Issue of August 15, 1874

THE BLACK HILLS

A Correspondent of the Inter-Ocean with General Custer's Expedition.

Realistic Narrative of "Life in the Open Air" of Dakota.

A Rainy Day in Camp—The Full Misery of Sogginess.

Relieved and Made Bearable by Reminiscence of an American Prairie Simoon.

Untamed Zephyrs Making A Night of It—They Way They Struck a Man of Peace.

Our Late Visitor the Comet, as Viewed Through the Lucid Air of the Plains.

The Baby Missouri and the Belle Fourche Rivers—The Place Where General

Raynolds Camped.

"Bloody Knife," the Tawny Cynic—A Geographical Indian by the Name of Goose.

From Our Own Reporter.

CUSTER'S BLACK HILLS EXPEDITION, IN CAMP OF THE BELLE FOURCHE RIVER, WYOMING TERRITORY, JULY 19, 1874.

A rainy day in camp. What visions of past misery rise in the mind of an old soldier. A cold, muddy earth; wet, dripping grass; damp clothing and blankets; soaked canvas, and everything in a condition of abject discomfort. A shower, either in camp or on the march, is one of the most refreshing things imaginable during such torrid weather as we have seen, but a whole day of cold, drizzling rain with no shelter but a low, narrow tent, tattered and leaky from age and, campaign violence, is enough to put a man in mood for murder. We have been unusually fortunate so far, this being our eighteenth day out and first "wet camp." We have had bright, dashing showers, just enough to wash the dust off us, and cool the atmosphere and have had a taste, too, of the dry prairie wind storms, and I suppose have little cause for grumbling for into such expeditions, as

Into each life, some rain
    must fall.
Some days must be cold
    and dreary.

The other night, camping on a high bluff near the edge of the Little Missouri "bad lands," we had one of those terrible dry storms that frontiersmen have described with so much horror—

THE SIMOOM (SIC) OF THE AMERICAN PRAIRIE

The day had been terribly warm and sultry, and as we had made a long march—as far as we could go and find grazing, so as to enter the clay desert fresh in the morning—the whole command were exhausted and disheartened. At sunset the sky was lightened up in the west with a strange crimson glow, that looked like the shadow of a burning world. The pulses of the air had ceased to beat, and it seemed as if some great wrong were brooding. Tired and sleepy, we hurried up our tents, gulped our supper down, and stretched our weary limbs upon our blankets. Sleep came and went for a few hours, but near midnight everyone awakened by the swaying and flapping of his tent, and terrible clouds of dust that drifted under the curtains with every gust. The whole heavens were covered with heavy, black-hooded, rifting clouds, broken momentarily by vivid flashes of lightning. The air was hot, dry and heavy, and the wind came in sudden gusts with a force that tore the tent pins from the earth as if they were leaves. Fancy the feelings of a man of peace, unused to bedding on the bare grass and rude awakenings at midnight. Fancy him gathering his bewildered senses to realize the situation and determine what is necessary to be done—whether to fall upon his prayer bones and beg protection from the raging elements, or to grapple them with his own puny strength. Another gust of dust decides him, and he rushes from under the shivering, flapping canvas and tottering poles to do or die. He seizes the fluttering ropes to draw the collapsed house into position, and drops them with torn and blistered fingers. Then he tries to hold the "flaps" down with his feet, and for a few moments, makes them fast while he cools the burning flesh in his mouth, but

the wind is stronger than he, and away goes the tent again with a gust. He shouts for aid, but his words are dashed in his teeth with a volley of

DUST THAT BLINDS AND STIFLES HIM.

He hears around him savage oaths, that assure him he is not alone in his misery, and as he sees in a glaring dash of lightning the uncertainty of the frail tenements around him, he gathers his courage in desperation, and makes another fierce essay. Catching the ropes, he winds them around his body, his naked limbs, and throws himself upon the ground, with vigorous resolves, but he strikes a cactus bed, and howling with anguish, he springs to his feet again, pours out the emotions of his soul in a few expressive words, and crawls back to his blankets. The tent collapses and comes down upon him, his "things"—and a citizen always has innumerable little ones that a soldier does not need—are scattered here and there by the tornado; but with reckless indifference he buries his head under the prone canvas, picks the cactus thorns out of his flesh, and lies till reveille. A few such nights will leave life little worth living for.

OUR COMET.

Usually the evenings and nights on the Dakota plains are such as one would always wish for. Nowhere have I seen such glorious sunsets, such cool, delicious night air, such brilliant stellar displays, and never has the moon seemed so clearly, purely beautiful. The sky is most always clear; the wind generally lies down to a soft, soothing breeze, and the atmosphere has that fairy-tale balm and pureness which has only to be breathed like a lotion to give sleep and pleasant dreams. Let it be understood that I refer only to the summer months; between November and May they tell me it is different. The pure atmosphere and clear sky have given fine opportunities to our scientific companions for astronomical observations, which have been sedulously improved. The comet, which is now, early in the evening, brilliantly apparent, receives its nightly attentions from pocket telescopes and field glasses, and is a treasure of scientific satisfaction if seen as plainly in "the States."

THE BABY MISSOURI.

Those who have been in the valley of the Little Missouri always associate it with disagreeable recollections. It is a rapid, turbid stream, in feature and in disposition like its larger namesake—a baby Missouri—turbid, miry, rapid in current, and full of rapids and whirlpools, uncertain at every point, and without one particle of that beauty which generally surrounds prairie streams and makes them a relief when one is tired of smooth, unbroken slopes, and treeless, trackless plains. There are, approaching it, tributaries which have afforded us the greatest camp comfort and which we remember as watering some of the most beautiful and fertile valleys we have seen, but no one will speak with respect or admiration of the Little Missouri.

THE BELLE FOURCHE RIVER,

on which we camped to-day, has opened up to us landscape of another and much more satisfactory nature. Its valleys being beautiful and verdant, full of pine and oak and cottonwood timber, and stream itself being pure and clear and rapid. It is the northern fork of the Sheyenne, which as the Indians say, has the Black Hills in its arms, and in distinction from the Sheyenne proper, which is turbid and miry, is called "Belle Fourche," or beautiful branch. The ridges that rise on either side are covered with black shale and clay beds, and the water of the springs in the valley is strongly impregnated with iron—as strongly impregnated as many bottled tincture that was ever dosed to an invalid. Our camp is on a beautiful grassy slope, shaded by grand old oaks, centuries old, under a ridge steep and stony, and covered with a dense growth of pine. The river encircles us, and its banks are groves of willows and cottonwood. Such perfect shelter, such a plentiful supply of water and wood, make this a favorite camping-place for the Indians, and our guides say the Sioux frequently spend their winters here, and make this place a sort of rendezvous during the hunting season,

leaving their families and wigwams, and whatever articles of value are not easily transported. They always make a stone-house of old mother Earth's bosom, and the goldless have been busying themselves during the rain today, digging in places where the soil appears to have been lately disturbed; but the old matron guards her trusts well, and nothing but a few arrows and worthless trinkets have rewarded the searchers.

GENERAL RAYNOLDS' TRAIL

It is a singular coincidence that General Raynolds, on his Yellowstone expedition, camped in this very place just fifteen years ago today, and one of our guides and interpreters, Louis Agar, (Agard) was with him at the time. His trail is well preserved, and a party under Colonel Ludlow have followed it up several miles. We cross it almost at right angles, our course being a little west of south. Over the river we see the Black Hills rising, and tomorrow's march will take us fairly into them. Far up the valley we see the Bear Butte, the highest peak in the Northern range; and far to the southward rises Inyan Kara, the highest in the southern, and, as far as is known, the highest of all. General Custer's plan is to march as directly as possible to the latter, the location of which has been accurately determined by General Raynolds, General Warren, and other explorers, and to go from there eastward, through an easy pass, which the Indians describe, into the unknown land. Our guides, so far, have proved trusty and competent, they have without exception led us to excellent camping grounds, have shown better roads than were anticipated, and although some of their stories and descriptions have proven superstitions or myths, they have even more than fulfilled expectation.

"BLOODY KNIFE"

especially deserves credit of honesty, faithfulness and frankness, qualities not proverbially credited to his race. He is the offspring of a matrimonial alliance between a Sioux chief and a Ree squaw, and although the two nations are hereditary enemies he seems to have lived in both, and wielded considerable influence. He has been

chief of the Unka Paupa tribe of Sioux, the worst of all in their enmity toward the whites, but becoming odious for some reason to his people was deposed, and took refuge among his old enemies. After the band of scouts was organized, General Custer appointed him sargeant (sic) and he is as proud of his stripes as a militiaman of his epaulets. His authority among his braves is that of a dictator, and he takes a burden of annoyance off Lieutenant Wallace's shoulders, for a hundred Indians are not the easiest company in the world to handle.

I went into Indian quarters one day, and found Bloody Knife gesticulating wildly, and talking in an angry tone to a group of warriors. Just as I approached, he was calling attention to the stripes on his arm, and as he looked toward me I gave him the customary salute. He caught the idea at once, and feeling strengthened in his authority by the acknowledgement of a pale face, proceeded all the more vigorously to enforce his orders. But notwithstanding his tyranny, he assumes to be the protector of his band, and is very careful to see that they are not imposed upon. One evening a couple of Sioux were put in the guard-house for carelessly shooting in camp, and that being the signal of danger, causing much commotion. Bloody Knife was not around when the penalty was inflicted, and it was two hours or more afterward before he learned of the indignity. Jumping upon his pony, saddleless and bridleless, he galloped furiously to headquarters, and found General Custer, who was sitting in front of his tent.

"Custer! Custer! Sioux; guard-house!" shouted he excitedly, using all the English at his command, but making himself perfectly intelligible by

A PANTOMIMIC PERFORMANCE,

which consisted of a succession of rapid motions in the direction of the guard-house, the holding up of two fingers, signifying the number interested, and the crossing of his wrists, to show that they were bound. General Custer is quite as good a contortionist as the native, and in a few moments by gestures and single words he showed his dusky sergeant the reasons and the results of the imprisonment. Bloody Knife gave a significant nod of his head, sprang upon his horse again, and lashing him furiously with the little buckskin thong the Indians always use as a goad, dashed back again to his quarters, and was soon vigorously supporting Custer's authority. In appearance he is a slender man, below the usual size, and has a decided stoop to his shoulders—the reverse of the beau ideal warrior—but a glance at his face shows that he is no ordinary man, for it bears few of the Indian characteristic features, being more of the Cuban or the Spanish type. His mouth and nose are small, the latter a smooth aquiline, and his lips are superbly cut, but wear, in repose, a sort of cynical curl, an index sign of his character, for Bloody Knife is

A TAWNY CYNIC,

and seldom allows himself to be caught like his fellows with the bait of tawdry finery or the cheap chaff which the white generally flings out to catch the red man's favor. He wears no ornaments—no rings in his ears, no beads braided in his heavy, long hair, no bracelets on his arms, or feathers in his scalp-lock,—nothing but a small steel horse-shoe hanging to his cartridge belt—the significance of which I have never been able to discover.

Every evening in camp General Custer calls his guides to headquarters to talk over the probabilities of the next day's march. Bloody Knife, or Goose, his associate, point out the direction of the march, tell what there is of interest to be expected, and answer the varied and frequently purposeless questions of the company that always attends this entertainment. Both the Indians and especially Bloody Knife, have a very fine sense of discrimination, and often answer a fool according to his folly, giving quite a spicy relish by their repartee and blunt sarcasm. Both are quite incredulous, and are loth (sic) to believe the stories we frequently tell them of the wonders of civilized life. The expression in Bloody Knife's face, after some extraordinary statement, is as full of cynical meaning as a chapter in Charles Lamb.

THE INDIAN AND THE MAP.

One evening General Raynolds' map of this country was spread before Goose, who looked at it curiously, but with indifference, until told what it was.

"Here," said General Custer, "is Heart River," indicating with his toothpick along its course, "and here is Fort Lincoln and the Missouri."

Goose looked silently a few moments, seized the map, and turning it around until he got the points of compass to agree, gave a "ugh," and began to tell the interpreter where we were going and where we had come. Following it along he came to Cannon Ball River, which he told the interpreter was not right, and a pencil being handed him he traced the course of several of its branches, and paused with his pencil on Slim Butte, which he placed at least fifty miles from where it stood on the map. General Custer showed him where the mountain was indicated. Goose looked at it a moment, and threw the map aside, with a sneering "ugh!"

"Perhaps it is not," explained the General, through the interpreter; "that map was made before anybody ever went there, and the men didn't know anything about it except what the Indians told them."

"The Indians were white Indians, I guess," said Goose. "You can make another map when you go there with me."

"Yes," replied the General, "that is what we are going for. I will give you a map if you would like one."

"My map is here," indicating his head with a haughty gesture; and after a few moments of silent meditation, he asked the General for an order on the sutler for a drink of whisky.

Goose is a Sioux, and was such a desperado in his tribe that they drove him out, and he took refuge among the more congenial spirits. Some of the timid in the command have suggested the idea that he might betray us to his tribe, or lead us into an ambush; but with Bloody Knife as his companion, that is impossible. We are beginning to see fresh Indian trails, and scouts report signs of large parties just ahead of us, but if they give

us no more trouble than they have, there will be little concern.

Curtis.

CHICAGO INTER-OCEAN
Issue of August 17, 1874

THE BLACK HILLS.

The Expedition Encamped at the Base of Inyan Kava, (sic), 6,600 Feet Above the Sea.

Disappointed Gold-Hunters—The Inexhaustible "Color" Proves to be Yellow Gypsum.

A Duel in the Wilderness—The First Two Graves—The Funeral Service—Lights are Out, All Out.

From Our Own Reporter

CUSTER'S BLACK HILLS, EXPEDITION, IN CAMP AT INYAN KAVA, (sic), WY. T., JULY 23, 1874.

We have entered the Black Hills, and are camping today at the base of the highest peak. So far we have seen nothing remarkable; the miners have discovered no gold; the geologists have whacked in vain for the fossil of the "missing link;" the naturalists have emptied their saddle pockets day after day without revealing the existence of any new wonders in life; the soldiers have fought no Indians, and so far the expedition, in a positive sense, has been unsuccessful. Where lie those treasures that contain the roots of the Indian jealousy of this land; where are hidden the glories that the poetic Sioux has painted, or the wonders which his legends have sung, is yet to discovered; and even the lynx-eyed Custer, the long-haired chief, as the Indians call him, may fail to reveal them to the world. There is something singular in the relation of facts in the Indian mind, which may account for a great deal of their untruthfulness. Metaphysicians have, of course studied the thing all out, and theorized it down to a point so small that the whole truth, like a thousand angels, could dance on the tip of a needle; but theory and observation are different things, like theory and practice. It is beyond the power of the imagination to suppose any

POETIC FIRE UNDER THE DIRTY SHIRT OF GOOSE,

our guide; but it is there, and creeps out occasionally in delicate beauty; the same lack of sympathy seems to exist between Bloody Knife's soldier's suit and the wonderful imagery of his language sometimes, and we have to drop our querying with the conclusion that the caged bird has not lost his song, or the tamed antelope his swiftness. Goose gave to the hieroglyphics at the cave a religious reverence; every stroke of the tracery had its solemn meaning to him, yet they were to us simply rude drawings by rough hands. Bloody Knife has woven words of wonder around some mysterious something in the Black Hills, which may develop into a similar disappointment; yet both seem to be so far civilzed as to understand the relation of things, and that certain causes belong to certain consequences. There is a little of Cooper's monarch left in the modern Indian—just a little— the poetic part. The murmur of a sea shell is still to him a sonnet; the pairing of birds and idyl—not as tedious as some of our idyls are; the tempest is a rough ode, without falsehood or rant; the stars a song of prophecy, and a summer, with its leaves and birds and flowers, an epic, subordinating a hundred minor parts.

IN THE BLACK HILLS.

We have been in the Black Hills five days. Crossing the Belle Fourche, we entered a country radically different than anything we had seen before. The hills were higher, full of limestone ledges, and covered with a dense growth of pine. The valleys were fertile, except where a stratum of red clay came to the surface, but water was very scarce, and we were obliged to depend upon the pools the late rain had left in the hollows. Occasionally a spring would be found, cold and clear, but strongly tainted with minerals. Immense beds of gypsum, as clear as crystal, came to the surface everywhere, and extend, as we have found by recent excavations, to a depth of ten or twelve feet; occasionally a layer of a yellow color is found, and this may have given the ground for the gold stories, for we frequently find pieces which resemble the pure

metal very much. I was talking to an old miner the other day about

THE PROBABILITIES OF FINDING GOLD

here, and he thinks they are small. The excitement of two years ago, he says, all orginated in a piece of yellow gypsum which was brought in to a trading post by some Indians, and exchanged as gold. Some ignorant charlatan examined it, pronounced it the true metal, found the Indian who brought it in, and learning from him that there were immeasurable quantities in the Black Hills, spread the report far and wide. Adventurers began to flock to Yankton, Fort Laramie, Fort Randall, and other

frontier stations, and expedition after expedition was proposed, all of which were stopped by a military authority, till finally the excitement died down. By a treaty with the Sioux nation miners cannot be permitted to enter the region, and were they so permitted it would be unsafe, unless they went in large numbers; and it is not probable that, even if the precious substance is discovered, it could be opened for operation for some years. The late General McCook, of Yankton, had for some years previous to his murder been ambitious to penetrate the country, and repeatedly sought permission of the government to make an exploration, and had he lived, he no

This picture, too, was probably exposed by Illingworth while the expedition was camped along French Creek. Once he had his chemicals mixed for wet plate processing it was his pattern to make several exposures in a particular area from one or more vantage points.

doubt, instead of General Custer, would be leading this expedition.

INYAN KAVA (sic), THE "MASK MOUNTAIN"

is called by our guides the highest peak among the Black Hills, and is by far the most imposing and beautiful of any we have seen. General Warren camped near it on his expedition in 1857, measured its altitude by angles, and gives an enthusiastic description of its beauties in his report. Today General Custer remained in camp in order to give it a thorough exploration, and the scientific corps have spent most of the day in investigation. Colonel Ludlow, by the barometer, finds its height to be 6,600 feet above the sea, and 1,600 feet above its surroundings. Its contour at a distance resembles the cover of an ordinary vegetable dish, with a high mound on the top for a handle, and before we knew its name it was always designated as "the Cover Butte." The greater portion of its surface is covered with thick pine, broken by occasional bald spots, where limestone crags jut out. In the stone were found large numbers of valuable fossils.

A SINGULAR CURIOSITY.

One of the most singular curiosities that has as yet been placed in our museum is the backbone of a buffalo in which a flint arrow head is imbedded so firmly that it cannot be drawn out. We have seen no traces of the late existence of the animal here, although the plains are covered with bleached bones.

Deer are getting plenty, and other game, so that our tables are constantly supplied with the rarest dainties. It is antelope for breakfast, venison for dinner, and a bit of hard-tack and bacon for lunch. One is scarcely able to appreciate venison till he eats it, fresh and juicy, broiled on a bed of pine coals. The slender slice that the resources of a city market house afford may be a dainty to those who do not know the luxury of the thing; but a slice of the tenderloin, cut while the savor is in it, and broiled as fast as it can be dropped and turned over, is something of which an epicure may fondly dream. Several of our scientific gentlemen—

THE BUG HUNTERS,

as the soldiers call them—are excellent shots, and after their explorations their saddles are generally well hung with venison; but it is getting a little unsafe to wander off from the command, and hunting will hereafter be enjoyed with an escort of cavalry.

In making this expedition complete, in gathering from many sources many men of many minds, there are of course human curiosities in the conglomeration. We have our silent men, and our talkative men; with hobbies, and men with opinions to suit all the nubs and niches in the opinions of others; positive men and negative men some who are a source of information, some a source of annoyance, and some a source of entertainment; but the one who heads the latter class is a big-bodied, big-hearted old fellow, a professor in a Western college, who is doing the botany. His character is noble, yet funny, for in it are mixed the most generous, manly notions, and a simple childishness it does one good to see.

THE PROFESSOR

—he alone, of the titled scientists, is exclusively known as such—is doing the botany; and to see him some in from a long day's march, with a benevolent smile playing over his sun-burned, half-peeled face, and wreathing itself in his whiskers, and a huge nosegay of flowers in his hand—to see him lower his corpulent form from the back of "Dobbin," slowly and carefully, so as not to jar the sensitiveness of his rheumatic back, and to hear his sigh of relief, breathed secretly under a cheerful, hearty greeting, is as good as a tonic. The Professor is very learned; his great stomach must be the storehouse of his memory, and it is full of dictionary words, for nowhere else in himself has he room to stow away the great sentences that always roll from his mouth, like mountains of lava from a crater. When he was new to us, when he was making his preparations for the expedition, the Quartermaster's people considered him a singular curiosity in human nature, and most of us joined in that belief; but now that we know him, the good old fellow's kind heart, unselfish motives, characteristic politeness, and

hearty enjoyment of everything make him a favorite everywhere, and, notwithstanding his pedantry, it cannot but seem that he is a great child enjoying a summer's holiday. I was touched last night by the flow of genuine sympathy— the real milk of human kindness— that the first shadow fate has cast on the expedition drew from his heart. Last night we made

TWO GRAVES IN THE WILDERNESS,

and one of the most impressive funeral ceremonies I ever witnessed took place. The day before, John Cunningham, of Company H., Seventh Cavalry, died of diarrahea (sic), superinduced by physical exhaustion; that morning, before daylight, Joseph Turner, of Company M., was shot and killed by a comrade. It was murder, the result of a long standing feud, and really an impromptu duel, for both had murder in their minds and arms in their hands—only Turner was a little the slower, and, to use his own words, "he got the best of me or I should have settled him." I need not unfold the long chain of circumstances that led to the affair, for both men are unknown, were desperate characters, and it is quite probable were serving under assumed names—a common thing in the army. Before he died Turner ordered his back pay and some effects sent to a man named Hughes in Jeffersonville, Ind., and that, probably, was his true name. Roller, the murderer, is under guard, and will be handed over to the civil authorities for trial when the expedition returns to Fort Lincoln.

SIMPLY HUMAN DRIFTWOOD— men who have committed crime somewhere, and are hiding in the service under assumed names; men who cannot brook the liberties and familiarities of society, and take refuge in military discipline; men who are disappointed, disheartened, and ambitionless, and find the lazy life of a soldier a relief. Cunningham was one of these classes, his own reticence making it difficult to decide which. He was intelligent, well-educated, and, from his silent courtesy to all, and a well-bred indifference to everything, was popular and influential, but let himself lie aimless, the foot-ball of fate, till he was kicked into an unmarked grave in the wilderness. Could any destiny be sadder?

The funeral was held after sunset, so that the attention of any scouting Indians might not be attracted, and the ceremony in the cold, pale light of the moon had an air of weirdness added to its awful significance. There was but one grave—a wide, deep hole on the hill-side, under a clump of cedar trees. The bodies of the men were folded in their blankets, wrapped in their tents, and sewn fast—

LONG, SHAPELESS LUMPS OF HUMAN CLAY.

The bier was a canvas litter; the hearse an ambulance; the bearers a squad of troopers; the escort the whole command—only mourners were missed. The band led the procession from headquarters to the grave, with a dirge, and the bodies were lowered silently down. Then an old Irish Sergeant, of H Troop, read the Episcopal service, slowly, and with a deep, rich brogue, crossing himself occasionally, after the Popish fashion, and the foundation words of all Christian creeds,

"I am the resurrection
and the life,"
sounded strangely beautiful, as heard in the silence that hovered around those lonesome graves.

When the service was read a volley was fired over the grave, and the trumpeter sounded "taps," the "good-night" call of the soldier, the theme of which and the words tradition has applied to it are singularly appropriate. I cannot reproduce the music in these columns, but the words are:

"Sun has gone, day is done,
Marching over, lights are out,
Lights are out.
All out."

The effect of the sound—simply a trumpet strain in a register of five notes—was such the Priests' March in "Athalia," or the "Ruins of Athens" march produces when Rubinstein plays it, and when the last echoes died away men forgot to swear, and chaff, but the camp was as still as if all the pulses in those long lines of tents had ceased to beat.

SERGEANT O'TOOLE'S DILEMMA.

But even the most serious circumstances have their funny side. A sentiment in an epitaph will seem ridiculous to some reader, and the most awful suspense is sometimes ludicrous in the extreme. The readers of the INTER-OCEAN will pardon me if I change my mood abruptly to tell a story that has a solemn connection with these funerals, although it is not so very solemn itself.

The commandant of the left wing of the expedition is Colonel Tilford, of the Seventh Cavalry, a genial gentleman, very popular in and out of his regiment, and well known in Chicago and some of its suburbs. Both of the deceased belonged to his division, and upon him devolved the duty of preparing the funerals. Sergeant O'Toole, an Irish Catholic of the troop, was selected to read the service, but he had no prayer-book.

COLONEL TILFORD'S STORY.

"It was just like my wife, I knew," says Colonel Tilford, when he tells the story, "to put one in my sachel, although I hadn't come across it yet, so I told O'Toole I thought I could get him one. Of course I found it when I came to look—my wife would have put it in if she had to leave out a shirt; and, by the way, that reminds me of a story I once heard of a fellow who was going out, and had a box of books taken out of his wagon, as he had no room for them. Pretty soon a man came along and said to him, 'I've got a barrel of whisky I've no room for?' 'Put it into my wagon,' said he; and that's just like my wife about the prayer-book. She always finds room for it, although I don't use it much. I've come to say," and the colonel went on—
"Well, you see O'Toole came to my tent, and I gave him the prayer-book. He went off with it, but pretty soon he came back and said,
" 'Be jazes, Colonel,' said O'Toole, 'I can't find it.' "
" 'Can't find what?' said I.'

" 'CAN'T FIND THE PRAYERS, SUR"

"Can't find the prayers?' said I in astonishment; 'can't find the prayers?'"

" 'Be G_d, Colonel, thaze not a d_d one of them in the book.'
"I took the book," continued the Colonel, "and I looked it over, and by George, sure enough it was some edition with the burial service left out, and as it was getting late, I was considerably puzzled what to do and I said to O'Toole:
" 'O'Toole,' said I, 'you go to Colonel Hale and see if he hasn't got one,' and he went. Pretty soon he came back, pinching a book like one would pinch a rattlesnake in the neck, with his fingers in the place.
" 'I've got it now, d_ m me, Colonel,' said he. 'Be jazes, I've got it now. I was afraid I'd have to repate it from memory,' and he started off to overtake the procession."
Curtis.

THE BLACK HILLS

Progress of the Custer Expedition Into the Hitherto Unexplored Country.

The Beauties of the Black Hills— Floral Valley—A Wonderful Stream—Professarial Hyperbole.

Indian Traces—Following a Trail—The Pipe of Peace— A Compact and its Violation— A Chase—Slow Bull in Limbo.

CUSTER'S BLACK HILLS EXPEDITION IN CAMP AT CASTLE VALLEY, DAKOTA TERRITORY, July 27, 1874

After leaving Inyan Kava (sic) we struck over the mountains eastward, cutting a road through the forests, and struggling with steep ascents and precipitous declivities, being able to make only ten miles on the 24th, although we were nearly fourteen hours in the saddle. "In the saddle," I say, using the words not with their ordinary meaning, for really we were on foot nearly all the time, leading our horses, clearing the brush and logs away, pulling up stumps, pushing the wagons up the hills, and holding them back with long ropes as they went down. It was perilous to animal life and property, but the same kind Providence that has guided us continually saw us safely through, and in the whole command there was no result more serious than blistered hands and scratched faces. Where is the historian to place our anabasis alongside of Napoleon's crossing of the Alps or the famous marches of Artaxerxes? None of us ever saw so dense or so extended a growth of pine. As far as we could see, from the highest peaks, rising and falling with the undulations of the country, the forests made an unbroken surface of the darkest green, almost a black, from which I supposed the hills were named. But the crossing was well made, for after cutting through eight miles or more we fell into

THE MOST BEAUTIFUL VALLEY REMEMBERED.

Narrow, nowhere spreading to a greater width than half a mile; hidden almost entirely by steep, wooded cliffs, which rose on either side, so that in the middle of the afternoon it was nearly as dark as twilight. The air was cool and fresh, while on the hills we had suffered from a sultry heat, with the thermometer at ninety-three, and was laden with the perfume of millions of flowers. The whole valley was a nosegay, and so rich was the soil that everything grew with the greatest luxuriance. Our eyes were opened then to the beauties of the Black Hills. Twenty days in a purgatory of bare plains, saline water, and alkali dust made us appreciate a paradise, and every man in the expedition stood silently to enjoy and admire. Watering the valley were numberless little springs, and a rapid, rocky trout stream, as clear as crystal and cold as snow, which singularly grew deeper and wider as we neared its source, until it became a dashing mountain torrent, booming over a bed of rocks. Some of the party followed it down the valley and saw it disappear suddenly in the earth, leaving not one trace to show that its course had ever been above ground. For miles further they sought its reappearance, but it did not come to the surface again, and as the valley rose rapidly, it was concluded that it had found an outlet under the mountains to the world beyond.

THE PROFESSOR'S HYPERBOLE.

The Professor, who accompanied the party down, came back with a wonderful story. "A hyperbole," he called it afterward, without any great scruplousness (sic) in regard to its truth.

The stream disappeared, he said, in the mouth of a mammoth serpent, twenty-seven feet from "ear to ear," which drank all the water, gulping it down when its mouth filled, three swallows a day.

"It will compensate you," he said to me, "to ascend the pinnacle of yonder elevation, and obtain an observation of the reptile."

The Professor's imagination is very fertile, and he entertains us frequently with the remarkable experience which he and "Dobbin" encounter. "Dobbin" is the "very excellent animal" which the Professor "equestrianizes"—a long, lank beast, very deliberate in his movements, but perfectly docile, and exactly to the Professor's taste.

"I was ruminating the other morning," said he once, "on the extraordinary good fortune which secured me the use of so excellent an animal. I have only one exception to make among his entire category of characteristics; and that is, that frequently he is not very foot-sure. Some times when we are passing over a territory at all imperfect in its surface he stumbles, and it does seem as if he would displace my lumbar verterbrae, or give me a hebidemeal rupture."

BUT MORE ABOUT "FLORAL VALLEY"

as we named it—very appropriately, too, for our botanist collected fifty-two distinct varieties of flowers in the limits of our camp, and twelve under the walls of his tent. Among them are several to which the authorities we have at hand make no reference, and it is thought they are peculiar to this section. Among them is a very beautiful white lily, not described in either Gray's or Wood's classification. A large number of bulbs were collected, and an attempt will be made to introduce it into the States. A very pleasant and nutritious berry, called the Savois berry, was also found in large quantities, and a few wild strawberries, the first fruit we have seen. No words that I can write would picture fully to the mind of the reader the beauty of this scene. No one who has not seen Indian Territory in April, or the Florida bottoms in their summer radiance can conceive to any degree of satisfaction how nosegay-like this valley of ours looks; one who has never seen colors mixed as nature mixes them, in her own rare conservatories like these, can realize the artistic effect that is produced; but let the reader imagine if he can such a valley as I have described, so narrow and deep that one glance will take in a long space of it, darkened by the heavy shade to the tinge of twilight, and illuminated—yes, fairly illuminated—by the gold, and the scarlet, and the blue of its flowers. But the picture is not finished. The regimental band is playing on a shelf of one of the walls, and the "Mocking Bird," "Garryowen," "Artist Life," "The Blue Danube," and snatches from "Trovatore," and other strains of

MUSIC FOR THE FIRST TIME HEARD IN PARADISE.

One wonders what effect the music will have upon these wonderful flowers; how long the echoes will remain in these cosy hills, and whether some straying savageling has caught the melody afar off, and will wonder for years hence where the sound came from, and whether it was the happy spirits singing in Paradise; and when the pale face invades this valley, and the savageling talks English, whether he will tell what mysterious noises he heard on the evening of July 24, 1874, or whatever year of our Lord the Indian chronicles call this.

HUNTING FOR GOLD.

So beautiful was nature outwardly; so rich was mother earth in the resources of vegetable life, that our miners imagined mineral treasures must be lying under our flower bed; and they dug for them —dug all one evening, and found— found a rich loamy soil, four or five feet deep, then a gravel bed on a stratum of limestone rock.

A REMARKABLE STREAM.

Everybody was sorry to break up camp after our first sweet step in the floral valley. The night was cold, almost frosty, and the morning air was really intoxicating. An early start was made, and we went up the river, finding new beauties and fresh gratifications at every step. The stream grew larger and more rapid as we neared its source, supplied by cold, deep springs that started out of the mountain side every few rods. This was the only stream any of us had ever seen that grew smaller as its supply became greater, and as it grew nearer its mouth; it was a new freak of nature, a strange one, but as the profane young man at headquarters said: "The d_d ground gobbled it up, I 'spose." Finally the creek disappeared entirely swallowed up in a cluster of springs, which were evidently its source.

At the summit, where half a dozen just such valleys as we had traveled met, was

A SMOOTH, FLOWERY PARK,

coverying (sic), perhaps, fifty acres, and hemmed in on all sides, except where the valleys broke the border, by a forest of pine and spruce and poplar, as thick and perfect as trees could grow. Conceive the effect of such a scene upon the senses, at sunrise—the senses of people only half awake, and under that indefinite sort of depression that early rising always creates. It is a favorite camping ground of the Indians, and the velvet carpet, with its ground work of green, and tracery of geranium, lilies, roses, and innumerable other floral designs, was marred in places by the ashes of campfires. Several relics of an ancient and memorable character were found, and immediately seized upon by the curiosity of hunters, and the wagons were soon laden with an only sheet-iron boiler, supposed to have been stolen from Raynolds in 1859, for he reports having lost a greater part of his outfit by Indian thieving; several worthless bows and arrows, and a number of old elk antlers. Choosing the valley that seemed to lie in the direction of our course, we entered

ANOTHER OF THOSE NARROW, GRACEFUL AVENUES,

like that by which we had approached, and followed it down, having the company of a dashing little trout stream, which opened out, wherever the valley swelled into wider proportions, into tiny little lakes, which were very beautiful to the eye but destructive to a wagon train. Bridges of corduroy were soon supplied, however, from the timber that skirted the edges of the water, and we went on.

The face of nature soon began to change. Our valley descended (sic) rapidly and our brook tumbled recklessly over little cataracts; on the tops and sides of the hills great lime-stone rocks began to creep out, which grew in proportions as we went further down, till they seemed like the battlements of some ancient race of giant warriors. The hills were steeper, the valley wider, and the timber thinner and more scattered. Our flowers were gone, but the soil seemed good, and the grass was very thick and nutritious.

FOLLOWING A TRAIL.

Traces of Indians began to be seen, and we found several places where there had been recent encampments. The trail grew more fresh as we went further on, and our scouts began, in their peculiar way, to show impatience. They unbraided their hair, rubbed vermilion on their faces, wrapped towels and white cloths around their heads, putting bunches of feathers in for a crest—all this in the saddle as we marched along—and hummed the dreary monotone of their warsong, the expressive words of which are:

Um ahaum, ahaum, um um um ahaum

Yah yah ahaum, yah yah ahaum, ahaum

Um um-m-m-m ahaum, ahaum, eu! eu!

The last two words are given as a subdued war-whoop. I do not give the song entire, but only one stanza, that the reader may catch its purport.

UNLEASHING THE HOUNDS.

General Custer caught Bloody Knife's eye, and gave him a significant nod, which the old chief understood, and he rode in front of the column as calmly as if there was not a Sioux in the country, and he hadn't the murder of a son to avenge. Pretty soon a thin, almost transparent, smoke was seen rising over a hill a mile or more beyond us, and the scouts fairly pranced with impatience. They stripped off their civilized garments, dashed streaks of red paint on their naked flesh in a moment, and when the General gave Bloody Knife permission to reconnoiter ahead, they rushed off after their chief. Until they reached the brow of the hill they rode like wild fire, then they stopped a moment, cocked their guns, and crept cautiously around the side of the knoll, single file. The camp was deserted, but traces remained to show a hasty and recent departure. The scouts were eager to pursue the trail, and it was with some difficulty that they were prevented, but as it lay in the direction in which we were going the General sent a couple on to reconnoiter, keeping the rest in the column.

On a wide, open "bottom," encircled by ridges of high pine hills, with towering palisades of lime-stone at their summits, we camped, and, after the tents were up, and the preparations for the night made, Bloody Knife and twenty-five Ree scouts were sent out to see where the trail led, with orders to attack no one, but simply to reconnoiter and report. It was the work of only a moment for the Rees to put themselves in war dress, and they were off,

CRAZY FOR A FIGHT.

A few days before we left Fort Lincoln, the Sioux attacked a Ree village near Fort Berthold; and a battle ensued, in which a son of Bloody Knife and a brother of Bear's Eye were killed, with several other warriors of the band we have with us. These deaths they were anxious to revenge, and the prospect of an opportunity gave us a glimpse of the old-Indian war-spirit.

The scouts were gone only a few moments, when Young Hawk, a handsome youth of 18, came hurrying back, with the news that they had found a village of five lodges, a large herd of ponies, and were waiting for orders behind a hill. General Custer immediately rode on himself, with two troops of horsemen and the remainder of the scouts, and found Bloody Knife and his party in the hollow of a hill, in all the glory of war paint and feathers. Goose and Bear's Ears, the most moderate of the crowd, with Agar (Agard) an interpreter, were sent on with

A TOWEL FLYING AS A FLAG OF TRUCE,

and entered the camp, the rest of us coming after at a slow pace. Our visit was evidently unexpected, and the camp was deserted by all the warriors except one, who, when he saw us, approached timidly with an extended hand, and the usual saluation—

"How!"

While the women and children scatted to the bushes, the General and several others shook hands with him, and he invited us to be seated, when an interpreter told him we were not come to fight, but to make peace with them, and ask them about the country, to which the warrior nodded significantly, and, filling a pipe, passed it

around, each member of the circle taking a whiff and blowing the smoke—if he could, and with killikinick tobacco it is not a very agreeable experiment — through his nose. Slow Bull, as he introduced himself, was a tall, slim fellow, with sharp features, and piercing gray eyes, resembling so much that it was immediately suggested by several of our party that old war horse of the Democracy, Dan Voorhees.

Being assured of our peaceful intentions Slow Bull called in the women and children, and sent for the other warriors who were hunting in the woods. They came, four of them. "One Stab," the chief, a wrinkled old man, at least 70, I should think, and "Long Arm," "Slim Bear," and "Young Wolf," lively young bucks—a good deal surprised to find a couple of hun-

dred horsemen in their camp, but quite confident. "One Stab" invited us into his lodge; his wife, a daughter of the famous chief "Red Cloud," brought us spring water in an old iron kettle, and we sat down for

A COUNCIL.

General Custer told them, through the interpreter, that the Great Father at Washington had sent him into the Black Hills to find out what sort of a country it was, and whether the Sioux had a good reservation. They had not come to fight, but only to see, and to make a map of the country, and he was glad to meet them, so as to ask some questions about the hills. He inquired who they were, and where they came from, and found they belonged to the Brule tribe of Sioux, from the Red Cloud

South Dakota State Historical Society

This picture and its twin on the facing page is another exposed by Illingworth while the Custer expedition camped along French Creek. Major George A. Forsyth, an aide to General Philip Sheridan, who accompanied Custer on the expedition wrote in his journal, "Have a beautiful camp, with abundance of grass, just opposite three beautiful mountains covered to their summits with pines."

agency. "One Stab" was hunting in the Black Hills for five months. The rest of his band was scattered in different portions of the hills, and some had gone back to the agency. He had twenty-seven people with him, but only five warriors. They had killed a great many deer, and were going back soon to receive their annuity. "One Stab" had always been a friend of the whites, he said, and was glad to be of any service to them. Inquiries were made about the country, and it was finally agreed that they should accompany the expedition several days as guides. General Custer invited them to his camp to get coffee and sugar, and bade them adieu.

The Ree warriors were not at all satisfied with the result of the conference, and Bear's Eye especially showed lively signs of hostilities, but the General ordered him under guard, and assured "One Stab" that none of his party would be harmed.

A SPECK OF WAR.

We were scarcely settled in camp again when "One Stab," "Slow Bull," Slim Bear," and "Long Arm" came after their rations, and another conference was held, in which they did not show the docile spirit that characterized the other interview, contradicting much of their previous information, and making altogether different replies to the same questions. "One Stab" expressed a fear of the Rees, and the General said he would send a troop of white soldiers to protect his lodges that night, and in the morning he could camp with us. To this they assented and started to leave. They were asked to remain until the white soldiers were ready to go, to which they consented, going to the Indian quarters to wait. The General was scarcely out of sight when "Slow Bull" rode out of our camp, hurriedly, in almost an opposite direction from that which he would naturally take, and the other three also started off. General Custer was notified and ordered a detachment of Santee scouts after them to ask them back, and if they refused, to bring them by force. Quite a chase resulted, in which the old man was captured, but "Slim Bear" showed fight, and

jerked "Red Bird," one of the Santees, off his horse, firing at him and galloping away. "Long Arm" also escaped. The chief was brought to headquarters, and the scouts sent after the fugitives. When they reached the village the lodges were all gone, and the trail led down to the valley toward the east. It seems that immediately upon our departure the whole outfit pulled up stakes and departed, the warriors coming to our camp to reassure the General of their friendship and willingness to be his guides, to get their rations, and then to follow on as fast as possible.

GIVE US "THE SHAKE" ENTIRELY.

Bloody Knife and his men were out five hours or more, but returned scalpless, having been unable to follow the trail in the dark, and there were howls of disappointment, and anger around the Indian camp, but the old man was a prisoner, and was placed under guard at headquarters. In an interview with the General he claimed to know nothing of the flight of his village, and explained it by saying the squaws must have been frightened. He received a lecture on truthfulness, and was told that he would be kept a hostage

South Dakota State Historical Society

The magnificent scenery of the Black Hills impressed not only Illingworth, but every member of the expedition. In one of his field dispatches, published in the CHICAGO INTER OCEAN, Custer said, ". . . the Black Hills consists of beautiful parks and valleys through which flows a stream of clear, cold water, perfectly free from alkali, while bounding these parks or valley, there are invariably found unlimited supplies of timber."

until we were out of the Hills, and must show us a good road. He was evidently quite relieved to know that he wasn't to be tortured and shot, but the expression on his lean, wrinkled face showed "there was trouble on the old man's mind," and he wrapped himself in his blanket, and silence for the remainder of the night.[23]

IN THEIR MIDST.

We are now about the center of the Black Hills, in the region marked park upon the map. Yesterday, for the first time, were found indications of gold, and today we remain in camp while parties have gone prospecting in every direction. We shall probably remain here several days. Explorations, east and west, will be made by small parties, as it is very difficult getting the wagons over the hills and through the timber, and the animals are fairly worn out.

This letter is sent by a carrier, who goes to General Sheridan with official dispatches, via Fort Laramie and the Union Pacific Railroad.

Curtis.

CHICAGO INTER-OCEAN
Issue of August 27, 1874

CUSTER'S BLACK HIILS EXPEDITION IN CAMP AT CUSTER PARK, DAKOTA, AUG. 3, 1874.

In the field thirty days or so, one begins to think of something else besides Indians, gold nuggets, or game. When he has gone through his "outfit," put on his last clean shirt, and used his last pocket handkerchief, and attempts a change to campaign haberdashery and soldier laundry work, he begins to think of the loved ones at home, and to count the number of days out and the date of the probable return. Without a calendar, and even with one, it is a somewhat difficult matter to determine the day of the week, and I heard an animated dispute this morning between two members of the West Point Alumni Association resulting in a wager, as to whether it is Saturday or Sunday. Some fellow who kept a diary said it was Sunday, and the Saturday party paid the drinks.

24. A mail will leave this command within the next 36 hours. Each comp. including officers will be allowed to sent not to exceed 3 ounces of mail matter. The mail from the different companies will be brought to these hq at an hour to be hereafter designated, by a non-commissioned officer.
Notice of mail run from exped.
Circular No. 23, Hq BHE, Camp. No. 27, Aug. 1, 1874. NA RG 393, Orders BHE, 1874.

23. STABBER AND SEVERAL INDIANS KILLED BY CUSTER'S MEN—THE EXPEDITION RETURNING—DISTURBANCE AT FORT GIBSON. I.T.
The following telegram was received at General Sheridan's headquarters yesterday:
Omaha, August 4, 1874
Colonel P. C. Drum, Adjutant General, Headquarters Division of the Missouri:
Colonel Smith, commanding at Laramie, telegraphs that Colonel Stanton, just arrived from the agencies, reports large numbers of Indians coming in from the north, who say that Stabber, a prominent Indian in the disturbances last spring at the agencies, and several others, were killed by Custer's men. There seems to be much feeling in consequence among the Indians.
E.O.C. Ord,
Brigadier General
CHICAGO INTER-OCEAN
Issue of August 5, 1874

Omaha, Neb. Aug. 12—An arrival from Spotted Tails Agency, today, says Spotted Tail's band refuses to move to the new reservation, as proposed by Bishop Hare and other commissioners, and are very indignant and much excited over it. It is probable that forces will have to be used to make them move. The Indians at both reservations are in a high state of excitement over the killing of Stabber and party, reported a few days ago. Custer's movement causes the Indians evident anxiety, fearing it is a movement to crush them between General Ord's and Custer's forces.
CHICAGO INTER-OCEAN
Issue of August 13, 1874

We passed the meridian of our summering the other day, and the people at headquarters began to talk about

SENDING A MAIL.[24]

This was the signal for letter writing, and everybody began to borrow paper and pencils. Married men remembered their wives and babies, and the fancy young veterans at the sutler's store hinted mysteriously about sisters and "friends" at home. The lieutenant in society and the lieutenant in camp are two entirely different individuals: one is on leave and the other in service; one talks poetry and the other swears. Fancy, oh, bespangled butterfly, your brass-buttoned, gold-laced chevalier in a faded flannel shirt, and trousers seated with canvas! Fancy him seated on the grass under the sutler's tent, leaning against a whisky barrel, and picking his teeth with a straw. Unshaven, the nose you thought so superbly molded covered with a white scaly crust, the mustache you thought "so military" lost in the scraggy growth of sun-bleached beard; those eyes that looked with such passionate fervor into yours, bloodshot and swollen by the heat and wind; those lips which—which whispered so fondly those sweet nothings, blistered and broken with great black patches; his faultless cravat exchanged for a red bandanna; that distingue foot covered with an army brogan and a pair of clanking spurs. This is your hero now, but he doesn't forget what he once was, and gets his letters ready for the mail. Each company is limited to four ounces of weight, and that's the reason he didn't write more.

Laramie was thought to be the nearest point of civilization, and General Custer decided to send the mail there; but who was to carry it—a hundred and fifty miles through an unknown, trackless region, right among the very homes of hostile Indians. Charley Reynolds was selected—

CHARLEY REYNOLDS, THE SCOUT,

and the sort of man one doesn't expect to find on the prairies. He would adorn a drawing-room if it wasn't for his diffidence, for he is one of God Almighty's gentlemen.

Born and reared in one of the aristocratic families of Kentucky, he went a few years before the war to Colorado—nobody knows why, for curiosity has never yet probed through his reticence on this point. With a singular aptness for scouting, and nerves that never quivered under danger, he became an important man in the war, and did signal service for the Federal army in the West. When peace came he went back to find a home that war had destroyed, and to realize himself alone in the world. His homelessness and a disposition which shrinks from fellowship with men drove him back to the frontier, and for several years he has been hunting and trapping in Montana and along the river, being occasionally employed by the government to do some service for which other men are too cowardly or incompetent. A short, stocky man, with a shrinking blue eye, and a face from which exposure has not yet effaced the beauty, a voice as soft as a woman's, and a manner unobtrusive and gentle—he doesn't seem like a hero, or a man that would deliberately look danger in the face, but they say—he never says so himself—that he has fought whole tribes of Indians single handed, and has lived whole winters in the mountains alone, without even so much as a horse or a dog to keep him company. This is Charley Reynolds—a man who has lived the best part of a lifetime on the plains and never learned the necessity of swearing; never smoked a pipe or a cigar before a camp fire, and never was known to drink.

A HERO'S MODESTY.

I asked him one day to tell me the story of his life. He blushed a little, laughed quietly, and said he didn't think it worth while.

"But they tell me you've had a remarkable experience," I suggested.

"Not so remarkable that it need be told," he said. "I guess you can find enough to fill your paper without publishing anything about me."

And that was all the romance I got out of Charley Reynolds.

Well, this man was chosen as courier, and he quietly went to work to prepare for a journey few men would have undertaken. He picked out a horse he thought would suit him; made some muffled shoes of leather and sponge that would make no sound and leave no trail: cleaned his rifle and filled his belt with cartridges; filled a haversack with bacon and hardtack, strapped a blanket on his saddle, and said he was ready.

A mail bag was made of canvas, and our dignified adjutant descended to a trifle, and labeled it as follows:

Black Hills Express.

Charley Reynolds, Manager.

Connecting with
All Points East, West,
North, South.

Cheap Rates; Quick Transit;
Safe Passage.

We are protected by the
Seventh Cavalry.

An engineering party, with an escort was going in his direction, so strapping his load of remembrances and longings to his saddle, he started off with them one morning toward the south. He rode all day with the escort, took supper with them, and at midnight started off alone into the dark. How he fared my readers know better than I.

The more I see of my frontier life, of men who, like Reynolds, make a home of the mountain wildernesses and the bare plains, who find society enough in solitude, and comfort enough in hunting and trapping hardships, the more do I become impressed with

A STRANGE PHILOSOPHY

which makes life less dear to men the less they have of it. I have not expressed myself as distinctly as I wish I could, but the point is this: The daily occupation of city life, filling every nook and crevice of the human mind, leave no room nor wish for anything beyond them—no men enjoy life more, and few fear death as much. One would suppose that the common period of human life spent in the factory, the counting house, or the wareroom would leave little desire for longevity; that a man, let him be ever so much of a glutton, would have had enough of decimal fractions and compound interest, would lay down his pen without a sign, and even for the sake of a little relaxation be glad to go into the next world. But there is nothing of the kind; your city man hates dying above all things; your frontiersman will look death in the face as calmly as he sits by his camp fire waiting the dawn of another day. He who sees the sun rise in an atmosphere, one breath of which is worth whole gallons of city air, and sees him setting over a glorious landscape of wood and glen, of field and valley, will leave his pure and beautiful world with fewer regrets than the denizen of some dark alley or some smoke-dried street in a metropolis. The love of life is in the direct ratio of its artificiality. The more men shut out nature from their hearts and homes surround themselves with the myriad little appliances of a factitious existence, the more do they become attached to the world.

THEY SAY THEY HAVE FOUND GOLD.

They found it just before Reynolds left, and he carried the news to the world. The INTER-OCEAN, I think had the privilege of telling it first, for Reynolds was to telegraph you the golden tidings from Laramie. The discovery was made on the 2d of August, in the bed of a creek we suppose is the French Creek of the maps, and the yield was about thirty-five cents in dust to three pans—a pretty good yield if one could keep it up for a year or so, and enough to assure our miners they have struck a lead. There are two of them—old veterans in the craft—who have been worth fortunes as many times as they have toes, and who know the names of every gulch west of the Rocky Mountains. Ross and McKay are their names, and General Custer employs them in the scientific corps as experts. Soon after we left Floral Valley, and as soon in fact as we struck the eastern ranges of the hills, quartz rock began to appear at intervals, and in time we saw huge mountains of it, as

BEAUTIFUL AS THE HILLS OF THE CELESTIAL CITY—

white and red and green and yellow crystal that fell under the hammer's blow into emeralds and rubies and opals and all sorts of precious stones.

"Now, by gosh," says McKay, taking a fresh quid of tobacco, "it begins to look like something."

And he went at work, with his pick and pan, every time the train stopped long enough for him to un-strap them. It wasn't very satis-factory prospecting, to leave a lead as soon as they got "the color" and they got it frequently, but the ex-pedition hurried on, and it was not until we went into camp here that a fair test was made. The farther north we go, they say, the better are the indications, and by the time we get to the plains again, I expect we shall be loaded down with nuggets.

"CUSTER PARK"

This is one of the many beauti-ful spots we found in the hills, a sort of parks they are, miniature prairies covered with a growth of grass that an Eastern farmer would gloat over, and the meadow is broken here and there by gar-dens of flowers—asters, gerani-ums, hare-belles, daisies, lilies, of a beauty that few excel, and dozens of exotics we know no name for. The park is watered by a swift-running stream that fed the "out-fit" with fishes for several days, and hidden by thick wooded hills so closely that one wonders how he got in. We have been in camp several days, while exploring par-ties have investigated the un-known to the south of us, and in honor of our leader this paradise, and the chain of paradises in which it is link, has been named Custer Park.

BECKER, A SOLEMN OLD SPECTACLED SERGEANT,

of the Engineer Corps, who rides in the awkward, two-wheeled "go-devil" that carries the odometers, and who is platting (sic) the map that gold-hunters will go by when they come here to defile this holy silence with their oaths, and call these beautiful valleys their char-acteristic names, has taken a won-derful fancy to this spot, has sur-veyed it, and staked out 160 acres which he says he will pre-empt. On a little shaded knoll, back of the line of the left wing, true to his nationality, he said he had laid out the limits of a lager-beer garden.

"And where," I asked him, "are you going to put the house?"

"D__m de'ow-us." he replied,

"dot will be times enough to dink of dot, anyhow."

I find a great many Germans in the army. They make excellent soldiers, and are generally well educated men, who have enlisted immediately after their immigra-tion, for the lack of something else to do. The Irish make better cav-alrymen, are better riders, and more bold and reckless, but for a good reliable infantryman, or "dough-boys," as the troopers call them, the Germans are the best. I have frequently spoken of what queer stuff the army is made of. Colonel Tilford told me the other day that he once had a son of Reverdy (sic) Johnson in his regi-ment, and but a short while ago the rolls of the Seventh Cavalry bore the name of a man who claimed to be, and was it is thought, a son of the late Richard Yates. He inherited many of his father's traits, among which were wit and a love for whisky, and a good story is told of him that il-lustrates both.

His Captain was also a disciple of Bacchus, and it came to pass that on one day both were pretty well inflated. The Sergeant re-ported Yates' intoxication to the Captain, who ordered him brought immediately to his presence. Yates came, and the Captain, looking at him for a few moments with his uncertain eyes, exclaimed:

"Drunk again, eh!"

"So am I, Cap'n," hiccoughed the private, "so am I, and if we don't look out they'll send us both to the guard house."

This was an exhibition of philos-ophy which struck the Captain, drunk as he was, as being singular; and he proposed to Yates that they "saw off," and each agreed not to get tight, except when he was sure the other was sober. Strange to say, the Captain remembered the agreement, and told it fre-quently as a good joke, till a few weeks after Yates was found drunk again. The officer sent for him and recalled to his mind the agreement.

"Dev'lish good contract, Cap'n," answered he. "But dev'lish bind-in' on the second party. I know I promised not to get drunk till you were sober; but d__n me, I thought my turn would never come."

Curtis.

GOLD!

The Land of Promise—Stirring News from the Black Hills.

The Glittering Treasure Found At Last . . . A Belt of Gold Territory Thirty Miles Wide.

The Precious Dust Found in the Grass Under the Horses' Feet—Excitement Among the Troops.

A Mining Company Formed and Notice Duly Given—"Aunt Sally" Takes A Claim.

The "Inter-Ocean" Reporter's Account of the Discovery

CUSTER'S BLACK HILLS EXPEDITION. IN CAMP AT CUSTER'S PARK. DAKOTA TERRITORY, Aug. 7, 1874

They call it

A TEN DOLLAR DIGGIN'S, and all the camp is aglow with the gold fever. In previous dis-patches and letters I have told of the discovery, but the place then hadn't reached the dignified name of a "diggin's," and only a few little yellow particles had been washed out of a panful of sand. This is the first opportunity our miners have had to make a really fair test of the "color," and it has yielded them abundantly. They scraped a little along the bed of a brook till they got the color, then with spade and pick began to dig beside it a hole about as long and wide and deep as a hu-man grave. From the grass roots down it was "pay dirt", and after a dozen pans or more had been washed out, the two persevering men who will be the pioneers of a new golden State came into camp with a little yellow dust wrapped carefully up in the leaf of an old account book. It was examined with the microscope; was tried with all the tests that the imagi-nations of fifteen hundred excited campaigners could suggest, and it stood every one. It was washed with acid, mixed with mercury, cut, chewed and tasted, till every-body was convinced and went to bed dreaming of the wealth of Croesus. At daybreak there was a crowd around the "diggins," with every conceivable accoutrement.

Shovels and spades, picks, axes, tent-pins, pot hooks, bowie knives, mess pans, kettles, plates, platters, tin cups, and everything within reach that could either lift dirt or hold it was put into service by

THE WORSHIPERS OF THAT GOD, GOLD.

And those were few who didn't get a "showing"—a few yellow particles clinging to a globule of mercury that rolled indifferently in and out of the sand. Officers and privates, mule-whackers and scientists, all met on a common level, and the great equalizer was that insignificant yellow dust.

The most excited contestant in this chase after fortune was "Aunt Sally," the sutler's colored cook, a huge mountain of dusky flesh, and "the only white woman that ever saw the Black Hills," as she frequently says. She is an old frontiersman, as it were, having been up and down the Missouri ever since its muddy water was broken by a paddle wheel, and having accumulated quite a little property, had settled down in Bismarck to ease and luxury.

"Money didn't done brung dis chile out hyar, now, I tells ye dat; dis hain't no common nigger, now, I tells ye: no it ain't", she says to me one day. "I'se got done workin fur money, I have, now hyar me; an ye wouldn't cotch dis gal totin' chuck out hyar now, I tells ye, if it hadn't bin for seein' dese hyar Black Hills dat Custer fetched us to. I'se here'd 'bout dese 'ere hills long 'fore Custer did. Now I'm talkin'. When I was on de Missouri—cooked on first boat dat ever run up dat stream, an' I hain't had no hard luck, neither, now, I tells ye folks. But I wanted to see dese Black Hills—an' dey ain't no blacker dan I am, and I'm no African, now you just bet I ain't; I'm none of yer common herd, I've got the money to back it, now I have, I tell you."

AUNT SALLY'S DREAMS OF GOLD.

Aunt Sally expected to find the Black Hills in some indefinite way or other adapted to the colored race, and was terribly disappointed; but the gold discoveries compensated for the lack of any distinctive mark of her race, and she joined in the developments with religious fervor. She talked incessantly about them from morning to night, and when she packed her mammoth body into a little wagon that was provided for her and her "traps," her dreams were of gold mines, and " 'ery thing dats good on dis hyar earth, now I 'low." She went to the stream when the strike was made, "scratched grabble," and staked out her claim, and she says she's coming here as soon as anybody, "now you hyar me."

The miners traced up the creek some distance finding color at every step, till the lead ran under a huge quartz mountain. Subsequent investigation proved that there was

A BELT, THIRTY MILES WIDE,

as near as they could determine, running from the southwest to the northeast, and embracing all these quartz mountains which we have looked at with so much admiration for their exterior beauty. Gold must be under them, the miners say, and the mineralogists add that it is strange if there is not—but in such a shape that we cannot reach it. No facilities for blasting or mining are at hand. We have no powder except what the little brass cartridge shells hold, and the earth will not unbosom itself to any other power; neither have we time to make the application, for more than half our time is gone and half our rations used, and much of the country to explore yet. But the expedition has solved the mystery of the Black Hills, and will carry back the news that there is gold here, in quantities as rich as were ever dreamed of. The method to reach it is yet to be provided. It is in the very heart of the Sioux territory—in their choicest hunting ground—and they hold the land with as holy reverence as the savage heart can feel. No one can come here with any safety, or with any legal right as long as the treaties that now exist hold good, and the wealth that we have found must be for several years yet under the ban.[25]

25. The Black Hills can be reached from Chicago in six days, and we should not be surprised to see a gold excitement springing up over this intelligence rivaling the California fever of '49. Already the frontier towns are in a tumult, and the excitement is spreading. Little is talked of or thought about save the discoveries in this wonderful land.

CHICAGO INTER-OCEAN
Issue of August 27, 1874

THE FIRST MINERS' MEETING IN THE BLACK HILLS.

An attempt to solve the Indian question was made around a camp fire the other night, and a conclave shook hands together to look fate in the face. It was a company of rough men; men—the most of them—who enjoy life on $13 a month and rations, but they feel that this expedition had in some dim wise opened a future for them, and they saw reflected in the gloss of that little gold dust great possibilities, and great hopes grew out of them for better things. Some who saw that meeting may laugh at me for this moralizing— but they saw nothing but the brown and hard faces of adventurers, and I thought I saw something more—ambition; not mercenary alone, but an ambition throbbing with pulsations of hope —and I imagined I saw in some of these a glimpse of something far beyond to be reached by this bridge of gold.

> All thought begins in
> feeling-wide
> In the great mass its base
> is hid.
> And narrowing up to thought
> stands glorified,
> A nerveless pyramid.
>
> Nor is he far astray
> who deems
> That every hope which
> rises and grows broad
> In the world's heart, by
> ordered impulse streams
> From the great heart
> of God.

The result of this meeting around a camp-fire among a cluster of wagons was the formation of

THE CUSTER PARK MINING COMPANY,

to be a working organization from that day forward, dividends to be paid annually until further notice. The company was dully formed according to the laws of the United States and the Territory of Dacotah, with authorized officers and Board of Directors, and the following notice was posted on the inside of a hard-tack box cover, out of the rain, and placed on the claim. I would like to give a fac-simile of the "Notice," but in these columns can only give its words:

DISTRICT NO. I, CUSTER PARK MINING COMPANY, CUSTER'S GULCH, BLACK HILLS, D. T., AUG. 5, 1874.

Notice is hereby given that we the undersigned claimants, do claim four thousand (4,000) feet, commencing at number eight (8) above, and running down to number twelve (12) below discovery for mining purposes, and intend to work the same as soon as peaceable possession can be had of this portion of Dakota Territory by the General Government.

And we do hereby locate the above claim in accordance with the laws of Dakota Territory governing mining districts.

H. N. Ross, 400 feet, discovery.
M. Smith, No. 1 below discovery.
M. Conner, No. 2 below discovery.
W. J. Kennelly, No. 3 below discovery.
W. T. McKay, No. 4 below discovery.
Dan Manning, No. 5 below discovery.
Henry Harvey, No. 6 below discovery.
Sarah Campbell, No. 7 below discovery.
D. Mathieson, No. 8 below discovery.
Harry Roberts, No. 9 below discovery.
J. Roach, No. 10 below discovery.
Tim Hayes, No. 11 below discovery.
G. Bosworth, No. 12 below discovery.
James McGee, No. 1 above discovery.
George McCabe, No. 2 above discovery.
Samuel O'Connell, No. 3 above discovery.
C. Bassett, No. 4 above discovery.
A. McBeth, No. 5 above discovery.
F. Weddell, No. 6 above discovery.
C. W. Freede, No. 7 above discovery.
Pat. Smith, No. 8 above discovery.

And thus were inaugurated the "mining interests" of the Black Hills. Thus were made, insignificantly, and illegally, perhaps, the incipient efforts toward the development of one of the most rich and beautiful pieces of Nature's embroidery on God's foot-stool.

EXPLORATIONS SOUTH.[26]

The train has been parked here, and the larger portion of the battalion has rested, while detachments of cavalry, with engineers and scientists, have explored the southern portion of the hills, it having been found impossible to climb the steep ridges with the wagon train, or to drop it into the deep rocky gorges and ravines that were frequently occurring. One party went southeast sixty miles, or more, to the Shyenne (sic) River, passing through the mauvais terres, or bad lands that lie between Harney's Peak and the stream. Another party went southwest to the same river, near which it forms its north fork, which is kncwn as the Belle Fourche, while another took the height and bearings from Harney's Peak, and still another traced several of the larger streams to their mouth, or so far as would determine their general direction and outlet. Nothing of special interest transpired, except those wonderfully-exciting things which are reached by logarathims (sic) in the engineers' note-books. One result of this expedition beside the discovery of gold and a general investigation of the country will be

AN EXCELLENT AND UNUSUALLY ACCURATE MAP.

The tracings that have been formerly made, and which have been used as a sort of base for our operations, were almost entirely founded upon guess work and information from the Indians. General Harney, General Reynolds (sic), Captain Warren, and others have been around the edges of the Black Hills, have seen something of the outline of the country, have questioned Indians and those unreliable hybrids called guides, and with their knowledge thus acquired have each made a map. The Engineer Department of the service has ingeniously joined the whole into a single map, harmonizing the contradictions as much as possible, but falling far short of reliability or accuracy in the result. For instance, Slim Butte—a long high hill on the plains—was placed more than fifty miles out of its real position, and this is only one of many similar errors. This expedition has had every advantage in the world for fulfilling the requirements the others have failed

26. Comments of the Press upon the Black Hills Discoveries.

Farewell now to the sequestered loneliness of the Black Hills, hitherto trodden only by the feet of the adventurous trapper and hunter, and the moccasins of the Sioux Indians, to whom the region had been set apart as an inviolate reservation in the days before the pioneers of the westward march of civilization suspected the wealth that blossomed and grew upon its surface, and the vast riches that laid concealed beneath its rolling stretches of meadow-land and timber-covered uplands. It has been some four or five weeks since 1,000 cavalrymen, sword by side and foot in stirrup, with Custer at their head, and a train of wagons in their rear, set out to penetrate this unknown land in Western Dakota; and now we are just getting back from the expedition such glowing and exuberant accounts of the glories of their discoveries as Ponce de Leon might have written from the shores of Florida, or as Johnson imagined when in "Rasselas" he wrote of the Happy County.—BALTIMORE AMERICAN.

CHICAGO INTER-OCEAN
Issue of August 29, 1874

to reach, and General Custer has taken a great deal of trouble to have the observations thorough and accurate. From some of the higher peaks the topographer has had an opportunity to take a bird's eye view of almost the whole country around him; could follow the rivers with his glass from their source to their outlet, and see the course of nearly all the prominent ridges of hills. Inyan Kara gave a view of nearly the whole Western range; from the top of Harney's peak the eye can photograph the country within a radius of fifty miles or more, and when we reach Bear Butte, as we shall do in a few days, its heights will be another Pisgah for this promised land.

HARNEY'S PEAK?

I do not remember whether I have described Harney's Peak or not—but it is worth a second description, if it has received a first. Although the Indians told us that the Inyan Kara was the Queen of the Black Hills, the former is higher by 2,000 feet or more, and tops the whole cluster. It is long, steep, and rocky—one of the most imposing mountains I have ever seen, and it was well to call it after such a grand old soldier as General Harney. He was the first to penetrate this region, and probably did more toward taming and conciliating the Northwestern Indians than any other man. His treaties are the finest; his battles were the most decisive, and he had what few have, the reverence of the red man. "Bears Ears," the solemn old fellow who ran away from his tribe because another fellow married his sweetheart, and who cut his finger off and lived among his enemies till he had killed his rival and eaten his heart, has said frequently that there lived in the Black Hills a medicine man that beat all the medicine men he had ever seen. He was very tall, he said, and had white hair and a long beard, and he had whole mountains of beads and bracelets and other things which made the Indian's heart good. And when he talked, old Bears Ears said, his voice seemed to come from a great cavern, so loud and so deep were its tones, and

THE WIND STOPPED TO LISTEN,

and the brooks and the deer stood still in the forest till he had finished speaking. He lived near Harney's Peak, but where he made his habitation, whether in the heavens above or in the earth beneath, or in the waters under the earth, old Bears Ears didn't know. But he had seen him, and had heard him talk long ago, when he was a young man and lived with the Sioux, and had a bracelet—a coil of brass—that the old gray-bearded medicine man had given him in these same black hills. And the superstitious old soul didn't know that he was talking of a simple retired soldier, who was at that very moment farming in an humble way down in Missouri.

We have now nearly finished the exploration of this portion of the hills, and tomorrow will strike northward toward Bear Butte. The country grows wilder and more rugged as we go on, and doubts are expressed as to the possibility of passing it with a wagon train. Game of all kinds is very abundant—deer especially abounding—but bear and elk are frequently shot. General Custer and Colonel Ludlow, with Bloody Knife killed the first bear—a mammoth grizzly, and the artist photographed them sitting around their prey.

"One Stab," the old Sioux that was captured the other day, has been released, and has gone to his tribe. Nothing has yet resulted from our little episode, although we see frequent signs around us.[27]

Curtis.

27. As we expected the exciting news of the gold discoveries, published exclusively in the INTER-OCEAN yesterday morning, occasioned a great furor in the city. It was the chief topic of conversation in all quarters, and men in almost every station in life went to bed last night dreaming of nuggets of gold and treasures of untold value. An immense edition of the INTER-OCEAN was printed, but before night the supply was well nigh exhausted, and the demand was still kept up. Old mining experiences came into play once more, and every man who had spent a season in the gold diggings of California, or in other places, who listened to with rapt attention by eager crowds. One thing seemed to strike everybody as particularly important in this discovery, viz.: the diggings were "get-at-able." Paying dirt had been found outside of the rocks, where expensive machinery is required to prosecute the work. The poor man seemed to have as good a chance as the capitalist—a pan and a spade being all the implements needed to commence business. Examination may prove that quartz mining is still more remunerative; but if the careful investigation of the gentleman attached to General Custer's command is to be accepted, it may be set down as settled that even the most primitive mode of obtaining this metal will prove satisfactory and yield a most valuable return in the Black Hills.

We publish this morning interviews on this subject with a number of gentlemen whose experience in, or knowledge of, the region in question makes their opinions of more than ordinary value. We also give the difficulties in the way of emigration, so that all may see the possible drawbacks of an early settlement of the country.

We yesterday cautioned the would-be gold seekers against preinitate action in the matter, and we repeat the warning today. At the same time we can not but admit that the inducements to emigration are, or are likely to soon become, very strong indeed. The accessibility of the region, its proven fertility, its healthful climate, the existence of other valuable minerals, which alone would warrant the immediate settlement and development of the country—all combine too inspire us with the belief that the discoveries of General Custer are of immense importance, and that they will and ought to be taken advantage of at once.

There could hardly be a more fortunate event for the country than the confirmation of these reports, and proof that the anticipations of those making the discovery are to be fully realized. It would give occupation to thousands who, from the dull condition of business, and now without work, and would stimulate trade and enterprise in every direction.

General Sheridan, as in duty bound, has issued an order forbidding parties from going into the reservation, and of course any occupation of the territory will be technically illegal; but it is likely that the risk will be assumed, and that we shall soon hear of the results of practical mining there. If, as is likely, Congress shall make provision for the opening up of the country, and an examination proves it to be as rich as reported, a railway from the Missouri River, a distance of only 155 miles, will be speedily built, and Chicago placed in easy distance of this important section.

CHICAGO INTER-OCEAN
Issue of August 28, 1874

(Authors' Note: In 1874, because of telegraph delays and other communication difficulties, news dispatches from the field frequently reached newspaper offices out of order from the sequence in which they were originally written. To preserve the chronology of events, we have arranged the dispatches in the order of their writing, which means that some of the issue dates appearing at the top of pages and in the columns will be out of calendar order).

CHICAGO INTER-OCEAN
Issue of September 5, 1874

THE GOLD FIELDS.[28]

Our Correspondent Tells of the Last Days of the Custer Party's Journey Through the Black Hills.

Speculations and Hopes— "What Will the Effect Be!"— The Excitement That Must Come.

"Our Jolly Old Pedagogue"—A Peculiar Old Gentleman Whose Back Became Sore.

The Consequence of His "Disagreement with Sergeant Clair in Reference to the Points of the Compass."

What Resulted from a few Amateur Attempts at Prospecting—Gold in Every Gulch.

Who will Formulate a Theory on the Question of Indian Rights?

From our own Reporter

28. An INTER-OCEAN reporter last evening interviewing Captain Thomas H. Russell, of Sioux City, with a view to obtaining particulars respecting the

FIRST EXPEDITION TO THE BLACK HILLS

country, of which he takes charge. Captain Russell is an old frontiersman, and was originally attracted to Sioux City by the glowing accounts he heard of the richness of the territory I recently explored. He is evidently a man of acute judgment, and will doubtless prove of immense service to an expedition of this kind. The result of the interview was as follows:

Reporter—I understand, Captain Russell, you are forming an expedition to the Black Hills country?

Captain Russell—Yes, sir; the expedition is partially organized, and my business in Chicago is to lay before the public our prospects of success.

R.—Before touching on that point, I should like your opinion as the the value of the reports lately published with regard to the mineral wealth of the country.

Captain R.—In answering that I can simply reiterate the statements already published in the INTER-OCEAN. It has been common knowledge for years on the frontier that gold in unlimited quantities existed there. Indeed, the rumors which have at times come to my ears have convinced me that in point of wealth the country has

NO PARALLEL IN THE WORLD.

There is a startling uniformity in the various statements, which invests them with no ordinary degree of truth; the accounts vary in nothing but quantity, and the most gloomy account is of such a golden hue that there cannot be the least doubt about the matter. If any doubt did exist, it has been totally annihilated by the result of General Custer's expedition.

R.—How has the recent news been received along the frontier?

Captain R.—With great excitement. It has set the people almost crazy, and they are impatient for the expedition to start. Mr. Goewey, of Sioux City, who arrived in the city today, informs me that the excitement there is on the increase, and every preparation is being made for the start.

R.—But is there no danger of the government interposing and stopping the expedition?

Captain R.—No; and for this reason: The Black Hills is neutral ground, and is open to Sioux, Cheyennes, and the other tribes alike. It may be a reservation, but it belongs to no particular tribe. Why should it not be open to energetic Americans? Besides there is very good reason for believing that a large portion of the gold region lies outside the reservation, to which the government edict does not apply.

R.—Are not the miners, however, likely to have trouble with the Indians?

Capt. R.—I think, we need apprehend no trouble between them. The Indians do not settle there; they stay in their several reservations. It is possible we may be bothered with straggling hunting parties on our route out, but they will be deterred by our numbers from the

redskins. Indians will rather attack soldiers any time than determined immigrants. At all events, that has proved my experience during 16 years of frontier life.

R.—Then you anticipate no

GOVERNMENT INTERFERENCE

at all?

Capt. R.—Not in the least particular. They would never have sent General Custer to prove the existence of gold there unless they wanted miners to rush in and work up the country. Besides, how are they going to stop them? Miners would laugh at any edict to keep them out of the country like this. Depend upon it, my idea is correct. The expedition is sent for a set purpose. Money is scarce, and the country needs gold. The sequence is obvious. There was a crisis in 1848-9; California was opened and helped us out. There was a crisis in 1857; in 1858 Colorado was opened and helped us out. There was a crisis in 1873, from the effects of which we have not yet recovered; the Black Hills will be opened, and pull us through.

CHICAGO INTER-OCEAN
Issue of August 31, 1874

Special Telegram to the Inter-Ocean.

Sioux City, Iowa, Sept. 5—In recognition of General Sheridan's last arbitrary orders against encroachment by prospectors on the government reservations, the Collins-Russell Black Hills espedition, with headquarters in this city, and branches in Chicago and other leading cities, have postponed further efforts to enter the Hills until Government permission can be obtained.

CHICAGO INTER-OCEAN
Issue of September 7, 1874

CUSTER'S BLACK HILLS EXPEDITION, IN CAMP NEAR BEAR BUTTE, AUG. 15.

Last night six scouts, coffee-colored, robust fellows, full of Indian instinct and roast venison, bare as to their lower limbs, and crowned with tufts of hawks' feathers, left for Fort Lincoln with the tidings that we were homeward bound.[29] Their ponies had been given an allowance of grain that fairly startled them; their saddles had been lightened of that accumulation of personal property an Indian always carries with him, consisting of "ole clo's" he has picked up around the camp, and at the brooks where the soldiers have been bathing, the skins of animals he has killed and is taking home for Mrs. "Lo" to tan and make into moccasins, haunches of venison half eaten and strapped to the saddle-tree for a lunch by the way, and almost every conceivable article that a white man would not think of carrying. Their saddles were unloaded of these things—the saddles of the six scouts—they were given six days' rations of hard bread and bacon, coffee and dried beef, a blanket or two, and a canvas bag containing official dispatches to General Sheridan and newspaper news, and were sent off at sunset. I always feel a tender regard for these bare-legged fellows; and there always seems to be a tender vein of sympathy between them and me that the world never can appreciate; I write the news and they carry it; they are servants of the public as I am: they are the embodiment of the mail, telegraph, and courier systems combined and unified, but they ride as unconscious as dogs in the sun. Sending out news to the world always awakens the query as to

WHAT NEWS THE WORLD WOULD SEND,

it (sic) could send news to us. Almost two months now have passed without even a rumor as to what is going on in civilization, and we wonder what is the latest scandal, where was the latest fire, and whether we are going to have a war with Spain or not; who is dead, and who has risen to the surface of society, to be talked and

29. Sioux City, Iowa, Aug. 19.—A report comes from Fort Sully this evening that the Indians, to the number of 4,000 made an attack upon Custer's expedition on the 15th, and were repulsed with heavy loss. Custer's loss is reported at fifty killed and wounded. This report was brought into Fort Sully by a mail rider, who states that he met one of Custer's scouts above Grand River and got the news from him.
CHICAGO INTER-OCEAN
Issue of August 20, 1874

30. The Sioux must leave their hunting grounds in the Black Hills. Pleasant as be the pastures in which their children have sported, the slopes that hold the bones of their dead, they must leave them for the land of the stranger, and stand not upon the order of their going. There is gold in the hills and rivers of the region, and the white man desires to take possession of it. What, to the roaming Yankee, are the links that bind the red man, to the home of his fathers? He is but an episode in the advance of the Caucasian. He must decrease that the new comers may grow in wealth. Happy for him the day when the last of his tribes shall fold his blankets around his shrunken limbs, and take his final sleep, to waken in eyes of the Great Spirit. If the story of the Black Hills expeditionaries are true, the mineral wealth of the land is but a trifle compared with its vast agricultural resources. But the latter consideration draws emigration slowly. California today finds her riches in the productiveness of her soil, and makes comparatively small account of the gold that continues to be raised in her hills. Yet it was the gold that gave the impetus to her population, and covered the Pacific with white sails stretching out to her harbors, and the Western plains with the wagons of hardy emigrants. A similar fever has already begun to manifest itself at the West, in regard to the Black Hills. The newspapers in that section are filled with stories telling of the wealth that is in prospect, and giving information as to the best means of getting there. Adventurers are already on the alert for a start as soon as the troops have returned in safety. But it will be advisable to maintain all undue enthusiasm. Gold-digging is tough work for hardy laborers, and is usually sure death to man unaccustomed to tool with their hands.—NEW YORK COMMERCIAL ADVERTISER.
CHICAGO INTER-OCEAN
Issue of August 29, 1874

written of, since we came away. General Forsyth, and Colonel Grant and I talk over Chicago matters, and prognosticate as to the probable culmination of certain events which about the middle of June were casting their shadows before, and it gives us an immense amount of pleasure to place ourselves alongside of fate, and discuss, like a trio of deities, how we would have things in the world below transpire. We wonder if there is an excitement in Chicago over the gold discoveries; if we won't meet an expedition coming out here as we go in; and then we go to thinking that if the people believe what we have told of the gold. That there is lots of gold here we are positive—that it lies both in and out of the lines that bound the Sioux reservation, and that with the pressure which certainly must be brought to bear on Congress, the whole country must soon be opened up to settlers. What a rush there will be here then; what a flood of humanity will flow in, washing out the treasure trove of these beautiful hills. One almost can regret there is anything to tempt such men as usually get the gold fever; one thinks such a natural paradise as this should be set apart for poets, like William Cullen Bryant and Waldo Emerson, who

"Can communion hold
with nature."

But with such inducements as are here displayed, there will be a rush next spring, we think, that even the California and Pike's Peak excitement did not impel. But it will not last long, the area is not very large, and 5,000 men will soon clean these gulches dry; yet the first who come will go away rich. Others will move on out into Wyoming or Montana, or somewhere else; but some will remain here, I hope, to cultivate these valleys, to cut this timber, and quarry this glorious building stone.[30]

A BIRDSEYE VIEW OF THE BLACK HILLS.

I do not know whether I have given the readers of the INTER-OCEAN a clear idea of the country. Seeing so much, the panorama passing so rapidly, and the opportunities for sending letters so few and far between, I have been able to give but a glimpse of what we have had broadened out into grand glorious pictures. Let me express, briefly and simply, a birdseye view of the Black Hills: Take a position on Bear Butte and look southward; you can see fifty miles or more over a succession of ranges of hills and a succession if interlying valleys, cutting the surface into dimples, and wrinkles, and deep brown scars; let your mind's eye reach further, and add what you remember to have seen from Inyan Kara on the west and Harney's Peak on the east, the other two corners of a triangle that will cover the best portion of the Black Hills. Around Inyan Kara were long wide valleys, stretching into slopes and miniature prairies, with here and there a gypsum bed jutting out, white and clear, lest the eye should tire with the constant green. Around Harney's Peak, sharp, rugged scenery, steep granite mountains, and rocks that are as imposing as the mosques of the Bosphorus. Narrow, cosy valleys, full of flowers and as cool as grottoes; rushing, babbling streams, and miniature cascades, as if the little brooks of the hills were trying to ape the noiseness of the mountain torrents. And the whole cluster, this beauty spot on an almost barren, totally desolate prairie, embraced by the two arms of the Shyenne. (sic).

THE EXTENT OF THE HILLS.

The Black Hills do not cover an area much larger than one-half of Massachusetts. A line drawn directly through from north to south would not measure more than 100 miles; another line from east to west would be less than 80. The sides of that triangle I alluded do not measure more than forty miles; and the majority of the intervening territory is wooded hills. The best way of entering the Hills, if you ever want to go to the gold fields, my reader, is to come here, to Bear Butte, and follow Custer's trail. It took him a long time to find a way out, and it will take you longer to find a way in, if you attempt it in this region. Another entrance can be made at Inyan Kara, at the southwest, if you start from the Union Pacific Railroad, and you will find gold almost from the very start. Gypsum will come first, then mica,

then the velvet valleys with their golden lining. These two courses are the most feasible, but of course trails may possibly be made elsewhere. The extreme Southern ranges, the ranges of the east and northwest, are almost impassible because of the steep declivities and the abruptness of the foothills.

A CHANGE OF NAMES.

General Custer has decided upon a change of names for several of the prominent localities and landmarks in the hills. The beautiful spot now called "Custer Park" in his honor will change on the military map and in the official reports to "Agnes Park," in compliment to Miss Agnes Bates, of Monroe, Mich., a charming friend of his wife; "Custer Gulch," where the gold was found in the largest quantities, will appear as Golden Valley. Shadow Park will be hereafter known as "Libbie Park," in honor of Mrs. Custer, and Elk Creek Valley was christened "Genevieve Park" because Colonel Ludlow's wife bears the name of Wordsworth's lady love. These changes will not puzzle gold diggers if any should ever come to this place, for they can find the yellow dust most anywhere, and even more plenty than ever, when the valleys and parks and gulches bear such sacred names.

I picked out a high, dignified peak that I wanted named after the old Professor, but nobody seemed to take the suggestion. I want to tell a story of him.

OUR "JOLLY OLD PEDAGOGUE"

"Good morning, Professor."

"Good morning, sir," replied he —one of the best natured, most benevolent old pedagogues that ever mouthed a sentence. "How is Mr. Curtis this morning? You look as bright as a dollar."

"Inwardly so, Professor, if not outwardly, thank you. How do you feel yourself?"

"A little fatigued from my long ride yesterday, but still qualified, I think, to meet all the requirements of the occasion. I was pondering this morning upon various subjects, and my train of thought was led into a channel which has become quite familiar to my meditations recently—that of thankfulness, or of congratulation. I may

be allowed to say—that I was permitted to accompany this reconnoissance. I have been recompensed triple fold, yea more, for all the hardship and exposure that had attended it."

"Then your back is better," I suggested, "those lumbar vertebrae were not dislocated after all?"

"Dislocated is an erroneous term in that connection, Mr. Curtis, if you will pardon my correction. Physiologically speaking, a dislocation of the lumbar vertebrae would be fatal, but if you refer to the complaints I have previously made, I am thankful to be able to say that my system is in excellent condition once more, and I think I am improving physically rather than otherwise under this vigorous campaign life."

"Thank you Professor"—and a half suppressed smile passed over the faces of our companions as we rode through the last valley of the Black Hills. However much enjoyment the Professor has obtained from our tent and saddle life, he has afforded his associates an infinite amount of pleasure. While his peculiarities and whims are tolerated and respected everywhere, his simple-minded enthusiasm over everything that is new and beautiful in his experience and his sublime ingenuousness have made him very popular among the officers and men, and a source of amusement a hundred blase wits could not have supplied. He is as near like that "Jolly Old Pedagogue" whom George Arnold immortalized as could be imagined:

"—His face was wrinkled, his gait was slow
But a wonderful twinkle shone in his eye,
And he sang every night as he went to bed,
Let us be happy down here below,
The living need happiness more than the dead
Said the jolly old pedagogue, long ago.
"He taught his scholars the rule of three.
Reading and writing, and history too,
And took the little ones up on his knee,
For a kind old heart in his breast had he,
And the wants of the littlest child he knew.

Illingworth recorded three views at the head of Golden Valley, east of Custer. This is a long shot. The "permanent camp" proved to be a great convenience to him, and it was here that he took the greatest number of pictures. In this view, the valley tends to be darker and more shaded than the granite mountains, which are abundantly illuminated by the sun. This exposure strikes a near perfect balance between the two elements whereas in the view of the facing page, the valley is properly exposed but the mountain in the background is light, or overexposed. In the third and final view on the following page, the valley is darker, because Illingworth underexposed the plate in order to allow the right amount of light to "bring in" the mountain.

"The rod was scarcely known
   in his school,
For whipping to him was a
   barbarous rule,
And too hard work for his
   poor old bones,
Beside, it was painful he
   sometimes said,
We must make life happy
   down here below
The living need charity more
   than the dead,
Said the jolly o ld pedagogue,
   long ago."
I wish I could give you

A PHOTOGRAPH OF THE OLD PROFESSOR

of his portly person, his comfort-able coat and vest, the large canvas patch on the baggy part of his pedagogical pantaloons, and his respectable straw hat with the vast pasteboard awning his ingenuity suggested, his mechanical skill created, and a few stitches of black thread attached to the brim. I wish I could metamorphose into language that "wonderful twinkle" that illuminates the little of his face which his long gray beard and heavy curling eyebrows do not cover—he has Deacon Bross' eye-brows and a little more than Dea-con Bross' beard—and I wish I could import Dobbin, the Profes-sor's reliable war horse, bodily into these columns, that my readers might see an "outfit" which we laugh at, but cannot revere. If I were an artist I would sketch the Professor for the benefit of those who love George Arnold's poem and for those who love good old men. I would sketch him as he is frequently seen, bent almost double in the ardor of scientific investiga-tion, the patch on his pantaloons exposed to the sun, gripping Dob-bin's bridle in one hand and whack-ing patiently at an obstinate relic of the palezoic age with his ham-mer in the other. For

THE PROFESSOR HAS NO-WHERE A COUNTERPART.

I had sought the old gentleman

to hear from him the story of his experience on the previous day, which, I was told, was interesting. He had been wishing, ever since we entered the game country, to shoot a deer, so that he might carry home a pair of horns and a hide perforated by his own bullet as a trophy, and, fearing he should soon lose the opportunity, had been out the day before with a hunting party under Sergeant Clair, of the color-guard, and I asked him—

"How did you get along yesterday, Professor? I understand you were lost."

"Yes," he replied, deliberately; "I experienced some very disagreeable sensations yesterday, and, having reflected upon them, I have resolved hereafter never to stray away from the main column, or at the most, I shall keep within the line of flankers."

"What was the trouble?" Colonel Grant asked, while the profane young man to whom I have before alluded inquired—

"What in h__l did you pike out for, anyway, old man; why d__n your old buttons didn't you know those Indians would tumble to you a d__n sight sooner than to anybody else in this outfit. Why _____ _____ me if they wouldn't rather have your old scalp tackled to their belly-strap than a hundred others."

"I must protest against your profanity, my young friend," answered the Professor, "but I confess I was somewhat imprudent. The circumstances were these: I had gone with Sergeant Clair and an escort of two men from the headquarter detail on a hunting expedition, in hopes of being able to secure a shot at a deer, and we had been out several hours without my having that privilege, although several had been killed by others of the party, when I began to thing it was time for us to return to the command. My suggestion was agreed to by my companions, but I disagreed with Sergeant Clair in reference to the points of the compass, and a dispute (for which I subsequently apologized) resulted. Both of us were positive in our opinions and we separated, I going alone in the direction I supposed the train to be.

THE OLD GENTLEMAN'S DILEMMA.

For some hours I wandered around among the hills, passing over a portion of the country which seemed to have suffered from a terrible blight, perhaps the fire fiend, for the vegetation was for the most part destroyed and the ground which I traversed was covered with fallen and half-burned timber — a disagreeable place to travel in whether on foot, or mounted as I was—till I became completely bewildered, and began to realize that my situation was one fraught with personal danger. I knew there were prowling bands of Indians about, and remembered General Custer's warning in reference to exposing ourselves to their attacks. I am no fighting man, neither am I any skirmisher, and I was in a state of indecision in regard to what course I should pursue in case I were attacked. I had heard that the conventional courtesies of warfare were not recognized by the Indians, and that if I were taken I might be exposed to the horrible tortures of which I have read, and which I consider

South Dakota State Historical Society

Correspondent William E. Curtis of the CHICAGO INTER OCEAN had a lyrical touch to his writing with which he seemed to capture in words what Illingworth recorded on film. In describing the Black Hills, he said, ". . . sharp rugged scenery, steep granite mountains, and rocks that are as imposing as the mosques of the Bosphorus. Narrow, cosy valleys, full of flowers and cool as grottoes; rushing, babbling streams, and minature cascades, as if the little brooks of the hills were trying to ape the noisiness of the mountain torrents."

even worse than death itself; so after a few moments' consideration I resolved to sell my life as dearly as possible, and surrender only with death. I took the revolver that Quartermaster Dandy, through Colonel Ludlow, had kindly loaned me from his holster, and examining it, to be sure that it was properly charged, placed it in my bosom, and rode on, keeping a sharp survey in all directions lest any person should approach me unawares. I wandered on for some time, utterly confused, till I came upon a trail which I knew at once was that of our train. My heart gave a throb of joy at finding myself where I knew my comrades had been, and I dismounted to see in which direction it led. After a close examination I was unable to decide satisfactorily to my own mind, but the indications seemed to point more in one direction than in the other, and I followed that, considerably faster than I had previously traveled. Much to my surprise, after several miles, it led me into your camp of the previous day—where the bear was killed, you remember, and although realizing that I had wasted much precious time and had traveled several unnecessary miles which I must retrace, I can assure you I was heartily grateful at being sure of my situation. I took a few moments' rest, then remounted "Dobbin" and rode as rapidly as was consistent with comfort along the trail. I finally came in sight of the rear guard, and it would be difficult to express fully the relief which I felt. As I remarked I shall not again stray away."

OUR LAST DAYS IN THE HILLS.

This was our last day in the Black Hills. Occasionally as we reached the summit of one of the border peaks we could see stretching away like an ocean, miles and miles beyond us, to where the brown earth and the blue sky seemed to meet, the hot, dry plains, that for days thereafter were to be our marching ground, and with much regret did we think of leaving the cool, shady valleys and fresh water for the hot and dusty prairies and alkali. The eastern and northern ranges of the hills are quite as beautiful, and fully as rich in every way as the other

parts, and will be, perhaps, more available for settlers when they are permitted to enter it, as the valleys are wider, the hills are generally lower and less abrupt, and the general face of the country more adaptable to agriculture. Frequently the valleys widen out into broad, level parks, large enough for a vegetable farm, and as fertile as a Rhode Island garden, which one could see in his mind's eye, laid out according to the rules and regulations of market men, "into all the luxuries of the season." It cannot be long before these imaginery pictures are realized; the future does not stretch far forward before it reaches the settlement and improvement of this oasis of the Dakota plains.

The miners continued their prospecting as we passed northward from Harney's Peak, and several times

FOUND THE COLOR OF GOLD,

but never succeeded in getting the metal. They claim that it is there that the belt stretches southeastward, and that their test was insufficient, as is no doubt the case, being hastily and hurriedly made. Frequent indications of iron were found, and large gypsum beds, like those that lie to the west of Inyan Kara. The deposits are pure and easily available, but unfortunately the demand for the substance is not sufficient to call for its mining. It is the gold, if anything, and the beautiful hills and valleys that will bring people to the Black Hills.

Those who are familiar with the Indian reports of the country claim that we have not seen the richest portion, that west of where we are now camped, in that district which lies between Bear Butte, and the southward bend of the Belle Fourche, which we have "straddled," to use a vulgar phrase, lie the treasures of which the Indian is so jealous; that the theme of all the fabulous stories are located, and that all the gold nuggets that Dame Rumor ever heard of were picked up where we have not been. But General Custer found the country impassable for his train, and led his train through that portion of the hills, although extremely difficult, was most easy to enter, and as his time was limited, the exploration of this El Dorado must be left for another

year. Already the expedition has done

MORE THAN WAS EVEN HOPED

of it by the most sanguine; more, even, than General Custer himself, who has never learned the use of the word failure, expected, and its direct results will be of great value on many accounts. The topography of Southwestern Dakota, Southeastern Montana, and the northeastern corner of Wyoming has been secured by the engineer corps to a degree of accuracy that is unusual; the course of all the streams has been determined, and all the progression of mineralogy, zoology, and botany has been applied to the investigation of a part of the country that was hitherto totally unknown, with a result that will be valuable as long as the star of empire westward keeps its way. The fact that gold and other mineral deposits exist here has been verified, and still further, the fertility of the soil and the healthful fragrance of the atmosphere has been found to equal any locality on Uncle Sam's farm. And from all the indications we have seen, it does not appear that the Indian need be jealous of this portion of his titled estate, nor will it be robbing him to deprive him of it. We have found no settlements in the Black Hills. All we have seen have been hunting parties for the Missouri agencies, who came up here for a little summer sport. There are few traces to show that they make this their home any portion of the year, or ever did, and the only temptation to draw them are the herds of elk and deer, which a few years of active hunting would exterminate. They cannot mine the gold or iron; the timber does them no good, and they will never make any use of the rich soil that has been waiting centuries to be utilized. But I am meddling with a question it is not my province to discuss. I will state the facts, and let other people formulate the theories. The great fact here is: one of the most valuable landscapes on the continent fenced in from all civilization— one of the richest storehouses ever filled with the gifts of the Almighty locked and barred by human legislation from those for whom it was meant. Wanted— A theory.   Curtis.

South Dakota State Historical Society

For his last exposure of this series of three, or perhaps it was the first, depending upon the sequence in which he shot them, Illingworth moved in for a closeup view of the end of Golden Valley. It was from this pleasant and comfortable setting that one of Custer's scouts, Charley Reynolds, left on August 3rd, with mail and dispatches for a hazardous 150 mile ride to Ft. Laramie, Wyoming. Reynolds made the journey successfully and one of the end results was that newspaper headlines across the land read, "GOLD."

CHICAGO INTER-OCEAN
Issue of September 1, 1874

THE BLACK HILLS.

Safe Arrival of the Custer Expedition at Fort Abraham Lincoln.

The Command in Excellent Condition to Take the Field at a Moment's Notice.

General Custer "Indorses Everything the 'Inter-Ocean' has Published."

A Consise but Comprehensive Report of the Gold Discoveries.

Silver, Lead, Galena, Plumbago, Iron, and Gypsum Found in Inexhaustible Quantities.

Our Own Correspondent Sends Additional and Exciting News.

Another Interview with Mr. Charles Collins of Sioux City, Iowa.

Better than Gold—He maintains that a Rich Quicksilver Mine Lies Hidden in the Black Hills.

No question but the Flush times of California are to be Repeated Nearer Home.

THE EXCITED WEST.

Special Telegram from Our Own Reporter

FORT ABRAHAM LINCOLN, VIA BISMARCK, D. T., AUG. 31.

The Black Hills expedition under command of General Custer arrived here this evening at sunset, having been absent about sixty days, and having traveled nearly 1,200 miles. The exploration of the hills was completed about the 17th of August, when the command left Bear Butte at the northern range of the hills, traveling northward at a remarkably rapid rate. The march was a very hard and exhaustive one, but was endured with wonderful fortitude.

THE RESULTS OF THE EXPEDITION

are even greater than had been hoped by its projectors, and the discovery of gold, alone is sufficient to recompense the government for the outlay. No serious difficulty was experienced from Indians interfering, and the command was unusually healthy during the entire reconnoissance, four men only being lost by death. The command is now in camp at Fort Lincoln, but will return to their various posts along the Missouri during the next few days.

The Black Hills expedition which arrived here last evening has

GONE INTO CAMP

temporarily, General Forsyth, Colonel Grant, and others from Chicago leaving this afternoon for their homes. Everybody was delighted with the trip, and the results are so satisfactory as to leave no cause for regret. The gold discoveries have awakened an interest second only to the great California excitement of '49, and parties on the frontier are already thinking of starting out as soon as an expedition can be formed and equipped. General Custer found on his arrival home hundreds of letters of inquiry from all parts of the country, and several persons of prominence concerning the results of the prospecting, and he gave me authority today to express

HIS INDORSEMENT (sic) OF EVERYTHING THE "INTER-OCEAN" HAS PUBLISHED

in reference to the matter. The fact that gold is there, he remarked, is certain as the law of gravity, and the fact of the discoveries were not carried to an extent greater than they were was owing to the brief time allowed the expedition. At a dozen or more different places gold was found. At one place in particular, Custer's Park, of which I have written, it yielded in paying quantities from the grass roots, down. A shaft eight feet deep was sunk several feet from the bed of a creek, and the excavations panned by hundreds of persons who had no experience and no tools except what their ingenuity suggested, and in no case did the color fail to appear, and frequently a generous amount would be gathered and carried off. Several pans yielded dust

ESTIMATED ABOVE A DOLLAR.

Practical miners who superintended the work declare that had the bedrock of the creek been reached the yield must have been marvelous, but although the greater part of the night was spent in digging, the place had to be left

in the morning for other parties to finish. Gold bearing quartz was found in perfect mountain piles, but we had no means of blasting, and whatever the rocks contained in their bosoms could not be reached. Several specimens of quartz gold, however, were obtained. General Custer is asked in the letters referred to whether the government will protect or assist the entrance of parties to the Black Hills. He wishes me to say that while he has no policy to dictate to the government in regard to the Indian treaties, he considers that the time has come when it must be decided whether the

DOG-IN-THE MANGER MODE

of the Indians will be tolerated. In his report he will express the opinion that the argricultural and mineral resources of the Black Hills are unsurpassed in the United States, and will advise an immediate decision upon the question of occupancy. General Forsyth, of General Sheridan's staff, coincides entirely with General Custer's opinion in regard to the Indian question; and, as to the gold, says he has himself seen evidence enough to convince him that the country within the Black Hills is as rich minerally as any portion of Montana or Colorado.

General Custer has been appointed Commander of the Division of Dakota, including a large portion of the Northwestern frontier, with headquarters at Fort Abraham Lincoln.[31]

Curtis.

31. The Chicago TRIBUNE has been a little behind in getting news from Custer's expedition, and has therefore taken no stock in the enthusiastic accounts of the prevalence of gold in the Black Hills, but it now backs water and says editorially:

Our correspondent confirms the reports of the wonders developed in the new country, which, he says, appears to be not only an Eldorado but a Paradise. As to the discovery of gold in large quantities there seems to be a little doubt. The deposits are fairly rich. This being the case, the government cannot too soon recognize the fact that there are not troops enough in the Northwest to give force to the order of General Sheridan, forbidding the invasion of the reservation. And as the government will be itself responsible in a measure for the gold-fever which is on the point of breaking out, its plain duty is to make immediate arrangements for the safety and indemnification of the Indians, who will inevitably be driven from the ground.

CHICAGO INTER-OCEAN
Issue of September 3, 1874

CHICAGO INTER-OCEAN
Issue of September 8, 1874

CUSTER'S ANABASIS.

How the Black Hills Expedition Came Home from Bear Butte.

The Resources of Indian Warfare—Sitting Bull Burns the Grass and Poisons the Water.

General Custer's Command Have a Hard March in Consequence—Incidents by the Way.

A Description of Indian Habits—The Capacity of a Word—Gold Excitement on the Frontier.

From our own reporter.

FORT ABRAHAM LINCOLN, D.T., AUG. 31.

The Black Hills expedition is a fact of history. Tonight the last "taps" will be sounded, and tomorrow the Seventh Cavalry will go from tents to barracks; from campaign to quarters; from marching to the idle routine of post life. Last night, just as the sun was setting, the pickets on the hills around Fort Lincoln reported a cloud of dust rising like smoke from the plains far away to the south. It is a herd of buffalo, perhaps, some one suggested; no, the buffalo have left the Missouri Valley forever. Perhaps a band of Indians, said another, and Colonel Poland sent an orderly to the different commandants to be ready for action. Perhaps the expedition returning—and the hearts of twenty women leaped for joy, and they rushed to the overhanging hills. Colonel Poland sat in his office at headquarters discussing, with Quartermaster Dandy, the probability of a return, and answering the anxious questions that came thronging in, when a breathless picket on a foaming horse rode down and said, with a salute:

"General Custer's colors, sir, bearing this way from the West."

"My horse!" shouted the colonel, and in a moment he was riding out to meet the campaigners. The ladies and children of the post ran frantically toward the direction the picket had mentioned, and when the command reached the out-skirting rifle pits, around the fort, they were met with an enthusiastic

"WELCOME HOME"

The band was playing "Garryowen"—the song of "Ours"—hurrying the quickstep upon the smooth, sweet echoes of "Home, Sweet Home;" the officers of the whole command formed a rusty, ragged, sun-bronzed, unshaven phalanx around the General, and tossed their campaign hats at their wives and babies as they rode along. The horses saw the stable and grain bins across the parade, and caught the inspiration of the moment, and the mules of the wagon trains lifted up their voices and wept for joy. It was a picture of the past repeated; a picture that every town and city in the Northern States saw in '64 and '65—the return of the boys in blue. Ask an old soldier the ideal of momentary joy, and he will answer, the return from a campaign. It was a curious pleasure to look along among the faces that lined the road side, to catch the expressions that played upon them. Some were anxious; in some eyes there was a painful longing that "something might not be so;" some were beaming with a happiness that was scarcely realized—they had seen the bronzed, bearded face they were waiting for; others were all expectation, confident, yet unsatisfied. As the General reached the gate he leaped from his horse, and it took just two jumps of those Custerian legs to clear twenty feet of door yard. The adjutant led the column to cavalry quarters, and the sergeant trumpeter sounded the retreat. It took less time to unsaddle, and stable those thousand horses than it ever took before—and such an after scene. Such hugging and kissing, and shaking of hands as has not been seen since—since the same regiment returned from their summer campaign one year ago. The expedition had been absent sixty-one days; had marched 1,080 miles, and had seen a country that white men had never saw before. The summer's work had been successful; the pleasure so unusally rare, and the general health and condition of the command so remarkably perfect that there was

REASON FOR CONGRATULATION ALL AROUND.

The march from Bear Butte northward was a very hard one;

more severe and exhausting than those old campaigners had ever known, yet only one man had died from exhaustion during the fourteen days, and Captain Smith had performed the startling, unheardof single act of Quartermasterial ability, of bringing home every wagon that he took away. The trail was marked with dead mules and horses, exhausted by overwork or empty stomachs, but the management of this portion of the expedition was so perfect that there has been no loss of stores or transportation. To look after rum is difficult; to deal out rations for an army of hungry campaigners is something that few people are fit to do. Imagine a man with 1,800 boarders on his hands, and then a livery stable of 1,000 horses and more than as many mules, with a clumsy wagon to every six of the latter. And Quartermaster Smith brought everybody home good-natured. True, he lost some of his stock, but as they say on tombstones, his loss with their gain, for the horse or mule heaven must be happier far than a prairie without grass or water, and only three and a half pounds of corn a day.

AN EPISODE ON THE MARCH.

From the Belle Fourche, which washes the foot of the Black Hills, to Fort Lincoln the grass had been burned entirely away, the water was very scarce, for the creeks were dry, and what little remained in the pools was unsafe to drink, for we did not know but it had been poisoned.

The day we reached Belle Fourche "War Eagle," a bright-eyed, handsome little scout came galloping to the General, and told him there were three or four horsemen riding far away to the north of us. The General sent Bloody Knife, Cold Hand, and his informant to meet them, and away they dashed, crazy for a recontre (sic). To civilized people the methods and customs of Indian warfare are very curious. We had little opportunity to see an exhibition, but occasionally our scouts had a chance to strip themselves to their fighting weight, and put on their war paint—and this was one.

THE WAR COSTUME OF THE INDIAN

consists mostly of moccasins and

This view and the one similar to it on the facing page were both recorded by Illingworth while Custer camped along French Creek. By slightly underexposing the wet plate, Illingworth was able to capture the mountains in the background, but this caused the foreground to darken, compared to the picture on the facing page. Sophisticated accouterments such as filters had not yet made their way into the then primitive science of photography.

feathers—the former at one, and the latter at the other extremity, with very little to speak of between, except streaks of red paint upon the chest, the ribs, and around the limbs, and a warrior can make his battle toilet on the full gallop as easily as a city belle can prepare for a party with a hair-dresser, a maid, and a dozen mirrors. Firstly, he lashes his horse to the length of his speed, with a stinging little cat-o'-nine tail he carries, then, guiding the animal with his knees, he commences to "peel." As fast as he removes the superflous clothing, he hangs it on his saddle, somehow, somewhere, unknown to the civilized mind, unbraids his hair, and throws it back upon his shoulders, gathering a few of the

front locks in what the ladies call a Grecian coil above his forehead, in which he places a cluster of painted feathers. Then, taking a little buckskin bag from some mysterious place, he dashes a coat of vermillion over his face, arms, chest, sides, and limbs, till he looks like a tattoed Sena-gambian—and he is ready.

APPROACHING AN ENEMY

for a battle. And did you ever see them approach an enemy? On the plains, where the ground is perfectly level for miles, they do it in a zigzag course; when the prairie is rolling, they dash through the valleys and up the hills till they reach the top, then dismounting and catching the lariat that always drags from their

pony's bridle, they creep cautiously up the hill, bending lower and lower as they near the top, and at last falling on their stomachs draw themselves like a serpent under the cover of a tuft of grass or shrub, and lie there till they have seen all there is to see, measured all the distances, and instinctively caught the intentions of their foes. Returning to their pony, they ride around, not over, the summit of the hill. This is the way Bloody Knife and his companions went after the strange horsemen. Their orders had been to talk with and not to fight them—but they couldn't help putting on their war paint, and they approach all strangers as they approach a foe. Coming in sight of the party they commenced to ride in a circle—a

In one of his field dispatches, which appeared in the CHICAGO INTER OCEAN, Custer, writing of the Black Hills, said, "In no portion of the United States, not exceeding the famous Blue Grass region of Kentucky, have I ever seen grazing superior to that found growing wild here in this hitherto unknown region." He went on to say, "The soil is that of a rich garden, and composed of a dark mould of exceedingly fine grain."

sign of peaceful intentions and an invitation to a conference. The strangers responded, and the two parties met. They were three Sioux warriors. In one of them "Cold Hand" recognized a nephew, fortunately, and because of this relationship we got more information than we could have otherwise.

WHAT SITTING BULL WAS DOING.

The strangers told our scouts six bands of Sioux were waiting for us in Prospect Valley; near the Little Missouri River—nearly 2,444 lodges, making something more than 6,000 warriors, General Custer calculated. They told them the grass had been burned so that our horses would have no grazing, and the water had been poisoned

so that we could have nothing to drink. They had been with the war party, but they got disgusted, and were on their way back to the agencies. In return for this really valuable information, Bloody Knife told them startling stories about the size of General Custer's command—larger, even, he said it was, than the Sioux party; with an infinite amount of thunder-iron, as they call artillery.

The Indians have a terrible fear of artillery. In fighting they depend quite as much upon their throats as their guns. Whooping makes their hearts bold they say, and if any one ever saw or rather heard an Indian battle he has a very clear idea of what the demons of the inferno are. But the "thunder-iron" can make more noise

than they, and it paralyzes them. Perhaps we are indebted to Bloody Knife's imagination for an uninterrupted march homeward, although the grass was burned all the way, and we had to seek river bottoms and the rushes that grew there for grazing, and running water to drink. Because of this General Custer had to make very long marches, averaging thirty-three miles a day for fourteen days, and at times the suffering of the animals and men was terrible. If anything will take the spirit out of a man it is a few days' experience like that we endured, and a large portion of the march was through those awful "bad lands." I have described them I believe, in a previous letter, but old General Sully expressed a volume of description in a few words when he compared them to "hell with the fires put out." It was

A TEST OF PHYSICAL AND MORAL ENDURANCE

such as few in life are called upon to bear. Even the good old Professor became humanized, and rode along on a yellow mule—for "Dobbin" had given out under the heat and burden of the day—and forgot to theorize and moralize and get enthusiastic over agates and petrified stumps. He called his mule "Patience," most appropriately, and said the swinging of "Patience's" ears as she trotted along reminded him of the wings of angels, and quoted poetry from authors no one had ever heard of before, appropos to the case. Said the Professor one day, as we rode along under the burning sun, tired, dusty and as thirsty as camels,

"I hope the throne of dullness is not vacant now, for I fear my friends might select me to fill it."

And the old gentleman was fond of quoting on very hot days those familiar and sonorous lines:
"Oh! for a lodge in some
  vast wilderness—
A boundless of contiguity
  of shade."

And when he came into camp at night, refreshed and rested, he used to put a camp-stool under the large canvas patch on his pantaloons, and remark from Willis,
"—And Abraham sat at the
  door of his tent
In the cool of the day."

General Forsyth, the ideal soldier that he is, rode along at the head of his column, as easily, as graciously, and, to all appearances, as comfortably as if he were sitting in the elegant headquarters of the Department of the Missouri, and looking out onto Washington street. Colonel Tilford would talk of that case of wine he was going to send for to Chicago, and if the day was very hot and the march very long, he would conclude to send for a barrel of whisky. Colonel Grant took it easily, but talked a great deal about the cool corridors of the Palmer House. General Custer is invulnerable to all the ills that other men are heirs to. He shot as many antelope and deer, he rode as far, and was as active, and dashing when the air was full of alkaline and the ther-

mometer 120 as he did when the grass was green and fresh and a breeze blowing a temperature that invigorated rather than enervated other men.

NOTHING REMARKABLE OCCURRED

on the homeward march. We were not attacked, and saw no Indians, although occasionally signs were visible. The course homeward was along the valley of the Little Missouri River northward to the Heart River, where the surveyed route of the Northern Pacific Railroad was overtaken, and followed eastward to Fort Lincoln. Every person in the command joins in one opinion that the expedition was the most delightful of any in which they ever took part. Although there were hardships, they are soon forgotten in the overwhelming enjoyment that was our general experience. Expressive of the universal opinion, I give an extract from a curious manuscript which has come into my possession, said to be an account of the expedition. The author is the petite band master of the Seventh Cavalry, and his knowledge of the English language has entirely been acquired since his return from a life-long visit in sunny Italy. I give it as it came to me. Its uniqueness has not been marred by a single pencil stroke. The reader can translate as much as he desires.

A SINGULAR SPECIMEN.

THE BLACK HILLS
PLEASANT EXCURTION,
BY 7TH U. S. CAVALRY,
COMANDET BY
GENERAL A. G. CUSTER
FORT AM. LINCOLN, D. T.,
1874.

It is very singolar to know that the Indians in thes yors, add ded leafth is reservation, and we told schore to met and citenzen was spoking about it, and som person was wery afred to ave larg trouble, becos we know very well hu is mester Indians, few nomth befor these try to steel 90 muls, but General Custer cary dem ferfuly, ontil som of those liff at to loss is on pony, wech one of the soldiers did captured the pony, and it is very good pony. I sopos is one of the best of all woth the Indians ther can rase.

I am requested to writhe oll woth consist in the Expedition by reason wy—I never tole no fols story. I only tole one, and is yost begining forty yars go, and is not corectudet yet bu hu know me dos trust wery Esey my words. I will try to Explin oll woth I cand, but it wery dificoltus for me, becos I dont writte moch ingles, the amateur of the Fors, peraps hi will Exusme in my mistakes, it is quite on anoigs story to tole all wath I see and wath it was occored on thes expedition but I well Breviet the story, for not anoing the amateur, the News Paper, hi con ave everyting by diferent mans, but I well yost tole the coreck and scort Report. we know is diferent writhers veek there lik ilustrat more and tole more wath realy it is. I gost past remark over all the trut, and comicaly nea I well related. I becos I am not a serios Ristocrats. But a comen Bock Private of the 7th U. S. Cavlry we know the soldiers as no brains mither comon sence, but the Ristocracy, sence wen the git brein or coin sence? were the gidet? Som of them are wery Brave in the pie time, wen hare in the setlors shop after wisky, but wen is business of wore, there pod is own tall dawn and no more noting to sead.

in the begenings of thes I dea, it was gost to see wath quality of contry and clima, becous the Indians ded represent great dificolty, in fact it was litle dificolty to go into, but General A. C. Custer hi tok the pleasure to entering in the enterior of the Blak Heels, wed out seing a Indians, in the wery first camp we alt, it was pleasant preiry, but Dray—the second camp it was wery moch beter ded Rein litle, gost and of to ave a good day travling, the terd camp, we begin to see wery beautiful grass and wather, the forth camp, a genuin honting grounds, it was wery moch ghems, but this gems it was noting else than grashoper, tru and fact, by the fifth camp, anoter wery good trawling prejery, fool of fruits, wech l was astonish to see somat but wath quality of fruits? Kakter over Kackter, week my Hors hi cod not wolk no more, I ad to desmont—every second and pick the Kackturs ove, I had wery moch trouble, but my Snoider hi di cam alon wery well, the sewent camp,

Although he had praise for the grass in Golden Valley, along French Creek, Custer was not totally pre-occupied with the pastoral aspects of the Black Hills. He did not hesistate to mention that his expedition had discovered gold. Custer had an interesting affectation in his writing style of feigning modesty or understatement and then casually dropping a literal bombshell. Such was the case in one of his field dispatches, published in the CHICAGO INTER OCEAN, where he wrote, "I omit all present reference to the portion of our explorations (for minerals) until the return of the expedition except to state what will appear in any event in public prints, that gold has been found at several places; and it is believed by those who are giving their attention to this subject that it will be found in paying quantities. I have upon my table forty or fifty small particles of pure gold, in size averaging a small pin-head, and most of it obtained today from one panful of earth."

litle wather and nod anof for the comand—the wiew of these preiry is plended and maganificent, also we cam acros few rivers, wetch we meth exelent wather, Sam time General Custer hi yuse Hant ewry days, and hi givs most is antilops to the Band—etcl, thes preiry it was all burnt bay Wolcanos—and before the fiars, it was a sea, weth smol (isola or isand) is wery comical scenering tru the preiry, but the beaty is on the bad Lanz, wech a man hi can see hau the fier it was burning and wath beatiful Heels hi leftn, thes Bad Lan contein burnt Coal, and Lava, etc.—

is no presietet ston mothver—all the rocks are burst and Derokated, and the soil is asches, and Red Kleys—thes Read Kley is Bakt by the it of the wokaney, after the bad lan, we Cros few more rivers very smol body of wottere, and are wery well Ruined by Reins and winds. no trouble to cosing. in ol outfet dont want a plea of tobako. I was realy desgosted, and so on, but more fhater is comicaly—I dont know mooch about of golds or silver, but seems to me is wery pover preiry—after som mor nockin, I understond from the Indian Interpret it is a grant Cave, wich

is cooled the Sle ivr Cave, in scort time we carrys wery close to—and oll the Soldiers went to Examin that Cave—the Cave is betwin a rovine and a bloff—the Entrance is probobly twenty foots af and Broad about gos the sam—gos daun by degres, and deminisching ontile beom a olls lik a Bakary fornaces—is no biuty in dat, but, it was representet a grand cave, were the indians uzo kip a withe man lleive for some time go.

* * *

the name of General Custer macke stand the Indians owe, and that little German Baud its is name for been so good and able to stand that fith of Beg Horns Deil 1873—that it was buly—and wery well don— the 7th U. S. Cavalry is a buly Reggt if is one. We can stand all consequences, and newes baking about. eneau wee are back in good prosperety and good health—the Expedition is noting more than a splendid summer Excortion of the beautiful Black Heels—of for General Custer.

Yurs, Respectful Servant

FELIX VINATERRI

Leader of 7th U.S.C. Band
Fort A. Lincoln, D.T.

———

my little Snider is Comback at Home all rithe

THE CAPACITY OF A WORD.

"My fellow contributor, the reader will see, if he has read the extract carefully, has made use of the word "Outfit" or "hout-feet" as he spells it. On that word in the frontier vocabulary hangs all the law and the prophets. It means a pair of shoes, a razor, a basket of chips, or a winter's supply of provisions. The little Italian was telling me his theory of the bad lands, and remarked that a "wolcano had busted, and blowed up the whole houtfeet up." A veterinary (sic) surgeon speaking of his little Italian's English vocabulary, and his use of the word beautiful, especially, said he meant to say a stone was a beauty, and got it "a beautiful"—he used "the whole outfit" remarked the Doctor. A fellow looks at your bootos, and wants to know where you got that "outfit," and again admiring the way a pack mule is laden, will call it a bloody good outfit. The word covers everything. If one want to speak of something, the name of which he does not remember, he calls it an "outfit." The expression is as useful as "whats-his-name," or "thing-um-bob."

THE GOLD EXCITEMENT.

Everybody at Fort Lincoln and Bismarck—the lively little frontier town over the Missouri where the Northern Pacific Railroad ends, is crazy over the gold discoveries. We haven't been in twelve hours yet, and the people

are already talking about another expedition. We wonder if it is so in the States. We wonder if wheat is low in the Chicago market, and if they are talking Black Hills gold on the Board of Trade. We have heard of the fire, and the Tilton-Beecher scandal, but nobody has told us that Chicago has the gold fever, although it does seem that Chicago should have the first of that Black Hills gold. An expedition fitted out there can get a boat at Sioux City, come up the Missouri to Bismarck, and get into the country so as to do an immense amount of prospecting this fall. Our miners have talked the matter over with me, and asked if the enterprise of the Garden City could reach so far. I told them I thought it could.

Curtis.

———

CHICAGO INTER-OCEAN
Issue of September 9, 1874

THE NEW ELDORADO

A Review of Custer's Last Achievement—The Exploration of the Black Hills.

How the Scheme Originated and How it was a Measure of Economy to the Government Besides Opening the Eyes of the World.

From Our Own Reporter.

FORT ABRAHAM LINCOLN,
D. T.,
SEPT. 1, 1874

THE HISTORY OF THE EXPEDITION.

"And he gave it as his oponion," says Gulliver of a man he met, "that whosoever could make two ears of corn or two blades of grass grow upon a spot where only one grew before, would deserve better of mankind and do more essential service to his country than the whole race of politicians put together"—and this sentiment applies exactly to a retrospective glance at what has been and what always will be known as "Custer's Black Hills Expedition." The scheme was Custer's own, although it had been suggested long ago, and an exploration attempted frequently. Congress made no appro-

priation, but instead of giving the army something of this sort to do, sat in its halls and talked about a "Reduction Bill." It was Custer's enterprise that originated it, and Custer's energy that carried it out. When the Northern Pacific Railroad was extended to Bismarck, it became important that a military post should be established near that place for its protection from the Indians that haunt that country, and the present site of Fort Abraham Lincoln was fixed upon. General George A. Custer, who was in the Southern Territories at the time, was ordered with his regiment, the Seventh Cavalry, to garrison it, and his jealous eye was immediately fixed up on a new field of conquest. That field he has won—not easily, but by that indomitable energy that has characterized his whole brilliant military career. He could not go into the Black Hills last season, for he had to follow Stanley up the Yellowstone; but no sooner was he established on his return from that campaign but he began to urge

THE IMPORTANCE OF HIS SCHEME

upon his official superiors. Congress was appealed to, but made no response. The Secretary of War was finally induced to allow a reconnoisance, if it could be made without expense to the government. In General Sheridan Custer found a sympathizing superior, and urged upon him the necessity of an exploration. But Sheridan's hands were tied, for the appropriations for his department would allow no such expenditure. Then Custer's ingenuity was called into play, and he discovered a method to meet all objections and carry his scheme into play. He calculated the expense of the expedition, and much to the astonishment of his superiors, he announced that he would make it, and save the government money. The estimate was suggested to General Sheridan, met his warm approval, and the Black Hills Exploration seemed a certainty. By the estimate it was shown that the government would save in forage more than enough to pay all the expenses of the expedition, and have a balance of $13,000! and subsequent developments proved that General Custer had been mistaken only in the amount of the balance, which was found on the return of the expedition to have been over $16,000. Thus the expedition was as General Custer claimed, a measure of economy in more senses than one. The peace commissioners then had to be satisfied that Custer had not blood in his eye, and did not mean extermination; but a formal message was sent to all the agencies announcing the expedition, and stating that the object was an entirely peaceful one. People claimed that the entrance of troops on to the reservation was an aggression, and objected on that score, but General Custer showed them that the treaty of 68 expressly provided for an exploration and topographical survey of the Black Hills.

THE RESULTS OF THE RECONNOISANCE.

Finally all difficulties were overcome, all objections answered, and the expedition moved on the 2d of July. How it went and saw and discovered has been duly told in the columns of the INTER-OCEAN, and it would be useless today to review the march. The country was found to be indescribably beautiful, and rich in all the gifts of the Creator. There is gold there in vast quantities, and the ground has simply to be caressed to yield up its treasures; there is iron, and perhaps silver; gypsum in large quantites, and timber suffiicent for all the uses the country may suggest. There is plenty of pure, cold water, and the soil is as rich as any on God's footstool. Although the valleys are very narrow, they are very rich, and the agricultural attractions are such as will tempt the best class of citizens.

A SITE FOR A MILITARY POST.

It was one of the duties of the commanding officer and the corps of engineers to select a feasible sight for the building of a military post, if such a protection should ever be required. General Custer made a careful survey with this point in view, but will state in his report that he found no location within the limits of the hills that would be adaptable; first, because of the extreme difficulty of entering them, and secondly, because there were no level places large

enough for the purpose which had all the natural requirements. But, however, he will advise a further investigation of the country near Bear Butte, on the Belle Fourche River, where he thinks a fit location can be found. If ever the country is opened to settlement it will be absolutely necessary for the establishment of a post, for the nearest military station is over two hundred and fifty miles away.

THE PROBABILITY OF SETTLEMENT.

To those who were in the hills, it scarcely seems possible that they should remain unoccupied long, and since the results of the exploration have been announced, the feeling of the country, if what I find here is an an indication, is such as to influence Congress to an abrogation of the reservation treaty immediately. We saw no indications of its occupancy by the Indians—the Black Hills are simply a summer hunting ground for small parties, and there is not sufficient game there to support a large tribe of Indians. As it is the country is useless—idle, when it might be utilized for the benefit of all mankind.

The people on this frontier are fairly crazy to push forward to this little Eldorado. Could the supplies be obtained I have no doubt there would be an expedition retiring in a week. The Bismarck paper, which lies before me, is fairly bristling with excitement, and its columns are full of such paragraphs as these:

Bismarck merchants are already laying in a stock of mining tools and miners' outfits. An expedition will undoubtedly leave this point this fall, intending to winter in the Hills, where there is an abundance of game of all kinds.

Gold in the grass roots, and at a depth of eight feet, is not bad, particularly when the amount yielded is $100 per day to each miner.

The best way for Montanians to reach the Black Hills gold region will be to come down the Missouri and take the government trail from Bismarck.

Mitchell's new atlas of the United States, sold in Bismarck by P. B. Gavitt, just published by Zeiglef and Curdy gives the correct location of Harney's Peak. Custer's

Gulch is seven miles south of it, on a little stream emptying into the south fork of the Cheyenne.

While the country south of the Black Hills is overrun by hostile bands for the Red Cloud, Whetstone, Yankton, and other agencies, their operations do not extend to the region north of the hills. That is neutral ground, and is seldom visited, and then only for hunting.

General Forsyth says, in his Black Hills report, that all attempts to enter the hills from the east or south would be futile: they can only be entered from the north or west. The Sioux City Journal says the country between Cheyenne and the Black Hills is barren, marked on the maps as sand hills, and proved to be barren and is therefore avoided by immigrants. The Journal alleges that via Sioux City is the nearest route to reach the Black Hills, and yet it admits that people must go from there several hundred miles up the river to Fort Randall, and when they get to Fort Randall they are ten miles further from the gold region than when at Bismarck.

Curtis.

CHICAGO INTER-OCEAN
Issue of September 2, 1874

THE GOLD COUNTRY.

The Excitement Spreading Along the Line of the Northern Pacific Railway.

Talk of a Return Expedition to be at Once Organized.

Effect of General Sheridan's Order Prohibiting Entry Upon Sioux Lands.

The Exact Location of the Gold Beds—They are in the Reservation.

But Extend South Into Wyoming—What an Expedition from the South might do.

Special Telegram from Our own Reporter.

FARGO, D. T., SEPT. 1.

Our party have reached this place on our return from the Black Hills, and expect to arrive in St. Paul tomorrow night. In all these beautiful little cities on the Northern frontier, we find the reports of gold discoveries have preceded us, and the Black Hills expedition and its results are the topics in conversation everywhere. Old frontiersmen are recollecting what they have heard the Indians say in years back, and have added fuel to the flame until it has already reached

A GLOW THAT WILL SOON BE FELT

all over the country. The border newspapers, especially those on the line of the Northern Pacific Railway, are full of gold stories, gold hopes, and plans for golden realizations. They have issued extras in which they proclaim the discoveries in trumpet tones, coupled with convincing arguments that

THE NORTHERN PACIFIC

is the only feasible and the shortest route to the Black Hills. There is no doubt but this is true, and it may give this country an impetus which will benefit not only the railroad and its towns, but the whole territory of the Northwest.

IN A CONVERSATION WITH ROSS AND M'KAY,

the practical miners who accompanied the expedition, and who are now at Bismarck, both expressed their intention of organizing as soon as possible

A RETURN EXPEDITION

to prospect the country more thoroughly. Chicago speculators can find no better field in which to plant the seeds of fortune.

The return trail of the expedition to Fort Lincoln leads directly to the gold country, and by the most direct and feasible route; and there is no doubt that Bismarck will be the point of general embarkation should expeditions be permitted to go. The indications that we saw in the Black Hills seemed to show that

THE WINTERS THERE WERE NOT AT ALL SEVERE,

and from the fact that there were no visible traces of freshets, we judged the fall of snow was usually light; and it may be that a party can start out this fall to spend the winter there.

Later.—General Sheridan's order

PROHIBITING ALL EXPEDITIONS

entering the Black Hills has just been received and creates considerable excitement. General Custer's opinion and plans on the subject have been previously telegraphed, and coincide with those expressed in the order. The question will now come up

WHETHER THE GOLD DISTRICT LIES WITHIN THE SIOUX RESERVATION.

There are decided differences of opinion among outsiders, although Colonel Ludlow, Chief of Engineers of this department, who accompanied the expedition, is positive that it does.

THE BELT OF GOLD

in which the discoveries were made runs northeastward, and leaving the reservation at latitude 43.20, longitude 104, enters Wyoming, which is not included in the reservation. "The color," to use a miner's phrase, was found several times in Wyoming, after hasty and unsatisfactory tests, but no metal. But the miners are positive that they could have reached it could they have had time to prospect thoroughly. An expedition coming northwest from Laramie, or some other point on the Union Pacific Road, would

AVOID ALL TREATY DIFFICULTIES,

and striking the hills near Inyan Kara Butte, might accomplish as much as one from the northward, although it would have to make a new trail, that portion of the country never having been explored.[32]

Curtis.

The Gold Regions being Invaded by Miners.
32. Sioux City, Iowa, Sept. 14—The Indian Agent at the Ponca Reservation, D.T., states that a few days since a party of Indians arrived from Spotted Tail's agency, near the head of White River, and brought a report that white men were coming into the Black Hills in large numbers from Montana and other Territories west.
CHICAGO INTER-OCEAN
Issue of September 15, 1874

Special Telegram to the Inter-Ocean.
Sioux City, Iowa, Sept. 26.—Within the past few days several parties of strangers have congregated here, quietly provided themselves with heavy canvas-covered wagons, ox-teams, and all the paraphernalia of miners, crossed the river into Nebraska, and are believed to be now en route to the Black Hills, though they denied that to be their destination. The character of the men and nature of their outfits indicated anything but landhunters, as some claimed to be when questioned.
CHICAGO INTER-OCEAN

Washington, November 27
The Secretary of War today forwarded the following telegram from General Sheridan to the Secretary of the Interior:
Chicago, Ill., Nov. 27.
To Brigadier General Townsend, Washington.
I wish to relieve the honorable Secretary of War from any apprehensions coming from the false statement going the rounds of some Eastern papers reporting miners at work in the Black Hills. It is possible the report may have originated from a recent discovery of gold forty miles north of Laramie City, on the Union Pacific Railroad, where many miners have gone. The place is at least 200 miles southwest of the Black Hills.
P. H. Sheridan,
Lieutenant General
CHICAGO INTER-OCEAN
Issue of November 28, 1874

Special Telegram to the Inter-Ocean.
SIOUX CITY, IOWA, Dec. 10.—Little Buckshot, one of the scouts who accompanied Custer's expedition to the Black Hills, has just returned from that place, where he went in quest of stolen stock. He says he saw between thirty and forty white men in camp in the lower portion of the hills. They had a good supply of cattle, wagons, etc., and had built a stockade about the entire camping grounds, which will afford ample protection against any sudden attack by Indians or others. The scout's description of the members of the party is so minute as to identify them as the party who left here in October last ostensibly for a hunting excursion on the railroad. He saw them prospecting on the streams and ravines, and thinks the Indians will not dare interfere with them in their present fortified position, and has no doubt but they will find gold.
CHICAGO INTER-OCEAN
Issue of December 11, 1874

NEW YORK WORLD

(Author's Note: Correspondent William E. Curtis is pictured on Page 97.)

In the summer of 1874 the NEW YORK WORLD was preoccupied with New York politics and not Custer's expedition to the Black Hills. And yet to make this statement would seem to conflict with the fact that it did arrange to have first hand coverage of the expedition. Furthermore, dispatches from its correspondent generally received front page preference and a variety of reports on the expedition were reprinted from frontier newspapers in the vicinity of the Black Hills region. But editorial comments were few and far between, and this reflected the fact that the WORLD'S editor was absorbed in the task of molding the platform of the New York Democratic party for the governorial election of 1874.

Within two years of its founding in 1860 as a one cent religious daily THE WORLD was bought up by Democrats and converted into an anti-war and pro-southern organ. Manton Marble was placed in charge of THE WORLD as editor and later became owner as well. Under Marble's leadership the paper achieved both notoriety and success. In May 1864, THE WORLD, along with a few other New York papers, published a bogus report that President Lincoln was calling up 400,000 additional troops. Federal authorities seized THE WORLD'S offices, suspended its publication for four days, and imprisoned Marble for a short time. In the remaining years of the sixties after Appomattox, Marble competed successfully with numerous rival newspapers through a combination of good management and able writing. It was in the morass of New York politics during the early 1870's that Marble gradually dissipated this earlier success.[1]

William March Tweed and his corrupt "ring" of political cronies dominated New York city and state government in the 1860's. And although Marble opposed corrupt government he neglected the opportunity to make THE WORLD the leader of a crusade to cleanse the Democratic party and New York of Tweedism. Instead he came to terms with the ring. In 1872 Marble returned to his editorial duties after a two year absence for health reasons and immediately plunged into New York politics. As a Democrat he urged the rebellious "mugwump" Republicans to join his party in nominating Charles Francis Adams to oppose Grant for the presidency. When the Liberal Republicans instead nominated Horace Greeley, editor of the rival NEW YORK TRIBUNE, Marble fought bitterly to prevent the Democrats from following suit. In the end Marble swallowed all the words he had hurled at Greeley and supported his candidacy, causing the credibility of the WORLD to suffer irreparable damage. During the subsequent two years Marble labored both privately and through the columns of THE WORLD to reform the New York Democratic party and groom Samuel J. Tilden for the governorship in 1874. It was this task which consumed Marble's attention in the summer of 1874

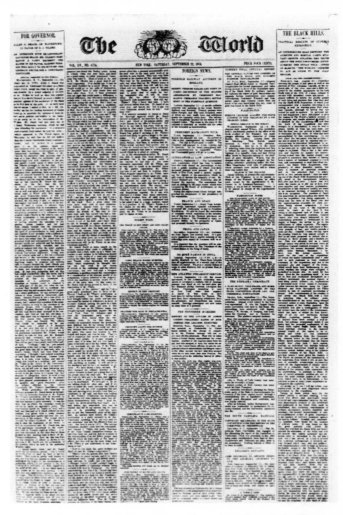

as he maneuvered in preparation for the state Democratic convention of early September.[2]

As an outspoken Democratic opponent of the Grant administration it is probable that Marble was unable to gain permission for a WORLD correspondent to accompany the Custer expedition. Consequently, he arranged to have William E. Curtis, special correspondent on the expedition for the CHICAGO INTEROCEAN, to free lance for THE WORLD as well. Thus while Curtis narrated Custer's exciting adventures as a member of the expedition, THE WORLD's own correspondent had to be content with reporting the speculations and wild rumors of its progress circulating in Sioux City, Iowa, and Bismarck. Both the facts and the rumors were published by THE WORLD, and it gave over much prime front page space to the Black Hills news. But only once and not until September ninth did Marble take notice of the subject in his editorial column. His tone was definitely one disapproving of the expedition itself when he opened with the comment that it would take more troops to protect "that supposed El Dorado" from eager gold hunters "than went with CUSTER to explore it." Though Marble termed Sheridan's proclamation against civilian expeditions to the Black Hills as "strong enough," he was confident that "the invasion of the Black Hills by white men bound to 'make money' out of them is only a matter of time."

The editor prophesized that "a heavy onset of gold-hunters" would soon occur in the wake of the fever developing in Bismarck and other frontier settlements. But he was less than sanguine that the reports of gold were reliable. "Possibly," he conceded, "some fortunes may be made by gold-hunters in the Black Hills; but if the present excitement continues," he warned his readers, "it is very certain to make paupers of many men who invest their all in the doubtful venture of gold-hunting." However, he stated in an almost disinterested sounding conclusion, "Disappointed and impoverished gold-hunters make pretty good farmers, and the soil of the Black Hills is said to be rich."[3]

Manton's editorial warning did not deter all his readers from being overcome by the gold fever. Some two weeks later the ST. PAUL DAILY PRESS reported that a party of New Yorkers were enroute to the Black Hills. The party, supposedly under the joint direction of two men "of long California experience," consisted of "young clerks who have been out of work," and as well as four or five men familiar with the frontier and mining. These adventurers had pooled what resources they possessed and received additional financial support from "somebody whose name is not given, who is to share in the loss or profit." Preparations were apparently well along with tools and weapons already headed for Chicago by rail. The DAILY PRESS had learned that the company was "prepared for adversity, both from Indians and General Custer. The former may have to be fought," the paper speculated, "while the latter must, if possible be evaded."[4]

Marble was completely successful in his political objectives in 1874. He largely wrote the state Democratic platform, and his man Samuel J. Tilden succeeded in being elected governor. But Marble's notable lack of interest in the more colorful and sensational news items like the Custer expedition proved to be the undoing of THE WORLD. The New York Democratic Party ceased supporting him and neither was Marble able to maintain the loyalty of the reading public. Circulation continued to decline as THE WORLD lost out in its competition with the more attention-getting journalism of the NEW YORK SUN. In 1876, after again supporting the losing candidate in a national election, Marble retired both from politics and the newspaper business.[5]

Ironically, while 1874 marked the beginning of the end for Manton Marble's NEW YORK WORLD, it was the auspicious beginning of William E. Curtis's career in journalism. The early dispatches which Curtis telegraphed to THE WORLD from Bismarck, while he and the rest of the expedition waited to get started, are similar to the ones he sent to the CHICAGO INTER-OCEAN at the same time. Perhaps, though there is nothing so remarkable about this similarity when one considers the limited items of interest to be found in a place such as Bismarck and nearby Fort Abraham Lincoln. Rather Curtis must be admired for the varied subjects he did search out and report upon. As the expedition got underway his letters to THE WORLD became a truly separate account which adds much to the information contained in his dispatches to the INTER-OCEAN. As special correspondent for the INTER-OCEAN Curtis's signed dispatches from Dakota Territory established his reputation for accurate and colorful reporting. Free-lancing for THE WORLD brought extra income which must have been welcome to the young reporter. It is evident that Curtis recognized the attractiveness of the opportunity, for he interrupted the courtship of his future wife in order to follow George A. Custer on his tour of the Black Hills of Dakota.[6]

FOOTNOTES

1. John L. Heaton, THE STORY OF A PAGE: THIRTY YEARS OF PUBLIC SERVICE AND PUBLIC DISCUSSION IN THE EDITORIAL COLUMNS OF THE NEW YORK WORLD, New York, 1913, pp. 2-3; Frank L. Mott, AMERICAN JOURNALISM: A HISTORY OF NEWSPAPERS IN THE U. S. THROUGH 260 YEARS: 1690-1950, New York, 1950, p. 351.
2. Sister Mary Cortona Phelan, MANTON MARBLE OF THE NEW YORK WORLD, Washington, D.C., 1957, pp. 75-89.
3. NEW YORK WORLD, Sept. 4, 1874.
4. ST. PAUL DAILY PRESS, Sept. 16, 1874, p. 3.
5. Frank L. Mott, AMERICAN JOURNALISM, p. 433.
6. Allen Johnson, ET. AL., DICTIONARY OF AMERICAN BIOGRAPHY, 20 Volumes, New York, 1928-1936, Vol. IV, p. 620.

NEW YORK WORLD
Issue of July 13, 1874

THE BLACK HILLS.
A GOLD HUNTING EXPEDITION TO THE SIOUX SACRED RETREAT.

A GOVERNMENT EXPEDITION BOUND FOR BEAR BUTTE—A FIGHT WITH THE INDIANS FULLY EXPECTED—THE SUCCESS OF THE EXPEDITIONS CONSIDERED CERTAIN—BISHOP HARE'S PROTEST—POSSIBLE SERIOUS RESULTS OF INVADING INDIAN TERRITORY.

(FROM OUR SPECIAL CORRESPONDENT.)

BISMARCK, Dak., June 30 — Who we are, whither we are going, and what we intend to do when we get there are the three things to be stated in this letter.

Beginning in medias res, our objective point is Bear Butte, "butte" being the common term for "hill" or "mountain" in this country. If you will look on your map for Dakota Territory you will find the Sioux country extending west of the Missouri River from the Nebraska line 43 deg. north to the line of 46 deg. north, a little above the mouth of Grand River. About midway of this the Big Cheyenne falls into the Missouri, flowing from the west and south. At a point just west of the one hundred and second parallel this stream divides into two forks, the more northerly, the Belle Fourche, flowing from the west; the other, the South Fork, from the southwest. Between these forks the map will show a film of mountains, from which radiate numerous rivers and creeks like the lines of a spider's web. Those are the Black Hills. As the reader of THE WORLD is probably at breakfast he can readily make a map by placing his carving fork at right angles with his knife. The knife is the Missouri; the handle of the fork the Big Cheyenne, the nearer tine the South Fork, that more remote the Belle Fourche. Put a bread crumb near the extremity of each tine on the inside. The nearer one will represent Harney's Peak, the farther one Bear Butte. From Bismarck Bear Butte is distant as the crow flies 200 miles.

The Black Hills enclose what may be called the earthly paradise of the Sioux, and from the mingled influences of superstition and selfishness they have guarded it with the utmost jealousy. All that we know positively is very little, and that little very vague. The geological features of the country are sufficiently interesting. The mesozoic rocks break from the Missouri along the valley of the Big Cheyenne into the prevalent consosic formation, and right in the heart of this mesosoic estuary is an island of metamorphic rock. Professor Hitchock considers the Black Hills the most conspicious of the interesting eozoic islands in the centre of the continent. This Laurentian area corresponding closely with that observed in Colorado, Utah, and Arizona, there should be found in it silver, gold, and gems.

In the jargon of this botantist the Black Hills be just within the western province of the prairie region, and are especially favored of nature. So far as we can judge by report, there is a range of hills so high as to be visible at a distance of sixty miles, bounding on every side a level valley of luxuriant vegetation. The hills are clothed to their summits with a thick growth of pines, and take their name from this sombre and shaggy growth. Rivers flow out from them to south and north like diverging spokes of a wheel. The soil is a deep, rich loam, and upon the water courses and lowlands are abundant forests of ash and oak, with the inevitable cottonwood. Both grasses are found in abundance, and thanks to the hills and forests, an exceptionally mild climate prevails. The Indians consider it a very paradise, free from extreme cold and drought and unswept by the bitter winds of the plains, and resort thither for pasturage, water, and fuel at all seasons of dearth.

The abundance of game is insisted upon by all competent witnesses. THE WORLD correspondent met Joe Belton (of whom more hereafter) at Sioux City some time since. He was emphatic on this point. "Bears and panthers," he said, "there were almost too many, and as for antelope, elk, white-tails, and black deer you will see more in a day than you could

miss in a year." Of fish there there (sic) are a good many in the mountain streams, but trout, I learned, do not choke up far-Western rivers save where these flow through guide books.

It is this quantity of game which I think, after due examination of all the facts of the case, induces the Sioux so highly to prize and jealously to guard the Black Hills. They sacredly preserve the game found within their boundaries so making of the country a combined deer park and Mecca.

At certain seasons they resort thither to hunt these seasons coinciding with the times of their religious celebrations. According to the evidence of Sitting Bull, the Indians had wont in former days to make their hunting there a mere accessory to—very possibly a part of—their worship. They hunted, but not for want or wantonness; but, if it were not a profane comparison, partook of the pleasures of the chase as sort of sylvan sacrament, an earnest here of the sport in the future hunting grounds. Even now when game is abundant elsewhere the Sioux hunting in the Big Hills is rather nominal than actual, and of late years the game laws, so to speak, have been made more and more stringent. The immemorial prohibition forbidding the permanent encampment of a band within the limits of the hills (a precaution against a regular and lavish destruction of game) has always been enforced, and within the past year or two—Indian chronology is of the most indefinite—it has been the custom of the visiting bands not to stop in the country more than one month nor then to camp for three successive nights within sight of the camp fire where the earlier stay was made. (This rude measure of distance is about a league and a half, and I am told by the French interpreters is commonly employed on the plains). Whether this was done in compliance with orders from the chiefs or was a regular custom the Arickarees could not say. Indeed they were not likely to know, as the Sioux are their hereditary enemies and keep the secrets of their councils sacred. It might be inferred, however, that at some remote day the medicine men have declared the Black Hills a holy ground wherein the ungalled hart (sic) should play and no stricken deer be moved to weep, and that at the present day the wisdom of the old men has induced them to revive as a piece of practical legislation the traditionary prohibition. The Indians have seen—notably within the past decade—the disappearance of the bison before the white man and the denudation of their hunting grounds. The tribes to the south have for the past two years been fretted to the verge of revolt by the whole-sale slaughter of the buffalo along the railroad lines, a similar peril menaces them from the north, hence the preservation of the Black Hills is absolutely necessary if they desire to live and hunt. All witnesses concur in stating that these Sioux are less wasteful than they were formerly in the hunting field, and it must have been a strong pressure of necessity or superstition that has made them provident.

Coupled with the desire to protect their national game preserve the superstitions of the savages concerning the Black Hills are the most powerful of incentives to opposition to opening up the country. For the Black Hills are holy ground of the very holiest sort. There they resort to hold their grand councils with the double advantage of perfect freedom from molestation or intrusion, and of having the decrees pronounced by the chiefs through their tools, the medicine men, obeyed most implicitly, for do they not come from the Sioux Sinai, the very antechamber of Manitou? There, too, takes place the annual sundance; most solemn of festivities. In the heart of the hills—I was going to say "are to be found," but, alas, they are not now to be found at all (so, at least the story-tellers feign)—the springs of immorality. The legend has it that a wonderful cave ran through the central hill from side to side. Difficulties and temptations of all sorts surrounded it and made entrance thereto so rare as almost to be impossible. Magic deer wooed the hunter to turn aside or back, and he who for a moment was diverted from his path and purpose was torn to pieces instantly by the panthers who guarded the approach. Traversing all these the

fortunate man, treading a subterranean pathway beset by perils as numerous and formidable as ever Christian encountered, came, in the very heart of the hill, to the sacred Wapka, or living river, a cascade that fell through the gloom from the bowels of the hill, and vanished in the darkness. Through this he who passed took a new lease of life till the eagles, whose eyrie was on the summit of the hill, entered another century of their eternal existence. Continues the fable: One early chief, to whom all later ones are but as children employed this stream to advance his Manitou-defying schemes, and during his added century of life sorely vexed earth and alarmed heaven. When he was about to apply for a further renewal of his life, already too long, the Great Spirit—I wish we could find a neat and new synonym for this being—resolved to punish him, and when he was in the bowels of the hill the mountain closed upon him and he never was seen again. Ditto the stream of life. The same as to the eagles, but the thunder remained as a perpetual sentinel to guard their nest. But a compensatory fountain poured out from the hill which still confers upon those who bathe in it the gift of invulnerability—it is a Dakotan Lethe. The candidate for immersion must go blindfold to the spring, bathe in it and drink of its waters, and—precisely as in Homer and the Nibelungen Lied—where the water does not touch him he is vulnerable. The Indians speak of their most successful warriors as men who have bathed in this spring, and attribute to its miraculous qualities their frequent and miraculous escapes from bullet and blade. Nevertheless, on questioning the narrator, he admitted that the most invulnerable of these warriors kept on the lee side of his horse as much as possible during a fight, and being pressed on the point he said that this was direction of the medicine men, whose patron spirit did not wish to have his favorites boast in an unseemly manner of the advantages he had conferred on them.

Those who were interested in myths can draw any deductions they please from that here transcribed. Instead of seeking a solution in the expulsion of Adam and

Eve, or some such remote event, I incline to believe that if we can get at the truth of the matter we shall find that a mineral spring and an extinct volcano had been taken advantage of by the medicine men and chiefs to impress their followers. That they have succeeded in convincing the Indians of the awful sanctity of the spot abundantly appears, for no Indian will venture near it.

Whether or not the Black Hill region is the residence of the spirits of good Indians preparatory to their final departure for the happy hunting grounds; whether, like the land of Havilah, there is gold there and the gold of that land is good, or whether there is a disinclination to permit the pale faces to violate the last hunting park left to the Indians, it is impossible to say. This much is certain, they have defended it and opposed entrance thereto as desperately as any Mussulman (sic) could guard the door of his harem. And hitherto successfully as the history of the past will show.

The pioneer of the Black Hills appears to have been a French half-breed trapper named Hercule Levasseur, who while trapping and hunting on the Upper Missouri, about 1855 or 1856, had heard the Sioux talking of the wonderful country west. Having married a squaw and been adopted into the nation he was on good terms with them and so was permitted to accompany his band to the hills for the annual council. Arrived there, however, entrance was refused him, on the ground that he was of white blood. Evading the guard left with him he must have attempted to enter and possibly succeeded. Anyway, he was killed on his way home. His hands were cut off and his tongue pulled out by the roots. This would appear to be the orthodox punishment prescribed for the profane who seek to enter this savage sanctum sanctorum, as several would be explorers have been treated in precisely the same manner.

Here let me contradict two statements I saw current among the papers ere coming here, which I am informed are utterly without foundation. In the first place, the Black Hills are not an especial place of sepulture like the Ganges to the Hindoo; on the contrary, the bodies of those dying there must be removed without the hills. In the second place, the hills are no sanctuary, or place where all the members of the nation are safe from private vendetta; on the contrary, the Dakota who is at feud will look forward anxiously to meeting and slaying his enemy when they meet there at council or feast.

To resume. In 1859 Lieutenant Warren tried to enter the country from the Big Horn country to the south by way of Powder River, but was ordered back by the Indians who were in such force that there was nothing possible but compliance. In 1861 General W. F. Reynolds, U. S. E., returning from the Yellowstone, passed near the Black Hills "between the forks of the Cheyenne, but was unable to do any exploring of consequence for reasons to be indicated. Since then several private expeditions have been made by individual explorers or small bands. Their history is invariably one of failure. As a rule the explorers have not returned at all; when they have come back it has been as chased and beaten fugitives. A Mr. P. H. Davy, an early settler of Minnesota, organized an expedition some years since which attracted a large number of adventurers allured by representations of the fertility of the soil, but the Government forbade its departure. A similar fate awaited the Sioux City explorers of 1873. General McCook tried last season to interest the General Government but permission was refused him. In February of this year an expedition 200 strong, with two guns, set off from Boseman, Mon., to try and make their way through Tongue River, but, after four pitched battles, had to return. Chris Gilson, an eminent citizen of Bismarck, who was introduced to me as "Mr. Gilson, the gentleman who killed Big Jack" (Big Jack having his lifetime been another eminent citizen with a professional penchant for poker and pistols), set out twice this year; but the stars in their courses fought against Chris Gilson: it rained heavily and blew hard, his mules stampeded, and he had to return. Joe Belton, of Sioux City, thinking that the Black Hills were worth having the little finger of his left hand chipped off upon a buffalo

skull, turned Indian, married a chief's daughter, lived two years among the Sioux, and came home, not having been permitted to set foot within the hills. This brings me down to the present expedition.

The magnet is of gold, as a matter of course, that has drawn so many adventures toward the Black Hills. Is there any metalliferous deposit there?

The most positive evidence on the subject I take to be the geological formation, which, as I said at the beginning of this letter, exactly coincides with that of Arizona, Utah, and Colorado. This insulated character of the outcrop of metamorphic rock makes this more certain. Local report—were it well authenticated all would be well, but on the frontier statements are loose and first sources of information not easily arrived at—declares that gold sand has been found in all the rivers springing in the Black Hill country, the Smoky Earth, Big Cheyenne, Owl, Little Missouri, Little Heart, &c. It is fact that on the Montana side one nugget of gold weighing four or five ounces was brought into Fort Laramie by a squaw, who claimed that it came from the hills; several times Indians have admitted the existence of gold, and their evasions at other times and the invariable opposition they have offered to exploration are also adduced in evidence. General Reynolds says in his official report of the exploration of 1861 that he found "very decided evidences" in the Big Horn Hills and the valley of the Madison, and "some indications" in the country between the forks of the Cheyenne, in the vicinity of the Black Hills. He, however, discouraged prospecting for fear that the men of the expedition would become frenzied with the gold fever beyond amenability to discipline. At the new Cheyenne Agency, near Fort Sully, a correspondent noted in 1869 or 1870 a necklace of rude flakes or scales that unmistakably were of pure gold, strung together by native workmanship. That is about all the evidence deserving of credence that has been noted.

There is no doubt but that the conviction, growing year by year to a fever among the frontiersmen, that the hills would prove a region of fabulous wealth, has induced

the Government to undertake the present expedition.

And this brings me to the next subject for consideration—Who we are.

The expedition consists of ten companies of the Seventh United States Cavalry—840 sabres in two columns—commanded by Major M. S. Tilson and Major George A. Forsyth, Ninth United States Cavalry, late aid to Lieutenant General Sheridan; Company G, Seventeenth United States Infantry, and Company I, Twentieth United States Infantry, under Captain L. H. Sanger, of the Seventeenth; sixty Arickaree Indians and thirty Santees to act as scouts, under Lieutenant J. W. Wallace and their chief, Bloody Knife. The artillery is commanded by Lieutenant Josiah H. Chance, and consists of three Gatling guns, each firing 250 balls a minute and carrying 800 yards, and a three inch Rodman, to be used in shelling woods on masses of Indians. The train consists of 150 wagons, drawn by 900 mules; 300 head of cattle, and the usual number of drivers, farriers, &c. The men are armed with the new Springfield rifle, a weapon of which great things are predicted and expected, and the new Colt's breech-loading revolver, whose cartridge, by the way, also fits the Gatling chambers. The engineers are commanded by Captain William Ludlow, Assistant Surgeon J. W. Williams is medical officer, and Captain A. E. Smith quartermaster. General Custer's adjutant is Lieutenant James W. Calhoun, Post Adjutant at Fort Abraham Lincoln, just over the river. Two forty-niners, William McKay and H. N. Ross, are attached to the staff as practical miners.

The "Pekins" are Professor Winchell, State Geologist of Minnesota; Professor George Bird Grinnell, of Yale and their assistants; and Mr. C. H. Huntington, of St. Paul, Photographer, besides three special correspondents. The guide and interpreter is Louis Agard. There are several other guides, including the Arickaree chiefs, Bear's Ears and Bloody Knife, and Charley Reynolds, a veteran scout.

I must not fail to state that Second Lieutenant Fred Grant, who is described in general orders as "Lieutenant - Colonel Fourth

Cavalry," accompanies us as acting aid.

The expedition, it will be seen, is not nearly so large, in fact not half so large; as that which, under Stanley, marched towards the Yellowstone last year; but is less unwieldy, and can move more rapidly and fight to greater advantage.

The Santees, I may say are Sioux of the lesser bands, and took part in the Minnesota massacres of twelve years ago. They have shown some reluctance to engage in warfare against their brethren, and only come forward when their presence was insisted upon. Superstition can have nothing to do with their reluctance, because they are all as good Christians as it is possible for Sisseton Sioux who were in the bloody work of 1862 to be, nor can there be much of that patriotism which ultimately moved Coriolanus to spare Rome in the case, for they were with Stanley in the fight on the Musselshell last year. I apprehend that the true cause will be found in their disinclination in the event of defeat to be taken by their brethren while participating in a campaign against the sacred country. Strong as our force is, splendidly equipped and well prepared for fighting, the Santees do not attempt to disguise the fact that a better expedition might possibly be thrashed.

"If so, and they take you," I said to one who understood English fully and spoke it fairly, "what will they do to you?"

He deliberated a moment, then remarked:

"Ugh!" relapsed into savage silence, said he didn't know, and changed the subject as if it were not the pleasantest in the world.

And finally, comes the question: How are we going to get there and what will we do when we are there?

Our official instructions are to push on to Bear Butte, or some point in its vicinity on the Belle Fourche. Once there a site will probably be selected for a future fort and post which will be temporarily occupied by a camp. From this as headquarters the cavalry will scour the country to the south, southeast, and southwest, examination of the country being carried on. The time allowed in orders is sixty days, so that we shall be a month or five weeks in camp in the hills, giving abundance of times for a thorough examination of the region. However, the General commanding is at liberty to turn back even before the Belle Fourche is reached, if, as the special order No. 117 delicately hints it, "any unforseen obstacles renders it necessary or advisable."

As the crow flies Bear Butte is about 200 miles distant; our route will make the march about 250. The road lies from the valley of the Little Heart south, and by west to the Belle Fourche. There are, of course, no maps save those of Reynold's expedition in 1861, which, as he passed to the south and west while we make our way from the north and east, are not specially available save as they are filled out by the experience and hearsay of the scouts and guides. One thing is certain; there are no "bad lands" to make marching difficult, such as we came across last year on the Yellowstone and Little Missouri. The Mauvaises Terres all lie south of the South Fork of the Big Cheyenne. We anticipate finding a country of prairie, belted with forest, cut deeply by rapid streams, with deep and wooded banks. Grass there is in abundance, and no scarcity of water is apprehended, though when we leave the clear lakes of Dakota for the muddy rivers across the Missouri the quality will seem worse perhaps than it is.

And now all that remains is to discuss the probability of resistance being offered us, its character, and extent.

There is no earthly doubt but that the Sioux will fight and are preparing for the conflict. That they should meditate resisting the Long-haired Chief—so General Custer is known among them, his chevelure being as noticeable as it was the day he dashed down the avenue at Washington in the grand review—with the Seventh Cavalry, a crack regiment, known to be perfectly armed and equipped, is sufficient proof, particularly after their whipping last year, that their blood is up. A rat will offer a desperate resistance if you pen him in a corner; much more an Indian. Naturally fond of fighting, hating the whites with an envenomed hatred, dowered with a pride—or a treacherous ferocity, call it which you will—that no amount of whipping can take out of them; sore from their last year's defeat and the encroachments of the railroad, the Sioux would be certain to fight, even if the expedition did not menace their last refuge and most holy land. Hence there is hardly a man who does not anticipate a very Gravelotte of savage warfare. This is the season at which the warriors all gather at the Black Hills to celebrate their annual festivities, so that there will be a total of from 4,000 to 5,000 warriors arrayed there perfectly armed. Five thousand Sioux actually in the field can be relied on to do as much mischief as we should think it would require twice their number to perform. Sitting Bull and other captains of the Sioux—a nation whose military leaders have always been of eminent capacity—have all the Napoleonic tactics, and by forced marches and rapid operations conducted over a wide extent of country, always leave the impression that their force is much greater than it really is. Sitting Bull has probably not more than 1,500 warriors and yet good soldiers have been ready to swear he must have 5,000.

The battle ground is expected to be all the way. The line of Grand River, from seventy to eighty miles south of here, is considered the first place where resistance is likely to be offered, and from there to the Belle Fourche we may have to work of the hottest sort. In a fair fight on the open plain, especially with the Gatlings, the expedition has nothing to fear, particularly, also, as the Indians never stand a charge. A serious ambuscade or night attack is extremely improbable, but the banks of the various rivers where they are high and wooded offer good defensive positions, and here the Sioux may do considerable injury to an attacking party, until they are shelled out or flanked. Long range fighting doesn't do much damage to any one, but this is likely, in General Custer's words, to be "a discouraging campaign for stragglers."

Though there is little doubt of the success of the expedition, it is none the less certain that the success will be, in all probability, dearly purchased. In the first place, the Sioux have been more than usually uneasy and for weeks a general Indian war has been predicted. The old pretence (sic) that they were only looking for Arickaree scalps has not been believed by any one. The cavalry has, of course, been concentrated here for the expedition; to replace it the infantry posts have been weakened, and even were it otherwise infantry are useless in a summer campaign. Over a month since officers at the various forts began to send home their wives and children, and General Custer wrote that the reservation Indians would certainly join the warlike bands in harrassing the expedition, and represented the imminency of a general Indian war, in which the troops would be at a disadvantage. Towards the end of April a large war party left the Cheyenne Agency (about midway between Bismarck and Yankton, at the mouth of the Big Cheyenne). Agent Bingham succeeded in turning them back but on the 26th of May they went out again 400 strong, and reinforced by 300 or 400 warriors from Grand River (midway between Cheyenne Agency and this point), attacked the Arickarees at Fort Berthold (eighty miles above here), killing six of them. This was a peculiarly sad affair, as the Rees are very peaceful and have been laboring diligently at agriculture for a year. They were warned of the danger that menaced them and applied to the commander for the loan of arms and ammunition to defend themselves, but these were refused, both at the fort and headquarters and so the Arickarees were left to meet as best they could with old mussle - loading smooth-bores the Sioux, each of whom carries one or two Spencers.

One result of this massacre has been the firing of the Arickaree heart, and the warriors who accompany the expedition are wild with excitement. They have painted and danced themselves into a fury and decline moving to their reservation, in the Indian Territory, till they have avenged themselves for their adversaries.

Rumors are, of course, all that we hear from the far posts, but these are all of one sort. Up along the Manitoba line the Indians are out, and they say that both up and down river they are stamped-

ing or killing their cattle, and leaving the reservations by scores. All of this is ominous. We can, and do, wish that civilization in this quarter may not be retarded for five or ten years, but our hope will be much stronger than our faith. "When the cat is away the mice will play," and with the Long-haired Chief and the Seventh far down in the plains, the opportunity to swoop down on the thinly garrisoned forts and the undefended settlements is a strong one. It is invariably a part of savage warfare to meet the enemy in the field with two-thirds of the force, and send the other third into his country to devastate the villages and slaughter the women and children. The Sioux have this advantage — their non-combatants are either on the reservations drawing rations, or up in the hills safe from any attack. I hope I am not a prophet of evil, but I fear that many a scalp with long hair or baby tresses will be taken in Dakota and even Minnesota this year, and that the ashes of many a humble home will be slaked in the blood of those it sheltered.

No need in this letter or in this correspondence to describe Bismarck, Fort Abraham Lincoln, just across the river, or the camp, a couple of miles away, where the expedition is waiting the order to march.

We have been in camp since the 19th to get our arrangements in gear. We had expected to set out on the 25th, but are delayed, waiting for the new Springfields.

The wires will keep the public informed of our movements days upon days before details are received by mail. New York papers, seven days old, are timely here.

BISHOP HARE'S PROTEST.

THE EXPEDITION SAID TO BE IN VIOLATION OF THE TREATY OF 1868 WITH THE SIOUX—SERIOUS TROUBLE FEARED ON THE FRONTIER.

(FROM OUR SPECIAL CORRESPONDENT.)

BISMARCK, Dak., July 1—The new Springfield arrived yesterday, and tomorrow we hope to move for the sacred land of the Sioux.

This, however, is of less interest

to the correspondents here and the public at large than the receipt of Bishop Hare's protest, and the enclandre generally raised in civilian circles about the expedition, its motives, rights, and objects. Inasmuch as THE WORLD correspondent is in a position to state pretty nearly the truth, which will differ largely from both the versions published ere this letter reaches you—possibly commented upon—the facts are here given with appropriate expression of impartial opinion. Of Bishop Hare I know something. He is the Missionary Bishop of Nebraska, an able man, zealously affected in all good works, and devoted to the interests of the Indians beyond question. He was the Chairman of the commission sent last March to investigate affairs at the Red Cloud and Spotted Tail agencies, and drew down a general storm of indignation upon himself by stigmatizing the sensational reports in the Wyoming press as wholly without foundation in fact, and only instigated with a view to enabling patriots with hay and oats to sell to dispose of the same to advantage on the buoyant market caused by an Indian war. It was that commission which, it may be remembered unearthed those gigantic beef frauds, and Bishop Hare is looked upon with horror in army circles as the gentleman who, when General A. J. Smith warned the Indians that, if a soldier were hurt or a cow stolen, he would "get some of them," stood up and told the Indians they were as good as and had rights as well as the soldiers —a speech indubitably founded in justice, but of doubtful expediency to be uttered in the presence of a crowd of such treacherous brutes as those upon the old military road.

Bishop Hare's protest, which has been referred from the President to the War Department, and in due course to Chicago, St. Paul, and Fort Abraham Lincoln, is based on the Laramie treaty of 1868, signed by Generals Sherman, Harney, Terry and others for the United States, and by all the prominent chiefs of the Sioux nation, like most of our Indian treaties, destined to be observed by neither of the contracting parties. This gave to the Sioux, and such other Indian nations as they might choose to admit among them, the reservation from the Missouri River to the 104th degree W., and the Nebraska line to the 46th parallel N., including—as will be seen by consulting the map—the Black Hills country. Indeed, it was only in consideration of the probable holding sacred of that region that they signed the treaty. In consideration of the surrender of this territory, with the reservations on this (the eastern) side of the Missouri, the right to hunt buffalo, so long as the buffalo abounded north of the North Platte and on the Republican Fork, and the definition of the Big Horn country as unceded Indian territory, the Indians gave up the right to build Pacific railroads. They were assured that no one but the agents of the United States, and "such officers, agents, and employes (sic) of the Governments as might be authorized to enter upon Indian reservations in discharge of duties enjoined by law, should ever be permitted to pass over, settle upon, or reside in the territory."

It is claimed by Bishop Hare and the Friends of the Indians that the Custer expedition is in direct defiance and violation of the treaty. It is further asserted that the whole expedition is characterized by still meaner motives and more selfish features. The absence of public discussion or preparation is insisted upon, though this really does not amount to much, as the reserved power of the War Department is sufficient for the purpose. The second objection, that, the great mass of the Sioux are peaceable, and that it is unjust to punish the many for the misdeed of the few, carries no weight with it. The only difference between the agency Indians and the roving Indians is that the former only take opportunity to misbehave, while the latter make opportunity. It is almost as certain that a Sioux will scalp a white man as it is that a white man will plunder a Sioux. It is precisely this absence of moral sense on both sides that makes negotiation so difficult and the most solemn truce only a farce. The Sioux from the reservations it was who butchered the Pawnees last year, and they regularly annoy the Mandans, Arickarees, and other tribes who never give them special cause. But the charge is further made that the whole affair has been "put up" by a small army clique, opposed by General Sherman, to give General Custer (who, remember, is only Lieutenant-Colonel of the Seventh, though by brevet a Major-General) an opportunity to earn a step and confer popularity on the Administration of General Grant by opening up a new gold region. Upon these points there are some grounds sufficient in these days of ours to warrant the erection of a sensation. Custer takes charge of the expedition while the Colonel of the regiment, Colonel Sturgis, remains in the empty depot at St. Paul without a platoon of men under him. But then Custer has a reputation among the savages, which in this sort of warfare is worth more than rank, and if this expedition were gotten up solely to promote him and glorify the father of our "Lieutenant-Colonel" it would be about as idiotic a piece of business as ever was devised. It is almost certain that we shall have a war and the very sort of a war which is unpopular, because it will involve the massacre—which can neither be prevented nor punished—of hundreds of women and children. It is also true that General Custer, when controverting General Hazen's publications about the lands in this section of the Northwest, significantly insisted on the mineral wealth of these lands, but what earthly connection have the Black Hills away in the south with Jay Cooke's schemes for future Congressional aid? The limited area of the Black Hills country, too, should show how absurd is the idea that the opening of that region or the discovery of gold there would exert an appreciable effect upon national politics or the currency. I have reason to know that General Custer considers himself entitled as an officer of the Government performing a duty of exploration to enter the country under the treaty, and that the whole question was discussed some weeks ago officially. While these adverse rumors have been largely set afloat and circulated by disappointed filibusters and sensation mongers, it has to be said further that if we had the right to do so it would have been but graceful to notify the Indians of our intention to exercise this right. We certainly have failed to do this and the Indians who have come in to protest have been informed that we were going to the Black Hills, peaceably if we could, but going in any case. This, at least, hardly consistent with the idea of a treaty between two parties, each having rights.

But I am inclined to do as people who live on the frontiers, and at the same time have no money to make out of an Indian war, generally do and consider the whole question as one wherein the expediency is to be weighed equally with, if not before, the principle. I doubt if our Indians and our Indian agents possess the capacity to observe any treaty whatever. While I am convinced that—admitting his right to go there at all and conceding his motives to be of the purest—Custer's expedition, in the way Indians go and our Indian affairs are managed, would be something comparatively harmless to all engaged except the few who get shot or scalped a little before their time, it is impossible to regress the conviction that at this moment the Black Hills expedition is worse than folly. If it were only a summer jaunt to enable a few officers to pick up steps, a few scientists to pick up fossils, and to give the President's son and the mule train a change of air, and if the Indians were at peace and the frontier protected, there would be nothing especially to censure. But with the whole Indian populations fevered and ripe for revolt from Mexico to Manitoba, it would be a crime to denude the posts and send every cavalryman on the frontier out to reach. We are goading the Indians to madness by invading their hallowed grounds, and throwing open to them the avenues leading to a terrible revenge whose cost would far outweigh any scientific or political benefit possible to be extracted from such an expedition under the most favorable circumstances. Those who can look after their own scalps; not so those who stay.

C.

NEW YORK WORLD
Issue of July 31, 1874

CUSTER'S EXPEDITION

ORGANIZATION OF THE COMMAND—THE TROOPS, THE SCOUTS, AND THE SUPPLY TRAIN—AN INDIAN WAR-DANCE AND ITS DISMAL SUGGESTIONS—SAVAGES IN SIGHT.

GENERAL CUSTER'S BLACK HILLS EXPEDITION, IN CAMP AT CANNONBALL RIVER, Dak.,

July 6—We have been out four days, having started from Fort Lincoln on the 2nd of July, just one week after the date originally appointed, and are rapidly becoming inured to the hardships of camp-life and the march. The weather has been terribly warm and dry, the thermometer having ranged constantly from 94 to 103 in our tents at the middle of the day, but the nights have been deliciously cool and bracing, so that by early marching and resting in the heated hours we have been able to get on right well, and having marked our seventy-fourth mile. General Custer is a rapid leader, and although our train is unusually heavy, he is hurrying forward so fast that we shall reach Slim Butte, the end of the first stage and the first point of interest, in about five days more. No white man has ever seen Slim Butte, and its attractions are at present quite indefinitely presented; but the Indians tell of beautiful scenery, remarkable caves, and rare minerals there. "Goose," our Sioux guide, to whom I shall have occasion to refer frequently, and whose remarkable history I have among the resources of my notebook, says there is one cave near the butte which the Indians regard as the abode of the evil spirits. It is entered, he says, only by a hole in the surface of the open prairie, and extends miles and miles— he cannot tell how far—being continually filled with the shrieks and wailings of the tormented damned. On the walls, he says, are carved great inscriptions on some unknown language, in letters as long as his arm, which even the medicine men of the Sioux have been unable to interpret, and to which have come also the wise men of all the tribes, but

with no better success. Sometimes, says Goose, the letters and figures shine as if they had been rubbed with fire, and then the shrieks and groans are the loudest, their echoes reaching even to the open air. These inscriptions; the Indians think, are the edicts of the Great Spirit against those in torment, and they shine like fire whenever they are renewed. The order of march General Custer has adopted is the same as is usual on these expeditions, the wagon train being in the center of a square formed by the advance guard, column of cavalry on each flank, and a battalion of infantry in the rear. General Custer himself leads, with his guides and the Indian scouts under Lieutenant Wallace, and carries a flag of red and blue, which he means to plant on the highest summit of the chain of Black Hills. The right flank is commanded by General Forsyth, of Chicago, and to left by Colonel Tilford, of Fort Rice. Thus it is seen Chicago is well represented in this expedition —represented by one of its most popular citizens and one of the noblest and bravest soldiers in the United States Army. But people do not appreciate General Forsyth till they see him in the field, and his admirers in society would congratulate themselves on their own good judgment could they see him among his soldiers on these hot, dusty marches—the model of patience, nerve, and soldierly courtesy. Campaigning under Custer is no sport. People who sit in cool, dark parlors and shaded offices may envy us, but if they consider seven and eight and ten and fourteen hours in the saddle, under a sun that raises the mercury 100 degrees and a parched, dusty plain, an experience to be envied, four days such as we have spent would convince them to the contrary. No one, so far, very fortunately, has felt fatally the terrible suffering, but the ambulances are full of poor soldiers who have fallen out by the day. The animals feel the heat and want of sufficient water even more than the men, and whenever the train stops the air is hideous with the braying of the poor, thirsty, tired mules. The most of the "bottom lands" in this region are covered with sediment of alkali, which is as fine as the finest powder, and

sifts through veils or any other protections a person can wear, and sifted through is very painful, getting into the pores of the skin, and burning and smarting till one imagines himself in the process of oremation (sic). The heat and wind parch and crack our lips and faces, and this dust, settling on the blistered flesh is about as serious torture as the strictest disciplinarian can desire. But nevertheless we enjoy it—the experience, not the dust—and lie down on our blankets at nightfall with the mind quivering with new thoughts and the strengthened pulses throbbing with the fresh vigor this glorious atmosphere instills.

SECOND LETTER.

IN CAMP AT "HIDDEN WOOD," Dak., Wednesday Evening, July 8, 1874—Our Indian scouts are curious characters. We have nearly one hundred of them, who form the advance guard— about forty Rees, fifty Santees, and a few Sioux. The Santees are regularly enlisted soldiers, are dressed in the regulation uniform, and most of them talk and write English; but the rest are the traditional aborigines — dirty, lazy, and singularly instinctive. They dress in the most fantastic fashion their imagination can suggest and their resources afford. Some have no clothes on—to speak of—although General Custer makes it imperative that something that cannot be mentioned politely be worn. Others have uniforms, and blankets ornamented and altered to suit the taste of the wearer, and their ideas of millinery or tailoring are exceedingly unconventional. Give one a pair of army pantaloons, for instance. The first thing he will do is cut away a large portion of the rear; then he will sew stripes of red flannel along the sides and around the bottom, and will end up by hanging on a few brass buckles or shells or beads.

In the Ree tribe there is a mysterious-looking individual clothed in a woman's frock, but wearing a warrior's scalp braid and accoutrements. He—or she—is the drudge of the camp—does all the cooking, brings all the wood and water, and looks after as many ponies as his—or her—duties will allow.

The braves look upon him—or her—with an air of superiority that cannot be mistaken and in one of the war-dances or other manly pastimes is he—or she—allowed to take a part; but the poor, begrudged indefinite drags out a miserable existence, neglected and forlorn, not even being allowed to ride with the column on the march, but being a perpetual straggler, generally having to lead three or four extra ponies belonging to the braves. I asked Bloody Knife about him—or her.

"The form of a man, but the heart of a woman," he replied through an interpreter, and then went on to explain that the indefinite was a man, but had not the courage to endure the tortures a young man must subject himself to before he can become one of the braves. So he had to live with the women and do a woman's work. Suffrage was not extended to such as he.

"Why does he come with you?" I asked of Bloody Knife.

"He wants to get rid of the frock," said the interpreter, without putting the question to the chief. "If he takes a scalp it comes off him."

Every night, before retiring, our Indians have a war dance. My tent is near their quarters, and I know it. To witness their singular ceremony once is quite interesting, but when one is kept awake half the night as a regular thing, and is expected to breakfast at three o'clock every morning, it loses its romance. The most amusing occasion of the kind was the night after the Santees joined the expedition, and the alliance of the tribes was celebrated. We were in camp at Fort Lincoln then, and a long, low, log-cabin was used as Indian quarters. In the center of the room, on the ground, was built a fire, the smoke of which, mingled with the odor that may naturally be expected to arise from seventy or eighty unwashed, naked, and perspiring savages, made the place almost intolerable for ordinary beings, and even the poor hungry dogs that always haunt an Indian lodge left the room disgusted, but the braves puffed their killikinnick, and breathed in the atmosphere with a relish. At the start two groups were formed, one of Rees and the other of San-

tees, either side of the fire. For a time they sat quietly smoking, till all the warriors were gathered, when some one brought in a drum and handed it to the Santees. They placed it in the center of their circle, and all who could reach it began to pound its head with sticks, their pipes, fingers, and everything available, humming a dreary monotone in the minor key. All Indian music is in the minor key. It was soft in tone, and grew into a sort of moaning, like the wind in the branches of a leafless forest, and lasted five minutes or so, ending with a few subdued shrieks. The pipes were relit and passed from one group to the other, each warrior taking a whiff or two and sending it along to the next. Then the Rees took the drum and went through the same ceremony, but with a different theme to their chant. It was then repeated by the Santees, a little louder and faster, and the shrieks at its close more decided and numerous. Then the Rees went at it again and the Santees for the third time interspersing lively little whoops between the measures of the song and pounding with decided emphasis on the drum. Then it was passed over to the Rees again, and two or three of the Santees rose to their feet, doing a sort of walk around, for which their brethren in the other group furnished the music. Then the others began to rise, one by one, and joined the dance, hopping up and down, first with one leg and then with the other, as if they were tramping down something each uttering a whoop at short intervals until the groups were broken up and the alliance was supposed to be formed. The pow-wow grew livelier, and drumming and moaning and whooping grew louder, and the atmosphere more vile as the dance went on, but a white man gets enough of it in a very short time and I could not remain after they got well agoing. It was my first war dance, and in it I saw something of which I had often read, but not the realization of my anticipations. It was certainly curious, a fantastic, a savage scene—naked men with painted bodies dancing in a dim, gloomy, flickering fire light. It was a scene for a painter—on canvas it would be poetic, legendary—but, bah! the

stench. The coming generations will not see war dances. The modern Indian hasn't animation enough to get up a pow-wow, and it's only old scarred braves who whoop as their fathers did. The modern Indian prefers peace to war; he prefers sleeping in the sunshine to hunting the antlered deer and the bounding antelope; he would rather steal than work. Shades of Cooper and Natty Bumppo, how the red man has degenerated! It is an open question whether Sitting Bull and his Sioux will attack us. Thus far we have had no trouble and have seen no Indians, although a scout reported having seen several the other day a mile or two from our column. The other morning about two o'clock the whole camp turned out at an alarm and several shots were fired, but it only proved to be a mule that had strayed out of the picket line during the night and was trying to stray back again.

NEW YORK WORLD
Issue of August 1, 1874

CUSTER'S MARCH PROGRESS OF THE EXPEDITION TO THE BLACK HILLS.

SEVENTEEN MILES A DAY, WITH THE THERMOMETER AT 90 DEGREES—THE MONOTONOUS LIFE IN CAMP—AN INDIAN DANCE—THE PROBABILITIES OF A FIGHT—NEITHER GOLD NOR INDIANS SEEN YET.

(FROM OUR SPECIAL CORRESPONDENT.)

CUSTER EXPEDITION, Camp No. 12, July 14.—To "place" us will not be easy work for the reader, whose maps show a dead blank extending between the Missouri and Little Missouri. Look, anyway, for the Grand and Owl rivers, two streams flowing into the Missouri, and about midway between them and on the hundred and third degree line west you will see "Slim Butte." We are a little west and south of that, about 160 miles in a direct line from Bismarck and perhaps 215 miles following our line of march. We have not moved quite as we at first intended, it having been in contemplation to approach Bear Butte rather more

South Dakota State Historical Society

This drinking party undoubtedly took place while Custer was away from camp, probably while the expedition was at Custer Park or Golden Valley in late July or early August. In a letter to his wife Elizabeth, Custer said, "There has been no drunkenness, no card playing on this trip." No identification has ever been handed down on this picture. Lt. Benjamin Hodgson may be the man on the far left. Third from the left could be the sutler, John W. Smith, who carried a supply of liquor. One theory is that the person standing fourth from the left is the sutler's black servant, Aunt Sally. The theory is apparently incorrect, as Aunt Sally was described by Correspondent William E. Curtis of the CHICAGO INTER OCEAN as being ". . . a huge mountain of dusky flesh" and another time he referred to her as having ". . . a mammoth body." The servant pictured is slender in stature. Pictured or not, Aunt Sally had the distinction of being the first black woman to enter the Black Hills. Fifth from the left is probably Capt. Fred Benteen. Sitting in the far right foreground appears to be Fred Grant, son of President Ulysses S. Grant. He bears a remarkable resemblence to early pictures of his father. Grant had a reputation for drinking. In a reminiscence 54 years after the expedition, one of the enlisted men, William R. Wood (see appendix) had this to say about Grant: "Fred Grant was a son of General Grant, and was drunk nearly all the time . . . The sutler had a wagon with liquor which he sold to the soldiers and everybody who wanted to buy it. Colonel Grant was a guest of Custer, he went along to see the country and have a good time." A good time was apparently had by all at this party as 15 bottles of wine (or chamagne) along with a bottle of liquor stand open on the table. An open box of cigars sets at the front corner of the table and both Grant and Hodgson are holding cigars in their left hands. If Illingworth partook of any wine, it was evidently a modest portion, as the picture is clearly in focus.

to the east of our present line, but our westward deviation to the Little Missouri Valley has been caused by the undesirable nature of the country on the head-waters of Grand River.

Precisely how to write up on one's "log" it is not easy to say. We sent back couriers from Heart River on our second day out; since then no news has been communicated to Fort Abraham Lincoln. Word has been passed that a courier will set out tomorrow morning, and the camp, or at least our section of it, has been turned into a writing school. After this probably no mails will be at our service till we return to what passes for civilization at Bismarck. If one were to send his diary in full he would fill more space than THE WORLD has at its command; besides thus far one day has not essentially differed from another day in its events. Nor have the events of all combined been of a thrilling or even moderately interesting character. We have neither scalped nor been scalped in the slightest degree; there has not been a scale of mica or a crystal of pyrites found; we are not yet within sight of the Black Hills. So slender a foundation of incident baffles any endeavor, however kindly, to beat it up into a sensational letter. Camp notes would read something after this wise:

Camp No. z., July yth—Marched z miles to-day. Weather hot. No Indians in sight. Grass scanty. Water brackish. Saw a herd of antelopes. Killed one.

And so on, and so on. The smallest of pocket diaries, with three days to the page, would suffice to reproduce our daily walk— or ride—and conversation, and there would be no need for any knowledge of stenography either. Probably, therefore, the end both of the reader and writer will best be attained by a brief and somewhat general letter, in which, when necessary, your correspondent will skip blank days and barren districts.

On the 29th of June our new Springfields arrived. So did a hailstorm of the severest description, accompanied by a deluge of rain and tempest of wind. Pelted with pellets as big as grapes, drenched with water, and driven by wind, tents went down, mules stampeded,

and the whole camp was temporarily thrown into confusion. By nightfall however, all had been righted. The 30th of June and 1st of July were devoted to giving the finishing touches to the column's fighting costume and saying goodbye to Bismarck and Fort Abraham Lincoln. Bismarck we parted with without much sorrow. It is the temporary terminus of a Pacific railroad, and has a military post just across the river—hence it may naturally be inferred that it contains a very rough adult male population, and an adult female population small but not select. Gambling hells, bagnios, rummills, furnishing stores, a newspaper office, and the railroad buildings make up the town. It stands on a bank of solid mud washed by a swirling river of mud, over which passengers are conveyed by a tottlish old ferryboat apparently of the consistency of mud as well as of its color. Fort Abraham Lincoln, tout au contrairie, is a spick and span new post. From a military point of view it is advantageously situated on a lofty bluff, commanding both the river and the prairies that undulate on all sides of it. The new barracks, the row of white cottages facing the parade park, the winding drives, the shade trees everywhere set out, to say nothing of the pleasant society, male and female after their kind, with the accessories of poker and pianos, and an excellent band (which we have with us), all these were a decided relief from things across the river, and so were duly appreciated during our two weeks of enforced leisure.

For the last few days at the Fort we lived in camp to become acclimated, as it were, and test practically all our arrangements, while it was yet possible to correct any defect. I cannot say that this life was enjoyable. The weather was hot and close by day and night, and at sunset the heron-billed vampires which are accepted hereaway as mosquitoes arose in clouds from the river bed, sat down on their victims, and waited until impending suffocation compelled them to put their heads out from under their blankets. Camp noises are sufficiently well-known to all correspondents—probably to many readers, and who that has

passed a night in the country is not aware of the sleeplessness to which the lungs and heels of domestic animals are subject? We had picketed in camp some 1,800 horses and mules and 200 cattle, and after dark the whole 2,000 accepted any sight or sound whatever, a falling star, a dog barking, a cock crowing, as a signal for a demonstration along the line, kicking with one end, and neighing, screaming, or bellowing with the other. Add to this the fact that our dusky allies of the Arickaree and Santee Sioux persuasion were enthusiastic and persistent in their war-dances, and it will be seen that the camp was not the sort of place that would have commended itself to Zimmerman.

Our Santee scouts, I wrote you once before, were converted and civilized Sioux, and evinced considerable reluctance at the outset about joining in the unholy alliance against their brethren. However, when they came to examine the Gatlings and arms of precision —probably no better-armed column was ever sent out than this—and to feel the ribs of the beef cattle, and to snuff the battle from afar off, the fighting spirit which is in all of us, and only needs adequate provocation, was awakened, and when the Arickarees came down, with their faces painted red and black, a scalp on a long pole for a flag, and a drum made of a big bowl of rawhide, they fairly fired, The Arickaree hate the Sioux with a hatred surpassing the hatred of woman. They are hereditary enemies in the first place. In the second place the Government has placed the Arickarees upon a reservation at Fort Berthold, where many of them are enaged in agriculture, and this serves as a sort of scalp preserved for the Sioux. Whenever they want a few scalps the Sioux go up to Fort Berthold and are certain to find their Mandan or Arickaree game easy to their tomahawk. Hence, when the Arickarees were offered a chance to scalp Sioux killed by soldiers— though General Custer declines to allow scalping, whenever a subject presents itself no one believes that it will be possible strictly to enforce the prohibition—they beat their drum, dug up the tomahawk, painted their faces, and came. The Santee fraternized with them at

Fort Abraham Lincoln, where a big log cabin was converted into a council chamber. At sundown a fire was kindled on the earthen floor in the middle, and on either side of it the Arickarees and Santees squatted on their hams. Nearly ninety warriors were present in various stages of dishabille and dirt, and what with ninety frowsy braves perspiring and the fumes of ninety pipes superadded to the acrid smoke of the fire that spread itself through the room, the eyes, noses, and stomachs. An eye-witness of a similar scene among the Gros Ventres, up on the Manitoba line, described for my benefit "what he had seen between coughs, winks, and vomits." Candor compels the acknowledgement that this was more accurate than delicate.

This council was much like all others. The Indians sat and puffed with the sullen sleepiness which is called imperturable dignity in the novels. Then a drum was placed in the centre of the Santee group, on which as many could reach it pounded and drubbed, all meanwhile moaning a song—if a rapid, shrill sighing. "Hain-ha-bain-ha," aborting in a sharp "Yeh, yeh!" can be called a song. The Arickarees then laid aside their pipes and drubbed and moaned. Each did this thrice, the performance becoming a little more marked in time and tone, and the sharp concluding cry rising to the regular "Hi! Yah!" of the excited savage. Then a few of the Santees, who, as the more numerous, assumed the initiative throughout the performance, rose and danced. As many Arickarees followed, then more Santees, and so on till all were dancing. The step is not so complicated as the Boston dip, but it displays more vigor. You hop into the air with one leg and kick with the other; on solemn occasions there is no restriction as to height, the disposition of your arms, or the pitch of your yell.

This sort of performance used to go on nightly at the Fort, and it is repeated nightly since we have taken to the plains. I don't know of anything more grotesque than to watch these dancers of a dark night from the smoky side of the fire with your fingers in yours (sic) ears. There is a smudgy glare—glare, however, is too

strong for one of those green wood fires in the open air—and about every five seconds a colossal shadow bounds madly across it, and vanishes into the dark whence he came. The absence of all noise makes this extremely odd. Fancy the apparition suddenly painted on the night of a big Indian, with a cavalry officer's hat stuck full of feathers and a pair of sky-blue infantry pantaloons cut off below the knee, and cut out all round the seat, his naked body painted, and a huge red sash flying behind his loins—fancy this creature, with arms and legs frantically spread, bounding six feet into the air, and vanishing to be succeeded by another in full regimentals, and a third naked, save for his breech-clot, or a fourth with his blanket flying round him like a thunder cloud.

I have overrun my trail and must "hark back," remarking ere I do that one of the wildest dancers of last night I noticed a few minutes since writing an English letter to his wife, beginning "Dear Jane."

On the 2d then as THE WORLD was advised by telegram, we set out about eight A.M. from the camp. Since then reveille sounds at five sharp, and as soon thereafter as may be we take the trail, our pace being necessarily slow, since we drive our beef cattle with us. Towards ten o'clock, or when the sun begins to exert his full power, a halt is ordered, and about three P.M. the march is resumed, the length of the evening spell being determined by the availability of camping ground. We are averaging about seventeen miles a day, which, with the heat and our cattle train, is very fair marching.

That is when we march, and this is how: Probably half a mile or more in front ride a dozen Indian scouts, who thoroughly beat over the ground, examining every ravine or depression of the ground, or rock, or clump of trees, or at the water-courses keeping an attentive eye on the fords, or for Indian sign. Then comes General Custer, with the Santees and Arickarees, under Lieutenant G. D. Wallace, and the guides. The General is as theatrical as ever in the saddle, and carries his little blue and red pennon, destined to be planted on the summit of Bear

Butte. After him comes the Gatling battery, Lieutenant Chance; then the wagon train, ambulances, and herd, Quartermaster A. E. Smith. Captain Sanger leads the infantry column behind this. On either flank, about eighty rods from the train, comes the cavalry, the columns being led by Major George A. Forsythe (sic) and Major J. G. Tilford. Captain N. Moylan with a company of cavalry covers the rear and small scouting parties are thrown out on either flank, rendering it impossible that a surprise would be made.. Scouting parties are on favorable occasions sent out two or three miles in advance or on either flank. It requires a special permit, very rarely given, to pass out of the lines; and to do our civilians and scientists credit, they are most amendable to discipline in this direction. We have had but one scare thus far, when a mule—first homesick and subsequently repentant—stole out of the lines and then returned rather demonstratively creating a sensation in camp till he was identified and anathematized, selon regle.

Setting out from Fort Abraham Lincoln, we first marched along the valley of the Little Heart River. The country did not vary materially from the characteristics common to Northern Minnesota and Dakota. A gently rolling prairie, with here and there a small stream furrowing its surface, with a low and narrow valley, grass scantily springing from the thin soil, an occasional shrub and a semi-occasional stunted tree, a deep and fertile soil, with, however, alkaline characteristics, near the river—this was the scenery. These northern prairies are of a lonesomeness infinitely superior to the prairies of the South. Instead of the dead level waving with lush grass on every hand, which resembles a sunset sea at rest, there is a rolling sea of light greenish billows, broken ground everywhere that fades far away into an apparent level. Never a hill nor a tree breaks the horizon with a faint blue shadow. Here and there may be seen the trails, cut deep and stamped hard as if by an old Roman engineer, of the extinct buffalo; his bones are everywhere to be found on the surface of the prairie in little bleached piles. Deer there were none of any consequence to be seen, but occasionally an antelope would appear, watch our movements with fear and fascination, and then scud away with the speed of the wind. Shy as these beautiful animals are, acute their every sense, and wonderful their speed, they do not elude Custer's hunters, who have regularly compelled them to appear at mess.

From the Little Heart we struck across to the Cannon Ball River, a tributary of the Missouri, narrow, shallow, and tortuous (sic), deriving its name from the presence of bowders of all sizes worn by attrition to perfect roundness. In our first four days we had made very nearly seventy-five miles, despite the terrible heat. Very rarely did the thermometer record less than 90 deg.; on the Fourth—a Fourth by no means glorious—it was 104 deg., no shade and never a breath of wind. Fortunately the nights were cool and we were spared the annoyance of the occasional alkaline dust that rising during the march made our thirst intolerable, eyes sore, and faces blistered despite veils.

Winding up the Cannon Ball we struck towards the waters of Grand River. On our seventh day out, Goose, our Sioux scout—his aboriginal name is something like Tobacco Chowchow—had an opportunity to display his skill as a guide, of which he had always been boasting. He had promised to lead us to the only timbered oasis within some fifty miles, and through a long twenty miles of what General Custer calls "varied monotony," over and up and down little coulees, and round and by innumerable buttes we wound, till after eight hours' dusty marching, with nothing like a tree in sight, and no evidence of the nearness of water save the high, shrill, almost human complaint of the keen-scented mules at every halt, we debouched into the promised oasis, a little lawn surrounded by hills so as to be invisible till you stumbled on it, with a clump of trees and a pearly stream of water. The old guide did not disdain a dignified chuckle as both novices and veterans in plain-craft acknowledged the beauty of the scene and his professional skill in reaching the spot. This endorsement of his competency was all the more valuable

as there is no map whatever in existence showing anything of the country after the Cannon Ball is left, and consequently, we must rely on Goose and Bear's Ears to track the route.

Progress, when we reached Grand River, was somewhat impeded by the alkaline character of the soil and water; nevertheless there was no lack of wood, water and grass. On the 11th we climbed the plateau out of the Missouri bottom and found what we had been promised—water abundant, timber plentiful and even dense along the streams, a soil yielding good pasturage and fairly adapted to cultivation. There is good water power, indications of gypsum and sandstone occur in the hills, and beds of lignite have been found across the last sixty miles. Moving at the pace and with the precautions we do, a thorough examination has as yet been impracticable. We have seen nothing to indicate gold, though as we have not yet reached the eozoic geological island on the further side of Belle Fourche we have no occasion to feel disappointed. Game has not, as yet, proved plentiful.

We have, it is true, found no gold, neither any scalps, but we have come across one of the sacred caves of which rumor had been so eloquent as I stated in a preceding letter, and Goose's character as a guide has again been signally endorsed. We came across it as he had predicted we should— near Slim Butte—and it was, as he had predicted, a subterranean passage opening from the prairie by a rugged and rocky entrance probably twenty feet square. It may be that, as he predicted, the cave extends beneath the earth for many miles and is the Sioux Erebus; our efforts to penetrate were not successful to that extent. We found, however, in about 100 yards all that he had promised in the shape of carvings and rude drawings cut deeply in the rock. A full description of these will be given in a letter going further into details than this one has gone. Suffice it to say, generally, that the work is clearly not that of any tribes of Indians now known here. The figures are very rude—as rude as any designed by Cheyenne, Sioux, or Mandan, but the depth of incision, the greater boldness of

the occasional curves, and the compactness of the whole work do not favor the hypothesis that any of these tribes wrought the work. Nor could the early mound-builders have been the authors, since no sign whatever of their occupancy of this part of the country has as yet been afforded. Rudely hazarding an opinion one would say from the selected situation and quality of the work, that its authors were of far Eastern origin, but if this were the case why should it occur at a point so far inland! If Custer's expedition, not having any particularly lofty aim, were to throw some light on the vexed question of our Indian tribes, that would be a notable instance of stumbling on an unexpected conclusion. As yet, however, the scientists are inclined to consider volcanoes and their thermal or mineral springs are real bases of superstitions concerning all these mystic caverns and hills of which we have heard so much natural phenomena improved to their own advantage by wily medicine men and chiefs.

We found in the cave heaps of objects evidently cast in as propitiatory offerings by passing bands—bows, arrows, cartridges, pelts, rattles, beads, knife-blades, &c, of which more anon, and the bleaching skull clearly of a Caucassian, perforated by a bullet-hole, in a manner making it probable that either he was sacrificed as a victim to the tutelary deity of the cave—which the scouts and interpreters concur in poo-poohing, as such a victim would not be shot, but certainly tortured by fire—or fell a prey, like many others, to the fascinating fables of the auriferous wealth of the Black Hills with which the frontier has rung for a quarter of a century.

Last, as to Indians. Within the next forty-eight hours we shall indubitably sight the Black Hills and reach them by the 20th at the latest. Yesterday we saw a small body of Indians away off on the left; they disappeared the moment that our flanking party moved to report their presence. This morning another small party appeared in the rear, evidently having moved round during the night, and as I write the signal so well known to old travellers through Colorado, Utah, and New Mexico, are visible behind us—three smokes, one considerably to the left of the other two, signalling the line of our march and the fact that there are no more of us coming. Sitting Bull, the guides believe, will certainly make a stand at the Hills. General Custer affects to disbelieve this, and his opinion is shared in by most of the officers. The fact is that there is considerable room for difference on not only this question, but others of greater gravity. Sitting Bull will not be a Sioux if he does not fight, and I incline to the belief that while the General has been pacific and cautious to the extreme of ostentation, he would very much like Sitting Bull to attack him. The column is considered about invincible, and Custer "owes Sitting Bull one," in common phrase, for the fight on the Yellowstone last year, wherein he gave the Long-Haired Chief his hands full till Stanley came up. At the same time the more that Bishop Hare's protest is thought about the less it is liked. According to the letter of the Laramie treaty we have no business here at all, and if there should be a fight and defeat, or a fight followed by a general outbreak and massacre, the blow would be fatal to the Grant-Sheridan Custer ring. Hence we find ourselves between two desires—to fight and not to fight. Another proof of this will be found in the fact that we shall make no such extended stay at the Hills as was at first contemplated. According to instructions the expedition was to be absent sixty days, and at least a month was to be spent in the Hills, which were to be thoroughly explored from Bear Butte. There is not the slightest doubt now that we shall not remain at the Butte more than ten days, but turn back at once and push for Bismarck as sharply as we have marched hither. The cause, of course, is a desire not to leave the frontier unprotected any longer than may be, but it will seem to the unprejudiced spectator that these reasons were of as urgent a character before we set out as they are now. If we have to hurry back, why come at all, especially since the exploring part of the work, which at the outset was so warmly insisted upon, has been entirely dropped.   C.

NEW YORK WORLD
Issue of August 2, 1874

CUSTER IN CAMP.
EFFECT OF THE COMET UPON THE SIOUX BRAVES.

A SIGN OF DEVINE DISPLEASURE AND IMPENDING WOE—PROGRESS OF THE MARCH—CHARACTER OF THE SOIL, FAUNA, AND FLORA—FOSSILIFEROUS REMAINS.

(FROM OUR SPECIAL CORRESPONDENT.)

CUSTER'S EXPEDITION, Camp No. 13, July 14.—Our Sioux and Arickarees tell us that the comet, which we have seen very plainly this last three or four nights up near the Dipper, may exercise a potent influence—whether beneficial or malign, they, however, are not decided—upon Indian affairs generally and our expedition in particular. Sifting their stories they come down to this: For the past year or so the prophets of the Sioux have been unrelentingly preaching a crusade of extermination against the whites, and adding as an argument, the further to influence their ferocity, that the spirits of the dead are upon the war-path. Thrilling accounts have been given of the nightly appearance of dear braves horsed on coursers of fire, lamenting the degeneracy of their sons who allow their places of sepulture to be violated by the whites and their hunting grounds to be taken away. This comet may be pressed into the service by some of the more artful of these prophets and be exhibited as a proof of the wrath of Manitou with the pale faces and an earnest of supernatural support in the war. On the other hand,—and the interpreters and hunters share in the belief,—it is stated that by the Indians, as generally by the ignorant, superstitions, and uncivilized, the comet is always accepted as a token of divine displeasure and impending woe, so that the comet is likely to prove our valuable ally. Anyhow, there it is, as I write, a nebulous streak upon the northern skies.

How lovely the skies are on these high plains! Filled as they are with millions of keen, sparkling stars seen through a cloudless atmosphere, and bending over a vast expanse unbroken by hill or house, the sight is not less splendid than that of the perhaps more brightly blazing southern constellations.

The health of our command has been singularly good, despite the intense heat of the first few days out. There was a great deal of straggling and falling out, particularly among the infantry; but no serious cases of exhaustion and none of sunstroke. To-night there are but three men in ambulance.

There is an inclination, particularly since we struck into the mauvaises terres, to taunt Bear's Ears with a failure to keep faith with us in the matter of the natural capacity of the soil, fauna and flora. He, however, claims that the Happy Land where the deer would have to walk on each other were they not so fat that they cannot walk at all, lies beyond the Belle Fourche, or northern fork of the Cheyenne. Qui vivra verra, as we shall reach that river in a couple of days. Thus far game has not been abundant, barring antelope, with which from the day we left Fort Abraham Lincoln our hunters have kept us steadily—sometimes lavishly—supplied. We have only seen a couple of deer; for all feathered game one flight of ducks, and no fish whatever.

The characteristics of the soil from the time we left Grand River have been described in another letter. We are now in the Bad Lands of Montana, near the Little Missouri, by whose headwaters we shall enter the Black Hills somewhat further west then we had at first intended. An adamantine clay, deeply scored by gulches and canyons formed by the power of water, with here and there a small stream, whose are waters are strongly impregnated with alkali, the lands, though less difficult to traverse than those further to the north and west, are utterly worthless for all purposes of civilization. There is no vegetation save in the cases and occasionally a bed of stunted, thorny cactus. The grasses are sparse; each tuft stands separate from the others, so that they do not cover the ground. Willows fringe the water-courses, with an occasional cottonwood. Briarroses are about the only attempt of nature in a decorative direction.

We have found a good many petrifactions some of them noticeable for oddity, some for size, but these are invariably of trees. But one "fossilferous remains" has been picked up—apparently the leg bone of an animal larger than any now existing in America, certainly than any that ever frequented this tract, which Mr. Greenwell found to-day. Of minerals we have as yet found none, nor any indications thereof, save occasional ferruginous stains in the clay.

I have already spoken of the sacred Washsum or spirit cave of the Sioux, found at Cave Butte, some little distance from Slim Butte. The butte itself is a rocky hill, about 220 or 230 feet high, and standing perhaps 100 feet over the highest of the knolls surrounding it and rolling up to it. Its summit was a perfect plateau, of 30 or 35 acres area, covered with a moderately abundant grass, and surrounded on every side by a continuous perpendicular wall of sandstone rock—a palisade almost as regular as if it had been made by architect and mason. There were salient angles and depressions in various places, and at each end the parapet rose into a rule tower, the whole giving the idea of a fortress planned by some Vauban centuries ago. Indeed, Captain Ludlow, our chief of engineers, was prepared to risk his professional reputation on the fact that this was no freak of exuberant nature, but a deliberate work of defence (sic). There was sufficient ground for this hypothesis for those fancifully inclined to accept it, but Mr. Winchell upset the theory in a moment by pointing out that the rocky out-crop was a regular occurence, and that while the clay and softer stone had been worn away by centuries of exposure, the sandstone had remained a fence around the boundary of the exposure through the softer clay.

The "cave" itself, which Goose found in a few minutes after having guided us unfalteringly to the butte, has been of interest to us rather because of the evidence it has furnished that the Sioux guide is competent, than because of its own inherent qualities. It isn't by any means a mammoth cave, but a crevice between two ledges of rock, sandstone forming the entrance and the walls further back being of limestone and clay. There are—as a survey of its interior for a distance of 130 or 140 yards, checked by the narrowness of its passage, proved—no chambers, neither any lateral expansions nor extensions. We found in it neither the souls of the damned nor the skeletons of the martyred, not even a bat or a snake.

Outside was picked up a skull with a round hole over the left eye, and two other fissures or fractures of less regular shape in the forehead. From the frontal angle, the surgeons declared it the skull of a white man, and at once a theory was set afloat that it was the skull of some unfortunate sacrified by the jealous Sioux to the deity of the cave. Inasmuch as the Sioux do not offer human sacrifices to their deities and employ fire in cases where formal torture is intended, the hypothesis goes for little, but the skull probably was that of some gold-seeker surprised and summarily shot. In the character of the wounds and the Indian name of the butte—"the place where the man was killed by a bull"—some of our philologists professed to find a clew (sic) to the fate of the owner of the skull and ascribed death to the attack of a bison; suggesting that the victim might have been a French trapper as were frequently received into Sioux tribes on the upper Missouri. On the other hand we have positive evidence that the Sioux never allowed their adopted members to enter their sacred places.

The engravings on the walls and roof of sandstone at the entrance were principally of animals and birds—horses, dogs, bears, deer, elk, and (probably) the eagle. The tracing was rude, but, as I have already said, the incision was deeper than is generally the case in these tracings, and the lines bolder and truer, particularly in the curves. One animal was considered by some of the party to be an extinct species of elephant or mammoth, being larger than the buffalo, the horns longer and straighter, the legs higher and much stouter, and the bulk of the maneless body more evenly distributed. About as high up on the wall as a man could reach was the impression of a human foot, probably four inches long, and unquestionably the work of an iron or steel instrument, for marks of the chipping were visible at the bottom of the mould. It was perfect in shape and finish. Two hands were sunk in the wall near it, possibly to a depth of a little less than an inch. This work was as admirably executed as the other, and its author and object as inexplicable, since while human figures often occur in these compositions on the rocks I have never known a part of the body to be reproduced. All around were marks rudely cut in the rock, some idle scratches done at random, others more deep and true and apparently with purpose. There was no particular evidence attainable in our hasty examination that there was any definite pattern or order, though the marking where it was most regular was distributed over two opposing faces of the rock with a rude semi-order or contrast. Nor could we say that the marks were hieroglyphics or written charatcers. It was certain, however, that the whole was the work of different hands, and was done at various periods, though in this atmosphere the traces of time are not easily read.

Goose stood without the cave while we were examining it stolid, silent, almost sad. He apparently thought that he had done sacrilege enough in guiding us to the sacred spot without assisting personally at its profanation. The younger braves were not so particular, and two or three of them ventured into the cave though not without evidences of vague apprehension. Goose grunted out that "Young men now were not like their fathers."

Of the heap of heterogeneous articles found in the cave I have already had something to say, at least as concerned their character. Apart from the weapons and ornaments of savage life, there were other articles evidently trophies of raids. A gold ring marked "A. L." or "A.E.," an old hair brush, the rusty blade of a table knife, the handle of a plated fork or spoon, and an old copper penny piece of Canadian coinage that had evidently been used for a medal or gaud, as it was pierced with a hole, in which was a wireshank, with a flint-lock horse-pistol two feet long (which the owner can have by proving property, paying expenses, and addressing G. A. Custer, Brevet Major-General, United States Army), were the prinicpal sorts of our curiosity-seekers. I asked Goose the object of these offerings, and he said they were made by bands of the Northern Sioux passing southward to hunt in order to obtain success in the chase.

C.

NEW YORK WORLD
Issue of August 16, 1874

THE BLACK HILLS. GENERAL CUSTER'S OFFICIAL REPORT.

AN AGRICULTURAL COUNTRY OF UNSURPASSED BEAUTY. THE REPORTS OF SURFACE GOLD FINDING FULLY CONFIRMED—A MARCH AMIDST FLOWERS OF EXQUISITE COLOR AND PERFUME—THE GARDEN OF AMERICA DISCOVERED—PROGRESS AND PROSPECTS OF THE EXPEDITION.

(FROM OUR OWN CORRESPONDENT.)

BLACK HILLS EXPEDITION, NEAR HARNEY'S PEAK, BLACK HILLS, Dak., August 2.— For many years great public interest, particularly in the West, has centered in this region, indefinitely known as the Black Hills. Many of your readers may not be familiar with the geographical location of this region, for their benefit I will state that the Black Hills, although sometimes understood to embrace a more extensive region of the country, are included in a series of ranges of hills lying principally in the southwestern corner of Dakota Territory, and extending in a northwestern direction into the territories of Wyoming and Montana, and situated between the 43d and 45th parallels of latitude and between the 103d and 105th meridians. This vast region as already stated, has for a long period excited greater curiosity and inquiry throughout the country, and particularly in the West, than any other portion of the public domain. This feeling originated and has grown, not only from the fact that the region referred to constitutes by far the most important, if not the largest, single tract of territory

South Dakota State Historical Society

This picture has long borne the caption "Sunshine and Shadow Mountain." The photograph was apparently taken sometime during the permanent camp along French Creek. Three men are pictured two in the right foreground and one at the middle far left, standing at the base of the tall tree. None is identified, however the profile of the man standing at the far right closely resembles that of Fred Grant.

remaining unexplored, and of which little or nothing was known. If there was but little actual knowledge concerning the Black Hills there has been no lack of rumors and opinions throughout the entire Western frontier as to the fabulous wealth of mineral stored in their recesses. Nor have these opinions and rumors been wholly chimerical. True, no white man has ever penetrated beyond the outer base of the elevated ranges which mark the termination of the surrounding plains, but Indian traders and men connected with the Indian Bureau have at various times approached the east-

ern boundary of the Black Hills, and from the Indians themselves and from other sources of information have derived the idea that the interior region inclosed by the Black Hills was rich in mineral wealth. It is stated, and upon unquestionable authority, my informant being an officer of the army of high standing and reputation, that years ago a squaw belonging to one of the bands of Sioux infesting this region came into one of our frontier posts along the Platte River and exhibited a large nugget of pure gold which she is stated to have found in the Black Hills. Of course this was ample foundation upon which to set all sorts of rumors afloat. The only practical result of the revelation made by this squaw, was a movement, begun by officers and others at the post referred to, looking to an elaborate exploration of the locality in which the gold was reported to have been found. An agreement was made with the squaw under which she was to guide a party to the desired locality. She, in the meantime, returned to her people, and the story goes that, acting in accordance with that policy which from time immemorial has induced the Indians to jealously guard all the approaches to the Black Hills, the Indians either made away with the squaw or so carefully guarded her that she has never been seen by white men since her departure from the fort. This is but one of the many stories, true or false, upon which the people of the western frontier have founded their belief that, inclosed within the Black Hills, were rich treasures of gold and silver which only await the advance of the white man to build up a wealth which, in belief at least, had become fabulous. Year by year added strength to this idea until the more important and more enterprising of our frontier population, unable to await the tedious action of the General Government in developing or at least exploring this pictured El Dorado, determined at various times to organize on a private basis parties to explore the Black Hills, and avail themselves of the hidden wealth confidently believed to be there. For years the Government has been forced, out of regard to its treaty stipulations with the Indians which forbid white men entering the regions of country for purposes of settlement or other purpose without the sanction of the Government, to issue orders positively forbidding these exploring parties to set out. No later than the past spring a project of this kind was set on foot in Dakota, the avowed purpose being to explore the Black Hills; but as such an organization was likely to become involved in difficulties with the Indians, and would probably exhibit but little regard for the rights of the latter, General Custer, who reported the proposed movement to the War Department,

was authorized to forbid its further progress, and to employ force if necessary to prevent the organization referred to from entering the Indian country. A similar expedition, acting with a similar purpose, was set on foot in Bozenan, (sic), Montana, the intention being to penetrate the Black Hills region from the west side. As soon as the authorities at Washington learned of the proposed movement instructions were telegraphed to the Territorial Governor to prevent the departure of the expedition, but the order arrived too late, the expedition, numbering 150 men, had started, and was already beyond recall. They had reason, however, to repent of the undertaking, as they had no sooner entered the Big Horn country east of the Yellowstone than they were beset by overwhelming numbers of Indians both by day and night, and after losing several of their number in killed and wounded, were forced to retrace their steps, arrriving at Bozenan (sic), the point of departure, in a miserable condition, and willing for the time being to leave the reputed treasures of precious minerals undisturbed in their rocky beds. Up to the present year the General Government has never attempted to determine the character of the Black Hills. The nearest approaches were made by exploring parties under Captain W. F. Raynolds, Topographical Engineer U.S.A., in 1860, (now General Raynolds, Engineer Department,) and by Lieutenant G. K. Warren, Topographical Engineers, in 1855, (now General Warren, Engineer Department, U.S.A.,) but neither of these officers made any effort to penetrate the Black Hills. They contented themselves with skirting along the exterior base of the outer ridge of hills, never even obtaining a glimpse of the country embraced within, except, perhaps, such as might be occasionally obtained from some outlying peak. Raynold, in the report of his explorations, states that when near the base of the Black Hills, and between the two main forks of the Cheyenne River which almost envelop the Black Hills on all sides, indications of the presence of gold were found. His report goes on to state that the very nature of the case, however, forbade that an

extensive or thorough search for the precious metals should be made by an expedition such as he commanded.

"The party was composed in the main of irresponsible adventurers, who recognized no moral obligation resting upon them. They were all furnished with arms and ammunition, while we were abundantly supplied with picks and shovels, and carried with us a partial stock of provisions. Thus the whole outfit differed in no essential respect from that which would be required if the object of the expedition had only been prospecting for gold. The powder would serve for blasting, and the picks and shovels were amply sufficient for the primitive mining of the gold pioneer, while the arms would be equally useful for defence (sic) and in purveying for the commissariat. It is thus evident that if gold had been discovered in any considerable quantity the party would have at once disregarded all the authority and entreaties of the officers in charge and have been converted into a band of gold miners, leaving the former the disagreeable option of joining them in their abandonment of duty or of returning across the plains alone through innumerable perils. It was for these reasons that the search for gold was at all times discouraged, yet still it was often difficult to restrain the disposition to prospect, and there were moments when it was feared that some of the party would defy all restraint."

This is probably the first and only reference officially made concerning the existence of gold in the Black Hills. This report was not made public until 1868, when Congress authorized its publication. The brief allusion to gold, although slight in itself, yet, accompanied as it was by the foregoing explanation showing that the search for gold was discouraged at all times, only served to strengthen all previous rumors and beliefs as to the existence of the precious metal in the Black Hills, and has since been referred to as corroborating testimony of that fact. For several years the sending of an expedition into the Black Hills has been contemplated by the Government, and has been a favorite idea with some of the higher officers of the army. To determine the existence or non-existence of the precious metals within the region referred to has not been the controlling object, however. The Indians, or those at least who could be induced to converse upon the subject, have at all times represented that this terra incognita was a region of unsurpassed beauty and fertility, inclosed by impassable ranges of hills or mountains that no white men had ever succeeded in penetrating this outer barrier of hills, and that few Indians, even, were at all familiar with the country inclosed. These descriptions and scraps of information, obtained at various times and from various sources, combined, with the prevailing belief of the existence of precious minerals and the increasembarrassment of the General Government in preventing the organization of irresponsible and unauthorized exploring parties, and the possible infringement of existing Indian treaties, to render it highly desirable that the true value and character of this much-talked of region of unknown, unexplored, country should be determined beyond reasonable doubt. Only in this way could the Government either quiet the vague rumors and beliefs concerning the wealth of the Black Hills and the most practicable route thereto.

In May last, under a letter of instruction from Lieutenant-General Sheridan to General Terry, the Department Commander, the present Black Hills Expedition was organized and equipped at Fort Lincoln, Dak., under the command of General Custer. The troops authorized to be employed embrace ten companies of the Seventh United States Cavalry, divided into two equal battalions, the first under command of Brevet Brigadier-General Geo. A. Forsyth, acting A.D.C. to General Sheridan, but temporarily acting under the orders of General Custer, the second battalion under command of Brevet Colonel J. G. Tilford, major, Seventh Cavalry; one battery of Gatling guns, commanded by Lieutenant Josiah Chance, Seventeenth Infantry; a detachment of sixty Indian scouts commanded by Lieutenant Geo. D. Wallace, Seventh Cavalry; and a battalion of infantry consisting of one company

of the Twentieth Infantry, Captain Wheaton commanding and one company of the Seventeenth Infantry, Captain L. H. Sanger, commanding the battalion. The expedition is expected to be absent from Fort Lincoln a period of sixty days. To transport the subsistence and forage required by this force, numbering in all about one thousand men, a wagon train of 100 and ten six-mule teams accompany this command, there are about one hundred civilians employed in the capacity of teamsters, wagonmaster, herders, &c. A beef herd numbering upwards of one hundred head of cattle is driven with the expedition. General Custer's staff is composed as follows: Acting Aid, Lieutenant-Colonel Frederick D. Grant, Aide-de-Camp to the Lieutenant General; Acting Assistant Adjutant-General, First Lieutenant James Calhoun, Seventh Cavalry; Quartermaster and Commissary, First Lieutenant A. E. Smith, Seventh Cavalry; Chief Medical Officer, Assistant Surgeon J. W. Williams, United States Army; Engineer Officer, Brevet-Colonel W. H. Ludlow, United States Engineers. The following named gentlemen accompany the expedition in the interests of science; Professor N. H. Winchell, of the Minnesota State University, as geologist; Professor A. B. Donaldson of St. Paul, Minnesota as botanist; and Assistant Geologist M. G.H. Grinnell, of Yale College (an assistant of Professor Marsh), as naturalist, Mr. L. H. North, assistant naturalist; Mr. Woods, assistant to engineer office; and Mr. Wm. H. Illingworth, of St. Paul, as photographer. The expedition set out from Fort Lincoln, on the Missouri River, on the morning of July 2, the intention being to pursue almost a southwesterly course for nearly 300 miles through a trackless region of country and strike the Belle Fourche River, the northern fork of the Cheyenne, somewhere near the 10th meridian. Knowing the dangers which beset a command when traversing a country infested by hostile Indians, independently of the peaceable objects and intentions of the expedition, the following order was published to the troops before the departure of the latter from Fort Lincoln:

HEADQ'RS BLACK HILLS
EXPEDITION,
JUNE 30, 1874

GENERAL ORDER NO. 3

First—The following order of march will be observed: The detachment of Indian scouts, Lieutenant G. D. Wallace, Seventh Cavalry, Commanding.

Second—The battery of Gatling guns, First Lieutenant Josiah Chance, Seventeenth Infantry, commanding.

Third—The ambulance and wagon train, the latter, when practicable, to move in four columns, the ambulances preceding the latter; company wagons to be formed in the outer columns in the order occupied by the respective companies, the pioneer wagon being in advance of one of the columns.

Fourth—The infantry battalion in two columns, Captain L. H. Sanger, Seventeenth Cavalry, commanding. The commanding officer infantry battalion will regulate the distance within 300 yards at which his command will follow the train.

Fifth—One company of the Seventh Cavalry as rear guard, to be designated as hereafter specified. The right battalion Seventh Cavalry, Major George A. Forsyth, Ninth Cavalry, commanding will habitually march on the right flank, and opposite the train, and at such distance, not exceeding 400 yards, as the battalion commander may direct. The left battalion Seventh Cavalry, Major J. G. Tilford, Seventh Cavalry, commanding, will habitually march on the left flank, and opposite the centre of the train, and at such distance, not exceeding 400 yards, as the battalion commander may direct. Each commanding officer of a cavalry battalion will cause flanking parties, consisting of a non-commissioned officer and three men from each company, to move opposite and to the right of their respective companies and at such distance from the latter as will most readily enable the flankers to give timely notice of the approach or presence of an enemy without unnecessary exposure of the flankers. The latter should not pass beyond the view of the range of the carbines of their respective companies. Each commander of a cavalry battalion will consider the entire flank upon which his command is moving as under the special protection of the latter, and will hold his command in constant readiness while on the march or in camp to repel, without further orders, any attack directed his particular flank of the main command.

The commanding officer of the infantry battalion will consider the train generally as under the protection of the latter, and in addition, will, while on the march, be in readiness to render suport to the rear guard should the latter be pressed or suddenly assaulted by a hostile force.

Lieutenant Wallace, commanding Indian scouts, will detail daily from his command ten scouts as the advance of the advanced guard. This advance will be instructed to precede the column, keeping within a thousand yards, a well as within sight of the latter. He will also send such special scouting parties to prominent points near the line of march as the commanding officer of the expedition may direct from time to time.

Line officers will not leave their respective commands without special permission to that effect from their battalion commander. The commanding officers of the battery and detachment of Indian scouts will habitually march at the head of their respective commands.

The acting quartermaster-sergeants of companies are authorized to march with their respective company wagons; all other enlisted men on duty with their company will march with the latter.

The non-commissioned staff, band, and other enlisted men on duty at these headquarters will march under the command of the Acting Assistant Adjutant-General near the head of the column.

Lieutenant A. E. Smith, Seventh Cavalry, Quartermaster of the expedition, will habitually march at the head of his train. He will also as Commissary of Subsistence require the beef herd which accompanies the expedition to be driven opposite and near to the train. The following assignments of medical officers of the expedition are hereby made: Assistant Surgeon J. W. Williams, United States Army, in addition to his duties as chief medical officer of the expedition, is assigned to duty with the right battalion of the Seventh Cavalry;

Acting Assistant Surgeon Allen, United States Army, is assigned to duty with the left battalion, Seventh Cavalry; Acting Assistant Surgeon Bergen, United States Army, is assigned to duty with the infantry battalion. The medical officers herein named will habitually march in the battalions to which they are assigned, and in camp will attend sick call and prescribe for the sick of their respective battalions. The chief medical officer of the expedition will, however, give a general supervision to the medical duties required in battalions other than that to which he is herein specially assigned. He will also provide medical attention and treatment for such cases of sickness as may require attention among the officers and men at these headquarters, and for the civil employees accompanying the expedition.

The general plan of camp will be that adopted in the present camp, the infantry battalion being advanced far enough from the nearest flanks of the two cavalry battalions to allow the wagon trains to be parked in its rear, and connecting the flanks of the right and left battalions of cavalry. Each cavalry company will occupy a front of fifty paces. The picket line will be stretched fifteen paces in front of the line of men's tents. All the latter will be on the company line except the tent authorized as a cooktent and two shelter tents for the use of company cooks. These tents will be pitched inside the picket line fifteen paces from the latter and near the company wagon. Company officers tents will be pitched outside the line of men's tents, fifteen paces from the opposite the centre of the line. Officer's cooktents will be pitched fifteen paces in rear of the line of officer's tents, the latter to face their respective companies. No tents other than those authorized by existing orders will be allowed to accompany the expedition. As soon as the camp ground to be occupied by their respective commands has been indicated by battalion commanders, the latter will at once, and before commencing preparations to go into camp, throw out a strong line of pickets to occupy a commanding line opposite to and several hundred yards, depending upon the

nature of the ground, from their respective commands.

The commanding officer of the detachment of Indian scouts will at the same time post such pickets in advance as will cover that point. The line of pickets about camp will be maintained until relieved by the picket guard at retreat. The latter under the personal direction of the officer of the day will be posted at retreat, and relieved by battalion commanders immediately after reveille by details from their respective battalions. As the utmost prudence will necessarily be observed to prevent the surprise of individuals or small parties of prowling Indians, no member of the command will go beyond the line of flankers while on the march, nor beyond the line of pickets while in camp, except by special authority from the commanding officer of the expedition, and then such parties will, when practicable, pass and repass the lines at the same point.

As a pistol or rifle shot will be the signal of danger, the discharge of fire-arms, within or near the lines, by day or night, is strictly prohibited. Firing at game from the column or from the vicinity of camp is prohibited, except under circumstances warranting special permission.

Hunting parties will only be organized under authority from these headquarters.

No horse will be grazed in camp without being secured by side lines and lariat. All horses will be fastened to the picket lines at retreat. Vicious horses will have side lines attached to them to prevent injury to other horses. The stable guard will also be instructed to act as pickets and promptly give the alarm in case of attack. Commanders of cavalry battalions will, in addition to the usual stable guard of three men and one non-commissioned officer, require an additional force of at least four men of a company, all under command of an officer, to be posted in good position at least three hundred yards beyond the herd dismounted. The Quartermaster of the expedition will cause the mule herd to be grazed under similar regulations as regards lariats, one teamster to every fourth team, and one wagonmaster to be constantly with the mule herd, which will be grazed as near to camp as the condition of the grazing will permit.

As the object of this expedition is a peaceable one, care will be taken not to molest or in any manner disturb any Indians who may be encountered on the march, unless the latter should first act in a hostile manner. As a matter of precaution, no party of Indians, no matter how small, will be permitted to approach the vicinity of the picket lines by day or night. Officers and men are particularly cautioned against being drawn into the trap usually laid by Indians— by the latter exposing a small number, endeavoring to induce pursuit. This command is about to march through a country infested by Indians, more or less hostile, and even should the latter, as it is hoped, not engage in general warfare and the usual acts of hostilities there is no doubt but that they will endeavor to make captures of stock and to massacre small parties found imprudently beyond the lines. To guard against this the utmost caution and prudence on the part of every member of this command will be required. While it is hoped that these admonitions will prove ample, the commanding officer of the expedition will promptly apply correctives of the most summary character in all cases of violation of the orders contained herein. Orders giving a list of trumpet calls will be furnished hereafter.

Sixth — While on the march reveille will be sounded at 2:45 o'clock. The general will be sounded at 5:15 o'clock, and the advance at 5 o'clock. The cavalry will not saddle up until the signal "boots and saddle" has been sounded from these headquarters. Tents will be left standing until the general has sounded. There will be two general roll calls daily—reveille and retreat—at both of which the men will fall in under arms, and the result of the roll-calls will be reported to the battalion commanders. In the case of the absence of officers from either roll call the fact will be reported by the battalion commander to these headquarters. The commanding officers of cavalry battalions will give their personal attention to the proper performance of stable duty, and will require the presence of company officers during the performance of this duty.

By orders of Brevot Major General Custer,
(Signed)

JAMES CALHOUN,
First Lieutenant Seventh Cavalry, Acting Assistant Adjutant-General.

Probably no expedition of anything like equal numbers ever began a movement on the plains so completely equipped and perfectly organized as this one. The mount of the Seventh Cavalry is equal, if not superior, to that of any regiment in the service, many of the horses having been purchased in Kentucky, so famous for the superiority of its horses. Many of the officers are mounted upon thoroughbreds, also purchased in the Southern States. The officers and men of this regiment are thoroughly inured to frontier service and campaigning against the Indians, having been almost constantly engaged in field duty on the plains since 1866. I speak particularly of the officers now serving with this regiment in the field, for it appears that only a small portion of the officers whose names appear in the army register as belonging to the Seventh Cavalry are serving with the regiment. Some, in fact, have never seen their regiment, but have been constantly on what those who perform their legitimate duty term "fancy duty," and are embraced in that noble army of patriots termed feather-bed soldiers. This, however, I believe, does not apply to but a small portion of the officers of this regiment who are not now with their command in the field. Many of them have been selected for their ability and former service during the war, and placed in positions of great trust. One captain is aid to General Sherman, another is aid to General Sheridan, a third captain is aid to General Pope. Thus there are three captains aids to three of our general officers. Another officer of this regiment is at the Artillery School at Fortress Monroe; still another is engaged in the Signal Bureau under Old Probabilities in Washington. These five officers have all been selected from reasons which, however detrimental to the regiment their absence may be, can only be regarded as complimentary to themselves.

There are other officers, however, not with their commands, whose absence whether regarded as detrimental to their companies or regiment or otherwise, have not the same complimentary reasons to cover their absence. Some officers prefer, as a lady once remarked to an officer of high rank now in command of a military department, to hunt the Comanche down Pennsylvania avenue. If report be true this remark is not without verification at the present. As evidence, see report of a recent interview with General Sherman, in which he is reported to have referred to a certain lieutenant who had been hanging around Washington for several months, in spite of the General's efforts to have him sent to his regiment. As the General did not name this lieutenant it may not be quite possible to identify him in so slight a description, but if no other regiment claims him I know of a regiment not a thousand miles from the Black Hills; the officers of which think they could name a party to answer the description without serious effort. But what has this to do with the Black Hills Expedition? About as much as some of the officers, to whom I have just referred with the military service of their country. No one fact, perhaps, has strengthened the confidence of the men belonging to the cavalry portion of the expedition more than that they were equipped with the recently adopted carbine, called the new pattern. It is a slight modification of what is known in the army as the Springfield pattern, the calibre being reduced from 50 to 45. It is said to be the most effective weapon ever yet placed in the hands of troops, and is remarkable both for its range and accuracy as well as rapidity of fire. Beyond the ordinary incidents attending upon a march on the plains nothing occurred worthy of record during the first few days. It required several days to get well under way. The men of the infantry were unaccustomed to field service, and many fell by the wayside the first day or two, rendering ambulances in great demand; but this little defect in their locomotive powers was soon overcome, and a few marches put them in such condition that they were able to rattle

South Dakota State Historical Society

The greatest excitement of August 7th was when Custer killed a large male grizzly bear. Preparations for camp were just beginning when, according to Correspondent A. B. Donaldson of the ST. PAUL PIONEER, "Bloody Knife exclaims motto! motto! (bear! bear!)." Four men apparently brought the bear down with six to eight rifle shots. Pictured from left to right they are Bloody Knife, Custer, Pvt. Noonan and Capt. William Ludlow. Later Custer wrote to his wife, Elizabeth, "I have reached the hunter's highest round of fame . . . I have killed my Grizzley."

In this second exposure, Capt. Ludlow was either invited or told to sit down. Custer extends his hand higher on his rifle barrel, throws his head back over his shoulder heroically and assumes a more dramatic pose. Bloody Knife maintains an impassive stoicism. The expedition's zoological report, referring to the bear, says, "The old veteran bore on his body the marks of many a conflict. On his back, just behind the shoulders, was a rugged scar 10 inches long and 2 wide; his face was marked in several places, and his sides and thighs were disfigured in the same manner." It went on to say, "In color it was everywhere a deep, glossy black, except on the head and on the lower part of the shoulders, and thighs, where there was a slight sprinkling of dark-gray hairs!" Later the same day, Santee scouts shot and killed the mate of this male grizzley.

off their thirty odd miles a day without flinching. On the 15th of July the expedition halted to rest one day, the time being taken advantage of also to prepare our letters for home. From this point two Indian scouts were despatched with the mail—the latter forming a small, compact parcel done up securely in canvas. This was confided to the two scouts, who set out on their perilous journey of 227 miles as soon as the darkness of night afforded a cover to their departure. Whether they reached their destination or not may be known to your readers, but as we are cut off from all communication from the rest of the world we must remain in doubt as to whether our scouts succeeded in eluding the vigilant eyes of the Indians then prowling about us or not.

From this point General Custer sent a brief despatch to the military authorities in the States giving a resume of our progress so far. As his despatch contains all that was of interest concerning our march and the country passed over up to that point I send you a copy:

HEADQ'RS BLACK HILLS EXPEDITION.

PROSPECT VALLEY, DAK., JULY 15, 1874.

Lon. 103 46W. lat. 45 29N.

Assistant Adjutant-General
Department of Dakota,
St. Paul, Minn.:

This expedition reached this point yesterday, having marched since leaving Fort Lincoln 227½ miles. We are now 170 miles in a direct line from Lincoln and within five miles of the "Little Missouri" River, and within about twelve miles from the Montana boundary, our bearing from Fort Lincoln being south, 62 deg. west. After the second day from Lincoln we marched over a beautiful country; the grazing was excellent and abundant, wood sufficient for our wants, and water in great abundance every ten miles. When we struck the tributaries of Grand River we entered a less desirable portion of the country; nearly all the streams flowing into Grand River being more or less impregnated with alkali, rending the crossings difficult. We found a plentiful supply of grass, wood,

and water, however, even along the portion of our route. Upon leaving the headwaters of Grand River, we ascended the plateau separating the watershed of the "Little Missouri" from that running into the Missouri, and found a country of surpassing beauty and richness of soil. The pasturage could not be finer, timber is abundant, and water both good and plentiful. As an evidence of the character of the country, we have marched since leaving Fort Lincoln on an average over seventeen miles per day, on day marching thirty-two miles; yet our mules and beef cattle have constantly improved in condition, the beef cattle depending entirely upon the excellent grazing we have marched over.

The health of my command is something remarkable, not a single man being on the sick report. Every one seems not only in good, health, but in excellent spirits.

Between the forks of Grand River we discovered a cave, to which the Indians attach great importance. The cave extends about four hundred feet underground, beyond which point it was not practicable to explore it. Its walls and roof are covered with rude carvings and drawings, cut into the solid rock, apparently the work of Indians, although probably by a different tribe than either of those now roaming in this region. Near the cave was found a white man's skull, evidently perforated by a bullet. It had been exposed to the atmosphere for several years. As no white man, except those belonging to this expedition, are known to have passed anywhere near this locality, the discovery of this skull was regarded with unusual interest.

The cave was found to contain numerous articles of Indian equipment which had been thrown into the cave by the Indians as offerings to the Great Spirit. I have named the cave "Ludlow's Cave" in honor of the engineer officer of the expedition.

Our march thus far has been made without molestation upon the part of the Indians. We discovered no signs indicating the recent presence of Indians until day before yesterday, when Captain McDougall, Seventh Cavalry, who was on the flank, discovered a small party of about twenty Indi-

ans watching our movements; the Indians scampered off as soon as discovered. Yesterday the same or a similar sized party made its appearance along our line of march, and was seen by Captain Moylan, Seventh Cavalry, who was in command of the rear guard, and soon after several signals of smoke were sent up which our Indians guides interpret as carrying information to the main body of our presence and movements. As I sent pacific messages to all the tribes infesting this region before the expedition moved, and expressed a desire to maintain friendly relations with them, the signals observed by us may have simply been made to enable the villages to avoid us. Our Indian guides think differently, however, and believe the Indians mean war. Should this be true, they will be the party to fire the first shot. Indians have been seen near camp today. Mr. Grinnell, of Yale College, one of the geologists accompanying the expedition, discovered on yesterday an important fossil. It was a bone about four feet long and twelve inches in diameter, and had evidently belonged to an animal larger than an elephant.

Beds of lignite of good quality have been observed at various points along our route by Professor Winchell, one of the geologists of the expedition. I do not know whether I will be able to communicate with you again before the return of the expedition or not.

G. A. Custer,
Brevet Major General U. S A.,
Commanding.

From Prospect Valley, from which General Custers despatch was written, the expedition moved on the 16th of July; for the incidents worthy of record from that date up to the date in which I send this letter, I will again refer you to General Custer's second despatch, or that portion of it completed at this point, as I believe it is the General's intention to proceed tomorrow morning with five companies of cavalry in the direction of Fort Laramie, and that the scout Charlie Reynolds, who is to carry our despatches to that point, will accompany this detachment as far as it moves in the direction of Fort Laramie, which will probably be as far as the south fork of the Cheyenne in a south-westerly direction from Harney's Peak, near whose base I am now writing:

HEADQ'RS BLACK HILLS[33] EXPEDITION, 8½ MILES SOUTHEAST OF HARNEY'S PEAK, AUGUST 2, 1874.

Assistant Adjutant General Department of Dakota:

My last despatch was dated July 15, and sent from Prospect Valley, Dak., longitude 103 deg. 46 min., latitude 45 deg 29 min. Two of my Indian scouts left as bearers of the despatch as soon as their departure could be concealed by the darkness. After leaving that point this expedition moved in a southwesterly direction until it reached the valley of the Little Missouri River, up which we moved twenty-one miles. Finding this valley almost destitute of grazing along our line of march I ordered the waterkegs filled, and a supply of wood placed on the wagons, and left the valley in search of a better camp ground. During our passage up the valley of the Little Missouri we had entered and were about to leave the Territory of Montana. Our course was nearly due south. After a further march of about nine miles we arrived before sundown at a point capable of furnishing us good grazing and water for our animals, having marched over thirty miles since breaking camp in the morning. From this point to the valley of the Belle Fourche we found the country generally barren and uninviting, save in a few isolated places. We reached the Belle Fourche on the evening of the 18th of July, encamping where good grass, wood, and water were abundant, and at a point a short distance above that marked ("15") fifteen on Raynolds's map, just west of the line separating Dakota from Wyoming. The following day was spent in camp. On the 20th we crossed the Belle Fourche and began, as it were, skirmishing with the Black Hills. We begun (sic) by feeling our way carefully along the outlying ranges of hills, seeking a weak point through which we might make our way to the interior. We continued

33. Custer to Elizabeth, July 2, 1874, from camp near Harney's Peak, Dakota Territory.
   Breakfast at four. In the saddle at five. First I have my official despatch at attend to, then a letter to the "World.'
   Marguerite Merington, THE CUSTER STORY, p. 272.

from the time we ascended from the valley of the Belle Fourche to move through a very superior country covered with the best of grazing and abundance of timber, principally pine, poplar, and several varieties of oak. As we advanced the country skirting the Black Hills to the southward became each day more beautiful. On the evening of the 22d we halted and encamped east of and within four miles of the base of Inyan Kara. Desiring to ascend that peak the following day, it being the highest in the western range of the Black Hills, I did not move camp the following day, but taking a small party with, proceeded to the highest point of this prominent landmark, whose height is given as 6,600 feet. The day was not favorable for obtaining distant views, but I decided on the following morning to move due east and attempt the passage of the hills. We experienced considerable delay from fallen timber which lay in our pathway. With this exception, and a very little digging, rendered necessary in descending into a valley, the pioneers prepared the way for the train, and we reached camp by two o'clock, having marched eleven miles. We here found grass, water, and wood of the best quality and in great abundance. On the following day we resumed our march up this valley, which I had explored several miles the preceding evening, and which led us by an easy ascent almost southeast. After marching nearly twelve miles we encamped at an early hour in the same valley. This valley in one respect presented the most wonderful as well as beautiful aspect. Its equal I have never seen, and such, too, was the testimony of all who beheld it. In no public or private park have I ever seen such a profuse display of flowers. Every step of our march that day was amidst flowers of the most exquisite colors and perfume. So luxuriant in growth were they that men plucked them without dismounting from the saddle. Some belonged to new or unclassified species. It was a strange sight to glance back at the advancing columns of cavalry, and behold the men with beautiful bouquets in their hands, while the head gear of their horses was decorated with wreaths of flowers fit to crown a queen of May. Deeming

South Dakota State Historical Society

This picture is believed to be of Custer Peak, located nine miles due south of the present City of Dead-wood. The peak was named in honor of General George A. Custer by Capt. William Ludlow, the chief engineer for the Military Department of Dakota. The peak rises 6,804 feet above sea level. The expedition passed by it on August 8th, during the return trip back to Ft. Abraham Lincoln.

it a most fitting appellation, I named this Floral Valley. General Forsyth, at one of our halting places chosen at random, plucked seventeen beautiful flowers belonging to different species, and within a space of twenty feet square. The same evening, while seated at the mess table, one of the officers called attention to the carpet of flowers strewn under our feet, and it was suggested that it be determined how many different flowers could be plucked without leaving our seat and at the dinnder table. Seven beautiful varieties were thus gathered. Professor Donaldson, the botanist of the expedition, estimated the number of flowers in bloom in Floral Valley at fifty, while an equal number of varieties had bloomed or were yet to bloom. The number of trees,

shrubs, and grasses were twenty-five, making the total flora of the valley embrace 125 species.

Through this beautiful valley meanders a stream of crystal water so cold as to render ice undesirable even at noonday. The temperature of two of the many springs found flowing into it was taken and ascertained to be 44 and 44½ deg. respectively.

The next morning, although loath to leave so enchanting a locality, we continued to ascend this valley until gradually, almost imperceptibly, we discovered that we were on the crust of the western ridge of the Black Hills; and instead of being among barren, rocky, peaks, as might be supposed, we found ourselves, in wending our way through a little

park, whose natural beauty may well bear comparison with the loveliest portions of Central Park. Favored as we had been in having Floral Valley for our roadway to the west of the Black Hills, we were scarcely less fortunate in the valley which seemed to me to meet us on the interior slope. The rippling stream of clear cold water, the counterpart of that we had ascended the day before, flowed at our feet and pointed out the way before us, while along its banks grew beautiful flowers, surpassed but little in beauty and profusion by their sisters who had greeted us the day before. After advancing down this valley about fourteen miles, our course being almost southeast, we encamped in the midst of grazing, whose only fault , if any, was its great luxuriance.

South Dakota State Historical Society

In this view, Illingworth has moved to his right, from his position for the picture on the facing page. It is possible with this pair of photographs and with a few of the others to overlap them or "match them up" to produce a wider panoramic view of the landscape. This may well have been Illingworth's intention with these pictures.

Having preceded the main column as usual with our escort of two companies of cavalry, "E" and "C", and Lieutenant Wallace's detachment of scouts, I came upon an Indian campfire still burning, and which with other indications showed that a small party of Indians had encamped there the previous night and had evidently left that morning in ignorance of our close proximity. Believing they would not move far, and that a collision might take place at any time unless a friendly understanding was arrived at, I sent my head scout, Bloody Knife, and twenty of his braves to advance a few miles and reconnoitre the valley. The party had been gone but a few minutes when two of Bloody Knife's young men came galloping back and informed me that they

had discovered five Indian lodges a few miles down the valley, and that Bloody Knife, as directed, had concealed his party in a wooded ravine, where they awaited further orders. Taking E Company with me, which was afterward reinforced by the remainder of the scouts and Colonel Hart's company, I proceeded to the ravine where Bloody Knife and his party lay concealed, and from the crest beyond obtained a full view of the five Indian lodges, about which a considerable number of ponies were grazing. I was enabled to place my command still nearer to the lodges undiscovered. I then dispatched Agard, the interpreter, with a flag of truce, accompanied by two of our Sioux scouts, to acquaint the occupants of the lodges that we were friendly disposed and

desired to communicate with them. To prevent either treachery or flight on their part, I galloped the remaining portion of my advance and surrounded the lodges. This was accomplished almost before they were aware of our presence. I then entered the little village and shook hands with its occupants, assuring them through the interpreter that they had no cause to fear, as we were not there to molest them. I invited them to visit our camp, and promised presents of flour, sugar, and coffee to all who would accept. This invitation was accepted. At the same time I entered into an agreement with the leading men that they should encamp with us a few days and give us such information concerning the country as we might desire, in return for which service

I was to reward them with rations. With this understanding I left them. The entire party numbered twenty seven. Later in the afternoon four of the men, including the chief, "One Stab," visited our camp and desired the promised rations, saying their entire party would move up and join us the following morning, as agreed upon. I ordered presents of sugar, coffee, and bacon to be given them; and, to relieve their pretended anxiety for the safety of their village during the night, I ordered a party of fifteen of my command to return with them and protect them during the night. But from their great disinclination to wait a few minutes until the party could saddleup, and from the fact that two of the four had already slipped away, I was of the opinion that they were not acting in good faith. In this I was confirmed when the two remaining ones set off at a gallop in the direction of the village. I sent a party of our scouts to overtake them and request their return; not complying with this request I sent a second party, with orders to repeat the request, and if not complied with to take hold of the bridles of their ponies and lead them back, but to offer no violence. When overtaken by our scouts one of the two Indians seized the musket of one of the scouts and endeavored to wrest it from him. Failing in this he released his hold after the scout became dismounted in the struggle, and set off as fast as his pony could carry him, but not before the musket of the scout was discharged. From blood discovered afterwards it was evident that either the Indian or his pony was wounded. I hope that neither was seriously hurt, although the Indians have their own bad faith as the sole ground for the collision. "One Stab," the chief, was brought back to camp. The scouts galloped down the valley to the site of the village, when it was discovered that the entire party had packed up their lodges and fled; and the visit of the four Indians to our camp was not only to obtain the rations promised them in return for future services but to cover the flight of their lodges. I have effected arrangements by which the chief "One Stab" remains with us as guide three days longer, when

he will take his departure and rejoin his band. He claims to belong to both Red Cloud's and Spotted Tail's agencies but has been to neither for a long time. He has recently returned from the hostile camp on Powder River and represents that the Indians lost ten killed in their fights with the Bozenan (sic) exploring party.

The creek which led us down into the interior of the Black Hills is bordered by high bluffs, on the crests of which are located prominent walls of solid rock, presenting here and there the appearance of castles constructed of masonry. From this marked resemblance I named this stream Castle Creek. The direction of Castle Creek having commenced to lead us more to the northeast than we were prepared to go, and the valley having become narrow and broken, I left this water course and ascended the valley of a small tributary, which again gave us a southeasterly course. After a march of fourteen miles we camped on a small creek, furnishing us an abundance of good water and grass. The direction of this creek was nearly west. On the 30th we moved in the continuation of our previous course, and through a fine open country, covered with excellent grazing. After a march of over ten miles we encamped early in the day about five miles from the western base of Harney's Peak, finding water, grass, and wood abundant, with springs of clear, cold water running through the camp. On the following day the command remained in camp, except the exploring parties sent out in all directions. With a small party I proceeded to Harney's Peak, and after great difficulty made the ascent to its crest. We found this to be the highest point in the Black Hills. From the highest point we obtained a view of Bear Butte in the north and of the plains to the east, five miles beyond the Cheyenne River. Our party did not reach camp until nearly 1 o'clock that night, but we were amply repaid for our labor by the magnificence of the views obtained. While on the highest point we drank the health of the veteran out of compliment to whom the peak was named. On the 1st of August we moved camp a few miles simply to obtain fresh grass, still keeping

near the base of the hills to the east of us. This morning I despatched two companies, under Colonel Hunt, in a southeasterly direction to extend our explorations with the south fork of the Cheyenne River. Tomorrow morning at 5 o'clock I will set out with five companies of cavalry and endeavor to reach the same stream in a southwesterly direction from Harney's Peak.

Reynolds, the scout who is to carry this despatch to Fort Laramie, will go with us as far as we go in that direction, when he will set out alone to reach his destination, travelling mainly by night. The country through which we have passed since leaving the Belle Fourche River has been generally open and extremely fertile. The main portion of that passed over since entering the unexplored portion of the Black Hills consists of beautiful parks or valleys, near or through which flows a stream of clear, cold water perfectly free from alkali, while bounding these peaks or valleys is invariably found unlimited supplies of timber, much of it capable of being made into good lumber. In no portion of the United States, not excepting the famous blue grass region of Kentucky, have I ever seen grazing superior to that found growing wild in this hitherto unknown region. I know of no portion of our country where nature has done so much to prepare homes for husbandmen and left so little for the latter to do as here. The open and timbered spaces are so divided that a partly prepared farm of almost any dimensions, from an acre upwards, can be found here. Not only is the land cleared, and timber, both for fuel and building, conveniently located, with a stream of fine water flowing through its length and breadth, but nature ofttimes seems to have gone further and placed beautiful shubbery and evergreens in the most desirable location for building sites. While on Harney's Peak I could contrast the bright, green verdure of these lovely parks with the sunburned and dried yellow herbage to be seen on the outer plains. Everything indicates an abundance of moisture within the space enclosed by the Black Hills. The soil is that of a rich garden, and composed of a dark mold of exceedingly fine

This picture has long been captioned "Pilot Knob on the right and Gold Quartz Mountain on the left." Pilot Knob is located slightly beyond the right edge of this photograph and is not visable. Illingworth shot this picture and then moved slightly higher for a second exposure.

grain. We have found the country in many places covered with wild raspberries, both the black and red varieties. Yesterday and to-day I have feasted on the latter. It is no unusual sight to see hundreds of soldiers gathering wild berries. Nowhere in the States have I tasted cultivated raspberries of equal flavor to those found growing wild here, nor have I ever seen them larger or in as great profusion as I have seen hundreds of acres of them here. Wild strawberries, wild currants, gooseberries, two varieties of pine berries and wild cherries are also found in great profusion, and of exceeding fine quality. Cattle could winter in these valleys without other food or shelter than that to be obtained from running at large.

As there are scientific parties accompanying the expedition who are examining into the mineral resources of this region, the result of whose researches will accompany my detailed report, I omit all present reference to that portion of our explorations until the return of the expedition, except to state, what will appear in any event in the public prints, that gold has been found at several places, and it is the belief of those who are giving their attention to this subject that it will be found in paying quantities. I have upon my table forty or fifty small particles of pure gold, in size averaging that of a small pinhead, and most of it obtained today from one panful of earth. As we have never remained longer at one camp than one day, it will be readily understood that

there is no opportunity to make a satisfactory examination in regard to deposits of valuable minerals. Veins of lead and strong indications of the existence of silver have been found. Until further examination is made regarding the richness of the deposits of gold no opinion should be formed. Veins of what the geologists term gold bearing quartz crop out on almost every hillside. All existing geological and geographical maps of this region have been found incorrect. This will not seem surprising when it is remembered that both have been compiled by guess-work and without entering the country attempted to be represented. The health of the command continues excellent. I will begin my northward march in four days from this date. I do not expect to arrive at

The peak of Gold Quartz Mountain can be seen in the center of this photograph, shot from a slightly higher elevation than the previous exposure. Illingworth continued to move to his right and next captured a picture of the famous Pilot Knob, on the facing page. The large rock to the right of this picture and the isolated cluster of trees on the right horizon appear at the left of the facing picture. Again, Illingworth probably intended for these pictures to be overlapped to form a panoramic wide angle view of the landscape.

Fort Lincoln until the 31st of August.

G. A. CUSTER,
Brevet Major-Gen'l,
comd'g expedition.

10:30 P.M., August 3, 1874.

P. S.—I left our main camp near Harney's Peak at 6 o'clock this morning, with five companies of cavalry, and after a march in a southerly direction of forty-five miles reached the South Fork of the Cheyenne River at the mouth of a creek flowing from the north, and emptying into the Cheyenne midway between the mouths of Hat and Horsehead creeks. From this point Reynolds the scout sets out in one hour with this despatch for Fort Laramie. I reached here

at 9 P. M., and will proceed to Harney's Peak by a different route tomorrow morning. The country between here and Harney's Peak is generally open and rolling, and, excepting the southern portion, covered with excellent grass.

G. A. CUSTER,
Brevet Major-General, U S A

The General will probably add a postscript to his despatch at the point from which Reynolds takes his departure. (This has been added.) If I can so arrange it I desire to accompany this detachment, and so will leave this letter open, to be concluded at the last moment. As will be seen by the despatches referred to, particularly the second, a magnificent

region has been discovered, a region blessed with everything required by the husbandman. The agricultural value and resources of the arable portion of the Black Hills—and this embraces a widespread area—is beyond all present estimate. This much can be said without exaggeration. No portion of the United States presents a more inviting prospect, so far as natural resources are concerned, to the farmer and stockraiser through the region of country just traversed by this expedition. I would go more into detail did I not believe that the official despatch of the officer commanding the expedition, of which I send you a copy, contains all that is important. That there is gold here, and perhaps throughout the Black Hills,

Pilot Knob rises in the center of this picture, as Illingworth made an upward ascent. It is located at the Pennington-Lawrence County line, just east of Highway 385 near the Merritt Ranger Station. N. H. Winchell included a sketch of what appears to be Pilot Knob in his scientific report of August 9, 1874. This is one of only three Illingworth glass plates in the South Dakota Historical Society collection that is damaged. The other 100 year old plates are in a near perfect state of preservation.

cannot be longer doubted. I have seen it in various small quantities as obtained in different localities, and under anything but circumstances favorable to a satisfactory examination. I have seen men after reaching camp go to the stream near by and return in a few hours with several small particles, almost nuggets, of gold mingled with the sand still remaining at the bottom of the basin with which the washing was done. That what I have seen was pure gold as obtains in nuggets, and that it was obtained along our line of march in the Black Hills, there is no manner of doubt. To what extent gold will be found in this region yet remains to be determined. One thing is certain, and that is that this question of the richness of the probable

yield throughout this region cannot be determined by an expedition which was limited in its absence from Fort Lincoln to sixty days allowing less than half that time to explorations within the limits of the Black Hills. The miners of practical experience who accompany the expedition express confidence that time only is necessary to enable them to find gold in paying quantities throughout the portion of the country thus far examined, but one must agree with them that moving as this command is compelled to move, in order within the allotted time to cover all the country intended to be examined, stopping not longer in one place than two or three days at furthest, is not a satisfactory way, nor does it afford a proper

opportunity to "prospect" a large tract of unknown country. Discoveries of silver and lead have also been made. The extent and value of these deposits remain to be determined. Now that it has been demonstrated that these hills and valleys contain the precious metals, the effort to reach this section of territory by private exploring parties will be more persistent than ever, and the embarrassment imposed on the government, in view of its treaty obligations with the Sioux, will be greater than ever before. Its best policy would be to follow this expedition with one of similar proportions early in the spring, care being taken to have it accompanied by as many practical miners as could be employed to advantage in taking a thorough examination of the mineral deposits throughout the entire region. Should the result of this examination disclose a mineral wealth sufficient to justify further development, the title of the Indians to this region—which is not occupied by them as their home, but as a sort of private backroom, a convenient hiding place, where hitherto, after the commission of some crime, they could quietly withdraw and await the return of quieter times—should be secured by proper treaty and compensation, if that is to be the policy of the Government, and in this way the Government would be taking the quickest, as well as the most humane road to what will surely be otherwise accomplished. For the fear of Indians alone is not going to prove sufficient to deter men seeking gold from entering and occupying a country in which they have reason to believe the precious metal lies stored. If the Government does not open the way, private enterprise, backed up by the courage of the Western frontiersman will. I believe by the former method the result could be accomplished without a drop of bloodshed; by the latter it would surely be accomplished in the end, but at a cost of many lives both to the red man and his persistent and more hardy opponent, the pioneer. The sixty days within which period the expedition is ordered by the powers that be to return to Fort Lincoln expire on the last day of August. Between this time and that date we must conclude our work here, and retrace our march of about three hundred miles through an unexplored country, as I believe it is the intention of General Custer to return by a new route. Upon inquiry of the General when the expedition would reach Fort Lincoln he replied that he had ordered dinner at Fort Lincoln at 6 o'clock the 31st of August, and he expected to be there by that hour. So mote it be.

It is rumored in camp that another courier or perhaps two of our Indian guides, will set out in about two days for Fort Lincoln with despatches; if so I hope to report our progress and results up to that date.

NEW YORK WORLD
Issue of August 19, 1874

THE BLACK HILLS.

CUSTER'S EXPEDITION ON ITS HOMEWARD MARCH.

DESCRIPTION OF THE MAGNIFICENT SCENERY OF THE REGION—EXTRACTS FROM THE LETTERS OF ONE OF THE SCIENTIFIC CORPS.

(FROM OUR OWN CORRESPONDENT.)

CUSTER'S EXPEDITION ON the South Fork, August 3—10 A.M. —After a forced march of over forty miles today from the camp near Harney's Peak, where the main body of the expedition is lying, we have reached the South Fork of the Cheyenne, near Horsehead Creek, about 103 deg. 30 minutes west of longitude and 43 deg. 20 min. of north latitude. This exporing force consists of companies, under Major Forsythe (sic), accompanied by Lieutenant Colonel Custer and his aid, Lieutenant Colonel Grant. This last stretch of country has been open and rolling, the grass disappearing as we approached the South Fork. Tomorrow we shall start homewards, descending the river, then striking north and by west to Harney's Peak, which we shall reach on the 5th. Charley Reynolds, one of Custer's scouts leaves in an hour or two for Fort Laramie with despatches and letters. All well.[34]

(SPECIAL DISPATCH TO THE WORLD). 34. SIOUX, Ia., August 3.—Four Indian runners arrived at Cheyenne Agency today, and report that they left the Custer Expedition on the evening of the 31st at Black Hills, near Bear Butte. They followed him from Fort Rice, and say he has had no opposition. These are the first Indians who have come on that have any knowledge of the expedition.
NEW YORK WORLD
Issue of August 4, 1874

NEW YORK WORLD
Issue of August 22, 1874

CUSTER'S PRIZE![35]

"THE WORLD'S" LATEST DESPATCH FROM THE BLACK HILLS EXPEDITION.

REVIEW OF THE WORK DONE. THE GOLD DISCOVERIES— AN AGRICULTURAL AND PASTORAL PARADISE.

GENERAL CUSTER'S LATEST OFFICIAL REPORT.

(SPECIAL DESPATCH TO THE WORLD.)

BEAR BUTTE, Dak., August 15[36]—The Black Hills Expedition having with its arrival at this point terminated the exploration of the Black Hills, a brief review of the work performed may now be made. The discovery of gold will no doubt at first be classed as the most important result attained by the expedition, but the true value and importance of this discovery will only be made evident after a development of the gold. This development should not be expected from an expedition of this character, compelled from the vast scope of country included within its operations to move rapidly and make but few and brief halts. Gold has been found at numerous points and of sufficient quantities to justify a high estimate to be placed upon this region as a rich mineral region. The miners who conducted the prospecting estimate many of the places examined as rich enough in this precious metal to yield $100 per day per man. Should anything like this prove true, it is easy to see that the longer exclusive occupation of this valuable territory by the Indians must cease at an early day. While the ultimate value of the newly explored country as a gold bearing region remains partly problematical the real and perhaps its greatest value has been already determined, viz, its character and desirability as an agricultural and stock-raising country. The interior of the Black Hills is divided into a succession of timbered hills and open parks and valleys.

The valleys are covered with a high, luxuriant pasturage, made up of a variety of the best grasses, and a different, but not less valuable, quality of pasturage extends

35. The command will not move camp tomorrow. A mail will leave this point for Ft. Lincoln tomorrow evening. The allowance of mail matter will be 3 ounces to each company. The mail will be received except between the hours of 5 and 7 p.m. All mail matter from each comp. will be delivered to the Lt. Maj. by a non-commissioned officer of the comp.

Mail run notice, Aug. 14.

Circular no. 25, HQ BHE, camp No. 35, Aug. 14, 1874. NA RG 393 Orders BHE, 1874.

36. SIOUX CITY, Ia., August 19.—A report comes from Fort Sully to-night that Indians to the number of 4,000 attacked General Custer's Expedition on the 15th, and were repulsed with heavy loss. Custer's loss is reported at fifty killed and wounded. This report was brought into Fort Sully by a mail rider, who states he met one of Custer's scouts above Grand River and got the news from him.

NEW YORK WORLD
Issue of August 20, 1874

CHICAGO, August 20 — Lieutenant-General Sheridan discredits the reports of a battle between the Indians and General Custer. From his knowledge of the locality and of the Indians he is confident that no such collision could have occurred. Moreover, the mail rider would have to ride 200 miles to carry the news to Fort Sully, whereas the scout from whom he professed to have obtained his information had only about sixty miles to travel in order to reach the nearest telegraph station. No official report has been received of any such affair.

NEW YORK WORLD
Issue of August 21, 1874

through the forests and covers the hillsides. So completely sheltered are these valleys from the winter storms by the outer boundary or belt of hills that the Indians who are familiar with this region say most excellent grazing can be obtained for cattle throughout the entire winter. The soil is beyond all doubt of the most fertile and inexhaustible character, and will richly repay the labor of the farmer or stock-raiser. Almost every hillside has its never-failing spring of pure water of almost any coldness and some of the springs are strong enough and have the requisite fall to render them available for water power. This country, although now in the possession of the Indians, who seldom visited and never occupied it, is surely destined at a very early day to become the home of a dense, thrifty and industrious population. This is inevitable, and the sooner the Government recognizes and acts upon this idea the better. All the available troops within the limits of this military department will not avail to keep out the enterprising frontiersman who is seeking a home for life, or the equally enterprising and indefatigable miner who is searching for gold. The military occupation of the country will soon become a necessity. In any event should the Government intend to maintain the present title of the Indians to the Black Hills region, troops will be necessary to keep out the whites, and should the country, as is to be hoped, be thrown open to settlement, the presence of troops will be necessary to prevent Indian hostilities and give safety and protection to the settlement. The country explored by the Black Hills Expedition is undoubtedly the most fertile and desirable portion of Dakota, not excepting even the famous Red River Valley. It is about 210 miles on a direct line from Bismarck, the present terminus of the Northern Pacific Railroad, and about one hundred and fifty miles from the nearest point on the Missouri River. Among the civilian employes (sic) of the expedition, numbering over one hundred persons, companies have already been organized, and claims in the gold district staked out looking to the future development of the mineral resources of the Black

Hills. These men have seen the precious metal taken with but little labor from the earth, and satisfied that it exists here in large quantities, they only wait the action of the Government to enable them to begin practical working of the mines. General Custer's official dispatch to his department commander, has been mailed, a copy of which I send you in advance, from which it will be seen that I have not overstated facts.[37]

NEW YORK WORLD
Issue of September 1, 1874

CUSTER'S RETURN.

THE BLACK HILLS EXPEDITION AT FORT LINCOLN.

A NEW REGION EXPLORED ON THE RETURN MARCH—NO HOSTILE INDIANS MET WITH —THE WORK OF THE EXPEDITION—PROSPECTS OF THE GOLD FIELD.

(SPECIAL DESPATCH TO THE WORLD.)

FORT LINCOLN, Dak., August 30, via Bismarck, Dak., August 31. —After an absence of nearly two months the Black Hills Expedition, which left this post on July 2, under command of General Custer, to explore the Black Hills of Dakota, returned to Fort Lincoln to-day, the explorations having been completed and all the instructions given to the commanding officer having been faithfully carried out. The return march from the hills to the fort was by way of the valleys of the Little Missouri and Heart rivers.

The valley of the former stream, the greater portion of which had never been visited by white men before the expedition entered it, was explored. The exploration resulted in the discovery of a magnificent region, including a large area of rich and valuable soil which is well timbered and promises splendidly for agricultural purposes.

Contrary to the the expectations that prevailed at starting, and fortunately for the uniform success of the work which the expedition was organized to perform, the command has met with no obstructions from the Sioux on its march, no hostile Indians having been encountered during the advance, or

37. Readers of THE WORLD will be duly advised of the intended departure of any expedition of gold-seekers. Single explores and small parties need not contemplate the trip, since they will only be saving the Sioux the freight on their scalps. Rumor hints that an expedition more formidable even that that which went out from
NEW YORK WORLD
Issue of August 26, 1874

Bozeman, Mon., this spring, will be organized, with from 200 to 300 men perfectly armed and having cannon with them. Nothing less than an expedition that can hold the country will do, and the objection to this expedition will be the difficulty of getting away without interference by the authorities. While the Government apparently does not scruple to break its own treaties, it is determined that its citizens—or, at least, those who are not in the ring—shall keep them. Hence it is almost certain that such expeditions would be forcibly stopped. And even if, as circumstantial rumor hath it, it was decided before the expedition set out to occupy the country, build a three-company post near Harney's Peak, to be christened after General Custer, and appease the Sioux by a new treaty throwing the Black Hills open next year, other rumors declare that a son of Secretary Delano, Mr. John Delano, accompanies the expedition with a land surveyor, and that whatever lands are particularly promising will in advance be pre-empted by the Washington ring. Altogether gentlemen of enthusiasm at the East will do well to wait til THE WORLD gives them the signal to set out, as it has now traced for them the route to pursue.
NEW YORK WORLD
Issue of August 26, 1874

on the return since it left this post.

Of what has been done since the departure of the command from Fort Lincoln THE WORLD has been full informed through letters and despatches sent at intervals of the march from trackless regions, and intrusted to the care of trusty Indian scouts, who have been compelled to ride hundreds of miles through perils arising from the presence of hostile Sioux to this post and Fort Laramie, to have the news forwarded by mail and telegraph.

The expedition returns to Fort Lincoln full of the half-military and half-adventurous spirit which guided it on its long and weary journey of 1,000 miles, and soldiers and civilians are no less enthusiastic over the beauties and richness of the Black Hills country than sanguine of the great results that must follow when by proper arrangements with the Sioux, to whose undisturbed possession this favored region is now guaranteed by treaty, the newly discovered localities shall be left free to the advent of the white man.

To summarize the results of the expedition briefly, it may be said that in accomplishing the discovery of the Black Hills and the Little Missouri lands the expedition has repaid its cost twenty-fold.

Starting hence on July 2, with instructions to be absent sixty days, General Custer, with his command of 1,000 soldiers, accompanied by perhaps a hundred civilians, scientists, teamsters, herdsmen, &c., reached the outskirts of the western range of Black Hills on the 20th, the number of miles marched daily averaging seventeen. The country traversed from Fort Lincoln to the Hills was variable in appearance, in the qualities of the soil, and in its condition as regards timber, pasture-lands, and running streams. On July 13 and 14 the first Indians were encountered, after a march of 227 miles from this post, the bearing being about south and west from here. The band, however, soon disappeared, and the only evidence of the presence of Indians after that was given in smoke-signals, which appeared along the line of march.

On July 15, from Prospect Valley, Dak., near which locality the Indians had been seen, the expedition moved southwesterly, first to the valley of the Little Missouri River, passing through a portion of Montana Territory, and then, in a southerly direction from that river, to the valley of Belle Fourche, a short distance from the dividing line between Dakota and Wyoming. This was on the 18th. From the 20th to the 22d General Custer was engaged in seeking the best passage into the interior of the hills. Ascending the valley of the Belle Fourche on the 23d, the command, before reaching the top of the western ridge, entered a most beautiful valley, through which for an entire day the men passed among flowers of delicate perfume and exquisite hue, which sprung profusely on every hand. Professor Donaldson found the flora of this valley—which General Custer appropriately named Floral Valley—to comprise 125 species, of which 100 are varieties of flowers. The water in two of the springs marked 44 degrees of temperature.

Descending the interior slope on the next day the expedition passed through another floral valley, scarcely less beautiful or rich in flowers than that met with on the day before. Proceeding for about thirty miles towards Harney's Peak, the highest point in the Black Hills, the command reached to within five miles of that mountain on the 30th. After a stay of two weeks in the Black Hills, which was passed in exploring the country lying between Harney's Peak and Bear Butte, on the northern side of the Hills, the command on the 16th of August, took up its march for Fort Lincoln, taking in on its way the large tract of country lying in the valley of the Little Missouri, which was up to that time unexplored, and of which mention is made in the first paragraphs of this despatch.

The interest connected with the work of the expedition just at present naturally centers in the question of the gold-bearing properties of the lands discovered. Making due allowance for fancy and exaggeration, the fact is patent that what has been related of the richness of the Black Hills in its deposits of gold, and in some localities, of silver and veils of lead as well, is fully sustained by the reports of investigations by the practical miners and the geologists of the expedition, as well as by

the casual "finds" of individuals of the party. It must be understood that no effort beyond the most cursory was made to elicit the exact truth in this matter, as the command was almost constantly on the move.

Gold has been discovered in quantities large enough to warrant the belief of the miners that the working may be made to pay in some places $100 to each individual for a day's work. Some of the streams were found to yield particles of gold in paying quantities from a single panful of earth while in one place, where a more determined effort than usual was made to reach the precious metal by digging a hole seven or eight feet in depth, a result was that enough gold was obtained to pay for the labor. In this case the gold particles were found from a point just under the surface to the bottom of the hole, showing a uniform richness of soil to that depth.

The specimens of the geologists are of course important in a consideration of this question. They are satisfied that unless all outward signs be fallacious, the presence of gold and the quartz veins that are seen on the hillsides must be admitted. In some of the "finds" the gold was in the pure state, as in nuggets. In every case the gold found was obtained with but the slightest labor.

The course of the Government in regard to the disposition to be made of the Black Hills country will now be eagerly awaited. Already have some of the civilians who accompanied the expedition staked out claims in the gold districts, and companies have been formed among them to work at the first favorable opportunity. Perhaps this fact is the best evidence of the belief entertained by those who have seen for themselves in the richness of the soil of the Black Hills.[38]

38. BISMARCK, Dak., September 7.—Despite the military precautions taken to keep unauthorized parties away from the gold region of the Black Hills, the authorities will find themselves outwitted probably within thirty days, for before that period shall have elapsed a party of fifty men, now preparing for the expedition, will leave here for the gold mines.

The men who are going and who are determined to get through to their destination in spite of the military in defiance of all laws to the contrary, and regardless of all risks from the peril of meeting the Sioux, are fully qualified to succeed in their enterprise.

They are not only hunters but men who have had large experience in the work of digging for the precious metal. They are familiar with the Indian mode of life and with their customs, and can adapt themselves when necessary to the wild life of the plains, and although they do not anticipate any trouble with the red men on their way they will go prepared for all emergencies.

The route hence to the Black Hills is one peculiarly favorable to the avoidance of meetings with the Indians. It lies inland, and far away from the lines of the agencies where and in the neighborhoods, the Indians would be most likely to be met with. And, besides, the journey would be a comparatively brief one, as the trip can be made in ten days.

The only possible trouble that might arise, the member of the expedition think, would occur en route if any strolling bands of Sioux should be encountered. Once in the Black Hills, they profess to have no fear of an easy and unmolested prosecution of their explorations for gold. As it is their purpose not to burden themselves with any unneccessary baggage or campequipage they will leave with nothing more than their arms and the usual utensils of primitive mining.

In the meantime General Custer, who is alert in the matter of these projected invasions of the country that he has opened up, has received strict orders to prevent the departure of parties for the Black Hills. He expects to be compelled to resort to heroic measures to check the rising tide of adventure in that direction; and as he is determined to do his duty and obey orders, if the expediton referred to above, and others, succeed in reaching the new El Dorado, it will not be his fault.

The fact that gold exists in paying quantities in the Black Hills—although exactly in what quantities remains to be seen—has so stimulating an effect on the frontiersman and the fortune-seeker of these regions to allow him to measure questions of law, or even of personal danger, with those of self-interest.

General Custer himself has declared the existence of gold, based on his own observations in the Black Hills, and the intense eagerness that now prevails here and all along the Missouri to enter this rich region is the natural result of the expectations that have been aroused.

NEW YORK WORLD
Issue of September 8, 1874

BISMARCK, Dak. September 2. — AS ALL ROADS ARE SAID TO lead to Rome, so do the thoughts of all men here, as well as at the military posts and trading agencies up and down the Missouri for a hundred miles and more on either side of Bismarck, tend to the Black Hills and the golden treasure they contain. Correspondents and the telegraph, as well as General Custer in his official report, have testified to the riches of that region; but, as returned members of the expedition, and especially the miners of experience who accompanied it, are often heard to say when speaking on the subject, "the half has not yet been told." In other words, if the word of these who should know best be accepted, the value of the gold discoveries in the Black Hills has been underestimated rather than overrated.

Under the impetus given throughout the country to the "gold fever," so to call it, by the accounts sent East from the expedition while en route and from this place since the expedition's return, it will not be surprising to know that many letters, telegraphic despatches, &c., are received here almost daily from parties in New York, Chicago, and other large cities of the Union, asking for additional details regarding the prospects of gold in the new El Dorado; also inquiries as to the shortest route and the best means of reaching the Hills, and the cost of the journey and of the necessary equipments. As far as is consistent with the secrecy which still is deemed necessary by those who have organized to start for the mines a few weeks, these inquiries are answered and from the replies received it is easy to perceive that, Sioux or no Sioux, the road between the Missouri and the Black Hills will be swarming ere long with gold-seeking adventurers.

The attitude of the military authorities, as is known, is against the furtherance of any individual schemes to enter the new country. This is as it should be so long as the honor of the country is pledged to abide by the treaty stipulations with the Sioux. But there can be no doubt that at the earliest moment practicable a change will be made in this regard, and that the gold region will be left free to settlers and gold-hunters.

NEW YORK WORLD
Issue of September 9, 1874

NEW YORK WORLD
Issue of September 12, 1874
THE BLACK HILLS.

PRACTICAL RESULTS OF CUSTER'S EXPEDITION. AN UNDERGROUND ROAD BETWEEN THE AGENCIES AND HOSTILE CAMPS— MILITARY OBJECTS OBTAINED —THE TRUTH ABOUT THE GOLD DISCOVERIES— EXTINGUISHING THE INDIAN TITLE—OFFER OF $4,000 TO "THE WORLD'S" COURIER TO ACT AS GUIDE TO THE GOLD REGIONS.

(FROM OUR OWN CORRESPONDENT.)

BISMARCK, Dak. August 31— Yesterday morning the people of this place as well as the garrison of Fort Abraham Lincoln, on the opposite side of the river, were not a little surprised by the sudden appearance on the high bluffs west of the river of a large column of cavalry with attendant trains and escort. A glance sufficed to inform the goodly people of both town and garrison that what they saw was the Black Hills Expedition, of which your correspondent was a member, returning to its resting as well as starting-point, Fort Abraham Lincoln, although its arrival was not looked for until to-morrow. In previous letters and despatches I have attempted to give the readers of THE WORLD a faithful account of the progress and results attained or sought to be attained by the expedition and now that the work of the expedition has been brought to a termination it may be well to glance briefly at what has been done not that the time has yet arrived to fairly weigh or determine the real value of what has been accomplished by this undertaking. In the first place the tax-payer who has so little to say and so much to pay in running this Government may be interested beforehand in ascertaining the extra cost or expense to which he has been put in order that the Black Hills might be explored. This is but a fair question and requires an equally fair answer. Having looked into the matter closely I am prepared to announce that instead of having been a matter of increased expense to Uncle Sam, and consequently to

each individual taxpayer, the Black Hills Expedition, independently of other desirable results, has been a measure of practical economy, and, on the principle that "a penny saved is two pennies earned," that the sending out of the Black Hills Expedition has actually saved to the Government between $20,000 and $30,000. I know this will strike the reader, as it did me at first, with some surprise, and may require explanation. Expeditions of this character usually are made at an immense increase of expenditure, but this is an exception. The question of funds was somewhat an embarrassing one about the time the expedition was being organized, it being near the close of the fiscal year and the appropriations available for such purposes being almost exhausted. It was doubted at one time if the expedition could be made at the time it was owing to the supposed lack of funds to pay the ordinarily increased expenses. General Custer, who was deeply interested in the undertaking, proposed a curtailment in the supply of forage, the saving to go to the defrayment of other expenses. The regulation allowance of forage for each horse is fourteen pounds of hay, and twelve pounds of grain per day. General Custer, relying upon the grazing, which he was almost certain to find on his route, proposed to reduce this allowance to three pounds and a fraction per day. This was adopted, and as a result enough money was saved to not only cover all additional expense rendered necessary by the expedition, but several thousand dollars besides; some thirteen thousand, I believe, was the actual amount. So much for the cost of the expedition. Of course the reader understands that I refer only to such expenses as were rendered necessary by the expedition, and not to the necessary pay and support of the troops, which would have been forthcoming in any event, whether the troops were occupied or permitted to remain idle. So much for that item. Now for the expedition itself. It was set on foot and conducted throughout as a military movement, the nominal objects at least being purely military viz., explorations to determine more direct means of communications between the stations along the Upper Missouri and those throughout the Platte country, in case of combined movements of troops. Also examinations of the country in and about the Black Hills with a view of selecting sites for military posts, the establishment of the latter being deemed necessary sooner or later, depending upon the various phases of the Indian question. The expedition was also a continuation of what has always been the policy of the Government, which has been to obtain the first knowledge of all our new territories through military exploring parties. But behind or beyond these there existed a well defined, but perhaps unexpressed belief, if not desire, that the proposed exploration of the Black Hills region might settle the long vexed question relating to the rumored mineral wealth of the region to be explored, and while no one connected with the expedition, from the Commanding General down to the lowest private soldier, openly acknowledged that the objects sought were other than I have named, scarcely an individual but secretly believed that valuable discoveries would be made of precious metals hidden away in the hitherto unvisited recesses of the Black Hills. In previous letters I have given the readers of THE WORLD an account of the organization of the expedition, from which it will be seen that men of scientific attainments, representing nearly all the departments of science necessary to a complete study of the natural features of the country, were connected with the undertaking. In addition to these, for men of purely scientific abilities are not always the most reliable judges of the questions which were to be determined, a few practical miners of many years experience accompanied the explorers.

As briefly as I can I will lay before your readers some of the most important results determined by the expedition.

Taking up those which have for the present purely a military bearing, it was found that direct and practicable routes of travel and communication between the military departments situated to the northward and southward of the Black Hills could be established thus rendering combinations of

military movements, hitherto desirable and necessary but deemed impracticable, of easy accomplishment—a fact of great importance in the conduct of military measures against the hostile Indians. Suitable and commanding localities were found for the location of military posts. It was found too that the great jealousy with which the Indian has watched the Black Hills and firmly opposed the admission of the white man was not because that region possessed any particular value or attraction in the red man's eyes; but it has served as a sort of covered way, a natural underground, or elevated railway, through which easy, safe, and undiscovered communication could be kept up between the hostile camps in the Powder River and Yellowstone country and the agency Indians located on the Missouri River. It was under shelter of the Black Hills that the young Indian bucks belonging to the various agencies on the Missouri River, and who are warlike disposed, could leave their fathers and mothers and families, those who had any, under the protecting care of their broad-brimmed, kind-hearted, easily duped agent, when they knew the latter, acting as the representative of the Great Father, would act the part of a bountiful provider, while they themselves being supplied through the kindness of Uncle Sam with arms and ammunition in ample quantities, would quietly steal away from their reservation, pass along by the northern or southern base of the Black Hills and ally themselves with the hostile camps during the time for active operations, at the termination of which they would return like so many prodigals to their agencies, and again become the recipients of their share of annuities. That this course has been pursued for years has been known to all on the frontier, and to none better than the agents themselves. The only point which has not been known was the routes by which this contraband system of intercourse was maintained. To occupy the Black Hills, either by a military force or by that better and more desirable method of peopling it with thrifty industrious settlers would be to break up in course of time this alliance, defensive and offensive, between the Indians who

acknowledge themselves as openly hostile and expect treatment accordingly and those who live off of the Government at their agencies and at the same time are prepared and constantly willing to join the hostiles in their depradations against the whites.

The topographical knowledge of the country which has been obtained, added to the geological and botanical features which have been determined, have been of great value and extent, nor can their importance be estimated at present. Passing over all preliminaries I presume the readers of THE WORLD who are interested in the subject of this letter desire to be informed of what economical value is the region recently explored by the Black Hills expedition. To give a correct and faithful answer to this question I will now apply myself. Omitting particular reference to that portion of the Plains passed over before reaching the Black Hills, and which possesses in the main the same characteristics of climate, soil, and productions as usually observed on the Plains elsewhere, I will confine my observations to the Black Hills and the valley of the Little Missouri River valley so far as covered by the explorations. As to the discoveries made of gold, upon this question I will be brief, at the same time guarded, in my statements. It is to be regretted that the limited time allotted within, which the expedition was compelled to complete its labors prevented other than an examination of the most superficial character at any one point, while a large portion of the interior of the Black Hills was not visited, or scarcely glanced at for want of time. No deposits of gold were found in quartz, although abundant quantities of the latter exist, and in the opinion of those who gave their attention to the subject it is more than probable that gold could have been found had the examination been made to extend over the quartz region. Frequent though limited examinations were made of the valleys and beds of streams and dry watercourses, and as the result of the examinations gold was found in numerous places, some of the valleys yielding what the miners term "color," or small particles of gold from every panful of earth examined. In the large majority of instances the yield of gold, considering all the circumstances, was not what would be termed "good pay" but in certain localities examined the miners were highly gratified with the results obtained, and pronounced entire valleys as rich enough to return "big pay," which reduced to figures expressed from $25 to $100 to each miner for each day's labor. All gold found, so far is generally known, or so far as I could ascertain, was obtained by the process known as "placer or gulch mining." No surprisingly rich discoveries were made, nor were any large nuggets found. To repeat what two of the principal miners said to me when exhibiting the bright, shining particles of gold obtained from a single panful of earth. "These diggings will not pan out like the California diggings where a man would have to work for a month or two, perhaps, and get nothing, and next day he might turn out ten or twenty thousand dollars. There one would find large nuggets, but not every day. Here the gold is more equally distributed, and in finer particles; one finds it all through the dirt; one panful is worth about as much as another, and it is all good pay. Still we have not reached the bed rock, and there is no telling how rich one might strike it if we once got down to the bed rock, but we stop so short a time in each place that there is no chance to dig but a few feet below our surface. One thing sure, considering the amount of work we do, we find more gold than they used to find with the same labor in California, and there is no getting around it. There is plenty of gold here if we only had the time to take it out." This, in substance, if not in actual words tells the miner's story as he told it to me, exhibiting the results of his prospecting, and this I believe is the substance of what is known concerning gold discoveries in the Black Hills.[39] Judging from all I saw and all I could learn from others, and having given close and careful attention to the developments made from day to day, I think the brief conversation just quoted contains all that could or ought to be said, even if page after page was written on the subject. If asked by a friend to state

to him my candid opinion in regard to this matter I would assure him that I felt confident gold could be mined in paying quantities in the Black Hills, and that I had every reason to believe that the slight examinations made failed as might reasonably be supposed, to discover the richest deposits, and that, according to my belief, still richer and more extensive deposits would be discovered in time. If that friend was a poor man, possessing but little of this world's goods, or occupying a position whose salary brought him a fair support, and he should ask me whether I would advise him to dispose of his little all or abandon his position and salary and seek his fortune in the prospective old mines of the Black Hills, my advice to such friend would be to remain where he is keep the little he has, and not risk all upon a very uncertain prospect. For while I have confidence in the correctness of the description first given of the gold discoveries in the Black Hills, I have not that confidence, until time for more elaborate and extensive examinations of the country are made, to advise a friend and such I will consider the reader, to abandon a sure support, a comfortable living, for the uncertainty of a fortune to be obtained from the gold deposits of the Black Hills. While writing this I feel confident that fortunes will be made in extracting the mineral wealth of the Black Hills. But in this particular instance my advice to all would be to make haste slowly. At the risk of misquoting I would say, "Better bear the ills we have than fly to those we know not of." While the discoveries of gold in the Black Hills have been rich and extensive, considering the hasty and imperfect examinations made, and while there is strong reason to believe that still richer deposits will be found, the knowledge thus far obtained is not sufficient to justify what is termed a rush to the gold diggings. He who goes to the Black Hills hoping or expecting to find a fortune in gold may or may not be doomed to utter disappointment, but he who goes to the Black Hills seeking a healthful, agreeable climate, a rich, fertile, and productive soil, a coun-

39. BISMARCK, Dak., August 19.—The evidence of Custer's scout, Charley Reynolds, is accepted as conclusive on the subject of the gold discoveries in the Black Hills, and Bismarck is already in a fever of excitement. People are again talking about organizing expeditions, but nothing will be done until the return of the column.

Mr. H. N. Ross, one of the practical miners attached to the staff, has written a private letter to a friend in this town cautioning him not to get unduly excited over the discoveries. They have, he says, found fair diggings, and he believes that if he had time he could find good mines. He is enthusiastic in praise of the physical features of the country.

NEW YORK WORLD
Issue of August 27, 1874

try posessing all the natural elements necessary to render a farmer's or stock-raiser's home comfortable, to produce crops, from the abundance of which fortunes may be slowly yet surely made—in other words, a country which will yield him rich returns for such labor as industry well-directed may bestow—to him I say with confidence but little risk is encountered in casting fortunes amid the Black Hills, whose beautiful valleys seem only waiting the coming of the frugal husbandman to produce in such abundance the fruits of the field. I write this, not recognizing the fact that at present the existence of a treaty between the General Government and the Sioux prevents the settlements of this most desirable region. Although the maintenance of the Indian claim to the Black Hills country is somewhat on the dog-in-the-manger principle, he neither derives benefit from the country himself nor is he willing that others should. But the remedy to this can easily be applied. The Government should promptly take steps to extinguish the claim of the Indian to the Black Hills, and in doing this and encouraging the settlement of the Black Hills by an industrious population, one very great and important step will be taken towards rendering the reservation system of managing Indians, at least on the Missouri River, a success; as by this step those of the Indians who are willing or who desire to remain peaceable will be effectually surrounded and cut off from the bad influences of those who are still determined to keep up their hostility. The further development of the Black Hills as to the mineral resources will soon be brought about. Companies are being organized at numerous points in the West with the intention of proceeding to the Black Hills as soon as practicable, and it will require the utmost vigilance upon the part of the military authorities to prevent a violation of our present treaty relations with the Indians. To show how extensive and earnest some of these enthusiastic fortune hunters are, one company on the Missouri River has offered Reynolds, the scout and bearer of one of my former letters to the WORLD, $4,000 to act as guide to the gold region.

NEW YORK TRIBUNE

Samuel J. Barrows

In 1874 the NEW YORK TRIBUNE, struggling to retrieve an earlier success, sought to win the allegiance of New Yorkers by bringing the excitement of the great American West to their breakfast tables. The colorful epics of frontier desperadoes, law men, and the activities of the United States Army were eagerly consumed by New York readers. Consequently, it was not unexpected that the TRIBUNE should arrange with General Phil Sheridan to have its special correspondent, Samuel J. Barrows, accompany Custer's expedition to the Black Hills of Dakota Territory that summer.

A year earlier a young writer for the NEW YORK TRIBUNE, visiting his boyhood hometown, had informed an old acquaintance that he was employed by the TRIBUNE. The man had replied in amazement: "With the Try-bune! Does it print yet? I thought Greeley was dead!"[1] This may well have been the reaction of many Americans, for Horace Greeley had created the TRIBUNE and so dominated it with his personality that readers had come to think of Greeley and the TRIBUNE as one-and-the-same. Now Greeley was dead, and the TRIBUNE struggled mightily to escape the fate of its founder.

The heir to Greeley's chair as editor of the TRIBUNE was his first assistant Whitelaw Reid. The TRIBUNE's new editor, like all newspaper men, was interested in seeking out the news. But Reid demanded more, and under his leadership the policy of the TRIBUNE was "the story better told; better brains employed in the telling." It was this formula rather than sensational journalism which he employed in his effort to make the TRIBUNE a success.

Until disenchanted with the corruption of the Grant administration, Greeley and his TRIBUNE had been staunchly Republican. It was in large part the leadership of the TRIBUNE which organized the anti-Grant Republicans into the "Mugwamps," and this insurgent group had acknowledged Greeley's inspiration by nominating him as their candidate for the Presidency in 1872. Unable to agree upon anyone better the Democrats also selected Greeley to lead their party in the election. Despite this combined effort Grant was reelected, and Greeley returned to his TRIBUNE to die a few weeks later. The political persuasion of the TRIBUNE under Whitelaw Reid continued to be liberal and anti-Grant Republican until after Grant left office. Thereafter Reid gradually revealed himself to be a political conservative who shared the outlook of major financial and political leaders. "Authority ought not to rest until it has swept down every resisting mob with grapeshot," he declared from the pages of the TRIBUNE during the great railroad strike of 1877.[3]

Whitelaw Reid was only thirty-six years old in 1873 when he took control of the TRIBUNE. While serving under Greeley, he had learned a great deal including as it turned out the ability to recognize writing talent. One such talented writer was young Samuel J. Barrows who had begun his career with the TRIBUNE in 1866 at the age of twenty-one. Barrows left the TRIBUNE the next year to become Secretary of State William Seward's private secretary and it was probably while accompanying Seward that Barrows, a native born New Yorker, first plunged into the intoxicating atmosphere of the American West. In Salt Lake City he witnessed a debate between the Morman leader Brigham Young and the Rev. John Philip Newman of the Methodist Episcopal Metropolitan Church of Washington, D.C. Barrows reported this dramatic confrontation for the NEW YORK TRIBUNE and after the debate while Barrows continued on to California his letters describing the places and people of the West were published as well.

**New York Tribune
Publisher Whitelaw Reid**

But it was religion rather than newspaper work or even the West which gradually became Barrows' preoccupation in succeeding years. In the fall of 1871 he entered Harvard Divinity School[4] and supported himself and his wife by working part-time as a private secretary to Professor Louis Agassiz, as a passport agent, and at other miscellaneous tasks, including being the Cambridge correspondent for the TRIBUNE.[5] With his wife expecting their first child in the early summer of 1873, Barrows quickly accepted an offer from the TRIBUNE to cover General D. S. Stanley's expedition to the Yellowstone that summer. The extra income was very welcome to the new family

of a struggling divinity student. On that summer outing, his wife states that Barrows became "a very intimate friend of General Custer."[6]

With his reporting ability now well established it was only natural that Whitelaw Reid should ask Barrows to spend the next summer chronicaling Custer's tour of the Black Hills. To Barrows it meant a long separation from his family, but even more important it meant enough money to support a years post graduate study in Leipsig, Germany, after finishing at Harvard in 1875.[7] In the fall of 1876, after a year abroad, Barrows was ordained as a Unitarian minister and served the old First Parish of Dorchester, Massachusetts. Later he was able to combine journalistic experience and talents with his religious vocation by becoming the editor of the weekly CHRISTIAN REGISTER. In 1897 the Tenth Massachusetts District elected Barrows to Congress as a Republican where he served only one term. Subsequently, until his death in 1909 Barrows was involved in prison reform work in the state of New York.[8]

The TRIBUNE published Barrows' reports from Dakota as they were received, but Reid withheld any editorial comment until the day after Barrows announced the discovery of gold. "The prose of reality," Reid declared, "even in official utterances surpasses the stories that were ascribed to fancy." Barrows' narrative of the discovery, wrote his approving editor, "read like a chapter of romance." Besides the gold, Reid reiterated all the other attractive features of the Black Hills—the rich pasturage, pure cold water, stone, wood, fuel, and 'lumber sufficient for all time to come,'" the fine climate and other minerals such as iron, plumbago, and gypsum. "We hear now nothing about Indian treaties, and the sacredness of the reservation," he observed. Instead, the cry from frontier inhabitants is "gold and gold and gold without end." Like other editors Reid expected a repeat of the California scenario unless the government took "prompt measures" to prevent the incursion of gold seekers.[9]

Three weeks later, after Custer's return and preliminary official reports had been published, Reid felt better able to accurately estimate the expedition's value than had been possible "when the first glowing dispatches from the new found territory" had been received. To Reid one of the most surprising features of the expedition had been the "utter failure of the evil prognostications made concerning it." It had been warned that the expedition would spark a general Indian war on the frontier. Indians had advised Custer that he would be attacked if the expedition proceeded and reports confirming these dark prophecies had been received while the expedition was in the field. But all dire predictions had proved erroneous. Not only were no hostile Indians encountered, but the Black Hills showed no evidences of being recently occupied.[10]

The official reports had clearly confirmed that the valleys of the Black Hills were attractive for agriculture, but what was not demonstrated certainly, announced Reid, was the presence of gold. It may be there, he admitted, "but Prof. Winchell, the Chief Geologist, says we must take the stories about it with a large grain of allowance." The editor mused that it would seem that a geologist should be "just the man to see the precious metals—where they exist." Interestingly enough, Reid's real concern was over reports that the Black Hills contained "many specimens of the work of the beaver, as yet untouched by man." It was his hope that the government would take appropriate action to preserve these for students of natural history. Not one word of concern did the TRIBUNE'S editor utter about the possiblity of disturbing the Indians.[11]

The TRIBUNE continued to wage its battle for survival in the keenly competitive field of New York journalism, and it persisted in its efforts to bring the action of the West to its readers. Early in 1876 as the army prepared to resolve the Indian difficulties in the region just to the west of the Black Hills, Whitelaw Reid again sought a reporter to accompany a Custer expedition. Samuel J. Barrows had returned from Europe that spring having lost what little money he had through a bank closure and with no parish immediately to assume. Thus, when Reid offered him the job of following Custer after Indians in Montana the money was tempting. Undoubtedly Barrows was forever grateful that his wife convinced him to decline the offer.[12]

FOOTNOTES

1. Harry W. Baehr, Jr., The NEW YORK TRIBUNE Since the Civil War, New York, 1936, p. 119.
2. IBID., p. 129.
3. Frank L. Mott, AMERICAN JOURNALISM, A HISTORY OF NEWS-PAPERS IN THE UNITED STATES THROUGH 260 YEARS: 1690 TO 1950, New York, 1950, p. 423.
4. Isabel C. Barrows, A SUNNY LIFE: THE BIOGRAPHY OF SAMUEL JUNE BARROWS, Boston, 1914, p. 68.
5. IBID., p. 86.
6. IBID., p. 87.
7. IBID., p. 87.
8. In addition to the biography written by his wife, shorter but more easily accessible sketches of Barrows' career can be found in THE BIOGRAPHICAL DIRECTORY OF THE AMERICAN CONGRESS, 1774-1971, Washington, D.C., 1971, p. 557; WHO WAS WHO IN AMERI-CA, vol. I, Chicago, 1943-68, p. 62; Obituary, NEW YORK TIMES, April 22, 1909.
9. NEW YORK TRIBUNE, Aug. 24, 1874, p. 4.
10. NEW YORK TRIBUNE, Sept. 14, 1874, p. 6.
11. NEW YORK TRIBUNE, Sept. 14, 1874, p. 6.
12. Isabel C. Barrows, A SUNNY LIFE, p. 91.

NEW YORK TRIBUNE
Issue of June 24, 1874

BLACK HILLS EXPEDITION.

GEN. CUSTER'S RECONNAISSANCE—ORGANIZATION OF THE EXPEDITION—THE RIGHT TO EXPLORE THE REGION RESERVED BY TREATY— WHAT IS KNOWN ABOUT THE HILLS—THE STORY OF BEAR'S EARS.

(FROM THE SPECIAL CORRESPONDENT OF THE TRIBUNE.)[40]

FORT ABRAHAM LINCOLN, D. T., June 11—When the Yellowstone Expedition started from Fort Rice last Summer, one of the pleasant but unauthorized dreams which a survey of the map created, was having penetrated to the heart of Montana, it might be possible to return to our starting point by way of the Black Hills. But the desire was only a dream. The plan was not comprehended in the official order, and geographically there was too much latitude in the way. It would have required a detour of many miles. The jaded condition of our horses and mules and the insufficiency of forage and supplies put the thing entirely out of the question. And so the primitive wildness of the Black Hills suffered no intrusion by the white man. What was not done last year because it did not come within the official and practical scope of the Yellowstone Expedition, is to be done this year, not merely in an incidental way, but by an expedition thoroughly organized and equipped for the purpose.

MILITARY ORGANIZATION.

The expedition or reconnaissance, as it is officially termed, is to be essentially a military one—military in composition but peaceful in intent. It is to be in command of Gen. George A. Custer, whose well-known and important exploits during the war, and more especially his subsequent and no less successful career on the Plains—in which he has been made familiar with every phase and exigency of frontier life, and with every possible attitude hostile, peaceful or diplomatic that an Indian can assume— are guarantees for his conducting such a reconnaissance to a successful issue. The general composition and objects of the expedition are

Sheridan to Custer, June 2, 1874, from Chicago. 40. Dear Custer—Forsyth and Grant will leave here next Sunday or Monday to join you. I have given permission to Whitelaw Reid to send a correspondent subject to such conditions as you may impose on him, expenses to be reimbursed to the Government. I have requested Prof. Marsh of Yale to go, but he cannot and will send an assistant, Mr. Grinnell, in his stead.
Marguerite Merington, THE CUSTER STORY, p. 271.

succinctly stated in the order creating it.

HEADQUARTERS,
DEPARTMENT OF DAKOTA,
ST. PAUL, MINN., June 8, 1874

Special Orders No. 117: In pursuance of instructions from the Headquarters of the Military Division of the Missouri, an expedition will be organized at Fort Abraham Lincoln, D. T., for the purpose of reconnoitering the route from that post to Bear Butte in the Black Hills, and exploring the country south, south-east and south-west of that point. The expedition will consist of the six companies of the 7th Cavalry now stationed at Fort Abraham Lincoln, the four companies of the same regiment now at Fort Rice, Company I, 20th Infantry, and Company G, 17th Infantry, and such Indian scouts from Fort Abraham Lincoln and Rice as the commander of the expedition shall select.

Lieut. Col. G. A. Custer of the 7th Cavalry, is assigned to the command.

The expedition will start from Fort Abraham Lincoln as soon after the 20th instant as may be practicable. Lieut. Col. Custer will proceed by such route as he may find to be most desirable, to Bear Butte or some other point on or near the Belle Fourche, and thence will push his explorations in such direction or directions as in his judgment will enable him to obtain the most information in regard to the character of the country and the possible routes of communication through it.

Lieut. Col. Custer will return to Fort Abraham Lincoln within 60 days from the time of his departure from it. Should, however, any unforeseen obstacles render it necessary or advisable for him to return from any point of his contemplated march, even before the Belle Fourche is reached, he is authorized to do so.

Capt. William Ludlow, Chief Engineer of the Department will report to Lieut. Col. Custer as engineer officer of the expedition; he will be accompanied by his Civil Assistant and three enlisted men from the Engineer Battalion.

The Chief Quartermaster of the Department will furnish such number of wagons and ambulances as with those now at Forts Abraham Lincoln and Rice will be sufficient for the expedition.

While the expedition is in process of organization and until it shall have commenced its march, Lieut. Col. Custer is placed in command of Fort Rice as well as of his own post.

By Command of Brig. Gen. Terry
O.D. Greene,
  Asst. Adj. Gen.
Official:
 Edw. Smith
  Capt. 18th Inf., A.D.C.

THE FORCE—THE STAFF—SCIENTIFIC AIMS.

The forces thus designated will be numerically as follows: 600 cavalry, 100 infantry, 100 civilian employes, and upwards of 50 scouts. There will be a section of Gatling guns, and a train of 150 wagons. Gen. Custer will be accompanied by Bloody Knife, who, with Clemmo, piloted the Yellowstone Expedition last year, and Bear's Ears, who is said to know more about the Black Hills than any available Indian on the river.

Gen. Custer's staff will be composed of the following officers: Acting Assistant Adjutant-General, James Calhoun, First Lieutenant 7th Cavalry; Quartermaster and Commissary, A. E. Smith, First Lieutenant 7th Cavalry; Chief Medical Officer, Assistant Surgeon J. W. Williams, U.S.A.; Engineer Officer, Capt. William Ludlow, Engineer Corps U. S. A., Acting Aids, Lieut.-Col. Fred D. Grant, A. D. C., and Major George A. Forsyth, A. A. D. C. to the Lieutenant General.

Gen. Custer will endeavor to make as thorough a scientific survey as possible and to this end is to have the company of George Bird Grinnell, an assistant of Prof. Marsh of Yale, who, aided by Mr. L. H. North, will secure as large a collection of fossils as the opportunity affords, and will make a report on the geology of the country. It is to be regretted that mineralogy, botany, and zoology are not to be specially represented in the Scientific Corps. A photographer, however, happily accompanies the expedition, and will bring to the outside world the first authentic representation of this unknown region.

The expedition this year will be less unwieldy than the one of last year, which contained twice as many soldiers and required a much larger wagon train. The object of that expedition was to determine the feasibility of a railroad route from the Missouri River to the Yellowstone and beyond. The survey was paramount and could not be delayed to satisfy our curiosity about the adjacent country. The present expedition has entire freedom. Gen. Custer will proceed as directly as possible to the Black Hills, which are on an air line about 210 miles distant, on a marching line about 250. Once there he can go when and where he pleases. The march to the Hills will occupy some fifteen days. Allowing the same time for the return, a whole month will be left to spend in the heart of the Black Hills. The infantry will be sufficient to guard the train. The cavalry, after having established a rendezvous, can move wherever the country seems to invite.

THE COUNTRY TO BE EXPLORED.

If the reader will take a recent map of the United States and find the point where the corners of Wyoming, Dakota, and Montana touch each other, and will there notice the great swarm of centipedes by which map makers are wont to indicate hills, he will know about as much of the Black Hills as the best geographer at present can tell him. For the chief thing about them is that they are there. In 1859, an expedition going west from the Missouri River skirted this range of hills and indicated Bear Butte and some of the streams which find their sources in the interior. But only so much of the country was seen as might be seen of a walled city by moving outside under a portion of the wall and noting a few of the domes and steeples from a distance. Of a vast area in the interior of the Black Hills we have no positive knowledge.

The truth is, that the Black Hills have long been the stronghold of large bodies of hostile Sioux, who have been and still are jealous of the approach and interference of the white man. Yet the reports of this region which have now and then been brought to the agencies

by friendly Indians have been such as to stimulate interest to the utmost.

From these reports the country is believed to be rich in minerals and game and beautiful in aspect. It would long before this have been invaded by the white man had not a treaty with the Sioux still in force conceded it as a part of the Sioux Reservation and had not the Indians willingly assisted the Government in enforcing the treaty. The present expedition, however, is entirely in accordance with the treaty. It is not intended to occupy the country, but simply to explore it, a right which the Government reserved for itself. No miners or adventurers will, however, be allowed to accompany the expedition.

TESTIMONY OF BEAR'S EARS.

Anxious to learn as much as possible of the country we are to enter by the kindness of Gen. Custer I was afforded an opportunity to meet and converse with Bear's Ears, before mentioned as the best authority on the river concerning the Black Hills. Through the mediation of Mr. F. F. Gerard, an accomplished interpreter, who has spent 26 years in this country and has an intimate knowledge of the Ree language, I was easily enabled to get the Indian's story in good English. Bear's Ears (Indian name, Coon-ough-et-ca-ta-wa) is an Arickaree Indian, coming from a point high up the Missouri River. As the Black Hills are far down in Dakota in the Sioux country, and the Sioux and Rees are traditional enemies, it was a matter of curiosity to learn how Bear's Ears had come to spend five years in Southern Dakota among the Sioux. I found that the man had a personal history which well accounted for this change in latitude. The loss of two of his fingers, which I readily discovered on shaking hands with him, was a perpetual reminder to the Indian of an early fued, the disgrace, the long-nursed revenge, the retaliation, and the self-banishment which ensued from it. Dressed up in ample suit of United States blue, devoid of ornament and war paint, Bear's Ears seemed friendly enough in appearance; but there was something in the piercing eye, the broad, heavy, rather Gothic features, the strong base to the brain covered by the long, black hair, which did not contradict his tragic history.

The Rees, like all other tribes of Indians, are divided into bands. Quarrels among different bands and their members are frequent, and Bear's Ears was not an exception to the rule. He himself became involved in a quarrel. The antagonist, pushing words to blows, took up a piece of wood from the fire and beat him over the body. Bear's Ears did not return the blows. His wrath was bitter, but discreet and patient. Had he been well supported by friends and relatives, he would have taken his knife and cut off, not the scalp, but the top knot of his foe—one form of Indian recompense. But he was not strong enough in friends to meet the consequences. Then he waited to see if his insulter would make reparation by sending him a horse, which, as a peace-offering to the injured Indian, covers a multitude of sins. But no horse came bearing the olive branch, and Bear's Ears took a silent vow of vengeance. He prayed to the gods. Every day for nine months he rose at day break, went off three miles, and there did penance and made offerings to his favorite deity, praying not that he might love his enemy, but that he might hate him more and more. In his terrible earnestness he cut off two of his fingers and gave them to the Great Spirit as a sacrifice. The following Winter his tribe went on a buffalo hunt. Bear's Ears and his foe were both in the party. They went a long way from home. The main party resolved to camp away from their village. Bear's Ears determined to return to it. Unknown to him his enemy made the same resolution, and being better mounted overtook him on the way. He was traveling in a narrow path, when suddenly he recognized the voice of his enemy calling to him to get out of the way. It was adding insult to injury. He turned aside as the other attempted to pass by, raised his gun and shot him dead. Cutting out the dead man's heart, he himself mounted in the vacant saddle and rode to his lodge. Telling his mother to pack up what things she wanted, he busied himself in preparing a vengeful meal. He cut open his enemy's heart, broiled it, and ate it. He had

hungered for this meal for many days. The two fingers he had given to the gods were cheap in comparison with the reward they had secured. Before daylight he was a refugee on his way to the Sioux camp. He was received as a friend and ally, and for eight years was a foe to his own household. During this time it was that he camped and hunted in the Indian's paradise, the Black Hills. Once more reinstated in his own tribe, he has with many of them enlisted as the scout of the Long-haired Chief—as the Indians call Gen. Custer—and has promised faithfully to lead him to his old haunts.

Taking a little stick in his hands, Bear's Ears, when he had learned what I came for, sat down and made a map in the sand. Carefully tracing out the streams and rivers, he placed his fingers on the Big Cheyenne and its fork, the Belle Fourche. "This," said he, "is the only way to the Black Hills. It is walled around on every side; here only is the gateway. Within this wall there is a large and fertile park. The Little Missouri River heads in close to the Black Hills, but there is no Bad Land, such as so vexed the Yellowstone Expedition, to be encountered. The bluffs on streams, however, are very high, and may give some difficulty to wagons. The country is heavily wooded. Ash, oak, and pine are found in addition to cottonwood, which abounds on the Cheyenne. Game is plentiful, especially elk, black and white-tail deer. Bears are numerous. Trout abound in the streams." The animal most feared by the Indian is the panther, of which Bear's Ears claims there are four kinds. The Indians know very little about minerals, but say there is iron there. There is a story that on one occasion a squaw brought a large piece of gold from the Hills to one of the agencies.

This region may be said to be the Indian's fable-land. It is invested with legends and superstitions. "Somewhere near the center," says Bear's Ears, "there is a great nest, like the nest of the eagle; this is the nest of the thunder." This spot even the Indians themselves do not visit because of fear. Perhaps the invincible Indians that Bear's Ears saw there had something to do with it.

"These Indians," said he, "you cannot kill, they will stand so close to a gun that the powder burns them yet the ball will not hurt them."

"Shall we meet these Indians?" I asked.

"Yes," said the guide, "they love that land, and why should they not fight for it?"

We shall see whether they will.

**NEW YORK TRIBUNE
Issue of June 26, 1874**

BLACK HILLS EXPEDITION

A PROSPECT OF HOSTILITIES
WHAT THE INDIANS THINK
OF CUSTER'S RECONNOIS-
SANCE—CONDUCT OF THE
MISSOURI RIVER SIOUX—
AN INDIAN EMBASSY—A
MULE CRUSADE—BANDING
OF THE SIOUX—A
FIGHT PROBABLE.

(FROM THE SPECIAL
CORRESPONDENT
OF THE TRIBUNE.)

FORT ABRAHAM LINCOLN, D. T., June 18—While expeditions are organized to find the North Pole, and others are pushing quests in Palestine, Turkey, Asia, and the interior of Africa, it would seem that a regiment of cavalry in the United States service could not be put to better use than in exploring a portion of our own country, concerning which, although the latitude of Boston, only 159 miles west of the Missouri River, we are as utterly ignorant as if it were the heart of Africa. This occasion, I have no doubt, is sufficient for the great mass of the people, but it does not seem to satisfy the Indian Ring any more than it does the Indians themselves. If the sentimentalists could countermand the order of the Department commander, from intimations already given, no doubt they would interfere. It is affirmed of this expedition more positively, but last as untruly as it was of the Yellowstone expedition, that it travels with a chip on its shoulders directly into the Sioux reservation. The destination assumed is correct, but the chip is a fabrication.

No doubt the reconnoissance may involve a fight with the Indians, but it does not invite one. If the expedition were purposely organized to single out and whip some of the the more insolent bands on the river, it could not indeed have morally a more sanitary object. But this is not its present purpose. The Indians now seem determined to make it so, however, and if they attempt to oppose the expedition, it may have that result. Gen. Custer has been ordered to the Black Hills. He will not go out of his proper route a step to find an Indian; but if the Indians go out of their way to meet him, he will still go to the Black Hills and thrash the Indians in the bargain. It is not difficult to make the friendly Indians understand this purpose of the reconnoissance and its conformity with treaty obligations; the hostile Indians do not wish to understand.

THE AGENCY INDIANS

Since coming here I have sought intelligence concerning the condition of the Indians on the river and their professed attitude toward the expedition, to supplement a personal inspection of all the Missouri River agencies made last Fall.

The Mandans, Rees and Gros Ventres are some 80 miles above Fort Abraham Lincoln. They are friendly to the Government and always have been, though the Government has never been very friendly to them. Being small in number, unitedly not exceeding a thousand, the government has no occasion to fear them, and therefore has not surfeited them with food and presents; but, on the contrary, has made them the victim of a starvation policy. If these Indians, who are of an entirely different lineage from the Sioux, had any virtuous way of supporting themselves, the indifference of the Government would not be material; but there is little game on that side of the river; the Indian has little inclination for agricultural pursuits, the soil is not readily productive, and the Sioux are too fond of coming up on the other side of the river to make hunting in small parties safe. From year to year they have lived a hand-to-mouth existence. Within the last year, however, the Government has been more just and generous in its issue of rations; and the chiefs of the tribes have just returned from a visit to the Great Father to arrange for their future prosperity. From 40 to 50 of these Indians have been engaged on the

expedition as scouts. Their friendship has long been tested. The news of the Sioux raid on their homes at Berthold has greatly exasperated them. They will fight desperately, but at the white man's side.

Going down the river from Fort A. Lincoln, there are six agencies of Sioux Indians within a distance of 400 miles. Of these the Yankton, Yanktonais, and the Santee Sioux agencies, numbering together about 4,500 Indians, are friendly, and though a few individual members of these tribes might lend moral encouragement to an expedition against Custer, the vast majority would give it no support whatever.

At Standing Rock, about 100 miles below Fort Lincoln, at the Cheyenne Agency, within 10 miles of Fort Sully, there are Sioux of three different varieties. There are first, the friendly Sioux, who have agreed to accept the Government bribe, considering it unsafe or impolitic to do otherwise; second, the "hostiles," who come to the agencies only from necessity or to foment mischief by inciting the better disposed Indians to insolence and violence. Their influence is powerfully bad, especially upon the young men, from whom their section is mainly recruited; thirdly, there are semi-hostiles, who vacillate between friendship and hostility, and whose mercurial temper cannot be relied on. Considerations of self-interest determine them to peace, but a strong influence from the hostile camp easily induces them to take the risks of war.

At Standing Rock there are some 8,000 or 9,000 Indians on rations. The number of young bucks who would like a chance to bother Custer in the Black Hills is pretty large. It would be necessary to divulge their intention to the agent. The Sioux have a neat euphemism which kindly reconciles him to their departure. They simply tell him they want to go off on a hunt. They say nothing about the game. The Indians here have made little or no real progress toward civilization. They have built no houses, have no schools among them, have made no attempt at agriculture; but when they are not eating their rations or

fighting the Rees or the Government, they are simply quiescent. Their principal chiefs are Two Bears, Running Antelope who looks more like an ox than an antelope), Fat Belly, Bear Ribs, and Long Soldier, six feet six inches in hight (sic). These Indians are largely of the Uncpapa and Ollagalla (sic) Sioux.

At the Cheyenne River agency there are about 5,000 Indians belonging to the Minneconjou, Sans Arc, Two Kettle, and a part of the Blackfeet bands of Sioux. Some of their principal chiefs are Long Manden, who is the head of the Two Kettles, Four Bear of the same band, Burnt Face of the Sans Arcs, Little Swan of the Minneconjous, and Little Black Feet. The Sans Arcs are perhaps the most numerous. The Two Kettles are the most industrious, and have built nearly forty houses. As at Grand River, they are powerfully influenced by the "hostiles," and their young men form a strong war party.

DECLARING INTENTIONS

The Indians have these two agencies, both by word and deed, have been very frank in declaring their intentions for the Summer. At Standing Rock an Indian came in during the Winter bringing a McClellan saddle, and openly boasted that he was the one who killed the cavalry doctor on the Yellowstone expedition. The sugar and coffee found in the deserted Indian camps last Summer proved that the Indians we were fighting had either come directly from the agencies or had been in contact with agency Indians. So that it would not be unreasonable to suppose that the "hostiles" may be considerably strengthened from this source. To leave no doubt about the matter, when news of the projected Black Hills expedition reached the Indians at Standing Rock, a delegation of about 200 came up to pay their respects to Gen. Custer and learn his intentions. Subsequently a party of 12 chiefs, and again about a half dozen of the same dignity, came up on the same errand. Two Bears was present with one delegation, and Running Antelope was the spokesman for each party. Gen. Custer in thinking of sending an exploring expedition into the Black

Hills simply to ascertain the character of the country; that this was the only portion of the country east of the Rocky Mountains that was not known, and that the Great Father wished to learn something about it; that the expedition was a peaceful one; that if we met any Indians he should meet them on friendly terms, unless they did some hostile act; that although we were going with peaceful intentions, we were going with a formidable force so as to be prepared for any emergency. The Indians replied that they came not only for themselves, but also for the hostile camp. Gen. Custer told them to send his reply to the hostile camp. Running Antelope then asked if he was going there to run a railroad through the country. Gen. Custer answered, No; that he would simply go through, make the exploration, turn around and come back again.

Running Antelope then claimed that he had been to Washington, and that the Great Father had said that no white man should go into the reservation. The treaty was produced, and Gen. Custer explained that in it the Great Father referred to three classes of persons; first the Indians, then white men, meaning settlers, who were excluded from the reservation: and thirdly, soldiers, who were under the Great Father's command and who could go just where the Great Father bid them. It was explained to the Indians that the soldiers by passing through their country could not acquire any title to their land. The Indians, however, did not feel satisfied, but said the white men wanted to go there to get rich, and that if the General went out he would leave a good many men there. The "hostiles" would see to that.

A RAID ON FORT LINCOLN.

One morning in the latter part of April another delegation came to the Fort. They did not ask to see the General. In fact they did not want to see him at all. They could conduct their business much better without him. They came with reference to 45 mules quietly grazing outside the garrison. The whole herd was stampeded. Their departure was observed and reported with speed to the commanding General. Gen. Custer immediately ordered a trumpeter to

sound "Boots and saddles!" In 19 minutes every horse was bridled, saddled, mounted, and flying over the plain in the wake of the absent mules, Gen. Custer on his thoroughbred leading the way. The chase was a long one and a hard one. A few of the horses gave out, but the rest bravely followed the sorrel throughbred. About 11 o'clock at night the gallant 7th came slowly marching home, bringing with them in addition to their tired horses 45 tired mules. Strange as it seem, and opposed as it is to the history of all previous stampedes, not one of the recreant mules was lost. To and fro it cost about 40 miles of traveling to secure this remarkable recapture. Gen. Custer had more than one message for the Indian delegation, but they waited not to receive them. An Indian pony alone stayed behind to receive a halter which its capturer would much more gladly have conferred on its original owner.

Some time after Two Bears sent word to Gen. Custer that it was a few of the young men of his tribe who had run off the mules, and by way of compliment he intimated that Gen. Custer was an old woman. Yet Two Bears and his mule-drivers are getting fat on Government rations, and no doubt laying in a stock of Government provisions to conduct his campaign in the Black Hills. Thus while the War Department is backing up the army the Indian Bureau is backing the Indians, while the country pays the cost for both.

The Cheyenne Agency Indians have been quite as enterprising during the Spring as the Standing Rock tribe. It was mainly from this agency that the 400 Indians were gathered who a few days ago attacked the Ree village at Berthold. Cheyenne is but ten miles from Fort Sully. Gen. Stanley, who has kept a close watch on the conduct of the Indians here, writing to Gen. Custer, and advising him of their departure for Berthold, says: "The time for soft words and moral supsion (sic) is passed; nothing but powder and cold lead will be of any avail."

As the opinions of an army officer this may be received with prejudice by people who have a horror of war in any form. But it has a strong confirmation from a

profession representing a spirit directly opposed to that wrongly attributed to the army. The Rev. Mr. Cook, an Episcopal clergyman at work among the Sioux, confessed to me last Fall that the only way to bring Spotted Tail's people under the influence of the Gospel was to give them a good thrashing. Last Sunday, in conversation with the Rev. Mr. Riggs, the author of the Sioux grammar and dictionary, who has been among the Sioux for 39 years, he expressed the same opinion, and added that if we met any of them this Summer he hoped Gen. Custer would give them a good whipping, whether they came from the agencies or from anywhere else. It is the influence of the hostile Indians which prevents much of the seed sown by missionaries from taking root.

A convenient rendezvous is afforded by the Black Hills not only of the Agency Indians on the Upper Missouri, who will only have to go 150 miles to reach it—a small journey for an Indian—but for the Northern Arapahoes and Cheyennes. For Spotted Tail's and Red Cloud's tribes, with which the Government has recently had a good deal of trouble, it would be a still easier journey.

According to Bear's Ears, our Ree guide, there are about ten bands of Indians there. The Uncpapas, Black Feet, Minneconjous, and Ogallallas are strongly represented. Our scouts have received word that the Indians of Two Bear's camp at Standing Rock have sent runners to all the other bands far and near advising them of the expedition and seeking an alliance. So that if the Indians mean war the Black Hills bands will be strongly re - enforced. Prominent among the chiefs of these bands are Eagle, an Ogallalla; Medicine, Bald Head, One Horn, Sitting Woman, Big Forehead, and a chief who rejoices in the unpoetic name of "Leggins."

A PRESS OF BUSINESS

An amusing feature of the diplomatic correspondence which has been carried on lately between Gen. Custer and the Indians in regard to the reconnoissance, was developed lately. It seems that the plans of the Government do not harmonize with those of the Indians. They had laid out other work for the Summer. They therefore seriously requested a postponement of the expedition for one year, saying that they want very much to go and fight the Crows this Summer, but they cannot attend to the Crows and the reconnoissance too. This furnishes a new argument against the expedition for the Indian attorneys at Washington. From the active measures the Indians are taking they have probably decided to defer their Crow campaign in favor of the expedition.

From what has been said of the conduct of the Indians on the river and others who have access to the Black Hills, it is evident that they do not need any provocation to hostility. If they have not a chance at a Government expedition they will prove their guns and horses by raiding on the posts and running off Government mules, or suddenly descending on the Ree villages, or preparing expeditions against the Crows or fighting among themselves in some way. All talk therefore about these Indians being driven by these expeditions to fight for their altars and their sires is simply bosh. If they fight at all it will be for the simple satisfaction of stealing our horses and killing our men, so that in times when their own history is becoming more and more dull and prosaic they may add a few more tales of bloodshed to the orgies of the dance and garnish their tottering wigwams with a few more trophies of their valor.

NEW YORK TRIBUNE
Issue of July 11, 1874

PREPARING FOR THE START.

ACTIVITY AT FORT LINCOLN—
A VIEW FROM THE HILL-TOP
—THE TREACHEROUS
MISSOURI—ORGANIZING AN
ARMY—VERSATILITY OF THE
AMERICAN SOLDIER—COST
OF THE EXPEDITION.

(FROM THE SPECIAL
CORRESPONDENT
OF THE TRIBUNE.)

FORT ABRAHAM LINCOLN, D. T., June 23—This fort is eminently adapted or quietude. Situated on the west bank of the Missouri River, some 500 miles west

of St. Paul, it is far removed from the turmoil and activities of civil life, and especially from its conventionalities. Bismarck, which lies flat on the plain on the other side of the river, does not materially alter the situation. It is only a little dot on the wide rolling green, scarcely noticeable in the great solitude. But just now Fort Lincoln is one of the busiest posts on the register. With 600 or 700 cavalry and several stirring trumpeters constantly quartered here, at no time is it very sluggish. There is a lively activity about cavalry quarters which does not pertain to those of the more easy-going infantry. Now, when a general order from the department headquarters has turned everybody's aspirations toward the Black Hills, the usual activity is doubled; but it is an orderly activity, without bustle or confusion. Everything moves by order before it moves in fact, and when the orders are well dovetailed and jointed to fit into each other, the plan of an expedition like this is soon realized.

THE FORT AND ITS
SURROUNDINGS.

A word in passing about Fort Lincoln itself. My parting impression of it last Fall was not a pleasant one. It was here in the cold, raw, wet close of September that the Yellowstone Expedition, having accomplished its mission, suffered a sudden and official collapse. Everything at once became disjointed. Men, horses, mules, wagons did not look as new as when they started out. Debris was a natural result of disintegration. Remnants of the expedition were scattered in every direction, and it looked as if it would take a geological period to clean things up. The quarters for the cavalry were just then building, which added to the confusion. Nine months have produced a great change. The only vestiges of the old expedition are found in the grass-grown trails which still may be traced over the hills. The reservation grounds are as clean and fresh as a new pasture. The cavalry stables, granaries, and store rooms and quarters for the officers and men are disposed on the bottom, arranged so as to bound a large rectangular space about 400 yards long by 250 wide. Everything looks neat, trim, and clean.

The officer's quarters are models of convenience; the apartments for the men are comfortable and roomy. The stables are large, well ventilated, provided with wells for Winter use when the river is frozen, and kept stringently clean. They are situated outside of the rectangle, about 100 yards in the rear of the company quarters. The interior of the rectangle thus formed by the buildings is laid out in a large parade ground, bounded by avenues broad enough for a column of cavalry to march in review. In front of the officers' quarters is what promises during the Summer to become a broad green lawn. The parade ground, which is intended for dismounted movements, is also sown with grass. During the Spring rows of cottonwood trees were set out along the avenues in front of the quarters and afford a prospect of good shade. A large post garden has been laid out and is strenuously cultivated, and if the multitudes of grasshoppers which have lately appeared will only spare it and give it a chance the garrison may rejoice in good crops.

Three-quarters of a mile up, on the hill, stand the infantry barracks, the hospital, magazine, and other buildings, which, until last Fall, comprised all there was of Fort Lincoln. The view from the hill is really delightful. Radiating from the observer for miles and miles, the open landscape has no secrets from his eye. North, east, south, and west are laid under tribute for the panorama. Nor is simple expanse. The broad stretch of country—for it seems rather an anomaly to call it plain— is molded, crimped, and corrugated into hills and hillocks, vales, and mounds, never prominent or broken, but always varied. At the foot of a long slope, dividing the circle of the horizon, flows the broad, swift, sun-burnished Missouri through treacherous banks heavily crowned with cottonwood. The river has a wayward course and is deeply dyed with stolen soil. It is one of the most inconstant rivers in the world. Its channel is in one place to-day, in another to-morrow, the day after in a third place. It is the puzzle and trail of pilots, who must trust to their wits and experience to guide them. A pilot last Summer came up the river. The channel had changed and bothered him. He thought he would mark it by a buoy to help him on his return down stream. He did so. Two weeks afterward he came down the river, and there was his buoy high and dry on a sand bank, while the river had cut out a new channel of uncertain depth. Let a man fall into this river with his clothes on, and he has little prospect of coming out. He may be a good swimmer, but the sand soon fills his boots and clothes, and he sinks inevitably. This was the unhappy fate of a cavalryman who, in watering his horse yesterday, ventured out too far. His horse plunged in the water. He slipped off, was carried down by the current, and was lost. The horse, freed from his rider, made his way to shore.

PREPARATIONS FOR DEPARTURE.

Few who are unacquainted with the minutiae of army organization are aware of the labor it involves. It is not fighting, even in war time, but eating and moving, which absorb the most time, labor, and expense in the army arrangement. Mobility in an army is not less necessary than courage and skill. An army needs legs as well as arms. It is a recognition of this act which has led a recent English military writer to declare that in the army of the future only mounted men would be used, simply to secure greater mobility.

It is the want of adequate transportation which delayed the expedition several days. Legs and wheels are in great demand. Let a few Indians make a raid on the post, and within ten or fifteen minutes after the sound of the trumpet the men who have been playing ball, or fishing, or lounging around the quarters are in the saddle in hot pursuit. A two or three days' march across the country does not present much difficulty either; but when it comes to two months, then visions of mules and white-bonneted wagons rise at once before the eyes of the commanders. To meet this want in the present case, requisitions have been made on Fort Abercrombie and Fort Rice. The personal baggage of officers and men has been reduced to the lowest quantity. The horses and mules will be put on a minimum amount

of forage and every expedient be tried to save weight. The trains have now arrived and will be loaded as soon as possible. The blacksmiths are busy shoeing the horses, carpenters and wheelwrights are repairing wagons, and the saddlers are mending harness and equipments. One car load of horses has already arrived, and another is expected by to-night to supply vacancies in the complement.

Not only on the march, but in the preparation of such an expedition as this, the versatility of the American soldier is well illustrated. If there be any trade or pursuit that is not represented in the army, it would be an item of news to find out what it is. And there is scarcely one of these trades that is not called into requisition either in garrison or campaign life. An officer who can furnish the raw material can have most anything he wants, from a saddle to a set of furniture. There is no lack of carpenters, blacksmiths, machinists, tailors, shoemakers, cabinetmakers, molders, and musicians. The 7th Cavalry band is made up entirely of enlisted men. There is plenty of material for good clerks, and now and then the professions are represented in the ranks. I have seen a graduate of the University of Edinburgh, acquainted with six or seven languages, thoroughly read and of excellent ability, in the ranks of a regular army. During the war such instances were of common occurence; but to-day, when there is little motive to enlist except the pay, and that would seem too small to be any inducement at all, these facts seem strange indeed.

Last winter it was feared life at Fort Lincoln would become monotonous. To guard against it the officers had frequent hops, sociables, and private theatricals. The enlisted men also determined to insure their own pleasure and so organized the Seventh Cavalry Dramatic Association. But they had no opera-house. Permission was obtained to build one. The men set to work with a will, and soon put up a large frame building sufficient to accommodate all the officers and men. What should they do for scenery? A painter and designer in the regiment solved the

difficulty. The canvas was procured and skillfully embellished, and with a sufficiency of shifts neatly executed to cover a good range of plays. A strolling company would have considered such a man invaluable. Three nights ago I had the opportunity of hearing the Dramatic Association in "Toodles" and "That Rascal Pat." Two of the regiment laundresses took the women's parts. Both plays, relieved between acts with some comic songs, were put upon the stage and performed in a manner which in the absence of much experience showed no little histrionic talent. The Association has performed in Bismarck with great success. The proceeds were very kindly devoted to the purchase of a tombstone for the grave of a dead comrade.

Such instances might be easily multiplied to show the resources of our army in matters of convenience, comfort, and taste, as well as of necessity. This resource saves not only army officers but also the Government itself considerable expense, especially in the field.

COST OF THE EXPEDITION.

While referring to the matter of expense I may say, to silence any croaking that the expedition, apart from the valuable additions to knowledge which it promises, which ought to be a sufficient justification for a liberal outlay, is in reality a stroke of economy. No extra expense for horses, mules, or wagons has been incurred. Arms and ammunition likewise do not come under the head of extras, while in the matter of forage there is a heavy balance on the side of the expedition. This may be easily illustrated. Making a calculation exactly in accordance with the allowance of forage fixed by the regulations, we have, as the cost of full grain forage, half corn and half oats.

Cost of full hay forage to same animals, including bedding allowance _____$	130.00
For 600 horses and 600 mules for one day _____	313.31
Total per day _____	443.31
Cost of four lbs. of corn per day, the allowance on the reconnoissance for the same number of animals	110.35
Saving per day _____	323.96

The saving in forage for sixty days would thus be _____ 19,437.40 Calculating now the extra expenses of the reconnoissance we have: Wages of 130 teamsters and cooks for 2 months   6,000.00 Leaving a balance in favor of the expedition of _____$13,437.60

Allowing $3,000 for contingencies, such as loss of mules or horses, wear and tear of wagons &c., we have still a balance of $10,000 on the forage allowance. Thus the expenses of the expedition are paid directly from the current appropriations, without any additional drain upon the Treasury of the maganimity of Congress. The gain to the service in efficiency secured by such an expedition, as compared with the routine life of a garrison, is something which cannot easily be computed in money. But is it the only real way to make soldiers that shall be worth something more than to cut a good figure on dress parade. As for Science, she properly scorns to put her achievements only in dollars and cents.

GOING INTO CAMP.

In order to find out what things are necessary in the way of minor camp equipage to give the men a preliminary taste of camp-life, and to have each man certain that he forgets nothing essential to the trip, Gen. Custer ordered the troops in camp on the 20th June. Camp was formed about a mile from the garrison. The horses are in excellent condition, if anything, a little too fat. The men are in good spirits and anxious to get off.

The following is a list of the company commanders: 7th Cavalry Company A, Capt. Moylan; Company B, Lieut. Ben. Hodgson; Company C, Capt. Hart; Company E, Lieut. McDougall; Company F, Capt. Yates; Company G. Lieut. McIntosh; Company H, Capt. Benteen; Company K. Capt. Hale; Company L, Lieut. Custer; Company M, Capt. French. The battalion of infantry is commanded by Capt. Sanger, 17th Infantry, and consists of his own company and a company of the 20th Infantry, commanded by Capt. Wheaton; battery commanded by Lieut.

Chance, 17th Infantry; Indian scouts by Lieut. Wallace.

Col. Fred Grant and Gen. Sands Forsyth, acting aids to the Lieutenant-General, and Col. Ludlow of the Engineer Corps, have arrived. Col. Grant will act as aid on Gen. Custer's staff. Gen. Forsyth was at first assigned to similar duty, but by a subsequent order has been assigned to the command of the left wing, consisting of five companies of the 7th Cavalry, Gen. Custer himself taking the right.

The Scientific Corps is to have a valuable addition to its force in the person of Prof. Winchell, State Geologist of Minnesota, who is daily expected. He will perhaps take charge of the botanical department also.

NEW YORK TRIBUNE
Issue of July 25, 1874

THE COMMAND REACHES SOUTHERN DAKOTA IN FOURTEEN DAYS—DESCRIPTION OF THE COUNTRY TRAVERSED—INDIANS WATCHING THE MOVEMENTS OF THE PARTY—NO HOSTILE DEMONSTRATIONS YET MADE—THE PROSPECTS OF A SUCCESSFUL RESULT ENCOURAGING.

BISMARCK, D. T., —July 24— A special dispatch dated July 15, received by scouts from the Black Hills Expedition, contains the following: "The expedition has been out 14 days; has made 228 miles, and is now in Southern Dakota, 12 miles from the Montana line, in lat. 45° 29', long. 103° 46'. A halt of one day is made here, near the Little Missouri Valley, to rest the stock. The route pursued has been generally south-west from Fort Lincoln, as far as the Grand River, when a westerly course was taken to and beyond Slim Butte, near this point. The expedition slightly diverted to visit a cave described by an Indian guide as very wonderful, and it was found to be without special interest. Within 50 miles of Fort Lincoln, the command passed over some very excellent grazing land. The country then gets deteriorated, and alkali swamps were encountered, and bad lands along the streams flowing into Grand River; but the expedition is now halted in a delightful valley, with excellent grass and water,

and the prospect ahead is very good. The skirts of the Black Hills, it is expected, will be reached in three days. The expedition will not go to Bear Butte, but will strike the Black Hills at a point further west, more accessible to the wagon train.

Indians were seen for the first time three days ago. They were in small parties of ten or twenty. They watch the movements of the expedition daily, but make no demonstration and have not been molested. Large fires were seen last night in the west which are supposed to be Indian signal-fires. The health of the command is good, not a single man being sick. The stock is in good condition; but one horse has given out thus far. Antelope have been killed in abundance. Only two woodless camps have been made, and water has been plentiful. One slight rain has been encountered and little difficulty has been experienced in moving the train.

Mr. Grinnell of Yale College found his first fossil of importance on the 14th. It was the humerus bone of an animal larger than an elephant. It was about four feet long and a foot in diameter. Thus far the prospects of a successful expedition are very encouraging. If no annoyance is experienced from Indians, the reconnoissance will be easily completed in the estimated time. The Indian guides say that the Sioux have gone off to fight the Crows, and that the command will not be troubled. Others think differently. Gen. Custer, in his official report to Gen. Terry, says:

As I sent pacific messages to all the tribes infesting this region before the expedition moved, and expressed a desire to have friendly relations with them, the signals observed by us may have simply been made to enable the villages to avoid us. Our Indian guides think differently, however, and believe the Indians mean war. Should this be true they will be the party to fire the first shot. Indians have been seen near the camp today. In the course of the march lignite beds of good quality were discovered.

ADDITIONAL ACCOUNTS FROM THE EXPEDITION— RAPID PROGRESS MADE.

NEW YORK TRIBUNE
Issue of August 20, 1874

BLACK HILLS EXPEDITION
ON THE MARCH IN
SOUTH-WESTERN DAKOTA

A CAPRICIOUS GOD OF THE
SIOUX—A DIVINITY WHO
BLOWS HOT WHEN IT IS
COLD AND COLD WHEN IT IS
HOT—A SETTLER'S OPINION
OF NORTHERN PACIFIC
RAILROAD LANDS—THE
REGION TRAVERSED—
GEOLOGICAL STUDIES
ALMOST ENTIRELY FAULT-
LESS—THE LEG-BONE OF A
MAMMOTH FOUND.

From the special correspondent
of the Tribune.

BLACK HILLS EXPEDITION,
DAKOTA, CAMP NO. 16, July 17.

—The Sioux are a people of a great
many gods. The popular presumption that supposes them with other
Indians to be essentially mono-
theistic worshippers of the Great
Spirit only, is entirely at variance
with the truth. Their gods are
numerous, but not always the best
quality. Some of them are unique
and peculiar. One of these, which
I adduce simply as an illustration,
is Ha-yo-ka; I know not what else
to call it in English but the God
of Paradox, or the God of Contradictions. It is a god who always
thinks and feels by opposites.
When it is warm, Ha-yo-ka always
conceives it to be cold, when it is
cold, Ha-yo-ka acts as if it were
warm. In the hot Summer moon
he wraps himself in buffalo robes
and builds a fire, and yet his teeth
chatter, and he shivers with the
cold. In Winter the perspiration
rolls down his face in great heavy
drops, and he fans himself to keep
cool, even when the mercury is
freezing. He requires of his de-
votees this same inversion or pretended inversion of thought and
feeling. They must always profess
a different mood from that which
you would most naturally expect.
Their religious life is spent in trying to convince the followers of
other gods that December comes
in July, and July in December—in
short, that our sensibilities are all
turned upside down.

A CAPRICIOUS CLIMATE.

Such a god very naturally originated in Dakota. Dakota is the
land of contradictions; and the Indians, who worship faults as well
as virtues, naturally recognized
and defied the fact. Ha-yo-ka has
visited us of the expedition more
than once this Summer. At the
close of a long hot day, for instance, we drop to sleep soon after
the sun goes down. The air is close
and sultry, and even one blanket
is too heavy for a coverlid. But in
a few hours Ha-yo-ka comes
around, and tries to persuade us
that it is nearly as cold as ice. He
easily converts the thermometer,
and, in its zeal for inversion, it
drops down to within eight degrees
of the freezing point. It is of no
use to dispute the fact when we
rise in the morning. It is of no
use to look at the calendar. It is
certainly the middle of July; but,
with the thermometer at 40 degrees, you are bound to shiver in
spite of yourself, and somehow
find yourself edging up to the
breakfast fire enveloped in a thick
blouse or Winter overcoat. At
noon you are again in your shirt-
sleeves, and the repentant thermometer at 100 degrees completes
the contradiction. Dakota, taking
it the year round, is a very dry
country. The umbrella trade would
languish and utterly fail did it depend on the rainfall of this latitude. But every now and then,
when you least expect it, Ha-yo-ka
summons the clouds, gorges them
with moisture, and fills them with
hail-stones, and then suddenly cuts
the tackling and drops them on
the earth like a wet blanket loaded
with bullets. When the storm has
subsided, the question which the
farmer with a tender growth in
his field finds it most difficult to
decide is whether or not the storm
has done more harm than good.

SHOWERS BY MOONLIGHT.

In studying Dakota climatology,
I have seen here what I have never
observed, to the same extent, anywhere else—a moonshower, or if
you prefer it, a shower by moon-
light. The dome of the heavens
was hung around with a deep
drapery of black; the wind blew
mightily, and the rain descended
in torrents. With difficulty we
kept our tents on its legs. It was
not a night that one would choose

for a lover's walk. And yet for full
half an hour of the storm's dura-
tion, and at the time of its intensest severity, the full moon was
sweetly shining in the door of my
tent. A long narrow avenue of
perfectly clear sky, just wide
enough for the pathway of the
moon had been cleanly cut through
the great black bank of clouds
from east to west, and left her
majesty space to move on, un-
challenged by even the faintest
haze.

Ha-yo-ka it must be that furnishes the soil with such strange
contradictions, so that a beautiful
plain of fertile grass is presently
succeeded by a great cactus farm,
with perhaps an intervention or
an intermingling of sage brush.
It is Ha-yo-ka perhaps who places
the solitary trees, here and there
dotting the timberless expanse, to
dispute the general uniformity.

Ha-yo-ka, for the benefit of
emigrants at least certainly deserves a place therefore in any
description of Dakota. Any emigrant who is unprepared for the
anamolies as well as the monotony
of Dakota may suffer disappointment. If Abraham and Lot for instance with their cattle herds
should enter Dakota from the east,
crossing triumphantly the Red
River as their posterity crossed
the Red Sea, undoubtedly they
would say, "It is a goodly land;"
perhaps in their first enthusiasm
they might exclaim, "It is a land
flowing with milk and honey." If
the same patriarchs, however, were
to enter it from the west, seeing its
maze of "Bad Lands," its alkali
swamps, its sage and cactus fields,
they would probably apply to the
whole country the expressive
language of Gen. Sully: "It is hell
with the fires put out." Unfortunately for the information of the
traveling public the Northern Pacific Road has written its circulars
only from the east end, presuming
in its ignorance, perhaps, that the
rather narrow strip of good land
along the Red River is a fair
sample of the country further
west.

A TESTIMONIAL TO
NORTHERN PACIFIC
RAILROAD LANDS.

I very much doubt even if the
Road would be willing to publish

South Dakota State Historical Society

This area is called Forsyth Dell, named after Major George A. Forsyth, an aide de camp to General Philip Sheridan, who accompanied Custer on his expedition to the Black Hills. Its exact location is not known. One man is kneeling at the top of the waterfall—perhaps Forsyth. The Major kept a detailed report (see appendix) and frequently mentioned water courses, but never specifically mentioned the one named in his honor. The July 25 entry in his journal may refer to this area, where he says, ". . . some six or eight beautiful springs bubbled up within a radius of 300 feet, forming at once a stream sufficient to turn a mill." The falling water is blurred because of the 10 to 15 second exposure time required by Illingworth's wet plate.

the testimony of one of its settlers whose chosen place lay between both extremes of Dakota latitude, viz., on the Missouri River, near Bismarck. Joshua—for like the renowned Hebrew, he was a pioneer and a military leader—thus summed up his experience for a year: "I built a fine ranch," said he, "and planted extensively. I had also a large garden intrusted to my care, and plenty of help to work it. I carried up water in barrels from the Missouri and irrigated the land. I had the satisfaction of seeing my crops come up. But no sooner had they got fairly started than the potato-bug made a fearful raid on the young growths. A terrible wind-storm and several extremely cold nights (Ha-yo-ka) jeoparded (sic) the whole crop. An immense army of grasshoppers then came and ate up what the potato-bugs had left; and last but not least, an extraordinary hail-storm beat to death the remnant which had survived the potato-bug and the grasshopper. To be sure, I have some corn left, but," said Joshua, taking great liberty of supposition, "if I were God I would just give every white man 10 days to get out of this country, and then I would sink the whole (elliptical) region and make a whale fishery out of it."

To many other hearers this did not seem a bad idea, and I think if a vote had been taken on the spot, Col. Joshua's sentiments would have prevailed.

The south-western part of Dakota, on a line from Fort Lincoln to the Black Hills, I am obliged to say is, however, generally a better region of country than that which extends due west from Lincoln on the line of the Northern Pacific Road. In each section there are tolerably large areas of good grazing land, and the country would be well suited for stock-raising, if water and timber were abundant. At the same time there are much larger areas of almost barren or cactus-covered alkali, utterly unfit for the residence of either man or beast. Even the best grass-growing districts, valuable for grazing-purposes, offer little inducement for agricultural purposes, the insufficiency of the rain fall being an insurmountable objection. The native grasses furnish no argument for the success of other grains, since like the cactus, they are peculiar to this latitude, and having become thoroughly acclimated, stand an amount of dryness which would be fatal to other growths. The alkali soil which contains a very large percentage of soda is found to a greater or less extent over the whole country. But now and then it breaks out in aggravated patches, destitute of all verdure and nearly as white as snow, which reflect the sun with a painful glare, and render water found in their vicinity utterly unfit for use.

THE COUNTRY TRAVERSED.

In a former letter I described our visit to Goose's Cave, and the disappointment which attended it. The intention which the General had originally entertained of lying over one day at the cave, was abandoned on account of the poverty of the grass. Our horses and mules are receiving but three pounds of grain per day. It is highly essential, therefore, that our camps, especially those where we take a day for rest, should have an abundance of good, nutritious grass. The command, therefore, pushed on. The visit to the cave was not without satisfaction, for from the top of the plateau which formed the roof of the cave we had a fine panoramic view of the surrounding country, and Col. Ludlow was enabled to take the bearings of many of the most prominent buttes. In furnishing the Indian names for these prominent buttes, Goose's aid was as invaluable as his knowledge was surprising. Most conspicuous among the landmarks were Rainy Butte to the north-east, and Whetstone Butte near by; Slim Butte to the east, and Slave Butte to the south, both of the latter already down on the map of Dakota. Off of the west lay the Short Pine Ridge, and to the west the "Rock with a Hole in it." Near the Short Pine Ridge was another long ridge dipping deeply into the prairie at its western end, and revealing to Goose through the naked eye, but to us only through the agency of the most powerful glasses, a faint line of blue beyond. This Goose informed us was the Black Hill range. It was 80 miles away, and we received the statement with some doubt, but afterwards found he was right. Down in the valley before us were the forks of the Grand River separating into many small fingers, which like the river itself, were only traceable by the sinuous strips of timber along their banks. The river itself here is only a creek, and its branches are now almost dry and serve only as branches in the Spring flood-time or after heavy rains. The cave plateau, though frequently cut in its length of several miles by deep ravines entirely insulating certain portions of it, resumes the same level after each interruption, and shows clearly its original unity. The rock, a yellowish sandstone, is uniform in disposition and structure, but is very susceptible to wind, and water action, and in some places is very much honey-combed. Off to the north of this ridge was a terrace covered with verdure and boasting a reasonable growth of pines, spaced with such regularity, however, as to suggest the intervention of art, while an outjutting mass of hard sandstone rising from the green and seen through the pine trees, furnished to the willing fancy an adequate figure of a house, the whole forming a refreshing picture of a desirable country residence.

GEOLOGICAL STUDIES.

The glacial drift which was noticed in a previous letter as of frequent occurrence within the first 75 miles of our journey, soon entirely disappeared, and a monotony of out-cropping unfossiliferous sandstone rocks succeeded. A large number of bowlders (sic), however, evidently of limestone, found on the tops of little knolls, and unaccompanied by any authentic foreign drift, were at first a little puzzling; but the surmise of Prof. Winchell that they originally formed part of a native limestone stratum, over-topping the sandstone, had been broken up into bowlders (sic) by the disintegration of the underlying rock, was afterward confirmed by careful observation. The limestone was naturally found in places, supported by two beds of softer and more perishable sandstone. At Wolf Butte, in our march along the Grand River, we found silicified wood in considerable quantities, the forest relics of a remote age. It affords little consolation to the travelers, however, to pick up a piece of this ancient wood on the plains in the excruciating noon of a Dakota sun, and reflect, as he broils in its glaring rays, that at some early antediluvian and ante-glacial time, Dakota, in addition to its tropical animals, was probably in possession of abundant forests which perished long before man was created to enjoy them. Carried down by floods, water-logged, then buried in sediment and embalmed in silica, more modern denudation has washed them from their resting places, broken them up, and scattered them far and near over the plain to torment the traveler by suggesting a shade which it is no longer in their power to confer. After leaving the Grand River this fossil wood entirely disappeared. We have seen none since, but are rejoicing in the prospect of timber of a more modern date.

Geologically our march through the country has developed no treasures especially new and important, nor do we expect fossil any more than mineral riches until we shall reach the more varied formations supposed to exist in the Black Hills or on their southern boundary. The discovery of a leg bone of a mammoth by Mr. Grinnell of Yale College, announced to you by telegraph, was very important, however, as an indication of the geological age of the country through which we have come. Studying geology without fossils is like substituting a blank book of different colored papers for a well-printed pictorial history of a town or country. The different layers of rocks are only the differently colored sheets; the fossils must furnish the historic illustrations. For instance, with cretaceous and tertiary periods which are geologically contiguous, and which in this country are frequently found overlapping each other, there is great similarity in the rock belonging to each era, and from the rock alone it is not possible to determine which period is represented at any particular locality.

A MAMMOTH'S LEG-BONE DISCOVERED.

Thus, for want of identification of characteristic fossils, which kept themselves out of sight, over 200 miles of the country, from Lincoln to the South-West, presented geologically a very ambiguous history. It was difficult to tell, lithologically, whether the tertiary or cretaceous epoch presented the best title-deed. At last, when 18 days from Lincoln, we struck a valuable item of this evidence. An aged mammoth, a great deal older than Methusaleh, and perhaps among his peers quite as respectable, had laid himself down to a final sleep, and, fortunately for us, had left one leg sticking out of the bed, or else some later water-flood had unkindly lifted the coverlid. Mr. Grinnell's ubiquitous eye had been looking for just such a phenomenon. Shovels and picks were at once procured, and the ancient remains of the great departed were tenderly removed to the scientific hearse. Nothing but the tell-tale leg was found to testify to the huge structure of which it had formed one of the prinicpal supports. Even this, after so many centuries of enforced seclusion, was too weak to endure its sudden exposure, and a large part of it crumbled to pieces. The bone was about four feet long and a foot in diameter at the larger end. The animal to which it had belonged must have been considerably larger than an elephant. Two or three turtle bones and the head of a small lizard had also found a resting place in the same locality. The bed in which they were found was of bluish clay capped with sandstone, the whole of which had been worn and carved by the water into an architecture so suggestive of medieval walls and turrets that we called it Castle Butte. The fossil remains were found some 80 to 100 feet under the surface. The evidence of these bones was suf-ficent to refer the locality in which they were discovered to the tertiary epoch, and though it would hardly be safe to make a sweeping generalization on the testimony of the two or three fossils, yet their discovery strongly favored the presumption that the greater part of the country we have traversed belong to the same period.

INDIANS, ACTUAL AND IMAGINARY.

Nearly every day since we departed Indians have been reported. The imagination of soldiers, especially the new recruits, is very active and easily invests a jut of sandstone or a solitary tree in the distance with life and motion. In this way the number of Indians seen each day has been from five to fifty. Habits of weighing evidence, easily acquired after testing a few soldiers' stories, lead one to reject about nine out of every ten stories of this kind that come to one's ears. But in our twelfth day out we had the best of evidence that Indians were watching our movements. Capt. McDougall, while out hunting with two of his men, met Raynolds [Reynolds], our special hunter, with a companion. While riding along together, an Indian, almost naked, was seen to start from a ravine about two thousand yards distant. He mounted his pony and rode off rapidly. Another was seen to follow him. A field-glass left no doubt that the Indian did not belong to our scouts. Soon after a band of twenty Indians were seen in the distance. The report was corroborated by Capt. French and also by our scouts. The Indian fires seen in the evening furnished additional evidence of the truth of the story. The effect of these reports has been to excite new caution. Stragglers and hunting parties are less frequent and pickets are less likely to yield to a temptation to sleep on post.

On Sunday, the 12th instant, winding through the tortuous gullies along the forks of the Grand River, we made a march of but seven miles in an air line, though our odometer justly registered eleven miles. The succeeding day we had better luck and made 15½ miles, though we were obliged to camp on a cactus plain, variegated with sage brush and sun-flowers. Indiscretions in the use of slippers around camp were dearly paid for. A great relief was the pleasant camp the succeeding night, which our surveyors named Prospect Valley, from the extensive and agreeable view it presented. Here Gen. Custer wisely determined to stay over one day, and every one, mules and horses included, rejoiced at the determination.

NEW YORK TRIBUNE
Issue of August 21, 1874

FROM PROSPECT VALLEY TO LITTLE MISSOURI RIVER.

A SABBATH IN CAMP—
PERILOUS MAIL CARRYING—
GUARDING AGAINST THE
INDIANS—SCIENTIFIC
RESEARCHERS AND DIVER-
SIONS—FIRST VIEW OF THE
BLACK HILLS—WAITING
FOR THE BUG-HUNTERS—
THE LITTLE MISSOURI.

BLACK HILLS EXPEDITION, LITTLE MISSOURI VALLEY, July 19.—Our rest in camp at Prospect Valley was one of those oasis experiences which in the popular metaphor furnish the memory with a green spot. We had marched 13 successive days, and made 223 miles, an average of 17¾ miles per day. We needed a Sabbath and we had one, though it came on Wednesday. Had we remained over at the Cave our Sabbath would have been identical with the Christian one, but so poor was the grass that our tired and hungry animals would have had to spend nearly all their time in hunting the material for a decent meal, and would have been compelled to take what rest they craved in the amenities of a cactus bed. Another object in lying over one day was to give officers and men time to write a few lines to the folks at home, the mail to be gathered and sent off in the evening by two scouts. The men chosen for the mission were two Ree Indians, both trustworthy men of experience and personal bravery. They were quite willing to undertake the work, and were perhaps rather glad than otherwise to have an opportunity to return to their wives and families at Fort Lincoln. They will not be required to rejoin the expedition. Mounted on good ponies, with their saddles well packed with a supply of coffee, hard tack, and sugar, they set out at sundown for their journey of 228 miles. If undisturbed by the Sioux, who if they should meet them would show them no mercy, they will probably shorten our trail, and reach Lincoln in four days.

PRECAUTIONS AGAINST SURPRISE.

The reports brought in by our scouts and flankers, as well as the signs of Indian neighborhood found along our line of march, have induced Gen. Custer to take additional precautions against a surprise. In order that the train may not be delayed on the daily march anymore than necessary, Gen. Custer, with his guides and one company of pioneers, has been accustomed to go on several miles in advance to pick out a road or make one when necessary. To pursue this desirable plan with safety, the advance guard has been strengthened by the addition of two companies of cavalry, one from each flank. These added to the pioneers and scouts make a formidable preliminary to the general advance, varying daily from 225 to 250 men, according to the strength of the companies detailed, while the train has still left for its protection a guard of 450 men. The change in programme will furnish no encouragement to Indians.

Leaving Prospect Valley Camp on the morning of the 16th of July, a neighboring ridge of hills offered for Col. Ludlow, our Chief Engineer, and his assistant, Mr. Wood, an observation opportunity not to be neglected. The other members of the Scientific Corps were invited, and with Goose, as guide, and Egard (Agard), the halfbreed, as interpreter, and under the protection of Company B, 7th Cavalry, Lieut. Ben. Hodgson, commanding, we separated from the main command for a little picnic on our own account. Ascending the hill at its gentlest slope we were soon out of sight of the train, and in a section of country distinctively different from that which we had previously passed over. A high range of hills with a broad table land on top abundantly supplied with grass, and furnishing more timber than we had seen during the whole extent of our trip, was an agreeable adjunct to Prospect Valley and a strong contrast to the region preceding. In our march from Lincoln we have passed over three sections of country each presenting marked physiographic contrasts. First the rolling, billowy land, which stretches out in shallow corrugations from Fort Lincoln to the west, and is characterized by occasional areas of fine pasture. Then succeeds the deterioration of cactus, alkali, and sage brush, with the attendant "Bad Lands" along the Grand River, which greatly change the whole aspect of the country and render it utterly unfit for civilization. Lastly, the hilly ridges of sandstone covered with pine, deeply cut with ravines, and their precipitous sides covered with the debris of crumbling sandstone. These hills were a glad relief from the level of rolling monotony which we had traversed for two weeks. There was an Eastern visage to the scenery which seemed natural and homelike.

FIRST CLEAR VIEW OF THE BLACK HILLS

From these hills we had the first clear and distinct view of the Black Hills which from the Cave Plateau had appeared only as a faint tangible line of distinct blue mist. Now their dark heavy wavy outlines, here and there sharply projected into a bold peak or butte loomed up in blue vesture against the sky over fifty miles away. Prominent to the South was the rounded crest of Bear Butte, one of the most conspicuous landmarks on the skirts of the Black Hills. Deer's Ears and Slave Butte again showed themselves from a different angle, and then Crow Butte, so called from a battle which occurred at this point between the Sioux and Crows in which ten of the latter were killed. Below us on the right stretched the valley of the Little Missouri, and the river course marked by the usual signature of trees, and the valley itself cut and furrowed into a thousand tributary gullies. We were glad, however, to see that the river at this point and further up toward its source was devoid of the vicious Bad Lands which disputed our wagon train last year on the Yellowstone Expedition, and which seem to grow worse as you follow the river to its mouth. "Ugh!" grunted Goose as we sat on the brow of the hill looking toward a distant knoll sparingly dotted with timber. None of the party could see anything except Louis Egard (Agard), the halfbreed, who gave a corroborative nod. Field-glasses were produced, yet even then only a few of the party could descry with their aid the little black ants miles away on the hill slope, who, with eyes as keen as Goose's, were probably watching their watchers. To our undisciplined gaze they were either trees or insects, we did not know which; but Goose, without moving his eyes from the spot on which they were fixed, simply said, "Sioux." We had too much respect for his opinion to contend for our theory. Then he pointed to a white wreath of smoke languidly floating in the distant sky, and said "Sioux" again, accompanying it with a look which could easily be translated, "Put this and that together." The wreath of smoke was an Indian bulletin. The crawling insects were a group of Indian reporters "interviewing" our observations to distant lodges in smoky clouds or ringlets figured on the sky.

A SCIENTIFIC DIGRESSION.

The topography of the country was soon transferred to our engineer's note-books, and, retracing a portion of our trail, we dismounted, and led our horses down the steep slope of the hill into the valley below. On this side of the ridge the geology was frank and communicative. The tall bluffs, bare of trees or verdure, in some places almost perdendicularly (sic) cut, presented an interesting disposition of sandstones, marls, and avenaocous limestones, regularly and horizontally stratified. Here Mr. Grinnell found a few saurian bones, but nothing rare or new. Two of our party, yielding to the scientific attractions of this hill, wandered far away from the escort, an imprudent habit, but a very natural one. The command was halted in the valley under the hot, glaring sun, and compelled to wait nearly an hour for their return from the hills. This time they were profitably spending in transcribing the testimony of the rocks. But enlisted men take but little interest in geology, and, suffering as they were from heat and thirst, were in no condition to endure patiently the delay. I have never heard more original profanity than the "bug-hunters," as the scientific corps are irreverently called, innocently excited on this occasion. A pious form of which concerning them, freed in a deluge

of oaths, was that they would immediately be surrounded be hostile Sioux, and scalped before aid could reach them. The men who uttered the wish would, in case of danger, be the first to go to their relief.

"Be easy now, Mike," said a philosophical sergeant; "they have only gone to take out a claim."

"Claim!" said Mike; "I wish that every one of the bug hunters would take out a claim six feet by two and enter it," putting considerable emphasis on the last two words.

But soldiers would not be soldiers if they did not have their daily grumble. A common form of morning salutation among enlisted men is "Have you had your grumble yet!" No man is considered to be in sound health of mind or body who fails to exercise this privilege.

It was 3 o'clock in the afternoon before we met the train again in the valley, and found water for men and horses. An hour later we struck the Little Missouri River. Here the train was halted, mules and horses unhitched and watered. Our water-kegs were filled, and a supply of dry wood placed in our wagons, the providential measures for a dry camp. The Little Missouri here was not more than from two to four feet deep, and ten yards wide. There were no Bad Lands along its banks, but good grass was scarce, and the lack of this induced Gen. Custer to push on till nearly 9 o'clock at night, when finding good grazing we made a dry camp. Dinner, though sadly displaced by our march of 34 miles, was served at 10½ o'clock. Weary of the long day, which had begun at 3½ in the morning, we wrapped the drapery of our army blanket around us and lay down to pleasant dreams. What did it matter that we had no roof nor canvas to shield us? With good Mother Earth beneath and the starry heavens above, who could wish couch more magnificent?

NEW YORK TRIBUNE
Issue of August 24, 1874

ARRIVAL OF THE CUSTER EXPEDITION AT HEENG-YA-KARA (sic).

NEARING THE END OF A LONG JOURNEY—WAYSIDE SCENES AND INCIDENTS— A NEW GEOLOGICAL AREA— JOY AT THE SIGHT OF TIMBER—THE VALLEY OF LA BELLE FOURCHE— BLOODSHED AND A DOUBLE FUNERAL.

From the Special Correspondent of the Tribune.

HEENG-YA-KARA (sic), Camp 20, July 20.—In the Black Hills at last! The great blue mists which for days have hung away under the horizon, gradually looming up into the sky and growing more and more formidable as we approached, have at last resolved themselves into massive, tangible rocks, rising in bold, mountain shapes above us. For more than two weeks, with faithful and pertinaceous inquisitiveness, we have been questioning guides, maps, compasses, and even the silent, far-distant stars, just to find this opportunity for self-gratulation, viz., the doorway to the Black Hills. Whether we have found the doorway remains to be seen; but at any rate, we have reached the Hills, the great unknown theater of our future quests. We have coiled a long trail around their feet; and thus binding our victim, we are now prepared to strike at its heart. When my last letter closed, we had made a dry camp in the Little Missouri Valley, within two days' march of the skirts of the Hills. Reveille, that cruel, merciless air, which the most skillful trumpeter cannot make attractive, roused us again after a four hours' sleep, and we pushed on till the middle of the afternoon. Halting on the top of a high bluff which formed the culmination of a gradual ascent from the valley, the prospect ahead for a wagon road was so discouraging that rather than attempt to reach the Belle Fourche that night, as originally purposed, Gen. Custer determined to make camp. Sufficient water and wood were found at the foot of the bluff. This camp is made hateful to our memory by

Thirty-eight members of Custer's officer and scientific corps assembled on the morning of August 13, 1874, at Custers order, to have their picture taken while the expedition was camped on the headwaters of Box Elder Creek. Identification of the men in this photograph has always been incomplete and sometimes conflicting. They are identified on the facing page as accurately as possible on the basis of current information.

a terrible dust storm, which besoiled everything in our tents and made life to the occupants utterly miserable. After this experience the subject of cremation was banished from conversation by common consent. Several tents were leveled by this dusty, disrespectful wind.

SEEKING A ROAD THROUGH AN UNKNOWN COUNTRY.

As we looked in the morning from the top of the bluff down into the vexatious maze of gulleys which seemed to cover the valley before us like a network, our pioneers and our wagon-masters grew faint-hearted. They were doomed to an agreeable disappointment. Like many other difficulties in life, those which threatened us proved

less formidable when actually encountered than when viewed at a distance. A wagon-way was found and followed without overtaking our pioneers. So it was for four or five miles. But there was a suspicious hill beyond which filled us with foreboding. We did not know what lay behind it. In fact, unless we are situated so as to command a view of the whole country, each day's march is an experiment more or less doubtful in its results. The hill proved to be another miniature Pisgah. I have no idea that any translation into words can convey to an unsympathetic reader a conception of the enthusiasm with which the view from the top of that hill was greeted. But let such a one travel for 16 days over a treeless plain, under a tropical sun, with no protection from its fierce

rays but the hat he wears on his head, and if he does not exclaim with joy when, just at noontide on the 17th day, a beautiful forest suddenly rises across his path, he is either a stoic or else is devoid of a thankful heart. Here and there we had seen scraggy timber on the hills, but none that furnished shade, or none that lay across our path. We had learned to appreciate at every halt on the march the shady side of a horse, only available, however, when the animal would stand still. But the prospect of having a real, live tree—a tree that would not tread on you just as you had dropped to sleep; a tree that did not need to be picketed, and would not move around to feed; a genuine, legitimate tree, such as we had seen in days gone by before we left the States—the

South Dakota State Historical Society

(1) Capt. William Ludlow, Chief Engineer; (2) Capt. George Yates, Co. F, Cav.; (3) 1st Lt. Thomas W. Custer, Co. L, Cav.; (4) 1st Lt. Donald McIntosh, Co. G, Cav.; (5) 2nd Lt. George D. Wallace, Co. G, Cav.; (6) 1st Lt. James Calhoun, Co. C, Cav.; (7) Capt. Thomas H. French, Co. M, Cav.; (8) 2nd Lt. Henry M. Harrington, Co. C, Cav.; (9) unidentified civilian—could be Boston Custer, youngest brother to Gen. George A. Custer; (10) unidentified military; (11) probably N. H. Winchell, geologist (holding rock hammer); (12) could be Luther North, scientist; (13) George Bird Grinnell, scientist; (14) Maj. John W. Williams, Asst. Surgeon; (15) Maj. George A. Forsyth, Battalion Commander; (16) A. B. Donaldson, scientist and correspondent for the ST. PAUL PIONEER; (17) Bvt. Maj. Gen. George A. Custer, Commanding; (18) 1st Lt. Thomas W. McDougall, Co. E, Cav.; (19) Bloody Knife, Custer's Scout; (20) Maj. Joseph Tilford, Battalion Commander; (21) unidentified military; (22) unidentified military; (23) Capt. Myles Moylan, Co. A, Cav.; (24) 2nd Lt. Frederick D. Grant, Acting Aide; (25) unidentified military; (26) unidentified military (almost concealed from view); (27) 2nd Lt. Charles Varnum, Co. A, Cav.; (28) Capt. Verling K. Hart, Co. C, Cav.; (29) Capt. Lloyd Wheaton, Co. I, 20th Inf.; (30) unidentified military; (31) 1st Lt. Algernon Smith, Quartermaster; (32) unidentified military; (33) Capt. Owen Hale, Co. K, Cav.; (34) 1st Lt. Benjamin Hodgson, Co. B, Cav.; (35) unidentified military; (36) Capt. Frederick W. Benteen, Co. H, Cav.; (37) 1st Lt. Edward S. Godfrey, Co. K, Cav.; (38) 1st Lt. Frank M. Gibson, Co. H, Cav. There are eight unidentfied members of the military in this picture. Ironically, there are eight names remaining on the roster of Custer's officer corps who are not already identified in the picture. The eight are: (1) Act. Asst. Surgeon S. J. Allen; (2) Act. Asst. Surgeon A. C. Bergen; (3) 1st Lt. Josiah Chance, 17th Inf.; (4) Bvt. Maj. Louis H. Sanger, Co. G, 17th Inf.; (5) 2nd Lt. Geo. H. Roach, Co. G, 17th Inf.; (6) 2nd Lt. J. Granville Gates, Co. I, 20th Inf.; (7) 1st Lt. Edward G. Mathey, Co. M, Cav.; and Michael Smith, Wagonmaster.

prospect was more than silence could bear, and we said "Hallelujah!" A timber preface to the Black Hills; how the mere fact of existence was elevated into a luxury by this chapter in our march!

Not only the rugged scrub oaks, the first we had seen on the trip, but the character of the soil and the changing aspect of the landscape showed that we were entering a different geological and topographical area. The low hills and ridges which anticipated the higher ones beyond, and introduced us to the Black Hill range were covered with a heavy deposit of loose shale, the result of disintegration from the underlying slate, which formed a bed below it of a hundred or more feet in thickness. This shale was almost entirely devoid of grass and all vegetation, except the lusty scrub oaks which seemed to find there a congenial home. In many places above the slate were beds of marl of an ashen gray color, and where this was not present the slate was generally concealed by the shaly debris already mentioned. Beds of impure limestone were also found on the tops of some of the bluffs.

IN THE VALLEY OF THE BELLE FOURCHE.

We had now left the plains behind us and were entering the approaches to the Black Hills. High hills and deep ravines compelled a tortuous route for the train, but following a mediatorial ridge with a sinuous but not difficult descent into a narrow valley, we found ourselves on the banks of a small stream which we knew to be the Belle Fourche or North Fork of the Cheyenne River, one of the two rivers—the other being the Little Missouri — which, through many tributaries, draw their waters mainly from the Black Hills. The north and south branches of the Cheyenne River are the two prongs of a water fork which clasps the base of the Black Hills. Each of these branches finds its ultimate sources in the Powder River Range west of the Black Hills, but flowing the one around the north and the other around the south base of the Hills, they derive the larger part of their volume from the small streams which drain the Black Hills, and uniting thirty miles east of them, form the Cheyenne River, which flows into the

Missouri River near Fort Sully, or about 275 miles above the northern boundary of Nebraska. At the point we struck it, the Belle Fourche is a small stream or creek with a rocky bottom, about fifteen yards wide at this time of year, containing but a small quantity of water, somewhat flavored with alkali, but still a great improvement on much of the water of previous camps. A considerable portion of the hills flanking the valley of the stream was covered on the surface with iron concretions, and a spring discovered in the course of the day's march was strongly impregnated with the same metal. The stream itself was well fringed with timber, the American poplar or quivering aspen and young growths of willow forming a large part of the wood. The valley was carpeted with good grass, figured strongly with sunflower and sage, but mostly exempt from cactus. This is an exemption from a camp carpet which we always accept with gratitude.

The following day was Sunday, and we did not break camp—less, I am inclined to believe, from religious motives than from a weather-wise discretion induced by a heavy fall of rain, which began before sunrise and continued with slight intermissions until afternoon. The ardor of the engineer corps, whose ambition always seeks the highest peaks, was not at all dampened by the heavy drench, and, with Capt. Hart's company as an escort, Col. Ludlow improved the halt by making a reconnoissance some eight or ten miles from camp. Striking an old timeworn trail not far from camp. Col. Ludlow pursued it sufficiently far to satisfy himself that it was the trail made by Capt. Raynolds, in 1859, on his trip to the Yellowstone and the upper waters of the Missouri, in which he skirted the Black Hills on their northern side by following the valley of the Belle Fourche. Fifteen years had not sufficed to obliterate the scars which the face of the valley had then received.

NORTHERN RIDGES OF THE BLACK HILLS

From our camp on the Belle Fourche to our present camp, at HEENG-YA-KARA (sic), we have marched 57 miles and consumed three days. Instead of following

Raynold's old trail and keeping along the Belle Fourche, we crossed that stream and pursued a general southwesterly direction, sometimes cutting deep into the hills and meandering through their valleys, then emerging and hugging the base of the inner range. On the north side there are many isolated hills, the outliers of the principal ranges. We generally succeeded in keeping well inside of these secondary ranges, and usually found a broad valley between them and the primary range, through which our train went without difficulty. Thus for three days we have had an opportunity to study the formation of the northern ridges of the Black Hills minutely for about 60 miles of their extent, while from objective points along the line of march our engineers have acquired an accurate idea of the topography for many miles on each side of our trail. Most noticeable thus far in the geological formation of the hills has been a bright red arenaceous stone, which seems to form the principal component of the northern and perhaps the eastern wall. The striking and peculiar aspect which these bright red exposures give to the general scenery has been noticed by Hayden, who accompanied Raynolds in the expedition before referred to. I have seen in the Little Missouri Bad Lands something of the same effect, produced by the red shale on top of the numerous bare-headed buttes of that fire-baked and water-troughed region. But in the Black Hills the color forms not merely a capping of the small conical hills or isolated buttes as in the Bad Lands, but as the legitimate and everywhere prevalent complexion of the rocks, which form the substance of the hills and rise frequently in massive, flaming red shapes from beneath their green coverlid. The frequency, boldness, and extent of these exposures invests the scenery everywhere with a strange, commanding brilliancy, almost gaudy in its effect, heightened by the complement which the red hue of the rocks finds in the fresh verdure of the hills. The suggestion derived from the landscape is that Nature, when she made her dress, was a little over-vain and rather "loud" in putting on the colors. Paint your Hudson

River Palisades a warm red color against a background of green, and reducing somewhat the perpendicularity of the bluff, you would have an apparent reproduction of the Jurassic exposures in the Black Hills. If the whole extent of the hills were made up of this formation, the "Red Hills" would be a more appropriate name than Black Hills. At a distance, however, much of this exposure is concealed by the heavy growth of pine, which, seen from afar, forms a black mantle to the hills and gives them the name by which they are now known. We have reason to believe also that in the interior of the hills this red arenaceous stone gives place to an older geological formation. Although no fossils have been found positively establishing the fact, Prof. Winchell agrees with Hayden in referring it to the Jurassic age. The stone much resembles that found in the Jurassic belts of New Jersey. The soil in the valleys, formed by trituration from the rocks, is of the same reddish hue so noticeable to a stranger on New Jersey roads in the districts referred to. We discover a marked improvement in the soil as compared with most of that over which we passed before reaching the hills. It is characterized by greater strength and fertility. Another peculiarity of the red arenaceous rock which should not be left unnoticed in the association with it of large quantities of gypsum, and, in smaller quantities, of salt. The same gypsum-bearing features are noticed in the corresponding geological formation in England, and assist in establishing the identity of the rock. The presence of this gypsum affected deleteriously the water found in its vicinity and threatened with sickness several of our men who used it. Good water was not difficult to find elsewhere, and some in springs discovered on our march was nearly as cold as ice.

A THOUSAND FEET ABOVE THE PLAINS.

A glance at the map and a determination of latitude and longitude show us that we are in the western portion of the Black Hills, at a point about one-third of their length, measured from the north. The barometer shows also that we have been constantly ascending from our camp on the Belle Fourche, and must be at present a thousand feet or more above the plain. We have had the good fortune to find an excellent wagon road, when the mountainous character of the country is taken into consideration. Only one day, the first day's march from the Belle Fourche, have we been obliged to cut a way through the woods. The timber has generally been avoided by following the bottom land between the hills. Our camps have uniformly been pleasant ones. At our first camp from the Belle Fourche, some 19 miles west of it, we had the pleasure on the 20th of July of eating strawberries without cream and cherries without pie crust. We left on the east side of the Belle Fourche the barren slates and scrub oaks. Burr oaks, larger and thriftier pines, better grass, and a more varied vegetation kindly took its place.

Our march has been made without special incident. Horses and mules seem to stand the trip well. A few of them are afflicted with sore backs and lameness, but none have failed from want of sufficient food. The sorebacked and lame are relieved from duty and led along slowly till they recover. One poor sorrel has been dropped by the wayside. He was judged too lame to keep up with the rest of the horses, and was turned loose. But the poor animal, although there was a plenty of grass and timber by the way, inviting him to rest, food, and shade, would not be abandoned. The cavalry horses are assigned to companies with reference to their colors. He knew where he belonged. His friends and companion horses were with the sorrels. They were marching at the head of the column. He was so lame he could hardly stand up, yet he painfully limped through a march of 19 miles to keep his place at the head of the column. The next day the sorrels were with the rear of the train. The old horse, with only three legs on the ground, was there too, doing his best to keep up. Rather than suffer the anguish of being left alone, with no companion to share the inviting pastures of the valley, he would endure the most intense physical torture. Every step made him wince, but never conquered his friendship and devotion. Poor old sorrel, it was a kind bullet which at last gave you an honorable discharge! A less pathetic incident of the march was the discovery by Major Hall of a rusty tin cup almost imbedded in the ground, where it had evidently been for years. The name of William Robinson was scratched on the outside. Mr. John Smith, our sutler, is acquainted with a half-breed of that name who makes his home among the Indians, and it is quite likely that the cup may have been dropped by him or by some wandering Indian who obtained it from him. Our march yesterday introduced us to some beds of carboniferous limestone, which lay directly in the line of our march, and the surface of which seemed to be broken up into large slabs. Our horses' feet clattered over them as if they were marching on a flag pavement. Several Indian trails were discovered during the day, one of them indicating a band of about 50 Indians. On our camping ground was abundant evidence of the former presence of Indians, though the signs were not of recent date. Camp was made at the foot of a large conspicuous spur of the western range of hills.

HEENG-YA-KARA (sic)

This range is called by the Indians Heeng-ya-kara. We had seen this landmark for several days and used it to steer by. It is one of the most prominent landmarks in the Black Hills, though not by any means the highest. Seen 40 or 50 miles away from the angle at which we approached it, it resembles in shape the cover to a soup tureen, and we called it "Cover Butte," a name which we rejected on identifying it with the Heeng-ya-kara, which signifies in the Sioux language. "Rocky Mountain goat." This peak was observed by Lieut. Warren in 1857, and is put down on the map as Inyan Kara. We have stayed over here today for the purpose of giving our engineers a chance to study the country from this mountain as well as to study the mountain itself. Unfortunately, the day has been too hazy to permit of extended observation, but the geological features of the mountain have well repaid the visit. The mountain, as before noticed, is shaped like a tureen cover, with a heavy knob on top. This knob is very steep, being inclined at an angle of 48 degrees, and is almost surrounded at its base by a sharp ridge of horse-shoe shape, separated from the knob by a deep ravine, except on a small portion of the northern side. The mountain is about two miles long and a mile wide; its height, about 1,200 feet. The mountain is evidently the result of an upheaval. The carboniferous limestone and the Jurassic red stone, which lie below the Kara, are of later date than Kara itself, which Prof. Winchell refers to the Lower Sirlurian. The knob is composed of metamorphic sedimentary rock, granitoid in appearance, but difficult to characterize accurately. The strata dip toward the east and west at an angle of 40 degrees. On the top of the ridge, small pieces of white quartz were found. As they had no geological business to be there, they were no doubt left there by the Indians, who are fond of making offerings to their gods from these lofty altars. Strawberries, raspberries, gooseberries and June berries were found growing plentifully on the mountain side. Our miners prospected for gold, but found none.

THE FIRST FUNERAL.

Added to its lofty oversight of hill and dale, its peculiar geological import, which give to the Heeng-ya-kara a special interest, it will always possess for us a sad memorial significance. It is the only monument of a double grave which last night we dug at its feet. When two days ago we moved into camp, but one day's journey from the Heeng-ya-kara, and the gold figure of the mountain rose before us, not one of the strong, robust men who saw it supposed that he was looking at his own tombstone. Little did poor Turner think, as the sun dropped down behind the hills and the darkness unfolded its pall, that the next time the familiar trumpeter sounded the "Good-night" call it would be over his own grave. But the next morning, just before we moved from camp, an altercation occurred between Turner and another soldier in the same company, named Roller. The dispute waxed warm, until the latter drew his pistol and shot his antagonist through the body. Roller was placed under guard, and Turner was put in an ambulance, and we started on our march; but the wounded man died before we reached camp. The other death was that of John Cunningham, another private, who died early the same morning of dysentery. The echoes in the hills for the first time in all their answerings mocked the mournful music of the dead march. Six hundred men, with not a single woman, formed a solemn square around the grave; service is read by a comrade; a squad fire a volley, which is repeated by the hills; then the trumpeter, who had so often given his comrades the signal for their evening rest, plants his foot on the mound of displaced earth and sounds the taps—the soldier's "good-night" — the only prayer which was offered at the grave. It was a solemn funeral, yet a funeral without a tear.

NEW YORK TRIBUNE
Issue of August 17, 1874

THE BLACK HILLS
A valley of Flowers.

THE BLACK HILLS
EXPEDITION IN EDEN—
SEVEN THOUSAND FEET
ABOVE THE SEA—
THE SOLDIERS SUCCUMB TO
THE BEAUTY OF THE SCENE—
THE HORSES DECKED WITH
FLOWERS AND THE SOLDIERS'
HANDS FULL OF NOSEGAYS—
THE MOST EXUBERANT
FLORA THIS SIDE OF
CALIFORNIA. A HIGHLY
FERTILE AND PRODUCTIVE
REGION.

From the special correspondent of the Tribune.

CAMP NO. 23, BLACK HILLS, FLORAL VALLEY, JULY 26. — An Eden in the clouds—how shall I describe it![41] I confess that I have too much pleasure in this lovely scene to make the attempt. As well try to paint the flavor of a peach or the odor of a rose as to turn this beautiful valley, nestled sweetly in the hills, 7,000 feet above the sea, with all its wealth of bloom and fragrance, into plain, prosaic printers' ink. Perhaps one poet in the world might translate into verse the mystery of this charm; perhaps the soul of Mendelssohn, in a new song without words, might phrase in sympathetic melody the sweet emotions which this little Eden awakens,

(Authors' Note: In 1874, because of telegraph delays and other communication difficulties, news dispatches from the field frequently reached newspaper offices out of order from the sequence in which they were originally written. To preserve the chronology of events, we have arranged the dispatches in the order of their writing, which means that some of the issue dates appearing at the top of pages and in the columns will be out of calendar order).

41. . . . Soldiering after this Cortez and Pizzaro style cannot be other than delightful. The reveille and retreat must sound like sweet musical interludes in a mid-summer dream gold-finding and berry-picking . . .
. . . A glorious discovery, and a felicious illustration of the Peace Policy with Indians. It ought to be named Happy Valley, where the Custer picnic encamped and went berrying. In comparison with the rough and riotous Modoc affair this is a perfect piece of art, or at any rate, of asthetics. It is such an episode in the current Indian was as our Quaker President himself, with his instinctive fondness for attractive pieces of real estate must envy his own son for having a part in. But it will be curious to read what Bishop Hare will say of these glowing accounts of a country whose exploration he denounced as a violation of a solemn treaty.
BOSTON POST
Issue of August 18, 1874

but only the greatest of painters with a brush inspired could convey to the imagination a picture of the vale itself. Yet what a task for a painter! It is not to paint the grand, the magnificent, the sublime; for the valley in which I write is none of these. The hills are lofty indeed, strong and bold in their bearing, and guard the vale beneath them with a jealous pride, which seemed to frown at our intrusion, as we trampled the lovely flowers beneath our feet and mangled their roots with our wagon wheels. But magnificent, grand, or sublime they are not. Nor is there anything here that is. There are no gushing geysers, as in the Yellowstone Park, sending their spray high in the air; no great rush and roar of waterfalls as at Niagara or St. Anthony; no colossal trees as in the grand primeval forests of California; nothing at all sensational. Each element in the picture—the lofty hills, the host of tall pines, the clear, pure stream of swift but almost silent water, and above all, the inexpressible wealth and eloquence of flowers to which all else seems to contribute—each of these is but a word in the utterance of the whole picture.

THE VALLEY AND ITS INDESCRIBABLE CHARMS.

It would not be very difficult to analyze the facts and elements in this scenic charm which extorts admiration and praise from even the most cynical of critics. Col. Ludlow could measure the hills and the valley and reduce them to figures and angles in his note book. Prof. Winchell with his hammer could catechise the rocks and transcribe their evidence. Dr. Williams could catalogue the exuberant flora if you gave him the privilege of naming a few of the flowers which have bloomed mayhap for centuries in this quietude unquestioned by the botanist. The soil, the atmosphere, the running stream, the bubbling, moss-lined springs, could all be enumerated. But what engineer, botanist, mathematician, or chemist could add up the elements and arrive at the beautiful unity into which nature has merged them all? As well try by counting the strands in a Gobelin tapestry to picture to the mind the interwoven design; as well attempt by

anatomy, physiology, and chemistry to reframe and reanimate the form which these have resolved. So right here in this heavenly valley science is baffled by a nameless beauty, which it can analyze and destroy, but cannot reproduce.

HARD CLIMBING.

At the Heeng-ya-Kara (sic) we found ourselves on the westerly range of the Black Hills, at a point not distant from the center. Gen. Custer then determined to bend to the east and enter the very heart of the whole range, with a view of finding the central park which the Indians had reported to exist there. The view from the Heeng-ya-Kara (sic) had failed to show us a pathway to the interior. Our Indian guides knew only the general direction, and but little else. They could point out no gap or pass which promised or even broached a way to the interior. The only authentic map of that section is a piece of blank paper. A wall of hills defended by a great army of pines threatened us if we attempted the most direct route. The valley we had followed seductively led in another direction as if intentionally to thwart our purpose. The odds of circumstance, therefore, were against us, but the odds of pluck and perseverance were in our favor. Gen. Custer boldly turned his column to the east. Capt. Yates, with his company of 9th Cavalry was ordered to charge on the pine brigade. His men advanced promptly with axes and slew them right and left. The hill was steep—a hard task for our mules; but they had had a day's rest and plenty of grass, and went at the hill with a good stomach. Their drivers' reputation for profanity and teamstership was staked on the occasion. So they lashed them hard with tongue and whip, and threatened their hearts with never-ending pain if they failed. Encouraged by the gross voice and whip, if not by the dismal theology, the poor "rat tails" pulled as if they were inspired. We reached the top of the hill and found that fires in the forest had saved our pioneers much clearing; but the brush was very heavy and annoying. A festive log in the way tipped over one of Lieut. Chance's Gattling guns by way of amusement, but hurt nothing or nobody. The flanking cavalry had to crash

their way through heavy underbrush and young poplar and pine. Hats were impertinently removed and clothes received a good brushing, and those in the advance marched at times more by faith than by sight. But we pushed on. Where we were going we did not know. We were on a crusade certainly, but like the unlettered enthusiasts of the first crusade, who expected to find Palestine next to Germany, all that we could certainly say was that we were going east and that the road was a hard one to travel. We could not turn well to the south, the only other direction which would have favored our course, without running into a valley with a heavier growth of timber than the one that opposed our progress. The prospect of getting "out of the woods" was not encouraging.

THE ENTRY INTO FLORAL VALLEY.

Was it by instinct, chance, or good fortune that somewhere about noon Gen. Custer caught a glimpse of the foot—I might almost say the little toe—of a small valley away down at the base of the lofty hills? Louis Egain, (Agard) our half-breed guide, thought it was by some sad calamity, for, said he, if we get down into that place we can never get out again. But the nearest problem was how to get down, and whether it would pay to make the descent. Gen. Custer, with a few followers, went on to explore. Soon after the word came to "advance." Our teamsters, when they heard the bugle and saw the cavalry lead down the steep hills, dropped the right foot from the stirrup and took an extra quid of tobacco at the prospect. The hill was never intended for a wagon road. If it was, the argument from design is a failure. The fate of Jack and Jill was written on every feature and lineament of this hill. We had discovered the hitherto unknown site of this great calamity, and mentally took the latitude and longitude. A certain newspaper instinct for "items" impelled me to sit at the brow of the hill and see history repeat itself. But somehow or other—no thanks to the law of gravity—the whole outfit, men, horses, mules, and wagons got down in safety, and neither Jack nor Jill, nor of any of the family suffered contusion. But Capt. Smith, our commissary and quartermaster, had to work like a beaver, and the men who held the ropes had to hold hard to secure this desirable result.

We had formed many anticipations connected with the Black Hills, had pictured the hills and dales, its forests and streams, its silver and gold. Nothing beautiful or desirable, we thought, had been left uninspected. But still, for all this, nature took us completely by surprise. We had expected everything but a bounteous floral welcome. We were almost startled by the unlooked-for array which met us as we descended into the valley. Such brilliancy, such beauty, such variety, such profusion! All the glories of color, form and fragrance which Flora could command had been woven into a carpet for our feet. The whole valley was a garden, teeming with the gladness and joy of a new creation. Yes, an Eden in the sky without the forbidden fruit. How we reveled in this new-found beauty. No one, from the commanding general down to the humblest private or the most profane teamster, could withstand the effect. The greed for gold was forgotten. We ceased to look for the nuggets which would make us suddenly rich. Beauty for the time seemed the only wealth, and men who had never picked a flower since their childhood days bent and paid the long-neglected homage. Cavalrymen and teamsters decorated their horses and mules; infantrymen plumed their hats; officers gathered nosegays; pocket-books and note-books were brought into requisition to press and preserve the free gift of the valley. There was something almost affecting in seeing rough, coarse men softened and refined by the sweetness of the flowers, taking out worn, tobacco-scented pocket-books and putting in a flower or two "just to send to the old woman."

THE MOST EXUBERANT FLORA THIS SIDE OF CALIFORNIA.

For once grumblers against camps and country were hushed by their own confession. I know no more powerful testimony to the charm of the valley than this general acquiescence, silent or expressed. It would be amusing, indeed, and an original contribution to criticism, to record the profane encomiums which illiteral enthusiasts bestowed on this new Florida The same inadmissible adjectives which were used as prefixes to the most blasphemous curses against the barren wastes of Dakota were now transferred to the dialect of praise. But there was no mistaking the difference in sentiment.

This side of California I have never seen such variety and abundance in a floral display. Lilies, roses, blue bells, asters, sunflowers, geraniums, flowering pea, monk's hood, lupen, flax, primroses, and many flowers that I cannot name, were mingled and repeated in artless and exuberant profusion. Scarcely moving from his seat on the ground, Gen. Forsyth collected seventeen different species of flowers. One of the commonest and most admired in the whole pasture is a beautiful white lily with a beaded throat, first noticed by Dr. Williams, which is not described in the botany books, and which none of us have met in the East. A bright pink and a white geranium, the former present in great abundance, seem to be undescribed varieties of the geranium maculatum. A number of other flowers found will have to be reserved until our return for exact classification. Nor had nature forgotten her function as caterer. Gooseberries, raspberries, juneberries (amelanchior canadensis), large and sweet, and occasionally a few strawberries were found on the hillsides and freely eaten.

Our camp last night was, by common consent, the loveliest of the trip, indeed the only one which, up to that time, deserved the title. Our tents were pitched on each side of the valley at the basis of the including hills, embowered in a grove of young aspens. This morning camp was moved at the usual hour. The thermometer was nearly down to freezing point when we sat down to breakfast at 3:30 o'clock. Thin ice was actually found on some of our rubber blankets. But still the flowers never seemed to droop or chill. They are better used than we to this mountain air. Huge camp-fires at night, and in the morning before sunrise, are not only comforts but necessaries. We find too, in this rarified air that any little exertion or climbing a hill makes us puff and blow like so many asthmatics.

MARCHING THROUGH THE VALLEY.

Our march of twelve miles up the valley today was simply delightful. The hills, which at the entrance of the valley almost shut it in, leaving but a narrow passage 75 or 100 yards wide, receded slightly from each other, but still greatly exceed in height the width of the valley. The flora seemed even to increase in richness and abundance. The little rill scarcely two feet wide at our camp last night, and which a little further down was lost in the soil, and only marked by a greener growth of grass, began to increase in size and volume as we ascended the valley. It seemed strange indeed that the stream should grow deeper, broader and more voluminous as we ascended than it was below. It was one of the enchantments of the valley. Prosaic observation broke the spell by noting that the sandy, porous stream bed of the lower valley gave place gradually to a hard, constant, smooth rock bed, over which the water flowed clear, cold and colorless, as perfect as water could be. About six miles up the stream we found a clear, beautiful spring with a temperature of 44½ degrees. Six miles further up the stream suddenly disappeared, but the disappearance was only temporary—a little game of "hide and go seek"— for we found it higher up dividing into several tributary rills, fed by mossy springs, the water a half a degree lower in temperature than the spring six miles below. As we ascended the valley, our band which favors us every morning with a variety of selections played "How so fair" and "The Mocking Bird." We forgot the mocking bird in listening to the mocking hills which played an echo fuge with the band. The effect was beautiful indeed. Never before had the echoes sung to Hoffmann or Flotow, but they never missed a note in their response. During our march a large male crane was seen on a rocky ledge. Presently it flew down into the valley. The column was halted and Gen. Custer with his rifle advanced under cover of the bushes

South Dakota State Historical Society

Bear Butte rises 4,426 feet above sea level and stands eight miles northeast of the present City of Sturgis. Illingworth took this photograph of it from the south, looking north. Bear Butte is a prominent landmark. It was recorded by the Warren Expedition in September of 1857. Capt. Raynolds passed north of it in July of 1859. The official military orders, issued by General Alfred Terry from the Headquarters of the Department of Dakota in St. Paul on June 8, 1874, specifically singled it out as an orientation point for the expedition. In part, the orders read: "Lt. Col. Custer will proceed by such route as he may find to be most desirable, to Bear Butte or some other point on or near the Belle Fourche, and thence will push his explorations in such direction or directions as in his judgement will enable him to obtain the most information in regard to the character of the country and the possible routes of communication through it." The Custer Expedition camped south of Bear Butte on August 14. Custer and other members of the expedition scaled it on August 15, by following deer and antelope paths to the top. Legend has it that at one time the father of Crazy Horse went to the top of this butte to perform the rites of a "mystic and seer." While he was there the Great Spirit appeared to him in the form of a bear and gave him power to overcome all obstacles and all peoples. The father asked that these powers might be transferred to his son. Because of the form the Great Spirit assumed, the hill was thereafter known as Bear Butte. During the course of the expedition, Custer climbed every major peak, including Bear Butte. If one believes in the Great Spirit and the legend behind the name, it is possible that it was on the summit of Bear Butte that the ultimate destiny of Custer was cast, for, in less than two years he and many members of his command fell before Crazy Horse at the Little Big Horn.

and read the poor bird his death warrant. His wings measured from tip to tip were nearly seven feet long. Soon after one of our Indians caught a young crane alive, which was added to our Central Park collection.

CAMPED WITHIN THE CLOUDS.

Camp was made by the advance at 11 o'clock. The train, having to bridge the stream many times, did not arrive till some four hours later. Meanwhile the turgid clouds above came down to visit us and bathed the hills in a heavy mist. We were really camped within the clouds. The barometer marks 23.17. We must now be nearly 7,000 feet above THE TRIBUNE counting-room. The clouds have gone again and the sun is glimmering on the hill-tops. I am sitting at the door of my tent, looking out upon this lovely vale, no longer nameless or unknown. Floral Vale is the merited title which Gen. Custer has conferred upon it. Myriads of lilies, bluebells, and geraniums vie with each other in beauty and abundance in the landscape before me. Two days ago this charm was unknown and untraversed by the white man. Only now and then an Indian trespassed on its quietude. Is Nature a spendthrift that she lavished so abundantly her treasures on this distant solitude? Is there sadness in the thought that so many flowers were "born to blush unseen, and waste their sweetness on the desert air?" No; there is no loss, no wastage, no unrequited beauty here. How sweetly Emerson, in his tribute to the flower which he found in the woods, has anticipated all questioning:

Rhodors, if the sages ask thee why
This charm was wasted on the earth and sky,
Dear, tell them that if eyes were made for seeing,
Then beauty is its own excuse for being.
Why thou wert there. O rival of the rose,
I never thought to ask, I never knew;
But in my simple ignorance suppose
The self-same Power that brought me there brought you.

NEW YORK TRIBUNE
Issue of August 18, 1874

SURPRISING AN INDIAN VILLAGE.

THE EXPEDITION THROWS A VILLAGE INTO COMMOTION—
A FLAG OF TRUCE DISTRUSTED—
THE REE GUIDES LONGING TO IMBRUE THEIR HANDS IN SIOUX BLOOD—
THEIR MURDEROUS INTENTIONS EFFECTUALLY RESTRAINED BY GEN. CUSTER—
MRS. SLOW BULL'S HOSPITALITY—
FEARS OF THE SIOUX, AND THEIR FLIGHT.

From the Special Correspondent of the Tribune.

CAMP NO. 24, July 28. — Our march up Floral Valley was marked on the third day by an episode which produced at first a little excitement, then still more satisfaction, and concluded with a good deal of disappointment. For a week or ten days we have crossed frequent Indian trails—most of them old, but some of them fresh. They were especially noticeable when we reached the Heeng-ya-Kara (sic). Had our object been an Indian hunt, we should not have lacked evidence of plenty of game, and instead of turning to the east from the Heeng-ya-Kara (sic), we should have followed these trails to secure it. But such was not our object, and we turned away from these trails to find and follow this beautiful valley. Indian signs are not wanting here. There was an old and well-marked trail up and down the valley, and here and there the sign of an old camp. On the second day of our entrance, Gen. Forsyth and Col. Ludlow, after a camp site was chosen, went on ahead for seven or eight miles to learn the prospects for the next day's road. Following the valley up which we had been traveling, they reached the top of a ridge or divide, which separated it from one on the other side, also well-watered, but the water running in the opposite direction. Here they noticed a fresh Indian trail and discovered a place on the bank of the little creek where ten or a dozen ponies had drunk the day before.

The next day, Sunday, the 26th of July, one of the most lovely days in the calendar of the trip, we continued our march according to the programme adopted on the previous day. In the twin valley on the other side of the ridge, we found a repetition of the floral wealth which had greeted us the two previous days. The enthusiasm for botany did not decrease, but rather seemed to grow with the opportunity spread out so lavishly before us. I think if anywhere the lilies predominated on this side of the valley; but the geraniums and compositae disputed the claim, and I should be at a loss to decide which deserved it. Following the valley to the south-east for several miles, we came to a point where it seemed to branch to the south and east. There are no guide posts in this country. We trusted to fortune. The road to the east, after a pursuit of two miles, suddenly became impassable, and we had to "right about" and go back and take the other branch. The Indian trail discovered here showed that we were on the right track. An abundance of lodge poles constituted the relics of an old hunting camp. Fresh pony tracks excited a still greater interest. After a march of fourteen miles we halted at another Indian camping ground—no doubt a favorite one from the lodge poles and pony tracks of different ages which marked it. This trail through the valley seemed to be an Indian highway, probably from the Red Cloud Agency to their hunting grounds, and this spot was probably a frequent halting place.

THE REE GUIDES EAGER FOR A FIGHT.

But what excited most interest among the evidences of the old camp was the presence of a small fire, still burning brightly, which had been abandoned but a few hours before. Indians, probably a small party, had plainly left that camp in the morning and moved further down the valley. Possibly our presence had been discovered and caused an alarm; possibly it was one element in an Indian decoy. As the site was an excellent one for camp, Gen. Custer concluded to halt here. Shortly after our advance scouts returned with the report that five Indian lodges were visible in the valley about three miles further up. Anxious, if possible, to give the Indians a proof of his peaceful intent and to secure their friendship, which might be useful in conducting his explorations, Gen. Custer sent forward Louis Egard (Agard), one of our half-breed guides, with a white flag, instructing him to go directly to the village and inform the Indians of our presence and object. To support him in the event of a repulse, a detachment of Indian scouts was ordered to follow at a proper distance behind him. Then mounting his horse, accompanied by Gen. Forsyth, Lieut. Calhoun, and myself, and escorted by a detachment of Co. E, 7th Cavalry, under command of Sergeant Hohmeyer, Gen. Custer followed the advance parties at a brisk gallop. After a run of about two miles along the valley we halted just under the crest of a hill which rose between us and the Indian village about three-quarters of a mile further on. Here, as previously directed, the advance detachment of scouts had halted to give Egard (Agard) time to reach the village. Our scouts are made up principally of Ree Indians, who have many reasons to remember the vengeful and merciless cruelties of the Sioux, and who themselves are not distinguished, any more than white people, by a practical love for the Christian law of forgiveness. As soon as the Rees had heard of the proximity of this Sioux camp they were wild with delight. They covered their faces with war paint, stuck eagle feathers in their heads, stripped their saddles of all unnecessary weight, and loaded their guns for the fray. They were only restrained from an immediate onslaught on the village with the greatest difficulty. They murmured not a little at the General's stern prohibitive. Had not the Sioux often attacked them and cruelly killed many of their kinsmen? had they not, just before the Expedition left Fort Lincoln, made a descent on the Ree village at Berthold and slain several of their brethren and made their hearts heavy? Here was a good opportunity to take revenge and make their hearts light. What a glorious scalp dance they could have after they had butchered this little village.

THE PEACE TO BE KEPT.

"Do not dare to fire a shot unless the Sioux attack you," was the General's only reply to this murderous breathing, said, however, in a tone which implied a penalty not expressed, and which the Rees did not dare to incur.

The Santee Sioux, mostly young, of whom we have about 20, have been long divorced from savage life, and, though their language is nearly like that of the other tribes, they have little in common with them. They are the friends of the white man. They perhaps liked the excitement of a little skirmish, but were not difficult of control. Goose, Cold Hand, and two or three other Sioux obtained by Gen. Custar (sic) from Grand River Agency, are, I believe, of the Unkpapa tribe. They have a free passport among the hostile Indians, and their own tribes are friendly or hostile to the whites as occasion may influence. About 25 soldiers from Company E, equally ready for peace or war, constituted the fourth element in this reconnoitering party lying under the hill.

Bidding this quadrangular party to lie in the hollow below and keep quiet, Gen. Custer crawled up to the top of the low wooded hill which formed our breastwork. Two or three of us followed. How pretty the little village of clean, white new-covered teepees looked in the nestling valley below.

The opposite side of the valley was flanked with a hill covered with a dense wood. What an opportunity this offered to conceal a foe. Gen. Custer sent an orderly back to camp telling Col. Hart to come up immediately with his whole company. The Sioux are wily enough. It was possible that the five teepees might only be a decoy. The precaution was well taken, but proved to be unnecessary.

Again cautioning the Rees against shedding blood, and sending the Sioux guides with them, Gen. Custer ordered both to advance to the village, presuming that the sight of a body of Indians coming down the valley would create less alarm than the approach of a body of cavalry.

A RUDE ALARM TO THE QUIET VILLAGE.

All was quiet and peaceful in the little village. The squaws were sitting in their teepees; the papooses playing around the door; the bucks had gone up in the woods to hunt. They were all alone in this beautiful valley with their wives and children. No harm could come to them for the white man was far away and so was the hostile Ree. Neither of them ever came to this lovely hunting-ground. So the village rested in fancied security. Imagine the surprise and fright of the unsuspecting women and children when a man, half Indian and half white, mounted on an Indian pony, with a white flag in his hand, came riding into the village, and close behind him, almost reaching the village before he had time to assure them of his friendly mission, a band of 25 Ree Indians dressed in war garb and looking murderously cruel. The children were struck with consternation and fled to the bushes. The squaws were almost dumb with fright. Egard's (Agard) words did little to reassure them. Slow Bull, one of their warriors, was near by and bravely came forward. But what was he against so many? Egard (Agard) pointed up the valley: "Here comes the White Chief himself," he said in Sioux, "the one in the blue shirt galloping at the head of the gray horses; he will protect you."

Fearful that the Rees might not be able to control themselves, we were coming down the valley at what a cavalryman calls "a rattling pace." Our gait and appearance were not calculated to allay alarm. And not until we had reached the village, and Gen. Custer, first off his horse, had said "How" and took the hand of Slow Bull, did the squaws breathe freer. Soon the children began to peep out of the bushes, and then timidly to come forward and look at the new comers. Slow Bull was hospitable, and after a little talk on the outside of the teepee, in which the pipe of peace was lighted and smoked, he invited us inside. Meanwhile some of the older children were sent to call One Stab, the chief of the band, and three other bucks who were in the woods hunting near a neighboring deer-lick.

MRS. SLOW BULL AND HER HOUSEKEEPING.

From Slow Bull we learned that

the party were mostly Unkpapas, from the Red Cloud Agency, which, as the Indians reckon, could be reached in about ten days by their lodges, or a man could go there on a pony in two days; from which we calculated that it was 60 or 80 miles away. He and his family had never been in this part of the Black Hills before. He could not tell us the name of the stream we were on, and did not think it had any name. They did not know that we were in the Hills, and had not even heard that we were coming. He did not think there were many Indians in the mountains. They had sent runners to the Red Cloud Agency a few days before to learn the news, but they had not returned yet.

Then we went into the teepee while Slow Bull went out to watch for the other Indians. Slow Bull's squaw we found was a daughter of Red Cloud. A not uncomely squaw she was, with a broad full face and a straight nose, a little hooked at the end, long black hair braided into a pair of "tails," dark, bright eyes, and a fine set of teeth, which just then were composedly chewing the gum of the pine tree. Mrs. Red-Cloud Slow Bull had with her neighbor squaws been very much frightened at first, but she had now recovered and was so glad that her husband and little ones were not going to be killed that she became very agreeable, and entertained us in the most lively manner. Her teepee was the cleanest and neatest of the five; in fact one of the few Indian teepees that invite an entrance. The family effects, such as were not needed for immediate use, were packed up in clean skins tied with thongs and disposed around the tent. Other skins were spread on the ground to lie upon. In one corner was a long dress or gown of buckskin, completely covered with beads, the evidence of great industry as well as vanity. Mrs. R. C. Slow Bull had given a pony for it. Therefore it was worth some $40 or $50. Mrs. Slow Bull is evidently a fashionable woman, though a very domestic one. She had an eye for the kitchen as well as the parlor, for one of the first things she told the General after the ice was broken was that she had not a bit of coffee and sugar in the house, and that her little children had been

crying for some days. The General promised that this deficiency should be remedied. Then she chatted the more freely, Egard (Agard) acting as interpreter. I amused myself by taking a phonographic report of the conversation, being the first phonographic report ever made in the Black Hills; and I am sure on looking it over that, in point of intelligence and interest, it is painfully superior to the senseless twaddle which so often distinguishes social entertainment in civilized circles. Mrs. Slow Bull than sent for some water. We all took a drink. Then the inevitable little dog came in and sat down in the middle of the people and went to sleep as though nothing had happened. Mrs. Slow Bull then took up one of her children and began to study its craniology with more minuteness than would be considered polite in good society in the presence of company; but no doubt the examination was necessary.

FRIENDLY TALK BETWEEN GENERAL AND CHIEF.

One Stab, the chief, an old man with a dilapitated felt hat which would have branded him as a pauper anywhere, a breech-clout and colored cotton agency shirt, came in, and we smoked the pipe of peace again. He told us all he knew about the country, the course of the streams, the bend of the hills, and gave us some suggestions about a road. He told us that there were twelve men and women and fifteen children in his village; they were going to move the next day.

"Tell him," said the General to the interpreter, "that we have come down on a friendly visit to look at this country, and that when we get through, which will be in a few days, we are going back home. We do not want to make war on anybody, and we do not want anybody to make war on us. Ask him if they do not want to go along with us for a few days. Tell him that we are making short marches, not longer than they make with their lodges, and if they will go with us until we get out of the Black Hills, I will give rations every day to all of the party. If they cannot all go, perhaps some of the men can go."

One Stab replied: "We have only five Indians here but if you want

me to send one of my young men today I can do it. I can show you the way clear up this creek here; and then you can go yourselves. I do not want to have any trouble with the white man; I have always been with the white man; I never stayed with the hostiles."

"I have seen a great many Indians," said the General, "but I have never seen any that have been with the hostiles."

One Stab continued: "My friends say that when I meet any Indians that steal any horses from the whites I always take them away and bring them back to the whites. When I meet a big chief like you I always tell him the best I can. My children were all much scared today because the Rees came; they would not have been afraid of the whites."

REE AND SIOUX HATREDS.

The General again asked if he could not give them a man for a few days, and if they could not stay over in camp for two or three days. One Stab at first hesitated, but Red Cloud's daughter said, "Yes, they could stay over a couple of nights as well as not," and One Stab assented. It was then arranged that the male Indians should come to our camp that afternoon and get some rations.

Then we left the teepee and took a look around the village. Thirty or forty Indian ponies were grazing near by. A good supply of venison had been cut up, and, hung on poles, was drying for Winter use. The skins were likewise stretched and pinned to the ground to cure in the sun. The village on the whole presented a very interesting and picturesque appearance.

The Rees and Santees were then sent off in advance, and, bidding the little village good-by, we followed, congratulating ourselves at the pleasant result of our peace mission.

Two or three hours after, One Stab, Slow Bull, and another Indian of doubtful name came to camp. They were kindly received. Their ponies were laden with sugar, coffee, pork, and hard-tack, and everything done to assure them of our friendship. Perhaps we should have had no difficulty in retaining their confidence, if it had not been for the close proximity of the Rees, who still looked upon them with an evil eye. The Sioux, too, looked askance whenever they saw a Ree. Slow Bull soon after went into the woods and did not return again. The General saw that the other Indians were uneasy. He determined to send a guard down to protect their camp, and ten men from Company E were detailed for the purpose. While they were saddling up, One Stab and the other Indian, who did not know of this intention, mounted their ponies and rode off. Gen. Custar (sic) immediately sent Goose, a Sioux, after them to tell them of the guard and ask them to wait for it. But the Indians were suspicious and would not heed him. Two Santees were then sent after them. They overtook them and told them of the General's wishes. But it was of no use; something had excited their fears; they would not return. One of the Santees then seized the bridle of the younger Indian's pony. The Indian at the same time grasped the Santee's gun and saying, "I may as well be killed today as tomorrow," tried to wrest it from him. The Santee dropped off his horse, still retaining his gun, and as the Sioux spurred his pony to escape, took aim and fired, the ball striking the pony. The Indian and his pony got away, however; but One Stab was taken and brought back to camp. When our guard from Company E reached the village soon after, they found that hours before the squaws had folded their tents like the Arabs and silently stolen away.

WHY THE SIOUX FLED.

Scouts were sent out to find the other Indians, but without success. One Stab was detained and asked for an explanation. He had nothing to do with it, he said. It was all the work of the young bucks. He did not know himself that the village was going to move. He had then a long private conference with Gen. Custer, which resulted in a mutual understanding. He is to remain with us and guide us through the Hills as agreed upon, and when we reach Bear Butte is to return to his people. He is well fed and treated with special kindness, and says he would be happy if his people only knew that he was alive and well cared for.

We all regretted this want of confidence in the Indians and the unpleasant consequences which it

produced. Gen. Custer did everything in his power to relieve the Indians of fear, and had it not been for the presence of the Rees and perhaps a guilty conscience in the breasts of the new-found Sioux, his efforts would have been successful.

The next day our scouts while out hunting discovered the saddle, blankets, and equipments of the Indian at whom our Santee had shot. He had evidently thrown them off to lighten his pony. The saddle and blanket were covered with blood, and one thickness of the blanket had been perforated by the bullet. The ball had probably entered the man's thigh and passed out in front of the saddle, inflicting probably only a flash wound. One Stab is still with us and, with the exception of a little anxiety about his family, is reconciled to the situation. We find him a very good guide.

NEW YORK TRIBUNE
Issue of August 10, 1874

A NEW GOLD COUNTRY.
Discoveries of the Black Hills Expedition.

INDICATIONS OF GOLD EVERYWHERE IN THE BLACK HILLS REGION— THE SURFACE SOIL WELL REPAYS WASHING— A COUNTRY OF GREAT BEAUTY AND PRODUCTIVENESS— NATURE'S EFFORTS FOR THE HUSBANDMAN— A DIVERSIFIED FLORA— THE HIGHEST POINT IN THE BLACK HILLS SCALED.

From the Special Correspondent of the Tribune.

Forwarded to Fort Laramie by special scout from The Tribune correspondent.

Headquarters Black Hills expedition, eight and a half miles southeast of Harney's Peak, Dakota Territory, Aug. 2. — The country which the expedition has traversed has proved to be one of the most fertile and beautiful sections in the United States. Indications of gold were discovered about a week ago, and within two days its presence in sufficient quantities abundantly to repay working has been established beyond a doubt.[42] How large an area the gold section covers

42. The pretext of Gen. Custer in running in the face of Gen. Sherman's frank opinion about the mode of fighting the Indians effectively is made to show its proportions in the despatch of August 2d, by way of Fort Laramie, from the headquarters of "Custer's Black Hills Expedition." It evidently is hoped that these roseate stories of gold and silver discoveries will condone the sheer independence of the commander of this auriferous hunt, at the cost of the Government, and so dazzle the general eye as to make accusation and criticism seem harsh and unwelcome in the universal gloating over the newly discovered treasure. The Black Hills region being the Sioux paradise, which they were averse by tradition to disclosing the existence of, it is simply daring them to battle to invade their country. But as a fresh triumph of gold discovery it cannot be claimed to by very much boast of when it is perfectly well understood that the surrounding territories and States are all a part of the same great metalliferous formation to which the Black Hills region belongs. Gen. Custer knew why he was going there before he started. He did not march off in that direction to suppress Indian hostilities so much as to invest his name with the charm of being a discoverer, as Fremont was, as Sutter was, and as it is not given to every living man to be.

NEW YORK TRIBUNE
Issue of August 10, 1874

Custer to Elizabeth, July 15, 1874, from Prospect Valley, Dakota Territory, twelve miles from the Montana line, 103° 46' west, 45° 29' north.
Keep Press notices of the expedition; they will be interesting, and of value, later . . .
Marguerite Merington, THE CUSTER STORY, p. 274.

Custer to Elizabeth, July 15, 1874, from Prospect Valley, Dakota Territory, twelve miles from the Montana line, 103° 46' west, 45° 29' north.
Capt. Smith is the best Quartermaster I ever had in the field, and wins praise from all sides for his management of the trains . . .
Marguerite Merington, THE CUSTER STORY, p. 274.

cannot be determined without further exploration, but the geological characteristics of the country, the researches of our prospectors, and all the indications point to valuable fields. So far we have obtained surface gold alone. Our miners hope yet to find a good quartz lead. The expiration of the Sioux treaty will open to settlement a beautiful and highly productive area of country, hitherto entirely unknown. Grass, water, and timbers of several varieties are found in abundance, and all of excellent quality; small fruits abound; game is plentiful. The valleys are well adapted for cattle raising or agricultural purposes, while the scenery is lovely beyond description. The flora is the most varied and exuberant of any section this side of California. In this respect it is a new Florida; it may prove to be a new Eldorado. The command is in good health and explorations are being rapidly conducted.

A VALLEY OF EXQUISITE BEAUTY AND MARVELOUS FERTILITY.

Black Hills expedition, Within two miles of South Fork Cheyenne River, Aug. 3—We have reached this camp by a march of 45 miles today. I send by Charley Raynolds, a special messenger, the following summary of Gen. Custer's official report, as made to date, covering the history of the expedition from July 15, starting from Prospect Valley, Dakota. Leaving this point, the expedition moved in a southwest direction until it reached the valley of the Little Missouri, up which we moved 21 miles. The valley was almost destitute of grass, and we left it in search of a better camping ground, making a march of over 30 miles and a dry camp. In order to secure camp during our passage up the Little Missouri, we entered the Territory of Montana for a short time. From the Little Missouri to the valley of the Belle Fourche the country was generally barren and uninviting. The Belle Fourche was reached on the 18th of July, and good grass, water, and wood were abundant. From this point just west of the line separating Dakota from Wyoming we began a skirmish through the outlying ranges of hills. The country was a very superior one, covered with excellent grass, and

having an abundance of timber, principally pine, oak, and poplar. On the 22d we halted and encamped within 40 miles of a prominent peak in Wyoming, called Inyan Kara, 6,600 feet high, which peak we ascended, lying over here one day. The expedition then turned due east, and attempted the passage of the Black Hills. After a short march we came into a most beautiful valley. "Its equal," said Gen. Custer, "I have never seen." Such, too, was the testimony of all those who beheld the panorama spread out before us. Every step of our march that day was amid flowers of the most exquisite color and perfume, some belonging to new or unclassified species. The total flora of the valley embraces 125 species. The water in the streams stood at 44 deg. This beautiful vale was named Floral Valley. We followed this valley to the top of the western ridge of the Black Hills, winding our way through a little park of great natural beauty.

A DIMINUTIVE INDIAN VILLAGE.

During our march through the valley, we came to a recent camping ground of a small party of Indians, and soon after discovered five lodges four miles beyond. To avoid a collision a party of Indian scouts were sent ahead to counsel with them, preceded by a guide bearing a flag of truce. Gen. Custer followed with an escort and, entering the village, assured them of his friendship and promised them presents if they would come to his camp. The village contained five men, seven squaws and fifteen children. The Indians promised to camp near us for a few days and assist us in our explorations. That afternoon three of them came to camp and secured the presents and promised to move their camp up near us in the morning to protect their camp from the Rees. Gen. Custer ordered a guard of soldiers to accompany them to their camp, but the Indians, who had not been acting in good faith, suddenly departed, and two scouts were sent after them with directions to request them to return, but to use no violence. The Indians refused, and one of them tried to wrest a gun from one of the scouts. The scout disengaged himself and fired

his gun, wounding both the Indian and his pony, though probably not seriously. The Indian who was hit escaped, One Stab, the Chief, being brought back to camp. The Indian village, during the visit of the chief to camp, had packed up and departed. One Stab has recently returned from the hostile camp on Powder River, and says that the Indians lost 10 killed in the fight with the Bozeman Exploring Party. He remains with us three days longer, when he will take his departure and rejoin his band.

GOLD FOUND IN PROMISING QUANTITIES.

On the 30th, we camped within four miles of the western base of Harney's Peak, which the next day Gen. Custer ascended with the engineers and a small escort. The peak was found to be the highest point in the Black Hills. Yesterday we moved to our present camp. This morning two companies under Col. Hart were dispatched to extend our explorations in a southerly direction to the South Fork of the Cheyenne. Tomorrow Gen. Custer with five companies of cavalry will endeavor to reach the same stream in a south-westerly direction from Harney's Peak, the wagon train remaining at or near the present camp.

In no portion of the United States, not excepting the famous Blue Grass region of Kentucky, have I ever found grazing superior to that which grows wild in these hitherto unknown regions. I know of no portion of our country where nature has done so much to prepare homes for husbandmen and left so little for them to do as here. Everything indicates an abundance of moisture within the space occupied by the Black Hills. Gold has been found in several places, and it is the opinion of those who are giving attention to the subject that it will be discovered in paying quantities. I have upon my table 40 or 50 small particles of pure gold, in size about that of a small pin-head. Most of it was obtained today from a single pan of earth, but as we have not remained longer at any camp than one day, it will be readily understood that there is no opportunity to make a satisfactory examination in regard to deposits of valuable minerals. Until further investigation is had regarding the richness of the deposits of gold, no opinion should be formed. Veins of what the geologists call "bearing quartz," crop out on almost every hillside. All existing geological or geographical maps of this region have been found incorrect.[43]

The northward march begins in a few days from this date, and Gen. Custer expects to reach Fort Lincoln by the 31st of August.

NEW YORK TRIBUNE
Issue of August 28, 1874

A PROMISING SURFACE YIELD.

GEOLOGISTS AND MINERS LOOKING FOR SIGNS IN THE ROCKS— FINDING THE FIRST GOLD— RICHNESS AND EXTENT OF THE GOLD AREA— NO GOLD-BEARING LEDGES FOUND— A GOOD-SIZED CLAIM STAKED OUT NOTWITHSTANDING THE TREATY— ADVICE TO ADVENTURERS.

From the Special Correspondent of the Tribune.

Black Hills, Aug. 10.—If Charles Reynolds, the bold and experienced hunter, who, at the risk of his life, undertook to carry dispatches from the Expedition to Fort Laramie, arrived there in safety, you have before this been informed by telegraph of the discovery of gold in the Black Hills. The Indian couriers who take this letter will carry additional dispatches. A more circumstantial account I have reserved for the mail.

It was a wise forethought which induced Gen. Custer to secure, in addition to the scientific corps appointed by the Department, the service of two skilled and experienced miners, who should supplement the accurate geological survey of Prof. Winchell by a minute and special research for valuable minerals. The men selected for this purpose were I. N. Ross and W. T. McKay of Bismarck, Dakota, who as prospectors and practical miners had served a long apprenticeship in California, Montana, and Nevada. They provided their own team, wagon, and mining outfit, and had liberty to prospect wherever they chose on the route of the Expedition. The result of their labors has

43. But Gen. Custer's explorers are too busy to pause to dig gold, remembering doubtless, as others should, that there have been El Dorados before which were El Dorados only in dreams and prophecy and never fulfilled the glittering anticipations of their discoverers. It is to be hoped that no popular excitement in neighboring regions will follow this announcement for the cessation and derangement of honest industry that necessarily ensue do more damage to the general prosperity than the richest placers can repair. More money can still be made on the average by any single laborer in digging potatoes than in digging gold. However, if the President still retains his curious notion about the possibilities of working off the national debt by the aid of gold mines, it is not unlikely that we may see considerable agitation at Long Branch.
NEW YORK TRIBUNE
Issue of August 10, 1874

justified this foresight, and converted a glittering fable into a glittering fact. The hints and surmises of geology have been tested and proved by the pick, pan, and scales.

As we left the Heenga-Ya-Kara (sic), and entered Floral Valley, we left the jurassic age with its flaming red walls, and came suddenly upon a calcareous chapter of the carboniferous age, in tables of stone which had been broken into fragments, the fractured slabs left lying on the older beds beneath. Between these two beds, thinks the Professor—the one of broken carboniferous limestone, the other a limestone of the upper silurian—a volume has been left out of the geological record. The whole devonian period, with its coral, fern, and ganoid chronicles, is missing. The history of a great age has in some way dropped out—more likely it was not stitched in at the bindery. I leave the solution to the geologists. Below this nether limestone—which, by the way, would make a very good quicklime and a fine building stone—was a hard sandstone of still earlier repute. As we proceeded up the valley and reached higher altitudes, the geological formation persistently becomes older. The discovery of some Linglua (sic) flags identified the Potsdam sandstone—the Lingula being the name of a small shell peculiar to this formation. Stratified rocks with their included fossils then gave place to metamorphic rocks, which, if less communicative to our geologists, were more communicative to our miners. Huge masses of mica schist protruded from the hills, inclined at an angle of 45 degrees, showing the effect of the great upheaval which produced the Black Hills.

THE FIRST GOLD.

Here, on the 26th of July, the day of our little Indian excitement, we found also the first good evidence of quartz rock. Our miners' experience chimed in with the surmise of the geologist. They began to prospect here, but did not find the glittering encouragement they sought. The discovery further on of large quantities of feldspathic and granitic rock, and ledges of gold-bearing quartz which, with alternation of mica schist, replaced all other exposures, set our miners to work still more diligently. What they most needed was not a field

The Heart River flows into the Missouri just north of Ft. Abraham Lincoln. The Custer Expedition crossed the Heart 12 miles west of the Fort. Custer's men laid at that location for one hour before assembling for a triumphal march into the Fort late in the afternoon of August 30, 1874. This was probably one of the last glass plates Illingworth was to expose in Dakota Territory.

but an opportunity. The discovery of gold was not the prime object of the expedition, and the other interests of the exploration could not be entirely sacrificed to the incidental one. Our marches were so long that after getting into camp, the miners had but little time to search. However, they made good use of their time, and worked with a patient and commendable industry. The sight of gold-bearing quartz to an old miner kindles hopeful ardor which is not easily discouraged.

At last this hope and patience were more tangibly rewarded. On the 30th of July we halted about noon in a pleasant valley, within 10 miles of Harney's Peak. One of our miners took his pan, went to the stream and washed out a pan or two of earth taken right from the grass roots. There was gold there, but it was merely a color, requiring careful manipulation and an experienced eye to find it. The few glittering grains, with a slight residue of earth, were carefully wrapped up in a small piece of paper and put in the miner's pocketbook. It was simply an earnest of what was to come. The discovery announced created a good deal of interest but little commotion, not half the excitement, indeed, that the blooming exuberance of Floral Valley produced. Perhaps many were still incredulous.

The next day the expedition remained in camp, and the miners had a chance to renew their search. The result was the discovery of a good bar, yielding from five to seven cents per pan, which could easily be made to pay if water were more plentiful there. On the succeeding day the expedition made a march of but five miles, and found another excellent camp, in which Gen. Custer decided to remain for four or five days. Ross and McKay, in a literal sense, found this their golden opportunity. Along the creek, running down the valley, very good colors were found in the loose dirt, none of which showed less than half a cent a pan, and some worth three of four cents. A hole was then sunk in a promising bar to the depth of six feet. Water intruded and embarrassed the work; but the earth panned out as high as ten cents. The miners were not able to reach the bed rock on account of the water. An

This scene was taken during the rest period along the Heart River just before the expedition assembled for its march into Ft. Abraham Lincoln. The prairie is covered with horses and wagons. In his journal Capt. William Ludlow was reflective when he wrote, "The whole country was once ranged over by enormous herds of buffalo whose trails are everywhere visable, but which are now seldom or never found east of the Little Missouri."

examination of the gulch for two or three miles showed the existence of a succession of gold bars of equal and some promise of greater value. Time proved insufficient, however, to test them all, or yet to define the limits of the gold belt even in this special locality.

VALUE OF THE GOLD YIELD.

To one unacquainted with the details and methods of mining the discovery of a gold field yielding anywhere from 8 to 15 cents a pan may not seem a very valuable discovery. It depends altogether, however, on the constancy and uniformity of the yield, and the facility with which it is worked. Many an old miner will prefer a digging which yields ten cents a pan to one which yields a dollar a pan, and will justify his preference by making ten times as much in a day at the former as he or any one else could make at the latter, the difference being that in one place it is rock, and the soil is excavated with difficulty, while in the pans are easily filled. Where the soil permits, a miner can shovel into a sluice 1,500 pans a day, which at ten cents a pan would yield $150 to the man. This is considered a pretty rich yield. The last pans taken out of Custer Gulch—for so the miners call it—averaged ten cents a pan, but this was from the rich bars. The general yield would average less. Mr. Ross is of the opinion, however, that the gulch where the whole was sunk would yield $50 a day to the man, and in some places $75. At the upper bar of the creek there are not five inches of water. By cutting across the stream and putting in a dam the miner could then get to the bed rock without much difficulty.

Thus far though we have found large quantities of quartz on the surface, no gold-bearing ledges have been found. Our miners feel sanguine, however, that they exist in the Hills, but they have neither had the time nor the machinery to prosecute the search. For miners of small capital placer mines such as these discovered offer the most inducement, and are attended with the least risk. The cost of machinery and outfit for a quartz mine would not be less than $50,000. For a placer mine all that is needed is a pick, pan, spade, and whip-saw. The sluice boxes are easily made. The remainder

South Dakota State Historical Society

This picture and the one on the facing page have long been identified as having been taken near the North Dakota-South Dakota border. That is probably incorrect. It is most likely that both of these photographs were taken at the end of the rest period along the Heart River, near Ft. Abraham Lincoln on August 30, 1874. This is probably a front view of the picture on the preceeding page. Illingworth's mule-drawn, enclosed spring wagon stands in the foreground, the photographer having carried his gear but a short distance from it. Custer is probably the mounted horseman just to the left of the front wagon in the right hand column. An extreme enlargement indicates that the rider is wearing buckskin, a Custer trademark. A dog, several of which belonged to Custer, sits farther to the left by the center column of the train. For such a finale, Custer would logically assume a central position in his command. In describing what must have been this scene, Correspondent A. B. Donaldson of the ST. PAUL PIONEER said: "Fourteen miles finds us resting on the banks of Heart River, only twelve miles from Lincoln and just concealed from view by rising ground between. The train closes up solid, stragglers all gather in, the company flags are all unfurled; and arrangements are all completed for taking the fort by surprise. A long line of mounted men extends across the prairie, just below the brow on the hill."

of the expense incurred is for personal outfit. It is usual for three or four miners to club together, the division of labor diminishing the expense and increasing the profits.

EXTENT OF THE GOLD AREA.

It is hardly possible to speculate with accuracy on the extent of the gold field. As already remarked our miners have had no such opportunity to explore as would have been afforded were the country free from Indians, and the time of the expedition less limited. Many valleys lying at right angles to or running parallel with the course of the expedition were left unnoticed, though apparently as favorable for prospecting as Custer's Gulch. In the latter place, so far as tested, the gold section had an extent of fifteen miles, running some eight or nine miles below camp, and about five miles above. In a stretch of about ten miles along the creek our miners report nearly a hundred bars, in some places three or four bars to the mile, in others eight or ten. These bars were not all "prospected," and those tested were not uniform in yield.

STAKING OUT CLAIMS.

Though the announcement of the discovery of gold created less excitement than might have been expected, a score of teamsters and wagon-masters were provident enough to locate claims in Custer

Following a now familiar pattern Illingworth exposed another glass plate before the expedition began its march forward. The correspondents who had accompanied Custer were universal in their praise of him and of the expedition. A. B. Donaldson said in the ST. PAUL PIONEER, "The expedition has been a complete success." Nathan H. Knappen writing in the BISMARCK TRIBUNE said, "It is useless for me to say Custer's Black Hills Expedition has been a decided success throughout—the fact is well known by all and may its memories live in the hearts of the American people." Samuel Barrows of the NEW YORK TRIBUNE said, "From a military point of view it was a complete success." Upon their arrival at Ft. Abraham Lincoln, the 7th Cavalry Band closed the expedition by playing "Garry Owen."

Gulch and recorded their priority in the following paper:

CUSTER GULCH, BLACK HILLS, D. T., AUG. 5, 1874.

Notice is hereby given that we, the undersigned claimants, do claim 4,000 feet, commencing at No. 8, above discovery, and running down to No. 12, below discovery, for mining purposes, and do intend to work the same as soon as peaceful possession can be had of this portion of the Territory by the General Government. And we do hereby locate the above claims in accordance with the laws of Dakota governing the mining districts.

Perhaps if this announcement were translated into Sioux, and copies sent to Red Cloud and Two Bears, this announcement would create more of a sensation than it is likely to make in Wall-st. At present the Black Hills are included in the Indian reservation, and are not eligible to white settlers; but sooner or later, say the claimants, the Government must remodel the treaty and open the doors to the white man.

A WORD TO ADVENTURERS.

A friendly bit of advice to these people may not be out of place in conclusion. The simple mention of the existence of gold in any new section of country is enough to fire

the imagination and unsettle the mind of a great many persons, who are always waiting for something to turn up. Somehow there is a fascination in digging gold directly from the earth instead of getting its equivalent by other forms of labor. The effect of the reports from the Black Hills, therefore, may be to create, especially in the West, a new gold fever, which, like all such diseases, must have its run. Reason and wholesome advice have little power to check the malady when once it has begun. Possibly they may be of use in preventing it.

To those, therefore, who contemplate an immediate rush to the

Black Hills gold district let me administer a friendly caution, based on two or three considerations. First, that the country is the recognized home of powerful bands of hostile Indians who have sworn to repel any intrusion of the white man. This country is a part of the reservation. Until it is purchased from them by the Government they have a prior claim and a perfect right to protect it. Be assured that they will do it. That they have not met and opposed the present expedition is nothing in the argument. They were informed of its object, which was not to settle but simply to explore. They knew also of its great strength, and feared an encounter. Small parties of whites entering the Hills in defiance of the red man's rights, as well as the laws of the Government, would find themselves between two fires, and would be pretty sure to be burnt by one of them. The scalp-dance is a favorite pastime of the Sioux, and a few unprotected miners might easily afford them material for this sport.

Secondly, though I have no reason to doubt the truthfulness and skill of our miners, and the correctness of their reports as to the extent and value of the gold field, yet it must be remembered that the yielding area, so far as determined, is not great; nor can it be said with any certainty how long it would last. The results thus far, though promising and satisfactory, have still been local and superficial. It would not be surprising if the field should prove both extensive and rich. But only further exploration and experiment can establish the fact. Those who seek the Hills only for gold must be prepared to take their chances. Let the over-confident study the history of Pike's Peak. The Black Hills, too, are not without ready-made monuments for the martyrs who may perish in their parks.

NEW YORK TRIBUNE
Issue of August 29, 1874

THE NEW GOLD COUNTRY. LAST DAYS IN THE BLACK HILLS.

BEAUTIES OF THE REGION TRAVERSED—INCIDENTS OF THE MARCH—A SOLDIER AND A GRIZZLY BEAR ON THE DEAD LIST—PASSING FROM THE HILLS TO THE PLAIN—FORTY-SIX DAYS WITHOUT A NEWSPAPER OR A LETTER.

(FROM THE SPECIAL CORRESPONDENT OF THE TRIBUNE.)

BLACK HILLS EXPEDITION, BEAR BUTTE, D. T., Aug. 15— The departure within a few hours of an Indian scout for Fort Lincoln leaves me time only to summarize the events and results connected with the expedition since our camp at Harney's Peak. Within six miles of this peak, in a beautiful park, the impediments of the expedition—did Caesar have such a wagon train?—halted and remained in camp for five days, only removing for change of grass. Using this point as a center, several detachments were sent out to the periphery of the Hills. Harney's Peak was the object of one of these scouts. It is not especially peakish in aspect, but is the culminating point of a high granite range which rises over 4,000 feet above the valley below and 9,000 feet above the level of the sea. Seen from the distance, the cap of the peak looks much like a little L-shaped country church. All through this granite section of the hills, the scenery is marked by the fanciful, peculiar, almost grotesque forms which these ridges exhibit. In one range the formation suggested a row of organ-pipes, and was so named. Castle Creek was also named from the Tudor-like shapes which rose above it. The outlook from Harney's Peak, is extended as well as grand. It is the most commanding peak in the Black Hills, and affords a panoramic view of the country for miles around. The party and escort, which was commanded by Lieut. Varnum, spent a whole day in making the trip, not reaching camp, indeed, until half-past twelve at

night. Their prolonged absence excited some alarm in camp, and signal fires were built for their guidance. They returned in safety, having simply overstayed the afternoon to enjoy the opportunity which the Peak afforded. On the 2d of August another detachment, consisting of Col. Hart's and Major Hale's companies of 7th Cavalry, with Lieut. Godfrey, 7th Cavalry, as engineer, took three days rations and explored the country from our camp to the Bad Lands on the south-east of the Black Hills. They were accompanied by Prof. Winchell, geologist, and our paleontologist, Mr. Grinnell, who hoped to find some tertiary fossils on the Bad Lands. Time proved insufficient for even a casual exploration of this section, and they were obliged to come home without bringing back any bones more ancient than those they took with them.

THE REGION ON THE SOUTH-WESTERN BOUNDARY OF THE HILLS.

Still another reconnoissance simultaneous with Col. Hart's was made by Gen. Custer from the same camp. At the head of five companies 7th Cavalry, viz., M. Company, Capt. French; F. Company, Capt. Yates; A. Company, Capt. Moylan; L. Company, Col. Custer; E. Company, Capt. McDougall, and accompanied by Gen. Forsyth and Col. Grant, and taking likewise three days rations, he proceeded in a south-west direction to explore the country to the South Fork of the Cheyenne River. After a hard day's march of nearly 50 miles, the South Fork was reached at 10 o'clock at night. Returning by another route, camp was reached about noon on the third day, and the detachment having marched a round hundred miles. In making the reconnoissance we passed through some of the finest portions of the Black Hills scenery, a noticeable feature of which was the prominence of an isolated butte of granite, its lofty head far above the tallest tree tops, so as to be seen for miles. We named it Turk's Head, from its top-heavy turban-like summit.

The country on the southern border of the Hills we found to be a counterpart of that bounding the northern and western portions. As we advanced south we gradually left the granite range and successively came into the micaceous limestone and sandstone formations which had introduced us to the Hills at the North. The red arenaceous gypsum-bearing belt renewed itself and then the alkali and cactus wastes of the Plains. The whole section of the Hills seems to be engirthed by the same geological formation. The Hills themselves are an oasis in the midst of a vast desert.

Though in the course of our march we dipped deep into Wyoming, and were within 40 miles of Red Cloud's Agency, yet we saw no signs of Indians, save here and there the relics of an old camp.

ONE STAB LEAVES.

On our return to the permanent camp, One Stab, the old Sioux chief, whom as related in a previous letter we came upon suddenly in Floral Valley, and who had formed part of the general's council ever since, was released from duty and sent on his way rejoicing. He could have been sent off when near the South Fork, but the Rees who were with us, his mortal enemies were on the watch for his departure, and would have overtaken and killed him. As it was, the Rees were deceived by his return, and he was sent off without exciting suspicion.

Leaving the Park near Harney's Peak we marched northward, recovering our old trail some 10 or 15 miles, and then boldly struck into the woods and made a new trail, which, though calling for some extra pioneer work, was a shorter and more direct route. Passing one or two of our old camps, we found that much of the grass had been burnt off through the carelessness of soldiers and teamsters in leaving fires burning when starting out on the march. A renewed order by Gen. Custer requires every camp-fire to be put out before starting, any company failing in this to be permanently detailed to pioneer duty.

An incident of the next day's march was the killing of a grizzly bear by Gen. Custer, assisted by Bloody Knife and Col. Ludlow. His bearship was discovered on the side of a hill about 75 yards away. A shot in the thigh from Gen. Custer's Remington caused him to halt, wheel about, and take an attitude defiant to the whole expedition. Another shot from Gen. Custer, and three more contributed by the General's companions, put an end to his career, and he consented to be photographed about 15 minutes afterward.

EMERGING FROM THE HILLS.

Though we reached a point within twenty miles of Bear Butte, the high hills in this direction forbade a passage out upon the plain, and we were compelled to find a passage further south. In this the General was at last successful, and we were all the gladder for the effort, because of a succession of short marches and delightful camps which this course afforded. Such green vales, such tall friendly pines, devoid of underbrush, casting their long shadows on the grass which stretches beneath them like a new-mown lawn; such lovely vistas, such castellated walls of granite, shedding pure, cool shy streams; such beauty and picturesqueness as we had not seen had we not been already in the Black Hills for three weeks and become somewhat prepared for its scenic revelations. A prosaic wagon-train never had such a poetic trail; now moving through the broad, green bottom-land, then entering narrow gorges, crossing embowered streams, winding its way up steep hill-sides, crashing through dense thickets, or, under escort of the pioneers who rive the pines and the echoes, slowly meandering through deep forests. Never were the hills and valleys surprised in this way before. Only one sadness marred the general gladness in our last days in the hills—another death from dysentery and another solemn, tearless funeral on the plains—private King, Company H, the victim.

Having emerged from the hills we are now resting for a day under the shadow of Bear Butte, on the east side of the Black Hills, about 300 marching miles from Fort Lincoln. This butte was visited by Capt. Reynolds in 1859. We shall cross his trail again on our homeward march, which begins tomorrow and we hope will terminate at Fort Lincoln on the 31st of August.

NEWS WANTED.

We have now been 46 days from Fort Lincoln. In all this period, though we have sent mail back two or three times by scouts, we have not heard a word from civilization, nor seen anything that could remind us of it, except the reminiscent outfit which we brought along with us. The lowing herd, "winding slowly o'er the lea"—prosaically one cattle herd, brought along to counteract a scarcity of game—is the most frequent domestic reminder. Otherwise, everything else is intense military.

We missed our daily paper at first. We are about reconciled to its absence now. Camp gossip, old stories, rumors of Indians, speculations of the General's intentions, and a variety of small talk supply the place of insufficient reading matter. We have been out so long that we have entirely forgotten the days of the week, and few men in the command could tell it at any time without considerable reckoning. The days of the month we faithfully count, but our calendar is mainly reckoned from the hegira at Lincoln—that is, we are so many "days out." Our odometer—when the horse does not run away to make distance—tells us daily how many miles we have made. This is always the first inquiry on reaching camp: "How many miles to-day?" just as Xenophon was asked no doubt, when he daily jotted down in his memorandum book the number of parasangs on his famous Anabasis. It takes a two months' experience with an expedition of this kind to appreciate the monotonous faithfulness with which Xenophon kept his record. They did not play base-ball in those days, but probably amused themselves in some equivalent way. At any rate, our Soldier's clubs, the Benteen and the Actives of the 7th Cavalry, felt justified in establishing a precedent, and played therefore the first game of ball ever played in the Black Hills, the Actives winning the first game by a score of 11 to 6, the Benteens winning the second by a score of 17 to 10.

By the time we reach Lincoln we shall have been gone sixty days. What has or will have taken place in civilization by that time may concern us then, but now, in our blissful ignorance, we are only concerned to know whether we shall have to make a dry camp on our next day's march.[44]

44. The urgency which Gen. Custer is said to exhibit in his final report to the War Department concerning the Black Hills will not, it is hoped, bring about any violations of our treaty with the Indians. Even if there were any pretext for overriding its provisions and breaking the pledged faith of the nation, it is an open question whether any material advantage would accrue to the eager frontiersman. A doubt as to the value of the alleged gold discoveries, coming from the geologist who accompanied the expedition, may be coupled with the fact that a good-sized thimble would easily cover all the gold that is actually known to have been found in the region. There is as yet no occasion for indecent haste.

NEW YORK TRIBUNE
Issue of September 1, 1874

NEW YORK TRIBUNE
Issue of September 14, 1874

THE RETURN OF CUSTER'S EXPEDITION

THE HOME ROUTE VIA THE LITTLE MISSOURI—INDIANS PROPHESY AN ENGAGEMENT—NO FOE ON THE FIELD—GRASS BURNED ON THE LINE OF MARCH—SAFE RETURN OF THE EXPEDITION—WORK ACCOMPLISHED BY THE SCIENTIFIC PARTY

(FROM THE SPECIAL CORRESPONDENT OF THE TRIBUNE.)

FORT ABRAHAM LINCOLN, D. T., Sept. 1—There is nothing like keeping your engagements. "Punctuality is the life of business," wisely said Poor Richard. "Sixty days, Custer, shalt thou be absent and do all thy work," said Gen. Terry, "but on the sixty-first thou shalt rest from thy labors." And it was so. Six hundred hungry horses, 700 hungrier mules, and 800 dusty sunburnt, weather-worn soldiers joined in the benedictory "Amen."

Lovely indeed were the Black Hills, a charming solitude beyond the grace of pencil or pen. "I should like to stay here the rest of my life," said one enthusiastic officer. The wish found a few dittoes. But when the band one day, as we were seeking an outlet from the hills, played with the best of intentions a wretched parody on "Home, Sweet Home," the charms of this delightful region had not so benumbed our affection that we could not recognize the sentiment concealed in the discord. I really believe there were some large drops in our tear sacs—for even soldiers have such an outfit—ready to roll down bronzed and dusty cheeks, had the imitation of the beloved air been more successful.

At all events, we were ready to "About face." We hated the dreary march across the plains, but the Missouri River had in our imagination an amiable flow, and we longed to watch it once more.

It was the 14th of Aug. that we climbed the last ridge of the eastward range of hills. A deep pine-fringed cleft in the ridge opened a wide vista to our view. We were in a lovely harbor; a great ocean rolled miles away, until it melted into the blue sky in the far distance. So it seemed to us. But it was a great land ocean, lacking most what it best imitated—an abundance of water.

It was with a great dislike that we launched upon this waterless ocean which many thousands of years ago lay at the bottom of the sea, and now boasts an altitude of 3,000 feet above its level. There are men who wish that this country was still at the bottom of the sea. It does not seem to have been much improved by elevation to its present position. If there is ever to be another flood, Western Dakota would offer an excellent site provided only that the second Noah could find timber enough there to build his ark. The thought that we were going home tinged our dislike with a joyful quality, which extinguished fifty per cent of our thirst.

OBJECT OF THE HOMEWARD ROUTE SELECTED.

A day at Bear Butte to collect ourselves, and then we struck out for Fort Lincoln via the Little Missouri River. This "via" was distasteful to not a few, and furnished a desired topic for grumbling. Such topics were rare, and therefore eagerly sought to satisfy a craving mental need of the soldier. "Fort Lincoln is 250 miles to the northeast—why not strike across country and go there directly instead of going 150 miles due north and then turning short to the east and marching the same distance?" Soldiers love a diagonal. But Gen. Custer had sufficient reasons. By traveling north and striking the Little Missouri, he hoped to make sure of water for his stock. When necessary to leave the Little Missouri we could then easily strike the head-water of the Heart River, which enters into the Missouri near Fort Lincoln. A second object was to give Col. Ludlow a chance to "locate" the Little Missouri River, the meanderings of which had never previously been properly traced and recorded. A third object was to give our palaeontologist, Mr. Grinnell, an opportunity to explore the Little Missouri Bad Lands for vertebrate fossils. The programme laid out was strictly pursued, though it compelled a few long hard marches not congenial to the health of our mules.

This is a view from Ft. Abraham Lincoln overlooking the Missouri River, taken by Illingworth just prior to or more likely just after the Custer Expedition to the Black Hills. Ft. Lincoln is closely identified with Custer. In addition to the 1874 Black Hills Expedition, it was from here that he led the fatal expedition to the Little Big Horn in 1876. The Fort was constructed in June of 1872, primarily to protect men working on the Northern Pacific Railroad. It reached its zenith under Custer's command. During the 1880's the Fort declined and after North Dakota was admitted to statehood in 1889, it was no longer needed. It was ordered closed in June of 1891 and abandoned a month later. It was completely dismantled in 1894. Partially reconstructed in the 1930's, it is now a state park in North Dakota, located just south of the present city of Mandan on Highway 6.

Though for sixty days we have been out of the reach and influence of all sensational and untruthful newspapers, we found on our first day's march from Bear Butte that we were not out of the reach of sensational and unconscientious reporters, though happily none of them were connected with the expedition. This time they were four wandering Sioux bound for the agencies, who crossed our trail and chanced upon Bloody Knife and our scouts. These Sioux, though they had their rifles cocked all the time they talked with the scouts, were instantly our friends. They had news of immense importance to every man in the command who was not bald-headed. They lost no time in divulging it, and then, for reasons best known to themselves, illustrated a cant Western phrase by "skinning out" as soon as possible. The news reported was in very large type and occasioned an unofficial camp bulletin at once, which was rapidly circulated from ear to ear with the following purport: "Two thousand Indians thirsting for our blood! Encamped on the Little Missouri waiting for a chance to drink it! Are determined to surround us before we get to Lincoln! They are well armed and equipped! A fight inevitable!"

NO OPPORTUNITY FOR FIGHTING.

The report created undoubted interest, though not a shadow of alarm, and served to relieve the monotony of a day's march. The ordered programme was not changed a whit. The military routine was not altered, only more strictly observed. We needed to make no preparations for Indians; both camp and march were in constant readiness for dusky visitors. I am not sure but some, perhaps a majority, of the soldiers were anxious to do a little professional work. But the opportunity did not come. The prophesized battlefield lay right in our line of march. We found there every element of a great battle except a foe. Had we been less well prepared to meet an enemy we should probably have found one. But the foe expected was not and had not been there. Somebody had lied. The general opinion condemned the four Indians who had warned us of our danger. Indians do not wear coats, but if they did I am certain that the four casual Sioux who started this report would have gone to Grand River laughing a little in their sleeves.

But if the hostile Indian was not there, he had left a black card behind him which excused his absence. A section of country from 50 to 75 miles square had been reduced to charcoal, the result of vast prairie fires which had consumed nearly every blade of grass within their range. There was just one advantage in this. It made an excellent road; the cactus had been consumed with the grass, and not a spine was left to torture man or horse. If the Indians burnt the country to destroy our grazing ground, on which we depended much, their success was annoying, but not disastrous. The prospect of finding camps with grass enough for a single feed seemed for two or three days almost as black as the country we traversed. But by making long marches and bending toward the Little Missouri, we succeeded in getting out of the "burnt district," and were fortunate enough to find grass and water for our depleted stock. At this season of the year prairie fires are very easily started, and it is possible that the burned country was the results of a casual spark from an Indian camp fire; more likely it was the product of a malicious torch.

For five days our marches averaged 30 miles a day, which was rather hard on mule flesh. Reaching the Little Missouri, the observance of Friday, by special dispensation, as a Sabbath day, was welcome alike to men and animals. We had learned last year something of the antagonism which these Little Bad Lands offered to road-makers. Gen. Stanley had conquered them last year. Gen. Custer had no desire to repeat the conquest. He kept his train out of there.

A FRUITLESS SEARCH FOR BONES

Mr. Grinnell, with a cavalry escort, renewed his search for long lost and forgotten bones, but without success. These Bad Lands were pretty well searched last year, but no verebrates whatever were found. The result of the exploration, both here and in the hills, confirms Gen. Sheridan's opinion that the "bone-yard" is bounded on the north by the Niobrara Bad Lands, though it may extend as far south as Kansas.

On the 23d of August, resuming our march, we struck Gen. Stanley's trail of 1872, and the next day came upon his trail of last year. From this point we were sure of a good road to Fort Lincoln, and know every camp we should make. Finding this trail was like striking an old familiar turnpike, though devoid of toll-gates and keepers. Concerning this trail, and the men who made it, your readers were informed in the Yellowstone correspondence of last year. Returning over this trail a second time for nearly 150 miles, I found that impressions of the country received last year were again renewed. Of the country traversed by that expedition, the section between the Big and the Little Missouri River, excepting occasional tracks along the Yellostone River and the Valley of the Mississippi River, was altogether the best. But even this offers few inducements for the settler, while the region west of the Little Missouri and west of the Yellowstone is hardly worth giving away. The admirable letter of Gen. Hazen to THE TRIBUNE last winter, giving a full and accurate description of the country in the vicinity of Fort Buford, well characterizes the region of which I speak. It is part and parcel of the same lot. Northern Pacific Railroad speculators are still making strenuous efforts to persuade emigrants of the fertility of this section of the North American desert. But while there are thousands of acres of good farming land still unoccupied, no one has a modicum of practical wisdom will select his homestead here. It is useless to deny that the country is a desert. The sad necessity of redeeming it has not yet arrived.

Rarely surprised himself, Gen. Custer is rather fond of surpising other people. He succeeded in surprising Fort Lincoln on the 30th of August. He was not looked for till the following day; but when the expedition reached Hart River Crossing, about 12 miles from Fort Lincoln, at noon on the 30th, the temptation to go in instead of camping was too great to be resisted. A halt for an hour and a half was ordered. A lunch was taken, and for the last time the familiar "To horse" and the "Advance" were sounded and we moved on the fort. A new order of march was adopted. The train was turned over to the tender mercies of the infantry. The cavalry were formed into a single column of fours, preceded by the company of scouts. Behind the scouts rode the band and the buglers. Officers' call sounded, and there was a rush of shoulderstraps to the front. Drawn up in a single line, with Gen. Custer in the center, 23 officers represented the commissioned authority of the expedition. Guidons were unfurled, and the band for the 120th time on the trip played "The Little German Band," and other classic pieces, reserving for the grand finale as we entered the garrison, Custer's favorite charging hymn, "Garryowen." For two months "Garry" had been corked up, waiting for an Indian engagement. The Indians failed to attend, and the tune was reserved for the expedition doxology. When the tune was concluded, the expedition had expired without a groan.

SUMMARY OF WORK ACCOMPLISHED.

So Custer's reconnoisance is over and dead, and its epitaph is alone to be written. From time to time, as opportunity permitted, your readers have been kept informed of all the results and discoveries of the expedition as they have been successively achieved. From a military point of view it was a complete success, none the less so because we met and conquered no Indian foe. If anything it is more to Gen. Custer's credit that the Indians, while they may have feared the result of an engagement, had sufficient confidence in his pacific promises to avoid precipitating one, than it would have been to have met and conquered them with

South Dakota State Historical Society

This is the last photograph Illingworth took while in Dakota Territory—or perhaps it was the first. It is of Fort Abraham Lincoln. Ironically, it is the only glass plate in the South Dakota Historical Society collection with a large piece broken off. Yet all of the other plates faced the hazard of a 1,000 mile mule drawn journey over prairie and hills, and survived, virtually unscathed. Someone is sitting in front of the wagon—perhaps an assistant—or perhaps Illingworth, with an assistant making the exposure. The large box beside the sitting man probably housed the camera. Illingworth had been hired by Capt. William Ludlow to take pictures of the expedition. Illingworth had agreed to provide six complete sets of pictures afterwards, but neglected to do so. Ludlow pursued the matter in court, but failed to gain a conviction. Ludlow commented tersely in his official report: "A photographer was engaged in Saint Paul, and furnished with a complete apparatus for taking steroscopic views. He agreed, in consideration of using government material, and being furnished with other facilities, to make six complete sets of pictures upon return from St. Paul to accompany the official reports. About sixty excellent views were taken, illustrating vividly the character of the country. But one incomplete set of pictures was furnished me, which is forwarded herewith. The photographer failed, and subsequently refused to furnish more, and an attempt to compel him to do so was defeated."

pistol and carbine. A supplement to Gen. Custer's reputation as a soldier needs to include his success as a peace commissioner. A Quaker garb indeed does not ill become him. It is no small matter of congratulation either that the commander was enabled to take a large train across a desert, and then through a country pronounced impassable for wagons, with so little loss of men, time and stock.

Scientifically, a valuable result will be the new and accurate map of this region from Col. Ludlow's survey, which will supersede all guess-work charts. It will be supplemented by the geological survey of Prof. Winchell, who through the enlightened liberality of the Regents of the University of Minnesota, was relieved from duty for the Summer in the latter State, and allowed to accompany the ex-

pedition at the State's expense. As the Government had made no provision whatever for a geologist or any scientific corps indeed, except as represented in the engineers, this action of the State of Minnesota deserves the thanks of the whole country.

Mr. Grinnell, our palaeontologist, found no opportunity in the metamorphic uplifts of the Black Hills to locate an antediluvian cemetery;

and without such a cemetery he could not find the bones he sought. But the large and valuable collection of birds and mammals made by him, transfers to the department of zoology the debt for his service. The collection of flowers made by Prof. Donaldson, and described by Dr. Williams, will add another floral chapter to the national herbarium.

To our practical miners belongs the credit of discovering gold—a discovery whose ultimate value can only be determined by future exploration. Though the quantity of gold taken out was not large, it must be remembered that it was washed from a few pans of earth. Nuggets and quartz lodes were not found, but should the creeks and gulches yet untested prove to contain dirt worth ten cents a pan, the value of the gold discovery will be certainly established. But the value of the Black Hills country will not stand or fall on the worth or continuity of its gold yield. It is pre-eminently fitted for the home of the farmer and stock-raiser. For them there is certainly gold in the soil, and I have no doubt that in the long run the most profitable way of extracting it will be with the scythe and the corral instead of with the miner's pan.

NEW YORK DAILY TRIBUNE
Issue of September 4, 1874

THE BLACK HILLS

GEN. SHERIDAN DETERMINED TO PREVENT EXPEDITIONS FROM ENTERING THE BLACK HILLS—SPECULATORS ENGAGED IN FOMENTING THE GOLD FEVER.

CHICAGO, Sept. 3—Gen. Sheridan, in an interview with your correspondent this evening, declared in the most positive terms that all expeditions to the Black Hills this Fall and Winter would be prevented. He is determined that the notice he has given shall be respected. He has sent orders to Gen. Terry at St. Paul and also to Gen. Ord at Omaha to seize and burn the outfits of any such expeditions, and to arrest those engaged in them next Spring. He will see all his influence to have the country properly opened to settlement by Congressional legislation. At present the Indian treaty must be respected. Reports come of expeditions secretly, fitting out at Sioux City, Iowa, and also at Bismarck. Every effort will be used to prevent them. Speculators in St. Paul and Bismarck in the interest of the Northern Pacific Road, are actively engaged in fomenting the gold fever. Dispatches are being published representing gold to have been found in unlimited quantities, when the truth is that all the gold actually discovered thus far, could be put in a thimble. Attention is also called to Bismarck as the nearest and best route to the Black Hills, when, in fact, this route is across a miserable section country, unfit for settlement.[45] Gen. Sheridan is confident, and the experience of your correspondent this Summer confirms it, that the best approach will be from the South, by way of Fort Laramie. Gen. Sheridan expresses himself as well satisfied with the results of Gen. Custer's expedition.[46]

45. The country from Bismarck to the Black Hills is well watered by streams whose banks furnish an abundance of fuel, and their valleys fine grazing. Unquestionably the route via Bismarck is the shortest, safest, and best.
BISMARCK TRIBUNE
Issue of August 26, 1874

NEW YORK DAILY TRIBUNE
Issue of September 4, 1874

ORDERS ISSUED FOR THE ARREST OF WAGON TRAINS AND THE DESTRUCTION OF THE OUTFITS OF PARTIES ATTEMPTING TO INVADE THE BLACK HILLS COUNTRY.

46. CHICAGO, Sept. 3—Lieut-Gen. Sheridan today sent the following order by telegraph to Brig-Gen. Alfred H. Long, at St. Paul, Minnesota:
Should the companies now organizing at Sioux City and Yankton trespass on the Sioux Indian reservation, you are hereby directed to use the force at your command to burn the wagon trains, destroy the outfit, and arrest the leaders, confining them at the nearest fort in the Indian country. Should they succeed in reaching the interior, you are directed to send such force of cavalry in pursuit as will accomplish the purposes above named. Should Congress open up the country for settlement by extinguishing the treaty rights of the Indians, the undersigned will give a cordial support to the settlement of the Black Hills. A duplicate copy of these instructions has been sent to the General commanding the Department of the Platte.
P. H. Sheridan,
Lieutenant-General

A party of New Yorkers are now en route for the Black Hills gold fields. They have accepted the favorable version of the mineral wealth of that tract which Gen. Custer has just explored, and have resolved to risk the hardships and dangers of the enterprise. The party is under the joint direction of Henry K. Stetson and Led. Barker, a miner of long California experience. The majority are young clerks who have been out of work; but there are four or five men in the expedition who are familiar with border life and mining. The money with which to pay expenses has been partly pooled by the adventurers and partly furnished by somebody whose name is not given, who is to share in the loss or profit. During two weeks the arrangements have been pushed forward; tools for surface operations and weapons for defense have been bought and sent to Chicago by freight transportation. The route thence has not been exactly fixed. The party, although it has probably been preceded by others from western points, will operate in an isolated field. They are prepared for adversity, both from Indians and Gen. Custer. The former may have to be fought, while the latter must, if possibly, be evaded. The latest news is that Custer, who is alert in the matter of these projected invasions of the country that he has opened us, has received strict orders to prevent the departure of parties for the Black Hills.

A journalist who went with Custer to the Black Hills is now in New York. He says that the mineral wealth of the country has been vastly exaggerated, and that the expedition did not find as much gold as could be held in a thimble. There is no doubt that there is gold in the Black Hills, just as there is in many of the eastern states; but there is yet not the slightest authority for believing that it can be found in paying quantities. The men who are now starting to hunt gold will probably find nothing to reward them, even if they escape Sheridan's soldiers and the bullets of the Indians.

ST. PAUL PRESS
Issue of September 16, 1874

The TRIBUNE has repeatedly warned people about seeking to enter the Black Hills from the south, as they would be compelled to pass through a country swarming with Indians, and beset with dangers on every hand. Below will be found an article clipped from the last Sioux City JOURNAL in which is detailed the troubles of Frank Stone and party. The Yankton party alluded to consisted of seven, one of whom was killed, one mortally wounded, and the remainder bruised and wounded as represented.

No such dangers as this will beset those who go to the Black Hills via Bismarck, for they will pass many miles north of the agencies and over neutral ground.

The article from the JOURNAL is as follows, viz:

F. W. Stone, a young gentleman from New York city, came here on the 10th of September, and on the 12th he, in company with two other plucky young fellows whom he fell in with here, started out with a mule team, well provisioned and well armed, for the Black Hills. Mr. Stone's party has returned. He informs us that he went within fifty miles of the Black Hills, and could have gone further had he been so inclined, but under existing circumstances the party concluded it would be policy to return. They saw Indians every few days, and sometimes the reds made it rather unpleasant for the boys, as they would hover about them in such uncomfortably close proximity as to interrupt their forward march and compel the party to throw themselves into a defensive attitude. Mr. Stone says that the Indians never attacked them during the night time, and this he attributes to the fact that he had with him two very large hounds that would scent the Indians afar off, and would keep up a deep baying while they were in the vicinity of the camp.

Mr. Stone and his companions were within two and a half miles of the scene of the fight between the Brule Indians and the Yankton party, and saw the Yankton boys after they got back home. They presented an altogether demoralized appearance, and every one of them bore some wound or bruise received in the engagement.

While Mr. Stone's party were at Niobrara, on their return trip, runners came in from Red Cloud's camp and reported about 3,000 warriors concentrated at that camp, with nearly double that number at Spotted Tail's Agency, all of whom were apparently equipped for service, and it was believed that they intended to make trouble for the expedition parties now scattered through that country, on their way into the Black Hills.

BISMARCK TRIBUNE
Issue of October 28, 1874

FINAL INTERVIEW

(Author's Note: After the expedition, General Custer was interviewed by the BISMARCK TRIBUNE. Although the story carries no by-line, we presume that it was the publisher, C. A. Lounsberry, who interviewed Custer).

BISMARCK TRIBUNE
Issue of September 2, 1874

CUSTER INTERVIEWED.
Results and Objects of the
Expedition.

Extent of Exploration and of
Gold Discoveries.
The Surrender of the Black
Hills a Military Necessity.

But the Treaty with the Sioux
Must be Respected.
The Policy of the Military
Toward Settlers.

The Best Route to the
Black Hills.

What Capt. John Smith Knows
About the Routes.

A Tribune reporter was dispatched yesterday to interview Gen. Custer relating to the Black Hills Gold Discoveries, the probable policy of the military authorities in relations to exploring parties seeking to enter the Black Hills prior to the extinguishment of the Indian title, the best route to reach the Eldorado, &c., &c., with the following result:

Reporter—Allow me to congratulate you, General, on your safe return. I presume, however, you were disappointed in not having a brush with the Sioux.

Custer—Yes I was somewhat disappointed for, though I had sent pacific messages and had taken every precaution to avoid hostilities, I had reason to anticipate trouble, I was disappointed, and am heartily glad of it. Some thought I courted an engagement —such was not the case, and I congratulate myself and the country on the return of the Expedition without bloodshed. An engagement, no matter how trifling, would have been magnified and misrepresented, and the good effects of the Expedition would have been to a great extent destroyed.

Minnesota Historical Society

One can perceive, by the expression in Custer's eyes, a sense of cocksureness. Indeed, he exhibits a great deal of self-confidence in this Brady photo taken in 1865. An expression and attitude comparable to this must have been borne by Custer when he granted a final interview to Bismarck Tribune Publisher C. A. Lounsberry at the conclusion of the 1874 Expedition to the Black Hills.

Reporter—I see you endorse fully the reports of the explorers and correspondents concerning the Gold Discoveries and therefore presume there can be no doubt as to the richness of the discoveries.

Custer—The reports are not exaggerated in the least; the prospects are even better than represented. I am familiar with and to somewhat extent interested in Colorado mines, and I saw localities in the Black Hills similar, as to formation, to the richest regions in Colorado, where the Geologists insisted the precious metals must be found, that were not explored by the miners at all. These localities were met with in my rambles along the valleys when the explorers were not within reach.

Reporter—What was the best prospect reported to you?

Custer—The product of one pan of earth was laid on my table which was worth not less than two dollars. It contained some fifty particles of gold, ranging from a color to the size of a kernel of wheat, averaging about the size of a pin head.

Reporter—Was gold found in localties other than in Custer's Park?

Custer—Yes at various points, though the explorers report the richest prospects there; but as I

State Historical Society of North Dakota

Main Street in Bismarck, looking west, 1874-75. Businessmen and other promoters saw Bismarck as the launching point for settlers heading to the Black Hills.

said before, the scientific gentlemen are satisfied that far richer discoveries will be made on further exploration. The miners also agree with this view of the case.

Reporter—Where did you first strike the gold country?

Custer—A long way this side of Harney's Peak we struck a country which gave unmistakable evidence of containing gold in paying quantities, and I am satisfied that a rich mining region will be found in the northeastern portion of the Hills.

Reporter—What is the best route to reach the Black Hills Mines from the Missouri River?

Custer—Unquestionably a direct route from Bismarck in the direction of Bear Butte.

Reporter—What is the distance from Bismarck to the Gold region, and the nature of the country?

Custer—The distance from Bismarck to Bear Butte is about one hundred and ninety-eight miles.

Harney's Peak is 35 miles southwest of Bear Butte. Custer's Gulch can be reached by a march of two hundred and forty miles over an excellent country, affording good grazing, a fair amount of timber, and abundance of water and everything essential to building up prosperous villages along the route. A route which offers absolutely no engineering difficulties should occasion demand the construction of a railroad from Bismarck to the hills.

Reporter—How many days will it require to reach the gold region from Bismarck with loaded trains?

Custer—The trip can be made without the least difficulty in eight days, though ordinarily it should take ten days.

Reporter—Are there no bad lands on this route?

Custer—None whatever. The bad lands, or mauvais terre are located along the Little Missouri and the Yellowstone rivers, and are

wholly barren of vegetation. Sully describes them as looking like the "bottom of hell with the fires out." Where the Northern Pacific crosses the Little Missouri they are only five miles in extent, and thirty miles south of the proposed crossing they disappear entirely. From the point of beginning they increase in extent until the mouth of the river is reached. The same is true of the Yellowstone river bad lands. They wholly disappear on its headwaters. The country along the route suggested is not a sage brush region even, but is in the main fair rolling prairies, with occasional tracts somewhat sandy, producing cactus, but these tracts are very limited in extent. On our recent trip from Bismarck to the Black Hills not a foot of land of this character was struck until we had devicated (sic) from our course eighty miles—eighty miles west of the route suggested a very inferior country is found, which was fully described in my official reports and in the letters of correspondents accompanying the Expedition.

Reporter—You speak of deviating from your course in marching to the Black Hills; why did you deviate?

Custer—My instructions and the objects of the expedition contemplated an exploration of as great an extent of the unexplored region as possible, and I made the deviation in order to take in a country wholly unexplored. I marched three or four days on a direct route from Bismarck to the Black Hills, then took a westerly course into Montana, then southeasterly into the Black Hills, entering them from the west.

Reporter—Are the hills accessible from other directions?

Custer—It is believed that all attempts to enter the Hills from the South or East will be futile. I made several attempts to pass through them southward but failed to find a passage. I had no difficulty in entering them from the west or in passing out toward the northeast.

Reporter—I see it is claimed that old Fort Pierre is nearer on the maps than Bismarck to the Black Hills region.

Custer—Referring to Reynolds, who passed over the route from Fort Pierre to Bear Butte in 1859,

I find that he pronounces against the country. On page 27 he says: "We have been out ten traveling days, and are one hundred and forty miles from Fort Pierre. The whole country traversed is entirely unfit for the residence of white men." This, as I understand it, is the trail that some parties have talked of taking. I do not think it a feasible route or one likely to be adopted. It cannot be compared with the direct route. I have suggested, running southwesterly from Bismarck, crossing at nearly right angles the following streams: Little Heart, Cannon Ball, Battle Creek, Grand River, Owl River and Cherry Creek, striking the Cheyenne at its forks. These streams are all small, and excepting one or two, afford good water and every facility for camping.

Reporter—Is there danger of interference on the part of Indians on the route suggested.

Custer—The country is neutral ground, and is not occupied by them, though small war or hunting parties pass over it occasionally. It is unquestionably the safest route; the Indians located at the agencies south and southeast of the Black Hills are very liable to give trouble to immigrants. Many outrages have occurred in that locality of late, while not a single outrage has occurred in my district during the past season except two cases of stock stealing.

Reporter—What is the probable policy of the military toward persons seeking to enter the Black Hills this fall?

Custer—The government has entered into a solemn treaty with the Indians whereby they agree to keep off all tresspassers (sic). This is a law of the land, and should be respected, and Gen. Sheridan has already issued instruction to the military to prevent expeditions entering upon the reservation and parties contemplating going have been warned to keep off.

Reporter—But, General, you are aware that you have a long line to guard and small parties may slip across the line and enter the reservation while the military is powerless to prevent it.

Custer—That is true to some extent but until Congress authorizes the settlement of the country the military will do its duty. When the Indian title is extinguished the military will aid the settlers in every way possible, I shall recommend the extinguishment of the Indian title at the earliest moment practicable for military reasons.

Reporter—What are those reasons General?

Custer—The Black Hills region is not occupied by the Indians and is seldom visited by them. It is used as sort of a back-room to which they may escape after committing depredations, remaining in safety until quiet is again restored. It is available in keeping up communication between the agency Indians and the hostile tribes located in the buffalo region northwest of the Hills, and if the Black Hills region is wrested from them this communication will be broken up and a fruitful source of trouble will be removed. The extinguishment of the Indian title to the Black Hills, and the establishment of a military post in the vicinity of Harney's Peak and another at some point on the Little Missouri will settle the Indian question so far as the Northwest is concerned.

Reporter—A region as valuable as the Black Hills are for agricultural purposes it would seem ought to be open for settlement. Their agricultural worth alone ought to be enough to cause the extinguishment of the Indian title were there no other reason.

Custer—Too much cannot be said in favor of the agricultural worth of the valleys in the Black Hills. No country in the world is superior for stock growing—the grazing is unsurpassed, the valleys are sheltered from driving storms, the snow fall is evidently light, the rain fall abundant. Think of those brooks in which the water is pure as crystal and only twelve degrees above freezing the warmest days in summer in connection with butter and cheese making. The valleys are not wide and yet they are extensive and the rich pasture extends not only throughout the valleys but well up on the pine clad ridges. Let the outer rim of a wash dish represent the outer rim of the Hills, then dent the bottom so as to represent the smaller hills and valleys and you have a very correct idea of the interior of the hills. Nature it would seem exhausted her resources in attempting to beautify and fit for the husbandman these delightful valleys. Man could ask no more at her hands.

Capt. John W. Smith was also approached in our interview. The Capt. has been freighting and trading on the plains for many years and is known to almost every one in Kansas, Nebraska, Western Iowa and Southern Dakota. In all of the Black Hills schemes originating below John W. Smith is referred to and his familiarity with the country admitted. He is a worthy and intelligent gentleman, a man in good circumstances, the trader of the recent Expedition, one whose statements are entitled to credit and will carry with them great weight where he is known. Capt. Smith endorses every word of Gen. Custer, as reported above, relating to the best route to reach the Black Hills. He is satisfied that the one suggested is nearly two hundred miles nearer than any other—nearer by one half than the route from Sioux City—while it has all the advantages claimed for it by Custer. A route from old Fort Pierre is suggested but Smith says the distance from Yankton to Fort Pierre is as great as the distance from Bismarck to the gold fields and from Fort Pierre to the mines is as much more. He has traveled over the route many times to within a few miles of the Hills, hauled freight over it and knows what he is talking about. As a quick and safe route Smith insists that the one from Bismarck is unequalled and that it must take the bulk of travel.

Custer's home at Ft. Abraham Lincoln. Original photo by Bismarck Photographer D. F. Barry. The Fort was abandoned in 1891 and dismantled in the winter of 1894.

Fort Abraham Lincoln as photographed by D. F. Barry of Bismarck, N. D. Built in 1872, the Fort achieved its zenith in 1876 and was abandoned in 1891.

Elizabeth B. Custer was photographed by Bismarck photographer D. F. Barry while she was stationed with her husband at Ft. Abraham Lincoln. Custer was approaching the pinnacle of his career at the time this picture was taken. After his death, Mrs. Custer spent her life perpetuating and glorifying his image.

Capt. Tom Custer, stationed at Ft. Abraham Lincoln, held two Congressional Medals of Honor from service in the Civil War. He accompanied his brother, George, on the 1874 Black Hills Expedition and died with him two years later at the Battle of the Little Bighorn.

The "good life" was led by Custer while he served as commanding officer at Ft. Abraham Lincoln. Custer is by the harp, while his sister Margaret plays the piano, with family and friends to the left. Original photo is imprinted "W. H. De Graff, Washburn, N. D."

Custer, his officers and family, assembled for the photo above at Ft. Abraham Lincoln in 1875, a year after the Black Hills Expedtion and a year before his death. Custer is standing third from the left. Mrs. Custer is the first woman on the left standing on the lower porch step. At the time of this picture, Custer's career was approaching its pinnacle. In stark contrast, the photo below shows the Custer home being dismantled in December of 1894 after Fort Lincoln was abandoned.

Epilogue

With the dust of travel scarcely brushed from his uniform, Custer granted an interview, published in the Bismarck TRIBUNE, September 2. And the feeling persists that politics is a silent but confident actor in the wings. Asked about the white encroachment upon Indian Territory, Custer is quoted as stating, "when the Indian title is extinguished, the military will aid the settlers in every way possible. I shall recommend the extinguishment of the Indian title at the earliest moment practicable for military reasons . . . . The extinguishment of the Indian title to the Black Hills and the establishment of a military post in the vicinity of Harney's Peak and another at some good point on the Little Missouri will settle the Indian question so far as the Northwest is concerned." The usual military reticence abandoned, this doughty statement was banner-headlined in the Bismarck TRIBUNE, September 2. Did it have a ring of thunder that reverberated farther than the success of the 1874 Black Hills Expedition?

The immediate consequences of the Expedition seem almost lost in the haste to scrutinize the rush of gold-pan and pickaxe-saddled parties bound for the Black Hills.

Some readers probably wondered, intrigued over the confusion, the charges and counter charges exciting the public of the time about: Custer's reticence regarding gold finds in his first dispatch and his eagerness to give out news on the rich discoveries in the interviews upon his return; the reservations of Prof. Winchell about the presence of gold in paying quantities in the Hills, his insistence that he saw no gold, and his charges that practical schemers "had brought gold in with them and then washed it in their pans" to show the credulous that there was "gold in the grassroots": Professor Winchell thought that in his position as state Geologist at the University of Minnesota, he ought not "to sanction by his silence, the wild fever that has now been excited."[1] Whatever his reservations, his reward was abuse and vituperation—"an ass and a Dogberry of the first water," howled the insulted Bismarck TRIBUNE as in dark headlines, it assailed Winchell: "As a Collector of Fossils He Is a Success, But as a Geologist He is Rather Thin, What He Don't Know About Gold in the Black Hills."[2]

Then there is the curious instance of Lieut. Fred Grant, the President's son, who with Custer, was labelled by the Boston POST as "one of the President's favorites." According to a reporter on the Bismarck TRIBUNE, Grant, on his return to Fort Abraham Lincoln, expressed himself as having no doubt about gold in the Hills,[3] but later on his return to Washington, he reversed himself, discounted the recent glowing accounts from the Black Hills as entirely unreliable; confronted with the opinion of Professor Winchell, maintained both the Chicago INTER-OCEAN and the St. Paul DAILY PRESS, "Grant reported that the rock supposedly containing gold, is of a metaphoric character, in which no precious minerals have ever been found." Then he added with a verbal sling shot: "not over three dollars worth was brought

under his observation during the entire expedition," he said, and added, "it is a question whether this was not imported into the section."[4] Thus he joined forces with Winchell. Outraged, the Bismarck TRIBUNE screamed, "Telegraphic accounts of pretended conversation with Fred Grant . . . . There is gold in the Black Hills and he knows it . . . . a score of affidavits can be furnished from as true men as ever lived, who saw it dug out of the earth or who dug it out." Appropriately the article was captioned: "There is gold in the Black Hills."[5] And strangely, soon after, Fred Grant is reported as having changed his mind again. He insisted he had been misquoted and agreed there was gold in the Hills.

One is reminded of the incident related in Dr. Edgar Stewart's excellent CUSTER'S LUCK.[6] In his account of the 1874 expedition, Stewart maintains that Custer and Fred Grant were good friends. Custer had boasted that there was no drinking or card playing in his column. Fred Grant, allegedly something of a tipster, aroused the ire of Custer one evening to the point where the General arrested the President's son for drunkenness. From this act Stewart infers that coolness between Custer and Grant began—a coolness that might have sent its chilling circles to the White House. Stewart cites W. M. Wemett in the NORTH DAKOTA HISTORICAL QUARTERLY[7] as his source. But Wemett recounts this incident without referring to sources. Nevertheless, the newspaper reports of Fred Grant's oscillations, if correctly quoted, are intriguing: his acquiesence to the general gold reports in Dakota Territory, where to defy the pitch of excitement, might have been hazardous, his repudiation of his Dakota statements and then his recantation of his own denial are bait to lure speculation. Did Fred Grant's changing attitude reflect White House dissatisfaction? Did Custer see the triumph of 1874 becoming tarnished contention and clash the rest of the year, all of 1875 and the months in 1876 before he was chosen to lead a wing of the army to march against the Sioux? Did he see his name, bold in headlines, diminish during the period over gold and Indian rights and violation of Indian territory? His name was still a household word but did June 26, 1876, promise another golden opportunity to lift higher and burnish more brightly the letters of his name and fame? It is possible that time and the prespective of history may show that in 1874 were woven also the black garlands of the prelude to glory that was to be Little Big Horn in June, 1876.

EPILOGUE FOOTNOTES
1. St. Paul DAILY PIONEER, September 10, 1874, p. 2.
2. Bismarck TRIBUNE, September 16, 1874, p. 1.
3. Bismarck TRIBUNE, September 30, 1874, p. 1.
4. St. Paul DAILY PRESS, Sept. 25, 1874, p. 1; Chicago DAILY INTER-OCEAN, September 25, 1974, p. 5.
5. Bismarck TRIBUNE, September 30, 1874, p. 2.
6. Norman, Oklahoma. 1955, p. 62.
7. Vol. 4, No. 4, p. 296.

Appendix

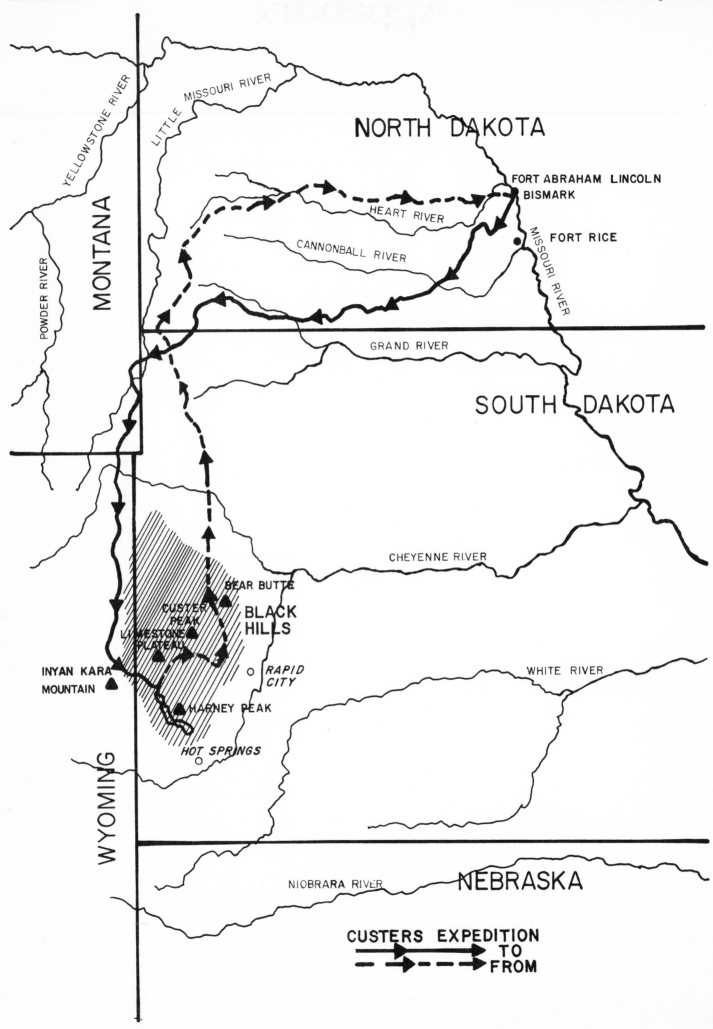

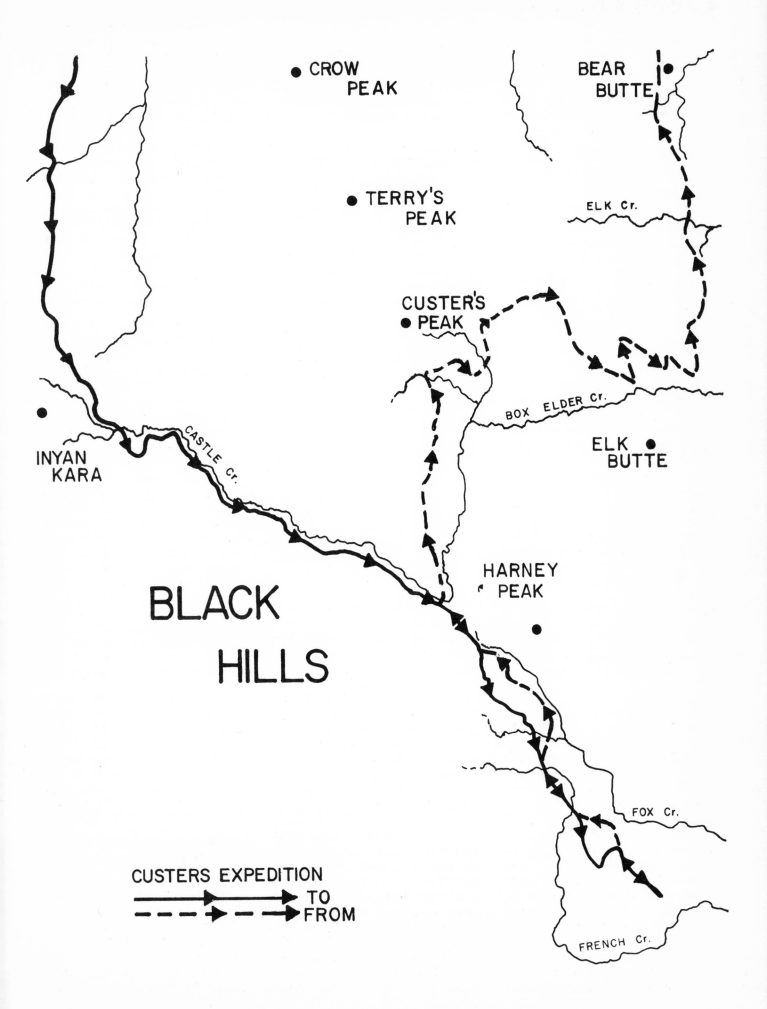

CROW PEAK

BEAR BUTTE

TERRY'S PEAK

ELK Cr.

CUSTER'S PEAK

BOX ELDER Cr.

ELK BUTTE

INYAN KARA

CASTLE Cr.

BLACK HILLS

HARNEY PEAK

FOX Cr.

CUSTERS EXPEDITION
→ TO
→ FROM

FRENCH Cr.

Custer's Report

(Author's Note: Custer's field reports and his final report were carried as items by the newspapers that covered the expedition).

CUSTER FIELD REPORT NO. 1

ST. PAUL DAILY PIONEER
Issue of July 30, 1874

BLACK HILLS EXPEDITION
Gen. Custer's First
Official Report.

The Command Moving Forward
—Hostile Indians Hovering
about the Column.

Discovery of a Sacred Cave—
A New Fossil Found—The
Expedition in Good Health
and Spirits.

Bismarck, D. T., July 24, 1874.

Headquarters Black Hills Expedition, Prospect Valley, Dakota, Longitude one hundred and three (103) degrees forty-six (46) minutes west. Latitude forty-five (45) degrees twenty-nine (29) minutes north.
Assistant Adjutant General
of Dakota, St. Paul, Minnesota.

SIR!—This expedition reached this point yesterday, having marched since leaving Fort Lincoln, two hundred and twenty-seven and a half (227½) miles. We are now one hundred and seventy (170) miles in a direct line from Lincoln, and within five miles of the Little Missouri, and within about twelve miles of the Montana boundary, our bearing from Fort Lincoln being south sixty-two degrees west after the second day from Lincoln.

WE MARCHED OVER A BEAU-
TIFUL COUNTRY.

The grazing was excellent and abundant. Wood sufficient for our wants, and water in great abundance every ten miles. When we struck the tributaries of Grand River we entered a less desirable portion of the country, nearly all the streams flowing into Grand River being more or less impregnated with alkali, rendering the crossings difficult. We found a plentiful supply of grass, wood and water, however, even along this portion of our route. Upon leaving the head waters of Grand River we ascended the plateau separating

the water shed of the Little Missouri from that running into the Missouri, and found

A COUNTRY OF SURPASSING
BEAUTY

and richness of soil. The pasturage could not be finer; timber is abundant, and water both good and plentiful. As an evidence of the character of the country, we have marched since leaving Fort Lincoln, on an average, over seventeen miles per day, one day making thirty-two miles; yet our mules and beef cattle have constantly improved in condition, the beef cattle depending entirely upon the excellent grazing we have marched over. The health of my command is something remarkable, not a sick man being on the sick report; every one seems not only in good health, but in excellent spirits. Between the forks of Grand River

WE DISCOVERED A CAVE,

to which the Indians attach great importance. The cave extends about four hundred feet under ground, beyond which point it was not practicable to explore it. Its walls and roof are covered with rude carvings and drawings cut in the solid rock, apparently the work of Indians, although probably by a different tribe than either of those now roaming in this region. Near the cave was found

A WHITE MAN'S SKULL,

apparently perforated by a bullet. It had been exposed to the atmosphere for several years, as no white man, except those belonging to the expedition, is known to have passed anywhere near the locality. The discovery of the skull was regarded with universal interest. The cave was found to contain numerous articles of Indian equipments, which had been thrown into the cave by the Indians as offerings to the Great Spirit. I have named the cave Ludlow's cave, in honor of the engineer officer of the expedition. Our march thus far has been made without molestation upon the part of the Indians. We discovered no signs indicating the recent presence of Indians until day before yesterday, when Captain McDougall, Seventh Cavalry, who was on the flank, discovered a small body of about twenty Indians, watching our movements.

The Indians scampered off as soon as discovered.

Yesterday the same or a similar party made its appearance, and was seen by Captain Connolly, rear guard, along our line of march. Soon after, several signals of smoke were sent up, which our Indian guards interpret as conveying information to the main body of our presence and movements. As I sent pacific messages to all the tribes infesting this region before the expedition moved, and expressed a desire to maintain friendly relations with them, the signals observed, by us may have simply been made to enable the villages to avoid us. Our Indian guides think differently, however, and believe

THE INDIANS MEAN WAR.

Should this be the case, they will be the party to fire the first shot. Indians have been seen near camp today. Mr. Grinnell, of Yale College, one of the geologists accompanying the expedition discovered yesterday an important fossil; it was bone, about four feet long and twelve inches in diameter, and had evidently belonged to an animal larger than an elephant. Beds of lignite of good quality have been observed at different points along our route by by Professor Winchell, one of the geologists of the expedition. I do not know whether I will be able to communicate with you again before the return of the expedition or not. G. A. CUSTER, Brevet Major General U.S.A., Commander of Expedition.

CUSTER FIELD REPORT NO. 2

CHICAGO INTER-OCEAN
Issue of August 15, 1874

GENERAL CUSTER'S REPORT.

Headquarters Black Hills
Expedition, 8½ Miles
Southeast of Harney's Peak,
Aug. 2, via Fort Laramie,
W. T., 8th August.

To Assistant Adjutant General,
Department of Dakota,
St. Paul, Minn.:

My last dispatch was dated July 15, and sent from Prospect Valley, Dakota, longitude 103 degrees and 46 minutes, latitude 45 degrees and 29 minutes. Two of my Indian scouts left as bearers of the dispatch as soon as their departure could be concealed by the darkness. After leaving that point, this expedition moved in a southwesterly direction, until it reached the valley of the Little Missouri, up which we moved 21 miles, finding this valley almost destitute of grazing.

ALONG OUR LINE OF MARCH

I ordered the water-kegs filled and a supply of wood placed in the wagons, and left the valley in search of a better camp-ground. During our passage up the valley of the Little Missouri, we had entered and were about to leave the Territory of Montana; our course was nearly due south. After a further march of about nine miles we arrived, before sundown, at a point capable of furnishing us good grazing and water for our animals, having marched over thirty miles since breaking camp in the morning. From this point to the Valley of the Belle Fourche, we found the country generally barren and uninviting, saving a few isolated places. We reached the Belle Fourche on the evening of the 18th of July, encamping where good grass, wood, and water were abundant, and a point a short distance above that marked fifteen on Raynolds' map, just west of the line separating Dakota from Wyoming. The following day was spent in camp. On the 20th we crossed the Belle Fourche and began, as it were,

SKIRMISHING WITH THE BLACK HILLS.

We began by feeling our way carefully along the outlying ranges of hills, seeking a weak point point through which we might take our way to the interior. We continued, from the time we ascended from the Valley of the Belle Fourche, to move through a very superior country, covered with the best of grazing and abundance of timber, principally pine, poplar, and several varieties of oak. As we advanced the country skirting the Black Hills to the southward became each day more beautiful. On the evening of the 22d we halted and encamped east of and within four miles of the cave Inyan Kara. Desiring to ascend that peak the following day, it being the highest on the western range of Black Hills, I did move camp the following day, but taking a small party with me proceeded to the highest

point of this prominent landmark, whose height is given as 6,600 feet. The day was not favorable for obtaining distant views. I decided on the following morning to move due east and attempt the passage of the hills. We experienced considerable delay by fallen timber which lay in our pathway. With this exception, and a very little digging, rendered necessary in descending into a valley, the pioneers prepared the way for the train, and we reached camp by 2 o'clock, having marched eleven miles.

We here found grass, water and wood of the very best quality, and in great abundance. On the following day we resumed our march up this valley, which I explored several miles the preceding evening, and which led us by an easy ascent almost southeast. After marching nearly twelve miles we encamped at an early hour in the same valley. This valley, in one respect, presented a most wonderful as well as a beautiful aspect. Its equal I have never seen, and such, too, was the testimony of all who beheld it. In no private or public park have I ever seen such

A PROFUSE DISPLAY OF FLOWERS

Every step of our march that day was amid flowers of the most exquisite colors and perfume; so luxuriant in growth were they that the men plucked them without dismounting from the saddle. Some belonged to new or unclassified species. It was a strange sight to glance back at the advancing columns of cavalry and behold the men, with beautiful bouquets in their hands, while the head-gear of the horses were decorated with wreaths of flowers fit to crown a queen of May. Deeming it a most fitting appellation, I named this "Floral Valley." General Forsyth, at one of our halting places, chosen at random, plucked seventeen beautiful flowers belonging to different species, and within a space of twenty feet square.

The same evening, while seated at the mess table, one of the officers called attention to the carpet of flowers strewn under our feet, and it was suggested that it be determined how many different flowers could be plucked without leaving our seat at the dinner table. Seven beautiful varieties

were thus gathered. Professor Donaldson the botonist of the expedition, estimated the number of species in bloom in Floral Valley at fifty, while an equal number of varieties had bloomed, or were yet to bloom. The number of trees, shrubs and grasses was estimated at twenty-five, making a total flora of the valley embrace 125 species.

THROUGH THIS BEAUTIFUL VALLEY

meanders a stream of crystal water so cold as to render ice undesirable even at noonday. The temperature of two of the many springs found flowing into it was taken and ascertained to be forty-four and forty-four and one-half degrees respectively. The next morning, although loth to leave so enchanting a locality, we continued to ascend this valley until gradually, most imperceptibly, we discovered that we were on the crest of the western ridge of Black Hills, and instead of being among barren heaths, as might be supposed, we found ourselves winding our way through a little park whose natural beauty may well bear comparison with the loveliest portion of Central Park. Favored as we had been in having Floral Valley for our roadway to the crest of the Black Hills, we were scarcely less fortunate in the valley which seemed to rise to meet us in the interior slope. A running stream of clear, cold water, the counterpart of that we had ascended the day before, flowed at our feet, and pointed out the way before us, while along the banks grew beautiful flowers, surpassed but little in beauty and profusion by their sisters who had greeted us the day before. After advancing down this valley about fourteen miles, our course being almost southeast, we encamped in the midst of grazing whose only fault, if any, was the great luxuriance. Having preceded the main column, as usual, with an escort of two companies of cavalry (E and C) and Lieutenant Wallace's detachment of scouts, I came upon

AN INDIAN CAMP FIRE,

still burning, and which, with other indications, showed that a small party of Indians had encamped there the previous night, and had evidently left that morning in ignorance of our close proximity. Believing that they would not move far, and that a collision might take place at any time unless a friendly understanding was arrived at, I sent my head scout, "Bloody Knife," and twenty of his braves to advance a few miles and reconnoiter the valley. This party had been gone but a few minutes when two of Bloody Knife's young men came galloping back and informed me that they had discovered five Indian lodges a few miles down the valley, and that "Bloody Knife," as directed, had concealed his party in a woody ravine, where they awaited further orders. Taking a company with me, which was afterward reinforced by the remainder of the scouts and Colonel Hart's company, I proceeded to the ravine where Bloody Knife and his comrades lay concealed, and from the crest beyond obtained a full view of the five Indian lodges, about which a considerable number of ponies were grazing. I was able to place my command still nearer to the lodges undiscovered. I then dispatched a guard, the interpreter with a flag of truce, accompanied by two of our Sioux scouts, to acquaint the occupants of the lodge that we were friendly disposed and desired to communicate with them!

TO PREVENT EITHER
TREACHERY OR FLIGHT
on their part, I galloped the remaining portion of my advance and surrounded the lodges. This was accomplished almost before they were aware of our presence. I then entered the little village and shook hands with the occupants, assuring them, through the interpreter, that they had no cause to fear, as we were not there to molest them. I invited them to visit our camp, and promised presents of flour, sugar, and coffee to all who would accept. This invitation was accepted. At the same time I entered into an agreement with the leading men that they should encamp with us a few days, and give us such information concerning the country as we might desire; in return for which service I was to reward them with rations. With this understanding I left them.

The entire party numbered twenty-seven. Later in the afternoon four of the men, including the

Chief "One Stab," visited our camp and desired the promised rations, saying that the entire party would move up and join us the following morning, as agreed upon. I ordered presents of sugar, coffee, and bacon to be given them, and to relieve them of the pretended anxiety of the safety of their village during the night I ordered a party of fifteen of my command to return with them and protect them during the night; but from their great disinclination to wait a few minutes till the party could saddle up, and from the fact that two of the four had already slipped away, I was of opinion that they were not acting in good faith. In this I was confirmed when the two remaining ones set off at a gallop in the direction of their village. I sent a party of our scouts to overtake them and request them to return; not complying with this request, I sent a second party with orders to repeat the request, and if not complied with, then to take hold of the bridles of their ponies and lead them back, but to offer no violence. When overtaken by our scouts, one of the two Indians seized the musket of one of the scouts and endeavored to wrest it from him; failing in this he released his hold, after the scout became dismounted in the struggle, and set off as fast as his pony could carry him, but not before the musket of the scout was discharge. From blood discovered afterward it was evident that either the Indian or his pony was wounded. I hoped that neither was seriously hurt, although the Indians have their own bad faith as the sole ground for the collision. "One Stab," the chief, was brought back to camp.

THE SCOUTS GALLOPED
DOWN THE VALLEY
to the site of the village, when it was discovered that the entire party had packed up the lodges and fled, and the visit of the four Indians to our camp was not only to obtain the rations promised them in return for future services but to cover flight of the lodges. I have effected arrangements by which Chief "One Stab" will be with us as guide three days longer, when he will take his departure and rejoin his band. He claims to belong to both "Red Cloud's" and

"Spotted Tail's" Agencies, but has been to neither for a long time. He has recently returned from the hostile river on Ponder River, and represents that the Indians lost ten killed in their fights with the Bozeman exploring party.

The creek which led us down into the interior of the Black Hills is bordered by high bluffs, on the crests of which are located prominent walls of solid rock, presenting here and there the appearance of castles constructed of masonry. From their marked resemblance, I named this stream "Castle Creek." The direction of Castle Creek having commenced to lead us more to the northeast than we were prepared to go, and the valley having become narrow and broken. I left this water course and ascended the valley of a small tributary, which again gave us a southeasterly course. After a march of fourteen miles we encamped on a small creek furnishing us an abundance of water and grass. The direction of this creek was nearly east. On the 30th I moved in continuation of our previous course, and through

A FINE, OPEN COUNTRY,
covered with excellent grazing. After a march of over ten miles, we encamped early in the day about five miles from the western base of Harney's Peak, finding water, grass, and wood abundant, with springs of clear, cool water running through camp. On the following day the command remained in camp, except the exploring parties sent out in all directions. With a small party I proceeded to Harney's Peak, and, after great difficulty, made the ascent to its crest. We found this to be the highest point in the Black Hills. From the highest point we obtained a view of Bear Butte, in the north part of the plains to the east far beyond the Cheyenne River. Our party did not reach camp till near 1 o'clock that night, but we were amply repaid for our labor by the magnificence of the views obtained. While on the highest point, we drank the health of the veteran out of compliment to whom the peak was named. On the 1st of August we moved camp a few miles simply to obtain fresh grass, still keeping near the base of the hills to

the east of us. This morning I dispatched two companies under Colonel Hart in a southeasterly direction to extend our exploration of the south fork of the Cheyenne River. Tomorrow morning at 5 o'clock I will set out with five companies of cavalry and endeavor to reach the same stream in a southwesterly direction from Harney's Peak.

Reynolds, the scout who is to carry this dispatch to Fort Laramie, will go with us as far as we go in that direction, when he sets out along to reach his desination, traveling mainly by night.

THE COUNTRY

through which we have passed since leaving the Belle Fourche River has been generally open and extremely fertile. The main portion of that passed over since entering the unexplored portion of the Black Hills consists of beautiful parks and valleys through which flows a stream of clear, cold water, perfectly free from alkali, while bounding these parks or valley, there are invariably found unlimited supplies of timber much of it being capable of being made into good lumber. In no portion of the United States, not excepting the famous Blue Grass region of Kentucky, have I ever seen grazing superior to that found growing wild in this hitherto unknown region. I know of no portion of our country where nature has done so much to prepare homes for husbandmen, and left so little for the latter to do as here. In the open and timbered spaces a partly prepared farm of almost any dimensions, of an acre and upward, can be found here. Not only is the land cleared and timbered for both fuel and building, conveniently located with streams of pure water flowing through its length and breadth, but nature oftimes seems to have gone further, and placed beautiful shrubbery and evergreens in the most desirable locations for building sites. While on Harney's Peak, I could contrast the bright green verdure of these lovely parks with the sun-burned and dry, yellow herbage to be seen on the outer plains. Everything indicates abundance of moisture within the space inclosed by the Black Hills.

THE SOIL

is that of a rich garden, and composed of a dark mould of exceedingly fine grain. We have found the country in many places covered with wild raspberries, both the black and red varieties. Yesterday and today we feasted on the latter. It is no unusual sight to see hundreds of soldiers gathering wild berries. Nowhere in the States have I tasted cultivated raspberries of equal flavor to those found growing wild here, nor have I ever seen them as large or in as great profusion. I have seen hundreds of them here. Wild strawberries, wild currants, gooseberries, and wild cherries are also found in great profusion and of exceedingly pure quality. Cattle would winter in these valleys without other food or shelter than that that can be obtained from running at large. As there are scientists accompanying the expedition, who are examining into the mineral resources of this region, the result of whose researches will accompany my detailed report, I omit all present reference to that portion of our explorations until the return of the expedition, except to state what will appear in any event in the public prints, that

GOLD HAS BEEN FOUND

at several places; and it is believed by those who are giving their attention to this subject, that it will be found in paying quantities. I have upon my table forty or fifty small particles of pure gold, in size averaging a small pin-head, and most of it obtained today from one panful of earth. As we have never remained longer in camp than one day, it will be readily understood that there is no opportunity to make a satisfactory examination in regard to deposits of valuable minerals. Veins of lead and strong indications of silver have been found. Until further examination is made regarding the richness of the gold, no opinion should be formed. Veins of what the geologists term gold-bearing quartz crop out on almost every hillside. All existing geological or geographical maps of this region have been found incorrect. This will not seem surprising, when it is remembered that both have been compiled by guess-work and without entering the country attempted

to be represented. The health of the command continues excellent. I will begin my northward march in four days from this date. I do not expect to arrive at Fort Lincoln until the 31st of August.

> G. A. Custer,
> Bvt. Major General U. S. A.,
> Commanding Expedition.

Postscript—10:30 p.m., Aug. 3.— I left our main camp near Harney's Peak, at 6 o'clock this morning, with five companies of cavalry, and after a march in a southerly direction of forty-five miles, reached the south fork of Cheyenne River, at the mouth of a creek flowing from the north and emptying into the Cheyenne midway between mouths of Hot and Horsehead Creeks. From this point Reynolds, the scout, sets out in one hour with this dispatch for Fort Laramie. I reached here at 9 p.m., and will proceed to Harney's Peak by a different route tomorrow morning. The country between here and Harney's Peak is generally open and rolling; and, excepting the southeastern portion, covered with excellent grass.

> G. A. Custer,
> Brevet Major General,
> Commanding.

CUSTER FIELD REPORT NO. 3
ST. PAUL PRESS
Issue of August 23, 1874

THE BLACK HILLS.

Official Report of General Custer News of the Expedition up to August 15th.

The Country Traversed by Custer's Command.

Pure Water, Splendid Pasturage and Mild Temperature.

Iron, Plumbago, Gypsum and Gold in the Hills.

The following is a copy of an official report received from Gen. Custer, and received at Department Headquarters yesterday. In view of the general desire to know something definite in regard to the terra incognita traversed by the expedition, Gen. Custer's report will undoubtedly receive more than ordinary attention; and as usual, the PRESS is the first to give the public the important information contained in this official dispatch:

HEADQUARTERS BLACK
HILLS EXPEDITION,
BEAR BUTTE, Dakota,
Aug. 15,
(via Bismarck.)

To Assistant Adjutant General,
Department of Dakota,
St. Paul:

My last dispatch was written on the 2d and 3d instant, and sent from the South Fork of the Cheyenne, from a point on the latter nearest to Fort Laramie. On the morning of the 4th instant I began my return march to our main camp near Harney's Peak, arriving there by a different route on the sixth. On the morning of the 7th the expedition began its march northward, Bear Butte being our next objective point. We advanced without serious obstacle until within ten or twelve miles of Bear Butte, when we found our further progress barred by a high range of impassible hills. We attempted to effect a passage through some one of the many valleys whose water courses ran directly through the hills in the desired direction, but in every instance we were led into deep, broken canons, impassable even to horsemen. Through one of these I made my way on foot and from a high point near its mouth obtained a view of the plains outside. Retracing my steps I placed the command in camp in a fine valley in which it had halted, and devoted the remainder of the day to a further search for a practicable route through the hills. The result decided me to follow down a water course which led us first toward the south, and afterwards towards the east. This stream proved to be Elk Creek, the valley of which, as well as the stream itself, proving at least equal in beauty and extent to any passed through during our march. We camped twice on the stream, and as far as we proceeded down its course we had a most excellent road; but finding that like nearly all other streams leaving the hills, its course would take us into a canon which could be barely made practicable for our wagons. I searched for and discovered a narrow gap in the rocky wall which forms the northern boundary of the valley, and which was conveniently large to allow our wagons to pass through. A march of an hour up a gradual ascent and through a pine forest, brought us to a beautiful park containing thousands of mores, and from which we obtained a fine view, in the distance, of our old acquaintance—the plains. Here we pitched our tents for the last time in the Black Hills; nearly every one being loth to leave a region which had been found so delightful in almost every respect. Behind us the grass and foliage were clothed in green of the freshness of May. In front of us, as we cast our eyes over the plains below, we saw nothing but a comparatively parched, dried surface, the sunburnt pasturage of which offered a most uninviting prospect to horse and rider, when remembering the rich abundance we were leaving behind us. A march of twenty-six miles gradually bearing northward, brought us to the base of Bear Butte, at which point I concluded to remain one day before beginning our return march. I propose to return by a different, although, perhaps, not shorter route than adopted in coming to the Black Hills. I am induced to make this change in order to embrace a larger extent of unexplored country within, the limits of our explorations, and particularly to enable us to locate as much as possible of that portion of the Little Missouri of which nothing is now known. I expect the expedition to reach Fort Lincoln on the 31st of August. The health of the command has been, and is, most excellent. This expedition entered the Black Hills from the west side, penetrated through the eastern and most southern ranges, explored the major portions of the interior, and passed out the most eastern ranges which form the boundary of the Black Hills. From the fact that in all our principal marches through the Black Hills, we have taken without serious obstacle a heavily laden train of over one hundred wagons, it may be inferred that the Black Hills did not constitute the impenetrable region heretofore represented. In entering the Black Hills from any direction, the most serious, if not the only, obstacles were encountered at once near the outer base. This probably accounts for the mystery which has so long existed regarding the character of the interior. Exploring parties have contented themselves with marching around the exterior base and from the forbidding aspect of the hills as viewed at a distance, inferred that an advance towards the interior would only encounter increased obstacles. In regard to the character of the country enclosed by the Black Hills I can only repeat what I have stated in previous dispatches. No portion of the United States can boast of a richer or better pasturage, purer water, the natural temperature of which in midsummer as it flows from the earth, is but 12 degrees above the freezing point, and of greater advantage generally to the farmer or stock raiser than are to be found in the Black Hills. Building stone of the best quality is to be found in inexhaustible quantities. Wood for fuel, and lumber sufficient for all time to come. Rains are frequent, with no evidence in the country of either drouth or freshets. The season perhaps is too short, and the nights too cool, for corn, but I believe all other grain could be produced here in wonderful abundance. Wheat would particularly yield largely. There is no doubt as to the existence of various minerals throughout the hills, as this subject has received special attention of experts who accompany the expedition and will be reported upon in detail. I will only mention the fact that iron and plumbago have been found and beds of gypsum of apparently inexhaustible extent. I referred in a former dispatch to the discovery of gold. Subsequent examinations at numerous points confirm and strengthen the fact of the existence of gold in the Black Hills. On some of the water courses almost every panful of earth produced gold in small yet paying quantities. Our brief halts and rapid marching prevented anything but a very hasty examination of the country in this respect, but in one place and the only one within my knowledge where so great a depth was reached, a hole was dug eight feet in depth. The miners report that they found gold among the roots of the grass, and from that point to the lowest point reached gold was found in paying quantities. It has not required an expert to find gold in the Black Hills, as men without former experience in min-

ing have discovered it at an expense of but little time or labor. As an evidence of the rich pasturage to be found in the region, I can state the fact that my beef herd, after marching upwards of 600 miles, is in better condition than when I started, being now as fat as is consistent with marching condition. The same may be said of the mules of the wagon train. The horses of the command are in good working condition. I have never seen as many deer as in the Black Hills; elk and bear have also been killed. We have had no collision with hostile Indians.
(Signed)

G. A. CUSTER,
Brevet Major General, U. S. A.
Commanding Expedition.

CUSTER'S FINAL REPORT
ST. PAUL PIONEER
Issue of September 1, 1874

BLACK HILLS EXPEDITION.
Return of Custer's Command
to Fort Lincoln.

The following dispatch was received from Gen. Custer at Headquarters in this city, yesterday:
Fort Lincoln, D. T., 30th.
Via Bismarck, August 30.

To A. A. Gen Dept. of
Dakota, St. Paul:

The Black Hills expedition arrived at this post at 4 p.m. today. Our route from Bear Butte having been by way of the Little Missouri river until the head waters of the Heart River were reached when we moved almost due east to this post. We explored and located that portion of the Little Missouri Valley hitherto unknown. We have marched about one thousand miles and my command with replenished supplies is in good condition to take the field tomorrow.

G. A. Custer,
Brevet Major Gen. Commanding.

Grant's Report

(Author's Note: Lt. Col. Fred D. Grant, was acting aide-de-camp to General Philip Sheridan. Grant accompanied Custer on the expedition to the Black Hills. At the conclusion of the journey, Grant filed this official report with the Army).

September 7, 1874
Grant, F. D.

Lt. Col. & A.D.C.
Submits report on his
observations on the
"Black Hills Expedition"

Hdqrs. Mil. Div. of the Mo.
Chicago, Septr. 16th, 1874

Respectfully referred to the
Chief Engineer of the Division
for his examination.
To be returned.

By Com'd of Lt. Gen'l Sheridan
R. C. Drum
Asst. Adj't General
Headquarters Military
Division of Missouri
Chicago, Illinois,
September 16th, 1874

Colonel R. C. Drum
Assistant Adjutant General
Military Division of
the Missouri
Colonel,

I have the honor to submit the following report of my observations upon the "Black Hills Expedition," in compliance with the provision of S. O. No. 41 dated Hdqrs., Military Division of the Missouri, Chicago, Ill., June 17th 1874, of which the following is an extract:

"1. Major George A. Forsyth, 9th Cavalry, and Lieut. Frederick D. Grant, 4th Cavalry, Aids-de-Camp, will proceed to Fort Abraham Lincoln, Dakota Territory and join the expedition now organizing at that post for the military exploration of the Black Hills country. On the return of the expedition they will report in person to the Lieutenant General at these Headquarters."

By Command of Lieut.
General Sheridan
(Signed) R. C. Drum
Assistant Adjutant
General

I left Chicago on the evening of the 18th of June and arrived in St. Paul on the evening of the 19th, where I had to remain over until the next morning (June 20th) when I started by the L. S. & Mississippi R.R., and arrived at Fort A. Lincoln the afternoon of June 21st, where we found the expedition in camp about two miles below the Fort. It was then the intention of the Commanding Officer to start on the 25th of June but owing to the delay of the arrival of the arms (the Springfield Carbines,) we were delayed until the 2d of July. On the morning of July 2d, at 8 A.M., the command moved from its camp and moved up a small valley to get over the hills that line the Missouri river. The expedition was commanded by Bvt. Major General G. A. Custer and consisted of ten (10) companies of Cavalry, two (2) companies of Infantry, 1 Battery of Artillery and sixty-eight (68) Scouts (Indians) —Twenty-eight (28) belonging to the Santee Agency, 34 Fort Berthold and Fort Lincoln Rees; with (6) Sioux from Fort Rice. Then there were some citizens—some of them old miners. Our Artillery was composed of one 3-inch Rodman gun, two 6-barreled and one 10-barreled Gatling gun. Our first three days' march was in a south-westerly direction, the next two days was in a westerly direction; then three days south-westerly again; then one day west; then two days a little West of South; then two days a little South of West. This brought us to Prospect Valley—very near Short Pine Butte and within ten or twelve miles of the Little Missouri River. Our next days' march (July 15th) was first a little South of West until we struck the Little Missouri, then a little West of South; and watered the stock in the Little Missouri, and then turned and went in a direction a little East of South. From this point we travelled two days almost due South and camped on the Belle Fourche near the place where Reynolds camped on the 14th of July, 1859— 15 years and one day before we did. After lying over one day on the Belle Fourche, the command started into the Black Hills and our route was in various directions— up and down valleys, over hills, &c.,—until the evening of the 22nd

of July when we arrived near the foot of Inyan Karra (sic) Mountain, which was almost due south of our camp on the Belle Fourche. From this point, for two days, our course was nearly east. Then we turned South-east until we went into Camp near Harney's Peak August 1st. Here the train went into camp until August the 6th. The 2nd of August, Capt. Hart of the 7th Cavalry started for the South fork of the Shyenne with (2) comp's of Cavalry and was to follow the creek on which we were encamped. On the morning of the 3d. Gen'l Custer, General Forsyth and myself started for the same river (South fork of the Shyenne) with (4) companies of the 7th Cavalry, but in a south-westerly direction and marched until half-past eleven that night and sent Reynolds, the hunter and scout, to Fort Laramie with the mail. We returned to where the wagon-train was encamped August 5th. On August 6th we broke camp again and, following our trail back (north-west) until we arrived at Elk-horn prairie, turned north, then south-east, then east, then a little west of north; and encamped on the evening of Friday, August 14th, near Bear Butte. Here we lay in camp one day; and General Forsyth and Colonel Ludlow made the ascent of Bear Butte. We broke camp at Bear Butte on the morning of August 15th, and marched in a direction a little west of north until we got to the Little Missouri. On the evening of August 19th, we crossed our old trail at the place we had camped July 14th and 15th. We lay in camp August 20th, and on the 21st we marched nearly north-east; 22nd., north-west; 23rd. north-east—into the "mauvais terre" of the Little Missouri and following the 1872 trail of Stanley into the bad land; August 24th, followed the trail of Stanley out of the bad lands to the head waters of the Heart river. At this point we were almost due West from Fort Lincoln and we marched in as straight a line for the Fort as the country permitted and arrived there about 2 o'clock August the 3rd.

The following distances marched each day and names of places where we camped; also the prominent points seen each day and incidents of interest. First call for reveille was always at 2:45 A.M.; five minutes after, second call; and at 3 A.M., was roll-call. We usually started on the march at 5 A.M., although sometimes a little sooner, and sometimes a little later.

REMARKS

Date July 2d. Thursday
Distance 13

Head of column commenced the advance at 8 A.M., crossed 2 streams —1 running water; got into camp at sundown; weather hot; 12 men in Infantry gave out, saw a few antelope and a good many curlew; streams crossed; tributaries to the Little Heart river.

3d. Friday. Dist. 14
Head of column commenced the advance at 7:45 A.M.; route very circuitous; weather very warm; 7 men in the Infantry gave out; distance gained about 7 miles. The soil of the country good; plenty of good grass; very good wood. Went into camp at 3 P.M. Sandstone on hills.

4th Sat'day. Dist. 15
Country very good. Crossed Stanley's trail of 1873, Reynold's trail and an Indian trail. Passed "Dog-teeth Buttes" and camped on Dog-teeth buttes creek. Country about the same as yesterday. Celebrated the 4th by going into camp at 12 M., & having the Band play the national airs.

5th Sunday. Dist. 17
Country not quite so good as usual until we got within 7 miles of where it was beautiful and is a sand-stone formation. The creek on which we camped is fed by very fine springs and is called by the Indians "the Creek where the Bear winters." It runs into the heart river and is full of fish (Chub). There were 2 crossings made this day. At the last one, one of the mules fell down and the wagon ran over the mule and driver but did not hurt either of them much. Could see Heart Butte today and passed "Dog-teeth Buttes."

6th Monday. Dist.—
The country very good; grass fine; a great deal of wild rye; weather very warm; thermometer 112° in the sun—and all of us had to be in the sun; went into camp at 12 M., on north forks of the Cannon Ball river, which is really a beautiful

stream for this country,—it has a valley of a quarter of a mile to several miles in width. A good many antelope seen and killed this day.

7th Tuesday. Dist. 30-35
A hard day's march on account of heat and alkali; some very bad crossings; country not near so good as north of the Cannon Ball river; crossed a wide alkali bottom at White Horse Creek. Went into camp on the Belle Pierre river. We found all along the route large pieces of silicious lime-stone with great hardness and would make good Burr Stone. Went into camp at 10:30 p.m.

8th Wednesday. Dist. 19
Just before Reveille had quite an Indian scare but saw no Indians. One of the men came in this morning and reported Indians in our last camp. We camped at a water-hole with plenty of wood, grass and water. The country contained a good deal of Marl which contained quite a large proportion of carbonate of lime. The place where we camped is called Hidden-wood creek and is a branch of Grand River. It was a hard day's march on account of the great heat. Went into camp at 4:30 P.M.

9th Thursday. Dist. 20
Made quite a crossing and marched until 1:45 P.M. Went into camp on Grand River which is quite a stream — running all the year round. Country quite poor that we passed through to-day, although we found more Gamma and spear grass than usual. Theromometer 100°.

10th Friday. Dist. 24
The country better to-day. Gamma and spear grass quite abundant. Crossed Lightning Creek and Buffalo Creek, besides crossing Grand River twice. Went into camp on Grand River (no wood but plenty of lignite) about 5 P.M. A great many antelope killed to-day.

11th Sat'day. Dist. 20
Passed near Slim Butte and by the hills where the Cave is—this cave is a great fraud. The country was quite poor. There is a good deal of timber on these hills—ash, elm, pine and cottonwood.

12th Sunday. Dist. 12.45
The country to-day was very hard to march through with a wagon-

train. Had a great many soft, miry, places to cross. Weather very hot. Found a good camp with plenty of wood and water; the country quite poor.

13th Monday. Dist. 15.60
Very hot. Thermometer 104° in the shade and 116° in the sun. Some Indians reported to have been seen. Country poor. Went into camp on a creek which I think was a tributary to south fork of Grand River.

14th Tuesday. Dist. 13.90
Marched through quite a rough country; had several bad crossings. Nobody on sick report; and all in fine spirits. All in hopes that we will have a fight in a day or so. Fires seen at night—supposed to be signal-fires to inform Big Horn Indians of our whereabouts. Went into camp in a beautiful valley which we named Prospect Valley. A good many Indians reported to have been seen to-day. One squad of fifteen (15) said to have been seen.

15th Wedn'day. Dist.—
Lay in camp to-day. Can see Short Pine Buttes. Indians reported to have been seen to-day. Sent mail out to-day by two Scouts "Bull-neck" and "Skunk's Head"—they started at sundown.

16th Thursday. Dist. 31.½
Marched until we got to the Little Missouri. Country very good up to that point. From here on the country was perfectly horrible— nothing grew except cactus. The ground had quantities of silinite (suephak of lime) through it. We made a dry camp as there was no water fit to use, neither was there any wood or grass.

17th Friday. Dist. 18.¾
The country marched through to-day better than yesterday. The Black Hills in sight. Crossed four ravines, the first drained for the Little Missouri and the other three for the Belle Fourche. Some grease-wood passed to-day. Went into camp on a bluff at the edge of some of the worst country I have ever seen. Grass very good, water poor, and no wood in camp. Had a storm during the night which blew all the shelter-tents down that were on the hill and a good many of the officers' tents also.

18th Sat'day. Dist. 17½
Marched directly towards the "hills" through a very mean country, filled with cactus and gullies. Then we came to a valley that looked very beautiful after the country we had just passed through. It had plenty of timber in it. We passed three large coule's that sent their waters into the Belle Fourche. The first had very bad water—salty and alkaline; the second had very good and pure water; the third had water strongly impregnated with iron and was very clear and cold. We passed large hills of hematite iron or with vast stratas of Slate-stone. We encamped on the Belle Fourche near the trail that Reynolds made 15 years ago. The Belle Fourche has high banks on each side. Passed a great deal of wood to-day —Burr-oak, pine, cottonwood, cedar, elm and willow. The grass is gamma grass and there is a great deal of it. The valley of the Belle Fourche is really a very handsome one and the water, although slightly alkaline, is very good.

19th Sunday. Dist.—
The command lay in camp to-day and built a crossing over the Belle Fourche. The wagon-train and Infantry crossed.

20th Monday. Dist. 14½
We crossed the Belle Fourche and marched directly into the Black Hills. The country was quite poor at first, with large quantities of hematite iron ore. Burr-oak at different places. Crossed over the hills and got on a long divide which looked like a large meadow—the grass as thick as in any hay field I ever saw. Crossed several ravines all of them draining towards the Belle Fourche. After going about 10 miles, we entered a valley beautifully timbered and having some wild fruit,—cherries, gooseberries and currants.

21st Tuesday. Dist. 15.48
The first part of the march to-day was through a beautiful valley, then passed into the valley of the Red Sandy which is very poor, red soil and contains vast quantities of gypsum. Water very bad but quite cold (45°).

22nd Wed'day. Dist. 22½
The country was bad that we passed through to-day until we got up to the head of the valley we encamped on last night where there was a very cold spring and the sulphate of lime changed into carbonate of lime. One man died this morning, named Cunningham; and one named Turner was shot in a quarrel and died just after getting into camp. Both were buried on a little hill near the Inyan Karra (sic) Creek. This stream has a great many fish in it, (Chub). Inyan Karra (sic) mountain was a little to the west of our camp and is nearly 6,500 feet high.

23rd Thursday. Dist.—
Lay in camp to-day and quite a party ascended Inyan Karra (sic). General Forsyth took his horse over the mountain—probably the only horse that has ever been over it.

24th Friday. Dist. 11½
Our course of march to-day was in an easterly direction and we passed over some very rough country where there was splendid water and good timber—some of the trees being as much as 3 feet in diameter. Our march was very slow on account of the roughness of the country and fallen timber. We went into camp in one of the most beautiful valleys I ever saw as it had a perfect carpet of flowers. There was no water where we entered the valley but as we ascended we came upon quite a stream which was very cold and hard water. The stream where we camped was about 3 inches deep, 2 feet wide and with a current of 1½ feet per second. Went into camp at 5 P.M.

25th Saturday. Dist. 11.85
Followed up the same valley, the stream becoming larger and larger, until it was quite a large mountain stream. Passed some very cold springs—temperature 44° and 44½°. The valley has been named "Flora Valley."

26th Sunday. Dist. 14
Continued our march up this valley (Flora Valley) until we got to the summit, which I should think was quite as high as Inyan Karra (sic) and was quite a park. There were two springs, very cold, on the summit. From here we took a valley which we call Castle Creek Valley and, after going several miles down it, we came upon large springs of water which made a very large stream. This was dammed up every few hundred feet by Beaver and at one place made quite a large pond. We passed quite a number of old Indian camps and places where they had been up to get lodge-poles. The place where we went into camp, we found a fire still burning and General Custer sent some scouts with "Bloody Knife" at their head to go down the valley and see if he could find any wild Indians. A report soon returned saying that there was a camp about 3½ miles below us and General Custer had the horses saddled up and started. The camp was soon surrounded. It had 5 Tepees and 27 Indians. They gave themselves up without firing a shot so no one was hurt. They promised to come to our camp that night and get rations. Four men did come, but soon after they got in one of them left. Pretty soon another did the same thing, so the two that remained were detained until we could give them rations. They left with some of our scouts, but hardly had they got out of sight when one of the Sioux grabbed at the gun of one of our scouts and fired at him. This caused a fight in which several shots were fired and one of the Indians got away. The other was caught and brought back to camp. At this camp a ledge of quartz-rock was found, which the miners claimed to be silver ore, but I could see nothing in it except a little mica schist and plumbago.

27th Monday. Dist.—
Lay in camp to-day and made up parties to explore the country. Found the saddle-blankets and rations of the Indian that got away yesterday with blood on them, so either he or his pony must have been wounded. A good many fish in the stream.

28th Tuesday. Dist. 10
We left this valley to-day and started across the hills until we got on Elk-horn prairie—so named on account of a large stack of Elk-horns. After going about six miles, the country was so rough, that we had to return part of the way and go back into "Castle Creek Valley" —about 3½ miles below where we camped yesterday and on the same ground that the Indian camp was. Quantities of mica schist.

29th Wedn'day. Dist. 14½
This was a very hard day's march. The country is a hard one to pass

over with a wagon-train and we were 24½ hours making it. We had pure, good water all day long. We left "Castle Creek Valley" where we broke camp, early in the morning.

30th Thursday. Dist. 12
The wagons got into camp at 4:30 A.M., this morning—after marching all night. After 2½ hours rest we started again; going into camp near Harney's Peak and on what we suppose to be French Creek. Some gold said to have been found.

31st Friday. Dist.—
Lay in camp all day. Several escorts sent out with Engineers. Quite a party ascended Harney's Peak. Gold and silver both said to have been found.

August 1st Sat'day. Dist. 4
Moved our camp down the creek where we could get more water and grass. Some more gold and silver said to have been found—but to me they looked like the same pieces that were shown to me yesterday and the day before yesterday.

2nd Sunday. Dist.—
Lay in camp with all but two companies of the 7th Cavalry which Capt. Harte (sic) took to follow down French Creek to the South Fork of the Shyenne.

3rd Monday. Dist.—
Four companies with General Custer started off in a southwesterly direction for the South Fork of the Shyenne, and after about a 50-mile march got into camp at 11:30 P.M.

4th Tuesday. Dist.—
After about a 35-mile march went into camp on some water-hole about 35 miles south of Harney's Peak.

5th Wedn'day. Dist.—
Marched into camp; distance: 20 miles. Capt. Harte (sic) also got back to-day.

6th Thursday. Dist. 23½
Took our old trail back for about 16 miles and passed through two of our old camps; then turned to our left; and went into camp at 9:30 P.M.

7th Friday. Dist. 16¼
We got on our old trail very soon and passed our last camp on Castle Creek. Followed the trail so as to get upon Elk-horn prairie. A

great deal of mica schist with quartz and some of it had a great deal of iron in it. Water strongly impregnated with iron. Two fine, large, grizzly bears killed; country quite rough; went into camp at 6 P.M. on a fine running stream.

8th Sat'day. Dist. 14¾
Very hard day's march on account of the mica schist which was on edge. We passed large beds of Potsdam sand-stone. Some of the mica schist had a large percentage of iron in it. A great many deer were killed. Had plenty of good water through this part of the country. Went into camp at 12 P.M.

9th Sunday. Dist. 7½
Went into camp at 1 P.M. to-day in a very pretty valley.

10th Monday. Dist. 7½
Marched through a most beautiful valley to-day; the stream the largest we have seen in the Black Hills. A great many deer killed and 3 elk—one with splendid antlers.

11th Tuesday. Dist.—
Lay in camp all day. Two companies went down the creek to make a road. 3 more elk killed.

12th Wed'day. Dist. 4½
Where we camped to-day is one of the most beautiful spots.

13th Thursday. Dist. 3½
Left the valley and went upon a prairie and camped there for the night. One man of "H" Co. died. General Forsyth, Lieut. Hodgson and myself each took a party of men and went out to see if we could find a road out of the Black Hills. All returned having found a good road.

14th Friday. Dist. 26¾
Went out of the Black Hills on to the plains and camped within five miles of Bear Butte. Passed a large valley to-day completely full of clear and very cold springs. Got into camp about sundown. Capt. Benteen before leaving camp this morning buried the man who died last night.

15th Saturday. Dist.—
Lay in camp to-day. A party ascended Bear Butte which is 1,500 feet above camp and 4,500 feet above the level of the sea.

16th Sunday. Dist. 29¾
Passed Bear Butte and crossed the Belle Fourche. The country fair,

with plenty of good grass. Just before reaching the Belle Fourche, we passed a fresh Indian trail and could see several ponies. So "Cold Hand" and "Bloody Knife" went after them and they told us that there were six bands of hostile Indians waiting for us in Prospect Valley camp on branch of Crow Creek.

17th Monday. Dist. 28½
Passed by Slave Butte and marched in the direction of Short Pine Buttes. All expect a fight with Indians to-morrow if not this evening. Passed several fresh trails. Country poor. Camped on headwaters of Owl river.

18th Tuesday. 29¾
Marched past Short Pine Buttes. Country miserable. Some of the horses and mules gave out and had to be abandoned on the road. No Indians found. Went into camp in Prospect Valley, near our camp of July 14th and 15th. Weather very warm.

19th Wed'day. Dist. 35
A hard day's march through one of the worst possible countries. Nearly all the grass had been burnt by prairie fires. A great many horses and mules gave out; some of them had to be shot. Weather very warm. Camped on headwaters of Grand River.

20th Thursday. Dist. 30
Country entirely burnt out. This was a very hard day on the mules and horses. Country miserable. Camped on the Little Missouri.

21st Friday. Dist.—
Lay in camp all day.

22nd Sat'day. Dist. 28½
Marched up the right bank of the Little Missouri. The ambulances not enough to carry the sick; some of the men very ill indeed. Country full of red baked clay buttes. Sentinel Buttes seen to the Northwest of us.

23rd Sunday. Dist. 18½
The march to-day mostly through the "Mauvais Terre" of the Little Missouri. Country burnt out. Entered the bad lands by Stanley's trail of 1872. Camped on Box Elder Creek. A great deal of lignite in this country.

24th Monday. Dist. 24½
Country burnt out. Camped on headwaters of Heart river—followed Stanley's old trail.

25th Tuesday. Dist. 18½
Country burnt out. A man of "L"
Co., died to-day. We passed the
grave of a man who was killed last
year by his wagon running over
him. 3 bears killed to-day. Camped
on Heart river.

26th Wedn'day. Dist. 31¾
Crossed the Heart river and went
into camp on a branch of the
Heart. Buried the man who died
last night. Country burnt out.

27 Thursday. Dist. 17 1/6
The day very foggy; country
burnt out. Went into camp on a
spring which was the best water
we have had since leaving the
Black Hills. From here we
marched into Fort Lincoln in two
days. None of the country burnt
over between here and that post.

Owing to the order, directing me
to proceed to Washington, I will
close this report with the following
about the gold discoveries in the
Black Hills:

We had several Miners along
who had nothing to lose and everything to gain; they all lived together and could concoct any plan
they wished. After we got near
Harney's Peak they said they
found gold. Now the country in
that region is full of Mica Schist
and a very coarse feldsparthie
granite. I have been in and around
a great many gold and silver mines
in my life and have never seen
this class of stone on mining
grounds. Also they came each day
and showed specimens and would
say "I got this from one pan of
earth to-day" and I noticed that
they showed the same pieces every
day. Then they told about what
could be produced saying that one
man could get from 10 to 100 dollars a day. I saw about all the gold
that was produced in the hands of
the different miners, and I don't
believe there was two dollars all
put together and that they took
out there with them. I washed for
gold once myself and could not get
a color. There is a small extent of
country around Harney's Peak in
which there is reason to believe
there could be some gold found
though there could not be much.
It is in the Indian country where
it would be dangerous for white
people to go. I don't believe that
any gold was found at all.
I am, Colonel,
Very respectfully,
Your obedient servant
F. D. Grant
Lieut. Colonel
and A.D.C.

Forsyth's Report

Major George A. Forsyth

(Author's Note: Major George A. Forsyth, an acting aide-de-camp to General Philip Sheridan was ordered by Sheridan to keep a diary of the expedition. His official report and diary appeared in the CHICAGO TRIBUNE).

CHICAGO TRIBUNE
Issue of August 27, 1874

THE BLACK HILLS.

GEN. CUSTER'S EXPEDITION THERETO.

Letter from Maj. Forsyth to Gen. Sheridan, and a Continuation of the Major's Diary.

The Country Offers Great Inducements to Farmers and Stock Raisers.

Gold Will Be Found in Abundance in the Eastern Hills.

"The Scenery Beautiful, Grass Splendid, Water Fine, and Climate Delightful."

* * *

BLACK HILLS EXPEDITION, NEAR BEAR BUTTE, Saturday, Aug. 15, 1874.

DEAR GENERAL: From the heading of the note, you will see that we are out of the Black Hills, near the northeast edge.

Entering the camp dated 15 on Reynold's route, we worked our way down to Inyan Kara, thence southeast to Harney's Peak, and from there pushed exploring parties down to the South Fork of the Cheyenne River. From Harney's Peak we moved north above the headwaters of Bear Creek, when, not finding a good road out of the mountains north of Bear Butte, we took down to the head of Box-Elder Creek, followed it down until the waters sank into the channel, and then left it and pushed directly across the mountains in an easterly direction, and moved north to our present camp.

Following this route on the map, you will see that we have taken a train of over 100 heavily-laden wagons throughout every part of the Black Hills, save in a little portion near Crow Peak.

The fact is, the interior of the Black Hills

OFFERS SPLENDID INDUCEMENTS

to farmers and stock-raisers of all descriptions. There are fine uplands and beautiful valleys, with good streams, and springs of pure water, and timber, and good building-stone, on nearly all the hills. As there are no indications along the streams of freshets in the spring. I conclude that the snowfall must be very light during the winter. The climate is delightful during the summer months. Wild fruit thrives in the valleys, the growth of grass is superb, and plentiful showers—even in the dry season—keep it always fresh and palatable.

Our animals, though worked all the time, are in capital condition, and we have only lost two men by sickness since we left Fort Lincoln.

The two miners we have with us tell me that they found "color" in every pan of dirt they washed near Harney's Peak; that the diggings there, in Custer's Gulch, will pay $10 per day in which to prospect, as we kept moving so fast, but that, in their opinion, when the eastern hills are rightly prospected,

GOLD WILL BE FOUND THERE IN ABUNDANCE.

I am inclined to think so, for the very roots of the grass would pan 5 cents to the pan in our camp near Harney's Peak.

From this point we start for Fort Lincoln, via the bad lands of the Little Missouri, to give Prof. Grinnell a chance at the fossils.

We expect to get in on the 31st inst. Very respectfully and truly yours,

GEO. A. FORSYTH,
Major and A.A.D.C.
Lieut. Gen. P. H. Sheridan,
Commanding Military Division of the Missouri.

I inclose (sic) further extracts from my journal.

F.

———

CHICAGO DAILY TRIBUNE
Issue of August 26, 1874

THE BLACK HILLS.

Gen. Custer's Expedition Thereto.

Extracts from the Diary of Gen. George A. Forsyth.

* * *

The following are extracts from the diary of Gen. George A. Forsyth, who accompanied Maj. Gen. Custer on the Black Hills Expedition:

CAMP No. 14,
Thursday, July 16, 1874.

Broke camp at 4:30 a.m. Moved west around a high bluff, sparsely covered with stunted pine-trees. Six miles out, crossed a deep ravine, and came into the

VALLEY OF THE LITTLE MISSOURI,

which is about 3 miles in width on each side of the river. The stream itself is slightly muddy, about 60 feet wide, from 2 to 4 feet deep, and easily forded. The water is good for drinking purposes, with possibly a shade of alkali in it. The land lying adjacent to the stream is quite poor; the grass, which only covers the ground sparsely, is of poor quality and intermixed with sunflowers and cactus. Went down to the river and watered at 5:30 p.m; then left the river, which here bends sharply to the north, and marched up to a high ridge; crossed a succession of hills, and made a dry camp at 8:30 p.m. The day was very hot, and the march long and tedious. Distance marched 30½ miles. Direction generally southwest.

* * * * *

CAMP No. 15,
Friday, July 17.

Broke camp at 4:45 a.m., took a southerly direction, which we held all day, marching over a high rolling prairie, with very poor grass, which was badly intermixed with cactus. Encamped at night on a high bluff overlooking

THE BAD LANDS

towards the Black Hills, which are in full view, about 25 or 30 miles distant. During the night, had quite a severe wind-storm from the west, which covered everything with dust and prostrated several of the officer's tents. Very hot during the day. Distance made 20 miles.

CAMP No. 16,
Saturday, July 18.

Crossed the Bad Lands without very much trouble, finding a good road through the clay and sand, and having only one bad ravine to cross, and then kept the crest of a series of hills or divides, until we finally, from the top of the highest one, came down into the Belle Fourche country. After coming into the first valley, where the grass was pretty good, we water at a ravine, where we found water at the bottom of a dry creek; and, when I use the expression "dry-creek;" I mean a water-course in which there are standing pools of good water, but which is not a flowing stream. Moving forward over a soiling country, of poor, sandy soil, and crossing a succession of low hills covered with stunted pines and a few scrub oaks, we finally came out on some high hills, covered with slate and sandstone ridges which overlook

THE BELLE FOURCHE

or north fork of the Cheyenne River. Descending these hills, we encamped in the stream, which we found to be about 30 feet in width, of good, pure water, though not as clear or transparent as we had expected. Coming from the plains, we fully appreciated our camp. Wood, principally pine and elm, in any quantity; grazing superb, and water in abundance. Among the hills today we found hematite iron ore in great profusion. Distance traveled 17 miles. Direction southwest.

* * * * *

CAMP No. 16,
July 19—10 a.m.

Commenced raining at 1 a.m., and, as there is every prospect of its continuing all day, we will not move until to-morrow. This will give the animals a much needed rest, and enable, the men to wash their clothes.

9 p.m.—It rained until 4 o'clock—was quite cool during the day; built a fire at the entrance of my tent and read the day through.

* * * * *

CAMP No. 17,
Monday, July 20.

Broke camp at 4:30 a.m., and the train having crossed the river the preceding afternoon, we got off in good shape, though the ground was rather heavy. Pushed up on to a high divide, thence down into a small valley running north and south, though heretofore they have all run east and west. Moved through this valley in a southerly direction, crossing a deep ravine, in which we found some good water and watered our train; thence through a piece of scrub-oak timber, over a succession of small hills covered with grass, and across a deep and rich-wooded ravine, to over a high rolling country, and finally on to a divide, which we followed for some miles, and from which we had an extended view of the adjacent country.

THE SIGHT WAS SUPERB:

we could see away to the north, east, and west, as far as the eye could reach. To the north of us, the Bad Lands, with their quaintly shaped clay and sandstone buttes, skirted by the Belle Fourche River; to the east and west, a succession of hills covered with fine grass, with here and there a valley slightly wooded with pines and oaks; while, to the south, the Black Hills loomed gravely up, shutting out an extended view in that direction. The Hills being our objective point, we left the divide, and, entering a ravine running in an easterly direction, we pushed on for about a mile, and then, turning south, we took up our route through the hills to our present camp on a dry fork of the Belle Fourche, but with plenty of water in its bed. The country passed over today is capable of producing grass and grain in abundance, and we came across wild cherries, black currants, and gooseberries. Distance marched 18½ miles. Direction southwest.

* * * * *

CAMP No. 18,
Tuesday, July 21.

Broke camp at 4:30 a.m., and

shaped our course in a southeasterly direction through a gap in the hills, with the intention of making our way through the mountain range, and, if possible, reaching the park which, rumor says, exists between the two outside ranges of the hills, or, more strictly speaking, the mountains. Following a roundabout road through the hills, and keeping our general direction as we may,—for our guides profess to be entirely ignorant of this part of the country,—Custer pioneers us through some bad ravines, then over a succession of high hills and along some elevated ridges. We find most of the hills covered, to within a few yards of the top, with bunch grass; in the summit of nearly all of them, the sandstone in regular layers crops out stark and bare, with here and there a scraggly pine shooting up out of the crevices. Some of the heads of the ravines we cross are filled with scrub oak and pine.

Crossing a pretty little tributary of

THE REDWATER RIVER, WHOSE COURSE THROUGH THE COUNTRY WE CAN EASILY DISCERN, OWING TO THE TREES WHICH FRINGE ITS BANKS, WE FINALLY ENTER A FINE VALLEY about 8 miles broad by 14 long, containing good grass, and having some good timber among the hills which skirt it. Passing over and descending a very high ridge, we come into our present camp in a dry fork of the Redwater, but with a splendid spring of very cold water running out of the sandstone ledges which crop out along its banks. Fuel is plenty, grass good, and water in abundance; so we put up our tents, and go to ? very well contented with our march without the aid of guides. Passed a number of red sandstone layers on the hills to-day. Some gypsurn (sic) and a little limestone were also found. Little game met with to-day. Direction southwest. Distance traveled 14½ miles.

* * * * *

CAMP No. 19,
Wednesday, July 22.

On Inyan Kara Creek, about 3 miles distant from the mountain of the same name, which is

ONE OF THE HIGHEST PEAKS

in the Black Hills. While at breakfast this morning, about 4 a.m., we heard a shot, and, within five minutes, one of the men of Company M. named Ritter, was brought in a prisoner, having shot and mortally wounded another man named Turner, of the same company. Almost at the same time, Dr. Williams announced the death of Private Cueminham (sic), of H Company, by dysentery. The General ordered his body to be brought to our present camp; and, just as we reached here this evening, Private Turner, who was wounded this morning, died also. They were both buried at sunset this evening.

We left camp at 4:45 a.m.; took a southwest course; moved up on to a high table land of red clay soil, with gypsum cropping out here and there; but notwithstanding the forbidding aspect of the country, the grass was good in both quality and quantity. Two miles from camp we crossed a pretty little streamlet, quite well-wooded; then moved steadily forward over a good grazing country, skirting some pine-covered hills on our left, and making for a pass in the mountains directly in our front, reaching our present camp at 5½ p.m. The march has been quite long, dusty, and very fatiguing. Direction southwest. Distance 21½ miles.

* * * * *

CAMP No. 19,
Thursday, July 23.

Command remained in camp all day, to give the Chief-Engineer an opportunity to

ASCEND INYAN KARA

and take observations. At 5 a.m. Gen. Custer and a party of five, myself included, started for Inyan Kara, and completed the ascent at 12 m. It was a hard task, and, owing to lowering weather and a smoky atmosphere, we did not get as good a view to the east and south as we wished. However, it was a sight well worth seeing, and repaid us for the trouble. The peak is something over 5,000 feet above the level of the sea.

* * * * *

CAMP No. 20,
Friday, July 24.

On a beautiful little stream in an exquisite little valley, which we

call "Floral Valley" from the profusion of wild flowers which completely cover the ground. We left Camp 19 at 5 a.m., and moved due east over hill and dale, passing through a beautiful little glen up a long hill into a burnt piece of pine woods, across them, and down a fearfully-steep hill into a little valley, in which was the dry bed of a little water-course. Thence up this valley, 5 or 6 miles to camp. As we came up stream it began to show signs of water, and pretty soon it was a beautiful, cool, clear stream, which keeps growing larger and larger as we ascend, and the valley keeps growing prettier and prettier, while the neighboring hills are covered with pine and aspen or poplar. Wild flowers abound in every direction, and our horses

WADE KNEE-DEEP
AMONG THEM

there are twenty or twenty-five different varieties, all in full bloom. The grass is good, and vegetation of all sorts luxuriant. We have had a hard days work, but are more than satisfied. Direction is a little south of east. Distanced traveled 11½ miles.

* * * * *

CAMP No. 21,
Saturday, July 25.

Still on or near the headwaters of Floral Valley Creek.

Moved at 4½ a.m. directly up the valley, crossing the creek— which kept growing larger all the time—no less than six times, as it seems to delight in meandering across the valley as often as possible. To-day's march has been the pleasantest I have ever yet made. The whole valley is carpeted with flowers. I have gathered seventeen varieties within 20 square feet. And the view along the valley, as it first widened and then contracted and widened again, with the murmuring waters of the brook constantly at our feet, has been exceedingly pleasant and attractive, and especially so when looking back at some of the hot, dusty days along the Little Missouri Valley and across the Plains. About a mile below our present camp, the stream suddenly stopped flowing, and, upon seeking for the cause, we found that

WE HAD REACHED THE HEAD.

Some six or eight beautiful springs

bubbled up within a radius of 300 feet, forming at once a stream sufficient to turn a mill, but which, 20 miles farther down, entirely disappeared by sinking into the sandy soil. Half a mile farther up we came to another spring, upon which we are now encamped. Wood and water are in abundance, but the vast quantity of flowers crowds out the grasses, and the grazing is only fair. We have traveled almost south to-day and made about 12 miles.

* * * * *

CAMP No. 22,
Sunday, July 24.

Broke camp at 4:45 a.m. Traveled up Floral Valley to the top of the range where it begins, passing through some of the most

EXQUISITE SITE OF
PARK-LIKE SCENERY

I have ever seen,—little open glades, with clumps of pine, evergreen, and aspen, on the low hills into which they ran, being constantly in sight. As we approached the head of the valley, the Hills grew smaller and smaller, until they would not average more than 50 feet in height. Upon leaving the crest of the watershed down which ran the creek we had last encamped upon, we found an old Indian trail, which we followed up through a rocky defile, which, after various windings, brought us into another valley, somewhat larger than the one we had just left, with a fine stream of water running in just the direction we wished, viz.; southeast, and in directly the opposite direction from the stream we had just left. Thus we followed down to our present camp, which is a very beautiful one, with good water and splendid grass in abundance. Throughout this valley, as far as we have come, there are any quantity of springs, and we begin to find quartz mixed with sandstone. Just after getting into camp, our Indian scouts, whom we had sent on in advance, having met with signs of Indians, came hurrying back with the information that there was a

SMALL VILLAGE OF
SIOUX INDIANS

encamped about 3½ miles on the stream below us. Taking the scouts and about 50 men with him, Gen. Custer moved quietly down upon them, and giving strict orders that they should not be harmed unless they showed fight, sent forward a white flag by one of the interpreters, and, following it almost instantly, succeeded in getting into their camp almost before they knew of our approach. The women and children were very much frightened at our Ree scouts, as the two nations are always at war; but they were soon reassured, and satisfied we did not intend to harm them. With a single exception, all of their men were out hunting, and he, "Slow-Bull," a fine-looking and plucky savage, made the best of the situation. The hunters were called in, and finally One-Stab, the Chief, came also. After a long talk, they agreed to come up to our camp and stay with us, showing us the country, in return for certain supplies which Gen. Custer offered them. We then left them, and, later in the day, One-Stab and three of his warriors came up after coffee and sugar. Two of the warriors soon made an excuse to go back and One-Stab and a young warrior awaited the arrival of the train with the supplies. Suspecting from their action that they might be

PLAYING A DOUBLE GAME,
Gen. Custer ordered some of the Indian scouts to go with them to their camp, and stay there as a sort of guard until they came up the next day, also charging them not to let One-Stab and his warrior out of their sight until they reached the Indian camp. While they were going quietly along, and within sight of our camp, the young Sioux suddenly attempted to wrest the gun of one of the scouts from him. In the struggle the gun was discharged, wounding either the Sioux or his horse, and One-Stab and his young man made off at full speed, followed by the guard. One-Stab was recaptured and brought back, but the young warrior escaped, and, when our scouts reached the village, that too had departed, and, night having fallen, it was impossible to pursue and overtake them. The whole party consisted of five lodges, six warriors, and twenty-one women and children. Distance marched to-day 14 miles.

* * * * *

CAMP No. 22,
Monday, July 27.

In camp all day. Four exploring parties out surveying and mapping the country. Miners with the party report

INDICATIONS OF SILVER
in quartz rock along the banks of the creek.

* * * * *

CAMP No. 23,
Tuesday, July 28.

Broke camp at 4:45 a.m. Moved over a low hill, through a small pine-wood, nearly due east, but on to a high, rolling prairie, surrounded in every direction by high hills densely covered by pine-woods. This opening was about 6 miles square, and, upon getting to the eastern edge of it, we were unable to find an available pass for our train, and so had to partially retrace our steps towards the valley we had just left, coming out again on Castle Creek about 4 miles lower down than our last camp was located, encamping a little below where the Indian villages had been, and upon a little stream emptying into Castle Creek from the south. Distance traveled, 10 or 12 miles.

* * * * *

CAMP No. 24,
Wednesday, July 29.

Broke camp at 4:45 a.m. Moving on

AN OLD INDIAN TRAIL
up the valley through which ran the little tributary to Castle Creek, upon which we encamped last night,—the general direction being a little east of south. This little valley opened out to quite a respectable size soon after leaving camp, and we moved up it about 6 miles, when it gradually ran into small hills, sparsely covered with pine, which we crossed, into, a high rolling prairie, covered with fine grass, similar to the one which we attempted to cross yesterday. Adhering to the Indian trait, it led us along over the prairie, through a small valley, across a wooded crest, and then up hill and down dale over one very fine stream of water, until we finally encamped 14½ miles beyond our former camp in a southerly direction. Owing to the number of springs along the route, it was slow work for the train to follow, especially as the pioneers had to

build several bridges. The result was, that all the train was not in at 4 a.m., when reveille sounded. Taken all is all, the country passed through to-day,

WAS VERY FINE,
offering many inducements to stock-raisers.

* * * * *

CAMP No. 25,
Thursday, July 30.

Broke camp at 7 a.m. Moved up the valley to a southwest direction, still following the Indian trail, which led us through the valley by a fine road, out into an open, park-like country, very beautiful, with vales and natural avenues in every directions, running between low hills covered with a fine growth of good pine, and with numbers of good springs in all directions. Grass most abundant and of good quality. Passed near the base of a range of mountains, which hid Harney's Peak from our view. Encamped about 3 p.m. in a fine open country, among a lot of low, wooded hills, with vales opening in all directions, on the bank of a still creek, with plenty of good water in holes, but it is not running water at this season of the year. Distance marched —.

* * * * *

CAMP No. 25,
Friday, July 31.

Command generally remained in camp all day. Four engineering parties went out in various directions to map the country. I accompanied Gen. Custer, Col. Ludlow, of the Engineers, and three other gentlemen in an

EXPEDITION TO
HARNEY'S PEAK,
crossing one range of mountains, we climbed the highest peak in site only to discover one still higher, upon climbing which we discovered somewhat to our surprise the veritable Harney's Peak nine miles away, towering up some 600 feet higher than the one we were then upon. Pushing forward we completed the ascents about 4:30 p.m. It was a hard climb but the view amply repaid us for one (sic) trouble. It was by all means the grandest I had ever seen and so said my companions in their own behalf. To the east were the almost impen ? mountains known as the Black Hills,—rugged, rocky, jag-

ged peaks of solid granite, with here and there a vein of glistening quartz, covered in many instances, almost to their summits, with a dense growth of pine, with now and then an aspen, whose lighter green looked all the brighter by contrast, and forming a solid barrier between us and the great plains, which, like a dead sea, stretched away to the east as far as the eye could reach. By the aid of a glass we could trace the course of the South Fork of the Cheyenne and the White River,—the trees along their banks marking their course as distinctly as if we saw the water. Far to the west we could trace a range of mountains, which we thought must be the Big Horn, and we could also overlook some of the open country we had just traveled over; while in the north and east, between 60 and 80 miles distant,

CROW CREEK AND BEAR BUTTE

loomed up like giant sentinels. On the north we could also see open country of the same character as that we have just passed over, which we intend taking on our way to Crow Peak, which will be our next objective point. After locating the peak and taking its altitude, we drank the health of Col. Harney out of our canteen of cold coffee,—all the fluid we had,—though our wishes for big long life were none the less hearty, and began the descent. Picking up our escort about half-way down, we started for camp, which we reached, after various mishaps, at 1 o'clock in the morning, a thoroughly tired out well-satisfied party.

* * * * *

CAMP No. 26,
Saturday, Aug. 1.

Moved 3½ miles down stream for fresh grass. Have a beautiful camp, with abundance of grass, just opposite three beautiful mountains, covered to their summits with pines. Remained in camp writing letters. Engineer mapping parties out in all directions. Rained very hard from 4 to 7 p.m.

* * * * *

CAMP No. 26,
Sunday, Aug. 2.

Mail leaves to-morrow. Have been writing all day. Two com-

panies have gone eastward towards the South Fork of the Cheyenne. Will return to-morrow night. Gen. Custer, with five companies, starts southward to-morrow for the

SOUTH FORK OF THE CHEYENNE,

to be gone three days. Col. Grant and myself accompany him. We are exploring the passes thoroughly, and will know something of the Black Hills when we return.

CHICAGO TRIBUNE
Issue of August 27, 1874

DIARY OF MAJ. GEO. A. FORSYTH (CONTINUED)

MONDAY, Aug. 3, 1874.

Leaving the main portion of the command in camp, Gen. Custer, with five companies of cavalry, the Chief Engineer of the expedition (Col. William Ludlow), the writer, and others, started at 5 a.m. for the South Fork of Cheyenne River. His object was the exploration of the country in that direction, and to give the scout, Reynolds, who was to carry dispatches to Fort Laramie, a good send-off, by putting him 50 miles nearer his destination and outside of the Black Hills.

Moving south over the hill and dale, through a beautiful grazing country, this whole region is

WONDERFULLY ADAPTED TO RAISING CATTLE AND SHEEP,—

we finally struck an old Indian trail, which we followed for 14 or 15 miles, until it finally led us through a pass out into the outlying hills beyond the main range of the Black Hills country. Pushwell out into these, we halted for a couple of hours to rest, and enjoy a thunderstorm, mixed with hail,—for the day was very warm, and the storm cooled the air perfectly.

Entering a deep ravine, we followed the course of a mountain-stream, which is not designated upon the maps, but which lies between Hat Creek and Horseherd Creek, and finally empties into the South Fork of the Cheyenne. Pushing on through brake and brier, we finally encamped near its mouth at 10½ p.m., having made 47 miles since morning.

The last dispatches were writ-

ten by the light of our campfires, and Reynolds started on his way, with our best wishes, a little after midnight, and if no evil befell him, probably reached Laramie within thirty-six hours.

* * * * *

TUESDAY, Aug. 4

Moved down 1½ miles, to the South Fork of the Cheyenne, at 5 a.m. Found it a good stream of clear, running water, over a pebbly or gravelly bottom. Water running slowly, and, from indications shown, I am inclined to think that, in some places,

IT SINKS IN ITS BED,

AND RISES AGAIN LOWER DOWN, SOMETHING LIKE THE SMOKY HILL RIVER in Kansas. Where we saw it, the banks were quite heavily fringed with cottonwood.

Left the river, and started up over the plains and foot-hills for our camp. Traveled northwest over a poor country until we reached the hills. Water was very scarce, and the day exceedingly hot. Had to abandon two horses, which gave completely out. Went into camp on a dry fork of the Cheyenne; found some good water in holes, though it was covered by a thick green scum. Grass good; wood in abundance. Distance traveled, 21 miles.

* * * * *

WEDNESDAY, Aug. 5.

Reached Camp No. 26 at 12 m., traveling 21 miles northwest over a very pretty country of hill and dale, crossing several very little creeks fed by springs gushing out of the hills.

Found all well at camp, but was a little disappointed to learn that the squadron sent out to the South Fork of the Cheyenne had returned without accomplishing its object, —the commanding officer giving as a reason that they had consumed nearly all their time in trying to find their way through a deep ravine, following a watercourse which they thought emptied into the river.

* * * * *

CAMP No. 27
Thursday, Aug. 6.

Started on our return trip, via Bear Butte, Crow Creek, and the Little Missouri, at 4:30 a.m. Moved back on our old trail, passing Camp

No. 25; thence moved away from the trail westward over some large hills, and finally encamped on a tributary of Castle Creek, where we found good wood and grass. During the night a very hard thunderstorm occurred. Distance 23½ miles northwest.

* * * * *

CAMP No. 28,
Friday, Aug. 7.

Started at 4:30 a.m. back on former trail passing Camp No. 24 in Castle Creek, and moved up and across Elkhorn Prairie, in a northerly direction, into a small valley with a beautiful stream of water through it, up a long ravine, over some pine-covered hills, down into another ravine, crossing another creek, and along the bank of this creek 6 miles west, and thence north over a high ridge, and into camp on a good stream, with grass and wood in abundance.

Just as he was selecting the camp, Gen. Custer started up

A LARGE ? BEAR

which, with the assistance of Col. Ludlow and Bloody Knife (a Sioux scout) he soon killed. It took five shots to bring him down; his weight was about 800 pounds. Distance made to-day, 16½ miles.

* * * * *

CAMP No. 29,
Saturday, Aug. 8.

Got off at 4:30 a.m. moving along the banks of the stream upon which we had camped, and moved away east of it, up a ravine, out on to a high rolling country, through an Immense extent of deadening—a place where the trees have been probably burned, and have then fallen or been blown down, crossing one another in every direction, with corpses of young populars here and there, sparsely covering the slate or sandstone which crops out in vertical ledges at the crest of the hills. The morning was so foggy that we halted a couple of hours until the sun dissipated it and enabled us to look out our course. Moved east into a small valley in which was a running stream, which we skirted for some miles; thence directly north up the hill into another deadening, across some stony, pine-covered hills, over another creek, and through some pine woods, into a small valley—making camp at

9:30 p.m. after one of the hardest day's marches we have yet made in the Black Hills. Distance 14¾ miles northeast.

* * * * *

CAMP No. 30,
Sunday, Aug. 9.

Moved at 4:45 due east along the bank of the creek upon which we had been encamped, passing three of the

LARGEST BEAVER-DAMS

I have ever seen; thence north, and again east, encamping upon a beautiful stream fed by an immense spring of the coldest water, save ice-water, I ever drank. Distance 7½ miles east.

* * * * *

CAMP No. 31,
Monday, Aug. 10.

We are now engaged in finding a practicable route through the outlying mountains to the plains, and thence to Bear Butte. Have explored two valleys, but cannot find a good wagon-road. Will try another route to-day. Upon leaving camp at 4:30 a.m., we moved due south over a small hill into a fine valley, about half a mile wide, with a splendid stream of water running through it, and covered with the finest kind of grass. Moved down this valley 7 miles along the creek, and went into camp at 12 p.m., where we intend remaining until the 12th inst., to give the engineers an opportunity to accurately determine the position of the principal peaks of these mountains, and to refit the command preparatory to our march to the Little Missouri River.

General Custer and myself made a careful exploitation for 12 or 15 miles down the creek, and found a

GOOD WAGON-ROAD
TO THE PLAINS.

* * * * *

TUESDAY, Aug. 11.

In camp all day, refitting. Sent forward two companies of pioneers to put the road in order for tomorrow's march. Day clear and beautiful; weather perfect.

* * * * *

CAMP No. 32,
Wednesday, Aug. 12.

We have finally concluded that the stream upon which we have

been encamped for the last three days is

THE BOX ELDER,

although it runs in a more southerly direction, and beads (sic) higher than it is shown to do on the map. Moving down the bank of the stream, crossing it now and then as it cuts into the bank on either side, we finally encamped 6 miles below our morning's resting place. We find an agreeable change in the foliage along the creek,—elm taking the place of pine, and any any quantity of hop-vines, in full bearing, running all over them. Just as we were unsaddling, a fine buck ran through camp, and no one dare shoot him for fear of hitting some of the men or horses. His ? proved his safety, and after our chagrin had subsided, we really enjoyed his feat. All along the route, since we have been in the Black Hills, we have found and killed deer in abundance; also a few elk, and one grizzly bear.

* * * * *

CAMP No. 33,
Thursday, Aug. 12.

Started at 2 p.m., and crossing the Box Elder moved east up the dry bed of a creek, which has forced its way through the limestone bluffs that just here loom up along the east bank of the stream in a solid wall, and pushed upon to an open prairie, or pass, about 100 feet above the creek, and moving south along the bank, encamped just below where the Box Elder sinks in its bed and disappears entirely, though we followed the dry bed down stream for several miles. Capt. Raynolds, in his report of the country adjacent to the Black Hills, mentions this as a curious fact, stating that nearly all of the large streams running out of the hills,

SINK AND DISAPPEAR
ENTIRELY

before finally emptying into the Belle Fourche and South Fork of the Cheyenne.

Just as we reached camp tonight, one of the men of Company H. James King, died of typhoid fever. He will be buried in the morning.

* * * * *

CAMP No. 34,
Tuesday, Aug. 14.

Started at 4 a.m., and moved directly east, across the outer range of mountains, finding a good road up on to their crest; thence across a very pretty, park-like country, and down a long divide, into a valley hemmed in by a few outlying hills of the range. Moved north for about 6 miles, finding some beautiful springs, and thence east across the foot-hills out on to the plains near the base of

BEAR BUTTE,

where we now are. We all leave the Black Hills with regret, for we have enjoyed them very much. The scenery is beautiful, grass splendid, water fine, and climate delightful. I hope to see the day when there will be any number of brave settlers and fine farms there.

Distance marched, 25¾ miles.

*   *   *   *   *

CAMP NEAR BEAR BUTTE,
Saturday, Aug. 15.

Went up the Butte this forenoon. Compared with the hills in the range, it is a pigmy, being only 1,140 feet above the level of the plains; but, standing alone as it does, it looms up quite grandly, especially when first seen by parties approaching the hills on this side.

To-morrow we start for Fort Lincoln, via the Little Missouri River, and hope to reach that post on the 31 inst., always providing Mr. Sitting-Bull don't interfere with our train.

Ludlow's Report

National Archives

Capt. William Ludlow

(Authors' Note: Capt. William Ludlow of the Corps of Engineers was the Chief Engineer of the Department of Dakota and had the responsibility of mapping the terrain covered by the expedition. His report was published in THE NEW YORK TRIBUNE and appears below.)

NEW YORK TRIBUNE
Issue of September 14, 1874

CHIEF ENGINEER'S
PRELIMINARY REPORT.

The Route Selected in going and Returning—Character of the Survey—Attractive Characteristics of the Black Hills Region.

To the Assistant Adjutant
General Commanding
Department of Dakota.

Sir: The expedition was organized for the purpose of exploring the unknown territory lying principally in the western and southwestern portion of Dakota and the eastern portion of Wyoming, with the view of discovering practicable interior military routes between Fort Lincoln in the Department of Dakota and opposite the terminus of the Union Pacific Railroad and Fort Laramie in the Department of the Platte, with that railroad for its base. In case circumstances should require the establishment of military posts in the region referred to, more knowledge of its resources than we possessed would also be required to guide in the selection of suitable sites.

I was directed by the department commander to accompany the expedition and act as engineer officer. Unable to obtain funds which would be available for the payment of salaries, I nevertheless secured the valuable service of Prof. N. H. Winchell of Minneapolis to act as geologist for the expedition, and of Mr. G. B. Grinnell, representing Prof. Marsh of Yale College, who kindly agreed to report upon the palaentology and zoology of the region traversed. Prof. Winchell would also make such report as his time afforded, upon the botany of the Hills, and Dr. Williams, Assistant Surgeon U.S.A. and chief medical officer of the expedition, promised to aid in the same department. A photographer was fitted out with apparatus and chemicals, and a spring wagon, constructed for similar use on the Yellowstone Expedition of 1873. In the surveying I had a detachment of engineer soldiers, consisting of two sergeants and four men, who were to keep two sets of notes of the route with prismatic compass and odometers while my assistant, Mr. W. H. Wood, and myself, would attend to the general topography and the astronomical observation for latitude and longitude.

The expedition left Fort Lincoln on July 2, and consisted of ten companies of the 7th Cavalry, one company of the 20th Infantry, and of the 17th Infantry, with a battery of three Gatlings and one three-inch Rodman gun, and a detachment of Indian scouts, guides, &c. The train consisted of over one hundred wagons. We were assured by the guides of two things in advance, first, that the expedition would be strenuously opposed by a hostile force of Indians, and secondly, that we could never penetrate the fastnezens (sic) of the Black Hills. They represented the difficulties in our way as being formidable for cavalry, and for wagons insuperable. Both predictions failed. The expedition returned to Fort Lincoln on Aug. 30, the sixtieth day out, with a loss of only four men, three from sickness, and one killed in a quarrel; having seen no hostile Indians during the whole trip of nearly 1,000 miles, and having explored the Black Hills from east to west, and from north to south.

The route pursued led us up the south side of Heart River, thence in a W. S. W. direction across the Cannonball, and up the north fork of the Grand River; thence southwesterly to a point which we named Prospect Valley, in about Lat. 45 deg. 30', and Long. 103 deg. 40'; thence up the east side of the Little Missouri River, and southerly to the north fork of the Cheyenne River, Belle Fourche. This point we reached on July 18, in about Long 104°, after 16 marches and 300 miles of travel. Hitherto the country had much resembled other portions of Dakota —an open prairie; wood scarce, and only found in the river valleys; water not always to be met in sufficient quantity, and frequently impregnated with salis, making it both disagreeable and injurious; but still a fair amount of grass and no serious difficulties presented to the traveler. All the country bordering on Heart River is good, that on Cannonball is fair; Grand River country is poor, as well as that near the headwaters of the Moreau or Owl River.

All the streams flow eastward, and head close up to the Little Missouri, which running northward at right angles to the others, has but a narrow and barren belt tributary to it on the east side. Its main support is from its branches bending in the Powder River range of hills. Our route led us in view of Slim Butte (which is rather a high steep cetaen than a butte), of Slave and Bear Buttes, and many others not hitherto located. The Black Hills, as we approached them looked very high and dark under their envelope of pine timber.

We crossed the Belle Fourche on July 22, and found ourselves in a new country. The whole character of our surroundings was changed. There was an abundance of grass, timber, small fruits, and flowers, and what perhaps was better appreciated than all, an ample supply of pure, cold water. These advantages, with a few exceptions, we enjoyed until we left the Hills for the return journey. Our course lay up the valley of the Redwater—a large branch of the Belle Fourche—to Inyan Kara, thence easterly and south-easterly into the heart of the hills. Valley leads into valley to the beautiful park country, always until now marked "unexplored" on the maps, of which we had heard so much, but hardly hoped to reach without wagons.

After arriving near Harney's Peak—a lofty granite mass with an altitude of over 8,000 feet above the sea, and surrounded with craggy peaks and pinnacles—a rapid reconnoissance was made to the south fork of the Cheyenne, nearly due south of us, with five companies of cavalry, and the exit from the interior was ascertained to be not difficult on that side.

Returning, the course lay northerly and north-easterly, looking for an exit near Bear Butte. Failing to find an easy one, we went southerly a short distance and discovered a pass near Elk Creek which led us out on the prairie. The change to the hot dry air and yellow grass of the prairie was wonderfully sudden and anything but pleasant. From Bear Butte the return journey led back past Slave Butte, touching the head waters of the Moreau, crossing the down trail in Prospect Valley, thence tapping the head of Grand River and following roughly the eastside of the Little Missouri northward and eastward to where the trail of the Yellowstone expedition crosses it, and thence into Lincoln, on the north side of Heart River. The return route was a much better one for a large force than the other. We had no difficulty in finding good camps, with plenty of water and grass. The country passed over, tributary to the Moreau, is barren, but the river valley itself is more favorable, and at the head of Grand River is much better country than lower down. From Grand River to above Heart River the grass had been thoroughly burned by the Indians. It caused some inconvenience, but we were always fortunate in finding a camp or some localities which the fire had spared.

With regard to the geology of the Black Hills, Prof. Winchell's report will be nearly exhaustive. Both Mr. Grinnell and he were as industrious as possible in collecting information, and I can only regret that the want of time prevented much opportunity for study. I call attention to the preliminary reports from both gentlemen presented herewith. Their detailed reports will be prepared as soon as possible, as well as one from Dr. Williams on the Flora of the Hills. It is a region admirably adapted to settlement, abounding in timber, in grass and flowing streams, with springs of pure cold water almost everywhere. The valleys of South Slope are ready for the plow; the soil of wonderful fertility, as evidence by the luxuriance of the grass and the profusion of flowers and small fruits; the climate entirely different from that of the Plains, giving evidence of being much more agreeable—cooler in Summer and more moderate in Winter—not subject to drouth, for the nightly dews are very heavy; not liable to excessive snow-fall, for in narrow valleys containing a large creek no indications of overflow could be detected.

The creeks confine their favor to the Hills. Upon reaching the exterior range they pass through rocky canons, sometimes of great depth, and arriving at the outer foothills sink into the ground and disappear.

Upon the mineral resources of the Hills Prof. Winchell's report will throw full light. No coal was found. Extensive deposits of iron ore of good quality exist. Immense beds of gypsum were met with. Specimens of gold were washed from the soil in the vicinity of Harney's Peak, and quartz in bed and bewider was visible in large quantities. A specimen of something which they discovered, believed to be silver, but which more resembled platinum, was shown. Plumbago was also found in small quantities. Any amount of excellent building-stone, limestones, sandstone, and granite are present. Some of the limestone, particularly in the vicinity of Inyan Kara, were fine enough for marbles and handsomely colored. The timber is mainly red pine and spruce of large size. Oak, ash, and elm are found on the exterior slopes. Game is abundant; bear, elk, and deer of two kinds were found and many killed. On the prairies antelopes were found in large numbers.

The complete report, accompanied by the reports of Prof. Winchell, Mr. Grinnell, and Dr. Williams, will be transmitted at the earliest possible day, together with a map showing the route pursued, with bordering country, from Fort Lincoln and return, and a special map on a larger scale of the Black Hills proper.

The photographer secured negatives for about sixty views, a set of which will accompany the report.

Respectfully submitted.
Wm. Ludlow
Captain of Engineers, U.S.A.,
Chief Engineer Department,
Dakota.

Winchell's Report

University of Minnesota

N. H. Winchell

(Author's Note: Professor N. H. Winchell accompanied the expedition as a geologist. His official report appeared in the NEW YORK TRIBUNE and is reprinted below).

NEW YORK TRIBUNE
Issue of September 14, 1874

CHIEF GEOLOGIST'S PRELIMINARY REPORT

Prof. Winchell's Opinion as to the Mineral Products of the Black Hills—He Thinks The Gold Discoveries Should be Taken with Many Grains of Allowance.

Col. William Ludlow,
St. Paul, Minn.

DEAR SIR: In accordance with your request I herewith give you a brief statement of the work done by me in the late exploration of the Black Hills by Gen. G. A. Custer, indicating at the same time some of the most important geological results that are likely to come from the reconnoissances. It is plain to see that in the absence of the specimens collected, none of which have yet arrived at Minneapolis, this report is based on field notes and impressions received in the field, and lacks that authentication that is desirable only from a careful study of the fossils.

In passing over the plains from Fort A. Lincoln on the Missouri River and the Black Hills, there was little opportunity to fix certainly the western limit of the Cretaceous, or to determine the area of the Tertiary. A few fossils were gathered near the Little Missouri River, and careful notes of exposed section of rock were taken at all accessible points. At a number of points beds of lignite were seen, and they will be indicated on the geological map, intended to accompany the final report. In crossing the plains the expedition traversed a district that had never been visited and reported on by any geologist. Dr. F. V. Hayden in a final report on the geology of Nebraska has however published a geological map showing the presumed areas of the Tertiary and Cretaceous in that portion of Dakota. Without intending here to deny the correctness of that map, I may state that the impression received from lithological evidence would reduce very much the area of the Tertiary, and increase relatively that of the Cretaceous. The Cretaceous area that Dr. Hayden represents along the valley of the Missouri River at Fort A. Lincoln, seems to extend much further west than has been supposed. Very important beds of lignite occur in it on both sides of the river in the vicinity of Fort A. Lincoln, and they seem not to be restricted to the Dakota group. On this question the fossils collected may throw some light when they shall have been examined. They have been submitted to Prof. Marah of New-Haven, Conn.

In entering the region of the Black Hills proper the evidences of disturbance began to appear on the plains about 20 miles before reaching the Belle Fourche, along our line of march. The shales and clays here begin to show a changeable dip and are more or less slaty, and deepened in color to a dark purple or black. A considerable clay ironstone is scattered over the surface, weathered from beds, and by drainage and erosion the rock, which is easily disintegrated, is wrought into a series of ravines and low bluffs. This aspect is most marked at our first crossing of the Belle Fourche, where the Fort Pierre group forms an exposed thickness of slate and slaty shale

of between 300 and 400 feet. From the Belle Fourche the formations passed over in entering the Hills came in the following order:

Feet.
1. Purplish or black slate, Pierre _____300-400
2. Sandstone, Dakota about _ 500
3. Green shale, Dakota ____ 45
4. Fossiliferous conglomerate 2
5. Purplish shale, toward the top _____ 10
6. Snow gypsum _____ 4-6
7. Red shale, massive or laminated _____ 75
8. Snow gypsum _____ 22
9. The same as No. 7 _____ 18
10. Snowy gypsum _____ 2½
11. The same as No. 7 _____ 30
12. Snowy gypsum _____ 2½
13. The same as No. 7 and slope _____ 35
14. Fine-grained limestone on which the last lies unconformably. This is known as the Carboniferous limestone, about ____ 100
15. Harsh, arenaceous magnesium, about _____ 75
16. White massive sandstone, about _____ 75
17. An immense limestone formation stretching over a large area in the northern portion of the Hills, capping hundreds of buttes and bluffs. This is a light-colored, often saccharoidal, variable limestone. It is hard and usually a compact texture. _____ 225
18. Hard red limestone with small, rounded quartz pebbles _____ 25
20. Red sandstone with glauconitic particles, perhaps 25 feet, seen only _____ 10
21. Conglomeretic sandstone, white _____ 30-40
22. Metamorphic schists and slate _____ —
23. White feldspathic coarse granite _____ —

Sections were observed in the southern portion of the Black Hills in which a reddish quartzite was conspicuous, immediately overly-the metamorphic slates, and forming the surface rock over the tops of a great many hills. In some places also a shaly sandstone is associated with No. 19 and 20, and contains obelilla and lingula.

In respect to the economical products of the rocks of the Black Hills, the following minerals exist in considerable quantities, and will ultimately be found very useful: Gypsum in unlimited quantities; variegated marble from the carboniferous limestone; iron ore in the south-eastern portion of the Hills; muscovite, talcose slate, useful for whetstones. There may be found also other products of the granite rocks; indeed, the miners that accompanied the expedition report the finding of gold and silver in some of the gulches in the south-eastern portion of the Hills, though I saw none of the gold nor did I see any auriferous quartz. I have taken the gold reports with a large grain of allowance.

The granite center of the Black Hills is in the southern and south-eastern portions. The whole of the region was explored as to determine the general geological structure, excepting a range of hills in the south-western part, the composition of which is presumed to be of the sedimentary rocks above the Potsdam. The hills die out toward the south much more rapidly than toward the north. The most practicable routes for entering the hills are from the north. A large part of the hills, especially in the north, are composed of slightly tiled sedimentary rocks, cut by erosion into bluffs, buttes, and ridges, separated by valleys that generally are well watered, often grassed and arable. The hills have a delightful climate, pure water, abundance of pine timber, and a sufficient quantity of arable land to sustain a thick population. Very respectfully submitted,

N. H. Winchell.
University of Minnesota,
Minneapolis,
Sept. 8, 1874

Grinnell's Report

National Park Service

George Bird Grinnell

(Author's Note: George Bird Grinnell accompanied the expedition as a paleontologist. His report appeared in THE NEW YORK TRIBUNE, and is printed below).

NEW YORK TRIBUNE
Issue of September 14, 1874

PRELIMINARY NOTICE
OF THE ZOOLOGY.

Game Abundant—One hundred deer killed in a Day—Elk, Bears, and Beavers—Ducks, Geese, and Grouse—A Region Attractive to Sportsmen.

Col. Wm. Ludlow,
Chief Eng. Dept. Dakota.

SIR: In accordance with your request made to me while at Fort Lincoln, viz.: that I should make such notes on the zoology of the region as I could, in connection with my other duties, I have to report that although my opportunities for zoological observation and collection were very limited, owing to the rapidity of our travel and the necessity of devoting all my time to the collection of fossils, I observed nearly 30 species of mammals, about 120 species of birds, and a few reptiles. A full ennumeration of the animals observed, together with such observations as I was enabled to make upon their habits, will appear in a detailed report, which I shall have the honor to make to you as soon as practicable.

As a game region the Black Hills will compare favorably with any locality in the country. Deer of two species are most abundant, the white-tailed deer especially being so numerous about the head-waters of Elk Creek that 100 were killed by the command in a single day. Elk, from indications, are numerous, although only a few were killed. Several bears were secured, and not a few exciting incidents occurred during their capture. No mountain sheep were obtained, although there were many indications of their presence and a single female was seen. Almost all the streams which we passed were dammed in many places by beaver and fresh tracks and signs were very plenty.

Game birds are well represented by several species of geese and ducks which are to be found along the various water-courses in and about the Hills, and by at least two species of grouse, the sharp-tailed and the ruffed. The former are numerous along the open valleys and in the sparsely wooded hillsides, and the latter among the dense pines of the higher land. Altogether, the Black Hills offer to the sportsman an abundance and variety of game, and if opened to the white man will be as much esteemed as a hunting ground by him as they now are by the Indian.

The fuller details which I shall present later will, I trust, be found interesting to the zoologist as presenting information on the fauna of a region of which so little has been told. Yours respectfully,

Geo. Bird Grinnell

PRELIMINARY REPORT
ON FOSSILS

Few Fossils Remains found—
Little opportunity for
investigation—The fossils
principally of
Vertebrate Types

Col. Wm. Ludlow,
Chief Engineer
Department Dakota.

SIR: The rapidity with which Gen. Custer's command traveled the long marches and brief halts, procluded any but a very hasty and incomplete exploration of the country passed through—No small camping ground would accomodate so large a force as the one in question, and, as might readily be supposed, the country best adapted for the discovery of fossil remains is that least fitted for camping purposes, on account of the lack of wood, water, and grass. Thus the very days on which the greatest degree of probability fossils might be expected were usually those on which the longest marches were made. Of course under such circumstances it was necessary to pass by many large areas of washed bluffs without even a cursory survey, and this was especially the case on the 14th of July, on which the day the first vertebrate remains were discovered. Enough, however, was seen to assure me that the localities traveled were by no means rich in fossils and that but limited collections could have been made even had I had more time to devote to their examination.

In the present brief notice I propose merely to touch upon the discoveries made reserving all scientific details for a future report, to be made as soon as the few specimens collected can be identified and their geological horizon determined with accuracy. This, is is (sic) hoped, may be accomplished in a few weeks.

Starting from Fort Lincoln July 2, and passing over a rolling prairie for about 20 miles, the first fossils were found July 8 near the summit of a small butte and just beneath the layer of triable, brown sandstone with which all the surrounding buttes are covered. These consisted mainly of a few cretaceous shallis, bivalves, gasteroped, and a cephaloped, all much weathered and so fragile as almost to crumble while being picked up. From this point until we left Ludlow's Cave, July 12, no "bad lands" were seen, but on the 13th several washes were visited and thoroughly explored, but all proved barren of fossils. On the 14th the country became much more rugged and barren. High bluffs and mounds of blue clay without vegetation were numerous, so much so that we were unable to visit all of them. At Castle Butte we found the first tertiary remains of the trip—a few turtle bones much worn by the weather and a single leg bone of a mammal of mammoth size, the latter so much cracked and shattered by pressure that I was unable to transport it to camp. On some very extensive bad lands at the northwest point of Short Pine Buttes, two large vertabrae were discovered, together with a few chalonian bones, and here I think was the most promising locality that we visited during the trip. But the time to examine them was wanting, and we were obliged to leave them without a proper exploration. While in the Black Hills a few palaeozoic fossils, chiefly brachlopods of various kinds, were found, which will be enumerated in a future report. Nothing however of general interest was observed until Aug. 17, when a few concretionary fossils were found in the black shale north-west of Slave Buttes. These were cretaceous bivalves and cephalopods, and the limestone concretious in which they were found lay in position in the shale. It is much to be regretted that the time allowed for investigation in this branch of natural science was so short, and it is earnestly hoped that another year a more thorough and careful exploration of this region may be made, and more interesting results obtained. In concluding this brief review I must heartily thank Gen. Custer and Col. Ludlow for their constant willingness to assist me in every way possible consistently with the best interests of the expedition.

Your obedient servant,

Geo. Bird Grinnell.

Zahn's Diary

(Authors' Note: One of the enlisted men on the expedition, William Zahn, kept a cryptic journal).

Scrap Book of Wm. Zahn
Black Hills Expedition[1]

June the 8, 1874
Monday — Started out from Grand River in route for Fort Rice. Marched 25 miles and encamped at the holes. Camp No. 1.

June 9, 1874
Struck tents early this morning and started on, marched 21 miles into Standing Rock, arrived there at eleven o'clock a.m. and laid over till two o'clock p.m. Started out and marched 5 miles to Battle Crick and Encamped There for the night Distance Traveled to Day 26 miles Camp No 2.

June 10, 1874
Broke Camp at half Past Five a.m. Started out for Fort Rice and a heavy rain all Day very Hard marching got into Rice at Three O'Clock P.M. marched 33 miles Campt Near fort Rice Camp No. 3

June 11, 1874
Thursday Laid over at Fort Rice. Pleasant to Day Camp No 3.

June 12, 1874
Laid over at Fort Rice Camp No 3.

June 13, 1874
Laid over at fort Rice. This Evening Prepare to Start for Fort Lincoln. Camp No 3.

June the 14, 1874
Broke Camp Early This morning and started for L. T. greens Camp arived there at Eleven O'clock A.M. Distance 19 miles Camp No 4.

June 15, 1874
Laid over all Day at Greens Camp

June 16, 1874
Laid over at greens Camp. Camp no. 4.

June 17, 1874
Laid over at greens Camp and got a Pass to go to Bismarck Camp no 4

June 18, 1874
Returned to Camp this morning Started for Fort A. Lincoln Marched to Lincoln Distance 5 miles Camp No. 5.

June 19, 1874
Laid over at Fort Lincoln till the 2nd of July then started on the expedition

July 2nd, 1874
Started out this morning in Rout for the Black Hills Marched 14 miles and camped Camp No. 1

July 3, 1874
Marched 22 miles and Made a Dry Camp no wood Camp No. 2

July 4, 1874
Marched 18 miles and Encamped on Alkali Creek Camp No. 3

July 5, 1874
Sunday Marched 17 miles and Camped on Bear Creek Plenty wood and water Camp No. 4

July 6, 1874
Marched 15 miles and camped on Cannon Ball Creek Plenty wood an water Camp No. 5

July the 7, 1874
Marched 31 miles and made a Bear Camp Hardly no wood and water Camp No. 6

July 8, 1874
Marched 21 miles good water no wood Camp No. 7

July 9, 1874
Marched 20 miles Encamped on Grand River Plenty of water But Poor wood Camp No. 8

July 10, 1874
Marched 22 miles and incamped on Grand River Camp No. 9

July 11, 1874
Marched 21 miles to the Cave Pirty good water and Pine trees Camp No. 10

July 12, 1874
Marching nearly all Day Distance 12 miles Encampt on the same range of Hills wood and water Camp No. 11

July 13, 1874
Marched 15 miles Encamped on a little Crick Hostile Indians around to Day Camp No. 12

July 14, 1874
Marched 15 miles and Encamped on a Branch of the Little Missouri River Plenty of wood But little water Camp No 13.

July 15, 1874
Laid over in Camp (15) Plenty wood But not much water Camp No. 13

July 16, 1874
Marched 30½ miles and wattered the stalk on the Little Missiourie and made a Dry Camp at night Camp No. 14

July 17, 1874
Marched 18 miles and Encamped on a Bluff no wood and very little water a Heavey Storm Camp No. 15

July 18, 1874
Marched 17½ miles and Encamped Belley Fourch or the north Fork of the Cheyenne River Camp No. 16

July 19, 1874
Laid over in Camp 16 on acount of heavy rain Camp No. 16

July 20, 1874
Marched 18½ miles and went in Camp on the Read Stone Crick Plenty wood and water we Have marched up to this camp 3.26 miles Camp No. 17

July 21, 1874
Marched 15½ miles Encamped at a Clear Spring Plenty wood and water Camp No. 18

July 22, 1874
Marched 22½ miles Encamped on Baise Bluff Creek good wood and water too Calvary men Buried at this plaise Camp No 19.

July 23, 1874
Laid over at Camp (19) name of this camp Inyan Kara Camp No (19)

July 24, 1874
Marched 11 Miles through Pine Woods in to Floral Valy and crosed last Creek Camp No. 20

July 25, 1874
March 11¾ miles still in Flower Valy Camped good water and wood Camp No. 21

July 26, 1874
Marched 14 miles still in flower valey name of Creek not know Five Lodges of Sioux Encamped Below us Fireing at an an other good place to Camp Camp No 22

July 27, 1874
Laid over in Camp (22) Camp 22

July 28, 1874
Started out and marched Back in to Flower valy good water wood Miles traveled 9¼ Camp No. 23

July 29, 1874
Marched 14¾ miles Had a hard road marching late at night Camp No. 24

July 30, 1874
Left Camp 24 at Seven O. C. a.m. marched 10 miles Camp No. 25

July 31, 1874
Laid over at Camp (25) Camp 25.

August 1, 1874
March 5 miles Encamped at Custers Park wood and water near

Auguest (sic) 2, 1874
Laid over in Custers Park 4 Companys of Cavalry left for to Scouting purpose? Camp Custer Park

August 3, 1874
Laid over in Custers Park

August 4, 1874
Laid over at Custers Park a slight rain this morning Custers Park

August 5, 1874
Laid over in Custers Park

Agst (sic) 6, 1874
Started homewards Past through Camp 25 and Camp 24 marched 23½ miles good water and wood Camp 1

August 7, 1874
Marched 16½ miles Past through Camp 23 incampt in a pirty valy general Custer Kill a Large Bair at This Camp Plenty wood and water Camp No. 2

Agust (sic) 8, 1874
March 14¾ miles through Dry Pine Timber Bad Road got in Camp at night Camp No. 3

August 9,1874
Marched 7½ miles Encamped in a valey good Spring Camp No. 4

Augst (sic) 10, 1874
Marched 7½ miles in a valey good Water and wood Camp No. 5

Augst (sic) 11, 1874
Laid over at Camp No. 15

Augest (sic) 12, 1874
Marched 5¾ miles Crossed the Creek and Encamped on the same Creek Camp No. 6

Augst (sic) 13, 1874
Laid over at Camp no 6 till ten oclock and then started and marched 4½ miles Encamped in a Big open Space in the Pine timber Camp No. 7

Augest (sic) 14, 1874
Broke Camp one soldier Buried at this Camp got out of the Black Hills to Day marched 28⅜ miles Encamped wood and water Encamped 5⅝ miles from Beare Bruts Camp No. 8

Augst (sic) 15, 1874
Laid over at Camp No. 8

Augest (sic) 16, 1874
Marched 29½ miles and past Bears Bute and crosed the Belley Fourch and camped on a high bluff Poore water no wood Camp No. 9

Augst (sic) 17, 1874
Marched 28⅛ miles Encamped on a High Bluff Good water and wood Camp No. 10

Augest (sic) 18, 1874
Marched 30⅛ miles past through Camp 13 wood and water scarce No. 11

Augest (sic) 19, 1874
Marched 35½ miles and got in Camp very late rain all night no wood plenty of water Camp No. 12

Augest (sic) 20, 1874
Left Camp Early in the morning and marched till sunset Encampt on the Little Missirre wood and water Plenty Camp No. 13

Augst (sic) 21, 1874
Laid over at Camp 13 raining to day Camp No. 13

Augst (sic) 22, 1874
Marched 28½ miles over Burnt Prairie and Camped on a Large Bluff water (1) mile away Camp No. 14

Agust (sic) 23, 1874
Marched 19½ miles and marched in Stanlys Old Trail of 1872. Past over one of His Old Camps Encamped above the Little Missoure a Branch of it Camp No. 15

Augst (sic) 24, 1874
Marched 24¾ miles on general stanlys trail Plenty wood and water Camp No. 16

Augst (sic) 25, 1874
Marched 18 Miles got in Camp at noon Plenty wood and water Camp No. 17

Augst (sic) 26, 1874
Marched 33½ miles got in to Camp at (5) oclock Plenty wood and water Camp No. 18

Augst (sic) 27, 1874
Marched 16 Miles a slight Rain this eavening Camp No. 19

Augst (sic) 28, 1874
Marched 1¾ miles still with the Rear gaurd got in Camp at noon water and wood along Distance away Camp No. 20

Augst (sic) 29
Marched 20 miles get in to Camp at noon wood and water along ways off Camp No. 21

Augst (sic) 30, 1879
Marched 23 Miles and stopped at Hart River and took Diner and then started for Fort Lincoln and got there at 3 PM and Camped on the river Bank Camp 22

Aug. 31, 1874
Laid Over at Fort Lincoln a hard wind and musterd at retreat Camp 22

Sep. 1, 1874
Laid at lincoln waiting orders to start for Grand River Camp 22

1. State Historical Society of North Dakota

Snow's Reminiscence

(Authors' Note: Fred Snow was one of the enlisted men on the Custer Expedition. Some 20 years after the journey he penned his recollections).

Black Hills Expedition 1874[1]

It has been my good fortune to know and enjoy the friendship of General Officers of the Army—who have won themselves undying fame by their Patriotism and Bravery—I refer to General Philip Sheriden (sic), Nelson A. Miles, O. O. Howard, Samuel D. Sturgis, Alfred Terry and George A. Custer—I have had the pleasure to serve with these since the close of the Rebellion on the Frontier in the capacity of Wagon Master, Forage Master, Packer, and Scout—

My last service with General Custer was during the Black Hill Expedition of July and August 1874—when I drove his private ambulance and had charge of his collection of Curiosities—It was on this Expedition I first met Boston Custer the Generals youngest Brother who had been appointed Forage Master and like myself was a Civilian Employee—

The Command left Fort Lincoln Dakota July 2d 1874—It consisted of the whole of the 7th Cavalry 12 companies and Co. "H" of the 17th Infantry — Colonels Ludlow and Grant accompanied the Expedition the former as Chief Engineer—

The Wagon Train was formed in 4 columns—The Cavalry divided upon either side with the Infantry in the rear—Pickets or Skirmishers were in advance and Flankers placed on both sides—These Flankers consisted of groups of four men who rode parallel with the Command and 100 yds. apart in sight of the Command—

On the 8th day of July the first Indians were noticed—some 20 in number and were discovered upon our left flank—but withdrew without any hostile demonstration. The following day we encamped upon a beautiful bottom on the north side of the Palanta Wak Paw Ree on Grand River. At the Forks of Grand River we discovered a Cave high up in the Bluffs—Clay Pipes Beads and an old Flint Lock Pistol were found in a nich (sic) of the Wall—

On the 13th Lieut. McDonald saw a small party of Indians South east of us and about one mile from the Flankers apparently riding parallel with the Command and watching our movements closely—The next day Fires were seen South and West of us and fresh Pony tracks near Camp—

On the 16th we reached the Valley of the Little Missouri—Indians were seen upon all sides of us during the day and in large members—From this point we obtained the first view of the Black Hills which appeared as a dark irregular cloud against the distant sky—Bear Butte was also faintly seen away off to the South East issolated (sic) and alone—standing on the Prairie like a grim Sentinel guarding the entrance to the Miners Paradise — The next morning Bloody Knife Chief of the Ree Scouts reported a large party of Indians as having crossed in front of us—dragging their Travoy (sic) Poles. This indicated a Village upon the move and not a War Party. They were headed for the Hills while we had been riding parallel with them.

Our Camp was made upon a high Butte overlooking the Surrounding Country—During the night a Dakota Zephyr visited our Camp and in our exposed position we felt it in all its severity—Tents were blown down and Horses stampeded—Some of the Infantry were made houseless in the early part of the night—and were drenched to the skin by the rain which followed the windstorm.

Two Soldiers Died and were burried (sic) in one Grave. A large fire was built over the Grave to obliterate all signs of the burial as Indians were known to have opened newly made Graves for the purpose of securing the Scalp—

Our next Camp in the North West corner of the Hills was made in a narrow but beautiful little valley—completely surrounded by almost perpendicular Bluffs — A bright sparkling little stream winds its tiny course through this Valley and is almost hidden by the heavy moss grown banks.

Large numbers of Flowers of innumerable Varieties dotted the Valley in all directions while sitting in front of my Tent. I counted nine different varieties within reach of my hand—As we advanced the Scenery became more beautiful and grand. The Flora was of the most brilliant kind—but what seemed remarkable was the absence of Birds—

Upon entering the Hills the Ree Indians in advance discovered an Indian Camp of 7 Lodges. The party was supposed to number from 20 to 30—A fire was still burning and there was every indication they had deserted the camp in haste—Scouts were sent in persuit (sic) and the Command went into Camp—An hour after a Scout reported a Camp directly in our front—General Custer and one Company left Camp and surprised a small party consisting of six Braves and five Squaws—The Chief of the party "One Stab" and one of the Braves were brought into Camp—They claimed to belong to a Hunting Party numbering Two Hundred of which One Stab is Chief.

General Custer after supplying them with Blankets and some Provission (sic) allowed them to return to their Camp and sent one of his Santee Indian Scouts with them to protect them from any straggling Indian belonging to our Command—When a short distance from Camp and in a secluded spot the Sioux Brave attempted to seize the Santees Gun during the struggle that ensued they were both dismounted—the Gun discharged—the Ball entering the Sioux body near the groin—All this time One Stab sat upon his Pony and took no part in the fight—he now rode toward the Santee who jumped upon his Horse and returned to Camp—Upon learning of the affair General Custer at once sent a party to the spot—who succeded in capturing One Stab but could not find the wounded Indian. The following day Custer himself found the Provissions (sic) and Blanket of the Sioux covered with blood but no trace of the Indian—

The first indication of Gold was found July 27, 1874—The first specimen being discovered by J. A. Ross and myself. General Custer had at his own expenses employed two practical Prospectors I had known for years—J. A. Ross and Charles McKay—who were supplied with all necessary Tools for Prospecting. For many years the

Sioux Indians had from time to time brought to the Trading and Military Posts on the upper Missouri Rich Specimens of Gold and Silver Quartz and many valuable Nuggets—To all questions they would reply—that they were plentiful in the Indians Hunting Land in the Black Hills—Ross, McKay and myself were mess mates—Tenting, eating and sleeping together and knowing from the Indians there was Gold in the Hills we improved every oportunity (sic) to prospect.

On the 27—the Command laid over. Ross and myself had passed the forenoon in Prospecting a small stream a tributary of Custer Creek above Camp but without success and were on our return to Camp when in crossing a Divide Ross picked up a small piece of Float or Blossom Quartz, before leaving the Divide we found several fine specimens and followed the croppings for more than a mile—

The first colors or Free Gold washed out in a Gold Pan was discovered in what is now Custer Valley upon the creek of the same name—The City, Valley and Creek are named in honor of General Custer—We encamped in this beautiful Valley for 3 days, and the discovery was made the first day—Aug. 2, 1874—We succeeded in washing out 15¢ to the Pan from the Grass roots down to a depth of 6 feet and did not reach bed rock—

Much of our route through the Hills was along the sides of mountains through heavily Timbered Ravines — across deep Goriges (sic) and Rivers—where it was necessary to cut down Trees build Bridges, and dig away Hill sides to make Roads for the Command and Wagon Train.

General Custer always took the lead with one Company of his Regiment as an Escort—and insisted that I should keep as near him with my Ambulance as the nature of the ground would permit. At all times I was in advance of the Pioneer Corps and main Command. While upon the Prairie I found but little difficulty in keeping the General in sight—but after reaching the Hills it was impossible to do so or even to follow upon his trail without great loss of time—for being an ardent Sportsman he would chase an Antelope, Elk or Deer

over Ground almost impassable for Horses—leaving nothing but an overturned stone along the Trail for my guide—Many times upon reaching a stream he had crossed I was compelled to leave my Team and search for more than a mile up and down the Stream to find a suitable place to cross with my Ambulance taking up the Trail again upon the oposite (sic) bank—

The General finally gave me the Head Quarter Detail of 12 men under charge of Sergent (sic) Frank Claire to assist me in different places—Time and again it was necessary to unhitch the 4 Horses from the Ambulance and lower it down the mountain side with ropes—at other times the men hung to upper side of Ambulance to keep it from turning over—If it were possible to drive across fallen Timber or Wash Out I did so leaving the Pioneer Corps to clear the way for the Command—One of the Gatlin Guns turned over, rolled down the mountain and was completely demolished.

The day after reaching Custer Valley General Custer, 5 Companies of Cavalry, the Professors and Bug Hunters—with a small Pack Train of Mules—loaded with 3 days Rations struck across the Mountain for the South Fork of the Cheyenne—The Route taken was impassible (sic) for Wagons and nearly so for Saddle Animals and during their 3 days absence the Men and Stock suffered terribly for Water—

Upon reaching the Cheyenne River Charles Reynolds the Scout was given Dispatches for Ft. Laramie—the distance some 150 miles through the heart of the Indian Country and frought with danger upon every side—At dark he bid adieu to his Commander and Friends and with the Stars for his guide started out alone upon his perilous undertaking having first taken the precaution to blind his trail by putting leather boots upon his Horses Feet—

Upon the return of the General we left the Hills by a North Easterly direction. One Stab whom the General had detained with the Command informed him he could proceed no farther with the Wagon Train in the direction we had been traveling. The Pioneer Corps were kept constantly employed cutting

trees, building Bridges across Ravines and deep Gourges (sic) and digging away Hill sides to make roads for the Command—

On the 14th day of August we reached the open Country and taking a North Easterly direction encamped near Bear Butte at the Confluence of Bear Butte and Spring Creek—souce (sic) 6 miles below the present site of Fort Meade—From the summit of Bear Butte a grand view of the Plains far over the Northern Divide can be had—Standing alone upon that bald barren Peak many hundred feet above the level of the Valley —you can look upon a scene of Natural grandure (sic) that is unequaled in all the Country east of the Rocky Mts.

Far to the North through the azure spread the flat dull Plains— The fringe of Timber along the serpentine banks of Grand River— winds its course like a tangled black thread towards the distant Missouri beyond the reach of the strongest glass—All the wild, weird region, is a vast lybraryuth (sic) of charred and blackened Mountains Verdaut and many tinted Valleys bright and Shimmering Rivers—with Harneys Peak to the South East penetrating the Clouds the Watch Tower of Dakotas Eldorado eternal in its majesty— Away to the South and West the earth was transformed into an exaggerated Map of the Moon—The rolling Hills and rippling ranges seemed the veritable semblance of a petrified Ocean—in every direction whichever way we turned our gase (sic) The Grand Panorama gave us vivid glimpses of new and startling forms, unequalled in beauty and matchless in sublimity.

After leaving Bear Butte the stock began to fail and a detail of Soldiers were sent to the rear with instructions to shoot all Animals that could not keep up with the command. This was done to prevent them from falling into the hands of the Indians—As we neared the Little Missouri River it was astonishing to see Horses and Mules that could scarcely move during the day—Trot and even run to the water. The stream was literally black with them. It was very shallow and many of them laid down and could not rise without assistance—The men were also worn out and the 4 ambulances were not sufficient to hold the Sick and many were crowded into army Wagons.

Returning to the Prairie from the Valley of the Little Missouri where we were compelled to lay over to rest men and Stock we passed over a portion of our old Trail—Many Horses and mules that had been shot lay as they fell food for Coyottes (sic)—In some instances the Wolves had already commenced their feast as could be seen by the mutilated carcasses (sic)—

The only good Indian found upon the trip was one discovered by Sergent (sic) Frank Clair while out hunting with me on the Belle Fouche (sic)—The Indian was in a Tree lashed upon a Frame Work of Willows. Tin Cups, a small Tin Pail and a Canteen containing a Red Liquor was placed at the foot of the Tree—and a Canteen was suspended from the frame upon which the body was placed—The Body was that of a young Brave—was wrapped in Gunny Sacks and tied with Shagganappi—or Raw-Hide thongs. From appearances he had been good but a short time.

The Expedition lasted 61 days. The total distance made by Wagon Train as marked by the Odometer was 894¾ miles which was accomplished in 49 traveling days at an average of 18¼ miles.

Taking into consideration the fact that no Teams or White men had ever penetrated the Hills before us and not one foot of the Route was known to anyone in the command General Custer being his own Guide It was one of the most remarkable trips on record and opened up one of the richest Gold and Mineral Fields in the United States.

Fred S. Snow
Antelope Fred

New Haven, Conn.
Feby. 12th, 1893—

1. Snow Reminiscence. Black Hills Expedition, package 31, E. B. Custer Collection, Custer Battlefield National Monument, Crow Agency, Montana.

Wood's Reminiscence

REMINISCENCE[1]
By William R. Wood (1927)

In 1874 I went to the Black Hills with Custer. We outfitted at Fort Lincoln near where Mandan is now, and struck southwest across the prairie. We had with us the war department maps of the explorations up to date. Captain Hardy of the Engineering Corps said he had heard of the Black Hills—he didn't go into them but he had marked them on his map. We were on the look out for signs of his party, but we didn't hit the trail all the way out. He had half a dozen army wagons with him, and they would make quite a trail because they follow one right after the other. One day, I think it was Ludlow who said, "Look at that!" There were two rows of sunflowers, just the gauge of the wagon apart, and as far as we could see, just an unbroken line of sun-flowers. We didn't follow the line of the flowers, we were crossing it at right angles. The horses and the wagons had broken the sod, what little sod there is out there — and the sod on that prairie isn't like ours; they probably went out in the time when the sunflowers were in bloom and scattering their seeds. The seeds that fell on the unbroken sod dried up — but the seeds that fell in the wagon trails sprouted. It was a pretty sight, the two lines of sun-flowers.

We crossed this line in the northeast corner of the Black Hills on the prairie. We went into the Black Hills at the north end, and we went through them to the south end, and it was pretty slow travel. We had a big train; we had about twelve hundred soldiers; calvary (sic), infantry and artillery — my impression is that we had twelve hundred men, and all their supplies for a two months' trip. It made a pretty big trail. I think we had one hundred army wagons. We didn't have time to hunt a trail, we just went in, and we had loads of trouble. Sometimes we didn't make more than four or five miles a day, we had to stop and pick a way for the wagons to get through. I have seen them go all night long,

once or twice — there was no let-up with Custer. He went ahead and picked out a camping place. One afternoon especially I remember, he picked out a camping place and said, "I guess they can come this far." they didn't get there until four o'clock in the morning — then they fed the horses and went right on.

During the afternoon Colonel Ludlow said, "Wood, let's go out and see if we can find a grizzly." There were plenty of them there, we had seen signs of them. So he and I went out, and we took his orderly with him. The three of us were mounted and we took rifles and went hunting. We left the camp, where there was considerable noise, and went down a little coolie where we thought there might be a spring, and in just a short time we found it — just at the foot of two hills, where the two hills came together. There was scarcely enough space for the horses to stand, the hills came together at such a steep angle. Sometimes we had to jump some fallen trees. Ludlow was in front, I was in the middle, and the orderly was behind. When Ludlow's horse jumped over a little place about two feet high, we were surprised to see a bear come out from under a tree to the left of us. He was surprised to see us too, and just stood looking. I was right beside the bear, so close to him if he had reached out with his paw he would have hit me. I saw Ludlow fingering his gun, and I said, "For God's sake, Ludlow, don't shoot." I was nearest the bear and I was afraid if Ludlow did shoot, the bear would have thought I was the aggressor. The bear stood still for what seemed like a few minutes, I suppose it really was only ten seconds, then he just turned tail and went up the hill.

Our horses could not go up that hill, but, we tried to find the bear again when we got on level ground; we were several miles from camp and though we looked for him all the way back to camp, we couldn't find him. But when we got back to camp, there was our bear lying on the ground, dead — Custer and some of his friends had gone hunting bear and got him. Before we got back to camp, Ludlow said, "Wood, Mike remember this: we have seen no bear."

Colonel William Ludlow was in the Spanish War, he was governor of Havana after we conquered Cuba. He was Captain of the engineers and then a brevet major when I knew him — he was a fine man.

We went on for some time toward the south end of the Black Hills. The engineer whose trail we saw had located Harney's Peak. He had estimated its height—it was a real peak, and the only peak in the Black Hills. It was a granite peak standing up above the rest of the mountains. One day Ludlow and three or four other men, and myself decided to climb Harney's Peak. It was quite a climb, we took out horses as high as we could, then tethered them and went the rest of the way on foot. Custer went too, but he took his horse a great deal higher then we did. Harney's Peak has an 8000 foot elevation, and we got a wonderful view of the surrounding country. I took a good many compass bearings of permanent places and then we turned around and went down. Custer's horse had a hard time getting down the steep peak—it was cruel, the horse's knees were bleeding, and he had a hard time to make the grade.

We came out of the Black Hills at the southern end not far from Harney's Peak, and went parallel on the prairie to go north and strike home again. We came back on the east side of the Black Hills so we were south and east of our going trail.

There was a captain in the calvary (sic), I wish I could remember his name, he was such a nice man. We two struck up quite a friendship, we rode parallel with the wagon trail, a little farther up — I suppose they were a quarter of half a mile on our left. While we were riding along one day we saw, not far away, a black tail buck, We both exclaimed, "I believe we could get a shot at him." I told the Captain to take the first shot at him, and he got down on his knees and shot, and missed. Then it was my turn and I got down on my knee and shot — I knocked the buck over, and took a second shot. That killed him. I thought that was pretty good shooting — we measured the distance later and it was just one hundred yards. We had a Colt forty-five revolver. Well, we cut his head off and took him back to camp and had his antlers cut off — they were still in the velvet and it was a nasty job. I kept those antlers for years, but they have finally disappeared.

I suppose that trip took six weeks or two months, from Fort Lincoln back to Fort Lincoln. The purpose of the trip was to explore the Black Hills — there were rumors that the Black Hills had gold in them. Custer took several gold hunters on that trip, and they found some gold. I saw those fellows pull up a bunch of grass and you could see the gold sparkling in the roots. It's a rich country, they are still mining gold there.

I made astronomical observations of the camp and kept a log with compass and odometer findings, of all the windings of our trail so we could map the country. The map I made, showing our trip and all the hills and streams, is now in the war department files.

Colonel Fred Grant was a guest of Custer, on that trip. Fred Grant was a son of General Grant, and was drunk nearly all the time. We used to start early in the morning, about six o'clock, and stopped anywhere from twelve to four. The sutler had a wagon with liquor which he sold to the soldiers and everybody who wanted to buy it. Colonel Grant was a guest of Custer, he went along to see the country and have a good time. He was in the army then, but he must have got a leave of absence. George Bird Grinnell, who was a young man just out of college, was on that trip. He was an ornithologist. The state geologist, Winchell, was also in the party, and Ludlow had a personal friends of his own, a civilian. There were four or five private citizens besides myself.

Grinnell and I became chums — we had a citizens' mess, you know. I was a civilian, Ludlow and Grant and Dana and Grinnell and myself — Professor Dana was one of the great geologists of this country, and this was his son. They were all twenty-five or twenty-six years old.

When we were coming home across the country — we always rode ahead with Custer and the horses were naturally faster than the teams, so about twelve o'clock we took out our lunch which we had brought with us. We unsaddled our horses, and sat down on the grass to eat, smoke. One day as we sat smoking we saw what looked like a hawk chasing a little bird, coming right toward us. Grinnell exclaimed that it was not a hawk but a Peregrine falcon. A falcon is different from a hawk, it's wings are longer and narrower. He was giving the little bird quite a chase, and as it came near to us, one of the men said it was a passenger pigeon. I was surprised, for I had an idea the passenger pigeons were all gone — that must have been about the last passenger pigeon in America, for I've never seen another. The little pigeon was putting up a good fight, but Grinnell was confident the falcon would get him in time.

When the pigeon flew past us, he flew quite low, down under the horse's belly. The falcon followed him, but he had a moment's rest. He got up and flew away again, the falcon after him, out of sight. He didn't get him, as far as we could see, either.

1. Minnesota Historical Society

Illustration Index

The Illingworth glass plates of the 1874 Custer Expedition to the Black Hills were acquired by the South Dakota State Historical Society in 1920, for the sum of $60.00. The then-secretary and superintendent of the society, Doane Robinson, was first approached in September of 1919 by Edward A. Bromley of Minneapolis, Minnesota, who owned the plates and was offering them for sale. Bromley had acquired the plates from Illingworth's son in 1900 and had held them for nearly two decades. In the correspondence with Robinson, Bromley said that "three-fourths of the Custer-Ludlow (glass plates) were still in excellent condition." Robinson had to wait almost a year before he was able to purchase the plates for the Society, because of a shortage of funds. Happily, they ultimately were acquired and have been carefully preserved by the Society ever since.

Illingworth offered only 55 stereo views of the Black Hills for sale. Apparently, he eliminated some of the duplicates. On the back of the stereos, he published this message:

"STEREOGRAPHS OF THE BLACK HILLS,

Comprising some of the most beautiful scenery to be found on the American Continent. The Hills, situated as they are in Latitude 40, abound in rugged grandeur; on the South and East sides the Limestone walls, and Granite Pinicles (sic), rising to the enormous height of 9865 feet, and enclosing the Hills in such a manner as to make it almost an impossiblity to penetrate the interior with conveyances, there being but two openings on the East side, and three on the South. The North may be considered the easiest route and, when at the highest elevation, you wind your way in almost any direction, through the beautiful fertile Valleys and delightful Parks, the latter looking more like being attended and cultured, than a wild and uncivilized region, magnificent trees, rich grass lawns, extending for miles.

"The Gold was found on the South and North side of, and in the vicinity of, "Harney's Peak." The Gold region extends about fifty miles square, amid scenery enchantingly grand, and for mineral wealth no territory can excel the Hills.

"The Views, in all, number 55. None genuine unless bearing my name on each end of the Stereo Card.

W. H. Illingworth"

Illingworth numbered his stereos 800-854. The list of slides was published on the back of each stereo and is captioned as follows:

800 Our first crossing of an Alkali Valley
801 Camp at Hiddenwood creek
802 Index Butte at Hiddenwood creek
803 Cannon Ball River
804 Ludlow's Cave, 450 feet deep
805 Inyan Kara, altitude 6,000 feet
806 Floral Valley
807 View from our first camp in the Hills, looking north
808 Castle creek Valley near the Divide
809 Wagon Train passing through Castle creek valley
810 Castle creek valley, looking east

811 Limestone Peak and Castle creek valley
812 Sioux camp in Castle creek valley
813 Camp in Castle creek valley
814 Headquarters in Castle creek valley
815 Limestone Peak in Castle creek valley
816 Limestone Peak in Castle creek valley
817 Elk Horn prairie
818 Gorge near Elk horn prairie
819 Harney's Peak at 10 miles distance, altitude 9,400 feet
820 Pulpit Knob, altitude 8,700 feet
821 Pulpit Knob, altitude 8,700 feet
822 Gold Quartz Mountain, altitude 3,600 feet
823 Turkey Rock
824 Illingworth Valley, near Harney's Peak
825 The Granite Range from Turkey Rock
826 Organ Pipe Range
827 Organ Pipes and Harney's Peak
828 From top of Beaver Mount over Agnes Park
829 Flora Park
830 Head of Golden Valley
831 Grant's Peak, 1,000 feet high
832 Sunshine and Shadow Mount
833 Godfre Peak
834 Genevieve Park
835 Agnes Park
836 Golden Valley Gulch
837 Golden Park, where gold was first found
838 Looking West from Granite Knob
839 Looking East from Granite Knob
840 Spectre Canon
841 The Organ Pipes and Golden Valley
842 Turret Rock
843 Permanent Camp in Agnes Park
844 Granite Knob and Harney's Peak
845 Gold Mountain Range and Headquarters
846 Permanent Camp in Agnes Park
847 Our First Grizzly, killed by General Custer
848 Red Sandstone in Elk Creek Valley
849 Top of Custar (sic) Peak and Elk Creek Valley
850 Forsyth's Glen
851 Bear Butte near Custer Peak
852 Custer's Expedition
853 Our Wagon Master
854 Custer's Expedition

The National Archives maintains a set of Illingworth stereos and carries the Illingworth numbers and captions as part of their identification number. Most of the photos in the National Archives files are identical to those in the South Dakota Historical Society collection, with one or two exceptions. The South Dakota State Historical society's collection is more extensive than the National Archives by 16 photos.

The State Historical Society of South Dakota carries a numerical list of Illingworth photos, totaling 73. Apparently, the numbers were arbitarily assigned at the time of the receipt of the glass plates in 1920, with no particular thought given to the sequence or relationship. In the Society's collection, no original glass plates, copy negatives or prints exist for numbers 35 and 64. Therefore, the actual South Dakota list totals 71 Illingworth pictures. Of the 71, 55 are full stereo negatives, ie., two 4 inch x 4 inch glass negatives side by side; 12 are ½ stereos, ie., one 4 inch x 4 inch glass negative; two are 5 x 7 glass negatives and two are copy negatives, apparently taken from original prints.

A detailed list of the South Dakota negatives appears below:

South Dakota
State Historical
Society

Official Number	Type of Negative	Page Number
1.	full stereo	65
2.	full stereo	59
3.	full stereo	36
4.	full stereo	31
5.	full stereo	57
6.	full stereo	20
7.	full stereo	173
8.	full stereo	172
9.	full stereo	16
10.	full stereo	23
11.	full stereo	19
12.	full stereo	109
13.	full stereo	218
14.	full stereo	221
15.	full stereo	199
16.	full stereo	48
17.	5 x 7 glass negative	89
18.	5 x 7 glass negative	87
19.	full stereo	176
20.	full stereo	49
21.	full stereo	15
22.	full stereo	38
23.	full stereo	137
24.	full stereo	35
25.	full stereo	143
26.	full stereo	68
27.	full stereo	85
28.	full stereo	83
29.	full stereo	37
30.	full stereo	47
31.	full stereo	225
32.	full stereo	18
33.	full stereo	44
34.	full stereo	219
35. no plate or picture exists		
36.	full stereo	21
37.	full stereo	27
38.	full stereo	84
39.	full stereo	50
40.	full stereo	211
41.	full stereo	88
42.	full stereo	134
43.	half stereo	117
44.	half stereo	168
45.	half stereo	86
46.	full stereo	90
47.	half stereo	74
48.	half stereo	123
49.	full stereo	113
50.	half stereo	157
51.	full stereo	163
52.	copy negative	34
53.	full stereo	53
54.	full stereo	58
55.	full stereo	140
56.	full stereo	25
57.	full stereo	82
58.	full stereo	91
59.	full stereo	141
60.	full stereo	227
61.	full stereo	22
62.	full stereo	175
63.	full stereo	14
64. no plate or picture exists		
65.	full stereo	108
66.	half stereo	220
67.	half stereo	122
68.	half stereo	169
69.	half stereo	17
70.	half stereo	75
71.	half stereo	135
72.	full stereo	177
73.	copy negative	204, 205

Illingworth pictures and other illustrations are listed in order of appearance.

Illustration	Page No.
Cover and Book Jacket by Don Steinbeck	
Frontpiece by Doug Jones	iii
President Ulysses S. Grant	1
Bvt. Maj. Gen. George A. Custer	3
Lt. Gen. Philip Sheridan	5
Brig. Gen. Alfred Terry	6
BISMARCK TRIBUNE front page	9
Bvt. Maj. Gen. George A. Custer	13
Cannonball River	14
Cannonball River	15
Hiddenwood Creek Camp	16
Hiddenwood Creek Camp	17
Rock Outcropping at Hiddenwood Creek	18
Wagonmaster Michael Smith	19
Ludlow's Cave	20
In Wyoming, South of Belle Fourche River	21
Inyan Kara	22
Inyan Kara	23
Inyan Kara	25
Floral Valley	27
Floral Valley	31
William H. Illingworth	33
Bvt. Maj. Gen. George A. Custer	33
Castle Creek Valley	34
Castle Creek Valley	35
Castle Creek Camp	36
Castle Creek Camp	37
Five Horsemen	38
Aris B. Donaldson	39
ST. PAUL PIONEER front page	39
Monument Butte	44
Monument Butte	47
Castle Creek Camp	48
Castle Creek Camp	49
Castle Creek Camp	50
Elk Horns	53
Harney Peak	57
Harney Peak	58
Harney Peak	59
Organ Pipes	65
Harney Peak	68
Illingworth Valley	74
Illingworth Valley	75

ILLUSTRATION INDEX

James B. Power	79
ST. PAUL PRESS front page	79
Near Needles-Harney Peak area	82
Custer Park area	83
Custer Park area	84
Custer Park area	85
French Creek Camp	86
French Creek Camp	87
French Creek Camp	88
French Creek Camp	89
French Creek Camp	90
French Creek Camp	91
William E. Curtis	97
CHICAGO INTER-OCEAN front page	97
French Creek Camp	108
French Creek Camp	109
Spectre Canyon	113
French Creek area	117
French Creek Camp	122
French Creek Camp	123
Golden Valley	134
Golden Valley	135
Golden Valley	137
French Creek area	140
French Creek area	141
Golden Valley	143
NEW YORK WORLD front page	147
Drinking Party	157
Sunshine and Shadow Mountain	163
Grizzley Bear	168
Grizzley Bear	169
Custer Peak	172
Custer Peak	173
Gold Quartz Mountain	175
Gold Quartz Mountain	176
Pilot Knob	177
Samuel J. Barrows	187
NEW YORK TRIBUNE front page	187
Whitelaw Reed	188
Forsyth Dell	199
Custer's Officer Corps	204, 205
Bear Butte	211
Heart River	218
Expedition at Heart River	219
Expedition Wagon Train	220
Expedition Wagon Train	221
Ft. Abraham Lincoln	225
Ft. Abraham Lincoln	227
Bvt. Maj. Gen. George A. Custer	231
Main Street in Bismarck	232
Custer's Home at Ft. Lincoln	234
Ft. Abraham Lincoln	234
Capt. Tom Custer	235
Elizabeth Custer	235
Custer Family and Friends (Interior)	235
Custer Family and Friends (Exterior)	236
Custer's Home at Ft. Lincoln	236
Route Map of Custer's Expedition (Complete Journey)	240
Route Map of Custer's Expedition (Black Hills)	241
Maj. George A. Forsyth	253
Capt. William Ludlow	260
N. A. Winchell	262
George Bird Grinnell	264

A

Agard, Louis (guide), 12, 24, 91, 209, 213
Alkali flats, 52
Arikara Indians: massacre, 153
Aunt Sally, 157

B

Badlands, 69, 76, 85, 111, 114, 202, 226, 232
Band plays, 23, 56, 60, 210, 226
Bare arm, (scout), 61
Barrows, Samuel J.: mentioned 4, 189; picture, 187; biography, 188
Baseball game: first game played in the Black Hills, 29, 92, 223
Bear Butte, 1, 3, 27, 28, 55, 74, 75, 93, 94, 95, 115, 179, 223, 232
Bear's Creek, 49, 94
Bear's Ears (Arikara): mentioned 69, 104, 191, 194; interview with, 191; makes a map, 192
Beaver Creek, 22
Beecher, Henry Ward, 3, 79
Belle Fourche River, 2, 22, 29, 56, 74, 75, 113, 115
Birds, observed on expedition: swallows, 52; owls, 52; sand-hill cranes, 60;blue crane, 70
Bismarck (D.T.) Tribune: mentioned 84, 144, 237; headlines, 5; Knappen to the hills, 9; chromo of Custer, 14; articles, 26
Bismarck, N. D.: mentioned 2, 41, 99, 146, 158, 182, 195; competes for settlers trade, 10; route via, 10, 30, 228, 232; crazy over gold discovery, 145
Bitter Creek, 22
Black Hills: mentioned 2, 61, 82, 85, 203; rumors of gold, 9; as lure to settlers, 6; geology, 7, 54; column enters, 54, 56; expedition to, 2, 1, 14, 46, 103; surrender of, 5; description of, 41, 56, 68, 71; exploration of Southwest Black Hills, 67; map, 149; paradise of the Sioux, 149; holy ground, 150; stronghold of hostile Sioux, 191; entering the approaches to, 206; southern border, 222; not occupied by the Indians, 233; agricultural worth, 233
Black Hills Expedition: Custer's Scheme, 145; topics in conversation everywhere, 146; organized, 165; return to Fort Lincoln, 180; measure of practical economy, 182
Black Medicine (scout), 61
Bloody Knife (Arikara): mentioned 2, 29, 55, 69, 73, 90, 94, 100, 115, 116, 173, 191; picture of, 168, 169; killing a grizzly, 223
Boston Post, 103
Bozeman Expedition, 11
Brule City, 30
Buckskin Joe (Mulewhacker), 107
Bug-hunters, 203
Bull Neck (scout), 55
Building Stone, 62

C

Cactus, 112
Calhoun, Lt. James, 12, 100
Cannonball River: mentioned 51, 81, 155, 160; valley of, 104
Castle Creek: mentioned 23, 61, 63, 94, 174; named, 222
Castle Valley, 23, 93
Cave Butte, 110, 155, 160, 170, 197
Chance, Lt. Josiah, 11, 24, 93, 100
Cheyenne Agency: Standing Rock, 193
Cheyenne Leader, 30
Cheyenne Agency, 93
Cheyenne River: mentioned 56, 60, 66; south fork, 178
Chicago, 2, 97, 145
Chicago Inter-Ocean, 2, 4, 5, 85, 97
Clear, Sergeant B. L., 68
Comet, 114
Congress, 233
Cook, Rev., 194
Correspondents, 3, 6
Courier, 66
Cunningham, Pvt. John, 24, 57, 208
Curtis, William Elroy: mentioned 80, 147; as correspondent 4, 85, 98; dispatches establish his reputation, 148
Custer, Elizabeth: mentioned 102; letter to, 6
Custer Expedition: mentioned 9; fight with Indians, 4
Custer, Gen. George Armstrong: mentioned 7, 26, 46, 61, 69, 73, 83, 85, 92, 94, 99, 104; described, 15, 44, 77, 101; assigned to expedition, 1; ordered into field, 11; prepares for expedition, 3; described by Curtis, 2; as hunter, 50, 82; and Indians, in Hills, 61, 81, 89, 91, 100; climbs Harney's Peak, 64; reports of finding gold, 24; kills grizzly, 28, 70; writes Elizabeth, 6; wood cut, 13; his dogs, 47, 81, 102; order against shooting, 50; names Prospect Valley, 54; inscription, 60; southwestern exploration, 67; description of the Hills by, 73; releases One Stab, 93; career, 102; rapid leader, 155; staff, 165; killed, picture, 168, 191; sent a brief dispatch, 170; letter from, 170, 190; assigned to command, 190; sent pacific messages, 6, 197; takes additional precautions, 202; enters Indian village, 213, 216; ascended Harney's peak; reconnoissance, 222; killing of a grizzly, 168, 223; surprising Fort Lincoln, 226; interviewed, 231; disappointed, 231; instructions, 232; grants an interview, 6, 237; arrests Fred Grant, 237
Custer's Gulch, 27, 219, 232
Custer Peak: picture, 172
Custer Park, 23, 26, 27, 63, 64, 67, 69

D

Dakota: mentioned, 198; land of contradictions, 198; climatology, 198
Dandy, G. B., 80
Davy, P. H., 151
Denver, 30

Denver News, 31

DeSmet, Fr. Jean-Pierre: mentioned 109; gold tales of, 2

Donaldson, A. B.: mentioned, 39, 40, 67, 77, 84, 172; collection of flowers, 228; his horse, 40, 64, 66, 102

Drinking Party, 157

Drum, R. C.: letter from, 1

Durfee (steamer), 46

Dust Storm, 204

E

Elk: mentioned, 60, 94; horns, 87

Elk Creek, 71-72

Elk Horn Park, 61, 94

Emigrant, 99

Expedition: mentioned, 100; "to winter in the Hills" (from Bismarck), 10; purposes of, 41; order to start; a measure of economy, 144; consists of, 151; instructions, 161; summary, 180; composition, 190; argument against, 195; preparations for, 196; cost of, 196; goes into camp, 197; return of, 224

F

Fargo, D.T., 144

Fishing, 93-94

Floral Valley: mentioned 23, 60, 87, 89, 172, 208; entry into, 209; marching through, 210; camped within, 212

Flowers, 23, 40, 60, 113, 171, 210

Forsyth, Gen. George A.: mentioned 3, 11, 59, 64, 80, 91, 100, 102, 105, 155, 222; Black Hills report, 144; plucked flowers, 172; assigned to the left wing, 197

Fort Abraham Lincoln: mentioned 2, 4, 10, 11, 16, 41, 76, 99, 158, 180, 225, 227; start of expedition, 190; Indian raid on, 194; description, 195

Fort Benton, 26

Fort Berthold, 42, 91

Fort Laramie, 13

Fort Randall, 30

Fort Rice, 72

Fort Sully, 72, 93, 95

Fossils, search for, 20

Fossil wood, 201

Fruit: mentioned 61, 64, 67, 88, 93; wild cherries, 67, 207; strawberries, 88, 207, 208; gooseberries, 88, 208; raspberries, 88, 208

Funeral: private King, 223; privates Cunningham and Turner, 24, 57, 208

G

Game: mentioned 28, 149, 161, 192; jack rabbit, 47, 95; antelope, 50, 51, 55; deer, 51, 60; prairie dogs, 52, 56; prairie wolf, 52; panthers, 60; elk, 60, 94; beavers, 61; bears, 71, 94

Gates, Lt. J. Granville, 84

Gatling Guns, 2, 11, 12, 42, 72

General Orders, 45

Geologists: with expedition, 2, 3

Geology, 94, 200

Gilson, Chris., 11, 151

Godfrey, Lieut., 72

Goeway, John, 5

Gold, in the Black Hills: mentioned 4, 5, 13, 24, 26, 27, 29, 30, 66, 73, 78, 81, 84, 164, 175, 183; discovery of, 67, 92; in quantities, 93; in valley of Madison and Big Horns, 100; evidence on, 151; nuggets, 11, 177; found at numerous points, 179, 183; gold-seekers, 180; indications discovered, 215; found in several places, 216; the first, 217; claims, 28, 220; found, 231; fever, 10, 181, 221

Goodhue, James M., 39

"Goose" (Sioux guide), 105, 155, 160, 200

Goose's Cave, 200

Grand River, 52, 75, 81, 160, 200, 201

Grant Administration, 1

Grant, Frederick Dent, 3, 12, 80, 85, 89, 100, 157, 163, 237

Grant Ulysses S., 98, 197, 222

Greeley, Horace, 147, 187

Grinnell, George Bird: mentioned 3, 191, 203, 222, 224; search for fossils, 12, 66; found his first fossil, 197; discovery of a leg bone of a mammoth, 201; search for long bones, 226; could not find the bones, 227

H

Hail Storm, 43

Hare, Bishop William H.: mentioned 161, 208; protests expedition, 2, 3, 153

Harney's Peak (Harney Peak), 55, 61, 64, 69, 163, 171, 174, 222, 232

Hayden, 206

Hazen, Gen.: letter to the Tribune, 226

Heart River, 76, 220, 224

Heeng-ya-Kara: See Inyan Kara

Hiddenwood Creek, 51, 105, 155

Hinman, Rev. S. D., 42

Hieroglyphics, 110

Horses, 167

Human Skull, 54

Hunting, 82, 93

Huntington and Co., photographers, 100

I

Illingworth, William: mentioned 33, 54, 80; embezzlement suit against, 35; as a hunter, 55; at Inyan Kara, as a photographer, 61, 66, 85, 94, 95; as the artist, 87; photograph of bear by, 94

Indian Bureau, 5, 194

Indians: mentioned 4, 46, 66, 82, 83, 103, 113, 167, 189; loss in battle, 4; dance, 15, 106; along the trail, 24, 51, 55, 71, 73, 90; village, 25; commence hostilities, 43; use of Hills, 78; encampment, 89, 90, 92; rights, 98, scouts, 11, 100, 106, 155; music, 106, 156; courier, 113, 222; guides, 115, 116; pow-wow, 156; campfire, 173; attacked General Custer's Expedition, 179; attitude toward the expedition, 193; seen, 197; trails, 207, 212; fight inevitable, 225; burn the country, 226; danger of interference, 233

Indian Ring, 103, 192
Indian Treaty, 228
Insects: grasshoppers, 69, 82, 200; mosquitoes, 82
Inyan Kara, 22, 58, 85, 115, 171, 207, 209

J

Jordan, Amos, 9

K

King, Pvt. James, 29, 72
Kluky, Emil, 103
Knappen, Nathan H.: as correspondent, 4, 9, 26, 84; credibility, 10; death, 10

L

Laramie Treaty of 1868, 153
Levasseur, Hercule, 150
LaVerendrye, Pierre, 1
L'Eglise, Jacques, 2
Lewis and Clark Expedition, 2
Lignite, 3, 51
Little Big Horn, 237
Little Heart River: mentioned 81, 159; valley of, 45
Little Missouri River, 3, 21, 29, 55, 75, 76, 115, 197, 203, 224, 226
Long Bear, 61, 62, 92
Lounsberry, Colonel Clement A., 9, 10
Ludlow, Col. William: mentioned 11, 33, 60, 69, 73, 94, 100, 110, 224; dispute with Illingworth, 35; picture, 168; engineer officer of the expedition, 190; making a reconnoissance, 206; killing of a grizzly, 223; survey, 227
Ludlow's Cave, 19, 54, 110, 170 (See also Goose's Cave)

M

MacIntosh, Captain, 93
Mad Bull, 69
Mail: dispatch of, 79, 170, 202
Mammoth's leg-Bone Discovered, 201
Marble, Manton, 147
Marsh, Professor, 3
McCook, General, 151
Menagerie, 60, 95
Mineral Wealth: exaggerated, 229
Miners: with expedition, 2; prospect for gold, 208; reports by, 222; discovering gold, 228
Minneapolis Tribune, 9
Minnesota, 39
Mitchell's new atlas of the United States, 144
Moorhead Advocate, 10
Missouri River, 9, 101
Montana, 54, 66, 113
Mosquitoes, 82
Mules, 49
Muleteers and mulewhackers, 49, 107, 112
Music and Musicians, Band plays (See Band)

McDougall, Captain, 81
McKay, William, 12, 24, 77, 93, 217

N

Newspaper Corps, 15
New Yorkers: enroute to the Black Hills, 148, 229
New York Tribune: Covers Expedition
New York World, 3, 103, 180
Northern Pacific Railroad, 9, 80, 99, 198, 226
Northern Pacific Road, 200, 228, 232

O

Odometer, 54
Official Instructions, 152
Official Roster, 43
One Stab (Sioux Chief): came to camp, 26, 61, 92, 174, 213; detained, 215; brought back to camp, 216; released, 69, 223
Order of March, 17, 45, 105, 165
"Organ Peaks", 64
O'Toole, Private, 64
Outfit, 145

P

Perham News, 10
Petrefactions, 20, 51, 52
Philippe, Louis, 1
Photographer (See Illingworth, Wm. H.)
Pilot Knob: picture, 175
Plan of Camp, 166
Poland, Col., 16
Power, F. W., 80
Power, James B., 80
Prairie fires, 76
Professor, 217
Prospect Valley: camp at, 2, 54, 120, 202; leaving, 202; letter from, 6

R

Railroad, 194
Rattlesnake, 19, 42, 49, 56, 95
Raynolds, Captain William: mentioned 2, 100, 164, 206; Bear Butte Expedition, 1; Yellowstone Expedition, 115
Red Bear (Santee scout), 94
Red River Star, 10
Red Water Creek, 22
Red Water Valley, Wyoming, 56
Ree, The: mentioned 24, 72, 192; scouts, 55, 61, 91; a man squaw, 106, village attacked, 194; guides eager for a fight, 212
Regiments of Infantry: the Sixth, 99; Seventeenth, 99; twentieth, 99
Reid, Whitelaw, 187-188
Republican (paper), 97
Return Route, 66

Reynolds, Charles: as guide, 12, 83, 170, 178, 185; rides with dispatches, 26, 67, 93, 216; gives information, 30; offer to act as guide to the gold region, 185; to carry dispatches, 217

Reynolds, General W. F., 151, 174, 223

Riggs, Rev., 194

Rollins, William, 24

Ross, Horatio N.: mentioned 12, 77, 217, 146; prospects in Hills, 24, 93, 218; letter to a friend, 184

"Running Antelope", 13

S

Saint Paul, 34, 80, 144

Saint Paul Pioneer, 3, 4, 79

Saint Paul Press, 24, 79, 80

Sanger, Major L. H., 11

Santees: mentioned 15, 72, 91, 106; scouts; 61, 158; Sioux agencies, 193

Scientific Corps, 197

Scribner's Monthly, 80

Sempker, Sergeant Chas., 76

Sepany, Dr., 47

Seventh Cavalry, 2, 11, 99, 196

Seventh Cavalry Dramatic Association, 196

Sheridan, Gen. Philip H.: mentioned 144; orders expedition to Hills, 1; receives Custer's Report, ; forbids entry into Hills, 73; limitations, 5; suggestion of abrogation, 5; support of Custer, 14; prohibiting all expeditions, 146; proclamation, 147; discredits the reports of battle between Indians and General Custer, 179; interview, 228; instruction, 233

Sherman, Gen. William T.: opposed to expedition, 154

Short Pine Creek, 21

Short Pine Hill, 55

Silver, 93

Sioux City, Iowa: mentioned 4; route from, 30; nearest route to Black Hills, 144

Sioux Indians: mentioned 203; divisions of, 41; protest expedition, 2; along the trail, 3; Ogilalah tribe (hunting party), 61; will fight, 152; gods, 198; village, 213

Sioux Reservation, 5

Sitting Bull (Sioux Chief), 2, 103, 107, 149

Skunk's Head (scout), 55

Slave Butte, 74

Slim Butte: mentioned 104; cave near, 105

Slow Bull (Sioux): mentioned 25, 61, 92, 213; came to camp, 214

Slow Bull, Mrs., 25

Smith, Captain A. E.; mentioned 12; endorses Gen. Custer's report, 233

Smith, Jedidiah: expedition, 2

Smith, John W., (late surveyor): mentioned 30, 80, 84; sutler, 207; interview, 233

Songs (of the men), 72

Springfield arm, 12

Standing Rock Agency, 193

Stanley, Gen. D. S.: mentioned 26, 42, 48, 188; trial of 1872, 19, 226

Stewart, Dr. Edgar, 237

Stone, Frank & party, 229

Sun Strokes, 18

Supply train, 46

T

Terry, Gen. Alfred: mentioned 191; as department commander, 6; letter to, 1, 3; letter from, 5

Tilford, Col. Joseph G.: mentioned 43; commands battalion, 155

Topography, 203

Treaty of 1868: mentioned 144; violation discussed, 5, 6

Turk's Head, 222

Turner, Pvt. George (James), 24, 208

U

Unepapa Tribe, 92

V

Valle, Jean, 2

Vinaterri, Felix, 145

W

Wagner, John C., 75

Wallace, Lt. George: commands Indian Scouts, 11, 62, 100

War Department, 3, 194

War Eagle (scout), 75

Warren, Lt. G. K., 2, 58, 100, 151, 164

Weare, P. D., 5

Wemett, W. M., 237

Wheelock, Joseph A., 79

Williams, Assistant Surgeon J. W., 12, 210, 228

Winchell, Newton H.: as geologist, 12, 54, 66, 73, 84, 100, 111, 188, 197, 207-208; geological survey, 200, 227; reservations about the presence of gold, 237; side trip to Bad Lands, 222

Windstorm, 114

Wood, petrified, 51

Wood, W. H. (engineer), 100

Wyoming: camp in, 56

Y

Yankton, D. T.: competes for mining trade

Yankton Agency, 193

Yates, Captain, 87

Yellowstone Expedition, 190, 195